International Tourism
Cultures and Behavior

Yvette Reisinger, PhD

ELSEVIER

AMSTERDAM • BOSTON • HEIDELBERG • LONDON • NEW YORK • OXFORD
PARIS • SAN DIEGO • SAN FRANCISCO • SINGAPORE • SYDNEY • TOKYO

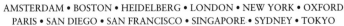
Butterworth-Heinemann is an imprint of Elsevier

Butterworth-Heinemann is an imprint of Elsevier
Linacre House, Jordan Hill, Oxford OX2 8DP, UK
30 Corporate Drive, Suite 400, Burlington, MA 01803, USA

Notice
No responsibility is assumed by the publisher for any injury and/or damage to persons
or property as a matter of products liability, negligence or otherwise, or from any use
or operation of any methods, products, instructions or ideas contained in the material
herein. Because of rapid advances in the medical sciences, in particular, independent
verification of diagnoses and drug dosages should be made

British Library Cataloguing in Publication Data
A catalogue record for this book is available from the British Library

Library of Congress Cataloging-in-Publication Data
A catalog record for this book is available from the Library of Congress

ISBN: 978-0-7506-7897-1

For information on all Elsevier Butterworth–Heinemann publications
visit our web site at books.elsevier.com

Printed and bound in the USA

09 10 11 12   10 9 8 7 6 5 4 3 2 1

Working together to grow
libraries in developing countries

www.elsevier.com | www.bookaid.org | www.sabre.org

ELSEVIER   BOOK AID International   Sabre Foundation

Contents

Preface   xvii
List of Tables   xxi
List of Figures   xxiii
Introduction   xxv
Acknowledgments   xxix

Part 1   International Tourism: The Global Environment

CHAPTER 1   Globalization, tourism and culture   3

Introduction   3
1.1   The concept and roots of globalization   3
1.2   Benefits and criticism of globalization   6
1.3   Globalization and the tourism industry   8
    1.3.1   The influence of globalization on tourism   8
    1.3.2   Forms and examples of globalization in
          tourism   9
    1.3.3   A new type of tourist   10
    1.3.4   A new type of tourism   13
1.4   Globalization and culture   15
    1.4.1   The emergence of globalized consumer
          culture?   15
    1.4.2   Global consumer and global products?   16
    1.4.3   Disappearance of local cultures?   16
    1.4.4   Cultural homogenization?   17
    1.4.5   Product standardization or customization?   18
    1.4.6   Cultural heterogenization?   19
    1.4.7   Cultural convergence or divergence?   19
    1.4.8   Cultural hybridization?   19
    1.4.9   Cultural commoditization?   20
    1.4.10   Cultural deterioration, loss, adaptation or
          change?   20
    1.4.11   Is consumerism a bad thing for tourism?   21
    1.4.12   Globalization and disappearance of local
          identity?   21
    1.4.13   Resistance to cultural change and emergence
          of local identity   22
    1.4.14   Glocalization   23

	1.4.15 Local internationalization and regional cooperation	23
1.5	Benefits and limitations of globalization in tourism	23
1.6	Challenges of globalization in tourism	24
1.7	The future of globalization: Americanization of culture, cosmopolitan culture, cultural hybridization, cultural disappearance or culture clash?	25
	Summary	27
	Discussion points and questions	28
	Case Study 1.1: The emergence of a global tourist culture? Disneyland resorts spread over the world	28
	Website links	29

CHAPTER 2   Cultural diversity   31

	Introduction	31
2.1	The concept of cultural diversity	32
	2.1.1 Definition	32
	2.1.2 Interpretation of cultural diversity	33
	2.1.3 How did the concept of cultural diversity develop?	34
	2.1.4 How does one measure cultural diversity?	34
	2.1.5 Is cultural diversity important?	34
	2.1.6 The benefits of cultural diversity	35
	2.1.7 The influence of cultural diversity on tourism and hospitality	35
2.2	UNESCO Universal Declaration on Cultural Diversity	37
2.3	The future of cultural diversity	39
2.4	Challenges for the tourism and hospitality industry	40
	Summary	41
	Discussion points and questions	42
	Case Study 2.1: American in Paris	42
	Case Study 2.2: Creativity in a tense situation	43
	Case Study 2.3: Promoting the "unpromotional"	44
	Website links	45

Part 2   Cultural Theories and Practices

CHAPTER 3   Intercultural theories   49

	Introduction	49
3.1	Communication Resourcefulness Theory (CRT)	50

3.2	Episode Representation Theory (ERT)	51
3.3	Expectations Theory (ET)	52
3.4	Cultural Identity Negotiation Theory (CINT)	53
3.5	Meaning of Meaning Theory	54
3.6	Network Theory in Intercultural Communication	54
3.7	Taxonomic Approach (TA)	56
3.8	Anxiety/Uncertainty Management Theory (AUMT)	57
3.9	Stranger Theory	59
3.10	Face-Negotiation Theory	59
3.11	Intercultural Adaptation Theory (IAT)	59
3.12	Communication Accommodation Theory (CAT)	60
3.13	Coordinated Management of Meaning Theory (CMMT)	63
3.14	Constructivist Theory (CT)	64
	Summary	64
	Discussion points and questions	65
	Website links	65

CHAPTER 4   Cultural practices and tourism impacts on culture   67

	Introduction	67
4.1	Erosion of local cultures	67
4.2	Cultural commoditization and transformation	68
4.3	Cultural hostility	68
4.4	Cultural arrogance	68
4.5	Authenticity of tourism experiences	69
4.6	Renaissance of traditional art forms	69
4.7	Marketing of culture and violation of rights to own cultural heritage	70
4.8	Culture change	70
4.9	Culture diffusion	71
4.10	Cultural borrowing	71
4.11	Cultural drift	72
4.12	Acculturation	73
4.13	Cultural adaptation	74
4.14	Cultural adjustment	75
4.15	Culture assimilation	75
4.16	Enculturation	77
4.17	Demonstration effect	77
4.18	Cultural conflict	78

Summary   80
Discussion points and questions   80
Case Study 4.1: Discovering the Maori culture   81
Website links   82

Part 3   Culture and Cultural Differences

CHAPTER 5   Culture   **85**
Introduction   85
5.1   Definition of culture   86
5.2   Culture as civilization   91
5.3   Cultures by region   91
5.4   Culture as religion   92
5.5   The world's major religions   92
5.6   Religion by region   96
5.7   Types and levels of culture   98
5.8   Civilization   101
5.9   Types of cultures in tourism   104
5.10   The purpose of culture   104
5.11   Characteristics of culture   105
5.12   Subcultures   106
5.13   Culture versus nationality   109
5.14   Culture versus country of residence   109
5.15   Culture versus country of birth   110
5.16   Cultural identity   110
5.17   Cultural distance   111
5.18   The impact of cultural distance on travel   112
5.19   The measurement of cultural distance   113
Summary   114
Discussion points and questions   115
Case Study 5.1: Micro-cultures of the United States   115
Website links   117

CHAPTER 6   Cultural variability   **119**
Introduction   119
6.1   Sources of cultural differences   119
        6.1.1   Cultural differences in communication   120
        6.1.2   Cultural differences in social categories   121
        6.1.3   Cultural differences in rules of social behavior 121

6.2   Cultural values   122
   6.2.1   Concept and definitions   122
   6.2.2   Culture and values   123
   6.2.3   Value system   123
   6.2.4   Value orientation   124
   6.2.5   Types of values   124
   6.2.6   Classification of values   124
   6.2.7   Measurement and analysis of values   125
   6.2.8   Value studies in tourism   127
   6.2.9   Cultural value dimensions   127
      6.2.9.1   Parsons' pattern variables   128
      6.2.9.2   Kluckhohn and Strodtbeck's
            value orientation   129
      6.2.9.3   Stewart's cultural patterns   132
      6.2.9.4   Hall's cultural differentiation   134
      6.2.9.5   Hofstede's dimensions of cultural
            variability   139
      6.2.9.6   Bond's Confucian cultural patterns   150
      6.2.9.7   Argyle's cultural differentiation   151
      6.2.9.8   Schein's, Trompenaars' and
            Maznevski's cultural differentiation   152
      6.2.9.9   Schneider and Barsoux's cultural
            assumptions   154
      6.2.9.10 Inglehart's cultural dimensions   155
      6.2.9.11 Minkov's World Value Survey   155
Summary   161
Discussion points and questions   161
Exercises   161
Case Study 6.1: The US culture   162
Website links   163

CHAPTER 7   **Cultural influences on intercultural communication   165**
Introduction   165
7.1   The concept of communication   166
7.2   What is intercultural communication?   167
7.3   Difficulties in intercultural communication   168
   7.3.1   Verbal signals   168
   7.3.2   Non-verbal signals   170
   7.3.3   Relationship patterns   173

	7.3.4	Conversation style	178
	7.3.5	Interaction style	180
	7.3.6	Values	183
	7.3.7	Time orientation	187
	7.3.8	Context orientation	187
7.4	Is intercultural communication possible?		190
7.5	Ethnocentrism		192
7.6	Stereotyping		192
7.7	Prejudices		194
7.8	Racism		195
7.9	Strategies for improving intercultural communication		195
7.10	The ethics of intercultural communication		196

Summary   196

Discussion points and questions   197

Case Study 7.1: Courtesy and politeness in Thailand and
Australia   197

Website links   198

CHAPTER 8 Cultural influences on social interaction   199

Introduction   199

8.1	The concept of scoial interaction		199
8.2	Social interaction in tourism		201
	8.2.1	The nature of tourist–host social interaction	206
	8.2.2	The context of tourist–host social interaction	206
8.3	Intercultural social interaction		209
	8.3.1	Dimensions of intercultural encounters	210
	8.3.2	Interculturalness of social interaction	210
	8.3.3	Degree of interculturalness	210
8.4	Types of intercultural interaction		211
8.5	Model of cross-cultural social interaction		211
8.6	Contact hypothesis		212
8.7	Contact hypothesis in tourism		213
8.8	Difficulties in cross-cultural interaction		214
8.9	Culture shock		215
	8.9.1	Symptoms of culture shock	215
	8.9.2	Types of culture shock	215
	8.9.3	How long does culture shock last?	216
	8.9.4	Culture shock and social interaction	217

	8.9.5	Culture shock in tourism	217
	8.9.6	Phases of culture shock	217
	8.9.7	Intensity and duration of culture shock	219
	8.9.8	Doxey's Irridex "Irritation Index"	221

Summary   222
Discussion points and questions   222
Case Study 8.1: Shanghai night or nightmare?   223
Website links   224

CHAPTER 9   Cultural influences on rules of social interaction   225

Introduction   225
9.1   Rules of social interaction   225
9.2   Orders and types of rules   226
9.3   Relationship rules   227
9.4   Cultural influences on rules of social interaction   227
9.5   Understanding rules of social interaction   228
9.6   Breaking rules   228
9.7   Cross-cultural differences in rules of
       social interaction   229
Summary   229
Discussion points and questions   230
Case Study 9.1: Universal and specific rules of social
       relationships   230
Websites   231

CHAPTER 10   Cultural influences on service   233

Introduction   233
10.1   The concept of service   233
10.2   Service encounter   234
10.3   Service classification   234
10.4   Key characteristics of service   234
10.5   Importance of service perceptions   237
10.6   Cultural differences in expectations from service   237
10.7   Service quality and value   238
10.8   Service satisfaction   240
10.9   Do cultural differences always matter?   240
Summary   241
Discussion points and questions   241
Case Study 10.1: Chinese travelers in France   242
Website links   242

CHAPTER 11 Cultural influences on ethics **243**

Introduction 243

The concept of ethics 244

11.1 Ethics in tourism 245

11.2 Ethics in a cross-cultural context 247

11.3 Cultural influences on ethical behavior 247

11.4 The most debatable business ethics issues 248

11.5 Conflicting ethical behavior and practices in tourism and hospitality: Ethical dilemmas 251

11.6 Theories and frameworks dealing with ethical dilemmas 254

11.7 Strategies for managing business ethical dilemmas 256

11.8 Global Code of Ethics for Tourism 257

Summary 257

Discussion points and questions 258

Case Study 11.1: Global Code of Ethics for Tourism 258

Website links 261

Part 4 Tourist Behavior

CHAPTER 12 Human behavior: its nature and determinants **265**

Introduction 265

12.1 The concept of human behavior 266

12.2 Environmental factors influencing human behavior 268

12.3 Theories of human behavior 270

12.3.1 Cause-Motive-Behavior-Goal Theory 271

12.3.2 Maslow's Hierarchy of Needs 272

12.3.3 Alderfer's ERG Theory 276

12.3.4 Herzberg, Mausner, and Snyderman's Two-Factor Theory 276

12.3.5 Expectancy Theory 276

12.3.6 Cognitive Dissonance Theory 277

12.3.7 Reinforcement Theory 277

12.3.8 Equity Theory 277

12.3.9 McClelland's Learned Needs Theory 278

12.4 Basic needs of human behavior 278

12.5 Factors influencing human needs 279

12.6 The concept of tourist behavior 279

12.7 The nature of tourist behavior 279

12.8	The meaning of tourist behavior	281
12.9	The importance of studying tourist behavior	282
12.10	The importance of studying tourist behavior in a cross-cultural context	283
12.11	Benefits of understanding tourist behavior in a cross-cultural context	284
	12.11.1 Tourism industry perspective	284
	12.11.2 Tourist perspective	285
	12.11.3 Local resident perspective	286
Summary		287
Discussion points and questions		287
Case Study 12.1: The Asian woman's shopping experience: New research from Thailand		288
Website links		288

CHAPTER 13 Consumer buying behavior — **289**

Introduction		289
13.1	Environmental factors	291
	13.1.1 Environmental stimuli	291
13.2	Buyer's factors	301
	13.2.1 Buyer's personal characteristics	301
	13.2.2 Decision process	305
13.3	Other theories of consumer decision-making	318
Summary		318
Discussion points and questions		319
Website links		320

CHAPTER 14 Cultural influences on tourist buying behavior — **321**

Introduction		321
14.1	Cultural influence on buyer's personal characteristics	322
	14.1.1 Gender roles	322
	14.1.2 Lifestyle and activities	323
	14.1.3 Personality	324
	14.1.4 The self concept	325
14.2	Cultural influences on buyer's psychological characteristics	326
	14.2.1 Motivation and needs	326
	14.2.2 Perception and image	326
	14.2.3 Learning and knowledge	328

14.2.4	Attitudes	329
14.2.5	Attribution	330
14.3	Cultural influences on buyer's decision process	330
14.3.1	Need recognition	330
14.3.2	Information search and choice of information sources	331
	14.3.2.1 The role of reference groups	332
	14.3.2.2 The role of opinion leadership	332
	14.3.2.3 Family decision-making	333
	14.3.2.4 Buying roles	333
	14.3.2.5 Level of decision-making	333
	14.3.2.6 Buying new products	334
14.3.3	Criteria and product evaluation	335
14.3.4	Purchase decision	337
	14.3.4.1 Purchase risk	337
14.3.5	Post-purchase behavior/decision	339
	14.3.5.1 Satisfaction	339
	14.3.5.2 Loyalty and commitment	339
	14.3.5.3 Criticism and complaints	340
	14.3.5.4 Product disposal	341
14.3.6	Beyond the purchase decision	341
	14.3.6.1 Memories and meanings	341
	14.3.6.2 Emotions and feelings	342
Summary		343
Discussion points and questions		343
Case Study 14.1: Japanese tourist behavior		344
Case Study 14.2: Cultural influences on tourist behavior		344
Website links		345

Part 5   Cross-Cultural Comparison

CHAPTER 15 Cultural differences among international societies   349

Introduction		349
15.1	Africa	349
15.2	Asia	350
15.3	Australia	357
15.4	Europe	359
15.5	India	364
15.6	Latin America	365

15.7   Middle East   366

15.8   North America   368

Summary   371

Discussion points and questions   371

Case Study 15.1: Managing in Asia: Cross-cultural
            dimensions   372

Website links   373

Part 6   Multicultural Competence

CHAPTER 16 Multicultural competence in a global world   **377**

Introduction   377

16.1   The concept of multicultural competence   378

16.2   Domains of multicultural competence   378

            16.2.1   Cognitive domain   379

            16.2.2   Affective domain   380

            16.2.3   Behavioral domain   382

            16.2.4   Environmental/interactional domain   383

16.3   Other factors influencing multicultural competence   384

16.4   Multicultural competence as a process   384

16.5   Multicultural competence development levels   384

16.6   Multiculturalism assessment techniques   385

16.7   An educational challenge   386

Summary   386

Discussion points and questions   386

Case Study 16.1: One practical solution to overcoming
            the language barrier   387

Website links   387

Conclusion   **389**

References and Further Reading   **391**

Index   **419**

Preface

There is no doubt that international tourism expanded significantly in the last decade. International tourism has also been forecasted to reach unprecedented numbers in the years to come. The consequences of such increased international travel can be very diverse. The question arises whether international tourism enhances understanding among people and the level of their enjoyment, or increases the likelihood of cultural misunderstanding and conflict. The argument of this book is that in order for the tourism industry to be successful in the future, managers and marketers need to be aware of, and sensitive to, cultural differences among international tourist markets. Learning about, understanding, and respecting the national cultures of others can prevent potential cultural misunderstanding and conflict in international tourism, significantly improve social contact between international tourists and local hosts, enhance tourist satisfaction with travel products, and generate repeat visitation.

There is a widely held assumption that tourism promotes understanding and peace. However, there is also evidence that individuals group themselves around the core values of their national cultures. Usually people who share cultural similarities understand and interact with each other more easily than people from different cultures. Those who are from different cultures do not understand each other well and may even be in conflict with each other. An increase in international travel and social exchanges among culturally different people may be a highly dividing force; social exchanges among culturally different individuals may increase interpersonal tensions and intolerance. It is very likely that increased contact between individuals from different cultures may in fact generate clashes of values, disharmonies, social barriers, and even very threatening experiences. This notion is supported by the distinctiveness theory from social psychology that holds that people do not define themselves by what makes them similar to others; rather, they define themselves by what makes them different from others. People want to distinguish themselves from others and be seen as unique. International travel and tourism create opportunities for social exchanges and emphasize peoples' cultural origins and identities, sometimes to the dissatisfaction of others. This establishes the grounds for undermining the others' values, exhibiting hostility toward the others' culture, breeding resentment, and even provoking rejection. However, these negative feelings can be avoided if people accept and learn to respect others and their cultures. This is the only way to successfully maintain the character of global international tourism, whose future will be determined by cultural factors.

This book alerts the reader to the fact that individuals' behavior is culturally bound. Culture and cultural values pervasively influence how individuals act and react. This book explains how deeply the national culture of the individual determines human behavior and how important culture is for understanding tourist behavior and the operations of the tourism industry.

This book focuses on the differences in behavior among international tourists and hosts. A tourist is defined in this book as a temporary visitor staying at least 24 hours in a region for the purpose of leisure (holiday, sport, study, or recreation), business, family (visiting friends and relatives), or meetings and conferences. However, the term *tourist* can have a range of meanings, depending upon categories of tourists that vary by the degree of institutionalization, type of encounter exchange, form of travel, traveler's status, and so forth. Some academics refer to tourists as sojourners. The definition of a tourist is further accentuated when one starts crossing cultural borders. For example, in many parts of the South Pacific tourists are treated as guests rather than tourists. Thus, for the purpose of this book a tourist is defined as a culturally different international visitor who sojourns at a destination for a minimum of 24 hours and a maximum of 12 months for the purpose of holiday, business, study, family, sport, or conference.

Hosts are defined either as (a) local residents, (b) people of the visited country, or (c) those employed in the tourism industry who provide a service to tourists. For the purpose of this book the *host* is defined as a resident of the visited country. This can be either an international resident of a destination or someone who is employed in the local tourism industry and provides a service to tourists (e.g. hotelier, front office employee, waiter, shop assistant, customs official, tour guide, tour manager, and taxi or bus driver). This type of host is often referred to as a 'professional host'.

This book explains how national cultures of tourists and hosts influence their social behavior and why tourists and hosts behave the way they do. In order to understand the behavioral differences among international tourists and hosts, one must learn about the concept of human behavior in tourism and the factors that influence this behavior.

There are many diverse definitions and theoretical approaches to the study of human behavior. The concept of human behavior is multidisciplinary. It has borrowed many ideas developed in other scientific disciplines, such as psychology, sociology, social psychology, anthropology, economics, marketing, and management. As a result, the concept of human behavior has different meanings in each discipline. In tourism, some concepts that define tourist behavior have also been borrowed from the above disciplines, as well as from recreation, geography, urban and regional planning, transportation, law, agriculture, and education. It is no surprise that defining tourist behavior is a complex and difficult process. In order to explain the concept and avoid any confusion caused by its multidisciplinary nature, there is a need to examine it in the context in which tourist behavior currently takes place or will take place in the future, that is, international tourism.

Today, a solid understanding of the influence of national cultures on tourist behavior and the identification of cultural differences and similarities among international tourist markets has become more crucial than ever before. The international tourism industry is facing globalization, and an increasing number of tourists from different cultures are crossing national borders. This creates challenges for an industry attempting to standardize its products and consumers globally. Tourist behavior is culturally bound. In order to successfully market the tourism product to international tourists, the industry must have a cultural knowledge of its target markets.

In the author's opinion, cultural factors have the most direct and influential effect on tourist behavior. Cultural factors are the most significant determinants of international tourist behavior. A detailed cultural analysis of the international tourist background gives a richer and more robust portrait of tourist behavior than any other discipline can provide alone. Understanding tourist behavior from the cultural point of view allows marketers and managers to better identify how national cultures influence tourists' purchases, choices, and experiences. Cultural variables can explain in a much better way many objective aspects of tourist behavior, such as the preferences for specific products and destinations, as well as subjective aspects of tourist behavior, such as the influence of emotions, beliefs, or customs on these preferences. Cultural variables can better explain the reasons for specific tourist reactions to the external environment. By using a cultural approach to understanding tourists and tourism, marketers and managers can make better strategic decisions.

Different cultural groups of tourists behave differently. They have different travel needs and motivation, engage in different search-and-learning processes, and are influenced by distinct internal and external environmental stimuli. Different cultural tourist groups develop different images and perceptions of travel products and assign different degrees of importance to product attributes. Culturally distinct groups of tourists also have different expectations and awareness, seek different benefits, and use different choice criteria. Culturally different tourists develop different attitudes; they have different opinions, emotions, and tendencies to buy. They not only have different preferences for travel lifestyle, accommodation, and food, but also color, numbers, and packaging. Their experiences and product evaluations differ, as well. Culturally different tourists select different destinations, respond to different communication practices, and are influenced by different promotional strategies and incentives. Culturally different tourists differ in how they communicate their reactions of satisfaction and dissatisfaction. They express different levels of loyalty and have different degrees of satisfaction with a product.

In summary, in order to be successful, tourism marketers should have cultural knowledge of their target markets. They must know and understand the major value orientations of their customers, and be aware of, and sensitive to, cultural differences among international tourist markets and local hosts. Tourism marketers and managers should learn, understand, and respect the influence of national culture on human behavior.

List of Tables

Table 1.1	Definitions of globalization	4
Table 1.2	Dimensions of globalization	5
Table 1.3	The influence of globalization on tourism	11
Table 1.4	Global values and new tourism products	13
Table 2.1	US labor force	40
Table 5.1	World's major religions	93
Table 5.2	The world's eight major civilizations	102
Table 6.1	Rokeach's instrumental and terminal values	125
Table 6.2	Kluckhohn and Strodtbeck's (1961) value orientation	131
Table 6.3	Characteristics of low- and high-context cultures	136
Table 6.4	Characteristics of in-groups and out-groups	137
Table 6.5	Evaluation of various countries on Hofstede and Hofstede's (2005) five value dimensions	141
Table 6.6	Ranking of various countries on Hofstede and Hofstede's (2005) five value dimensions	144
Table 6.7	Ronen and Shenkar's country clusters and Hofstede's cultural dimensions	148
Table 6.8	A comparison of distinct cultural orientations towards the world and people	156
Table 7.1	Verbal signals affecting intercultural communication	170
Table 7.2	Non-verbal signals affecting intercultural communication	172
Table 7.3	Relationship patterns in communication affecting intercultural communication	176
Table 7.4	Conversation styles affecting intercultural communication	179
Table 7.5	Styles of interaction affecting intercultural communication	182
Table 7.6	Values affecting intercultural communication	185
Table 7.7	Time orientation as it affects intercultural communication	188
Table 7.8	Context orientation as it affects intercultural communication	189
Table 8.1	Major features of social interaction	200
Table 8.2	Typology of a tourist	201
Table 8.3	Symptoms of culture shock	216
Table 9.1	Types of rules of social interaction	226
Table 13.1	Future consumer segments and their buying needs	294
Table 13.2	Future important market segments	296
Table 13.3	Factors influencing pre-purchase information search	308

Table 13.4	Criteria used to evaluate tourism destinations	311
Table 13.5	Example of ratings for hypothetical destinations	311
Table 13.6	Destination purchase decision: attribute criteria	312
Table 13.7	Types of risk associated with tourism	316
Table 15.1	Cultural differences between Mandarin-speaking tourists and Australian hosts	351
Table 15.2	Cultural differences between Indonesian tourists and Australian hosts	353
Table 15.3	Cultural differences between Japanese and Australian characteristics	355
Table 15.4	Cultural differences between Thai and Australian characteristics	358
Table 15.5	Evaluation of the European countries on Hofstede and Hofstede's (2005) cultural dimensions	360
Table 15.6	Major values and orientations of the US population	369
Table 16.1	A self-evaluation form for assessing multicultural competence	385

List of Figures

Figure 3.1	Communication Resourcefulness Theory (CRT)	50
Figure 3.2	Episode Representation Theory (ERT)	51
Figure 3.3	Expectations Theory (ET)	52
Figure 3.4	Cultural Identity Negotiation Theory (CINT)	54
Figure 3.5	Social Network Theory (SNT)	55
Figure 3.6	Taxonomic Approach (TA)	56
Figure 3.7	Anxiety/Uncertainty Management Theory (AUMT)	58
Figure 3.8	Intercultural Adaptation Theory (IAT)	61
Figure 3.9	Communication Accommodation Theory (CAT)	62
Figure 3.10	Coordinated Management of Meaning Theory (CMMT)	64
Figure 4.1	Acculturation-assimilation continuum	76
Figure 5.1	The concept and elements of culture	90
Figure 5.2	Major religious groups as a percentage of the world's population in 2005	95
Figure 5.3	Map of prevailing religions in the world	95
Figure 5.4	Abrahamic and Indian religions in the world	96
Figure 5.5	Christian and Muslim religions around the world	96
Figure 5.6	Levels of culture	100
Figure 5.7	Relationships between dominant culture and minor subcultures A-G	108
Figure 5.8	Cultural differences among cultures and subcultures according to Samovar and Porter (1991)	113
Figure 6.1	Key dimensions of culture	160
Figure 7.1	Communication model	166
Figure 8.1	A continuum of interculturalness	210
Figure 8.2	The cross-cultural interaction model	212
Figure 8.3	The U-curve and W-curve of cultural change and adaptation over time	219
Figure 8.4	The acculturation curve	220
Figure 8.5	Doxey's Irridex "Irritation Index"	221
Figure 12.1	Major aspects of human behavior	267
Figure 12.2	Levels of the environment influencing human behavior	269
Figure 12.3	Categories and sources of motivation	270
Figure 12.4	Cause-Motive-Behavior-Goal model (Leavitt et al., 1990)	271
Figure 12.5	Maslow's Hierarchy of Needs (original 5-stage model)	272

xxiii

Figure 12.6	Maslow's Hierarchy of Needs (8-stage model)	274
Figure 12.7	Maslow's Hierarchy of Needs and information sought at different needs levels	275
Figure 12.8	Factors influencing human needs	280
Figure 13.1	Consumer buying behavior process	290
Figure 13.2	The influence of buyer's personal and psychological characteristics on decision process	306
Figure 13.3	Types of products from which consumers make selection	310
Figure 16.1	A conceptual model of multicultural competence	378
Figure 16.2	The cognitive domain of multicultural competence	379
Figure 16.3	An affective domain of multicultural competence	381
Figure 16.4	A behavioral domain of multicultural competence	382
Figure 16.5	An environmental domain of multicultural competence	383

Introduction

The modern tourism environment is experiencing an increasing internationalization and globalization. Advances in technology, communication, and transportation are enhancing people's mobility and travel, and leading to their exposure to culturally different societies, social interactions, and cultural exchanges. This book argues that it is imperative for the tourism and hospitality industry representatives, who operate in the international business environment and deal with international tourists on a daily basis, to understand the national cultures of the tourists and the influence of these cultures on tourist behavior. Tourism and hospitality graduates who will work in a very complex multicultural tourism environment must understand how national culture affects the relationships between guests and hosts, the quality of services expected by the guests, their perceptions of tourism products, their vacation experiences, their satisfaction, and, ultimately, their repeat visitation.

The culturally different tourist is the target of the international tourism industry. Currently, Asia is the major international market generating tourism around the world. New emerging markets are Central and Eastern European, as well as Latin American. The business challenge will be to better understand the cultural diversity of these tourist markets, and to determine how these markets will experience and perceive the outside world and engage in cultural exchanges. It is imperative that a new class of tourism managers, marketers, and industry professionals enter the industry with multicultural skills. Cross-cultural competencies are critical as the tourism and hospitality industry moves into the 21st century. Ignoring cultural differences among international tourist markets and the impact of tourists' national cultures on their behavior and travel decision-making will undermine tourism destinations' efforts in achieving their objectives.

Although the number of cross-cultural studies investigating the influence of national culture on consumer behavior has increased in the last decade, information on cultural differences among international tourist markets is not yet readily available in the tourism literature. The concept of culture is very complex. The analysis of culture in a multidisciplinary tourism context and the application of the concept of culture to the abstract psychological concepts of perception, attitude, or satisfaction, all of which have different meanings in different cultures, create problems. Consequently, more information is required on the influence of cultural characteristics on international tourist behavior. With tourism businesses becoming more global and with thousands of professionals hosting international guests, it is becoming increasingly important to analyze and understand the cultural differences among international visitors and the impact of these differences on tourist behavior. Such analysis should allow for identification of similarities and differences among international tourists, as well as locals and decision-makers in different countries. It should also contribute to more adequate and effective tourism marketing and management.

Given all of the above, it was felt that the most effective and appropriate response to the current and future international tourism needs was to prepare a textbook that would focus on cross-cultural differences in tourist behavior and explain the influence of cultural differences on international tourist behavior.

This book is intended to complement the Elsevier title *Cross-Cultural Behaviour in Tourism: Concepts and Analysis,* written by Y. Reisinger and L. Turner for the graduate market. This graduate version is primarily a research reference book that provides in-depth insights into concepts, definitions, and measures of cultural components and that focuses on the statistical tools for analyzing cultural differences and testing substantive theories. The graduate-level book was written under the assumption that many readers do not use quantitative methods due to statistical complexity. The current book is a simplified version of the graduate-level book. It is designed specifically for the undergraduate market. The current book does not replicate the graduate version. The statistical material has been eliminated and new chapters added. Because of the enduring nature of the subject, some concepts (e.g. culture, values, social interaction, rules of social behavior, service quality) have been retained. The chapters discussing these concepts have been rewritten and efforts have been made to include the newest approaches to the concepts.

Aims

The major aims of the current book are:
1. To explain the impact of globalization on international tourism and culture
2. To present the role and the importance of cultural diversity to the tourism industry
3. To understand major cultural theories and their applications to tourist behavior
4. To explain major cultural practices and the impact of international tourism on the tourist and host culture
5. To discuss the concept of national culture and cultural differences
6. To identify major cultural differences among the international tourist markets such as Africa, Asia, Australia, Europe, India, Latin and North America, and the Middle East
7. To show how cultural differences among the international tourist markets influence tourist behavior and, in particular, communication, social interaction, perceptions and satisfaction with service, and buying decision process
8. To explain the importance of cross-cultural awareness, sensitivity, and competency skills for international tourism managers and marketers
9. To understand the need for a cultural approach to destination marketing.

Scope

The book can be used in the following disciplines:

Tourism – The book determines how national characteristics of international tourist behavior contribute to the development of tourist experiences.

Marketing – The book shows that understanding the cultural background of international tourists helps in formulating marketing strategies that promise to respond to the cultural needs of these tourists; indicates the importance of a cultural approach to marketing in order to increase international tourist visitation; and allows for direct comparison of cultural orientations of international tourist markets.

Management – The book helps to understand which cross-cultural skills need to be acquired by future tourism and hospitality managers to enable them to understand, effectively deal with, and motivate international tourists to visit a destination.

International business – The book implies which strategies need to be applied by today's international business professionals to be able to work effectively within multicultural tourism environments.

Cross-cultural communication - The book broadens knowledge of the theory and practice of the cross-cultural encounter and communication by suggesting specific skills necessary for an effective interaction and communication with culturally different tourist markets.

Reader benefits

This book presents definitions and explains the cultural factors that influence tourist behavior in an international tourism context. It gives a theoretical understanding of the abstract concepts of culture and cultural differences. It summarizes the most frequently used cultural value dimensions and explains their influences on intercultural communication and interaction. It presents models of tourist behavior and explains cultural influences on tourist purchasing behavior. The book explains what to do with all this cultural theoretical knowledge.

This book also discusses the practical implications of the cultural influences on international tourist behavior for tourism marketing, management, and communication strategies. The book describes the psyche of the average tourist; identifies major cultural characteristics of the main international tourist markets, such as Asia, Australia, Europe, Latin America, the Middle East, and the United States, and gives guidelines on how to meet the needs of these markets.

This book should be a loud wake-up call for those who underestimate the significance of cultural differences in tourism. It addresses the current debate about how to respond to the needs of culturally diverse tourists in a globalized world. The book offers a solution to this debate by emphasizing the importance of being culturally aware and sensitive to international tourist markets' needs and understanding how the cultural background of these markets influences tourist experiences. As a result of being able to understand the tourists' cultural needs, the industry's managers and marketers may be able to differentiate their products, deliver those products more effectively and efficiently, and improve their social relations with international tourists.

This book is also a hard hit at those who operate with preconceived cultural assumptions, or form their own cultural perspective. For those who are already sensitive to cross-cultural issues, the book provides a valuable checklist of what one should bear in mind.

Moreover, this book is a vital piece in the jigsaw puzzle of tourism impacts because it indicates potential outcomes of tourist behavior in the cross-cultural context and explains how, and under what conditions, these impacts occur and manifest themselves.

The structure of this book allows for it to be used as a textbook for tourism students worldwide. The author hopes the book will have good longevity, as it does discuss aspects that do not change in the short term.

General market

The most suitable academic level is first-, second-, and third-year undergraduate-level courses in tourist behavior, tourism marketing and management, tourism analysis, and cross-cultural communication. The book can also be used as a reference text for graduate tourism and hospitality students, those with undergraduate degrees in areas other than tourism, university academics, and researchers involved in all aspects of travel and tourism.

The secondary market comprises tourism practitioners who interact and communicate with culturally different international tourists. Providing detailed information about the fundamental cultural differences between tourists from various countries, the book allows practitioners to improve their managerial, interpersonal, and communication skills. Industry people will find the presented mini cases to be particularly useful as benchmark practices. However, this book should not be considered a handbook or a "know-how" manual for practitioners.

The book has an international orientation; it can serve the various international student, academic and industry markets that can access books written in English. The book provides case studies which are all international in nature. Despite a "Western-world" orientation that is due to the origin and experience of the author, the text was written with the intention of benefiting readers from various cultural backgrounds.

The author hopes the book will be popular for a long time to come. Although it has been written for academic readers, the author recognizes that many of its readers will be from various industries as well as a variety of businesses.

The author hopes she can better serve your needs.

Yvette Reisinger

Acknowledgments

I would like to acknowledge and thank Professor Frederic Dimanche from CERAM Business School, Nice, Sophia Antipolis, France for his comments on the initial draft of this book. I owe gratitude to some of his students for permitting to use portions of their assignments and converting them into mini case studies.

Yvette Reisinger

International Tourism: The Global Environment

1

Part One discusses the concept of globalization, its impacts on international tourism, and the changes it brings in culture and tourist behavior. The importance of cultural diversity in tourism is highlighted.

Globalization, tourism and culture

1

The aim of this chapter is to explain the concept of globalization and its impact on international tourism and culture.

OBJECTIVES

After completing this chapter the reader should be able to:
- Understand the concept of globalization
- Identify benefits and criticism of globalization
- Understand the impact of globalization on tourism
- Understand the impact of globalization on culture
- Explain the challenges and future of globalization

INTRODUCTION

Today, there is a trend in the tourism sector towards globalization. Many tourism organizations are global organizations operating across national borders. But what is globalization, and how does it affect tourism and consumer behavior in tourism? This chapter explains the concept of globalization and its impact on tourism, tourist behavior, and culture.

1.1 THE CONCEPT AND ROOTS OF GLOBALIZATION

Globalization is a complex and multidimensional process. There are five key related definitions of globalization that significantly highlight different elements. According to Scholte (2000), globalization should be defined in terms of internationalization, **3**

Table 1.1 Definitions of Globalization

Globalization as internationalization

A process of developing cross-border relations between countries and international exchange and interdependence between people in different countries; describes a growing flow of trade, capital, and goods beyond the border of a national economy to a stronger, globalized economy.

Globalization as liberalization

A process of removing government-imposed trade barriers, capital controls, and restrictions on the flow of goods between countries in order to create an open, borderless world economy or so-called ''free-trade'' economy.

Globalization as universalization

A worldwide process of spreading objects and experiences to people at all corners of the earth (e.g. spreading computing, television, etc.).

Globalization as Westernization or modernization

A process of Americanizing the economy; a dynamic process that spreads the social structures of modernity, such as capitalism, rationalism, and industrialism around the world, destroying pre-existing cultures and local self-identity.

Globalization as deterritorialization

A process of spreading supraterritoriality; reconfiguring geography so that territorial places, distances, and borders do not exist; linking distant places in such a way that what is happening locally is determined by events occurring many miles away.

Source: Scholte, J. (2000). *Globalization. A critical introduction.* London: Palgrave.
Source: http://www.infed.org/biblio/globalization.htm.

liberalization, universalization, Westernization or modernization, and deterritorialization. The explanation of the above terms is provided in Table 1.1.

Globalization has powerful economic, cultural, social, environmental, political, and technological dimensions, and as such should be viewed from different perspectives. However, most definitions refer to globalization in economic terms as the process that merges national economies into an interdependent global economic system. This process includes forming regional economic trading blocs, growing local internationalization through developing economic ties, deepening multinationalization by multinational firms, introducing global norms and standards, developing global markets and strategies, and growing firms with no specific national operational base. The phenomenon of globalization has increased interconnectedness between societies in various areas of life (Saee, 2005). Various dimensions of globalization are explained in Table 1.2.

The concept of globalization has often been used in the past. For decades people referred to the process of globalization in terms of decentralizing production to different countries, and internalizing capital and labor markets, export, and imports. The concepts of modernization, capitalism, and economic interdependence have also often been used to understand the precursors of globalization. However, today, the form of globalization has changed. While in past decades globalization has been described as flows of goods and population, now globalization is described by the movements of

Table 1.2 Dimensions of Globalization

Economic dimension

From the economic point of view, globalization is the process whereby the world economies are becoming increasingly integrated and interdependent, market-oriented approaches to development are spreading, the notion of state provision of privatization and deregulation are being withdrawn, trade and investment are being liberalized, and increased penetration of transnational corporations in life is being encouraged.

Cultural dimension

From the cultural point of view, globalization is the process of increasing homogeneity of lifestyles and aspirations via media, TV, films, tourism, etc., combined with the rapid spread of different views and greater opportunities for marginalized voices to be heard.

Technological dimension

From the technological point of view, globalization is the process of rapid innovation and increasing inter-connectivity, particularly for information and communication services, and biotechnologies. This is the process in which knowledge is the most important factor determining the standard of living, more than capital or labor. Today's most technologically advanced economies are truly knowledge-based (World Bank, 1998).

Social dimension

From the sociological point of view, globalization is the process of incorporating people into a single world society. The world is becoming a "global village."

Political dimension

From the political point of view, globalization is the new process of shifting the power from national governments in directing and influencing their economies, to global institutions, such as the World Bank, the European Union, the European Central Bank, the World Trade Organization, the World Health Organization, and the World Tourism Organization. In order to survive, national governments that can no longer manage their national economies must increasingly manage national politics by adapting them to the pressures of transnational market forces.

Environmental dimension

From the environmental point of view, globalization is the process of increasing inter-linkages between ecosystems, accelerating biological invasions, simplifying and homogenizing natural systems, and intensifying pressure on global commons.

Source: Saee, J. (2005). *Managing organizations in a global economy: An intercultural perspective*. Australia: Thomson.

services and flows of information and capital. Today, societies are services oriented and embrace new elements of globalization, such as information technology and experiences. Globalization is not just about modernization or Westernization and liberalization of markets; it is more than internationalization and universalization. Today, globalization is about an intensification of worldwide economic, socio-cultural, political and environmental relations. These relations link distant places in such a way that local events are determined by international events, or in other words, what is happening locally is determined by what is happening globally (Saee, 2005).

1.2 BENEFITS AND CRITICISM OF GLOBALIZATION

Several benefits of globalization have been identified, such as

- Increased spread and connectedness of production and communication technologies across the world.
- Diffusion of ideas and practices around the world.
- New developments and technological improvements.
- Development of the knowledge economy.
- Growth and expansion.
- Increased economic and cultural activity.
- Gains in productivity and efficiency.
- Increases in revenues, profits and returns on investment, and raised incomes.
- Job creation.
- Growth in economies of scale achieved by centralizing the marketing and production activities.
- The rise of global brands and products that can be sold everywhere (e.g. Coca Cola, Nike, and Sony have become part of the lives of large numbers of people).
- Increased understanding of geography and experience of localness.
- Increased understanding of the world (Saee, 2005).

Some of the major benefits of globalization, such as the new developments in the life sciences and digital technology, have opened vast, new possibilities for world production and exchange. Innovations such as the Internet have made it possible to access information and resources across the world. Access to knowledge and the knowledge itself have become the most important factors determining the standard of living, beyond labor and capital of production. Knowledge generates new ideas, turns them into commercial products and services, and increases revenues and incomes of those who know how to use it. Those who have knowledge can develop, grow, and succeed. All technologically advanced economies are knowledge based. Knowledge makes the nations and their economies truly competitive and successful.

Unfortunately, not all nations and economies can benefit yet from globalization, developments in new information technology, and access to knowledge. Globalization is perceived by some as discriminatory and moving against human rights. Critics of globalization claim that globalization brings

- *Decline in the power of national governments and an increase in the power of multinational corporations and supranational organizations.* National economies become dependent on activities of the major multinational corporations that have the capital and technical expertise.

- *An increased polarization of the world in favor of the stronger economies.* Poorer countries become dependent on activities in major economies, such as the United States. The gap dividing rich and poor nations is rapidly increasing. Rich and powerful nations have capital and technology; poor and powerless nations do not have access to capital and information technology. Those with capital and technology do not allow for generating and spreading information and knowledge equally among the other nations. Large corporations claim intellectual property rights over new discoveries in physics, chemistry, biology, for example, in genetic research, and receive large profits from licensing their knowledge to others. There are doubts whether modern economies are indeed knowledge economies.
- *Supraterritoriality.* Although most employment is local or regional, the strategic activities have been spread around the world. What happens in a local neighborhood is increasingly dependent upon the activities of people and systems operating in different countries and on different continents. People's lives and their activities across the globe have become increasingly interdependent and interconnected.
- *Negative impact on local communities.* The big multinational companies usually operate in regions where they can exploit cheap labor and resources. Although profits flow into the local communities, the local industries are taken over by multinational corporations. This generates social and economic inequalities, large unemployment, low wages, and generally poor working conditions. Since children and young people represent the cheapest source of labor, they are economically exploited. Also, multinational companies have significant influence on the provision of infrastructure, such as hospitals, roads, and housing, which are built mainly to meet corporate demands rather than public needs.
- *Delocalization and outsourcing.* Many of the activities that were previously local are now being performed across great distances and national borders. Banking, telecommunication, and retailing have adapted new technologies that allow them to operate in different parts of the world with less customer–seller face-to-face interaction and thus reduce the cost of their operations. They serve local clients on different continents. Similarly, local bakeries, restaurants, and boutique shops have been closed in favor of opening big, cost-effective shopping malls. The result of economic and social activities leaving local regions and cultures in pursuit of cheap labor over the border has been this: a significant de-localization in world operations.
- *Separation of work from the home.* Technology has allowed people to communicate and make transactions between different places, spaces, and communities. As a result, the work place has been separated from the home place. People move between cities, regions, states, countries, and continents in search of jobs. They relocate to different geographic and time zones.
- *Decline in social capital and civic community.* A large segment of tourism activities has been converted into commercialized and privatized activities. Many public parks, outdoor recreation areas, land where children could play, beaches, fields and plantations have been purchased or rented by developers to build new housing complexes, apartments, or shopping malls. These events have seriously decreased the quality of life and sense of well being within communities. The features that first attracted

people to a local community, such as isolation, natural beauty, and peacefulness of landscape, have been gradually eroded by new developments and a faster pace of life.

- *Imitation of Western culture*. A large number of consumers, mainly from developing countries, have developed an interest in and demand for products and services that reflect the standards of the developed countries. They seek to imitate Western consumption patterns to enhance their social status and self-esteem.
- *Standardization of the tourism product and disappearance of local standards*. The process of globalization has led to the homogenization of consumption of such globally marketed goods and services as food, clothing, music, and travel products. Many communities follow global ideas and demand global products, in turn losing their local consumption patterns, distinct qualities, and sense of being different.
- *Environmental degradation*. The global industry has exploited the natural environment and radically changed its quality. The land, sea, and air have acquired commercial value. Many farming and fishing centers have been converted into new developments, resorts, shopping malls, or entertainment centers. These changes have often been irrevocable; they have turned the environment into places that cater to developers rather than local communities, causing alienation of locals and loss of their distinct qualities.
- *Considerable risk*. Technological and economic progress have generated high production risk across the globe. New diseases, viruses, and substances that threaten life on Earth are produced every day. They can quickly spread beyond their immediate context. The more that dangerous goods are produced on this Earth, the more peoples' lives, properties, and commercial interests will be put at risk (see http://www.infed.org/biblio/globalization.htm).

1.3 GLOBALIZATION AND THE TOURISM INDUSTRY

Tourism is one of the world's largest multinational economic activities (Friedman, 1995); it ranks among the top five export industries for 83% of countries (Fayed & Fletcher, 2002). Tourism involves the greatest flows of goods, services, and people on the surface of the earth, and it is, therefore, the most visible expression of globalization. Although the role and share of tourism in international trade is constantly increasing in importance, trade in tourism services has been concentrated mainly in the developed countries, such as North America and the European Union. The share of developing countries in total world tourism is comparatively low, although rising significantly.

1.3.1 The influence of globalization on tourism

Globalization has opened new opportunities for developments in tourism. Globalization has facilitated growth in tourism through developments in electronic technology, communication, and transportation. It has affected worldwide suppliers and computerized information and reservation systems, which have become more flexible and cost-effective; decreased costs of air travel; and offered easier access to destinations (Peric, 2005). The rapid spread of information technology has improved the efficiency of the industry's operations as well as the quality of services provided to consumers. It has also generated increased demand for new travel services, such as computerized hotel and car bookings, online reservation services, teleconferencing, video brochures, smart cards, and electronic funds transfer. The increasing use of the Internet in destination marketing, direct sales, and bookings has given rise to electronic tourism markets.

The development of sophisticated websites has allowed for the direct dissemination of travel information to potential clients. The Internet has made travel products globally accessible at much lower costs. As a result, customer demand has become more technology- and Internet-driven. In fact, the Internet has become the most sought-after amenity in hotel rooms, airports, travel information and entertainment centers, and educational institutions. The impact of technology and the Internet has dramatically affected all operations of the travel industry and significantly reduced the need for travel intermediaries.

1.3.2 Forms and examples of globalization in tourism

Globalization in tourism has taken many forms. The examples of globalization in the airline sector have included the liberalization of air transport that allowed for market access for private carriers, the formation of international alliances, privatization, restructuring of government-owned airlines, investment in foreign carriers, airline consolidations at the national level, joint ventures between airline companies or between airlines and equipment manufacturers, and outsourcing. The three major airline alliances have been Star Alliance, Oneworld, and SkyTeam (Dimanche & Jolly, 2006). These alliances have cooperated in marketing and promotion; standardization of equipment, services, and suppliers; development of a common brand; and sharing of frequent-flyers programs (Peric, 2005). Large air carriers developed computerized reservation systems, such as CRS and GDS, which facilitated the flight reservations process and became the main distribution and marketing tools in international tourism.

Examples of globalization in the accommodation sector have included hotel cooperation and chain creation, joint ventures, franchising, management contracts, and consortia of independent hotels. Major international hotel groups include Intercontinental Hotels (the United Kingdom); Accor (France); and Cendant, Marriott, and Starwood Hotels and Resorts (the United States). These hotel corporations are involved in various countries worldwide. For example, Marriott International bought more than 50% of Renaissance Hotel Group and is presently managing more than 1300 hotels of different brands worldwide. Strategic partnerships provided Marriott International with access to 40 new markets, including Russia, China, Japan, India, Italy, and Turkey. Four Seasons Hotels used the strategic partnership with Regent International Hotels Ltd. to take over the management of hotels in Bangkok, Hong Kong, Kuala Lumpur, Melbourne, and Sydney (Knowles et al., 2001).

Examples of globalization in the retail sector include partnerships, integration, and franchising. Tour operators and travel agencies entered into partnerships and/or integrated with hotels, charter airlines, retail distributors, and cruise companies. American Express developed a range of products in various sectors of the industry. Since it focuses on the activities of 3200 travel agencies, it has become the largest tour operator in the United States, Australia, Canada, Mexico, and France (Knowles et al., 2001). Franchising and management contracts are used as management strategies by food-service companies. Another example is the German group TUI, leisure tourism world leader. This integrated company owns travel agencies, tour operators, airlines, cruise ships, and hotels in more than 30 countries.

Large firms have exerted their influence on the operations of local firms by, for example, obliging local authorities to comply with certain laws and imposing conditions on local suppliers. Some tour operators have exerted a strong influence on the ways hotels operate and the prices they charge. For example, one adventure tour operator from the United Kingdom, strongly committed to protecting the environment of the destinations it features, ensures that local suppliers comply with environmental protection rules and use environmentally friendly equipment, products, and materials (Peric, 2005).

1.3.3 **A new type of tourist**

Globalization and the new political and economic world also brought changes to the tourist profile and preferences for products and services. In the eighteenth and nineteenth centuries, scientific and technological advances led to mass production and the development of mass markets with similar attitudes and tastes. The consumer demanded mass-produced goods and services at a low price. This led the producers to mass produce products and services that had a universal appeal, such as fairly standardized mass-market package holidays. They offered good value products, though quality was sacrificed for price. This process has often been described as ''McDonaldization'' (Ritzer, 1993).

New consumers have shown a completely different behavior pattern. They have become more globally oriented. As a result of developments in communication and information technology, and increased social and economic exchanges, they have been exposed to different cultures and developed new ideas and viewpoints. They have multiple demands, often borrowed from other cultures. They have become more dependent on information technology, self-service, and personal reservation tools. The new self-sufficient consumer has become more individualistic and requires more customized and highly developed products; greater choice, quality, and variety; and good value for money. Consumers have also begun to demand easier access to information technology, lower-cost transportation, and greater flexibility in travel (Akpinar, 2003).

Moreover, after September 11, 2001, the fear of the unexpected, such as wars, political conflicts, terrorism, or incurable diseases, has increased consumers' desire for safety, social stability, and order. Consumers have begun to re-evaluate their consumption behaviors, use of time, and attitudes toward leisure. They have chosen a new balance between career and family, and work and play. They have developed a new ''wait and see'' attitude, facilitated by ''last-minute-purchase'' web sites, resulting in late bookings. Also, the emergence of ''search for experiences'' as a travel motivator, as well as increased environmental awareness, has led travelers to modify their behavior and to look for alternative forms of travel. These changes in consumer behavior have generated demand for new experiences. Consumers have begun to demand authentic and genuine experiences. A new type of tourist called the "experiential" tourist has emerged. This type of tourist is interested in novelty, "strangeness," authenticity, and all that is different and that creates unique experiences. As a result, the industry has striven to organize tours to various localities that have something unique and specific and that set them apart from other destinations with their scenic beauty, festivals, or art works.

The new tourist has also developed new, intrinsic travel motivations and cultural needs, such as seeking new identity, self-actualization, and self-development, rather than physical recreation and rest. As a result, the suppliers must pay more attention to what the new tourist thinks and feels.

Such a shift in consumption preferences has begun to produce a new tourist who demands new products, variety, flexibility, and personalization. New tourists have also begun to develop new values and worldviews that stress the importance of family and ecology. It is hoped that in such a world, traveling will come to be more about developing social relations, preserving natural resources, becoming educated, and maximizing the quality of experience than about the quantity of products purchased. In fact, more and more tourists are seeking the fulfillment of intrinsic needs and finding self-expression in culture, ethics, and morality; understanding the importance of intellectual, emotional, and spiritual well-being; and becoming more concerned about the planet, its resources, and its inhabitants all coexisting in peace.

Such changes in consumer behavior have also brought changes to destination marketing and called for the development of more targeted and customized products. A number of new lifestyle segments, such as single-parent households; "empty nesters" (couples whose children have left home); double-income couples without kids (DINKS); baby boomers; and generations X, Y, and M, have became prevalent in tourism and signaled the need for a more differentiated approach to targeting. The identification of the specific needs of the individual customer have called for product diversification, customization, and exploitation of niche marketing. Table 1.3 shows the examples of the influence of globalization on tourism.

Table 1.3 The Influence of Globalization on Tourism

Culture
- Creation of global village
- Globalization of culture
- Global uniform culture
- Global tourist; uniform tourist behavior
- Culture change
- Resistant to change in culture
- Emergence of local identity
- Emergence of local consumer behavior
- Glocalization

Table 1.3 (*Continued*)

Ecology
  Ecological degradation
  Climate changes and their effects on destinations
  Global warming and its effect on tourism businesses

Economy
  Horizontal and vertical integration strategies of tourism enterprises
  Foreign investments in hotels and tourist attractions
  Global players and strategic alliances (air companies, hotels, tour operators)
  Global tourism management
  Global competition of vacation resorts

Politics
  Increasing importance of international tourism organizations
  Necessity for global coordination and regulation of passenger circulation
  Sustainable development as quality and dominant idea

Technology
  Global booking systems
  Global distribution networks
  Web 2.0 tools
  Mobile phone technology
  Standardized technologies in transport systems

Tourist behavior
  Global orientation
  Dependence on information technology
  Use of self-service and personal reservation tools
  Demand for new experiences
  Increased uncertainty and fear
  New intrinsic travel motivations
  Wait-and-see attitude
  Sensitivity to price
  Travel cost-cutting
  Individual travel, do it yourself
  Travel by car/coach/train instead of plane
  Accommodation other than hotel (apartments, country houses, bed and breakfasts)
  Visiting family and relatives

Note. Some items adapted from Peric, V. (2005). Tourism and globalization. In the *Proceedings of the 6th International Conference of the Faculty of Management*, Koper Congress Centre Bernardin, Slovenia, 24–26 November 2005.

1.3.4 A new type of tourism

Changing values of the new consumer have created a demand for new products and provided a driving force for the development of new types of tourism. Traditional mass tourism, although still prevalent, is evolving into a ''new tourism,'' often called *responsible*, *soft*, *alternative*, *green*, or *sustainable* tourism. The new types of tourism that hold a great potential for the future tourism market are cultural tourism; health, wellness and spa; nature-based; educational; wildlife; geo-; genealogic; gastronomic or food and wine; photographic; volunteer; virtual; experiential; space; ethical or moral; community; and para tourism. These new types of tourism require tourism product customization, which has begun to play an important role in the industry and tourism marketing. The industry is facing the challenge of catering to the individual tourist's needs, and it is therefore transforming itself from being focused on the mass market to becoming diversified and focused on individual tourists' needs. Table 1.4 shows the global values and future demand for new tourism products.

Table 1.4 Global Values and New Tourism Products

Values	General Features	Relevance to Tourist Behavior
Community	Public service	Demand for products that create a sense of community and connect with the community (social events, social tourism)
Culture	Culture more important than money and material possessions	Demand for cultural products (art, music, film, museums, galleries, concerts, cultural tourism, ethnic tourism)
Ecology	Importance of saving, conserving, and protecting natural resources	Demand for products that protect fragile environment and nature (eco-friendly products, ecotourism, geotourism, nature-based tourism, wildlife tourism)
Education	Education is the best investment	Demands for products that encourage learning experiences (books, guides, videos, educational tourism, cultural tourism, wildlife tourism, interpretation services, special interest tourism, food and wine tourism)

Table 1.4 (*Continued*)

Values	General Features	Relevance to Tourist Behavior
Family	Importance of family relations, support and love	Demand for products that bond family together (games, sport and fishing products, family vacations, group activities, genealogy tourism, community tourism)
Friendship	Importance of friendship, friends are forever	Demand for products that allow people to spend time with friends and show appreciation (games, card, gifts, wine, tea, jewelry, visiting friends and relatives, community tourism, volunteer tourism)
Harmony	Social harmony	Demand for products and services that create social harmony (social events, social tourism, ethical tourism, moral tourism)
Humanitarianism	Caring for others, empathy, human rights	Demand for products that compete with commercial market leaders (products for elders, disabled, unemployed, fund-raising events, donations, voluntary tourism, tourism for those with special needs, subsidized vacations, non-profit tourism)
Love	Importance of feelings, ethics and morality	Demand for products that generate and teach feelings (poetry, music, art, romantic cruises, nostalgic tourism, nature-based tourism)
Safety and security	Importance of safety, security, social stability, and order	Demand for risk-free products and products that reduce risk (comfortable and safe clothing, transportation, sport and kitchen equipment; translating, guiding and interpreting services; insurance)

Table 1.4 (*Continued*)

Values	General Features	Relevance to Tourist Behavior
Spirituality	Importance of inner values, inner peace, satisfaction	Demand for spiritual and religious products that allow people to understand their inner self and the purpose of life (stones, crystals; tarot cards; bibles; religious books; spiritual retreats; pilgrimages; health, wellness, spa tourism; religious tourism; experiential tourism; trips to sacred sites)

Source: Reisinger, Y. (2006). Shopping in tourism. In D. Buhalis & D. Costa (Eds.), *Tourism business frontiers: Consumers, products and industry.* Oxford: Elsevier.

1.4 GLOBALIZATION AND CULTURE

1.4.1 The emergence of globalized consumer culture?

It seems that the world's consumption patterns are following a global consumer culture characterized by a high level of desire for, and consumption of, material possessions (Ger & Belk, 1999). This is accompanied by the acquisition and display of goods and services which is a source of destructive envy and resentment but also desire and admiration (Belk, 1988) and fuels consumers' needs (Ger & Belk, 1999), even in countries where purchasing power does not allow access to goods and services. High levels of consumption are generally believed to be a symbol of the good life. Also, global consumer culture dictates that people strongly believe in the unlimited ability and achievements of science and modern technology. Modern technology has produced and disseminated information and images that convince people of its ability to solve all human problems, such as disease, hunger, and poverty, and to offer the means to a better and bigger future. These images have led to the desire to possess everything, enjoy freedom, and make change. Global consumer culture is thus characterized by high purchasing power, high individualism, individual freedom, a strong focus on material achievements and possessions, a belief in time as a scare commodity, a tendency to devalue the past in favor of a future orientation, and enthusiasm for change and innovation.

Consumption has become a necessity in order not to be behind the time, to live like a human being of the contemporary world, and to achieve major economic growth and liberalization (Ger, 1992). However, in some cultures consumption and materialism are generalized symbols that stand for evil (Wuthnow, 1994) and are seen as being foolish, wasteful, and shallow. It is believed the excessive consumption and materialism create humanistic, social, environmental and religious discourses. For example, one of the environmental concerns that is typical of global culture and is caused by excessive consumption patterns is the increased level of pollution and the depletion of the ozone layers.

1.4.2 Global consumer and global products?

Some argue that in a new global world consumers have become increasingly similar in their values and behavior patterns despite their national cultural characteristics; global consumers are increasingly eating the same food, wearing the same brands, and watching the same TV programs (DeMooij, 2004). It is argued that it is even possible to identify consumers on a worldwide basis. For example, one can create segments of consumers with a similar global profile and attitudes. These segments can be targeted without reference to their national characteristics. For example, marketers can easily distinguish among the European, American, or Asian consumers who share particular characteristics; they have similar lifestyles, incomes, and interests. These segments can be targeted with global products. The global products are of similar nature and are produced for similar consumers (rather than consumers demanding them). For example, global business travelers can be targeted with global brands from a wide variety of duty-free shops. Global products are advertised and sold in many countries around the world. In 2007, Amadeus, a world leader in technology solutions for the travel industry, published a report that identified four major ''traveler tribes'' that may emerge in the next 10–15 years and potentially transform how the airline industry delivers its products and services. These tribes include global executives, active seniors, cosmopolitan travelers, and global clans (www.amadeus.com). According to Amadeus, these tribes will be recognized across borders and cultures.

However, there is also an argument that there is no such thing as a global consumer. One cannot distinguish among European, American, or Asian consumers because of the differences in their lifestyles across continents and countries as well as at the local, regional, and national levels. For example, although there are clear differences between the EU countries, there is also a fundamental disparity in their value systems and lifestyles (Wierenga et al., 1996). Numerous studies suggest that a global tourist does not exist (see Reisinger & Turner, 1999a, 2002a, 2002b). Very different people live in the different countries of the world. They have different cultures and behavior patterns. For example, Asian consumers cannot be clustered into one group because Japanese differ from Thais, Thais differ from Indonesians, Indonesians differ from Chinese, and Chinese differ from Koreans. Similarly, there are differences among European consumers: German consumers differ from French, British, and Italians. Because there are these cultural differences among consumers from different countries, the marketing mix must also change to suit the national characteristics.

1.4.3 Disappearance of local cultures?

It is argued that global consumption patterns and global consumers do not exist. The true globalization of consumption patterns and global consumers could occur in a genuine global world only. This would happen only when French consumers develop a real taste for peanut butter, American women decide to wear kimonos, and Australian men swap their shorts and thongs for Bavarian lederhosen (Usunier, 2005). This, however, is not possible. Local cultures and their consumption patterns do not disappear. For example, both Americans and Europeans like their coffee, but the Americans treat their coffee as a morning necessity, while the Europeans treat their coffee as a social and leisure event. Similarly, Americans and Australians have different eating habits (fast food versus slow food).

It is possible that consumption patterns could be globalized if everyone were to adapt others' ways of life and cultural values. However, a direct adaption of others' ways of life and values might not be effective. In fact, the potential for one society to adapt the values and consumption patterns of another is limited. For example, the adaption of the American (or Westernized) style of life would be difficult to implement in other countries (e.g. developing countries) with different tastes and preferences. Some countries might be resistant to a change and disapprove others' technological developments and adaptation of ideas (e.g. China, Japan, and France often oppose US ideas).

Further, although some people might share global values that transcend national borders (e.g. teenagers wear jeans or watch MTV), they often have to give up on these values and re-adapt nationally accepted values. For example, when Japanese young people join the workforce or start a family, they are expected to follow culturally appropriate behavior. Significant elements of local culture, such as dress, social relations rules, or language patterns, must be followed.

1.4.4 Cultural homogenization?

There are arguments that globalization leads to cultural homogenization. The growing economic and cultural interdependency has accelerated the homogenization of consumer demands for, and universal acceptance of, global products such as food, drink, clothing, music, and film. The new developments in technology and media communication, such as the Internet, television programs, travel documentaries, and online newspapers and magazines, have allowed people from different regions and cultures to contact each other, communicate, expose themselves to other cultures, and export their own. The cumulative effect of the communication media and of tourists bringing in new ideas and products reflecting urban, Western ideals is additional cultural exposure and exportation. The end result is that similar products are consumed throughout the world, especially by teenagers, who quickly adapt the same fashions, jargon, music, or entertainment preferences. Thus, globalization significantly accelerates cultural homogenization (McLeod, 2004) and convergence toward a common set of cultural traits and practices.

Those who believe in a continuous cultural homogenization also believe that global culture follows the global economy and so-called ''McDonaldization'' and ''Coca-colonization.'' The notion of ''McDonaldization'' refers to the worldwide homogenization of societies through the impact of multinational corporations, cultural Westernization, and, in particular, Americanization of the entire globe. Other nations have followed the US pattern of buying cars, home electronics, and fast food. People around the world identify themselves with McDonald's and Coca-Cola. The homogenization of culture around the world began with the McDonaldization of society.

Consumption has been built upon a standardized brand image, mass production, advertising, and the high status attached to Western products and services, particularly US products. The global consumer has been targeted by the images of non-utilitarian values, such as dreams of affluence and personal success, rather than the utilitarian convenience of global products. Societies have become very consumption oriented.

Over the years, the process of cultural homogenization has been strengthened by the rise of the Internet and other information technologies. Companies such as Yahoo! Microsoft, Google, and Motorola have become more important cultural icons than McDonald's and Coca-Cola. Also, Western education and knowledge have disseminated Western standards and created similar values that have influenced international organizations, such as the World Bank, the International Monetary Fund, the United Nations, and many other multinational/global corporations. This, of course, has given rise to the emergence of similar interests of global elites.

1.4.5 Product standardization or customization?

It seems that consumer purchasing patterns are becoming similar across the world. The US purchasing patterns are followed by others. However, the emergence of a global consumer culture implies a certain standard to follow. This standard means that (1) the same product is offered to everybody, everywhere, all the time; and (2) the product's quality is also the same. This standardization has four benefits: (1) it implies efficiency of production and delivery to a consumer; (2) it allows for quantification based on measured criteria; (3) it guarantees predictability (the consumer has access to the same product across different places and times); and (4) it guarantees the following of strict production and delivery rules, and allows for control. This standardized consumption pattern has often been criticized for not being good and useful to people in all cultures. The meaning of standardization and its implications for the consumer might differ in various cultures. For example, the fast-food concept and product standardization have been successfully adopted in the People's Republic of China, where consumers praise shorter waiting time and fast service. However, it has been received with criticism in France, where consumers seek distinctiveness and identity.

The issue of standardization has been debated in the American market context, mostly. The United States is the ultimate example of a homogenous country where one finds the same types of hotels, shops, fast-food restaurants, etc., all over the country. The country does not have cultural differences shaped by many centuries of inhibited communication and exchange between different regions (Wierenga et al., 1996). Since global consumers increasingly follow the American consumption patterns, shopping malls, hotels, airports, banks, and even gambling casinos are quickly becoming indistinguishable, whether they are in the Americas, Australia, Europe, or Asia. Only the world religions, languages, and currencies continue to show major differences among nations. It is possible, however, that these differences will also disappear. Fortunately, evidence suggests that cultural differences between regions of the United States are significantly increasing instead of diminishing (Kahle, 1986).

1.4.6 Cultural heterogenization?

Some believe that the process of globalization has led to a culture of heterogenization. Heterogeneity is developed through an increasing emphasis on local cultural elements, such as language, education, religion, traditions, art and crafts, food, shared history, or the role of family. These elements are created and brought by the arrival of different people from a wide variety of cultural backgrounds. As a result, people become exposed to various cultures and are made increasingly aware of their differences.

However, the process of cultural heterogenization is limited. Global foreign brands, theme parks, films, and television programs have different meanings and impacts in the world. The American soap operas are interpreted very differently among Japanese, Israelis, Algerians, and Americans (Liebes & Katz, 1990). Likewise, the Western clothes, soft drinks, cigarettes, liquor, films, and books that flooded Eastern and Central European countries significantly differed from the ethnic clothing and foods, and thus were not always popular on the local markets.

One may also argue that the processes of cultural homogenization and heterogenization occur simultaneously, albeit at different levels. The homogenization of the consumption patterns occurs at the international level, whereas the efforts to maintain cultural uniqueness and distinctiveness occur more at the regional and local level.

1.4.7 Cultural convergence or divergence?

The concepts of cultural homogenization and heterogenization have led to two theories, one claiming that the world's cultures are converging and others diverging. The first theory claims that since the world is under pressure to become global and more homogenized, it converges to commonality. As more and more people cross national borders, trade goods and assets, and exchange ideas and cultures, the planet is getting smaller, and its cultures are converging (mainly economically and technologically). The second theory claims that the flows of goods, assets, and knowledge are directed towards the main centers of capital and knowledge only. Societies that do not have access to electronic technology and cannot communicate with each other across the globe remain uninformed and thus lack accurate and adequate knowledge of the world. As a result, according to Burns, these societies and their cultures are diverging (mainly in social relations) (cited in Wahab & Cooper, 2003).

1.4.8 Cultural hybridization?

There are also arguments that increasing interconnections between people and places have caused the partial convergence of cultures and led to new forms of culture called *cultural hybridization* (Meethan, 2001). Cultural hybridization implies the incorporation of cultural elements from a variety of sources within particular cultural practices.

For example, the McDonald's in Moscow mixes an American fast-food restaurant into a Russian market. American students living in Toronto eat at a Vietnamese restaurant. Japanese women wearing kimonos use the bank's automated teller machines. Cultural hybridization can develop through migration or bio-cultural marriages allowing for the combination of two identities, two languages, and two cultures. Hybridization is the solution to cultural polarization (homogenization versus heterogenization). Hybridization allows for movement and negotiations between the cultures.

1.4.9 Cultural commoditization?

As a result of globalization and the attempt to respond to tourists' demands for cultural experiences, culture is often commoditized and transformed into a new form (commodity) in order to sell it. Cultural commoditization is done by creating inauthentic cultural artifacts, specifically designed for tourist consumption, and adapting them to the needs of tourists. They are accepted by many tourists as being traditional cultural products. Many would argue that cultural commoditization is the worst effect of globalization on culture. Turning authentic cultural products into commercialized commodities for tourist consumption strips these products of their original quality and meanings; they have nothing to do with the traditional and genuine ways of their production and are far from the traditional way of life that produced them (Richards, 1996).

Although cultural commoditization is unavoidable, it is not necessarily a bad thing. Cultural commoditization can be the solution to local cultural deterioration. By becoming cultural artifacts for tourists, local products are recognized and traditional values enhanced. Cultural commoditization can be a means of cultural conservation and preservation, provided that local communities maintain control over their own products.

1.4.10 Cultural deterioration, loss, adaptation or change?

There is a belief that globalization has led to cultural commoditization and erosion of cultural forms. Since culture has been commodified and commercialized for the purpose of sale to mass tourists, many elements of culture have deteriorated and even significantly eroded. Also, the increasing contact between peoples from different cultures has caused some communities to change their local values and traditions. In fact, some communities have lost their traditional values by adapting to foreign values. As a result, pristine, genuine, and authentic elements of local culture have disappeared.

The development of new technology has become a major threat to cultural authenticity. The media and communication technology that created the demand for the unfamiliar have homogenized culture. For example, the development of tourism in Bali that generated demand for commodified forms of the local culture caused cultural pollution, disappearance of genuine local traditions, and a threat to the Balinese people. Likewise, the development of tourism in the Caribbean and Goa brought commoditization and deterioration of the local culture (Meethan, 2001).

Some argue that globalization has not homogenized and deteriorated culture. Increasing interconnections between people and places has caused the convergence of cultures and cultural change. Culture changed through cultural contacts, cultural borrowing, and adaptation. Cultural elements, both material and non-material, are being transformed between places, adjusted, and adapted for more localized forms of consumption. As a result, cultures have become so intermixed that there is no longer any pure or authentic culture distinct from others. For example, hybridization of culture has brought a loss of cultural ''purity'' and authenticity. Thus, one also can no longer assume that cultures are territorially bounded and self-contained wholes (Meethan, 2001).

However, the spread of globalization does not always have to cause a loss of cultural purity. In some regions culture adapts itself to foreign themes. The production of local products is adapted to tourist consumption. This is an example of cultural change (local consumption change through differentiation) but not an example of a loss of cultural authenticity or purity through commoditization (Meethan, 2001).

1.4.11 Is consumerism a bad thing for tourism?

One of the universal results of globalization is consumerism, defined by an increasing demand for high consumption of a variety of products and services. Consumerism affects tourists by exposing them to the attitudes of the consumer-oriented society, with its modern, urban lifestyle, expectations of high service levels, and an understanding that everything is for sale. It is often believed that consumerism destroys culture and generates environmental and social problems such as congestion, overcrowding, and queues at attractions, museums, and restaurants. For example, the overwhelming influx of tourists in Venice has produced a growing number of negative environmental and social impacts. Venice is essentially ''full'' of tourists. The invasion of visitors in St. Mark's Basilica has caused serious damage to the frescos through the condensation of the visitors' breath. Also, the stones underfoot have been worn away by the stream of visitors. However, these environmental problems are often accepted by tourists and seen as being an important part of their experience (Richards, 1996).

Tourist consumption does not necessarily have to destroy culture. High tourism consumption creates high demand for cultural preservation and conservation. Tourism consumption revitalizes local traditions and authenticity, promotes cultural awareness, and creates new systems of values and power. One must only know which elements of culture are for sale and tourist consumption, which are not, and which need to be preserved.

1.4.12 Globalization and disappearance of local identity?

McLeod (2004) believes that globalization destroys socio-cultural identity of the local community and its native values, traditions, and way of life. Today, the land and sea are often acquired by developers who turn farms and fishing centers into tourist resorts, and cut off fields and forests to build apartments and commercial centers. Modern hotels, expressways, and bridges lack the previous local uniqueness and appeal. Everything that initially attracted tourism, such as the beauty of the landscape, peacefulness, or isolation, including the qualities of life, are gradually eroded by tourism developments and the faster pace of life. Fishermen become shopkeepers and tour guides, young women seek financial independence and emotional liberation, locals reinterpret traditional roles and events, and all follow different patterns of life and values. The meaning of local culture is dissolving. Tourists now go fishing in ''real'' fishing boats while fishermen work in supermarkets, and locals eat ''local'' dishes in modern restaurants while watching themselves performing traditional dances in promotional videos (McLeod, 2004). This results in locals becoming alienated from their natural and local surrounding. With the increasing influx of foreigners, new technology, and modern lifestyles, opportunities for maintaining local identities become smaller and even disappearing. Also, as more infrastructure and apartments are built, and locals follow global life patterns, the experiences of visitors and locals are getting lower. Consequently, globalization and tourism development destroys local identities, the quality of tourism, and tourism itself (McLeod, 2004).

1.4.13 Resistance to cultural change and emergence of local identity

There is growing evidence of local resistance to the forces of globalization that have destroyed local cultures. In Europe, which is culturally very fragmented, the process of resistance to global cultural influences is in progress. European countries pay particular attention to their cultural identities, origins of artists, rituals, art works, buildings, and even whole landscapes. Cultural differences are increasingly emphasized. Cultural differences are what attract tourists to a particular place. The most attractive are the differences that are unique, authentic, and place bound. Thus, in an increasingly globalized and culturally homogenized world, there is a growing need to establish local difference. However, the degree of difference must not be too great because it would cause disturbance and friction between the local population and tourists.

Local resistance to globalization also gives rise to nationalism. Through the means of mass communication and increased social contacts, people and nations realize that they can strive for cultural sovereignty and identity. Individual communities often fight for their cultural recognition, history, and distinct qualities. For example, despite the European Union's increasing involvement in the lives of its countries and an increasing number of arrivals of foreign nationals, European countries have not lost their identities and sense of themselves (McLeod, 2004). Numerous European communities guard their national borders and currencies and preserve culture and language. It is hoped that the national identities of many European communities will not disappear. According to Hall (1990), it is not likely that globalization destroys national identity of distinct communities. People will search for local roots and go to various lengths to preserve the national, state, community, and individual values.

1.4.14 Glocalization

One of the important means of preserving local/regional identity is *glocalization*. Glocalization represents a blend of globalization and localization, and it means that globalization is adapted to local conditions (Robertson, 1995). One example of glocalization is the Moscow McDonald's that varies from its American counterparts by catering to Moscow's consumers. Although McDonald's is an increasingly global corporation, it survives only by catering to local tastes and needs. Another example of glocalization is global advertising of goods and services differentiated for local markets and consumers. The success of such glocalization depends on the in-depth understanding of the target markets and their expectations.

It is often argued that it is not so much cultural homogenization, but a global localization that develops as a result of globalization. McDonaldization does not represent a form of cultural homogenization; rather, it is a form of intercultural hybridization (intermingling between cultures). Firms like McDonald's have abandoned product standardization and developed marketing and product strategies that are as numerous as the variations of consumer demands in different markets.

Glocalization is the result of the relationships between the global and the local. These relationships allow the global and the local to reinforce and complement each other rather than compete with each other. Although markets, customers, and products may be global in many contexts, they are local in their designs and content.

1.4.15 Local internationalization and regional cooperation

Another important means of preserving local identity as well as differentiation in a global tourism market is local internationalization and regional cooperation that promote direct investment, lower transportation and transaction costs, and reduced production and distribution costs through developing economies of scale. Local internationalization and cooperation facilitates and secures regional economic development and competitiveness. For example, in East Asia a number of regional growth areas have been established to maximize cross-border movements of goods, services, and human capital; to attract investment and technology; and to compete with much larger countries, such as China and India. Similarly, Europe and North America established sub-regional growth. According to Hall, examples in North America include cross-border relations between the United States, Canada, and Mexico (cited in Wahab & Cooper, 2003). These sub-regional areas not only provide a more competitive environment, but also allow the regions to develop their own uniqueness and distinctiveness.

1.5 BENEFITS AND LIMITATIONS OF GLOBALIZATION IN TOURISM

Globalization has brought great benefits to tourism. For example, globalization has increased trade, capital, and human flows; generated growth; and created thousands of jobs in developed and emerging economies. Globalization has boosted the development and progress of the tourism industry by encouraging investments in new tourism infrastructure, particularly in underdeveloped regions, and improving their positioning in the international market. Globalization has raised incomes of consumers, as well as the quality of their material life in terms of increased product choice (Saee, 2005). Tourism has benefited from globalization by following global principles of socio-economic, ecological, and culturally sustainable development, thus contributing to the betterment of the world as a place in which to live and work. However, globalization has also polarized the world. Developing countries have little influence on global institutions and their activities. Globalization largely benefits advanced societies and creates new forms of colonial control. World trade is responsible for uncontrolled environmental problems. Globalization continually invades the biosystem. Developing nations that believe they have a right to their natural resources build factories that pollute the air and water. Globalization in tourism also means standardization of a tourism product and the loss of national, regional, and local character. Globalization helps to create homogenous tourist resorts, food and beverage establishments, theme parks, and events, thereby erasing local standards. It offers impersonal service standards, superficial communication, and poor content. Globalization causes the loss of competitive advantage; it renders a tourism product standardized and unrecognizable, and can even make it disappear. For this reason tourism destinations have to differentiate themselves from others clearly and follow strict local cultural standards, balanced with the global service standards that customers have come to expect.

Supporters of globalization assume that benefits associated with globalization far outweigh the perceived drawbacks. Generally, globalization has been beneficial to nearly all countries around the world, resulting in increased real living standards, as measured by per capita GDP. No nation can afford to ignore it since it can be beneficial to nations involved in international trade (Saee, 2005).

1.6 CHALLENGES OF GLOBALIZATION IN TOURISM

Globalization presents the world and the tourism industry with a new set of challenges. The most important is that businesses operating in foreign host countries with different cultural, political, economic, technological, and legal practices must adapt to the local environments. Practices and strategies that are perfectly acceptable in one country can be taboo in another country. Complexities of globalization call for understanding and accommodating different worldviews, variations in employers' business practices, and differences in national cultures of employees and consumers. Global tourism managers and marketers must develop high levels of intercultural communication and competencies and make appropriate adjustments to their business practices to suit a particular international environment. Global tourism managers must effectively deal with communication difficulties, control legal and political decisions. They must accommodate the structure and composition of the workforce and its requirements to culturally different business practices. They must develop international human resources policies; provide cross-cultural raining in the accommodation, transportation, and catering sectors; and develop awareness of the different cultural norms, for example, in work and leisure patterns, health, safety and occupational standards, as well as hiring, dismissal, discrimination, and workers' rights.

Employees' worldviews and attitudes toward work will vary, as will consumers' needs and preferences. To accommodate their employees and customers, global managers and marketers must therefore learn about cultural differences in religions, customs, work ethics, languages, and behavioral codes and standards. For example, when McDonald's entered India, its menu had to accommodate the cultural tastes of locals.

Globalization has also created new challenges for destination marketing. Cultural differentiation, market disaggregation, and segmentation – not cultural convergence and market aggregation – are important future targeting tools that will determine destination competitiveness. Global tourism marketers must become aware of the cultural needs of particular markets and use the knowledge of these needs to develop destination marketing plans for international tourists. Marketers must distinguish between global, international, and sub-national cultures, and differentiate their approach to destination marketing accordingly. Destinations must create unique cultural identities that differentiate themselves from other destinations in the global marketplace.

Also, since tomorrow's global consumers are today's children, the challenge will be to develop their interests in the local communities and pride in their identities. Today's children are familiar with the Internet and influenced by a variety of global advertising. They are accustomed to desiring global products such as McDonald's or Disney from an early age. Whether these children will follow traditional versus global values when they become older will depend on their intellectual, ethical, and practical reasons for protecting local cultures from globalization (Usunier cited in Swarbrooke & Horner, 2007). The challenge will be to develop their interest in the local environment and pride in own cultural identity.

1.7 THE FUTURE OF GLOBALIZATION: AMERICANIZATION OF CULTURE, COSMOPOLITAN CULTURE, CULTURAL HYBRIDIZATION, CULTURAL DISAPPEARANCE OR CULTURE CLASH?

The term "globalized world" often refers to a "global village" and suggests that the world in which we live is a peaceful place where people live together and follow commonly accepted rules that help them organize their lives. However, DeSebastian (2005) argued that globalization is not a peaceful, orderly, equitable process. The world is without law and order, dominated by the influence of the United States, the largest and strongest economy in the world, with the best technology, most well equipped universities, and unparalleled expertise. American consumerism has changed values and patterns of peoples' behavior; the societies which were integrated and lived peacefully have begun to follow American patterns of consumption. This increased demand for self-conscious consumption has brought acts of violence, kidnapping, looting, assault, and drug trafficking. It has created tension between what globalization offers and what the lower classes are capable of actually obtaining (DeSebastian, 2005).

The power of the American film industry – Hollywood images, music, and fashion – pervades the whole world and generates an identity crisis among the poor nations. Millions of people reject the good elements of their own cultures to follow the American way of life and its modern culture. Many risk losing their identities; they do not know who they really are or where they belong. For this reason, many people resent the power, world dominance, and influence of US culture on other cultures (DeSebastian, 2005).

However, the strong associations of globalization with Americanization of culture might be overstated. There still remain strong cultural relationships between the former colonizing nations (e.g. the United Kingdom and France) and their former colonies (e.g. India and French-speaking Africa). Also, although Americanization of culture is criticized and rejected by many, it seems that Indonesianization may be more worrisome than Americanization, as Japanization may be for the Koreans, Indianization for Sri Lankans, and Vietnamization for Cambodians (Huntington, 1996).

Moreover, although globalization spreads American culture throughout the world, the United States does not represent a cultural power or a world culture with which all others are homogenized. There are multiple cultural powers, not one strong, dominant culture in the world. A real global culture is a cosmopolitan culture that represents a symbiosis of all elements of the many other existing cultures (DeSebastian, 2005). The creation of a cosmopolitan culture implies, however, accepting cultural differences and a common universe of difference. Cultural hybridization, that creates transcontextual and less cosmopolitan cultural forms, rather than globalization may facilitate this process. Since different cultures are transcontextual (not cosmopolitan) and intermixed, there is not and will no longer be any pure or authentic culture that is distinct from others.

If the world does not respect all cultures and the process of hybridization does not develop on a larger scale, the process of globalization will continue. As a result, we may experience a separation and even disappearance of certain cultures. Cultures that are the weakest and most vulnerable, such as small Indian populations in the Amazon, Mexico, the Patagonia, and other remote parts of Latin America, Aborigines in the Pacific, or the pigmies in Central Africa, might be gradually eradicated from the face of the earth. The modern communication and technology will not reach them. They will be cut off from markets, and their societies will gradually die out. In addition, if ethnic minorities are excluded from advances in science and disconnected from progress, their cultural biodiversity might also suffer (Huntington, 2003).

It is also likely there will be a clash of major cultures or even civilizations. The beginnings of this are already taking place in the world today (Huntington, 2003). The weak cultures that are unable to compete due to a lack of opportunities or education, will feel threatened, overpowered by wealth and the rich life of the strong cultures. As a result, they would like to free themselves from the influence of the global consumption and fight for social and economic justice.

In summary, if cultural homogenization is occurring, it is not an Americanization of the cultural world. Other Western and non-Western cultures have risen to cultural powers. Too great a focus is placed on the Western hemisphere as shaping the rest of the world. If the world is to survive, we must represent and accept various powers and we must see it as multicultural.

SUMMARY

Globalization has important economic, cultural, social, environmental, political, and technological dimensions. Although numerous benefits of globalization have been identified, globalization is perceived by some as discriminatory and moving against human rights. In tourism, globalization has opened new opportunities for growth through the developments in electronic technology, communication, and transportation. Globalization has brought changes to the tourist profile, created preferences for new products and generated demand for new experiences. A new type of tourist with new values and worldviews has emerged. A new approach to destination marketing which focuses on more targeted and customized products is required.

It is argued that in the new global marketplace, consumers have become increasingly similar in their consumption patterns. However, many believe that there is a fundamental disparity in their value systems and lifestyle such that global consumption patterns do not exist. The truly global consumption patterns and global consumers occur in a genuine global world only. There are and will be cultural differences among consumers from different countries. In fact, evidence suggests that cultural differences among countries and regions are significantly increasing.

There are also arguments that increasing interconnections between people and places creates the convergence of cultures and leads to cultural hybridization, which implies a loss of cultural ''purity'' and authenticity. One of the worst effects of globalization on culture is cultural commoditization; culture is modified for tourist consumption and transformed into a new inauthentic form in order to sell it. However, tourist consumption does not necessarily destroy culture; high tourism consumption creates demand for culture preservation, conservation, and revitalization of local traditions. It is also argued that globalization destroys local identity and native values As a result, there is growing local resistance to globalization and a need for establishing local differences. Glocalization represents a means of preserving local identity; globalization is adapted to local conditions.

Globalization presents new challenges in tourism. Priorities include understanding and accommodating different worldviews and cultural differences among consumers and employees, and developing intercultural communication competencies to suit a particular international environment. The cultural approach to destination marketing, and in particular cultural market disaggregation and segmentation, are important targeting tools.

Although American consumerism has changed values and patterns of peoples' behavior around the world, the strong associations of globalization with Americanization of culture is overstated. The United States does not represent a cultural power or world culture; there are multiple cultural powers. If the world is to survive, we must accept it as being multicultural. A real global culture is a cosmopolitan culture; a symbiosis of all elements of the many other existing cultures which accepts cultural differences and a common universe of difference.

DISCUSSION POINTS AND QUESTIONS

1. Critically discuss the advantages and disadvantages of globalization for the nations involved in globalization.
2. To what extent has the Internet affected globalization?
3. What does it mean to be truly global in tourism?
4. What impact does globalization have on tourists and their consumption patterns?
5. Why has marketing to international tourists become an opportunity and challenge?
6. Do you agree that the global consumer exists? Develop arguments for the emergence of a global consumer and identify reasons against it.
7. What impact does globalization have on local cultures?
8. Do changes brought by globalization lead to the eradication of cultural differences and the replacement of cultural heterogeneity with a global culture characterized by homogeneity?
9. Does the process of globalization lead to cultural heterogenization or homogenization? What are the pros and cons for cultural homogenization versus heterogenization?
10. To what extent should cultural products be commoditized and to what extent should local communities retain control over their own culture?
11. What is the impact of globalization on destination marketing?
12. What is the future of globalization? Do you think the world will continue to be dominated by the influence of the United States?

CASE STUDY 1.1 The Emergence of a Global Tourist Culture? Disneyland Resorts Spread Over the World

Over the years Walt Disney Co. has tried to apply global tourism and global consumption patterns to its theme parks. It has attempted to ''Disneyize'' society and promote the mass consumption of its products. However, mass consumption does not mean a global consumer culture.

The spread of Disney resorts throughout the world started fifty years ago with the launch of the concept in California. Since then four more attraction parks have been built around the world. The launch of the Hong Kong Park represented an attempt to reach the Chinese market and reinforced the idea that the company could be successful everywhere because international tourists would adapt to the product. Disneyland has become a ''top of mind awareness'' attraction park and is now part of the culture of every tourist in the world.

Disneyland has penetrated different countries in terms of culture. With the increasing brand consciousness in people's minds, Disneyland has become a destination by itself. The global culture has led tourists to buy the concept rather than the product itself; tourists became attached to the concept more than to its concrete application. Such behavior was in line with Disney's initial idea: to sell the same concept everywhere. However, tourists did not react in the same way to the product concept as to the product itself. International tourists were not completely adapted to the Disneyland product; parks and resorts had to be developed to suit the tourists' needs. The Disney company made an effort to adapt to tourists' cultural needs. For example, in Hong Kong the company did not build Western-style attractions because they were not part of the Chinese culture. The existing attractions were also managed differently. It was believed that tourists who enjoyed Disneyland in California might not enjoy Disneyland in Hong Kong to the same degree; the former would react differently in Hong Kong. For example, Disneyland in Paris was not appreciated as much as Disneyland in Tokyo. While Disneyland in Paris suffered from a bad image, long waits, and language problems (only French was spoken), Disneyland in Tokyo was perceived as being clean and customer friendly. Tokyo's lines were short, and English was spoken. Since tourists demanded more tailor-made experiences, had more diverse needs and tastes, and no longer wanted mass-standardized and rigidly packaged vacations, Disneyland resorts provided them with a broader range of products, each for different customer groups (e.g. hotels of every possible category, restaurants with different types of food, and different attractions adapted to every age).

Although Disney's concept can be sold everywhere in the world, the product must be sold in different ways. Although the global tourist culture emerged, every park has had to adapt its product to the specific needs of consumers.

WEBSITE LINKS

1. Mass customization in the hospitality industry: Concepts and applications, http://www.hotel-online.com
2. Definitions of globalization, http://www.infed.org/biblio/defining_globalization. htm
3. Accor Hotels, http://www.accor.com/gb
4. Amadeus, http://www.amadeus.com
5. TUI, http://www.tui-group.com/en

Since in globalized world the tourism industry will hire more workers and serve more guests from diverse cultural backgrounds, the next chapter will discuss the concept of cultural diversity and its importance to the tourism industry.

Cultural diversity

2

This chapter explains the concept of cultural diversity and how it can enrich people and organizations and provide competitive advantage for tourism businesses.

OBJECTIVES

After completing this chapter the reader should be able to:
- Understand the concept of cultural diversity
- Learn how cultural diversity enriches a tourism business environment and provides it with competitive advantage
- Understand why managing a multicultural workforce in the tourism and hospitality industry presents both opportunities and challenges

INTRODUCTION

In a globalized world, hotels, restaurants, and travel organizations will hire more workers and serve more customers from diverse cultural backgrounds. Understanding those who are culturally different will present a global challenge to the tourism and hospitality companies that compete in a global marketplace. This chapter explains the concept of cultural diversity and its importance to the tourism industry.

2.1 THE CONCEPT OF CULTURAL DIVERSITY

2.1.1 Definition

The concept of *cultural diversity* can be defined in numerous ways. Cultural diversity is most often referred to as

- The variety of human groups, societies, or cultures in a specific region, or in the world as a whole
- The mosaic of individuals and groups with varying backgrounds, characteristics, values, beliefs, customs, and traditions
- Differences in race, ethnicity, nationality, religion, or language among various groups within a community, organization, or nation
- The variety or multiformity of human social structures, belief systems, and strategies for adapting to situations in different parts of the world.

Culturally diverse groups of people can be small and limited to one country only. However, these groups can also be large, encompass varieties of people, and extend over large geographical areas with numerous nations and cultures. Different races, ethnic groups, languages, and religions can be found among people living in these areas. For example, a wide variety of people with different characteristics, religions and beliefs can be found in the United States: African-Americans, Native Americans, Caucasians, Hispanics, Middle Easterners, Asian-Pacific Islanders, Koreans, and Chinese Americans, to name but a few. All these people have their identities and ways of life, speak different languages, and have different experiences. A wide variety of subcultures can also be found in India, China, Asia, Australia, Europe, and Canada. Culturally different behaviors and values of locals encountered in these countries reflect a wide cultural diversity.

In the United States, one third of the most populous counties are occupied by various groups of people classified as multicultural or multiethnic. Currently, the largest sites of multicultural groups in the United States are large international cities, such as Chicago (with Asian populations), Washington (with Hispanic populations), and Houston (with African-American populations). The other large sites of multiethnic groups are fast-growing suburbs. The new wave of multicultural immigration spread to the suburbs and transformed them into so-called ''majority minority'' places. Hispanic people, in particular, are increasingly attracted to areas outside major metropolitan centers because of job opportunities and lower costs of living. While between 2000 and 2006, the total population in small towns and rural areas increased by 3%, the Hispanic population in these counties grew by 22%, from 2.6 million to 3.2 million. The largest increases in Hispanic population were noted in Los Angeles and Riverside, California; Dallas and Houston, Texas; and New York.

Although African-American populations declined in New Orleans, San Francisco, Los Angeles, San Diego, and New York, the biggest increases were noted in Atlanta, Houston, Dallas, Miami, and Washington. The growth in Atlanta, Houston, and Dallas was partially attributed to the influx of refugees from Hurricane Katrina. The highest growth rates among Asian populations were experienced in Napa, California; and Ocala, Naples, Cape Coral, and Port St. Lucie, Florida. The greatest numerical increases were in New York, Los Angeles, Washington, San Francisco, and Chicago (http://diversityspectrum.com/index.php?option=com_news_portal&task=section&id=16&Itemid=1038).

These trends indicate that the United States is a very diverse country in terms of human cultures. The minority cultural groups are increasingly spreading across the continent, making it one of the most culturally diverse countries in the world.

Considerable differences are also recognized in peoples' physical characteristics, social class, economic status, age, and even gender. A wide variety of people of different demographic and socio-economic characteristics can be found in every country or region of the world. The large differences among people indicate that they do not represent a homogenous group; rather, they belong to different groups with different characteristics. There are hundreds of millions of people in the world who claim to belong to one or even more than one specific group of people. For example, one can claim to be Caucasian, European, Catholic, female, Irish, middle class, and young.

There are also significant variations among people depending upon the way societies organize themselves, that is, in their conception of morality, ethics, freedom, and loyalty, and in the way they interact with their environment and show concern for its resources. Some of these differences arise from human migration, and some are products of human evolution. This book examines the variety of people in terms of the differences in their cultural backgrounds; it does not examine differences in peoples' physical characteristics, or their demographic or socio-economic characteristics. The book focuses solely on the cultural diversity of human groups.

2.1.2 Interpretation of cultural diversity

The concept of cultural diversity has different meanings and interpretations because culture is differently defined by various nations and ethnic groups. The modern anthropological definition of culture refers to common knowledge, perceptions, and values that constitute the foundation of social, economic, and religious institutions in a society (Svanberg & Runblom, 1988). According to this definition, culture is a historically formed system of meanings that gives significance and direction to peoples' lives. Peoples' customs, food, dress, traditions, and perceptions of the world give their life meaning. Since culture has no national borders, those customs can differ between and within social communities, between generations, and even between men and women. This means a person can have multiple cultural identities and belong to different cultural subgroups. Since there are hundreds of millions of people in the world who claim to belong to different cultural groups, their interpretations of culture and what cultural diversity means differs from one to another. Consequently, the differences between people indicate that people are not homogenous; rather, there are groups of different individuals with different characteristics.

The term cultural diversity is sometimes used to refer to multiculturalism (http://en.wikipedia.org/wiki/Cultural_diversity). *Multiculturalism* is an ideology advocating that society should consist of, or at least allow and include, distinct cultural and religious groups, with equitable status. Some countries have official multiculturalism policies aimed at preserving the cultural identities of immigrant groups. In this context, multiculturalism advocates a society that extends equitable status to distinct cultural and religious groups, no one culture predominating. However, the term is more commonly used to describe a society consisting of minority immigrant cultures existing alongside a predominant, indigenous culture. Often, multiculturalism is interchangeably used with the term *interculturalism*. Which term is used depends on what language is spoken by the people. For example, English-speaking European researchers usually use the term multicultural, while non-English-speaking researchers use the term intercultural (Gundara, 2000). It is also argued that multicultural describes the nature of the society whose members are from different ethnic and religious groups, while intercultural describes their interactions, negotiations, and processes. Another view is that intercultural refers to two culturally different groups of people, and multicultural refers to more than two culturally different groups of people. Therefore, the term multicultural is acceptable when referring to multiple cultures.

2.1.3 How did the concept of cultural diversity develop?

There is a consensus among anthropologists that since humans first emerged in Africa about 2 million years ago, they spread throughout the world, adapting to different conditions and climate changes. As a result, many separate societies, significantly different from each other, emerged around the globe. Many of the differences among these societies persist to this day.

2.1.4 How does one measure cultural diversity?

Cultural diversity is difficult to measure. A good indication of cultural diversity is the number of races, nationalities, religions, and languages spoken in a region or in the world. For example, by using the language measure, one can notice that the world's cultural diversity is declining. Less than 10% of the languages currently spoken in the world will still be spoken in 100 years' time. One language becomes extinct every two weeks (David Crystal, Honorary Professor of Linguistics at the University of Wales, Bangor). The reasons for this decline in languages are immigration and imperialism. International organizations, such as Survival International and United Nations Educational, Scientific and Cultural Organization (UNESCO), work towards protecting threatened societies and cultures, and preserving and promoting cultural diversity and intercultural dialog.

2.1.5 Is cultural diversity important?

Cultural diversity is vital for the long-term survival of humanity on earth. According to UNESCO, the conservation of many different cultures and, in particular, indigenous cultures, is as important to humankind as the conservation of species and ecosystems to life. However, this argument is rejected for several reasons. First, it is argued that the importance of cultural diversity for survival cannot be proved or disproved. Second, it is unethical to preserve "less developed" societies and their cultures, because this denies their members the access and benefits of technological developments and medical advances enjoyed by those in the "developed" world. Finally, there are many people with strong religious beliefs who are convinced that it is in the best interests of individuals and humanity to reduce cultural diversity and support only one model of society to which all other societies would conform.

2.1.6 The benefits of cultural diversity

By paying attention to the cultural differences in their workforce, a company can raise their levels of comfort and capitalize on employees' different skills and abilities as a major asset to the company's productivity. The wider the range of cultural differences in the workplace, the richer the organization and the more excellent its performance. The ability to utilize cultural differences and manage cultural diversity can provide the company with competitive advantage. Cultural diversity stimulates greater innovation, creativity, and responsiveness to consumer demands and changing environments. It also contributes to the reputation of the work place and more effective competition.

The ability to attract and manage cultural diversity can also develop greater sensitivity to, and satisfaction from, different consumer markets. Product development proposed by people from different cultures is more likely to be successful among the wider variety of consumers and suit the different tastes of consumers than when it is proposed by people from a single culture. People from different cultures are more likely to understand the needs of different consumers and fulfill these needs. Products that meet the different needs of consumers draw consumer attention and generate higher demand.

2.1.7 The influence of cultural diversity on tourism and hospitality

Because of cultural differences, the management of companies operating in the global tourism and hospitality environment might have trouble relating to their employees' work style, expectations, and ethics. Problems may arise because of a lack of communication and differences in work style and ethics. Someone's values and beliefs may preclude the understanding of others' behavior and attitudes. Many of the misunderstandings among people from culturally diverse groups may be due to ethnocentrism, which is assigning primacy to one's own culture and assessing others according to it. Ethnocentrism and limited knowledge about another's culture may prevent objective assessment and understanding of culturally different people. This lapse can pose serious consequences for the work environment.

In order to manage culturally different employees and attract culturally different customer markets, it is necessary to know the surrounding culture of that employee and consumer, learn their established cultural practices, and understand why they act the way they do.

In tourism and hospitality, cultural misunderstanding often occurs when delivering services to customers. Often customers are disappointed with service because of their cultural bias. For example, a European traveler to the United States does not want a glass of water to be totally filled with ice cubes, and an American traveler get frustrated when traveling in Europe if her/his glass of soda contains only two ice cubes! Cultural misunderstanding may affect service staff, as well: American waiters may develop negative attitudes toward European tourists who do not tip. In Europe, tipping is usually not practiced; a 15–20% gratuity is always included in the check. European travelers need to be reminded about the practice of tipping in the United States, and US providers need to be explained the different tipping practices in Europe. ''To forget to tip'' may create bad impressions of European tourists in the United States and negatively affect guest–host social relations. Likewise, to demand a tip from European customers may also create a bad impression of American providers.

Many of the cultural mistakes can be avoided if tourists, locals, and industry professionals are made aware of the cultural differences among them. Since quality of the social contact between customers and employees influences customers' perception of service quality and their ultimate satisfaction with the product, tourism and hospitality representatives should pay increasing attention to managing cultural differences in personal relations between providers and customers. Being aware of the cultural differences and learning how to face and manage them will be one of the keys to success in the future tourism marketplace. The following two examples present the strategies implemented by two European organizations to better satisfy Chinese tourists.

In 2005, over 31 million Chinese traveled abroad. Maison de La France, the French National Tourism Organization, commissioned a study to determine France's potential as a destination for Chinese tourists. The study suggested that France was the top overseas country in terms of intention to visit in the next five years. Realizing the challenge that numerous Chinese travelers would present to hospitality businesses, Maison de la France published a practical handbook titled *Les touristes chinois: Comment bien les accueillir? (How to properly welcome Chinese tourists)* that was made available to various tourism-related businesses intent on attracting and satisfying this new market segment. This handbook presents some very practical advice to help tourism professionals satisfy Chinese travelers.

Anticipating growing demand from Chinese travelers, Accor, the leading European hotel company, implemented a product-development strategy for its European hotels: Accor put in place various training strategies for its hotel managers, chefs, and staff so that they could better understand and respond to Chinese travelers' specific needs and expectations. For hotels that wanted to go further and be recognized as ''Chinese friendly,'' Accor proposed a ''Chinese Optimum Service Standard'' certification. Those hotels provide Chinese-speaking staff, Chinese newspaper, Chinese TV channel, hot water point or a kettle in the room, and Chinese breakfast with rice soup and noodles.

2.2 UNESCO *UNIVERSAL DECLARATION ON CULTURAL DIVERSITY*

In 1945, UNESCO recognized the importance of cultural diversity. One of its missions is to encourage mutual knowledge and understanding between peoples by promoting the free flow of ideas, encouraging education, and spreading culture and knowledge. The UNESCO Universal Declaration on Cultural Diversity states that intercultural dialog and respect for cultural diversity and tolerance are essential to building world peace. The Declaration recognizes that globalization, together with rapid advances in information and communication technologies, presents a threat to cultural diversity but also creates conditions for dialog among cultures and civilizations.

The Declaration was adopted in Paris in 2001. It lays down general guidelines on how to live in a more open, creative and democratic world. The Declaration raises cultural diversity to the level of humanity's common heritage, which is a source of exchange, innovation, and creativity, and is as essential for humankind as biodiversity is for nature. According to the Declaration, cultural diversity should be protected for the survival of humanity and the benefit of both present and future generations, and should be considered a basic human right. According to the Declaration, cultural diversity is a process that must guarantee and prevent segregation and fundamentalism. Each individual must acknowledge the plurality of his or her own identity within societies that are themselves plural. Cultural products and services are the symbols of identity, values, and meaning, and must not be treated as commodities or consumer goods. Cultural diversity is expressed through cultural industries and can be a strong contributor to sustainable development. According to the Director General of UNESCO, Mr Matsuura (2001), the Declaration is an outstanding tool for development, capable of humanizing globalization. Below are some statements from 11 articles of the Declaration.

Article 1 – Cultural diversity: the common heritage of humanity

Culture takes diverse forms across time and space. This diversity is embodied in the uniqueness and plurality of the identities of the groups and societies making up humankind. As a source of exchange, innovation and creativity, cultural diversity is as necessary for human kind as biodiversity is for nature. In this sense, it is the common heritage of humanity and should be recognized and affirmed for the benefit of present and future generations.

Article 2 – From cultural diversity to cultural pluralism

In our increasingly diverse societies, it is essential to ensure harmonious interaction among people and groups with plural, varied and dynamic cultural identities as well as their willingness to live together.

Article 3 – Cultural diversity as a factor in development

Cultural diversity widens the range of options open to everyone; it is one of the roots of development, understood not simply in terms of economic growth, but also as a means to achieve a more satisfactory intellectual, emotional, moral and spiritual existence.

Article 4 – Human rights as guarantees of cultural diversity

The defense of cultural diversity is an ethical imperative, inseparable from respect for human dignity. It implies a commitment to human rights and fundamental freedoms, in particular, the rights of persons belonging to minorities and those of indigenous peoples. No one may invoke cultural diversity to infringe upon human rights guaranteed by international law, nor to limit their scope.

Article 5 – Cultural rights as an enabling environment for cultural diversity

Cultural rights are an integral part of human rights, which are universal, indivisible and interdependent ... All persons have therefore the right to express themselves and to create and disseminate their work in the language of their choice, and particularly in their mother tongue; all persons are entitled to quality education and training that fully respect their cultural identity; and all persons have the right to participate in the cultural life of their choice and conduct their own cultural practices, subject to respect for human rights and fundamental freedoms.

Article 6 – Towards access for all to cultural diversity

While ensuring the free flow of ideas by word and image care should be exercised that all cultures can express themselves and make themselves known. Freedom of expression, media pluralism, multilingualism, equal access to art and to scientific and technological knowledge, including in digital form, and the possibility for all cultures to have access to the means of expression and dissemination are the guarantees of cultural diversity.

Article 7 – Cultural heritage as the wellspring of creativity

Heritage in all its forms must be preserved, enhanced and handed on to future generations as a record of human experience and aspirations, so as to foster creativity in all its diversity and to inspire genuine dialog among cultures.

Article 8 – Cultural goods and services: commodities of a unique kind

... particular attention must be paid to the diversity of the supply of creative work, to due recognition of the rights of authors and artists and to the specificity of cultural goods and services, which, as vectors of identity, values and meaning, must not be treated as mere commodities or consumer goods.

Article 9 – Cultural policies as catalysts of creativity

... cultural policies must create conditions conducive to the production and dissemination of diversified cultural goods and services through cultural industries that have the means to assert themselves at the local and global level.

Article 10 – Strengthening capacities for creation and dissemination worldwide

... it is necessary to reinforce international cooperation and solidarity aimed at enabling all countries, especially developing countries and countries in transition, to establish cultural industries that are viable and competitive at national and international level.

Article 11 – Building partnership between the public sector, the private sector and civil society

... promotion of cultural diversity ... is the key to sustainable human development.

2.3 **THE FUTURE OF CULTURAL DIVERSITY**

The importance of cultural diversity for global business will grow in significance. There are several reasons for this.

(1) Increasing multicultural work force. The tourism and hospitality industry is becoming global. Companies are diversifying and developing their operations abroad to expand their market possibilities. Many companies from the United Kingdom, Japan, and the United States send managers and executives to work overseas. Some countries that do not have the necessary skilled personnel locally send their hospitality managers to gain experience abroad.

(2) Growing international ownership. The increase in international ownership throughout the world, together with European economic integration, has resulted in increasing numbers of managers and employees working outside their native country. For example, in the last decade Japanese companies made significant purchases of US corporations, including hotel companies. Australia accounts for a significant amount of foreign direct investments overseas.

(3) Increasing migration. Many people migrated to other countries to improve their living conditions. For example, more than 2 million people from East and South East Asia have left home to work elsewhere in the region. Many have entered hospitality and tourism as flight attendants and cooks. Furthermore, it is estimated that up 500,000 Eastern Europeans may migrate each year. Thus, tourism and hospitality businesses will increasingly rely on employees who are of a different nationality and culture than those of existing managers or employees.

(4) Changes in demographics. Demographic projections indicate businesses in the United States will face a drastically different worker base beyond the year 2010. The workforce will grow more slowly, becoming older and comprising more females and minorities. Women, non-whites, and immigrants will comprise more than 50% of new additions to the workforce. The current proportion of an increasing ethnic and racial diversity in the United States is 72% white, 13% African-American, 11% Hispanic, 3% Asian, 1% Native American and Eskimo (2005). It is predicted that the Hispanic group will become the largest minority group in the United States by 2010. For example, the Hispanic population of Florida recently earned the right to use Spanish as an official language in governmental affairs. Currently, Hispanics represent more than 65% of Miami's population. The African-American group is expected to increase to up to 15% of the population. These proportions will dramatically increase in the next 20 years. Other minority groups, such as Asians, Pacific Islanders, and Native Americans will also grow in the next decades. The white, non-Hispanic population is not growing as fast as other groups. Consequently, the United States is moving towards a mix of cultural minorities with no majority. Moreover, some minorities will become new majorities.

The changing demographics, growing international ownership, increasing migration, and multiculturalism will have numerous repercussions for the structure and composition of the workforce. For example, in 2005 all minorities represented more than 50% of the total workforce. It has been predicted that the importance of women and Hispanics will significantly increase by 2020. In 2005 women constituted 48% of the US workforce; by 2020 they will represent 68% of the work force. Likewise, Hispanics represented 11% of the workforce in 2005 and will equal 14% by 2020. The contribution of Whites, non-Hispanics will decrease from 73% (2005) to 68% (2020) (see Table 2.1).

Table 2.1 US Labor Force

	Percentage 1995	Percentage 2005	Percentage 2020
Whites, non-Hispanic	76%	73%	68%
Women	46%	48%	68%
Hispanics	9%	11%	14%
African-Americans	11%	11%	11%
Asian-Americans	4%	5%	6%

Workforce 2020, Hudson Institute.

2.4 CHALLENGES FOR THE TOURISM AND HOSPITALITY INDUSTRY

A truly multinational organization is one that is able to utilize cultural diversity as its competitive advantage. Cultural diversity derives from human resources of different backgrounds, with different values and expectations. The challenge is to respond to the demographic trends in the workforce, understand the cultural background of the human diversity, and effectively utilize it to drive the company's profitability and competitiveness. Unfortunately, not many companies think about cultural differences as a source of competitive advantage. They utilize diversity mostly by integrating women and people of different ages into the workforce. Cultural diversity and the skills of multicultural and multiethnic groups are often ignored.

Cultural diversity cannot be ignored. Tourism and hospitality companies that operate in an international environment need to learn about their culturally diverse workforce and how to manage it. The effective management of culturally different people is of critical importance for the success of the tourism industry. Tourism managers must pay more attention to cultural human resources management.

Cultural diversity and differences in peoples' cultural orientation impact people's attitudes to innovation and learning, acceptance of failure, functioning in teams, evaluation of performance criteria, communication style, group affiliations, acceptance and use of technology, attitudes toward challenge, loyalty, and work and leisure ethics. Knowledge of the culture of the company's employees and customers is important to an understanding of how the employees and customers will behave and how to manage and market to them. Culture defines the appropriate behavior of different social groups, the roles their members play in the workplace, the relevance of social status, goals, and behavior that gain social approval, and ways of meeting the socially acceptable needs. Culture defines social rules, establishes conventions in terms what is appropriate and what is not, and affects peoples' orientation to time and activities.

The tourism and hospitality industries have to adapt to the multicultural environment of its workforce; otherwise the relationships between customers and employees may be threatened. For example, cultural differences in service expectations or communication may lead to frustrations among personnel and dissatisfaction among customers. Thus, training of employees in recognizing culturally different customers may be required.

Culturally different markets will be the future of the tourism and hospitality industry. Most of the tourists will be international tourists from different cultural backgrounds who are not always fluent in English. In particular, there will be an increasing number of travelers from Eastern Europe and Asia. Since these travelers represent a culturally diverse pool of potential customers, a cultural approach to marketing and providing services will be required. It will be imperative for tourism managers, supervisors, and other employees to understand how their clients differ. *Cultural competence* will be the key term for the future success of the tourism industry. Those with language skills other than English and cultural awareness and understanding will succeed. Opportunities should be given to people from different cultures and with languages other than English to teach the management of international markets.

In conclusion, the tourism and hospitality industry is people based. This is an industry run *by* people and *for* people. The real potential for the tourism and hospitality companies lies in their people. Each person's differences bring unique and special gifts to the organization. Cultural differences among employees and customers can make or break the industry. If the industry is to flourish in the future, the managers of tourism's multinational companies need to be flexible and adapt to the growing number of people from culturally diverse groups. Tourism industry representatives need to be able to identify unique individual and cultural skills and utilize them appropriately.

SUMMARY

A wide variety of people with different demographic, socio-cultural, and economic characteristics, religions, and beliefs live in different countries and continents. Differences in their behaviors and values reflect a wide cultural diversity in these countries and regions. In the United States, one third of the population is represented by multicultural or multiethnic groups of people. The three major ethnic groups living in the United States are African-Americans, Hispanics, and Asian-Americans. Cultural diversity often refers to multiculturalism, which describes the nature of a society whose members are from different ethnic and religious groups. Cultural diversity advocates equal status and rights for these groups.

Cultural diversity is important for the long-term survival of humankind on earth. Its importance has been recognized by UNESCO's *Universal Declaration on Cultural Diversity,* adopted in 2001. Cultural diversity brings numerous benefits to the workplace, including greater innovation, creativity, and responsiveness to consumer demands, increased productivity, and more effective competition. Cultural diversity determines management styles and practices of tourism and hospitality organizations. Knowledge of the culture of the company's employees and customers is important to understanding how they will behave and how to manage them.

The importance of cultural diversity for global business will grow in significance due to the increasing multicultural workforce and migration, growing international ownership, and changes in demographics and the structure and composition of the workforce. The major challenge for the tourism and hospitality industry is to utilize cultural diversity as its competitive advantage.

DISCUSSION POINTS AND QUESTIONS

1. What are the major reasons for increasing cultural diversity around the world?
2. Does the concept of cultural diversity mean the same as multiculturalism?
3. Why has managing an intercultural workforce in the tourism and hospitality industry become an opportunity?
4. Why has managing an intercultural workforce in the tourism and hospitality industry become a challenge?
5. What are the major statements of the UNESCO *Universal Declaration on Cultural Diversity*?
6. Identify hospitality companies that have properties and workers in more than one continent.

CASE STUDY 2.1 American in Paris

In the last few decades international companies have grown larger. In the tourism industry, huge travel conglomerates have been formed with offices on most continents of the world. People of different nationalities and different cultural backgrounds work together for the same company. This diversity in human resources can lead to communication problems, different perceptions of projects or tasks, and different attitudes toward work and work methods.

To illustrate this we take as an example an American's view of the French while going to a meeting in Paris.[i] An American, a representative from the sales offices of a large tour operator in the United States, is going to meet with his counterparts from the offices in France to decide about ideas for a new ad campaign. The meeting is set for 9 a.m. on Monday. The American decides to fly to Paris on Sunday and come back home on Monday night. In his mind, one day is more than enough to discuss business affairs with his French counterparts; he even plans to visit the Eiffel Tower before he leaves for the United States.

At 9 a.m. on Monday the American arrives at the meeting place in Paris and realizes that the people he is supposed to meet are not there yet. Finally, at 9:30 a.m., all the participants arrive and assemble in the meeting rooms. Now everyone starts with a cup of coffee and a chat about what they did over the weekend, followed by a long and heated discussion about where to have lunch. After only a few minutes' discussion of the ad campaign, the clock turns 11 a.m., and someone exclaims that it is time to go to the restaurant "in order to beat the traffic." To ease the young American's mind, the French manager tells him not to worry; they will continue with the meeting over lunch. However, during lunch the topics of conversation are football, wine, and world news; everything except the topic of the meeting.

At 2 p.m. they return to the meeting room, the French bringing their laptops. Now a half-hearted discussion starts on the topic at hand, as the majority of the attendees are busy reading their e-mails or chatting on the Net. Then at 4:30 p.m. the French manager announces that they will have to conclude their meeting over dinner at 8 p.m., "as the most important decisions in business are usually done over dinner, anyway." Now the American rushes to the phone to postpone his flight back home by one day and book a hotel room for one more night; he doesn't want to miss this important dinner meeting.

Over dinner they discuss the campaign while enjoying excellent food and good wine. The young American, who had arrived in Paris with a clear vision of the project at hand and who had been used to a more focused meeting agenda, left France the following day with an unclear understanding of whether or not a decision had been made on the business topic. The American was confused about the way the French conducted the meeting. He was used to focused agendas, clear visions, and directions, whereas "in France *deciding* is giving the broad guidelines without getting into implementation details."[ii]

It is important to an international company to understand and teach its own employees about cultural and social differences in doing business in different countries. What may seem to be a necessity in one country may be considered unimportant in another; what one nation describes as being focused might be considered too detailed in another; what one society looks favorably upon as being authoritative might be condemned as being arrogant and dominating in another.

i Adapted from Hall, E., & Hall, M. (1990). *Understanding cultural difference*. Yarmouth: Intercultural Press.
ii Messier, J.M. (former CEO of Vivendi). Retrieved from www.understandfrance.org/France/ Intercultural3.html

---

CASE STUDY 2.2 Creativity in a Tense Situation

A US firm has a major investment in an international project headquartered in Moscow, Russia. They send an engineering team that includes Trina, an African-American woman, 32; and three men: Brian White, a European American, 26; Bob Velasquez, a Peruvian-American, 29; and Derek Chan, a Chinese American, 28.

After arriving in Moscow, Trina finds that Brian, Bob and Derek tend to do things without inviting her, and she sometimes feels excluded in casual conversations. She turns her attention to her foreign colleagues, who include Russian, Austrian, and Italian professionals. She determines to make an extended effort to get to know them and to learn and experience as much as she can during her stay in Moscow. Her efforts are more than rewarded when the Russians organize a special tour of excavation sites in the Kremlin as well as other excursions to places otherwise unavailable to visitors. She feels welcomed and celebrated and quickly develops several friendships.

Her US colleagues notice Trina's success and the invitations she is receiving. They are rarely approached by non-US colleagues, except in work conversations. They become resentful and start calling her ''Chechen Rebel'' in public places. With the ethnic tensions running high in Moscow, such an ethnic joke could become a security issue for Trina. Trina calls her boss in the United States and asks for help.

Please explain how you would handle the situation:

A. This is a security issue; it must be handled quickly and efficiently. Brian, Bob, and Derek should be reprimanded. Security and safety policy should be reviewed to include breaches of professional conduct.

B. This is a racism and sexism issue, and should be managed as such. Domestic diversity training should be integrated into international assignments.

C. This is an issue of trust. The group does not know and trust one another. Team-building training should be conducted to enhance the employees' performance and repair relationships.

D. This is a business issue. Trina uses a creative relationship-building strategy that allows her to integrate into the international team and provides a competitive advantage for her company. Her efforts should be rewarded and used as the best example for future projects of this type.

E. Other explanation.

Adapted from Cameron, C., Fertelmeister, T., Yuzhakova, S., & Hofner S. D. (2004). *The cultural detective: Russia.* www.culturaldetective.com. Also http://www.diversityhotwire.com/learning/diversity_dilemma.html.

CASE STUDY 2.3 Promoting the ''Unpromotional''

A major international company has operations in the United States, Russia, Somalia, and Japan. After reviewing promotional statistics in the organization, the senior vice president in charge of diversity and equity is dismayed to find that the organization tends to promote European Americans to key management positions at a rate three times greater than that of Asian-Americans, African-Americans, Hispanics, Somalis, Russians, and Japanese.

The vice president does not fully understand why this is the case. He has implemented major equity programs in the company, worked with human resources around diversity concerns, and required key management to attend diversity and EEO-related training programs.

The general response among (largely European American) top management is that many of the non-dominant (United States, Russian, Japanese, Somali) applicants for managerial positions do not want a promotion, lack appropriate interpersonal and leadership skills, or are simply ''not ready'' yet for promotion to key management positions.

The president of the company has requested that the vice president provide a set of recommendations to increase promotional rates among Asian-American, African-American, Hispanic, Russian, Somali, and Japanese employees. Among the recommendations were: (a) management development training for employees; (b) training for management around the cultural differences in identifying professional role; (c) assumptions and expectations, developing key guidelines for promotion; (d) strengthening the performance and promotion system; (e) workshop for all management worldwide to reduce prejudice. What would you recommend?

Adapted from Hammer, M. www.http://www.diversityhotwire.com/learning/diversity_dilemma.html.

WEBSITE LINKS

1. UNESCO Global Alliance for Cultural Diversity
2. International Network for Cultural Diversity
3. Foundation for Endangered Languages
4. Cultural diversity in WikEd
5. Diversity central (''resources for cultural diversity at work'')
6. Broadcasting regulation and cultural diversity
7. CEN/ISSS cultural diversity focus group
8. Accor Hotels: http://www.accorhotels.com

Since in a globalized world there will be increased opportunities for communication and interactions between culturally different persons the next chapter will discuss theories related to intercultural communication and interaction.

Cultural Theories and Practices

Part Two summarizes current theories designed to explain social interaction and communication in the cross-cultural context. This part also presents the cultural worldwide practices and their impacts on the host culture and culture change. The purpose of this part is to alert the reader to various cultural theories and practices before the concept of culture and its influence on tourist behavior is discussed.

Intercultural theories

3

The aim of this chapter is to present theories of intercultural interaction and communication.

OBJECTIVES

After completing this chapter the reader should be able to:
- Identify theories related to intercultural interaction and communication
- Identify variables that influence intercultural interaction and communication
- Understand the influence of culture on social interaction and communication
- Draw the models of intercultural interaction and communication

INTRODUCTION

Intercultural interaction and communication refer to interaction and communication between persons who are distinct from one another in cultural terms. This is in contrast to interpersonal interaction and communication between persons who are distinct in terms of their person-specific qualities. Intercultural interaction and communication theories seek to understand how people from different countries and cultures interact, communicate, and perceive the world around them. Most of these theories relate to the management of social interaction and communication for the purpose of creating meaning across cultures. The theories developed can be, and have been, applied to many fields of studies, such as consumer behavior, marketing, advertising, and website design. As businesses become more international, it is important for them to learn how to interact and communicate with customers and employees. Intercultural theories are now used within education, health care, and other public services due to growing multicultural populations. Intercultural theories are of **49** particular importance to international tourism due to the rapid increase in the number of tourists from different cultural backgrounds.

3.1 COMMUNICATION RESOURCEFULNESS THEORY (CRT)

The Communication Resourcefulness Theory (CRT) (Spitzberg & Cupach, 1984) refers to the ability of the individual to use three types of resources – cognitive (knowledge), affective (motivation) and behavioral (skill) – in order to communicate appropriately and effectively in diverse social situations (see Figure 3.1). Knowledge means knowing what behavior is best suited for a given situation. Motivation means having the desire to communicate in a competent manner. Skill means having the ability to apply the best-suited behavior in the given context. The CRT explains how people can approach social interaction with culturally different strangers. Some individuals treat an inter-cultural encounter with others as a source of knowledge, challenge, and learning (use cognitive resources), while others develop fear and become anxious about it. Some individuals can be motivated by self and self-ego (use affective resources); others can focus on others. Some people can develop a wide range of verbal and non-verbal skills (use behavioral resources) to respond to strangers and learn from them. Others can be unresponsive and unwilling to learn about and from strangers.

Culture plays a major role in developing knowledge, motivation, and skills for intercultural encounters. For example, members of individualistic cultures usually are self-oriented and develop skills that help them to meet their individual needs. On the other hand, members of collectivistic cultures are usually other-oriented and develop skills and activities aimed at caring about others. Similarly, members of the high-uncertainty-avoidance cultures are cautious about strangers and foreigners and thus experience difficulties in learning from strangers and foreigners. In contrast,

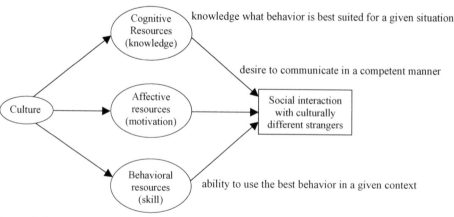

Figure 3.1

Communication Resourcefulness Theory (CRT)

members of the low-uncertainty-avoidance cultures are open, willing to accept strangers and foreigners, and learn something new from them.

3.2 **EPISODE REPRESENTATION THEORY (ERT)**

The Episode Representation Theory (ERT) (Forgas, 1983) assumes that those who are involved in intercultural encounters and communication differ in terms of cognitive representations of social episodes such as the degree of intimacy, involvement, friendliness, self-confidence, activity, evaluation of each encounter, the importance of task-versus-relationship orientation, anxiety, and values (see Figure 3.2). Cultural differences play an important role in how people think about the social episodes. The greater the cultural differences between interactants and communicators, the more difficult it is for them to understand the social episodes. For example, members of collectivistic cultures (e.g. in Asia) perceive social episodes in terms of collective values, while members of individualistic cultures perceive the same social episodes in terms of competitiveness and individualism. Similarly, members of high-power-distance cultures perceive social episodes in terms of usefulness, as opposed to members of low-power-distance cultures that perceive these episodes in terms of pleasure and joy.

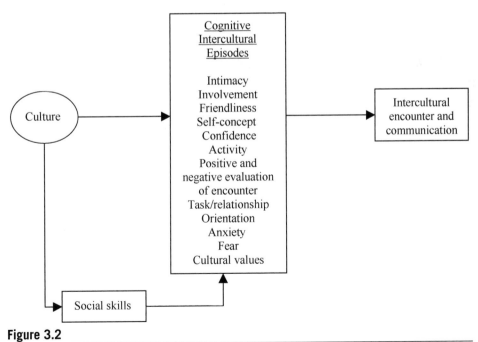

Figure 3.2
Episode Representation Theory (ERT)

The degree of differences in social episodes and difficulties experienced in intercultural interactions is determined by a person's social skills. For example, those with highly developed social skills treat social episodes positively and see them in terms of high involvement, intensity, and friendliness, while those with poorly developed social skills treat social episodes negatively and develop fear and anxiety.

3.3 EXPECTATIONS THEORY (ET)

This theory argues that social behavior and communication are influenced by people's expectations about others' behavior, in particular how others who receive their message will respond to what they say (Miller & Steinberg, 1975). People's expectations are determined by their knowledge, beliefs/attitudes, stereotypes, self-concept, social roles, prior interaction, and social status (Berger & Zelditch, 1985) (see Figure 3.3). The more accurate the knowledge and information people have about others, the fewer stereotypes, prejudices, negative attitudes, and expectations they develop. In order to gain accurate information about others, people must interact directly with members of other cultures; they must ask questions, share and exchange views, and not be afraid to self-disclose.

People's concept of self (the way they define themselves) and their social roles influence how people relate to one another and what they expect from another persons' behavior. For example, when people define themselves as unique and distinct individuals, their interaction and communication with others is interpersonal, whereas when they define themselves as members of a group, their interaction and

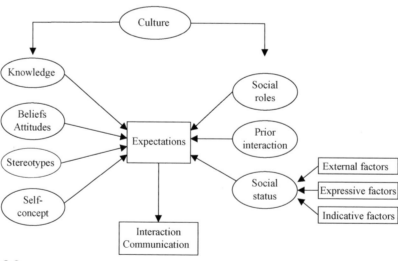

Figure 3.3

Expectations Theory (ET)

communication with others is called inter-group. In inter-group interaction and com-munication, people's expectations about others' behavior are influenced more by their beliefs about and attitudes toward people than by one-on-one relationships.

Social status also determines expectations about others. Social status is determined by external factors (e.g. race, ethnicity, gender, attractiveness, education, occupation, income), expressive factors (e.g. eye contact, speech style, dialect), and indicative factors (someone's statement that he/she grew up in a high/low status family). Culture plays an important role in how people assess their status. For example, in high-power-distance cultures (e.g. Japan) professional status is very important; people need to know in advance the professional position of the person they are about to interact with in order to determine how to address that person correctly. The introductory business cards (*meisihi* cards) that are exchanged at the beginning of each social encounter and conversation indicate the owner's status. On the other hand, in a low-power-distance society like Australia, attempts to assess someone's professional status are regarded as rude.

Expectations of others' behavior are not always met. If person A does not have knowledge of, or has inadequate knowledge of, person B's culture, the expecta-tions of person A's own culture prevail. As a result, person A can develop ethnocentrism, stereotypes, or prejudice towards person B. According to the Expectancy Violation Theory, when communicative norms are violated, the vio-lation may be perceived either favorably or unfavorably, depending upon the perception that the receiver has of the violator. Thus, when person B's behavior is in accordance with person A's expectations, person A assesses person B usually positively. However, when person B's behavior violates expectations of person A, person A negatively evaluates person B. In inter-cultural encounters in which participants are from different cultural backgrounds, there is a higher rate of negative evaluations of partners than in intra-cultural encounters (Hoyle et al., 1989).

3.4 CULTURAL IDENTITY NEGOTIATION THEORY (CINT)

The Cultural Identity Negotiation Theory (CINT) (Collier & Thomas, 1988) refers to communication between people of different cultural identities. In the process of intercultural communication and contact with others, people form, compare, judge, ascribe, negotiate, confirm, and challenge their cultural identities. This theory argues that by interacting and communicating with those who are culturally different, people negotiate stereotypes, opinions, norms, and meanings of, for example, concepts of time, feelings, or activities, which differ from one culture to another. Cultural identities influence interpretations of the meanings. When people identify with cultural groups, they are able to manipulate and understand systems of symbols and beliefs and are able to enact culturally appropriate and effective behavior with members of that group. The successful intercultural encounter is characterized by reaching an agreement as to the negotiated meanings and norms. Once the agreement is reached the individuals' cultural identities are positively enhanced (Collier, 1988) (see Figure 3.4). The CINT can be very useful in identifying similarities and differences in interpretations of rules, norms, feelings, and symbols. The theory also assumes that all individuals have many cultural identities. Cultural identity is dynamic and fluid because it is rendered in interaction. However, it also is transmitted from generation to generation, or from cultural group member to newcomer. One or more particular cultural identities may be salient in a given encounter.

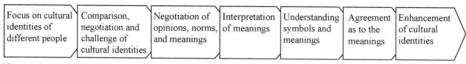

Figure 3.4

Cultural Identity Negotiation Theory (CINT)

The CINT has its origin in the Social Identity Theory (SIT), a theory formed by Tajfel (1978) and John Turner, which assumes that individuals seek positive social identities in inter-group encounters. According to the SIT, individuals (1) put others (and themselves) into categories and label them as *Muslim, Turk* or *piano player*, (2) identify with certain groups (or in-groups) which help them to boost self-esteem, (3) compare their groups with other groups, and (4) desire their identity to be distinct from that of others.

3.5 MEANING OF MEANING THEORY

The Meaning of Meaning Theory (Richards, 1936) argues that misunderstanding takes place when people assume words have direct connections with their referent. However, words alone mean nothing. Meaning is created by the way people use words. In order to understand meanings, people use definitions, metaphors, language, or examples. Similar cultural background, a common past, history, and traditions facilitate understanding the meaning and reduce misunderstanding.

3.6 NETWORK THEORY IN INTERCULTURAL COMMUNICATION

Network Theory in Intercultural Communication (Yum, 1988) has its origin in the Social Network Theory (SNT), which suggests that individuals are embedded in a structure or network of social relationships and are tied by their values, visions, ideas, friends, kinships, race, ethnicity, gender, dislikes and likes, conflicts, jobs, sexual relations, work relations, etc. Positions and social relationships, rather than beliefs and norms, are the main focus of the network. The social networks are very complex (see Figure 3.5). There are many networks because there are many types of social relationships among individuals. Social networks operate on many levels, from families up to the level of nations. Members of the local networks share the same values, information and their communication style converges. Members of the national or regional networks diverge in the communication.

Precursors of SNT in the late 1800s were Emile Durkheim and Ferdinand Tonnies. They argued that individuals could be linked by shared values and beliefs (*gemeinschaft*) or impersonal, formal, and instrumental social links (*gesselschaft*). For example, individuals L, M, and N form *gemeinschaft*; they are closer to each because they may share cultural values and beliefs and be family members or in-group members. On the other hand, individuals C, D, and F form *gesselschaft*; they are more distant from each other because they may have only formal relations (e.g. work). George Simmel (1908/1971) pointed out the importance of nature and network size, and their influence on social interaction. Personal interactions occur when the network is small and ties are strong, whereas formal and official interactions occur when the network is larger and ties are looser.

The Network Theory in Intercultural Communication (Yum, 1988) is based on the assumption that intercultural communication is more heterogeneous than intracultural communication. Intercultural networks are less dense, less likely to be multiplex, more likely to consist of weak ties than strong ties, and have weaker effects on social relationships. Networks with many weak ties and social connections are more open and likely to have new ideas and seek new experiences than close networks with many redundant ties. In other words, a group of similar people (e.g. culturally similar) who have close networks and only interact and communicate with each other is likely to have the same and limited knowledge and opportunities. On the other hand, a group of people who have open networks, with connections to other social networks (e.g. culturally different social networks) is likely to have access to a wider range of information, more and broader knowledge, and opportunities.

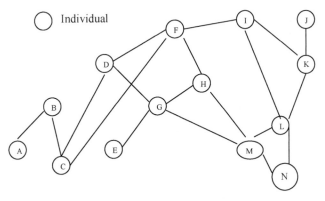

Figure 3.5

Social Network Theory (SNT)

3.7 TAXONOMIC APPROACH (TA)

The Taxonomic Approach (TA) to intercultural communication (Sarbaugh, 1988) establishes similarities and differences among participants in communication. The degree of difference is referred to as the level of homogeneity/heterogeneity of the participants and is used to classify the differences along a continuum of homogeneity/heterogeneity. This continuum indicates the levels of interculturalness of communication (see Figure 3.6). When participants are highly homogenous/similar in their (1) worldviews (beliefs about the nature of life, the purposes of life, people's relationships to the cosmos), (2) normative patterns (beliefs and actions pertaining to what is involved in being a good person), (3) code systems (verbal and non-verbal codes, including time and space), and (4) perceived relationships and intent (compatibilities of goals, hierarchy of relationships, positiveness or negativeness of feeling toward the other person), then the level of their interculturalness is low, and communication requires minimal effort and is very accurate. On the other hand, when participants are very heterogeneous or different on the continuum of the above variables, their communication requires greater effort, and communication can be inaccurate.

The TA to intercultural communication allows for creating numerous combinations of variables from groups (1), (2), (3), and (4). Also, it is not just the presence or absence of difference that influences the intercultural communication, but the degree of difference. The amount of difference may range from undetectable to the most extreme. Differences might be small in one dimension of the taxonomy and large in another. The question is which differences on which dimensions have the most influence on communication outcomes.

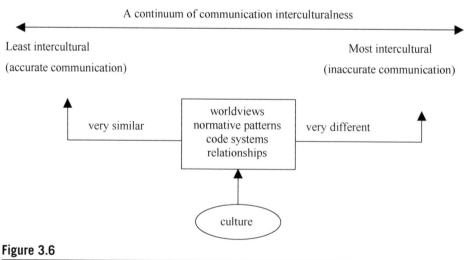

Figure 3.6

Taxonomic Approach (TA)

3.8 ANXIETY/UNCERTAINTY MANAGEMENT THEORY (AUMT)

The Anxiety/Uncertainty Management Theory (AUMT) (Gudykunst, 1988) proposes that intercultural encounters, particularly in their early stages, are characterized by high levels of uncertainty and anxiety, especially when cultural differences are large. In order to communicate effectively, individuals attempt to manage their anxiety and reduce uncertainty about themselves and the people with whom they are communicating and interacting. The AUM theory shows what encourages and inhibits effective communication and what takes place during this communication.

The AUMT has its origin in the Uncertainty Reduction Theory (Berger & Calabrese, 1975), according to which individuals seek information to reduce uncertainty. Berger and Calabrese (1975) suggested that as levels of non-verbal behavior (e.g. showing warmth, smiling, touching, eye contact), information sought, intimacy level, self-disclosure, reciprocity, similarity, and liking increase, uncertainty is reduced, and the amount of communication increased. The higher the similarity between individuals, the lower the uncertainty and the greater the amount of communication. Likewise, the higher the dissimilarity between individuals, the higher the uncertainty and information seeking and the lesser the amount of communication.

In a cross-cultural context, the AUMT (Gudykunst, 1988) refers to communication between strangers, usually those from different cultural groups. Individuals experience uncertainty because they are not able to predict others' culturally determined attitudes, feelings, and beliefs. When the individuals experience uncertainty at too high a level, they feel uncomfortable and try to reduce uncertainty by searching for information about the strangers. They also may avoid encounters with strangers and even end the interaction. As a result, the individuals may develop stereotypes and use them to predict other people's behavior. This leads to misinterpretation of messages and misunderstanding. On the other hand, when the individuals experience uncertainty and anxiety at too low a level, they may be bored and not pay attention to interaction with strangers. Consequently they may miss important cues and behave ineffectively. In general, effective communication is achieved when the levels of uncertainty and anxiety are between too high and too low. However, in interactions with strangers who are culturally different, the levels of uncertainty and anxiety are usually too high to achieve effective intercultural communication.

Several strategies can be used to reduce uncertainty, such as information seeking, controlling anxiety, or adapting to new situations and people. In terms of information seeking, people can adopt three strategies: (1) passive strategies – observe personally or through mass media or do nothing and hope that things will become clearer, (2) active strategies – seek information about others from outside sources (e.g. ask other strangers about the group), and (3) interactive strategies – seek direct interactions and communication with people about whom uncertainty exists to obtain information about them and be able to predict their behavior (Berger, 1979).

Figure 3.7 shows that intercultural communication is influenced by anxiety and uncertainty that in turn are influenced by a large number of variables, such as self-concept, motivation, cognitive capacity, social categorization, situational processes,

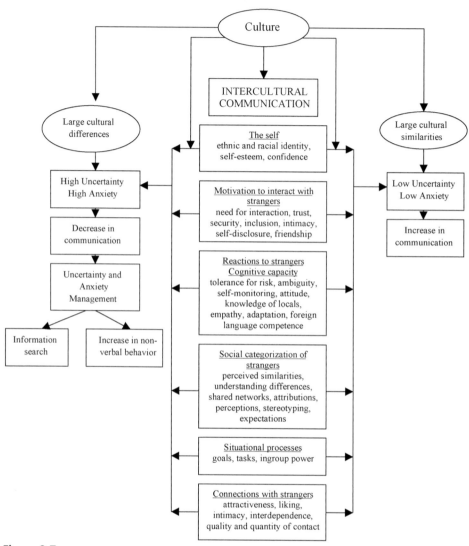

Figure 3.7

Anxiety/Uncertainty Management Theory (AUMT)

Source: Adapted from Gudykunst, W. (2005). An anxiety/uncertainty management (AUM) theory of effective communication. In W. Gudykunst (Ed.), *Theorizing about intercultural communication* (p. 292). Thousand Oaks, CA: Sage; Guirdham, M. (1999). *Communication across cultures* (p. 211). Houndmills, Basingstoke, Hampshire: MacMillan Press.

connections to strangers, and mindfulness. A change in one of these variables affects anxiety and uncertainty and thus intercultural communication. For example, having poor knowledge of locals and their traditions and customs, as well as experiencing foreign language difficulties, decreases a sense of security and emotional stability of tourists and make their intercultural interaction and communication with locals less effective. However, an increase in similarity, attractiveness, and liking of locals reduces uncertainty and anxiety of tourists and makes their intercultural communication more effective. In high-uncertainty-avoidance cultures, people are usually highly anxious about interacting with strangers, whereas in low-uncertainty-avoidance cultures people are not threatened by uncertainty and are willing and able to adapt communication when interacting with strangers.

3.9 STRANGER THEORY

The Stranger Theory (Gudykunst, 1985) is a sub-theory of Gudykunst's AUMT (Gudykunst, 1988). The Stranger Theory claims that strangers are more inclined to notice and stereotype members of the host society. For instance, a stranger from the United States in Japan may claim that all the Japanese buy too many gifts. Strangers tend to overestimate the influence of cultural identity on peoples' behavior in a host society, and disregard individual differences. As a result, cultural conflicts appear.

3.10 FACE-NEGOTIATION THEORY

According to a Face-Negotiation Theory (Ting-Toomey, 1985), whenever two people from different cultural backgrounds meet for the first time, they develop feelings of uncertainty and anxiety. As a result, they develop strategies to avoid conflict that could be generated by these feelings. Members of collectivistic high-context cultures, who are concerned about others, saving mutual face and belonging to a group, try to avoid conflicts or seek compromise. People from individualistic low-context cultures who are concerned about the self, self-face, and independence, try to dominate and solve a problem.

3.11 INTERCULTURAL ADAPTATION THEORY (IAT)

Intercultural adaptation is the process through which people in cross-cultural situations change their behavior to facilitate understanding. In other words, intercultural adaptation refers to the adjustment of behavior to decrease the probability of being misunderstood by someone from a different culture. For example, a British conversing with another British can facilitate understanding by adjusting his/her communication style in response to perceived miscommunication. Adaptation that occurs between people of different cultural backgrounds requires more adjustment to reduce miscommunication than adaptation that occurs between individuals of similar cultures. For instance, in conversations, people of the same culture may only need to repeat a particular sentence or word to understand each other, whereas people of different cultural backgrounds may need to use body language and other non-verbal cues to compensate for their inability to convey message through verbal means.

People adjust their behavior during initial stages of cross-cultural interactions, where there is a perception of "foreignness." If there is no perception of "foreignness," adaptation is not likely to occur. One may perceive the other person to be foreign based on that person's voice quality, skin color, or non-verbal cues. Also, if individuals believe that they are interacting with a person who is foreign, they usually perceive that they share limited or no knowledge with this person, including language, which will likely result in miscommunication. Thus, potential misunderstandings are usually occurring when interactants lack shared knowledge of each other. So, as perceived "foreignness" increases, perceptions of shared knowledge decreases, the probability of miscommunication increases and understanding decreases, and vice versa (Cai & Rodriguez, 1997).

The Intercultural Adaptation Theory (IAT) (Ellingsworth, 1988) describes the conditions under which individuals interacting in a new cultural environment make changes in their identities and behavior (adapt or not). The theory argues that the process of adaptation is goal driven; individuals are interacting and communicating to accomplish some goals. Various factors influence intercultural adaptation, including participants' motivation and power in the interaction (Ellingsworth, 1988) (see Figure 3.8).

According to the IAT, people adapt their behavior when they have a specific purpose in an interaction and are motivated to make it successful. If people have the same purpose (e.g. they need to cooperate or agree on something) they adapt their behavioral style, regardless of their differences. If both persons have the same purpose, then both persons adapt. However, if only one person has a purpose, then only that person adapts. Similarly, when one person has more power than the other (e.g. has a territorial advantage or more social status), then the other person adapts. The more the people adapt, the more they change their attitudes to and perceptions of themselves and others and the culture they represent. During the adaptation process people learn about themselves and others and modify their cultural perceptions and stereotypes. The knowledge they gained during the adaptation process influences their future intercultural behavior.

3.12 COMMUNICATION ACCOMMODATION THEORY (CAT)

The Communication Accommodation Theory (CAT) (Gallois et al., 1988) examines the way individuals change their communication style while interacting during cross-cultural encounters. The theory analyzes the motivations and consequences of what happens when two speakers change their communication styles. The theory argues that communication involves a constant movement towards and away from

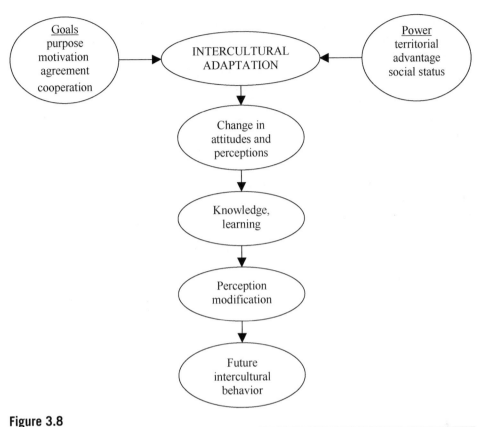

Figure 3.8

Intercultural Adaptation Theory (IAT)

others; people change their communication styles and try to accommodate or adjust their style of speaking to others. This can be done in three ways: convergence (decreasing communicative distance), divergence (increasing communicative distance), and maintenance (maintaining communicative distance) (see Figure 3.9). Communication convergence involves changing one's linguistic behavior (language, dialect, speech style, vocabulary) or paralinguistic behavior (tone of voice, speech rate) to improve communication clarity and comprehension and decrease communicative distance and thus become similar in communication style to the partner and gain approval. The more a speaker converges to his partner, the more favorably the person is likely to be evaluated by the listener. Communication divergence involves the opposite: speakers seek differences between their communication styles to increase communicative distance and emphasize their uniqueness. The more a speaker diverges from his partner, the less favorably the person is likely to be evaluated. Communication maintenance refers to continuing one's own speaking style.

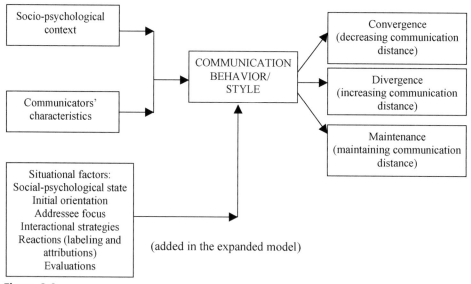

Figure 3.9

Communication Accommodation Theory (CAT)

Source: based on Gallois, C., Franklyn-Stokes, A., Giles, H., & Coupland, N. (1988). Communication accommodation in intercultural encounters. In Y. Y. Kim & W. B. Gudykunst (Eds.), *Theories in intercultural communication*. Newbury Park, CA: Sage; based on Guirdham, M. (1999). *Communication across cultures* (p. 211). Houndmills, Basingstoke, Hampshire: MacMillan Press.

The communication movement depends on the social and psychological contexts and communicators' characteristics. For example, strong individuals or people with strong ethnic or racial pride often use divergence strategy to emphasize their identity. On the other hand, powerless individuals who have strong need for social approval use convergence strategy.

An expanded model of the CAT indicates that communication accommodation depends upon additional variables, such as situational factors, the interactors' initial orientation, the social/psychological states of speakers, addressee focus, interactional strategies, reactions, and the evaluation (see Figure 3.9). Situational factors decide whether communication occurs in high-status and high-threat situations (business meetings) or low-status and low-threat situations (party with friends, vacations). Intercultural (intergroup) communication usually occurs in high-status and high-threat situations. In these situations people evaluate the behavior of others negatively and follow strict norms of group behavior. Social/psychological state refers to the speakers' perceptions of the communication as having potential for conflict, and motivations to accommodate to others. Initial orientation refers to the differences in the way the individuals view their situation, either as being a member of a dominant ethnic majority or a subordinate ethnic group.

Addressee focus refers to the way speakers pay attention to the needs or behavior of each other (e.g. conversational needs, skills, and competence of the partner). They can converge or diverge in their communication, depending on their needs. If they focus on the skills and competence of the partner, they can slow the speech, use more questions, and select familiar topics for conversations to ensure the partner understands what is said and achieve mutual understanding. If they focus on the partners' conversational needs, they can share a topic of choice. If, however, they emphasize their roles in the communication, they may interrupt each.

Speakers' reactions to one another modify the communication moves. When speakers seek social approval, focus on self-presentation or own social status or role-played in relations, they decrease communicative distance, and communication convergence occurs. When speakers desire to communicate their unique images, dissociate from the other speaker and emphasize differences between speakers (e.g. in experience, knowledge, status, style) they increase communicative distance, and communication divergence occurs.

Evaluations of the communication behavior (positive or negative) of the other speaker (accommodating or not accommodating) influence the changes in communication moves. These evaluations also have impact on future communication encounters.

3.13 COORDINATED MANAGEMENT OF MEANING THEORY (CMMT)

The Coordinated Management of Meaning Theory (CMMT) (Cronen & Shuter, 1983) is based on theory of Pearce and Cronen (1980) that argues that people who are interacting socially construct the meaning of their conversation and see the social world depending on specific situations and contexts. According to the CMMT, the meaning can be created and understood by attaining some coherence and coordination. The meaning can be created on six contextual levels: (1) *Verbal and non-verbal behavior*: how clearly people understand one another's speech, gestures, posture, signals, eye movement, words, (2) *Speech acts*: the way meaning is attached to forms of address such as status or level of formality or respect, (3) *Episodes*: sequence of behavior, rituals, arrangements for eating, sightseeing, tipping, or gift giving, (4) *Relationships*: nature of social bonds, rights, and expectations, responsibilities, formation of friendships, development of business relationships, (5) *Life script*: the way people perceive themselves in action, their relationship to others and physical environment, social and cultural institutions, and (6) *Cultural pattern*: the way the larger community is defined, what is perceived as honesty, guilt, justice or equity within a society, freedom of speech, spiritual beliefs, attitudes to gender (see Figure 3.10). These different contextual levels play key roles in how people create meanings and understand messages. People choose which contextual level is most important in the situation and behave accordingly. These six contextual levels need to be heeded in order to solve the problem of cultural misunderstanding. Successful cross-cultural encounter and

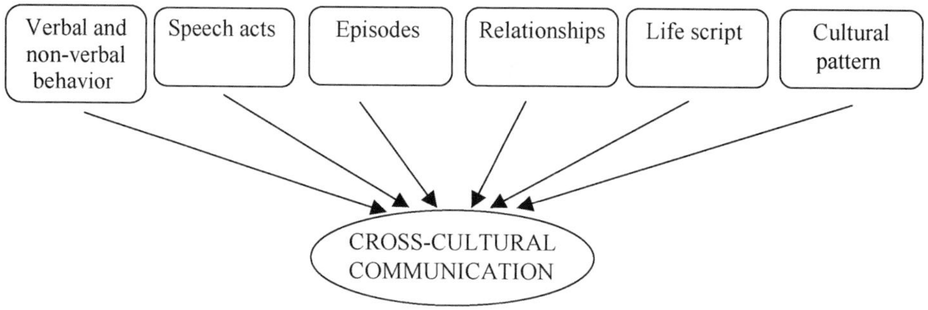

Figure 3.10

Coordinated Management of Meaning Theory (CMMT)

communication are characterized by understanding the exchanged messages at all levels. It is possible to analyze every single element of cultural misunderstanding at each contextual level.

3.14 CONSTRUCTIVIST THEORY (CT)

Constructivist Theory (CT) argues that through processes of accommodation and assimilation to a new environment (e.g. new cultural environment), individuals develop new experiences, learn, and construct new knowledge. When individuals assimilate to a new environment, they incorporate their new experiences into their existing beliefs. When individuals' new experiences contradict their beliefs they may change their perceptions of the experiences and knowledge of the external world. Thus, by accommodating to a new environment, developing new experiences and changing beliefs and the perceptions of how the world works, the individuals learn and construct new knowledge. They become richer, more understanding, and more open to the outside world.

SUMMARY

Several intercultural theories can be used to explain communication behavior in international and global contexts. However, these theories are of Western origin. It is questionable whether they can be applied in all cultures. Each theory stands alone; no effort has been made to integrate them. There are many more variables that could be included in each model to explain the concept of successful intercultural communication and encounters. More theories from disciplines such as psychology, social psychology, intercultural communication, marketing, or management should be drawn to arrive at one intercultural communication and interaction theory that international researchers and theorists can agree upon. More reference should be made to cultural differences in the various models.

DISCUSSION POINTS AND QUESTIONS

1. What do you understand by cognitive, affective, and behavioral communication resources, and how do they influence communication effectiveness?
2. What are the major assumptions of the Uncertainty Reduction Theory and AUMT?
3. What are the three communication accommodation strategies, and what factors influence the communication movements?
4. Under what conditions will people interacting in a new cultural environment adapt their communication style?
5. Explain how six contextual levels of cross-cultural encounter facilitate understanding exchanged messages and cultural understanding.

WEBSITE LINKS

1. The Intercultural Communication Institute: http://www.intercultural.org.
2. Intercultural theories: http://www.uky.edu/~drlane/capstone/intercultural.

Since many countries and destinations experience changes in culture as a result of contact between tourists and hosts of different cultures the next chapter will discuss the impacts of international tourism on the host and tourist culture.

Cultural practices and tourism impacts on culture

4

This chapter investigates the impacts of tourism on culture and the consequences for tourist and host societies.

OBJECTIVES

After completing this chapter the reader should be able to:
- Explain the impact of tourism on culture
- Explain worldwide cultural theories and practices related to culture change

INTRODUCTION

The results of numerous empirical studies show that many countries and destinations experience cultural changes due to tourism development. The larger the numbers of tourists the more significant are the changes. This chapter explains tourism impacts on native cultures and shows what happens when tourists step into hosts' lives when each other's value systems are different.

4.1 EROSION OF LOCAL CULTURES

It is often argued that with an increase in international travel and excessive demand for tourism products many societies experience erosion of local cultures and traditional ways of life and customs, including indigenous cultures. In order to keep up with tourist demand for local arts, the non-traditional craftsmen are given tasks to create pseudo-native artifacts, called ''original art.'' The original art forms become **67** replaced by unsophisticated mass produced forms, often sloppily and carelessly made. As a result, the quality of the traditional artistic designs and forms deteriorates and their artistic and symbolic values and meanings disappear. The traditional art forms become substituted for meaningless pseudo-traditional arts promoted for the purpose of sale.

4.2 CULTURAL COMMODITIZATION AND TRANSFORMATION

Traditional culture is being packaged and treated as commodity for sale over which tourists and entrepreneurs from the tourist culture, rather than locals, have rights. Superficial non-authentic art forms are produced to create quick impressions of what art once was and provide tourists with ephemeral and superficial experiences. As a result, the local culture is commercially exploited and the rights of locals to own cultural heritage are lost. Examples abound of mass produced and distributed ''local'' souvenirs or artifacts that can be found in various regions and countries, and that bear little resemblance to original and local artwork.

4.3 CULTURAL HOSTILITY

Since tourism often destroys traditional ways of life and local economies, creates dependency and low-skilled unsecured jobs, and harms indigenous peoples, local hosts develop hostility to tourists. Cultural hostility is a form of cultural rejection or denial, often associated with anger and aggression. It refers to refusing to accept others' views of the world and forcing others and the world to fit their views regardless of the cost. The larger the number of tourists visiting the destination, the greater the hosts' hostility towards tourists. If hosts are not involved in setting the guidelines for tourism development, they may resent tourists and tourism development.

4.4 CULTURAL ARROGANCE

Confronted with an influx of mass tourists, host populations often stage cultural experiences in order to compensate tourists for the lack of real experience. Staging cultural experiences is done by creating backstage areas, where locals continue their meaningful traditions away from the gaze of tourists, and front stage areas, where locals perform a limited range of activities for tourist audiences (MacCannell, 1973). Displaying superficial local traditions and customs to tourists is a form of cultural arrogance. However, this is done to protect and insulate local culture from the impact of mass tourism. Staging cultural experiences diverts tourists from authentic local culture, relieves pressure upon it and thus helps its preservation.

Designing international hotels in Western styles and showing little respect and appreciation for the local traditions is another example of cultural arrogance. In order to avoid being called culturally arrogant, some hotels incorporate local features in hotel interiors, exhibit work of the indigenous painters or sculptures, and display symbols of local lifestyle, such as crafts and dress.

4.5 AUTHENTICITY OF TOURISM EXPERIENCES

In order to satisfy mass tourism, pseudo-artifacts are produced and commoditized creating standardized and inauthentic products. Some scholars argue that tourists like commoditized, inauthentic products, imitations, images, and so called ''staged attractions'' (Boorstin, 1961).

However, it is debatable whether tourists are able to actually experience what is authentic in foreign cultures, as most of what they are offered is pseudo-experience. In order for tourists to experience an authentic foreign culture, they need to get away from the main streets, shopping centers, and attractions where only staged authenticity is present. False back stage areas are often set up to deceive tourists; they could be more inauthentic than staged front regions. Thus, commoditization and globalization destroy the authenticity of tourist experiences (MacCannell, 1989).

However, some believe that what is promoted to tourists is assumed to be authentic (Culler, 1981) and what is inauthentic may become authentic over time (Graburn, 1976). For example, tourism products that are initially regarded as inauthentic (e.g. Disney World) eventually get incorporated into local culture and perceived as authentic (Cohen, 1988).

Tourists are often willing to perceive tourism products as being authentic because they are ''symbols'' of authenticity, not because they are originals or represent reality (Culler, 1981). Tourists like to take home from Mexico sombreros with Mexican designs on them as authentic evidence of their destinations. Although these objects are made for the mass market and promote *inauthenticity* (Errington, 1998) traditional techniques may remain unchanged (Cohen, 1993).

Many tourists are not concerned with authenticity and the origins of attractions as long as they enjoy them and the products transformed by the commoditization remain authentic in the tourists' eyes. Also, many tourists accept superficiality of tourism products as long as it helps to protect the original culture (Cohen, 1995). Tourists understand that commoditization of cultural products may change or add new meanings to them (Cohen, 1988; Grunewald, 2002). Most tourists accept commercialized objects as authentic as long as they are convinced that these objects have traditional designs and have been made by members of an ethnic group (Cohen, 1988).

4.6 RENAISSANCE OF TRADITIONAL ART FORMS

In some cases tourism enables a rejuvenation of particular forms of art and craft. The exposure to other ethnic groups can often result in the adaption of their art traditions, forms, and designs (e.g. pottery, jewelry). By borrowing from one culture, modifying and refining the original local art, new forms of traditional art can develop. For example, refining highly demanded Indian and Aboriginal arts and crafts allowed for developing new ideas and creating new designs. Thus, in the process of commoditization (mass) tourism may help to maintain and revive original traditions, and art designs and forms (Cohen, 1988).

4.7 MARKETING OF CULTURE AND VIOLATION OF RIGHTS TO OWN CULTURAL HERITAGE

By treating traditional culture as a commodity for sale and making it commercially exploited, culture is turned to paid performance. Traditional ceremonies and festivals are pre-arranged and treated as daily entertainment rituals for sale (e.g. hula girls greet tourists at Honolulu airport; Maori perform daily dances in Rotorua, New Zealand). As a result, the tourists see the visited country through superficial experiences that are selective, pre-arranged, and distorted from reality. The commercialization of culture proves that the traditional culture can be treated as a commodity over which locals lose their rights.

The discussed above cultural practices are usually responsible for culture change.

4.8 CULTURE CHANGE

Culture change occurs as a result of (1) evolutionary changes occurring within a society, (2) changes in the way people live, and (3) contact between societies and groups from different cultures (e.g. hosts and visitors). All cultures are changing in response to the changes in social environment, institutions, technologies, politics, and ideologies. One of the major reasons for culture change is frequent contact between societies. Cultural elements such as values, ideas, or scientific developments are spread all over the world by travelers, immigrants, business people, guest workers, diplomats, and students. Culture is also carried by film and literature. The spread of these cultural elements among societies is a two-way process. Visitors bring their ideas to the host country, and hosts expose visitors to their values and perspectives. As a result of cultural contact between their members, both cultures (host culture and visitor culture) influence each, and affluent society has more influence on the non-industrialized and developing society. For example, the Western industrialized nations have more influence on Third World countries than the Third World countries have on developed Western nations. Those with more power significantly influence the culture of those with less power.

Tourism significantly influences the changes induced through contact between societies with different cultures. Many studies show that the interaction between locals and tourists creates significant changes in cultural (as well as social, economic, and political) value systems. Tourism is a medium for cultural transformation. In particular, tourism can initiate irreversible changes within the cultures of host communities (Robinson, 1998). Tourists are viewed as agents of cultural changes (Pearce, 1995).

4.9 CULTURE DIFFUSION

Cultural diffusion refers to the spread of cultural elements such as ideas, styles, food, religions, technologies, etc., between individuals and groups within a single culture or from one culture to another. For example, the new fashion items and dressing styles, such as blue jeans, Nike shoes, or Movado wristwatches; technology products, such as the Apple ipod or Dell personal computers; foods, such as pizza, spaghetti, or sushi; ideals, such as democracy or human rights, have spread rapidly around the world in the last several years. The spread of cultural elements across different cultures is called inter-cultural diffusion, and it usually happens through migrants and trans-cultural visitors such as tourists, diplomats, soldiers, business people, scientists, actors, trans-cultural marriages and media (letters, books), all of which carry their culture with them. The effect of culture diffusion is changing local cultural features (dressing, styles, food) and traditions; creating new products, services, and jobs; changing beliefs and ideas and improving the quality of life. In tourism, culture diffusion refers either to the tourist or the host populations who spread and adapt cultural elements of one another. The cultural elements that are spread through tourism can be gastronomy, dress, language, traditions, art and music, handicrafts, architecture, religion, and leisure activities.

Various theories explain the origins of culture diffusion. According to the helio-centric diffusionism theory, all cultures originate from one culture. Culture circles diffusionism (*Kulturkreise*) theory teaches that cultures originate from a small number of cultures. Evolutionary diffusionism theory assumes that societies and their cultures are influenced by other societies and their cultures, and that all humans are equally able to create new ideas and innovate. Biblical diffusionism theory argues that the universe and all cultures started with Adam and Eve. The cultural evolutionary diffusionism theory states that new cultural items appear simultaneously and independently in several different places when certain items are diffused to the respective communities. For example, the inventions of the portable computer and cell phone spread simulta-neously all over the world.

Although the concept of cultural diffusion is often used to explain similarities among cultures, it has been criticized for implying that various cultures would not be capable of development if it were not for cultural diffusion. Also, diffusion is difficult to prove; it can be proved only when it leaves some tangible traces, such as arche-ological traces. In addition, the theories of cultural diffusion fail to explain why some cultural elements have not been diffused between countries and continents.

4.10 CULTURAL BORROWING

Cultural borrowing occurs when two cultures come into contact and borrow each other's traditions, customs or values. Borrowing is not symmetrical; it depends on the nature and the duration of the contact, its purpose, context, characteristics of the interacting individuals, and the differences between individuals and their societies. Those who are from less wealthy and influential societies borrow from those who are from wealthier and influential societies. For example, hosts from developing countries are more likely to borrow from tourists who are from developed countries.

Host destinations that support tourism development borrow cultural elements from tourists' cultures in order to follow the standards of their culture. As a result of cultural borrowing in developing countries, the original culture of the host societies becomes weaker (they develop a Western style of society) and the culture of the tourist societies becomes stronger.

The effects of cultural borrowing may be positive and negative. Cultural borrowing may lead to learning elements from other cultures, better understanding of other people and to some extent influencing people's patterns of life. Sometimes both cultures become similar. When the host culture lags technologically behind, cultural borrowing can revitalize its cultural features (art, culture, etc.) (Pearce, 1995). However, cultural borrowing may also lead to cultural collision: natives, for example, may replace their traditional costumes with cheap imitations of the city tourist's dress (t-shirts and jeans), while the tourists may adorn themselves with expensive imitations of native costumes (Gee et al., 1997).

4.11 CULTURAL DRIFT

Cultural drift refers to a temporary and random cultural change. A good example of cultural drift is a temporary change in language; over time, pronunciation, vocabulary, spelling and even grammar can change. Although some of these changes occur as a result of changes in education and technology, most of them are caused by the changes brought by different cultures, especially a continuous interaction between societies. In tourism these changes are brought by contact between tourists and locals. Since their contact is often seasonal and brief, the changes may be temporal.

The temporary contact between tourists and hosts can result in visible changes in their behavior (phenotypic behavior). For example, the host can develop an attitude of servitude toward tourists. Since tourists visit the host's culture for the purpose of leisure, and hosts are at work, both strive to achieve different goals: tourists strive for personal satisfaction and hosts for financial gains. This often results in exploiting each other and the host environment.

Cultural drift assumes that the hosts' and tourists' behavior is changed temporarily for the duration of the tourist stay. The hosts and tourists may return to their original values and lifestyle when tourists leave. However, the changes in the host behavior may also be permanent. As the number of visitors to a destination increases and the contact between hosts and guests is more continuous, hosts may need to adjust to the needs of the tourists on a more permanent basis. Their values, norms, and standards are permanently changed and passed from one generation to the next. These reflect the changes to hosts' genotypic behavior. The larger the contrast between the host culture and the tourist culture, the more significant the changes.

4.12 ACCULTURATION

Acculturation ''results when groups of individuals from different cultures come into continuous first-hand contact, which causes changes in the original cultural patterns of either or both groups'' (Redfield et al., 1936). During the acculturation process, cultural elements of each group or individual are exchanged. As a result of this exchange, the original cultural patterns of either or both groups may be changed, but the groups remain culturally distinct (Kottak, 2007). Those who come to a new environment learn the behaviors, attitudes, and values of a culture that is different from their culture of origin (Lee, 1988). During the acculturation process, both changes of phenotypic and genotypic behaviors occur.

The process of acculturation is not balanced. Acculturation occurs when contact takes place between a stronger culture and a weaker one. It is more likely to occur between the developed and the developing world. For example, tourists from powerful, developed countries influence locals from poorer, developing countries.

Historically, acculturation was believed to be a one-way process whereby the individual coming to a new culture learned its values and norms. Acculturation can affect one or both groups. However, it influences one group more than the other (Berry & Sam, 1997). For example, although both the newcomer culture and the host culture undergo changes, the impact of the host culture on the newcomer culture is relatively stronger compared to the influence of the newcomer culture on the host culture (Kim, 1985). The newcomers need to adapt more to the host culture than the hosts need to adapt to the newcomer culture (Ogden et al., 2004).

Traditionally, it was believed that in order to adapt to a culturally different environment individuals had to lose their cultural characteristic and gain characteristics of other cultural groups. Today it is believed that individuals may maintain their culture of origin while gaining characteristics of other cultural groups (Berry, 2003). Individuals themselves determine the amount of cultural characteristics and contact needed with the dominant culture to successfully adapt. Individuals who are not able to make this decision often experience stress resulting in reduced mental health (Berry, 2003; Burnham et al., 1987).

Acculturation occurs at both individual and group levels. On the individual level, newcomers learn new values and develop new perceptions, attitudes, and personality (Berry, 1980). On the group level, acculturation occurs through socialization, social interaction, and mobility (Olmedo, 1979). Individual acculturation is called *transculturation* and occurs on a smaller scale and has less visible impact. It mostly occurs to long-stay visitors and first-generation immigrants, for whom the process is very difficult, due to the lack of precedents in the family. The degree of acculturation varies, depending on the individual's interests and the motivation. An example of individual acculturation is learning regional vocabulary by a traveler who spent some time in a foreign country.

The group acculturation occurs on a larger scale and is more visible. The group acculturation occurs due to the inflow of new technology, modernization, and advancement. For example, due to continuous contact, cultures exchanged foods, recipes, music, clothing, and technologies. However, the group acculturation may have damaging impact on the indigenous culture, leading to total assimilation of the indigenous people with the dominant culture. For example, many Native Americans of the United States, Taiwanese aborigines, and Australian aborigines have nearly lost their traditional culture when it was replaced by the dominant new culture.

Acculturation is measured by the extent to which a person has adapted to a new culture and changed his or her own behavior as a result of the contact with a new culture. In the early 1900s many of the European migrants successfully assimilated and adapted American culture. However, the new immigrants to the United States (e.g. Hispanics) do not desire to be fully assimilated. Many of them want to maintain their own cultural identities.

One of the most important indicators of acculturation is the extent to which new-comers (1) speak their native language versus host language, (2) become aware of the cultural heritage, identity, and social behavior of a new culture versus their culture, and (3) are culturally affiliated with a new culture and do not feel discrimination.

Acculturation can be voluntary or forced. Acculturation is voluntary when the individuals voluntarily come to a new culture and learn its values and beliefs. Acculturation is forced when the individuals are forced to come to a new culture for political or economic reasons. Voluntary acculturation is quicker and easier because individuals are motivated to learn the host language, become familiar with the preferences and lifestyle of a new culture, and become affiliated with a new culture. Forced acculturation is difficult and it takes longer time.

The process of acculturation is often referred to as the ''Macdonaldization'' of global cultures (Mason, 2003). Due to globalization, access to new technology and advancements in communication customers, regardless of their location, learn about new products and share common tastes and preferences on a worldwide scale. Homogenized products and global standards that imitate and assimilate patterns of social behavior, language, dress, and, cuisine are spread around the world (Ritzer & Liska, 1997). This standardization of products around the world blurs cultural lines (Jafari, 1996) that results in cultural homogeneity and standardization of tourism destinations.

4.13 CULTURAL ADAPTATION

Cultural adaptation refers to adaptation of elements of other culture. Hosts need to adapt some elements of tourist culture in order to meet tourists' needs. Host communities are usually pro-active and adapt to different categories of tourists despite stereotypes (Sofield, 2000). The process of adaptation depends on the duration of the tourist's visit, duration and intensity of interaction between tourists and hosts, the strength of their cultural affiliations, and capacity to withstand the influences of each other. The process of hosts' adaptation to tourists' needs often leads to commoditization and commercialization of local culture.

There are various adaptation models developed. For example, according to Doxey (1976), the resident population (hosts) changes their behavior and attitudes to tourists over time. When tourists first visit the destination, hosts greet them with euphoria and then over time as the numbers of tourists and their impacts (positive and negative) grow, hosts' attitudes move through stages of apathy and annoyance to a level of aggression towards the visitors (Mason, 2003).

4.14 CULTURAL ADJUSTMENT

Cultural adaptation is often referred to as cultural adjustment. Trivonovich identified four different stages which every visitor may have to go through when adjusting to a new and different culture: (1) honeymoon stage, (2) hostility stage, (3) integration/acceptance stage, and (4) home stage (http://www.cgu.edu/pages/945.asp). In the honeymoon stage visitors are excited and fascinated with everything new. They are happy, interested in a new life and other people, and willing to please and cooperate. In the hostility stage the visitors become anxious, judgmental, fearful, and often depressed. They are frustrated about new rules of life and customs. They are easily upset by small and unimportant things, are not able to sleep and eat, and suffer from headaches, indigestion, and other illnesses. They blame the new environment for own discomfort and unhappiness and reject it. Visitors become hostile to all that is new and foreign; they lose motivation and often withdraw. In the integration stage visitors begin to feel comfortable and relaxed in the new environment. They smile and joke, and are not concerned with minor misunderstandings which previously caused hostility. They make friends and start seeking more information about the new environment. In the home stage, visitors feel at home and treat their new culture as their native culture. They have successfully adjusted to the customs and standards of the new environment and are able to live successfully in both cultures (http://www.cgu.edu/pages/945.asp). Sharp (1992) identified similar stages of adjustment, such as (1) initial enthusiasm and excitement about visiting a new destination, (2) withdrawal and loneliness due to difficulties caused by cultural problems, (3) re-emergence and adjustment, and (4) achievement and enthusiasm after adapting to a new culture.

There are several techniques that can be used to ease cultural adjustment. These include (1) being humble and having a genuine desire to meet and talk with local people, (2) expecting different things when traveling, (3) being open minded and not taking things seriously, (4) not letting others get on one's nerves, (5) enjoying the experiences and being a good ambassador for one's country, (6) learning about the new country to be visited, (7) not judging others by the people one has trouble with, (8) listening and observing, (9) understanding that other people may have different thought patterns, (10) being aware of what may be offensive to other people, and (11) reflecting on new experiences (http://www.cie.uci.edu/world/shock.html).

4.15 CULTURE ASSIMILATION

There is some ambiguity between the concept of acculturation and cultural assimilation. Consequently both terms are often used interchangeably. However, there is a difference between these two concepts. Acculturation refers to cultural borrowing when some elements of the other culture are added without abandoning the native culture (individuals gain characteristics of another cultural group while maintaining their original culture, causing changes in the original cultural patterns). When contact between tourists and hosts is temporary, hosts get back to their traditional values and lifestyles after tourists leave. If the contact is very short, a host society can experience cultural drift. On the other hand, assimilation occurs when a person fully adapts mainstream values of a new culture and gives up his/her cultural heritage (Berry, 1980; Padilla, 1980). Assimilation is about the replacement of one set of cultural traits by another one. It is a very intense process of integration and absorption of members of a cultural group (typically immigrants) or minority groups into another one. During this process many cultural characteristics of those who try to assimilate can be lost.

The differences between acculturation and assimilation can be presented on an acculturation–assimilation continuum. At one end of the continuum is the unacculturated extreme, where the individual's cultural heritage strongly influences his/her behavior. At the other end is the acculturated extreme, where the individual is fully assimilated to the host culture and has fully adapted the values and attitudes of the host population (Hair & Anderson, 1972). At this end, assimilation rather than acculturation occurs (see Figure 4.1).

Acculturation   Assimilation

Figure 4.1

Acculturation–Assimilation Continuum

Similarly to acculturation, assimilation can be voluntary (in the case with long-term visitors and immigrants) or forced upon an individual or group. When individuals or national groups are forced to assimilate for political or economic reasons they may strongly resist it. Sometimes governments put extreme pressure and even use force to assimilate the minority groups to a dominant culture. In this process some minority cultures can be exterminated and even physically eliminated because they usually do not have political power and are not in a formal position to impose elements of their culture on the dominant culture.

Different individuals assimilate in a different way. Some can assimilate quickly (e.g. young and motivated), while others cannot assimilate at all (e.g. the elderly). Children born in host countries to long-term visitors, such as guest workers, diplomats, soldiers, or immigrant parents, do not have trouble assimilating. These children easily associate with the host culture on a regular basis and treat the culture into which they have been born as their native culture. However, new long-term visitors and immigrants and their children have to adapt first before they assimilate to the host societies; they retain or modify elements of their native culture depending on how the host culture meets their needs.

Individuals try to assimilate with the new environment by learning the language of the host country, making new friends, finding a job, or going to school. Host societies also try to adapt to newcomers by accepting them as their own, providing them with language classes, helping to find schools and jobs, and giving them preferential treatment over themselves.

The effects of assimilation may be positive and negative. Assimilation may lead to learning, understanding, and accepting a new culture and its people. However, it may also lead to the minimization of the distinctive features of the native cultures and even their total disappearance.

4.16 ENCULTURATION

Enculturation refers to the learning of what is contained in culture. It is the process of learning the accepted norms and values of the culture or society in which the individual lives, what is and is not permissible within that society's framework, and the individual role within society. Enculturation also involves learning the language and ways of life of other people and their countries. Enculturation is about learning from other people how to behave. Thus, enculturation results in behavioral similarities and differences across societies.

Much of learning occurs through communication (speech, words, and gestures), observation of others and emulating their behavior (e.g. using different slang, expressions, and dress), education, and socialization (through social events and behaviors that prevail in a particular culture). Thus, enculturation also refers to socialization (Segall et al., 1990). Parents play a very important role when a child is learning a culture. Enculturation is a life-long process. It can be conscious or unconscious. Individuals are usually unaware of how much they learn. People who are most thoroughly enculturated are the least aware of their culture's role in influencing them (Segall et al., 1990). Enculturation is sometimes referred to as acculturation, a word which originally referred only to exchanges of cultural features with foreign cultures.

4.17 DEMONSTRATION EFFECT

Demonstration effect is the effect on the behavior of individuals caused by observation of the actions of others and their consequences (http://en.wikipedia.org/wiki/Demonstration_effect). The example of demonstration effect includes individuals or countries that adapt cultural elements and policies used by those who have been successful in adapting them. The purpose of demonstration effect is to emulate the success of others.

In tourism, demonstration effect refers to local residents adapting the styles and manners of visiting tourists. Locals notice the superior material possessions of the visitors and wish to have the same. One of the positive effects of demonstration effect is that it encourages residents to better work and productivity. Particularly, in developing countries hosts can be motivated to perform better because they can see in tourists the standard of living they want to follow. However, the expensive cameras and watches carried by tourists can not only be the objects of admiration and motivation to work harder, but also a source of anger and even threat. Demonstration effect can be disruptive; locals can become resentful of visitors because they are unable to obtain the goods and lifestyle demonstrated by them. The exposure of the host society to tourists' goods or ways of living can create unhappiness of hosts with what they previously regarded as acceptable. Demonstration effect can often generate jealousy, resentment, and even hatred of tourists in the developing host countries, especially, when locals see they cannot be as wealthy as tourists and have the same standard of living.

Demonstrating the Western way of living, either through travel and tourism or media, to host countries that have not reached the same level of development and wealth, may be a sign of egoism on behalf of tourists. However, international travelers from developed countries are not always aware of the socio-economic situation of the host countries in which they travel and thus do not always understand the effects of their behavior on the local population. Consequently, tourists are not always to be blamed for their behavior. Demonstration effect is most often brought by commercial and media activities which are to be blamed.

Young people are particularly susceptible to demonstration effect. Demonstration effect encourages young people to leave their families and home land, especially rural areas, and move to urban areas or even overseas in search of the better ''demonstrated'' lifestyle. Demonstration effect may be responsible for social divisions between the young and old members of a society, and conflicts rather than learning and cooperation (Mason, 2003).

4.18 CULTURAL CONFLICT

Cultural conflicts are created by cultural contacts. Conflicts arise because those in contact (individuals or groups) are from different cultures. Culture is a major factor in culture conflict. In particular cultural differences that cause misunderstanding and value clashes, cause culture conflicts. People are cultural beings, and culture is part of their identity, the way they perceive and act in the world and the way they interact. Culture affects their relationships, how they develop meanings, create identities, understand their roles and responsibilities, and argue and negotiate. Culture is an important component in human conflicts. Human conflicts are cultural conflicts. In all human conflicts tensions develop due to inaccurate communication or stressed relationships, which are due to differences in culture. Even conflict resolutions are influenced by culture. For example, the Kosovo conflict or Israeli–Palestinian or Indian–Pakistani conflicts are not about territory and sovereignty issues; they are also about making different meanings, perceiving the world, and acknowledging and legitimizing own cultural identities and ways of living.

Societies as well as individuals who share cultural similarities understand each other, develop mutual relationships, and group themselves around their values. Those who do not share cultural values and preferences have difficulties with understanding each other and are not successful in developing relationships; thus they are increasingly in conflict with each other. The question is whether global tourism will be characterized by increasing cultural understanding or conflicts? What is the likelihood of cultural understanding and conflicts between people?

Whether international travel traffic has increased its impact on human contact and relationships is often debatable. It is generally assumed that international tourism reduces the probability of cultural conflict and leads to cultural understanding and peace. However, there is not much evidence to confirm this assumption. In fact, to the contrary, there is much evidence that increasing contact between people from different cultures may be a highly divisive force for international tourism (see Chapter 8). One may even say that it is unlikely that increasing contact between people from different cultures will ease international tensions or promote greater international understanding and good relations among countries. Even economic benefits that tourism brings cannot foster understanding and peace among nations. Increased communication, trade, and travel multiply interactions among cultures, and increasingly encourage people to pay attention to their cultural uniqueness and identity. For example, two Europeans: one German and the other French, interacting with each other, identify each other as German and French. However, when interacting with two Arabs: one Saudi and the other Egyptian, they define themselves as Europeans and Arabs. Consequently, in an increasingly globalized world there will be a very strong focus on cultural, ethnic and even civilizational identity. People will increasingly desire to emphasize their identities which may be a determining force for generating future cultural conflicts.

Cultural conflicts are more dangerous than conflicts between social or economic classes. Vaclav Havel, a former president of the Czech Republic stated that ''cultural conflicts are increasing and are more dangerous today than at any time in history'' (Havel, 1994). Nations who share similar culture, values, social relations, customs and philosophical assumptions and have similar outlook on life usually support ethnic conflicts, tribal wars, and violence between groups from different cultures. Thus, it is expected that future conflicts between nations and individuals will be generated by cultural factors rather than by economics or ideology (Delors, 1993). In today's increasingly multicultural world, global tourism will be characterized by increasing cultural conflicts (Huntington, 1996). Cultural differences will be undoing the world. The more the world will become globalized, the more pressure there will be on societies and individuals to become culturally unique and distinct. The existence and nature of the cultural conflicts will greatly depend upon understanding and accepting the cultural differences as differences rather than deficiencies. As a result, those who want to avoid conflicts and function more effectively in a new global world will require cultural competency (see Chapter 16).

SUMMARY

With an excessive demand for tourism products many societies experience erosion of local cultures. Traditional cultures are being commoditized and commercialized, exploited over which locals lose rights. Although commoditization destroys authenticity of local culture it also helps its conservation and preservation.

Culture change refers to changes in culture due to contact between culturally different groups. Cultural diffusion defines the spread of cultural elements from one culture to another. Various theories failed to explain why some cultural elements are not being diffused. Cultural borrowing occurs when two cultures borrow each other's traditions, customs, or values. Although cultural borrowing may lead to learning other cultures, it may also generate cultural collision. Cultural drift refers to a temporary and random cultural change. The tourist–host contact can result in temporary and visible (phenotypic) or permanent (genotypic) changes in behavior. Acculturation refers to adding some elements of the other culture to one's native culture and causing changes in one's original cultural patterns. Acculturation is measured by the extent to which a person has adapted to a new culture. Cultural adaptation refers to adaptation of elements of another culture. Hosts need to adapt some elements of tourists' culture to meet tourists' needs. There are various stages of cultural adaptation or adjustment and techniques for easing cultural adjustment. Culture assimilation occurs when a person fully adapts mainstream values of a new culture and gives up his/her cultural heritage. The differences between acculturation and assimilation can be presented on an acculturation–assimilation continuum. Acculturation and assimilation can be voluntary or forced. Although assimilation may lead to learning a new culture it can also lead to a total disappearance of native cultures. Enculturation refers to the learning of what is contained in culture; it often results in behavioral similarities and differences across societies. Demonstration effect refers to local residents adapting the styles and manners of visiting tourists. Demonstration effect frequently creates jealousy and hatred of tourists in the developing host country. Culture conflicts are caused by misunderstanding and value clashes and are more dangerous than conflicts between social or economic classes. Global tourism will be characterized by increasing cultural conflicts.

DISCUSSION POINTS AND QUESTIONS

1. What is the effect of cultural commoditization and transformation on local traditions and customs?
2. Find in the literature examples of products that are sold to tourists as ''local and authentic'' although they may be mass produced elsewhere.
3. How important is authenticity of tourism experiences?
4. What is the difference between acculturation and cultural assimilation?
5. What strategies do you use in your own life which aid your adaptation in foreign country and reduce cultural stress?
6. Give three examples of demonstration effect in tourism.

CASE STUDY 4.1 Discovering The Maori Culture

I arrived in New Zealand on the 20th of October 2004. This country has always fascinated me. At that time I didn't know much about Maori culture. The only image of New Zealand I had was the entrancing ceremony made by the New Zealand rugby players before a match. I also saw a film *Once Were Warriors* on failed assimilation and destruction of indigenous cultures. When visiting New Zealand I wanted to experience the cultural practices of its indigenous people. I hoped the Maori culture had not been transformed into some kind of tourist attraction.

After a few days in Auckland, I headed off for Rotorua – the cradle of Maori culture and the birthplace of tourism in New Zealand. My first confrontation with the Maori culture was through the visit of the New Zealand Maori Arts and Crafts Institute (NZMACI), a carving and weaving school. Arts and crafts are very important in Maori culture. ''Like the pictures of a book, arts and crafts are the pages of the Maori culture. It's how stories were told and passed down through generations; how traditions and genealogy were preserved. History was carved and woven'' (http://www.nzmaori.co.nz). Through the visit of this living museum, Maori people can preserve their culture and share their art with the tourists.

After this very interesting introduction to the Maori culture, I attended a Maori show in the evening. I was never interested in staged tourist attractions, because I would rather experience real cultural practices. I felt that by participating in this show I was consuming culture like any another product; I could pay for a piece of the Maori cultural heritage. However, I also knew that I wouldn't be able to experience the Maori culture if I didn't attend the show. I wanted to learn more about the Maori culture, so I decided to attend the show.

The performance took place in the Maori village at *Te Puia*, literally ''the land of Maori ancestors.'' After a traditional welcome, the show began with a challenge by fierce warriors, following an hour of song and dance inside the *Marae*, the ''sacred meeting house.'' Being surrounded by the carvings of ancestors, I could enjoy the seductiveness of the *Poi* dance and the ferocity of the *Haka*, the war dance. After the show, the performers shared with us a food provided from the traditional *Hangi*, where food is steam cooked on hot rocks of the earth.

I left the village with the impression that I knew a little more about Maori culture and that those people were proud of their heritage and willing to share it with the tourists. According to Zeppel (1997), ''The experience of presenting Maori people as part of a living culture is a success for both the tourists and the hosts. Maori staff recreate a traditional lifestyle, the *hangi* and concert provide an educational experience of Maori culture for visitors, and Maori employees are motivated to learn about their own culture and to share it with the visitors.''

The Rotorua region and its people are known for their hospitality. They naturally accept the tourists coming to share their cultural practices. Their shows not only generate incomes and work in the community, but also better educate tourists about Maori culture and keep their traditions alive. It is important that the Maori people and tribes continue to be involved in all instances of the planning and further developments of tourism in New Zealand.

Zeppel, H. (1997). Maori tourism conference Te Putanga Mai. *Journal of Travel Research 36* (2), 78–80.

WEBSITE LINKS

1. Cultural change: http://en.wikipedia.org/wiki/Culture
2. Culture change: http://anthro.palomar.edu/change/default.htm
3. Cultural diffusion: http://en.wikipedia.org/wiki/Diffusion_(anthropology)
4. Cultural drift: http://www.mentalwanderings.com/gulch/2003/12/cultural_drift.html
5. Acculturation: http://en.wikipedia.org/wiki/Acculturation, http://www.encyclopedia.com/doc/1E1-accultur.html
6. Cultural adaptation: http://www.temple.edu/studyabroad/students/cultural_adaptation.html
7. Cultural adjustment: http://internationaloffice.berkeley.edu/multiple_use/cultural_adjustment.php, http://www.uazone.net/Adjustment.html
8. Cultural assimilation: http://en.wikipedia.org/wiki/Cultural_assimilation
9. Enculturation: http://en.wikipedia.org/wiki/Enculturation

Since the aim of this book is to explain the impact of culture on tourist behavior, the next part will discuss the concept of culture and cultural differences.

Culture and Cultural Differences 3

Part Three explains the concept of culture and identifies major cultural differences in core value patterns among international societies. This part also discusses the influence of national culture on communication, social interaction, rules of social behavior, and service. The discussion is placed in the context of ethics.

Culture

5

The aim of this chapter is to provide a detailed explanation of the concept, elements, and characteristics of culture.

OBJECTIVES

After completing this chapter the reader should be able to:

- Understand the concept, elements, and characteristics of culture
- Identify different types and levels of culture
- Explain the concept of subculture
- Distinguish between national culture, nationality, country of residence, and country of birth
- Learn about the importance of cultural identity in this world
- Understand the concept and measurement of cultural distance

INTRODUCTION

In an increasingly multicultural tourism context, the question of the similarities and differences in tourist behavior across cultural borders is gaining in importance. More and more people are traveling around the world, and their countries are being integrated into global markets. Therefore, tourism marketers and managers operating in this environment need to understand the concept of culture and the role of national culture in influencing tourist behavior.

5.1 DEFINITION OF CULTURE

Many people generally believe that culture manifests itself in music, literature, painting, sculpture, theater, and film (Williams, 1976). Others describe it in terms of consumption and consumer goods (Berger & Smith, 1971). However, the concept of culture is very difficult, perhaps even impossible, to define because it is a theory and/or abstract name for a very large, complex, multidimensional phenomenon. Hundreds of definitions of culture have been developed under different conditions under which different scholars have worked. These scholars have all had different views about what constitutes the concept and meaning of culture.

Originally, the term *culture* derived from Latin *cultura*, which means to cultivate. The term refers to patterns of human activity and the symbolic structures that give such activities significance and importance. Anthropologists, in particular, point to the human origin of culture. Functionalists refer to culture as a set of rules that gives direction to people, informs them how they should behave and what means they should use to meet their needs. Cognitive anthropologists view culture as cognitive knowledge. Symbolists refer to culture as a system of symbols and meanings that help to communicate. Social anthropologists emphasize the importance of social relationships and practices of human consumption processes. Cultural anthropologists focus on human norms and values. Archaeologists concentrate more on the material remains of human activity. Marketers refer to culture as a set of important assumptions that members of a particular community share in common. These different definitions reflect different theoretical bases for understanding the concept of culture and criteria for evaluating human activity. Such a division of thoughts also shows difficulties in arriving at one central definition. As a result, culture is ambiguously defined, and no single consistent and integrated definition of culture has been proposed. Yet, the term is used as if its meaning was clear.

The section below presents more detailed explanations of culture. The definitions presented range from the view that culture is an all-inclusive phenomenon (e.g. culture is everything) to the view that it takes a narrow perspective (e.g. culture is about people's way of life). Sir Edward Burnett Tylor, who described culture from the perspective of social anthropology, defined culture as "that complex whole which includes knowledge, beliefs, art, morals, law, customs, and any other capabilities and habits acquired by man as a member of society" (Tylor, 1874, p. 1). This classic definition of culture emphasizes the inclusive nature of culture (many variables are included).

A view of culture from a narrower perspective points to different aspects of the concept and reflects its essential features. These definitions are not mutually exclusive. Accordingly, culture refers to the:

1. *Human environment.* Culture has been created by humans; it is a part of a human-made environment that holds human groups together.
2. *Social heritage and traditions.* Culture refers to the history of a nation, region, or group of people, and its traditions, customs, art crafts, architecture, music, and painting.

3. *Way of life*. Culture is a way of life of a group of people or an entire society; it shows how to live and what standards and criteria to use to decide what to do in life and how to do things.
4. *Behavior*. Culture is about human behavior; it influences human behavior and shows how people should behave. It determines the patterns of behavior associated with particular groups of people, and the conditions and circumstances under which various behaviors occur. Culture also helps to interpret, understand, and predict others' behavior. People's behavior depends upon the culture in which they have been raised. Culture is the foundation of human behavior.
5. *Rules of social life*. Culture represents a set of rules that gives direction concerning how human beings should behave in their lives. These rules also allow for a better understanding of others' behavior and predicting how others will behave and why. These rules need to be followed to maintain harmony and order in a society.
6. *Dress and appearance*. Culture dictates how people should dress. It determines what clothing people wear for a business or casual meeting, as well as at home. To be socially accepted people dress appropriately for the occasion. Cultural customs and traditions determine the dress code and color, the length of hair, the jewelry to be worn, and the amount of makeup to be used. Some cultures accept jeans worn by youth and elders (e.g. in the United States), others favor traditional dress, (e.g. Japanese kimono or the sarong in Southeast Asia). Culture determines a sense of aesthetics.
7. *Food and eating habits*. Culture determines how food is prepared, cooked, presented, and consumed. For example, in some cultures people eat beef (e.g. in the United States), while in others beef is forbidden (e.g. India). In some cultures people use forks and knifes to eat (e.g. Europeans), while in others, people use chopsticks (e.g. Chinese), or their hands (e.g. Indians). Culture determines table manners. For example, one can distinguish between Europeans and Americans by observing how they hold forks and knives at the dinner table.
8. *Sense of self*. Culture gives people a sense of identity and self-esteem. Culture provides meanings and directions, and shows people where they belong. Culture also provides answers to those who feel lost due to globalization, industrialization, urbanization, new technology, and rapid economic developments.
9. *Relationships*. Culture impacts personal relationships, businesses, corporations, and government. Culture indicates how people should behave in a group, relate to each other, and treat others, for example, friends, elders, teachers, supervisors, minorities, and special needs groups. For example, in some cultures, elders are honoured, respected, and allocated the best rooms in the house (e.g. Korea). In other cultures it is common to send elders to special care facilities (e.g. the United States). Culture influences attitudes towards genders, gender roles and responsibilities, marriage, social relationships, and work. The concept of culture can explain various systems of a society, such as social, political, economic, financial, educational, kinship, religious, health, and recreational systems.

10. *Values and norms.* Culture dictates the priorities people should attach to certain values; it indicates what should be the most important and least important values. In some cultures individuals are concerned with work, personal achievements, and material things (e.g. the United States), whereas in other cultures people are expected to share, obey, and be concerned about others (e.g. Asia). Culture helps to reaffirm values, cope with difficulties, and find solutions to problems. Culture includes systems of values, and values create culture.

11. *Beliefs and attitudes.* Culture defines people's beliefs, views, opinions, perceptions, and attitudes towards themselves, others, and the world. Culture determines religious practices, beliefs in life and death, and the difference between good and bad.

12. *Ways of thinking and doing things.* Culture is the socially acquired way of thinking, feeling, and doing things. Culture is the means through which human beings communicate their thoughts and values and fulfil their needs.

13. *Work and leisure habits.* Culture determines attitude towards work, work habits and practices, accomplishments, assessments, promotions, incentives, responsibilities, work ethic, worthiness of activity, loyalty to employer, commitment to quality of work and service, and ways of making decisions. In some cultures people ''live to work'' (e.g. the United States), in others, people ''work to live'' (e.g. Australia, France). Culture also determines attitudes towards leisure, travel habits, frequency and seasonality of travel, preferred modes of travel and accommodation, sources of information used, spending patterns, length of stay, and destination selection. For example, tourists from the United States and Europe like to travel independently, whereas tourists from Asia prefer to travel in groups.

14. *Time.* Culture determines attitude towards time. In some cultures punctuality and promptness are expected (e.g. Germany). In others, people do not bother about time, instead they manage their life by sunrise and sunset, and by winter, spring, summer, or fall. For example, in India or in Latin America, being late for appointments and not adhering to time schedules are accepted.

15. *Cognitive knowledge.* Culture is a system of cognitive knowledge, classifications, and categories existing in the minds of people and shaped by the human brain. Culture is often described as ''the collective programming of the mind, which distinguishes the members of one group or category of people from another'' (Hofstede, 1991, p. 5). For example, rules for human behavior are created by a culturally patterned mind.

16. *Mental process and learning.* Culture is about how people organize and process information, how they learn and adapt to the surrounding environment, and how they suffer the consequences of not learning certain information and not adapting to new circumstances. For example, some cultures favor straightforwardness, logic, cognition, and intellectual skills (e.g. Germany), others stress circular logic, conceptualization, abstract thinking, and emotional communication (e.g. Japan).

17. *Information and communication.* Culture is information, and information is communication. Thus, culture is a communication system. It uses verbal and

non-verbal cues that distinguish one group from another. Language is a guide to communication and culture. Language helps to transmit people's values, beliefs, perceptions, and norms. It facilitates the development of attitudes and perceptions of the world. Differences in languages and verbal cues create different ways of expressing beliefs, values, and perceptions. Non-verbal cues, such as gestures or body language, also differ by culture. For example, in some cultures, interruptions in discussions are common (e.g. Brazil), in others, they are regarded as rude (e.g. Japan). So, different cultures have different communication systems. In some societies people speak several major languages (e.g. in Switzerland people speak German, Italian, and French). Within one language group there may be various dialects, slang, jargons, or accents. People who speak the same language with the same accent or jargon distinguish themselves from others.

18. *Symbols and meanings*. Culture is a system of symbols, meanings, ideas, and emotions that influence people's experiences. Members of the same culture rely on the same symbols (e.g. letters, signs) to frame their thoughts, expressions, and emotions (e.g. joy, sorrow). Symbols help people communicate, develop attitudes towards life and others, and understand socially accepted behavior. Symbols make culture possible and readable. Although meanings cannot be observed and measured, they can help to understand others' behavior. For example, in some cultures patting a child on the head is unacceptable because the head is considered to be the center of intellectual power (e.g. Malaysia), while in other cultures head patting is acceptable. In Poland, for example, patting a child on the head is considered to be a caring and protective gesture.

19. *Perceptions*. Culture is a way of perceiving the environment. Culture is ''the sum of people's perceptions of themselves and of the world . . ..'' (Urriola, 1989, p. 66). The similarity in people's perceptions indicates the existence of similar cultures and the sharing and understanding of meanings (Samovar et al., 1981).

20. *Differences and similarities between people*. Culture is about differences and similarities between people. Culture is often referred to as differences between groups of people who do things differently and perceive the world differently (Potter, 1989). These differences indicate the existence of different cultures. It is important to understand how cultural differences affect human perceptions of the world. Figure 5.1 illustrates the concept and elements of culture.

The definitions of culture that were presented cover a very wide range of meanings. However, they do not exhaust the many uses of the term *culture*. In 1952, Alfred Kroeber and Clyde Kluckhohn compiled a list of 164 definitions of culture. As a conclusion of their extensive analysis, they suggested a comprehensive and all-inclusive definition of culture: ''Culture consists of patterns, explicit and implicit, of and for behavior acquired and transmitted by symbols, constituting the distinctive achievements of human groups, including their embodiments in artifacts; the essential core of culture consists of traditional (i.e. historically derived and selected) ideas and especially their attached values; culture systems may, on the one hand, be

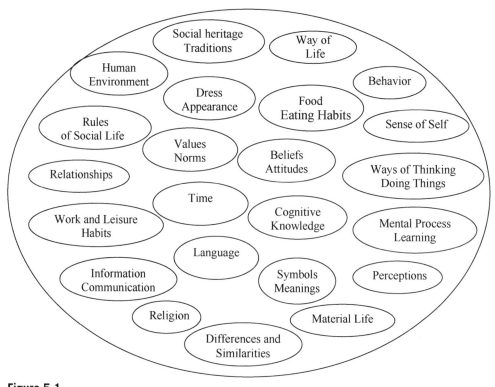

Figure 5.1

The Concept and Elements of Culture

considered as products of action, on the other as conditioning elements of further action'' (Kroeber & Kluckhohn, 1952, p. 181). This definition is consistent with Malinowski's (1988, p. 74) more concise definition of culture as ''the sum of goods, of rights and duties, of ideas, beliefs, capabilities, and customs.''

Culture, as these definitions suggest, represents a system of tangible and intangible components. Tangible components of culture represent material culture and comprise productive forces and physical elements necessary to support human life, such as clothing, tools, food, buildings, paintings, and many other cultural objects and artifacts. Intangible elements of culture represent non-material culture and refer to values, beliefs, attitudes, morality, ethics, spirituality, traditions, and customs.

In recent years Herbig and Dunphy (1998) defined culture in terms of human experiences and their interpretation. They referred to culture as ''both explicit and implicit rules through which experience is interpreted'' (p. 11). Pizam, cited in Pizam and Mansfeld (1999), referred to culture as ''an umbrella word that encompasses a whole set of implicitly, widely shared beliefs, traditions, values, and expectations that characterized a particular group of people'' (p. 393). More recently, the

United Nations Educational, Scientific and Cultural Organization described culture as the set of distinctive spiritual, material, intellectual and emotional features of society or a social group that encompasses, in addition to art and literature, lifestyle, ways of living together, value systems, traditions and beliefs (UNESCO, 2002). It appears that the basis of all human behaviors and beliefs is the group's specific value system. Values represent the core of any culture (Rokeach, 1973; Kroeber & Kluckhohn, 1952) and comprise psychological, spiritual, and moral phenomena (Kroeber & Kluckhohn, 1967; Trompenaars, 1993).

5.2 CULTURE AS CIVILIZATION

Culture was also compared to civilization (Tylor, 1874). According to this notion, some countries and nations are more cultured or civilized than others. Similarly, some people are more cultured and civilized than others. It was noted that the word *cultured* describes people who know about or take part in the elite activities such as museum art and classical music (Bakhtin, 1981). These activities are called ''high culture'' and are pursued by the ruling social groups. High culture differs from mass culture or popular culture (pop culture), which is pursued by the masses (non-elites). However, today masses also engage in cultured activities as elites.

The word *cultured* is often assigned to the Western world; some believe that the Western culture is more civilized and cultured than non-Western culture. This assumption is wrong. Non-Westerners are just as civilized and cultured as Westerners, albeit in a different way.

5.3 CULTURES BY REGION

Different geographical regions are characterized by different cultures through the influence of social contacts, colonization, trade, travel, migration, religion, and mass media. For example, African culture, especially sub-Saharan African culture, has been influenced by European colonialism and Arab and Islamic culture, especially in North Africa. The American culture has been shaped by the cultures of the people of Africa, Europe, and Asia, who arrived either through the slave trade or the waves of immigration from Europe, (e.g. Dutch, English, French, German, Irish, Italian, Portuguese, Scandinavian, or Spanish), Latin America (e.g. Cuba, Mexico, and Nicaragua), and more recently Asia (e.g. China, Korea, and Vietnam). The North American culture is known as a ''mixed culture'' because it has adapted different cultural elements from different cultures and races. Asian cultural traditions were influenced by Buddhism and Taoism, especially in East Asia, and the social and moral philosophy of Confucianism. Hinduism and Islam influenced the culture of various parts of South Asia. The influence of Chinese and Chinese writing on Korean, Japanese, and Vietnamese languages is well known. The countries of the Pacific Ocean have been influenced by their indigenous cultures as well as European culture. For example, Australian and New Zealand cultures have been shaped by European settlers and indigenous Australian and Maori (New Zealand) cultures. The Polynesian culture was strongly influenced by Christianity. The European culture has been mostly influenced by ancient Greek, ancient Rome, and Christian cultures. The Middle East has been influenced by Arabic, Persian, and Turkish cultures. This region is predominantly Muslim, although a large number of minorities (Christians and others) live there. Arabic culture has influenced the Persian and Turkish cultures through Islam, affecting their languages, writing systems, art, architecture and literature. The Iranian culture influenced Iraq and Turkey (http://en.wikipedia.org/wiki/Culture#Cultures_by_region).

5.4 CULTURE AS RELIGION

Religious beliefs are integral to a culture. Religion is defined as a set of beliefs, practices, and moral claims, often codified as prayers, rituals, and religious laws, all of which are shared within groups. Religiousness is referred to as adherence to the beliefs and practices of an organized church or religious institution (Shafranske & Malony, 1990). Religion teaches people to search for an external God. Religion often dictates behavior, as in the case of the Ten Commandments of the Judeo-Christian tradition, or the five precepts of Buddhism.

5.5 THE WORLD'S MAJOR RELIGIONS

The world's major religions are classified into Christianity (33% of the world's population), Islam (20%), Hinduism (13%), Chinese folk religion (6%), and Buddhism (5–6%). These religions can be combined into larger groups, or smaller sub-denominations. The larger groups are represented by (1) Abrahamic religions, which include Christianity, Islam, and Judaism (and sometimes the Bahá'í Faith), (2) Dharmic religions (or Indian religions) which include Hinduism, Buddhism, Sikhism, and Jainism, and (3) Far Eastern religions (or East Asian, Chinese, or Taoic religions) which include Shinto, Taoism, Confucianism, and Chinese folk religion. Conversely, the major religions may be parsed into denominations such as (a) Christian denominations (Catholicism, Eastern Orthodoxy, Protestantism, Oriental Orthodoxy, and Nestorianism), (b) divisions of Islam (Sunnism, Shi'ism, Sufism, and Kharijites), (c) Hindu denominations (Shaivism, Vaishnavism, Shaktism, Smartha and others), and (d) schools of Buddhism (Theravada, Mahayana, and Vajrayana). About 4% of world's population follows indigenous tribal religions. About 12% of the world's population is irreligious. Table 5.1 presents the world's major religions.

In 2005 the majority of the world's population adhered to Abrahamic religions (53.5%), Indian (19.7%), Far Eastern (6.5%), tribal religions (4.0%), and new religious movements (2.0%). More than 14% of the world population was irreligious. Figure 5.2 shows the major religious groups as a percentage of the world population in 2005.

Table 5.1 World's Major Religions

Religion	Beliefs and concepts
Christianity	Christianity is a religion centered on the life and teachings of Jesus of Nazareth. Christians believe Jesus to be the Son of God and the Messiah (or Christ) prophesied in the Old Testament.
Islam	Muslims believe that God revealed the Qur'an to Muhammad, God's final prophet, and regard the Qur'an and the Sunnah as the fundamental sources of Islam. They do not regard Muhammad as the founder of a new religion, but as the restorer of the original faith of Abraham, Moses, Jesus, and other prophets.
Hinduism	Hinduism is a religious tradition that originated in the Indian subcontinent. Hinduism is often referred to as Sanātana Dharma, a Sanskrit phrase meaning ''the eternal path'' or ''the eternal law''. A conglomerate of diverse beliefs and traditions, Hinduism has no single founder.
Buddhism	Buddhism is a set of teachings described as a religion. One point of view says it is a body of philosophies influenced by the teachings of Siddhartha Gautama, known as Gautama Buddha. Another point of view says it is teachings to guide one to directly experiencing reality.
Sikhism	Sikhism, founded on the teachings of Guru Nanak Dev and nine successive gurus in fifteenth century Northern India, is the fifth-largest religion in the world. The principal belief of Sikhism is faith in Vāhigurū – represented using the sacred symbol of ēkoarikār, the Universal one God. Sikhism advocates the pursuit of salvation through disciplined, personal meditation on the name and message of God.
Judaism	Judaism is the religion associated with the Jewish people. It is based on the principles and ethics embodied in the Hebrew Bible (Tanakh), as further explored and explained in the Talmud.

Table 5.1 (*Continued*)

Religion	Beliefs and concepts
Bahá'í Faith	The Bahá'í Faith is a religion founded by Bahá'u'lláh in 19th-century Persia, emphasizing the spiritual unity of all humankind. According to Bahá'í teachings, religious history has unfolded through a series of God's messengers who brought teachings suited for the capacity of the people at their time, and whose fundamental purpose is the same.
Confucianism	Confucianism is an ancient Chinese ethical and philosophical system developed from the teachings of the Chinese philosopher Confucius. It focuses on human morality and good doings. Confucianism is a complex system of moral, social, political, philosophical, and quasi-religious thought that has had tremendous influence on the culture and history of East Asia.
Jainism	Jainism, traditionally known as Jain Dharma, is one of the oldest religions in the world. It is a religion and philosophy originating in ancient India. The Jains follow the teachings of the 24 Jinas (conquerors) who are also known as Tirthankars.
Shinto	Shinto is the native religion of Japan and was once its state religion. It is a type of polytheism, and involves the worship of *kami*, spirits.

Source: http://en.wikipedia.org/wiki/World_religion; retrieved 18 February, 2008.

The prevailing world religions are Catholicism, Eastern Orthodoxy, and Protestantism, followed by Islamic religions, Chinese religion, Buddhism and Hinduism. Figure 5.3 shows the prevalence of the major world religions by continents.

The prevalence of Abrahamic (dark) and Indian (light) religions in each country is shown in Figure 5.4.

The relative proportion of Christians (dark) versus Muslims (light) in each country is shown in Figure 5.5.

Over the last 100 years, there has been an increase in the proportions of the world population adhering to Islam and Christianity. It has been predicted that the proportion of Christians will decline to about 25% of the world's population by 2025, and the proportion of Muslims will continue to increase to 30% (Huntington, 1996).

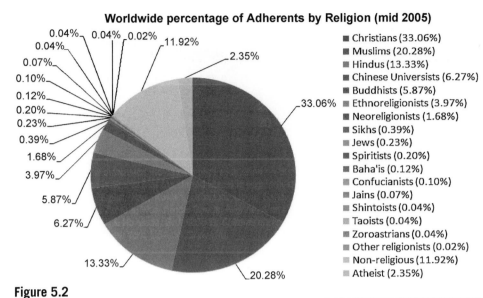

Figure 5.2

Major Religious Groups as a Percentage of the World's Population in 2005

Source: http://en.wikipedia.org/wiki/World_religion.

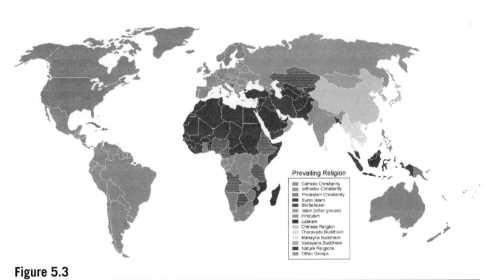

Figure 5.3

Map of Prevailing Religions in the World

Source: http://en.wikipedia.org/wiki/World_religion.

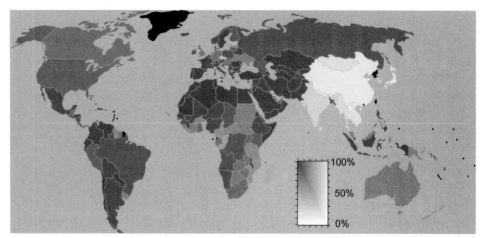

Figure 5.4

Abrahamic and Indian Religions in the World

Source: http://en.wikipedia.org/wiki/World_religion.

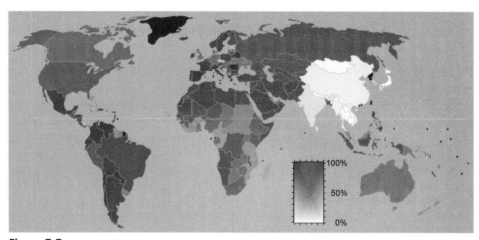

Figure 5.5

Christian and Muslim Religions Around the World

Source: http://en.wikipedia.org/wiki/World_religion.

5.6 RELIGION BY REGION

Most Africans adhere to the Abrahamic religions, either Christianity (Egypt, Ethiopia, Eritrea) or Islam. Islam is the dominant religion in Northern Africa, and it is also prominent in western Africa (Côte d'Ivoire, northern Ghana, southwest and northern Nigeria), northeastern Africa and along the coast of eastern Africa. Christianity and

Islam are often adapted to African cultural contexts and indigenous belief systems. Many also practice African traditional religions and folk religion (http://en.wikipedia.org/wiki/World_religion).

Asia is the birthplace of Hinduism, Judaism, Buddhism, Sikhism, Confucianism, Taoism, Christianity, and Islam, as well as many other beliefs. Roman Catholicism is the second largest religion in Vietnam.

The majority of Chinese people adhere to Buddhism, followed by Taoism and Chinese folk religion. Mahayana Buddhism represents the largest organized religion since its introduction in the 1st century. Some Chinese consider themselves both Buddhist and Taoist. Minority religions are Christianity (3-4%), Islam (1.5-2%), Hinduism, Dongbaism, Bon, and a number of new religions and sects (particularly Xiantianism and Falun Gong). In 2005, 14% of the Chinese population was irreligious (http://www.adherents.com/).

In India 80% of the population follows Hinduism and 13% follows Islam.

Religion in North America is dominated by Christianity (Mexico: 94%; the United States: 80%; Canada: 75%). Canada (16%) and the United States (15%) have the highest number of irreligious people (atheists, agnostics) and account for roughly 10% of the North American population. Islam is practiced by only 2% of the Canadian population, 0.6% the US population, and 0.3% the Mexican population. Judaism is practiced in the United States by 1.4% of the population. Also, Voodoo is practiced in the back islands of North and South America (http://en.wikipedia.org/wiki/World_religion).

The United States is one of the most religious countries due to the nation's diversity and multicultural makeup. Most US citizens adhere to Christianity (78.5%). About 15% of the population has no religious affiliation, which is still less than in Britain (44%) and Sweden (69%). Judaism is the second major religion (less than 3% of the population), followed by Islam (less than 1%), Buddhism (0.5%) and Hinduism (0.4%) (http://en.wikipedia.org/wiki/World_religion).

Most South Americans (90%) are Christians: 81% are Roman Catholic, 9% are of other Christian denominations. Altogether South Americans account for about 19% of Christians worldwide (http://en.wikipedia.org/wiki/World_religion).

In Australia, over two-thirds of the population is Christian and over one-sixth is atheist. The remaining population (less than one-sixth) represents a diverse group which includes all the world's main religions (http://en.wikipedia.org/wiki/World_religion).

Religion in Europe has a rich and diverse religious history. Predominant religions in Europe are Roman Catholicism, Eastern Orthodoxy, and Protestantism. The vast majority of religious Europeans are Christians. Roman Catholicism is one of the largest denominations, with adherents existing mostly in Latin Europe, Ireland, and the Visegrád Group, and also the southern parts of Germanic Europe. Protestantism and Eastern Orthodoxy are divided into many churches, the largest of which are Eastern Orthodoxy (Albania, Belarusia, Bulgaria, Greece, Romania, Russia, Serbia), and Protestantism, including Lutheranism–Zwinglianism (Denmark, France, Belgium, Germany, Hungary, Sweden, Switzerland), Anglicanism (England,

Ireland, Scotland, Wales, Spain), Calvinism-Presbyterianism (England and Wales, Scotland, Ireland, Netherlands) and Anabaptism–Baptism (Great Britain, Sweden). These various faiths have influenced European art, culture, philosophy and law. Islam, Hinduism, Buddhism and Judaism exist in much smaller numbers. Europe has also the largest number of irreligious, agnostic, and atheistic people in the Western world, with a particularly high number of non-religious people in the Czech Republic, Estonia, and Sweden (http://en.wikipedia.org/wiki/World_religion).

Europe has no Islamic tradition, except for the Balkans region, which was formerly part of the Ottoman Empire, and the Iberian Peninsula, which was part of the Arab Empire before the Reconquista. The Muslim population in Europe today is mostly a result of migration, accounting for about 10% of the population in France, 6% in the Netherlands, 5% in Denmark, just over 4% in Switzerland and Austria, and almost 3% in the United Kingdom. In comparison, in the Balkans, Muslims make up 70% of the population of Albania, 40% in Bosnia and Herzegovina, more than 30% in Macedonia, about 20% in Montenegro, and more than 10% in Bulgaria (http://en.wikipedia.org/wiki/Islam_by_country).

Religion in the European Union is also diverse, however predominantly Christian. Although the European Union is secular, there are state churches (typically Protestant), for example the Church of England.

In Southwest Asia and North Africa the majority of the population is represented by Muslims. In the majority-Muslim countries, Islam dominates politically. There exist many divisions in Islam, for example, the Sunni–Shia split. However, the Muslim (or Islamic) community spreads across many other different nations and ethnic groups. It represents roughly one-fifth of the world's population (http://en.wikipedia.org/wiki/World_religion).

5.7 TYPES AND LEVELS OF CULTURE

The term culture often refers to national culture. However, nationality alone does not define culture. People's behaviors and preferences are influenced by several other cultures: global environment, ethnicity, race, religion, occupation, family, friends, and even individual value systems. For example, people everywhere are influenced by political and social systems as well as economic development. Business people are influenced by industrial, organizational, and professional culture. Socially people are, of course, influenced by family and friends. Accordingly, the following types of culture can be identified:

- *Universal culture* refers to culture of all nationalities and humans, their ways of life, behavior, values, morals, and ideas.
- *Civilization culture* refers to culture of a particular civilization, which comprises different nationalities with similar political systems, economic development, ethnic roots, and religious values.

- *Ethnic culture* is culture of an ethnic group of people who share a language, color, history, religion, descent or heritage, or another attribute of common origin.
- *Race culture* refers to culture of a specific race, such as African-American, Asian-American or Hispanic-American.
- *National culture*, which is the focus of this book, refers to culture of a national group, sometimes called ''country'' culture. National culture can be defined in this way as long as nation and country have clearly defined regional boundaries. However, this is not always the case. Different nationalities may coexist within the geographic boundaries of a single country and have different cultures. For example, several different nationalities: Serbs, Croats, Montenegrins, Muslims, Slovens, Albanians, Hungarians and Macedonians, each with a different culture, lived in a one single country, the former Yugoslavia.
- *Regional culture* is the culture of a particular geographical region, such as the Southeastern culture of the United States (casual, relaxed) or the Northeastern culture (formal, busy), each with different values, priorities, and lifestyles.
- *Generation culture* refers to the culture of a particular generation. For example, generations of Baby Boomers and Generation X have different values, preferences, and needs.
- *Industry culture* refers to the culture of a specific industry. Industries such as tourism, banking, construction, retailing, or pharmaceuticals have their own specific cultures because they share different worldviews on how to organize and manage a business. For example, the tourism industry culture is more customer-oriented than the banking culture. On the other hand, the banking industry is more customer-oriented than the construction culture.
- *Professional culture* refers to the culture of a specific profession. Distinct occupational and professional groups (e.g. doctors, lawyers, engineers) have their unique cultures because they differ in their task requirements, beliefs, and values, have distinct codes of conduct, and even have unique dress codes.
- *Organizational/corporate culture* refers to the culture of a specific organization. Organizations and corporations have different cultures because they are influenced by the different nature of the industry, business, products, and services. Some are involved in information technology; others sell real estate, cars, or insurance.
- *Functional culture* refers to the culture of a specific department within an organization. Different departments and sections in organizations (e.g. finance, production, marketing, research, and development) are characterized by distinct cultures: they have different functions to perform, time frames for achieving objectives, and customers to serve. For example, the department of research and development tends to take a more down-to-earth approach, whereas the advertising department is more creative.
- *Family culture* refers to the family's structure and cohesion, the nature of the relationships between its members, roles and responsibilities of wives and husbands, as well as orientation towards religion, politics, or economy.

- *Individual culture* refers to an individual's value system, beliefs, ideas, expectations, actions, attitudes, and intentions, all of which are often influenced by demographic characteristics (e.g. gender, age, income, years of formal education) and personality (e.g. motivations, knowledge, etc.).

The above presented conceptions of culture can be regarded as different levels of culture. As a result, one may distinguish several levels of culture (see Figure 5.6). At the bottom of the pyramid and at the lowest level of culture is individual culture, characterized by values and standards of the individual. The second level is represented by organizational and family cultures that are shared by the smallest social groups, for example, organizations, families or clans. The third level comprises industry and professional cultures, which are shared by groups or communities, for example, a professional group or industry such as physicians or the pharmaceutical industry. The fourth level refers to nation, origin, or residence cultures that are shared by people of the same nationality, country of origin, or country of residence. The fifth level is represented by civilization culture and comprises different nationalities with similar political systems, economic stages of development, ethnic roots, and religious values. Finally, the sixth level is represented by universal human culture. This highest level represents culture of all nationalities and humans, their way of life, behavior, values, ideas, and morals.

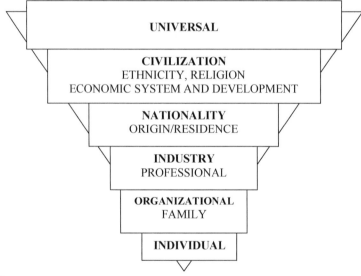

Figure 5.6

Levels of Culture

These various culture levels are interdependent and influence each other. For example, a national culture is influenced by the economic system and development, ethnicity, and religion of a civilized culture. In turn, national culture influences industry and professional cultures, as well as organizational cultures and family traditions.

5.8 CIVILIZATION

A civilization is the highest cultural grouping of people (after nationalities, ethnic groups, and religious groups) and the broadest level of cultural identity people have. For example, a resident of France can define herself/himself as being French, Catholic, Christian, European, and Western. The Western civilization to which the French resident belongs is the broadest level of identification with which s/he identifies.

A civilization distinguishes humans from other species. Civilization represents an advanced stage of human development characterized by a high level of art, religion, science, and social and political organizational development. A civilization is a culture. Each civilization encompasses many nations, political units, governments, and states. The key cultural elements which define a civilization are the blood, language, history, religion, way of life, worldviews, social structures, institutions, and self-identification of its people.

Civilization differs from race; there may be people of different races united by the same civilization, or there may be people of the same race deeply divided by civilization. For example, Christian and Islamic civilizations encompass societies comprising people from a variety of races. The major distinctions among human groups relate to their values, beliefs, institutions, and social structures, not their physical appearance, head shapes, and skin colors.

Civilizations evolve through time, adapt, appear and disappear, and are the most enduring of human associations. Civilizations differ in size and importance. A civilization may involve a very large number of people, such as the Chinese, or a very small number of people, such as the former Cretan civilization. There are major and peripheral civilizations. People can change their identities and thus the composition and shape of civilizations.

Today at least 12 civilizations have been identified, seven of which no longer exist (Mesopotamian, Egyptian, Cretan, Classical, Byzantine, Middle American, Andean) and five of which do (Chinese, Japanese, Indian, Islamic, and Western) (Melko, 1969). In the contemporary world, to these five civilizations one has to add Orthodox, Latin American, and African civilizations (see Table 5.2).

The Buddhist areas of Bhutan, Cambodia, Laos, Mongolia, Myanmar, Sri Lanka, Thailand, Arunachal Pradesh, Kalmykia, parts of Nepal, parts of Siberia, and the Tibetan government-in-exile are identified as separate from other civilizations. Huntington (1996) does not identify them as a major civilization in the sense of their international importance. In some cases, the Sinic, Hindu, Buddhist and Japonic civilizations are merged into a single civilization called Eastern World.

The foundations of major civilizations are the world's major religions. Religions determine characteristics of civilizations. For example, the four major world religions associated with major civilizations are Christianity, Islam, Hinduism, and Confucianism. The fifth major religion, Buddhism, has not been the basis of any major civilization because it was separated into Confucianism and Taoism and suppressed. The great religions of the world were produced by non-Western civilizations. The Western civilization has never generated a major religion (Huntington, 1996).

Table 5.2 The World's Eight Major Civilizations

Civilization	Characteristics	Nations
Sinic	A single distinct Chinese civilization dating back to 1500 B.C. and perhaps a thousand years earlier, or two Chinese civilizations in the early centuries of the Christian epoch. Although this civilization is often labeled "Confucian," it encompasses more than Confucianism.	The common culture of China in Southeast Asia and elsewhere outside of China, cultures of Vietnam, Korea, Singapore, Taiwan
Japanese	Distinct civilization which was the offspring of Chinese civilization, emerging during the period between 100 and 400 A.D.	Japan
Hindu	Existed on the Subcontinent since at least 1500 B.C., referred to as Indian, Indic, or Hindu; the core of Indian civilization.	India, Nepal
Islamic	Originates in the Arabian Peninsula in the 7th Century A.D. Many distinct cultures or subcivilizations exist within Islam, including Arab, Turkic, Persian, and Malay.	North Africa, Iberian Peninsula, Central Asia, Southwest Asia; cultures of Afghanistan, Albania, Azerbaijan, Bangladesh, Indonesia, Malaysia, Maldives, Pakistan, Somalia, parts of India
Orthodox	Centered in Russia, distinct religion, 200 years of Tatar rule, bureaucratic despotism, limited exposure to the Renaissance, Reformation, Enlightenment and Western cultural experiences.	Armenia, Belarus, Bulgaria, Cyprus, Georgia, Greece, Montenegro, Republic of Macedonia, Romania, Russia, Serbia, Ukraine

Table 5.2 (*Continued*)

Civilization	Characteristics	Nations
Latin American	Offspring of European civilization, different from Europe and North America; has authoritarian culture; Catholic only; incorporates indigenous cultures which vary in importance; often considered as a subcivilization within Western civilization or a separate civilization affiliated with the West. A question is as to whether it belongs in the West.	Mexico, Central America, Peru, Bolivia, Argentina, Chile
Western	Historically it is European civilization. In the modern era it is Euroamerican or North Atlantic civilization.	Europe, North America, Australia, New Zealand
African	Most scholars do not recognize distinct African civilization. North Africa and east coast belong to Islamic civilization; Ethiopia has its own civilization; South Africa has multi-fragmented European (Dutch, French, English) culture; south Sahara has Christianity.	South Africa is possibly its core state

Source: Melko, M. (1969). *The nature of civilizations*. Boston: Porter Sargent; http://en.wikipedia.org/wiki/Clash_of_Civilizations

The major differences in civilizations are due mostly to the differences in religions associated with them. Differences in religions create conflicts between people and nations. Often, those who share ethnicity and language may differ in religion, and slaughter each other, as happened in Lebanon, the former Yugoslavia, and the subcontinent (Tiryakian, 1974). The current world conflicts occurring between major civilizations (Western versus non-Western) are due mostly to religious and cultural differences.

Currently, Western civilization's influence is declining. Asian civilizations (e.g. Sinic, Japanese) are expanding their economic, military, and political strength. The Islamic civilization is exploding demographically and appears to be having destabilizing consequences for some Muslim countries and their neighbors. Non-Western civilizations are reaffirming the value of their own cultures (Huntington, 1996). Thus, globalization is bringing cultural revival in Asian and Islamic countries generated by their dynamic economic and demographic changes. The era dominated by Western ideology may come to an end; the world is moving into an era in which multiple and diverse civilizations will interact, compete, coexist, and accommodate each other (Sakakibara, 1995).

5.9 TYPES OF CULTURES IN TOURISM

In tourism, one can distinguish among different types of culture: tourist culture, host culture, and tourism culture.

The *tourist culture* refers to the country culture that tourists bring with them when visiting other countries, whether for business or for vacations. The tourist culture influences and contributes to explaining tourist behavior. However, since tourists behave differently when they are away from home, the tourist culture depends on the "residual culture," which explains how tourists from different cultures behave (Jafari, 1987). Also, since both "touristic cultures" (the culture of groups of tourists, backpackers, etc.) and national cultures influence tourists of different national cultures, it is important to understand the extent to which "touristic cultures" are free of national cultures and are reflected in the behavior of all tourists regardless of nationality (Pizam, 1999, cited in Pizam & Mansfeld, 1999).

Host culture is the culture of the host country with which tourists are in contact (Jafari, 1987). It is the national culture of those who provide local offerings and services to tourists.

Tourism culture refers to the outcome of the behavior of all participants involved in the tourism process, that is, the behavior of tourists and those who offer tourism and hospitality products and services. Tourism culture is a result of mixing together tourist, host, and residual cultures. It is a special type of culture created at each destination. Tourism culture is distinct from everyday culture of tourists and hosts because tourists and hosts behave differently from the way in which they behave at home, without the presence of the other group (Jafari, 1987).

5.10 THE PURPOSE OF CULTURE

The purpose of culture is to teach people how to live, do things, and think. Culture guides people through life. Its purpose is to establish ways of behavior, standards, and criteria of performance, and ways of dealing with interpersonal and environmental relations that will reduce uncertainty, increase predictability, and promote survival and growth among the members of any society. Culture influences human behavior and determines which behavior is appropriate and socially accepted; which is helpful and should be rewarded; and which is unacceptable and harmful, and should therefore be discouraged (Herbig, 1998). Culture tells what is correct, good, true, honest, valuable, and important (Kraft, 1978). Culture teaches significant rules of behavior, rituals, traditions, customs, and procedures. It dictates what clothes to wear, what kind of food to eat, what to say, how to serve guests, and what to do at a dinner party. Culture dictates ideas and sets the rules that the majority of society obeys. It regulates human behavior by offering order, direction, and guidance (Herbig & Dunphy, 1998). Culture teaches relationships with others, and how to form and maintain relationships (Dodd, 1998). It determines relationship patterns and encourages a specific interaction style. Cultural rules and norms help to achieve and maintain harmony in society. Without these rules and regulations, society would be in chaos (Jandt, 1998). Culture simplifies everyday life decisions. Culture provides the means for satisfying physiological, psychological, and social needs (Herbig & Dunphy, 1998).

Culture also makes it possible for human society to communicate using verbal and non-verbal codes of communication. Culture explains how a distinct group understands received information (Herbig & Dunphy, 1998). Culture determines a particular communication, negotiation, persuasion, and discussion style. Culture shapes perception, and develops attitudes, feelings, images, and stereotypes (Dodd, 1998).

Culture structures the governmental bodies. It influences the social, political, economic, financial, educational, kinship, religious, health, and recreational systems of a society. Culture influences family, social, and work relationships.

Culture binds people together (Dodd, 1998); it determines the identity of the group of people. Culture identifies the uniqueness of the social group, its values, beliefs, and thoughts (Leavitt & Bahrami, 1988). Members of the same culture share similar thoughts and experiences. Shared experiences, values, and norms give the members of a society a sense of their common identity (Herbig & Dunphy, 1998). Culture helps to define who they are (Jandt, 1998).

5.11 CHARACTERISTICS OF CULTURE

The following section provides a set of characteristics for culture.

1. *Long term perspective*: Culture was developed thousands of years ago and is the sum of accumulated experience and knowledge.
2. *Collection*: Culture is a collection of beliefs, values, habits, norms, and traditions.
3. *A social phenomenon*: Culture arises out of human interaction and is unique to human society.
4. *An environmental phenomenon*: Culture is influenced by various environmental factors (micro, e.g. peer or organizational rules; and macro, e.g. economy, politics, geography).

5. *Political phenomenon*: Culture is influenced by various political and legal factors (e.g. legislation, laws, regulations, bills)
6. *Learned*: Culture is learned, not inherited genetically, not innate, it is successively learned from other members of the society by people who enter the society. It is possible to learn new cultural behavior and unlearn old behavior.
7. *Shared*: Culture is shared by a large group of people and is particular to that group.
8. *Functional*: Each culture has a function to perform and a purpose that provides guidelines for behavior of a particular group of people.
9. *Influential*: Culture influences human behavior. The nature of its influence on life, economics, politics, and human behavior can vary from one period to another.
10. *Prescriptive*: Culture prescribes acceptable behavior.
11. *Arbitrary*: Cultural practices and behaviors are arbitrary; certain behaviors are acceptable in one culture and not acceptable in other cultures.
12. *Value laden*: Culture provides value, indicates what has most and least value, and tells people what is expected of them.
13. *Facilitates communication*: Culture facilitates verbal and non-verbal communication.
14. *Adaptive/dynamic*: Culture is constantly changing to adapt to new situations and environments; it changes as society changes and evolves. If a specific standard of conduct does not fully satisfy the members of a society, it is modified or replaced. Thus, culture continually evolves to meet the needs of society.
15. *Satisfies needs*: Culture helps to satisfy the needs of the members of a society by offering direction and guidance.
16. *Implicit*: Culture can be expressed by its intangible forms, such as beliefs, values, and ideas.
17. *Explicit*: Culture can be expressed by its tangible forms, which involve architecture, painting, and music.

5.12 SUBCULTURES

Large societies often have subcultures, or groups of people with distinct sets of behaviors and beliefs that differentiate them from a larger culture of which they are a part. A subculture can be distinguished based on its members' race, nationality, tribe, religion, geographic region, ethnicity, social and economic class, age, gender, occupation, politics, and sexual orientation, or a combination of these factors. Each culture consists of several subcultures.

There are different categories of subcultures:

- *Racial subcultures* often refer to groups of people with similar biological characteristics, mainly the same color and /or physical type. Different racial categories can be characterized by different physical features, such as skin color or shape of the eyes. Racial subcultures may also refer to a group of people descended from the same ancestors, sharing the same history, language, customs, for example, the German race. Race recognizes the evolution of the world. Various racial categories have evolved in history. For example, many western European countries include people of the Caucasian race.

- *Nationality subcultures* refer to groups of people who share a common history and usually a language, but may not always live in the same area, for example, the Indian national subcultures of North America and the United Kingdom.
- *Tribe subcultures* refer to groups of people, smaller than nations, sharing the same customs and usually the same language, and often following an ancient way of life, for example, a wandering tribe of hunters in the Amazon forest.
- *Ethnic subcultures* refer to a wide variety of groups of people who share a language, region of origin, history, religion, descent or heritage, and pheno-typical characteristics (e.g. skin color, hair color), or other attribute of com-mon origin, and identify themselves as a distinct nation or a cultural group. Ethnic cultural traits are passed on to children. The examples of the ethnic groups are Anglo-Americans, Blacks/African-Americans, Middle Easterners, Southeast Asians, Hispanics, Philippinos, or Jews. In former Yugoslavia, there were numerous ethnic groups (e.g. Serbs, Croats, or Muslims), each with its own culture, who were forced to live as one nation, following the Second World War.
- *Religious subcultures* refer to a wide variety of groups of people who are identi-fied on a basis of the differences in their religious beliefs and worship.
- *Geographical* and *regional subcultures* refer to geographic differences within countries or similarities between countries. Regional subcultures refer to subcul-tures that evolved due to differences in geography, history, politics, economics, language, and religion (within and beyond national borders). Each geographic area or region develops its own culture, values, and lifestyle. For example, the South-west of the United States is known for its casual lifestyle, outdoor entertainment, and active sports. The Southwest also appears to be more innovative when com-pared to the conservative region of New England.
- *Economic* and *social subcultures* are identified on a basis of the differences in the socio-economic standing of people (differences in income and wealth). For exam-ple, the urban African-American subculture in the United States has often been associated with low income, drugs, and educational deprivation.
- *Age-based subcultures* are identified on a basis of the differences in the age. Each age group develops its own culture. For example, younger people have different preferences for clothing, food, music, shelter, cars, and leisure activities than older people. Young people prefer to spend heavily on fashionable clothes, music, and entertainment; elders prefer to spend more on comfortable clothes, medicine, and insurance.
- *Gender-based subcultures* are identified on the basis of the differences in gender. Each gender develops its own cultural habits and customs.

As a result of regional, demographic or socio-economic differences, each subcul-ture provides its members with a different set of values and expectations that tell people how to behave, interact, and think within these subcultures. Each subculture exhibits different patterns of behavior that distinguish it from others within a dominant culture. Therefore, the major dominant culture differs from minor variant subcultures.

Figure 5.7 presents a model of the relationships between various subcultural groups (A–G) and dominant culture. Each subculture has its own unique pattern of values, beliefs, and expectations, yet all groups share dominant cultural patterns. While dominant culture determines the form of public, socially accepted behavior, the minor subcultures indicate the forms of private social behavior. Consequently, the behavioral patterns of the individuals who are from the same dominant culture may not be the same because they may be members of various subcultures.

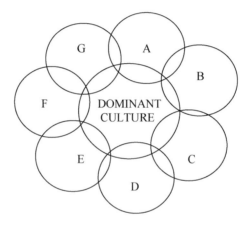

Figure 5.7

Relationships Between Dominant Culture and Minor Subcultures A–G

Subcultures can be represented by a small or large group of people. People can be members of many different subcultures at the same time. A person might identify with being a white, Irish-American female, a Catholic, a member of the middle class, with high annual income, and age of 25.

Distinguishing a dominant or typical cultural pattern for any culture is extremely difficult or even impossible. Many societies are culturally highly diverse. A wide variety of ethnic groups can be found in many countries. For example, the United States, Australia, and Canada have British, Germans, Italians, Greeks, Turks, Serbs, Croatians, Poles, and many other nationalities. The United States contains over 125 ethnic groups and nearly 1200 different religions (Samovar et al., 1998). Thus, the analysis of culture of a specific country must be limited to the dominant culture of this country.

The focus of this book is on the dominant national culture of the tourists and hosts. The minor subcultures and private patterns of social behavior are not analyzed.

5.13 CULTURE VERSUS NATIONALITY

Nationality refers to a relationship between a person and its state of origin, or a membership of a nation by a person. Usually, nationality is established at birth by a child's place of birth and/or bloodline. Nationality may also be acquired in life through naturalization. The legal sense of nationality, particularly in the English-speaking world, may often mean citizenship, although it does not mean the same thing everywhere in the world. For example, in the United Kingdom, citizens have rights to participate in the political life of the state of which they are citizens (voting or standing for election). However, nationals need not immediately have these rights; they may often acquire them in due time.

One can have the nationality of a country and live somewhere else. For example, one can have British nationality and live in France. Nationality also refers to a large group of people with the same race, origin, and language. For example, people from different nationalities (e.g. Latvian, Ukrainian, and Belarusian) live in the former USSR.

Often, no distinction is made between culture and nationality as long as culture and nationality of a group are clearly defined by geographical borders. However, this is not always the case. In today's world, people of different nationalities and different cultures live within the same geographic boundaries (e.g. Mexican, Russian, and Brazilian nationals live in the United States). Thus, in order to avoid confusion between the concepts of culture and nationality, the term *national culture* should be used; it is more precise for describing the particular groups of people.

Nationality cannot be used as a single factor to explain cultural differences among people. Individuals may possess multiple nationalities, their culture can be different from their nationality, and many can be bicultural. For example, one can be a US national who is Russian but follows a French cultural pattern. Also, some nationals of the United States, Australia, and Canada may be conversant in more than two cultures because they originate from other cultures. In addition, those nationals who migrate to a new culture may possess a nationality different from the culture to which they migrate.

5.14 CULTURE VERSUS COUNTRY OF RESIDENCE

Country of residence refers to a country where one permanently lives. Country of residence can be but does not have to be the same as someone's national culture. For example, one can live in Spain and be an Australian national with an Australian cultural pattern. Thus, national cultures differ and cannot be determined by a country of residence (''where you live''). Some people may live in another country for a long time and have no time or desire to adapt to its culture; they maintain and follow the patterns of their national culture.

5.15 CULTURE VERSUS COUNTRY OF BIRTH

Country of birth refers to a country where one was born. Country of birth can be but does not have to be the same as someone's national culture. Many people move to a new culture (immigrants) and experience a process of acculturation and deculturation, they learn new cultural patterns and unlearn childhood cultural patterns of the country in which they were born. Thus, their national culture can change although a country of birth is still the same. Also, the country of birth can be but does not have to be the same as someone's country of residence. For example, one can be born in Italy and live in New Zealand. Thus, someone's culture differs from, but cannot be determined by, a country of birth (''where you were born''), or country of residence (''where you live''), or even citizenship (''your nationality'').

In conclusion, the concepts of culture, nationality, country of residence, and country of birth are different. Some people might be born and raised in one country and live in another. Foreign nationals (born in one country and raised in another) and those who were born and raised in one country and lived in another for extended periods of time may behave differently than those who were born and raised, and live, in the same country all their lives.

5.16 CULTURAL IDENTITY

Cultural identity is the (feeling of) identity of a group, culture, or individual as far as this individual is influenced by his or her belonging to the culture. The issue of cultural identity and self-definition is of growing importance in a globalized world. As more people travel, take new jobs, migrate to new countries, become separated from their ancestry roots, and become exposed to new socio-economic and cultural environments, they increasingly search for new sources of identity, values, morals, and image. People need to know who they really are, who they are not, where they belong, and where they are heading.

People define their identity in terms of their occupation, education, material possessions, wealth, social classes, kinship, place of residence, ideology, ancestry, language, history, values, customs, institutions they work for, and even politics. However, the most important distinction among people is not political, economic, social, or ideological, but cultural. Cultural identity is dramatically increasing in importance compared to other dimensions of identity. People identify themselves with cultural groups such as tribes, ethnic groups, religious communities, nations, and, at the broadest level, even civilizations. They like to use symbols of their cultural identities, including traditional clothing, music, food, flags, crosses, head coverings, and colors. Cultural identity is what is most meaningful to most people. It is the major factor that gives people the sense of self and belonging, provides meanings and directions, helps to reaffirm values, defines beliefs and views, and develops attitudes towards world politics, the economy, and the environment.

Cultural identity gives strength to those who are lost through globalization, industrialization, urbanization, and rapid economic and technological developments.
The question "Who are we?" is important not only to individuals and societies
but to all nations. Most nations identify themselves not by economic wealth or
military power but their cultural values. Thus, today more and more nations are
seeking their cultural identities.

However, in recent years there seems to have begun a global identity crisis. As the
world has brought everyone closer, people and nations are renewing their desire to
maintain their identities; they want to return to the differences. People and nations
want to distinguish themselves for their cultural differences, not commonalities.
According to the distinctiveness theory in social psychology, people define themselves
by what makes them different from others, not by what they have in common. Thus,
they search for different ancestry, religion, language, and values to distance themselves
from others. In a global culture what counts the most is that people and nations want to
define themselves in cultural terms. Having a strong cultural identity allows people to
enhance their relationships with others and makes their position in the world stronger.
Those who do not have a cultural core will lose their culture and become part of
another one.

Unfortunately, the increasing need of people and nations throughout the world for
differentiating themselves in cultural terms also means that conflicts between different
cultural groups are inevitable; these conflicts may present a central problem to global
tourism and could prove very destructive.

5.17 CULTURAL DISTANCE

Cultural distance (CD) refers to the extent to which national cultures differ or to which
a cultural gap exists among different cultural systems. Large CD can be a source of
friction and potentially disrupt all economic, social, or political relations between
countries. The CD construct can be applied in international tourism and defined as
the extent to which national culture of the originating region (tourists) differs from that
of the receiving region (local hosts). The CD construct has implications for interactions
between tourists from one culture and visiting another culture. The larger the CD
between international tourists and hosts, the higher the probability tourists will experience difficulties in the host culture.

The extent of CD between tourists and host national cultures may range from very
small to extreme. When national cultures of tourists and hosts are very similar to one
another, the CD between tourists and hosts is very small; it may even not exist, whereas
when national cultures of tourists and hosts are very different from one another, the CD
between tourists and hosts is very large.

It can be argued that cultures are distant from one another because every culture
has different values and norms and consists of multiple different subcultures. However,
it is not just the presence or absence of difference between national cultures, but the

degree of difference between the culture that influences CD. As the degree of difference increases, the CD increases.

Depending on the degree of differences between national cultures, one can distinguish several categories of CD:

(1) When national cultures of tourists and hosts are the same or similar, the CD between tourists and hosts is very small or non-existent.

(2) When national cultures of tourists and hosts are different, but the differences are small and/or supplementary, the CD between tourists and hosts is small.

(3) When national cultures of tourists and hosts are different, and the differences are large and/or incompatible, the CD between tourists and hosts is large. In this case, tourists and hosts have no cultural commonalities, and experience difficulties in their interaction. As the differences in national cultures increase, tourists and hosts can experience misunderstanding, friction, anxiety, and often conflicts (Sutton, 1967).

In light of the above, CD can be defined as the degree of difference in national cultures of people; if CD is large, it can distort people's perception of each other and lead to conflict. CD between national cultures of tourists and hosts is usually large in the destinations where the majority of tourists are foreigners. Consequently, conflicts between culturally different tourists and hosts are inevitable and may present a major problem to global tourism.

Samovar and Porter (1991) presented a scale that allows for examining the degree of cultural difference between nations along a minimum–maximum dimension (see Figure 5.8). The largest CD was found between Asian and Western cultures. This means that visitors from Asia to the West or vice versa have the least commonalities with each other; their interaction can be very difficult, and they can get involved in cultural conflict. Although some cultural groups may seem to be similar (e.g. United States American/English/Canadian), they may also be culturally dissimilar due to a different variety and size of ethnic groups found in these cultures.

5.18 THE IMPACT OF CULTURAL DISTANCE ON TRAVEL

The distance between a tourist and a host national culture influences intentions to travel and visit specific destinations. Many tourists like to travel to destinations that share the same cultural background. For example, Hong Kong nationals frequently travel to mainland China because of its similar cultural background and very small, if any, CD. Saudi tourists prefer to visit Muslim countries (Yavas, 1987). Visiting culturally similar destinations with low CD reduces the extent of cultural conflicts and increases the likelihood of positive experiences. Although the above is true, cultural differences, rather than similarities, can also attract tourists to destinations. Culturally dissimilar destinations provide an attractive travel environment for the young, adventurous, and educated market segments.

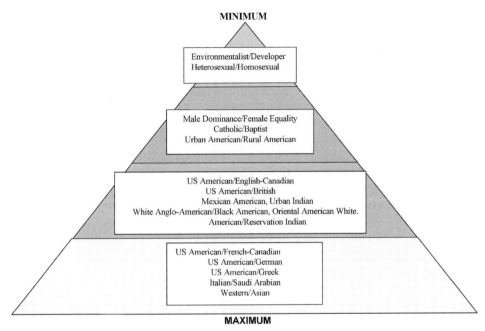

Figure 5.8

Cultural Differences Among Cultures and Subcultures According to Samovar and Porter (1991)

Source: Reisinger, Y., & Turner, L. (2003). *Cross-cultural behavior in tourism: Concepts and analysis* (p. 29). Burlington, MA: Butterworth-Heinemann; based on Samovar, L., & Porter, R. (1988). *Intercultural communication: A reader*. Wadsworth, Belmont, CA.

5.19 THE MEASUREMENT OF CULTURAL DISTANCE

There are several measures of the perceived CD between countries.

Cultural diversity index

Jackson (2001) measured CD between 50 countries included in Hofstede's (1980) research and the base country (Australia). He ranked these countries from 1 to 50. He calculated the absolute rank difference between each country from the base country for each of Hofstede's cultural dimensions (power distance, uncertainty avoidance, individualism/collectivism, and masculinity/femininity). He produced the cultural diversity index by summing all four absolute rank differences (for four dimensions). The index ranged from very similar (4) to very dissimilar (196). Although the index is simple and easy to use, it is based on work-related values obtained between 1968 and 1972, and thus does not capture individuals' perceptions of cultural differences today.

Cluster analysis

Clark and Pugh (2001) calculated CD by using cluster analysis. They discriminated between countries on the basis of language, religion, and geography, and identified five clusters: Anglo, Nordic, Germanic, Latin (Latin European and Latin American), and the Rest of the World (Near Eastern, Far Eastern, Arab and the independent clusters). They calculated each cluster's distance from Great Britain by coding countries in the same cluster as Great Britain as 1, countries in the Nordic cluster as 2, countries in the Germanic cluster as 3, countries in the Latin cluster as 4, and countries in the Rest of World as 5. Their index of CD was criticized for its scoring based upon a subjective identification of clusters, rather than on empirical observation, and thus not reflecting real cultural differences.

Self-rating

Boyacigiller (1990) and Rao and Schmidt (1998) used self-rating to measure perceived CD. In a survey, respondents were asked about their perceptions of the cultural differences between their countries and a set of other countries using a low-to-high distance scale (''How large are the cultural differences between your country and XYZ country?''). The mean score was used as a measure of CD to their home country.

Linguistic distance

Measuring distance between national cultures offers only a limited approach to measuring CD because culture does not necessarily correspond to national boundaries. Many countries consist of multicultural groups, are characterized by regional differences, and welcome people of multiple nationalities (e.g. with different country of birth, residence, and nationality). Since culture is often defined within linguistic, ethnic, or religious boundaries, linguistic, ethnic, and religious distance could be much better tools for evaluating the extent of cultural differences among nations. West and Graham (2004) proposed a linguistic distance as a measure of CD. Their measure is based on language genetics or common ancestor, and implies grammatical similarity. West and Graham (2004) measured 50 countries for linguistic distance from English-speaking countries and found it to range from 0 (lowest distance) to 7 (highest distance). Linguistic distance in multilingual countries was calculated on the weighted average of the official languages spoken in that country.

SUMMARY

Culture is a very difficult and complex multidimensional phenomenon to define. There is no consensus definition of culture. The term generally refers to patterns of human activity, and to the way people life and behave. Culture is compared to civilization and religion. The Western civilization is declining in its influence, and non-Western civilizations are strengthening the value of their cultures. There are different types and levels of culture. Culture also serves different purposes. There are intangible and tangible elements of culture. Large societies consist of various subcultures. National cultures cannot be determined by a country of residence, country of birth, or citizenship (nationality). Cultural identity is becoming of growing importance in a globalized world. CD, or the extent to which national cultures differ, is an important index in international tourism, influencing travel intentions and destination choice. The largest CD is between Asian and Western cultures. CD can be measured by using the cultural diversity index, cluster analysis index, self-rating method, and linguistic distance index.

DISCUSSION POINTS AND QUESTIONS

1. Define culture and explain its major elements.
2. What are the purposes of culture?
3. Can cultural elements completely distinguish among different cultural groups?
4. What are the major levels of culture? Which level, in your opinion, is the most important?
5. Why is culture compared to civilization?
6. Identify and describe regional, religious, geographical, ethnic, racial, socio-economic, age-based, and gender-based subcultures in the context of your national culture.
7. Explain the differences among the concepts of nationality, citizenship, country of residence and country of birth. Can these concepts determine national culture? If not, why not?
8. Why is it important to understand the concept of cultural distance in international tourism?

CASE STUDY 5.1 Micro-Cultures of the United States

African-Americans

African-Americans represent 13% of the US population, and their buying power is projected to reach $1 trillion by 2010. Their economic standards and buying power are relatively lower than white Americans. African-American consumers in the United States are price conscious and shop at neighborhood stores. Despite this, there has been a rapid growth of the black middle and upper classes. African-Americans are now emerging as an attractive market for expensive products, such as cars, large appliances, electronics, telecom, entertainment, travel services, financial services, insurance, and computer-associated hardware and software. They also spend relatively more on clothing than white consumers. African-Americans are arbiters of popular culture; they influence the purchasing choices of the greater marketplace in high-image categories such as cars and alcoholic beverages, and in youth products, such as fashion and entertainment. African-Americans are trendsetters who enhance brand volume among all consumers.

Hispanic-Americans

Spanish-speaking Americans represent the world's fifth-largest Hispanic nation. Hispanic or Latino Americans are the second largest and fastest-growing US minority. They represent more than 10% of the US population, and their buying power will soon reach $1 trillion. The group is very diverse in terms of history, wealth, and class. Some are wealthy, whereas others are hard-working migrants who have low-paying, low-status jobs. The majority are Roman Catholics who support family values. The first generation of Hispanics is generally Spanish-speaking and extremely curious and enthusiastic about products and services available in the United States. The second and third generation Hispanics, born and educated in the United States, are bilingual and bicultural. The ability to work and live in English and Spanish gives them a very distinct competitive advantage. Some desire to retain their own language, cultural values, and traditions of Spain, Mexico, Central and South America, and Cuba, as a complement to American values. Hispanic Americans represent a very lucrative and influential market not only for food, beverages, and household appliances, but also for upscale consumer products, such as computers, photography equipment, travel, recreation, and financial services. Hispanic-Americans are brand- and quality-conscious and are easily reached through a growing network of Spanish language TV, radio, and print media. Hispanics have access to approximately 250 Hispanic television stations across 12 Hispanic television networks, 650 Hispanic radio stations, and 433 Hispanic newspapers, magazines, and newsletters. They are very heavy adapters of new media. Effective Hispanic marketing must focus on emotional connections with consumers in order to motivate them to purchase. By the year 2015 the Hispanic population will increase by 75% and will reach 96 million by 2050.

Asian-Americans

The Asian-American market is uniquely attractive. Asians are experiencing the fastest population growth rate of all racial groups in the United States. They have the highest median household income of all groups, more than $9000 ahead of non-Hispanic White households and far ahead of Hispanic and African-American median incomes. Asians also have the highest level of education of all groups in the United States, with 44% of Asians holding an undergraduate degree or higher. In addition, they have disproportionately high rates of business ownership. They are heavy consumers of international calling, banking, and financial services. They buy new cars and luxury products such as fine spirits, cosmetics, computer hardware/software, and travel and leisure packaged goods. According to the US census, the Asian-American population will more than double in size to 23 million by the year 2020. By 2050, Asian-Americans are projected to account for a full 10% of the total US population.

African-Americans, Hispanic-Americans, and Asian-Americans constitute almost one-third of the total US population. They are the fastest-growing populations in the country. They also represent 50% of California's population.

Source: Gitlin, S. (2000, May–June). The Asian-American market: An updated opportunity for America's marketers. *Archives Multicultural Marketing News*; Buford, H. (2007). Simple truths for maximizing your share of the African American market. In L. Skriloff (Ed.), *The source book of multicultural experts 2006/07*. New York: Multicultural Marketing Resources; Gitlin, S. (2007). The Asian-American market: Heading towards Census 2010. In L. Skriloff (Ed.), *The source book of multicultural experts 2006/07*. New York: Multicultural Marketing Resources; Lopez Negrete, A. (2007). Is Espanol still enough when marketing to Hispanics? In L. Skriloff (Ed.), *The source book of multicultural experts 2006/07*. New York: Multicultural Marketing Resources.

WEBSITE LINKS

1. Culture: http://www.en.wikipedia.org/wiki/Culture
2. Nationality: http://www.en.wikipedia.org/wiki/Nationality
3. Residency: http://www.en.wikipedia.org/wiki/Residency
4. Cultural identity: http://www.en.wikipedia.org/wiki/Culturalidentity
5. Major religious groups: http://en.wikipedia.org/wiki/Major_religious_groups
6. Certificates of non-citizen nationality: http://travel.state.gov/law/citizenship/citizenship_781.html

Since there are many cultural differences among various nations, the next chapter will identify major dimensions along which national cultures differ.

Cultural variability

The aim of this chapter is to introduce the concept of cultural differences and identify major cultural dimensions along which national cultures differ.

OBJECTIVES

After completing this chapter the reader should be able to:
- Understand major sources of cultural differences
- Understand the concept of value system and values orientation
- Identify different types and measurements of values
- Describe major value dimensions
- Identify major cultural differences in values among international communities

INTRODUCTION

Cultural differences influence human behavior. Cultural values predict human behavior. Cultures differ along major value dimensions which provide ways to understand how people behave and communicate across different cultures, how they develop social relationships and what perceptions they develop of others. This chapter identifies major cultural value dimensions along which cultures differ and demonstrates the ways in which these dimensions affect human behavior.

6.1 SOURCES OF CULTURAL DIFFERENCES

Triandis (1972) argued that the main elements of culture are values, perceptions, attitudes, stereotypes, beliefs, categorizations, evaluations, expectations, memories, and opinions. Various cultures perceive these elements in different ways. Those who **119** are of a similar culture perceive these elements in the same way; they have similar values, norms, rules, beliefs, expectations, behaviors and language. On the other hand, those who belong to different cultures perceive these elements in different ways; they have different values, norms, rules, beliefs, attitudes, and often languages. They perceive things differently and behave differently.

Scollon and Scollon (1995) argued that the major areas of cultural differences are (a) ideology, including history, beliefs, values, religion; (b) socialization, including education, enculturation, acculturation, learning; (c) verbal communication, including information, relationships, negotiation, group harmony, individual welfare; and non-verbal communication, including kinesics (body movement), proxemics (the use of space), and concept of time; and (d) social organization, including kinship, the concept of self, in-group–out-group relationships and Gemeinschaft and Gesselschaft.

Others identified sources of cultural differences in language (spoken and written), economic and political systems, religious beliefs, social institutions, classes, family structures, values, attitudes, manners, customs and traditions, aesthetics, education, and material items (Czinkota & Ronkainen, 1993; Hofstede, 1991; Trompenaars, 1993).

6.1.1 Cultural differences in communication

Cultures differ in the way they communicate:

(a) Different patterns of verbal communication (language and paralanguage: intonation, laughing, crying, questioning), and

(b) Different patterns of non-verbal communication (body language, such as facial expressions, head movements, gestures, use of space, use of physical distance between people) (Bochner, 1982).

Differences in verbal communication and, especially the manner by which language influences the ways in which people think are due to:

(a) Variations in vocabulary (different words are used to express the same meaning). For example, the word *chips* is used in the United Kingdom or Australia, whereas Americans say *French fries*.

(b) Variations in linguistic grammar (due to differences in time, social hierarchy, and cultural characteristics).

(c) Linguistic relativity and intercultural communication (differences occur due to ethnic, social class, generational and political reasons; different dialects, accents, and jargon) (Whorf, 1956).

Differences in verbal communication are also reflected in the (a) differences in sound (phonology), (b) differences in meaning units (morphology), (c) differences in meanings of words (semantics), (d) differences in the sequence of the words and their relationships to one another (syntactics), and (e) differences in effects of language on perceptions (pragmatics) (Lustig & Koester, 1993).

Differences in non-verbal communication are reflected in:

- Body movements (*kinesics*), such as gestures (emblems); visual representation of the verbal message (illustrators); facial and body movements (affect displays); synchronizers of conversation, such as head nods, eye contact (regulators); and body movements as a reaction to an individual's physical or psychological state (adaptors).
- Space (*proxemics*), such as use of personal space (intimate, personal, social, public), and territoriality.
- Touch, such as the meanings of touch, and differences in whom, where, when, and how often one can touch.
- Time, such as orientation towards the past, present, and future; orientation towards time systems (technical or formal/informal time); time perceptions (long/short time); and use of time (time commitment/no time commitment).
- Voice, such as vocal communication (high/low, fast/slow, smooth/staccato, loud/soft).
- Other non-verbal codes, such as natural body odor, tears, sweat, smells (chemical code system); blushing, blanching (dermal code system); facial features, skin and hair color, body shape (physical code system); and clothing, buildings, furnishing, jewelry, lighting, cosmetics (artifactual code system) (Lustig & Koester, 1993).

Cultural differences are also reflected in:

- Persuasion style (presentational/analogical).
- Argumentation style (evidence, warrants, claims, conclusions).
- Conversation structure (topics discussed, the ways topics are presented, value of talk and silence, rules of conversations) (Lustig & Koester, 1993).

6.1.2 Cultural differences in social categories

The other major aspect in which culture differs is social categories: social role, status, class, hierarchy, attitudes towards people, natural environment, activity, time, relationships between individuals, standing, looking, perceiving sense of shame, feelings of obligations, responsibility, saving face, avoiding embarrassment, confrontation, taking initiatives, responses, and external appearance (Argyle, 1967, 1978; Damen, 1987; Dodd, 1987; Gudykunst & Kim, 1984; Hall, 1955, 1959, 1976, 1983; Taylor, 1974; Thiederman, 1989).

6.1.3 Cultural differences in rules of social behavior

The third major aspect in which cultures differ is rules of social behavior: ways of defining and attributing importance to social relations, ways of establishing and maintaining social relations, greetings and self-presentations, beginning a conversation, degree of expressiveness, showing emotions, frankness, intensity, persistency, intimacy, and volume of social interaction expressing dissatisfaction and criticism, describing reasons and opinions, exaggerations, moral rules about telling the truth, joking, asking personal questions, complimenting and complaining, expressing dislike, showing warmth, addressing people, apologizing, farewelling, expressing negative opinions, and gift giving (Argyle, 1967, 1978; Jensen, 1970; Nomura & Barnlund, 1983; Triandis, 1972; Wagatsuma & Rosett, 1986).

6.2 CULTURAL VALUES

6.2.1 Concept and definitions

There are many definitions of value. Every person has a unique set of values. The values that permeate a culture are called *cultural values*, and they inform about what is good and bad, right and wrong, true or false, positive or negative, and the like. Values define what ought to be or ought not to be, what is useful and useless, appropriate and inappropriate, what types of events lead to social acceptance and satisfaction. However, there is also a lack of consensus about what exactly constitutes value. For example, values have been defined as the core of culture (Kroeber & Kluckhohn, 1952); world-views (Redfield, 1953); system and core of meaning (Kluckhohn, 1956); specific beliefs about preferences (Baier, 1969); standards and criteria (Rokeach, 1973); attributes of individuals (Barton, 1969) and collectives (Kluckhohn, 1951). Important definitions of value are presented below.

Values are principles that define life situations, selection, and decision-making, and create social order. Values are attributes of people; they have affective, cognitive, and conative elements (Kluckhohn, 1951). Value is ''a conception, explicit or implicit, distinctive of an individual or characteristic of a group, of the desirable which influences the selection from available modes, means and ends of actions'' (Kluckhohn, 1951, p. 395).

Value is ''an enduring belief that a specific mode of conduct or end-state of existence is personally preferable to an opposite mode of conduct or end-state of existence'' (Rokeach, 1973, p. 5). Values are ''beliefs about desirable goals and modes of conduct'' (Rokeach, 1979, p. 41), such as to seek truth and beauty, and to behave with sincerity, justice, compassion, humility, respect, honor, and loyalty. These desirable modes of conduct are abstract ideals, which represent ideal existence, such as security, happiness, freedom, equality, state of grace, and salvation (Rokeach, 1973). Values are ''means and ends'' (Rokeach, 1973). Values are socially shared, and are conceptions of the desirable (Rokeach, 1973) and they are standards or criteria (Williams, 1970, 1979). Values are criteria that we ''employ to guide action, . . . to guide self-presentations, . . . to evaluate and judge ourselves and others by; to compare ourselves with others . . ., not only with respect to competence . . . but also with respect to morality. We employ values as standards, . . . to decide what is worth and not worth arguing about, worth and worth persuading and influencing others to believe in and to do . . . We employ values to guide. . . action, thought, and judgment. Thus, the ultimate function of human values is to provide us with a set of standards to

guide us in all our efforts to satisfy our needs and at the same time to maintain and ...
enhance self-esteem ... to make it possible to regard ourselves and to be regarded by
others as having ... morality and competence'' (Rokeach, 1979, p.48). Therefore,
values determine social behavior (Rokeach, 1973).

Values play an important role in judging, praising, or condemning (Smith, 1969).
Values are preferences for actions and have strong affective components (Kluckhohn,
1951; Triandis, 1972; Williams, 1979). Values are abstract categories (Triandis, 1972).
Values are individual attributes that can affect people's attitudes, perceptions, needs,
and motivations (Bailey, 1991; Kluckhohn, 1951).

6.2.2 Culture and values

Culture and values held by its members are related (Hofstede, 1980). Values are the
core of culture (Kroeber & Kluckhohn, 1952) and depend on culture (Fridgen, 1991).
Culture represents a system of shared values of its members (Bailey, 1991); culture
is rooted in values (Hofstede, 1980). Values are psychological variables that characterize people within the same culture. People with similar values belong to a similar
culture. People with different values belong to different cultures (Segall, 1986). Differences in values indicate differences among cultures, such as differences in thinking,
acting, perceiving, understanding of attitudes, motivations, and human needs
(Rokeach, 1973). Differences in values involve not only differences in the importance
members of a particular culture attach to values but also the extent to which members
of each society adhere to particular values, the degree to which the values are accepted
in a society, and the emphasis which each society places on particular values
(Williams, 1979).

6.2.3 Value system

Values can be organized and prioritized (Rokeach, 1979) systematically
(Rokeach, 1973). A value system is an organization of beliefs concerning preferable
ways of behavior (preferable modes of conduct) or end-states of existence along a
continuum of their relative importance. A value system is the *system* of criteria by
which one can evaluate one's own and others' behavior and apply sanctions to it; it is a
system of socially accepted guidelines that show the cultural norms of a society and
specify the ways in which people should behave, a system of standards that permits
individuals to make decisions about relationships with self, others, society, nature, and
God (Rokeach, 1973).

A value system is relatively stable over time but may change and be rearranged in
the long-term. Changes in values affect people's thoughts, beliefs, and actions. Differences in value systems may create disagreements and even conflicts. For example, on
an individual level, a person may feel a conflict about being polite and friendly versus
being dishonest, whereas on a societal level, members of different cultures may feel a
disagreement on the importance of values. When people are from different cultures,
differences in their values may jeopardize their social relations. Violations of a value

system by someone from a different value system can often produce conflict, hurt, and even insult.

6.2.4 Value orientation

There is a distinction between value and value orientation. *Value orientation* refers to ''complex but ... patterned-rank ordered principles, ... which give ... direction to the ... human acts ... the solution of common human problems'' (Kluckhohn & Strodtbeck, 1961, p. 4). Differences in value orientations are the most important cultural differences and the central focus of the structure of culture (Kluckhohn & Strodtbeck, 1961). People's value orientation is a critical variable to examine when comparing cultures (Zavalloni, 1980). Cultures differ along major value orientations. Human behavior, standards, and criteria for behavior differ in these cultures. The major value orientations are discussed later in this chapter.

6.2.5 Types of values

In general, there are two types of values: *instrumental* and *terminal* (Rokeach, 1973; Kluckhohn 1951; Kluckhohn & Strodtbeck, 1961). Instrumental values are preferable modes or means of behavior (to be honest, obedient, ambitious, and independent; to love). These values may be moral and socially accepted (to behave honestly; to be helpful, loving), or may be concerned with personal competency or self-actualization (to be ambitious, self-controlled, logical, imaginative). Terminal values are goals (salvation, world peace, freedom, comfortable life, true friendship). They may be personal (individual security, freedom, happiness, salvation) and social (national security, social recognition, true friendship). People's attitudes and behavior depend on whether their personal or social values have priority (Rokeach, 1973). Instrumental values are means to terminal values (ends). For example, being ambitious is a means to social recognition. Table 6.1 identifies terminal and instrumental values from the Rokeach's Value Survey (RVS) (Rokeach, 1973).

The number of values is limited by a person's biological and socio-cultural characteristics and needs. A person possesses about 18 terminal values and between 60 and 72 instrumental values (Rokeach, 1973).

Further, values may be applied to individuals and groups. By examining personal values it is possible to identify cultural values of a particular group or society, although individual values need not to be identical or similar to dominant cultural values of a group or society.

6.2.6 Classification of values

Values can be classified according to their importance within a society. There are *primary*, *secondary*, and *tertiary* values (Samovar & Porter, 1988). Primary values are the most important and are at the top of the value hierarchy; they specify what is

Table 6.1 Rokeach's Instrumental and Terminal Values

Instrumental values	Terminal values
Ambitious (hard working, aspiring)	A comfortable life (a prosperous life)
Broad-minded (open-minded)	An exciting life (a stimulating, active life)
Capable (competent, effective)	A sense of accomplishment (lasting contribution)
Cheerful (lighthearted, joyful)	A world at peace (free from war and conflict)
Clean (neat, tidy)	A world of beauty (beauty of nature and the arts)
Courageous (standing up for your beliefs)	Equality (brotherhood, equal opportunity for all)
Forgiving (willing to pardon others)	Family security (taking care of loved ones)
Helpful (working for the welfare of others)	Freedom (independence, free choice)
Honest (sincere, truthful)	Happiness (contentedness)
Imaginative (daring, creative)	Inner harmony (freedom from inner conflict)
Independent (self-reliant, self-sufficient)	Mature love (sexual and spiritual intimacy)
Intellectual (intelligent, reflective)	National security (protection from attack)
Logical (consistent, rational)	Pleasure (an enjoyable, leisurely life)
Loving (affectionate, tender)	Salvation (saved, eternal life)
Obedient (dutiful, respectful)	Self-respect (self-esteem)
Polite (courteous, well mannered)	Social recognition (respect, admiration)
Responsible (dependable, reliable)	True friendship (close companionship)
Self-controlled (restrained, self-disciplined)	Wisdom (a mature understanding of life)

Source: Rokeach, M. (1973). *The nature of human values*. New York: Free Press; Rokeach, M. (1979). *Understanding human values: Individual and societal*. New York: Free Press.

worth the sacrifice of human life, or worth dying for. Secondary values are very important, but they are not strong enough for the sacrifice of human life. Tertiary values are at the bottom of the value hierarchy (e.g. hospitality to guests may be a tertiary value). Whether a value is primary, secondary, or tertiary depends upon the national culture of an individual.

6.2.7 Measurement and analysis of values

Values can be measured directly and indirectly. The direct measurements include surveys; people are asked to rank values according to their importance (Rokeach, 1973), or to rate them on a disagreement/agreement Likert scale (Milbraith, 1980; Moum, 1980). The indirect measures include asking people about their desired and desirable values, or by describing other people. People's perceptions of other people are influenced by their values. Values can also be examined through open-ended questions or essays; by observing people's choices, interests, types of rewards and punishments; and by analyzing historical documents, and reading about art, myths, and legends.

Values were measured by different techniques: Ways to Live Test (Morris, 1956), Survey of Interpersonal Values (Gordon, 1960), Personal Value Scales (Scott, 1965), ranking procedures (Kohn, 1969; Rokeach, 1973), Value Survey of Rokeach (1973), and a variety of questionnaire measures and procedures developed for specific purposes (Mirels & Garrett, 1971; Scott, 1965). Not all of these techniques gained universal acceptance. For instance, Morris's (1956) Way of Life Test was criticized for being suited to highly educated respondents only. Scott's (1965) Personal Value Scale used forced-choice format. One of the best available tests is the Allport–Vernon–Lindzey's (AVL) Test (Allport et al., 1951, 1960). Also, value surveys are very useful in studying adult values. The value surveys were praised not only for measuring a person's value but also for perceiving others' values.

The Rokeach Value Survey (RVS) (Rokeach, 1973) is found to be the best available survey instrument for measuring human values. Rokeach introduced two lists of 18 alphabetically arranged instrumental and terminal values (see Table 6.1) accompanied by short descriptors. Rokeach (1973) asked the respondents to arrange values in order of importance to them from 1 to 18. He found that the three most important terminal values are a world of peace, family security, and freedom, whereas the three most important instrumental values are honesty, ambition, and responsibility.

The RVS was found to be an excellent tool in differentiating various political, religious, economic, generational, and cultural groups (Braithwaite & Law, 1985). The RVS has been used in many studies to measure human values. It identified cultural differences in values between Western and Asian countries. The RVS was also used to construct the "List of Values" (Kahle & Timmer, 1983) that included a sense of belonging; fun and enjoyment; warm relationships with others; self-fulfillment; being well respected; and having a sense of accomplishment, security, self-respect, and excitement.

The value surveys were also criticized for not allowing for explanations of cultural differences. Some value surveys are inappropriate for less developed societies and groups with low verbal comprehension. Certain values may be misunderstood or irrelevant to some cultures and thus should not be included in surveys. Although the ranking procedure allows for developing a hierarchy of values understandable to groups with little education, the meaningfulness of the ranking procedure was questioned. Consequently, the most recent value studies apply a rating rather than a ranking system.

In summary, it is difficult to measure and examine values: values are abstract constructs, difficult to translate into different languages. Their interpretations depend on the cultural backgrounds of respondents and researchers. Often the evaluation of the behaviors of others is based on the values and belief system of the observers. Moreover, values can be confused with other concepts, such as attitudes or interests. It is often difficult to determine which particular values should be measured. Usually the values that are important to the individual receive high rankings, for example, love, family, and friendship are given a higher priority than economic values; leisure values are ranked lower. One of the best techniques to assess values is to focus on values that are less individualistic, more cultural. Further, the choice of technique to measure values creates problems. Each measuring method (direct/indirect, surveys, ranking/rating) has its own advantages and disadvantages. Studies that use multiple methods of measurement of values give the best understanding of cultural values.

6.2.8 Value studies in tourism

Not many value studies have been conducted in tourism. Shih (1986) used a Values, Attitudes, and Lifestyles (VALS) technique to assess whether personal values affect the selection of Pennsylvania as a holiday destination. Pitts and Wood-side (1986) used values to describe visitors to tourist attractions versus non-visitors, and identify ''a value profile'' of each group. They noted that differences in cultural values can predict visitation to tourist attractions. Pizam and Calantone (1987) examined a value scale related to tourist vacation behavior. They used different scales to measure values such as the RVS, Scott's Personal Values Scales (Scott, 1965), and others. Pizam and Calantone (1987) noted that values predict travel behavior. Muller (1991) found that different segments of American tourists in Toronto had different values and thus attached different importance to destination attributes. Madrigal and Kahle (1994) identified differences in vacation activity preferences among English-speaking tourists to Scandinavia; these differences depended upon the different importance tourists placed on four value domains. Based on the above studies it appears that values are important variables in predicting tourist behavior and destination visitation.

6.2.9 Cultural value dimensions

Many elements differ among cultural groups. Can these elements completely and adequately distinguish between all cultures? How many of the cultural elements need to be different in order to determine cultural differences? Which cultural elements are the most significant to indicate cultural differences? Which cultural elements have the most significant effect on human behavior? To what degree should these cultural elements be different in order to indicate cultural differences between people and nations? Which elements should be used to be able to successfully compare cultures?

Among the elements on which cultures differ, the most frequently used are the Parsons' (1951) pattern variables, Kluckhohn and Strodtbeck's (1961) value orientations, Stewart's (1971) cultural patterns, Hall's (1960, 1966, 1973, 1976, 1977, 1983), Hall and Hall's (1987), Hofstede's (1980, 2001) and Hofstede' and Bond (1984) dimensions of cultural variability, Argyle's (1986), Schein's (1992), Trompenaars' (1984, 1993), Trompenaars and Hampden-Turner's (1994), Maznevski's (1994), and Schneider and Barsoux's (1997) cultural dimensions. These dimensions provide ways to understand how people behave and communicate across different cultures, how they deal with social life and human relationships, what difficulties they may have in relating to others, and what perceptions they may develop of others. These dimensions also indicate how the major cultural differences may influence the social relations between international culturally different tourists and hosts. The ways cultures differ for these major cultural dimensions are discussed below.

6.2.9.1 Parsons' pattern variables

Parsons (1951) identified six pattern variables that differentiate cultures: universalism–particularism, ascription–achievement, diffuseness-specificity, affectivity–affective neutrality, instrumental–expressive orientation, and self-orientation–collective orientation. The *universalism–particularism* dimension differentiates between cultures depending upon the way people describe each other and the objects and rules they use for this purpose. In cultures with a *universalistic* orientation, people use universal and general rules and standards to describe themselves and objects. People also interact and communicate with others in the same way regardless of social situations and circumstances. In cultures with a *particularistic* orientation, people describe themselves and others in specific categories that are unique to the situation. People's interaction and communication patterns with others differ depending upon situations. For example, the United States and Canada are the most universalistic cultures on earth, whereas Japan, Singapore, Hong Kong, China, Thailand, and South Korea are more particularistic (Ballah et al., 1985).

The *ascription–achievement* dimension differentiates between cultures depending upon how people assess each other. In the *ascription* orientation people, assess others on the basis of the inherent qualities (e.g. gender, family heritage, race, ethnic group), and predict others' behavior on the basis of qualities ascribed to them (India, China, Japan, Indonesia, France). In the *achievement* orientation, people judge others and objects on the basis of the performance and measurable results, and predict others' behavior on the basis of their efforts, occupational status, and achievements (the United States, the United Kingdom).

The *diffuseness-specificity* dimension differentiates between cultures depending upon how people categorize others and objects. People categorize others and objects in a holistic manner within a wider context by searching for patterns, structures, and theories (collectivistic cultures). In the *specificity* orientation, people categorize others and objects according to specific facts, tasks, and numbers, and respond to a particular aspect of a person or an object only, for example, role or responsibility assigned (individualistic cultures). Japan, Thailand, Malaysia, China, Hong Kong, Singapore, and Nepal are holistic oriented, whereas Canada, Australia, France, Germany, the United States, Netherlands and the United Kingdom are more specifics oriented (Hampden-Turner & Fons-Trompenaars in Joynt, 1996).

The *affectivity–affective neutrality* dimension differentiates between cultures depending upon the nature of the gratification people seek, their emotional and non-emotional responses, and the way their decisions are made. In the *affective* orientation people look for immediate gratification; their behavior and decisions are guided by emotions (Latin American cultures such as Spain, Italy, or Mexico). In the *affective neutrality* orientation people express self-restraint; their behavior and decisions are guided by cognitive information and facts (the United States, Australia, the United Kingdom).

The *instrumental–expressive* dimension differentiates between cultures depending on the nature of the goals people seek to achieve in their social interactions. In the *instrumental* orientation social interactions are important because they help to achieve certain goals (the United States), while in the *expressive* orientation, social interactions are valued for their own sake (Latin America, Arab cultures). In the expressive orientation, people value friendships more than in instrumental orientation (Gudykunst & Kim, 1997).

The *self-collective* orientation dimension differentiates between cultures by identifying those cultures that focus on the needs and rights of individuals versus those that care about the welfare of others and the community. In the *self-oriented* cultures the individual goals are emphasized, people look after themselves and take initiatives (the United States, the United Kingdom). In the *collective* cultures people are concerned about the interests and well being of others (Asia). Americans and Canadians are the most self-oriented and individualistic nations on earth; the Chinese, Singaporeans, Hong Kong, Malaysians and Koreans are more concerned with the group of people with whom they work or interact socially (Hampden-Turner & Trompenaars, 1996).

6.2.9.2 Kluckhohn and Strodtbeck's value orientation

Kluckhohn and Strodtbeck (1961) compared cultures on the basis of people's beliefs about the character of human nature, the relationship of human kind to nature, the value placed on human activities, orientation toward time, and the relationship of people to each other.

Orientation toward human nature deals with inner character, which is good, evil, or a mixture. Western societies perceive a person as good, while Eastern societies (e.g. Chinese) perceive a person as good or bad. This orientation has a significant impact on people's attitudes toward each other, including trust, and their interpersonal contact. Humans can also be viewed as able to change (mutable) or not able to change (immutable). As a result, there are numerous combinations of various aspects of human nature. Humans are categorized as evil but mutable, evil and immutable, neutral with respect to good and evil, a mixture of good and evil, good but mutable, and good and immutable. The US Americans see human nature as evil but mutable; they use discipline and self-control to change their nature.

Orientation toward nature deals with the way humans treat their environment. Humans can have mastery over nature, live in harmony with nature, or subjugate to nature. Western societies believe they can control nature and that all natural forces can and should be overcome (e.g. floods, storms). Eastern societies believe people should live in harmony with nature and worship it. Asian societies see nature as a creation of God, and life as God's will. They regard members of Western societies who seek out alternatives for God and spiritual dimensions, as barbaric, untrustworthy, unintelligent, and biased. Latinos believe people should be subjugated to nature; nothing can be done to control nature if it threatens. The orientation towards nature affects people's attitudes toward religion, aesthetics, material possession, life quality, and interpersonal relations.

Orientation toward human activities deals with people's attitudes toward activity. People can be either doing, or being or being-in-becoming, oriented. Societies that are ''doing'' and ''action'' oriented (Western cultures, such as the United States or Germany) emphasize activity, task completion, goal achievement, getting things done, and competition. They believe that activities are tangible and can be measured. For example, a common question in the United States is, ''What do you do for living?'' The *being* orientation is the opposite of the *doing* orientation. People engage in spontaneous activities, indulge in pleasure, and show their spontaneity as an expression of their personality, for example, Latin cultures. The *being-in-becoming* orientation is concerned with spiritual more than material life. The focus is not on what you own, but on self-development, contemplation, meditation, and self-improvement (e.g. Hinduism, Zen Buddhist monks). In both being and being-in-becoming cultures, people emphasize passivity and defensiveness; they strive for social harmony in interpersonal relations at the expense of efficiency. These cultures are people oriented and social-harmony oriented.

Eastern cultures are either being or being-in-becoming oriented. Eastern cultures stress humility, tolerance, peacefulness, individualistic obligations to society, group harmony, warm relationships, and gift-giving (Beatty et al., 1991). An understanding of the activity orientation gives insight into the people's decision-making. In the being-oriented societies, decisions are emotional and people oriented, whereas in the doing-oriented societies, decisions are economically driven and task oriented. The activity orientation dimension has a significant influence on interpersonal relations.

Orientation toward time deals with people's attitudes toward time. People can focus either on the past, present, or future. Western societies are future-oriented. They perceive time as a scarce resource and try to use it effectively. They value change and see the future as ''bigger and brighter'' (e.g. the United States). Eastern societies, on the other hand, are past- and tradition-oriented; they worship ancestors and have strong family traditions (e.g. China, Japan). They attach relatively less importance to time schedules, appointments, and punctuality. They perceive time as circular rather than linear (e.g. Indonesia). However, in Western-influenced Hong Kong, the majority of Chinese act according to precise time schedules. Present-oriented societies believe that the moment has the most significance. The future is vague and unknown; what really matters is ''now.'' People pay relatively little attention to what happened in the past. People believe they must ''enjoy their moment.'' People of the Philippines, Mexico, and Latin America are usually present-time oriented. Also, present time predominates among the Navajo Indians of northern Arizona. Time orientation has a significant impact on people's attitudes to tradition, ceremony, etiquette, and interpersonal relations.

Orientation towards other people appears to be the most crucial in governing human relations and is the most differentiating between Eastern and Western cultures. There are three types of orientations towards other people: (1) *individualistic* (individual goals take primacy over group goals); (2) *collateral* (the individual is part of a social group which results from laterally extended relationships; and (3) *linear* (stresses the continuity of the group through time in succession) (Kluckhohn & Strodtbeck, 1961).

Western cultures (the United States) emphasize individualism, personal goals that enhance social status, competition, self-image, and informality. Eastern cultures, on the other hand, emphasize both collaterality and linearity (hierarchy). Collateral (collectivistic) relationships are characterized by the strong and smooth relationship between an individual and a group, group harmony, consensus, agreement with group norms, and concern for the welfare of others. For example, the important Chinese values are politeness, thrift, and saving face; causing someone else the embarrassment of losing face is regarded as inappropriate behavior (DeMente, 1991). Smooth interpersonal relations, the importance of being together, emotional closeness with the family, and friendly relations outside the family are also vital to the Philippinos (Hollnsteiner, 1963; Jocano, 1966; Lynch, 1964). Similarly, Thai emphasize smooth interpersonal relations, being polite, kind, pleasant, and conflict-free (Komin, 1990). Smiling is an important element in Thai interpersonal relations (Gardiner, 1972). Also, the Vietnamese frequently display affection and are ready for social contact with strangers (Forrest, 1971).

Linear interpersonal relations are characterized by the hierarchy of society; obedience, and loyalty to authority; feelings of duty, responsibility, and submission to the group, elders, and those in superior positions; desire to comply; and being respectful. The major Confucian values teach people to behave modestly and refrain from challenging one's superiors (Leung, 1991). For example, in Chinese culture politeness and deference to authority are considered to be virtues (Ettenson & Wagner, 1991). One of the important Confucian values of the Chinese people is the giving of unquestioning respect to parents and the elderly through understanding and expectations of authority (filial piety) (Huyton, 1991). Deference to age and authority; face saving; connections (Yau, 1988); and maintaining harmony, prestige, and social respect (Huyton, 1991) are important to the Chinese. The Chinese believe that it is better to perform acts of self-effacement rather than break the group harmony. Submissiveness to authority, the desire to comply, and filial piety also characterize the Vietnamese culture (Forrest, 1971). Similarly, conformity, endurance, and deference with regard to interpersonal relations is important to the Philippino (Lynch, 1970). In general, Eastern societies are more conforming, and people depend more on each other than Westerners do (Doi, 1981). Table 6.2 shows Kluckhohn and Strodtbeck's value orientations and their characteristics.

Table 6.2 Kluckhohn and Strodtbeck's (1961) Value Orientation

Character of human nature	Evil	Mixture	Good
Relationship of humankind to nature	People subject to nature	Live in harmony	Master nature
Orientation toward activity	Being	Being-in-becoming	Doing
Orientation toward time	Past	Present	Future
Relationship of people to other people	Authoritarian	Group	Individualistic

Importance of social harmony

Eastern cultures emphasize harmony in interpersonal relations, self-restraint – the avoidance of negative emotions, criticism, negative opinions, complaints, and conflicts in all interpersonal relations. Members of Eastern cultures try to ''save face'' and avoid embarrassment to maintain harmony in interpersonal relations. Openly disagreeing or saying ''no'' is considered rude and damaging to social harmony. For instance, in China one confirms a negative statement with a ''yes'' (Leung, 1991). In Japan there are several techniques for politely saying ''no.'' Philippinos avoid social disruption, embarrassment, or disagreement because these can bring shame (Lynch, 1970). The Philippine and Indonesian concept of shame is very similar to the Chinese and Japanese concept of ''saving face.'' In Eastern societies, criticizing in public makes people lose face and damages their relationships with those who criticize. Thus, in order to protect the individuals from loss of face, peoples of the East rarely criticize or admit failure. For example, the Thai response to criticism, where criticism is rare and face saving common, is rigidity and withdrawal (Foa et al., 1969). The most acceptable expression of anger by Thai people is ''keeping calm'' (Gardiner, 1968). For the Japanese, good human relationships are more important than money (Ellis & Ellis, 1989). In Japan, social relations are seen as mutual responsibilities, and the smallest favors put the receiver in debt. Similarly, harmony in social relations is paramount for the people of Hong Kong (Huyton, 1991). In contrast to Eastern societies, Western societies see interpersonal relationships as opportunities for friction; Westerners are less concerned with apologies, and more with self-esteem. For example, the Westerner's reaction to failure or criticism is an attempt to improve performance and an increased cognitive flexibility (Foa et al., 1969). The Eastern concept of shame also appears to be in contrast with the Western emphasis on truthfulness and forthrightness, which often cause disagreement, social disruption, and embarrassment.

Importance of apology

In order to maintain social harmony, people in Eastern cultures apologize frequently. The Japanese apologize by acknowledging their fault even when they are not at fault, in order to indicate their will to maintain or restore relations (Wagatsuma & Rosett, 1986). Americans, on the other hand, blame others even when they know they are at fault. Further, the Japanese, who are sensitive to fulfilling their social obligations, apologize frequently for not meeting their obligations (Coulmas, 1981). The Japanese tend to apologize if repayment is not possible and offer compensation for the other person in order to maintain harmony in relations. Americans, on the other hand, give explanations and justify their behavior (Barnlund & Yoshioka, 1990).

6.2.9.3 Stewart's cultural patterns

According to Stewart (1971), cultures can be differentiated according to their members' orientations to activity, social relations, the self, and world.

Activity orientation is similar to Kluckhohn and Strodtbeck's (1961) activity orientation; it differentiates between cultures on the basis of how people view human activities and how they express themselves through activities (doing/being/becoming). *Doing* cultures value action and "getting things done"; people seek change and want to control their lives (Euro-Americans). *Being* cultures focus on non-action (African-American, Greek); people believe that all events are determined by fate (Hindus from India). *Becoming* cultures see human beings as evolving and changing (Native Americans, South Americans).

The activity orientation determines the pace of people's life. *Doing* cultures are governed by time schedules and appointments, and are characterized by a fast pace of life. *Being* and *becoming* cultures are characterized by a slower and more relaxed pace of life (Lustig & Koester, 1993). The activity orientation also determines how people measure their own success. In *doing* cultures, people set the goals for their activities and evaluate the results of their activities by measurable criteria. In *being* and *becoming* cultures, the process is more important than the final result. Further, the activity orientation influences the relationship between work and play. In *doing* cultures, work is separated from play: employees are supervised and controlled. In *being* and *becoming* cultures, work is a means to an end, and there is no clear distinction between work and play. Employees mix together and socialize. Moreover, *doing* cultures challenge and solve problems that arise. *Being* and *becoming* cultures accept the difficulty rather than challenge and eliminate it. Further, in *doing* cultures, interpersonal interaction and communication focus on accomplishing specific tasks and solving problems. In *being* and *becoming* cultures, social interactions focus on being together.

Social relations orientation is similar to Parsons' (1951) self-and-group orientation and Kluckhohn and Strodtbeck's (1961) individualistic–collateral and linear relationships. It differentiates cultures on the basis of how people relate to one another (formal/informal; egalitarian/hierarchical; direct/indirect). In *formal* cultures people follow rules of social hierarchy and address others in an official way by using appropriate titles (Japan, Germany). In *informal* cultures social relations are based on equality, and people interact and communicate informally (the United States, Australia). *Egalitarian* cultures (European and the United States) emphasize equality, evenness in interpersonal relationships, independence, and a minimum number of obligations and responsibilities (the United States, Australia, the United Kingdom). *Hierarchical* cultures (Korea, Japan, Mexico) emphasize status differences between individuals, obligations, and dependence (Japan, China). The degree of dependency in hierarchical cultures depends on the social status and formality that exists between individuals. *Direct* cultures emphasize directness and openness in interpersonal interactions and communication (Europe, the United States). *Indirect* cultures emphasize ambiguity and the use of third parties or intermediaries (Japan, Korea, Thailand, China, Africa) (Lustig & Koester, 1993).

Self-orientation is similar to Parsons' (1951) self-orientation and Kluckhohn and Strodtbeck's (1961) individualism–collectivism orientation. Self-orientation differentiates between cultures depending upon how people view themselves and form their identities; whether their nature is changeable; what motivates their actions; and who is valued and respected (self/group orientation). In *self-oriented* United States and Europe the emphasis is on the individual self. Children are encouraged to make their own decisions and be independent from an early age. People seek innovation and change. Alternatively, in *group-oriented* Asian cultures people define themselves through their association with others. An individual cannot exist without the group. People depend on each other at work, school, and home. Members of the group are motivated by loyalty to a group, duties, and responsibilities (e.g. family, company). They also seek advice from senior members who have valuable life experience and knowledge.

World orientation is similar to Klukhohn and Strodtbeck's (1961) orientations toward nature and time. World orientation differentiates between cultures on the basis of how people relate to the spiritual world and nature (subjugation/harmony/control). Europeans, the US Americans, and Canadians believe in the power of an individual to control, manipulate, and change nature. They also believe in separate physical and spiritual worlds. Reality is what can be tested and proved, as opposed to spirituality. On the other hand, Latino cultures view humans as having very little power to control the forces of nature and, thus, being subjugated to nature. They also place a great value on spirituality. Eastern cultures focus on living in harmony with nature. The world orientation also determines the way people view time. While the US Americans and Europeans are future-oriented, Native Americans and Latinos are present-oriented (Stewart, 1971).

6.2.9.4 Hall's cultural differentiation

Hall differentiated cultures on the basis of different communication style and orientation toward the world and people.

Communication style

Hall (1976, 1983) distinguished between cultures according to how communication takes place: (low/high context), information flow (covert/overt messages), language (low/high context), and the handling of personal space (public, private).

Context

There are the *low-context* cultures (LCC) and *high-context* cultures (HCC) depending upon the level of information included in a communication message (Hall, 1976). In the *low-context* cultures most of the information and meaning is contained in verbal messages, very little in the contextual message. Messages have clear meanings and line logic; explicit direct verbal communication and clear intentions are emphasized. Western cultures (Germany, Sweden, Switzerland, Australia, the United States, France) belong to LCC, where there is a need for explicit instructions, signs, and procedures that explain how to behave. In the *high-context* cultures very little information is coded in the verbal message; most information is coded in the non-verbal and contextual message. All events can be understood only in context; meanings vary depending upon circumstances, and categories can change. Emphasis is on spiral logic, implicit imprecise and indirect communication. Intentions are not clearly specified and discretion in expressing opinions is exercised (China, Japan, Korea, Taiwan, Vietnam, Latin

America, Mexico). The HCC value face saving, honor shame and obligations, avoid confrontations, and use smoothing strategies to manage conflicts in interpersonal relations. Members of HCC are also more careful in initial interactions and make assumptions based upon a stranger's cultural background. They ask more indirect questions (Gudykunst, 1983); direct questions are considered to be rude (Elashmawi, 1991). Those who belong to HCC (the Japanese, Chinese, Southeast Asians, Indonesians, Micronesians, and Indians) expect others to sense the rules of behavior (Dodd, 1987).

Information flow

Cultures are distinguished on the basis of the structure and speed of messages between individuals. Members of high-context cultures use *covert messages* that are high in context. The focus is on non-verbal codes and implied meanings. People know the meanings of particular messages in specific situations, and they do not need to be explicit. Little is left for interpretation. In low-context cultures, members use *overt messages* that are low in context. People send explicit messages, which include clear instructions to convey exact meanings. Precise verbal codes and words are used to transmit the meanings.

Language

Different cultures dictate how language is used. Language determines appropriate subjects of discussion (family, politics, religion) and the degree of expressiveness. For example, in high-context cultures being direct and open, using many verbal codes, and expressing emotions or showing feelings is considered a sign of immaturity. In order to maintain social harmony and not to threaten the face or self-esteem of the others, one must be silent and reserved. In low-context cultures it is acceptable to express anger, show excitement, be noisy and appear confident. Table 6.3 presents major characteristics of low- and high-context cultures.

In-groups and out-groups

In low- versus high-context cultures there is a distinction between in-groups and out-groups. In high-context cultures there is a strong emphasis on *in-groups* and a clear distinction between those who belong to a group (in-groups, insiders), such as families, friends, neighbors, and work groups, and those who do not (out-groups, outsiders), for example, non-members, clans, organizations, and foreigners. Individuals identify themselves with only a few groups, with which they have strong binding ties (Japan, Korea, China). People know how to behave according to the rules and situations and what to expect from the behavior of the others. In contrast, in low-context cultures, where the emphasis is on *out-groups* (the United States, Europe), people belong to many different groups throughout their lifetimes. Membership in these groups is temporary; people change groups (e.g. change jobs and companies) and

Table 6.3 Characteristics of Low- and High-Context Cultures

Low-context cultures	High-context cultures
Overt and explicit communication	Covert and implicit communication
Verbal messages	Non-verbal contextual messages
Explicit and precise instructions, signs, rules	Imprecise
Clear intentions, meanings	Not clear intentions; meanings depend upon circumstances
Line logic	Spiral logic
Conflict and confrontation are natural	Avoidance of conflict and confrontation
Importance of action and solution	Value of face saving, relationships with others, social harmony
Protecting own dignity and self-respect even at the expense of others	Desire to be acknowledged and approved by others
Discussions and arguments, revealing	Smooth strategies to manage conflict, concealing
Reactions on the surface	Reserved reactions
Equality	Importance of obligations, status, position and power
Highly organized time	Flexible time
Flexible in-groups and out-groups	Distinct in-groups and out-groups
Short-lasting relationships, casual, fragile, low involvement	Long lasting relationships, commitment, loyalty, trust, high involvement
Diffused authority, difficult to pin down one's responsibility	Importance of authority and responsibility

do not feel committed and loyal to others. Table 6.4 identifies major characteristics of in-groups and out-groups.

Space

Cultures can differ depending on the ways people handle their communication space. In *public-space* cultures, people are suspicious of activities conducted in secret, social closeness is needed, and public meetings are valued. In *private-space* cultures, members respect personal space, value privacy, and keep social distance.

Orientation toward the world and people

In terms of the orientation toward the world and people, Hall (1960, 1966, 1973) and Hall and Hall (1987) distinguished between cultures on the basis of orientation toward human nature (agreements), human relationships (amount of space, possessions, friendships, authority), time (past, future, monochronic, polychronic), and activity (change/no change).

Table 6.4 Characteristics of In-Groups and Out-Groups

Out-groups	In-groups
Casual expectations for behavior	Fixed expectations for behavior
Fragile bonds between people	Strong bonds between people
Weak identification with a group	Strong identification with a group
Low commitment between people	Strong commitment between people
Define themselves in relation to self	Define themselves in relation to the members of the group
Responsibility to oneself	Responsibilities to others
Independent	Interdependent
Short-lasting loyalty to family and members of social and work groups	Long-lasting loyalty to family and members of social and work groups
Temporary membership in the group	Permanent membership in the group
Frequent changes of social networks	Seldom changes of social networks

Orientation toward human nature

In high-context cultures, agreements between members tend to be *spoken* rather than written. Written contracts are not binding and can be changed depending on the circumstances. In low-context cultures agreements tend to be *written* rather than spoken. Written agreements are final and legally binding.

Orientation toward human relationships

Cultures differ in the way people use *space*. There are four spatial distance zones: *intimate* (for loving, comforting, protecting or fighting); *personal* (for conversations with intimates, friends); *social* (for impersonal and social gatherings); and *public* (for lectures, speeches, concerts, ceremonies, plays) (Hall, 1966). By understanding the rules of space, people know how far to remain from others in different social situations without interrupting the conversations and jeopardizing privacy. Space distances are culture-specific. For example, people living in colder climates (Germany, Scandinavia, the United Kingdom) use larger physical distance when they communicate. They also expect others to keep their distances. People living in warm weather climates (Italy, Greece, Spain, Africa) display closer distances.

In various cultures, people differ in their attitudes toward *possessions*. Individualists are motivated by material possessions, such as cars, clothes, and homes, as well as high social positions and power. Collectivistics are motivated by a responsibility and duty to a group, loyalty, and social harmony.

In high-context cultures relationships are relatively long lasting, based on the individual's commitments to each other, loyalty, and trust. Stable and long relationships are needed for developing *friendship*. In low-context cultures, relationships are relatively shorter in duration and more casual, the bonds between people are fragile, and the extent of involvement in a long-term relationship is low. Deep personal involvement with others is valued less.

In high-context cultures *authority* is respected; people are personally responsible for the actions of subordinates; in low-context cultures authority is diffused and personal responsibility is difficult to establish.

Orientation toward time

Cultures differ in the importance attached to *past* and *future*. Americans are not concerned about the past; they believe the past is relatively unimportant. In contrast, Europeans and Asians have a long history and deeply rooted traditions; thus, they pay attention to the past and follow traditions. In high-context cultures time is viewed as open, less structured, more responsive to the needs of people, and less to external goals. In low-context cultures, time is highly organized so that people are able to live and work with others.

There are *monochronic* and *polychronic* cultures (Hall, 1983). *Monochronic* cultures, such as Anglo-Saxon (the United States, Canada, Australia, the United Kingdom) and northern European cultures (Sweden, Norway, Finland, Germany), are task-, time-schedule-, and procedure-oriented. They see time as a long ribbon that can be sliced into segments. Time is used in a structured, sequential, linear fashion. Activities are scheduled according to time and can be stopped when ''time is up.'' So, time is treated as money, which can be spent, saved, borrowed, lost, or even killed. People are concerned about punctuality, time slots, and appointment schedules. They believe that only one thing can be done at a time; there is a need for completing a task or coming to a conclusion before beginning something else. Human relations depend upon time. On the other hand, *polychronic* cultures, such as southern Europe (Spain, Italy, Portugal), and the Middle East believe time is unlimited, non-linear, and can be expanded to accommodate various activities at the same time. Members think of time in terms of pictures or configurations. Punctuality is not as important; being late and interruptions are excusable. The focus is on relationships rather than task completion within time schedules. People have time for each other. Time can be sacrificed (Latin America, Arab states) for the sake of the relationship. As a result, the polychronic cultures are more effective in developing and maintaining relationships and solving human problems (Schein, 1992). Further, Asian cultures believe in the cyclical concept of time: time is in phases rather than in circular form. One season follows the next; one life leads into another (Sithi-Amnuai, 1968).

Orientation toward activity and change

Time orientation influences orientation towards activity and change. In high-context cultures people are cautious of change. In low-context cultures people desire change; they live faster and change their behavior faster. For example, the US Americans tend to view change as good and desirable, they constantly search for new and better ways of doing and improving things. Europeans tend to view change as risky since it can threaten their traditions. In Asia change may be seen as dangerous since it brings uncertainty, which needs to be avoided (Schneider & Barsoux, 1997).

6.2.9.5 **Hofstede's dimensions of cultural variability**

The most widely utilized dimensions of national culture that allow for differentiating among cultures are those identified by Hofstede (1980, 2001). Geert Hofstede (1980) conducted perhaps the most comprehensive study of how values are influenced by culture. He analyzed a large database of employees' values scores collected by IBM between 1967 and 1973 and covering more than 70 countries. First he used only the 40 largest; afterwards he extended the analysis to 50 countries and 3 regions. He initially identified four distinct cultural dimensions: Power Distance (PDI), Uncertainty Avoidance (UAI), Individualism (IDV), and Masculinity (MAS). He scored each country using a scale of roughly 0–100 for each dimension. The higher the score, the more that dimension is exhibited in society. The description of Hofstede's (1980, 2001) cultural dimensions is presented below.

The *Power Distance (PDI)* dimension refers to the extent to which a society accepts the unequal distribution of power in relationships and institutions. In *high PDI* cultures (Malaysia, Guatemala, Panama, Philippines, Mexico, Venezuela, China), people are not equal but everyone has a rightful place. Power and authority are facts of life. Status, rank, obedience, conformity, supervision, and co-operation are valued. In *low PDI* cultures (Austria, Israel, Denmark, New Zealand, Ireland, Sweden) inequality is minimized. People value independence, consultancy, and personality, instead of autocratic decision-making; there is a strong ethic of competition. Australia, the United States, and Canada scored relatively low on the PD scale.

The *Uncertainty Avoidance (UAI)* dimension refers to the extent to which a society feels threatened by uncertain and ambiguous situations and tries to avoid them. In *high UAI* cultures (Greece, Portugal, Belgium, Japan, France, Peru), societies feel anxious in situations which they perceive as unstructured, unclear, and unpredictable; they believe that such situations, and any other ambiguities in life, are threats that must be fought. Therefore, they avoid conflict, disapprove competition, remain emotionally restrained, display nationalism and suspicion toward foreigners, reject strange behaviors and new ideas they are not familiar with and consider dangerous. People seek stability and security in life, desire law and order. They have many formal, written rules, guidelines, and strict codes of behavior that dictate to them how to act in order to avoid risk. Societies are characterized by a high level of anxiety, loyalty, consensus, and group decisions, which help to reduce risk. Japan scored the highest among all Asian countries on the UAI dimension (92/100). The Japanese definitely avoid ambiguous and uncertain situations. In *low UAI* cultures (Singapore, Denmark, Sweden, Hong Kong, the United Kingdom, Ireland, India), societies accept the uncertainty inherent in life conflict, tolerate ambiguity, and take more risk. People accept foreigners with different ideas; new ideas are not threatening. People are more flexible, do not need many rules. They believe in common sense and less in expertise. They are less stressed. Societies focus on advancement and competition. Australia, the United States and Canada scored relatively low on the UAI dimension.

The *Individualism (IDV)* dimension refers to the extent to which people emphasize their own needs. *Highly individualistic* cultures (the United States, Australia, the

United Kingdom, Netherlands, New Zealand, Canada, Italy) value individualism, independence, uniqueness, self-actualization, self-development, freedom, autonomy, challenge, initiative, activity, achievement, financial security, self-orientation, and privacy. The social ties are loose. *Highly collectivistic* cultures (Guatemala, Ecuador, Panama, Venezuela, Colombia, Pakistan, Indonesia, Peru, Taiwan, Thailand), emphasize group goals, rights, decisions, consensus, and cooperation. Individual initiative is discouraged, and people are ''we'' oriented. The social and family ties are tight. There is a distinction between in-groups and out-groups. The in-group members look after the other members in exchange for absolute loyalty. Friendships are predetermined by long, stable relationships. East Asian countries are particularly high on collectivism, and English-speaking countries are particularly high on individualism.

Individualistic and collectivistic cultures also differ according to whether relations among people are horizontal or vertical (Triandis, 1995). In *horizontal* cultures people are treated equally; focus is on equality. In contrast, in *vertical* cultures, people see themselves as different from others; equality is not valued highly. In *horizontal collectivistic* cultures little value is placed on freedom; members of that culture are not expected to stand out in the group (e.g. Japan). In *vertical collectivistic* cultures individuals are expected to fit into the group and allowed to stand out in the group (e.g. India). In *horizontal individualistic* cultures (e.g. Sweden, Norway) people are expected to act as individuals, and at the same time, not stand out from others. In *vertical individualistic* cultures (e.g. the United States, the United Kingdom, France, Germany) people are expected to act as individuals and stand out from others.

The *Masculinity (MAS)* dimension refers to the extent to which a culture values ''masculine'' behavior, such as assertiveness, acquisition of money and material possessions, and lack of care for others, as opposed to ''feminine'' behavior and the quality of life, and the extent to which gender roles are differentiated. In the *highly masculine* cultures (Japan, Hungary, Austria, Venezuela, Italy, Switzerland, Mexico), societies value money and material possessions. Emphasis is on performance, growth, ambition, living to work, successful achievement, excellence, dominance, and assertiveness. People accept the company's interference in their private lives. There is high job stress. Gender roles are differentiated and unequal. Japan scored the highest on the masculinity index 95/100 among all other Asian countries. In the *high feminine* cultures (Sweden, Norway, Netherlands, Denmark, Finland, Chile, Portugal, Thailand) society's focus is on quality of life, welfare of others, caring and nurturing behavior, and sympathy for the unsuccessful. Gender roles are equal. People also believe in the importance of the environment. Australia and the United States scored relatively high on the masculinity index, Canada scored between high and low. Table 6.5 presents evaluation, and Table 6.6 presents a ranking of 74 countries on Hofstede and Hofstede's (2005) five value dimensions.

According to Hofstede's model, Malaysia had the highest PDI score (104), Greece the highest UAI score (112), the United States the highest IDV score (91), Japan the highest MAS score (95), and China the highest LTO score (118). On the other hand, Austria obtained the lowest PDI score (11), Singapore the lowest UAI score (8),

Table 6.5 Evaluation of Various Countries on Hofstede and Hofstede's (2005) Five Value Dimensions

Country	Power Distance	Uncertainty Avoidance	Individualism	Masculinity	Long-term Orientation
Arab countries	80	68	38	53	
Argentina	49	86	46	56	
Australia	36	51	90	61	31
Austria	11	70	55	79	31
Bangladesh	80	60	20	55	40
Belgium total					38
Belgium Flemish	61	97	78	43	
Walloon	67	93	72	60	
Brazil	69	76	38	49	65
Bulgaria	70	85	30	40	
Canada total	39	48	80	52	23
Canada – Quebec	54	60	73	45	30
Chile	63	86	23	28	
China	80	30	20	66	118
Colombia	67	80	13	64	
Costa Rica	35	86	15	21	
Croatia	73	80	33	40	
Czech Republic	57	74	58	57	13
Denmark	18	23	74	16	46
East Africa	64	52	27	41	25
Ecuador	78	67	8	63	
El Salvador	66	94	19	40	
Estonia	40	60	60	30	
Finland	33	59	63	26	41
France	68	86	71	43	39
Germany	35	65	67	66	31
Great Britain	35	35	89	66	25
Greece	60	112	35	57	
Guatemala	95	101	6	37	
Hong Kong	68	29	25	57	96
Hungary	46	82	80	88	50
India	77	40	48	56	61
Indonesia	78	48	14	46	
Iran	58	59	41	43	
Ireland	28	35	70	68	43

Table 6.5 (*Continued*)

Country	Power Distance	Uncertainty Avoidance	Individualism	Masculinity	Long-term Orientation
Israel	13	81	54	47	
Italy	50	75	76	70	34
Jamaica	45	13	39	68	
Japan	54	92	46	95	80
Luxembourg	40	70	60	50	
Malaysia	104	36	26	50	
Malta	56	96	59	47	
Mexico	81	82	30	69	
Morocco	70	68	46	53	
Netherlands	38	53	80	14	44
New Zealand	22	49	79	58	30
Nigeria					16
Norway	31	50	69	8	44
Pakistan	55	70	14	50	0
Panama	95	86	11	44	
Peru	64	87	16	42	
Philippines	94	44	32	64	19
Poland	68	93	60	64	32
Portugal	63	104	27	31	30
Romania	90	90	30	42	
Russia	93	95	39	36	
Serbia	86	92	25	43	
Singapore	74	8	20	48	48
Slovakia	104	51	52	110	38
Slovenia	71	88	27	19	
South Africa	49	49	65	63	
South Korea	60	85	18	39	75
Spain	57	86	51	42	19
Suriname	85	92	47	37	
Sweden	31	29	71	5	33
Switzerland					40
French	70	70	64	58	
German	26	56	69	72	
Taiwan	58	69	17	45	87
Thailand	64	64	20	34	56
Trinidad	47	55	16	58	
Turkey	66	85	37	45	
The United States	40	46	91	62	29
Uruguay	61	100	36	38	

Table 6.5 (*Continued*)

Country	Power Distance	Uncertainty Avoidance	Individualism	Masculinity	Long-term Orientation
Venezuela	81	76	12	73	
Vietnam	70	30	20	40	80
West Africa	77	54	20	46	16
Zimbabwe					25

*A high score on a dimension indicates a high evaluation on that dimension. For example, a score of 91 on the IDV dimension indicates that the United States is very individualistic.
**Arab countries: Egypt, Iraq, Kuwait, Lebanon, Libya, Saudi Arabia, United Arab Emirates; East Africa: Ethiopia, Tanzania, Zambia; West Africa: Ghana, Nigeria, Sierra Leone.
Source: Hofstede, G., & Hofstede, G. J. (2005). *Cultures and organizations: Software of the mind* (Revised and expanded 2nd ed.). New York, USA: McGraw-Hill.

Guatemala the lowest IDV score (6), and Sweden the lowest MAS score (5). People in the United States and the United Kingdom have low LTO scores.

The drawbacks of applying Hofstede's theory

Hofstede's (1980) theory of cultural differentiation can be of great use when analyzing a country's culture. However, there are a few things one has to keep in mind. First, the dimensions have been chosen for comparing countries, and the measuring instrument was meant for use at country or geographical level only. The averages of a country do not relate to individuals of that country. The dimensions cannot be used for comparing the values of individuals. For example, a person can be a highly individualistic even though the person's national culture is strongly collectivistic. Although Hofstede's theory proved to be quite correct when applied to the general population, not all individuals or even regions with subcultures fit into the theory. The identified dimensions should be used only as a guide to understanding the difference in cultures between countries, not as law set in stone. Second, the data have been collected through questionnaires. In group-oriented cultures, the context of conducting a survey is very important; individuals might respond to questions as if they were addressed to the group they belong to, not the individual. In contrast, in individualistic cultures, the responses will most likely be perceived through the eyes of that individual.

Next, Hofstede assumed that a country (geographical territory) corresponds with a cultural group. While this is valid for many countries, it does not hold in the countries where there are many strong subcultures based on ethnicity of origin or geography. For example, in Canada there is a distinct French-Canadian culture that has a different set of norms compared to English-speaking Canada. In Italy, the northern part of the country has a distinct culture compared to the southern part; both parts would score differently on the masculinity dimension.

Table 6.6 Ranking of Various Countries on Hofstede and Hofstede's (2005) Five Value Dimensions

Rank	Country	PDI	Rank	Country	UAI	Rank	Country	IDV	Rank	Country	MAS	Rank	Country	LTO
1-2	Malaysia	104	1	Greece	112	1	USA	91	1	Slovakia	110	1	China	118
1-2	Slovakia	104	2	Portugal	104	2	Australia	90	2	Japan	95	2	Hong Kong	96
3-4	Guatemala	95	3	Guatemala	101	3	Great Britain	89	3	Hungary	88	3	Taiwan	87
3-4	Panama	95	4-6	Uruguay	100	4-6	Canada total	80	4-5	Austria	79	4-5	Japan	80
5	Philippines	94	4-6	Belgium Flemish	97	4-6	Hungary	80	4-5	Venezuela	73	4-5	Vietnam	80
6	Russia	93	4-6	Malta	96	4-6	Netherlands	80	6	Switzerland German	72	6	South Korea	75
7	Romania	90	7	Russia	95	7	New Zealand	79	7	Italy	70	7	Brazil	65
8	Serbia	86	8	El Salvador	94	8	Belgium Flemish	78	8	Mexico	69	8	India	61
9	Suriname	85	9-10	Belgium Walloon	93	9	Italy	76	9-10	Ireland	68	9	Thailand	56
10-11	Mexico	81	9-10	Poland	93	9-10	Denmark	74	9-10	Jamaica	68	10	Hungary	50
10-11	Venezuela	81	11-13	Japan	92	11-13	Canada Quebec	73	11-13	China	66	11	Singapore	48
12-14	Arab countries	80	11-13	Serbia	92	11-13	Belgium Walloon	72	11-13	Germany	66	12	Denmark	46
12-14	Bangladesh	80	11-13	Suriname	92	11-13	France	71	11-13	Great Britain	66	13-14	Netherlands	44
12-14	China	80	14	Romania	90	14-16	Sweden	71	14-16	Colombia	64	13-14	Norway	44
15-16	Ecuador	78	15	Slovenia	88	14-16	Ireland	70	14-16	Philippines	64	15	Ireland	43
15-16	Indonesia	78	16	Peru	87	14-16	Norway	69	14-16	Poland	64	16	Finland	41
17-18	India	77	17-22	Argentina	86	17-18	Switzerland German	69	17-18	South Africa	63	17-18	Bangladesh	40
17-18	West Africa	77	17-22	Chile	86	17-18	South Africa	67	17-18	Ecuador	63	17-18	Switzerland	40
19	Singapore	74	17-22	Costa Rica	86	19	Germany	65	19	USA	62	19	France	39
20	Croatia	73	17-22	France	86	20	Switzerland French	64	20-21	Australia	61	20-21	Belgium total	38
21	Slovenia	71	17-22	Panama	86	21	Finland	63	20-21	Belgium total	60	20-21	Slovakia	38
22-25	Bulgaria	70	17-22	Spain	86	22-24	Estonia	60	22	New Zealand	58	22	Italy	34
22-25	Morocco	70	22-24	Bulgaria	85	22-24	Luxembourg	60	23	Switzerland French	58	23	Sweden	33
22-25	Switzerland French	70	22-24	South Korea	85	22-24	Poland	60	24	Trinidad	58	24	Poland	32

25–27	31	Austria
25–27	31	Australia
25–27	31	Germany
28–30	30	Canada Quebec
28–30	30	New Zealand
28–30	30	Portugal
31	29	USA
32–33	25	Great Britain
32–33	25	Zimbabwe
34	23	Canada
35–36	19	Philippines
35–36	19	Spain
37	16	Nigeria
38	13	Czech Republic
39	0	Pakistan

25–27	57	Czech Republic
25–27	57	Greece
25–27	57	Hong Kong
28–29	56	Argentina
28–29	56	India
30	55	Bangladesh
31–32	53	Arab countries
31–32	53	Morocco
33	52	Canada total
34–36	50	Luxembourg
34–36	50	Malaysia
34–36	50	Pakistan
37	49	Brazil
38	48	Singapore
39–40	47	Israel
39–40	47	Malta
41–42	46	Indonesia
41–42	46	West Africa
43–45	45	Canada Quebec
43–45	45	Taiwan
43–45	45	Turkey
46	44	Panama
47–50	43	Belgium Flemish
47–50	43	France

25	59	Malta
26	58	Czech Republic
27	55	Austria
28	54	Israel
29	52	Slovakia
30	51	Spain
31	48	India
32	47	Suriname
33–35	46	Argentina
33–35	46	Japan
33–35	46	Morocco
36	41	Iran
37–38	39	Jamaica
37–38	39	Russia
39–40	38	Arab countries
39–40	38	Brazil
41	37	Turkey
42	36	Uruguay
43	35	Greece
44	33	Croatia
45	32	Philippines
46–48	30	Bulgaria
46–48	30	Mexico
46–48	30	Romania

23–25	85	Turkey
26–27	82	Hungary
26–27	82	Mexico
28	81	Israel
29–30	80	Colombia
29–30	80	Croatia
31–32	76	Brazil
31–32	76	Venezuela
33	75	Italy
34	74	Czech Republic
35–38	70	Austria
35–38	70	Luxembourg
35–38	70	Pakistan
35–38	70	Switzerland French
39	69	Taiwan
40–41	68	Arab countries
40–41	68	Morocco
42	67	Ecuador
43	65	Germany
44	64	Thailand
45–47	60	Bangladesh
45–47	60	Canada Quebec
45–47	60	Estonia
48–49	59	Finland

22–25	70	Vietnam
26	69	Brazil
27–29	68	France
27–29	68	Hong Kong
27–29	68	Poland
30–31	67	Belgium Walloon
30–31	67	Colombia
32–33	66	El Salvador
32–33	66	Turkey
34–36	64	East Africa
34–36	64	Peru
34–36	64	Thailand
37–38	63	Chile
37–38	63	Portugal
39–40	61	Belgium Flemish
39–40	61	Uruguay
41–42	60	Greece
41–42	60	South Korea
43–44	58	Iran
43–44	58	Taiwan
45–46	57	Czech Republic
45–46	57	Spain
47	56	Malta
48	55	Pakistan

Table 6.6 (*Continued*)

Rank	Country	PDI	Rank	Country	UAI	Rank	Country	IDV	Rank	Country	MAS	Rank	Country	LTO
49–50	Canada Quebec	54	48–49	Iran	59	49–51	East Africa	27	47–50	Iran	43			
49–50	Japan	54	50	Switzerland German	56	49–51	Portugal	27	47–50	Serbia	43			
51	Italy	50	51	Trinidad	55	49–51	Slovenia	27	51–53	Peru	42			
52–53	Argentina	49	52	West Africa	54	52	Malaysia	26	51–53	Romania	42			
52–53	South Africa	49	53	Netherlands	53	53–54	Hong Kong	25	51–53	Spain	42			
54	Trinidad	47	54	East Africa	52	53–54	Serbia	25	54	East Africa	41			
55	Hungary	46	55	Australia	51	55	Chile	23	55–58	Bulgaria	40			
56	Jamaica	45	55–56	Slovakia	51	56–61	Bangladesh	20	55–58	Croatia	40			
57–59	Estonia	40	57	Norway	50	56–61	China	20	55–58	El Salvador	40			
57–59	Luxembourg	40	58–59	New Zealand	49	56–61	Singapore	20	55–58	Vietnam	40			
57–59	USA	40	58–59	South Africa	49	56–61	Thailand	20	59	South Korea	39			
60	Canada total	39	60–61	Canada total	48	56–61	Vietnam	20	60	Uruguay	38			
61	Netherlands	38	60–61	Indonesia	48	56–61	West Africa	20	61–62	Guatemala	37			
62	Australia	36	62	USA	46	62	El Salvador	19	61–62	Suriname	37			
63–65	Costa Rica	35	63	Philippines	44	63	South Korea	18	63	Russia	36			
63–65	Germany	35	64	India	40	64	Taiwan	17	64	Thailand	34			
63–65	Great Britain	35	65	Malaysia	36	65–66	Peru	16	65	Portugal	31			
66	Finland	33	66–67	Great Britain	35	65–66	Trinidad	16	66	Estonia	30			
67–68	Norway	31	66–67	Ireland	35	67	Costa Rica	15	67	Chile	28			
67–68	Sweden	31	68–69	China	30	68–69	Indonesia	14	68	Finland	26			
69	Ireland	28	68–69	Vietnam	30	68–69	Pakistan	14	69	Costa Rica	21			
70	Switzerland German	26	70–71	Hong Kong	29	70	Colombia	13	70	Slovenia	19			
71	New Zealand	22	70–71	Sweden	29	71	Venezuela	12	71	Denmark	16			
72	Denmark	18	72	Denmark	23	72	Panama	11	72	Netherlands	14			
73	Israel	13	73	Jamaica	13	73	Ecuador	8	73	Norway	8			
74	Austria	11	74	Singapore	8	74	Guatemala	6	74	Sweden	5			

* PDI – power distance; UAI – uncertainty avoidance; IDV – individualism; MAS – masculinity; LTO – long-term orientation.

** A high position (Malaysia) on PDI indicates the country prefers a large power distance; a low position (Austria) means the country prefers a small power distance.

*** Arab countries: Egypt, Iraq, Kuwait, Lebanon, Libya, Saudi Arabia, United Arab Emirates; East Africa: Ethiopia, Tanzania, Zambia; West Africa: Ghana, Nigeria, Sierra Leone.

Source: Hofstede, G., & Hofstede, G. J. (2005). *Cultures and organizations: Software of the mind* (Revised and expanded 2nd ed.). New York, USA: McGraw-Hill.

Further, the data in Hofstede's study were related to work values and collected in a single industry (computer industry) and a single multinational corporation (IBM). The list of countries examined was not exhaustive. Finally, although it is assumed that the dominant culture of a country is stable, it may change over a long period of time because it is influenced by various internal or external forces. Thus, although Hofstede's dimensions proved to be valid, the country's values may change over the longer period of time.

The strengths of Hofstede's theory

Despite its shortcomings, Hofstede's (1980) study made it possible to compare among national cultures (Mead, 1998). Ronen and Shenkar (1985), for example, developed a set of country clusters based on Hofstede's study. While there is considerable variability within each cluster, these clusters provide a sense of what to expect in a given part of the world (see Table 6.7).

The clusters were derived from the following countries: Nordic (Denmark, Finland, Norway, Sweden), Germanic (Austria, Germany, Switzerland), Anglo (the United States, Australia, Canada, New Zealand, the United Kingdom, Ireland, South Africa), Latin European (Portugal, Spain, Italy, Belgium, France), Latin American (Colombia, Peru, Mexico, Chile, Venezuela, Argentina), Far Eastern (Thailand, South Vietnam, Indonesia, Taiwan, Singapore, Hong Kong, Philippines, Malaysia), Arab (Abu-Dhabi, Oman, Bahrain, United Arab Emirates, Kuwait, Saudi Arabia), and Near Eastern (Turkey, Iran, Greece).

Further, Hofstede's cultural dimensions were accepted around the world as distinguishing among major cultural groups. They were found to be applicable not only to work-related values but also to values generally, and accepted as being cross-culturally universal. Hofstede's (1980) study has been replicated numerous times and the results confirmed on different samples.

In 2001 Hofstede replicated and extended his study on different international populations. The scores for 74 countries and regions confirmed the 1980 results. Hofstede (2001) demonstrated that there are national and regional cultural groupings that affect the behavior of societies, and are stable across time.

Many studies have been done based on Hofstede's (1980) cultural dimensions. For example, Hofstede's dimensions were found to be very useful in identifying differences among British, Hong Kong, Malaysian, and Indonesian cultures (Wright et al., 1978; Wright & Phillips, 1980) as well as Chinese and Australian cultures (Kroger et al., 1979). Chinese culture was characterized by high power distance and authority differences, with strong collectivistic social structure, accepting inequality, solidarity, and group orientation. The Australian culture was characterized by small power distance and strong individualism, low tolerance of inequality and authority, loose social networks, and weak sense of social obligations. The Chinese also seemed to emphasize social values in human interactions, while Australians stressed competitiveness and individualism.

The IDV dimension was assessed as the major dimension differentiating cultures (Chua & Gudykunst, 1987; Gudykunst & Nishida, 1986; Hui & Triandis, 1986; Kim

Table 6.7 Ronen and Shenkar's Country Clusters and Hofstede's Cultural Dimensions

	Power Distance	Individualism	Uncertainty Avoidance	Masculinity
Nordic: Denmark, Norway, Sweden, Finland	Low	Medium–high	Low–medium	Low
Germanic: Germany, Austria, Switzerland	Low	Medium–high	Medium	High
Anglo: UK, USA, Canada, Australia, New Zealand, South Africa, Ireland	Low–medium	High	Low–medium	High
Latin European: France, Belgium, Italy, Portugal, Spain	High	High	High	Varies
Latin American: Spain, Portugal	High	Low	High	Varies
Far East: Pakistan, India, Taiwan, Hong Kong, Thailand, Philippines, Singapore	High	Low	Low–medium	Medium
Near East: Greece, Iran, former Yugoslavia, Turkey	High	Low	High	Medium

Source: Nation clusters taken from Ronen, S. (1986). *Comparative and multinational management* (pp. 262–265). New York: John Wiley & Sons; Ronen, S. & Shenkar, O. (1985). Clustering countries on attitudinal dimensions: A review and synthesis. *Academy of Management Review, 10,* 435–454.

& Gudykunst, 1988; Kluckhohn & Strodtbeck, 1961; Marsella et al., 1985; Schwartz, 1990; Ting-Toomey, 1985; Triandis, 1988). The IDV dimension explains the cross-cultural differences in interaction patterns (Hui & Triandis, 1986) and predicts implications for social interactions (Triandis, 1988). For example, cultural variations in individualism and collectivism determine how members of cultures see themselves and behave, for example, whether they feel a part of the social relationship or emphasize the self (Markus & Kitayama, 1991). Individualists are concerned about the self, and feel responsible for their own successes and failures (Hui & Triandis, 1986); they are concerned with self-face maintenance (Kim & Gudykunst, 1988) and thus they experience separation and distance from their in-groups (Hui & Triandis, 1986). On the other hand, collectivistics emphasize harmony in relations with others (Hui & Triandis, 1986), consider the implications of their behavior for others, share material and non-material resources with others, are concerned with reciprocal obligations, and are controlled by shame (Kim & Gudykunst, 1988). Therefore, they experience closeness with their in-groups. It was found that collectivistics (Indonesians) adapt to the group (Noesjirwan, 1978), whereas Australians (individualists) ''do their own thing'' even if they must go against the group.

The dimension of IDV can also explain communication differences among cultures (Schwartz, 1994; Triandis et al., 1988). Low- and high-context communication styles are a function of individualism/collectivism (Gudykunst & Ting-Toomey, 1988). For example, members of individualistic cultures are more emotional and expressive, whereas members of collectivistic cultures are more restrained, concerned with avoiding conflict, hurting, and imposing on others. Also, in order to accomplish their goals, members of individualistic cultures use direct requests as the most effective strategy for accomplishing their goals, while members of collectivistic cultures perceive direct requests as the least effective strategy (Kim & Wilson, 1994). There is much evidence of cultural differences in communication between collectivistic Japanese and individualistic Americans (Barnlund, 1989; Gudykunst & Nishida, 1983; Okabe, 1983).

Other studies which used Hofstede's (1980) cultural dimensions showed that different cultures place different values on interpersonal relationships (Argyle, 1972). Individualistic cultures are concerned with individualized relationships, whereas collectivistic cultures are concerned with group relationships (Hui & Triandis, 1986; Triandis, 1988). In the collectivistic cultures such as Japan and Hong Kong, maintaining harmonious relations is of high importance (Argyle, 1986; Argyle et al., 1986). In Japan and Korea human relations are also treated as more personal than in individualistic cultures (Gudykunst et al., 1987). In Japan, for example, there is a distinction between the *omote* (public, formal) and *ura* (private, informal) style of interaction (Okabe, 1983). Interpersonal relationships in Japan differ depending on the role of the individual and group interaction (Damen, 1987). In-group relationships are more intimate in collectivistic than in individualistic cultures (Gudykunst & Nishida, 1986). The importance of time invested in building trustful relationships is crucial to the Japanese (Elashmawi, 1991).

Different cultures develop social networks differently. For example, collectivistic Asians develop close networks; Confucianism provides them with basic rules for social relationships (Yum, 1985, 1987). Establishing a personal bond between participants and carefully maintaining personal ties are prerequisites for successful relationships. Western cultures have loose social norms. Different cultures have different attitudes toward self-presentation (Tu, 1985). In individualistic cultures (e.g. Australia) self-presentation is of importance, whereas in collectivistic cultures (e.g. China, Korea, and Japan) self-presentation depends upon the situation. Different cultures accept different degrees of self-disclosure. Members of individualistic cultures who use open communication systems tend to self-disclose more intimate topics than members of collectivistic cultures (Ting-Toomey, 1991). For instance, the Japanese are more discrete in relationships than Americans, as they put emphasis on group harmony and cohesion (Ting-Toomey, 1991). Different cultures have different attitudes toward interacting with strangers and in-group members (Leung & Bond, 1984; Triandis, 1972); they also experience different emotions (Schrerer et al., 1986). For instance, collectivistic Asians experience greater anxiety in interaction with strangers compared to members of individualistic cultures, regardless of whether they are less assertive or not. The reason for this is that they are concerned with preserving harmony in relationships, particularly in those that involve conflict and that are threats to interpersonal harmony (Zane et al., 1991). Further, in different cultures people feel a different degree of responsibility for the other people (Argyle, 1972). In individualistic cultures people help those who depend on them; in collectivistic cultures helpfulness implies reciprocity (Berkowitz & Friedman, 1967). There are also differences in accepting compliments. In collectivistic cultures people maintain social harmony by complaining less often and are less likely to accept compliments than in individualistic cultures (Barnlund & Araki, 1985). Finally, different cultures develop different perceptions of social interactions. In collectivistic China social interactions are perceived in terms of social usefulness, as opposed to Western individualistic societies that perceive social interactions in terms of competitiveness, self-confidence, and freedom (Kim & Gudykunst, 1988).

6.2.9.6 Bond's Confucian cultural patterns

In order to evaluate Hofstede's findings and overcome a possible Western bias developed by other European or the US scholars who measured cultural values, Michael Bond, with a group of researchers from Hong Kong and Taiwan called the Chinese Culture Connection (CCC) (1987), developed a Chinese Value Survey. This survey was developed on the basis of 40 important Chinese values and was administered in 23 countries of the world. The CCC found four dimensions of cultural variability: *integration* (social stability, tolerance, harmony with others, non-competitiveness, interpersonal harmony, group solidarity, intimate friendships), *human heartedness* (patience, courtesy, compassion, sense of righteousness, kindness toward others), *moral discipline* (restraint, moderation, keeping oneself disinterested and pure, having few desires, prudence), and *Confucian work dynamism* (persistence, thriftiness, a sense of shame, status differences, ordering relationships, reciprocation, protecting face, importance of tradition).

The first three dimensions of CCC corresponded to the cultural dimensions described by Hofstede. The integration dimension was related to Hofstede's (1980) IDV and MAS dimensions, the human heartedness dimension was similar to Hofstede's (1980) MAS dimension, and moral discipline was correlated with Hofstede's PDI. Only the Confucian work dynamism did not relate to any of Hofstede's (1980) four dimensions. The values of the Confucian work dynamism describe patterns that are consistent with the teachings of Confucius (social order, unequal relationships between people, importance of family, proper social behavior, education, hard work, modesty, patience, perseverance).

According to Hofstede, four of the Confucian work dynamism values positively associated with the dimension – ordering relationships by status and observing this order, thrift, persistence, and having a sense of shame – characterize people who have a *long-term orientation* toward life. The CCC argued that these values reflect a hierarchical dynamism present in Chinese society. The other four values negatively associated with the dimension – protecting the face of self and others, personal steadiness and stability, respect for tradition, and reciprocation of greetings, favors, and gifts – reflect distractions from the Confucian work dynamism, and thus characterize people who have a *short-term orientation* toward life. After finding that people in Asian countries with a strong link to Confucian philosophy acted differently from people in Western cultures, Hofstede added a fifth dimension based on Confucian dynamism, Long-Term Orientation – LTO, to his model. The six major countries, which scored highly on Confucian values dimension, are China, Hong Kong, Taiwan, Japan, South Korea and Brazil (Hofstede, 1991).

6.2.9.7 Argyle's cultural differentiation

Argyle (1986) differentiated cultures according to the degree of formality in the interpersonal interactions and an acceptable level of physical contact between people.

Formality

Cultures range from very formal to very informal (Argyle, 1986; Samovar & Porter, 1988). In *formal* cultures (Japan, Korea, China, Egypt, Turkey, Iran, Germany) all human behavior, including greeting, addressing, dressing, talking, sitting and even eating, reflects adherence to the strict rules of social etiquette and status differences. For example, people use formal titles to identify others and their positions in society. In *informal* cultures (the United States, Australia) little attention is paid to formal rules of behavior; people treat each other informally, address each other by first names, dress casually, and do not pay attention to social hierarchy.

Structural tightness

In formal and *tight* cultures there are many rules and constraints imposed on social behavior (Triandis, 1994). The rules and norms are clear, and people are expected to follow them (Pelto, 1968). Sanctions are imposed on people who violate the rules. Japan is an example of a tight culture in which one must follow ''all the rules of good behavior'' (Benedict, 1946, p. 225). In informal and *loose* cultures there are few rules and constraints; rules and norms are vague and flexible; people are allowed to deviate from them. The sanctions for violating rules in loose cultures are not as severe as they are in tight cultures (Pelto, 1968). Thailand is an example of a loose culture where the behavior of people lacks discipline and regularity (Phillips, 1965).

Touch

In *contact* cultures people touch more, face each other more directly, and stand closer (Western societies). In *non-contact* cultures people touch less, face each other less directly, and stand further apart (Asian cultures). For instance, in Japan people do not look each other in the eye much (Morsbach, 1973). Too much gaze is regarded as disrespectful, threatening, or insulting (Argyle & Cook, 1976). However, too little gaze is interpreted as not paying attention and being impolite, insincere, dishonest or shy.

6.2.9.8 Schein's, Trompenaars' and Maznevski's cultural differentiation

Schein (1992) distinguished cultures on the basis of the following dimensions: human nature (evil, good, mixed), relationship with nature (subjugation, harmony, control), human activity (doing, being, being-in-becoming; work, family, personal), human relationships (individualism, groupism; participation and involvement; role relationships), time (planning, development; discretionary time horizons (function, occupation, rank); temporary symmetry, pacing; past, present, near or far-future; monochronic, polychronic), reality and truth (physical, social, individual; high/low context, moralism, pragmatism), and space (intimacy, personal, social, public, high/low status). These dimensions are described below.

The *human nature* dimension defines what it means to be human and describes the attributes of human beings; it is similar to that of Kluckhohn and Strodtbeck (1961). Western and Asian societies have very different concepts of self. Asians are less focused on separating the individual from the group and pay less attention to self-actualization, whereas Western societies have a strong sense of the individual and the self (Redding & Martyn-Johns, 1979).

The *relations with nature* dimension defines what is right for humans to do in relation to the natural environment; it is similar to the perspectives of Kluckhohn and Strodtbeck (1961) and Stewart (1971). People can control nature (the Western tradition), live in harmony with nature (the assumption of Oriental religions and societies), or be subjugated to nature (the assumptions of Southeast Asian societies).

The *human activity* dimension defines the appropriate level of human activity (doing, being, being-in-becoming), and the relationship between work, play, family and personal concerns; it is similar to concepts of Kluckhohn and Strodtbeck (1961) and Stewart (1971).

The *human relationships* dimension defines cultures based on their assumptions about the right way for people to relate to each other, distribute power, and love. This dimension resembles Parsons' (1951) and Kluckhohn and Strodtbeck's (1961) work in defining individualistic and competitive (the United States), groups; collateral and cooperative groups (Japan); and linear, hierarchical, and authoritarian (Latin countries) orientations. This dimension also relates to Hofstede's (1980) PDI dimension and its focus on social hierarchy, as well as Stewart's (1971) hierarchical relationships and self- and group-orientation. Schein (1992) distinguished among different levels of participation and involvement in decision-making and the use of authority, as well as different roles played: autocrative, paternalistic, consultative, democratic, participative, and power sharing; and delegative and abdicative relationships.

The *nature of time* dimension explains the basic concept of time, its types, importance, and measurement. Monochronic cultures are characterized by time *planning;* people believe they can plan time and treat it as an object to be manipulated. Polychronic cultures are characterized by *development* time; people believe that time can be developed; things will take as long as they will take; time cannot be slowed down or speeded up. Time does not have any limit and can be extended into the future. Also, people in different cultures have different attitudes toward time; they measure and evaluate it in different ways. Attitudes toward time differ by people's function, occupation, and rank. The period of time depends on the time needed to do a job at different ranks and levels. Time is also determined by the way activities are paced and the degree of this pacing at different occupations, ranks, and levels. As a result, "being on time" or "right away" may mean different things depending on situations.

The *reality and truth* dimension distinguishes cultures on the basis of their assumptions about what constitutes reality and truth. Reality can exist at physical, social, and individual levels, and the assessment of what is real depends on scientific tests, social consensus, and individual experience. *Physical reality* refers to what can be logically proved by science. *Social reality* refers to the things that members of a cultural group agree upon, i.e. group identity, its values, the nature of relationships, the distribution of power, the meaning of life, ideology, religion, and culture itself. *Individual reality* refers to what an individual has learned from experience and believes to be the truth. For example, the Anglo-Saxon culture believes in physical reality, or truth that exists in facts and figures and can only be logically proven and assessed by scientific tests. Other cultures (Brazil, Asia) rely more on feelings, intuition, and spirituality and believe in the spiritual world as reality. Members of *moralistic* cultures seek truth in a philosophy, moral system, religion, and tradition; *pragmatic* cultures seek truth in their own experience, knowledge, and wisdom based on authority and a legal system. Europeans were found to be more moralistic, whereas Americans tended to be more pragmatic.

The *space* dimension differentiates cultures on the basis of their assumptions about space: How it is allocated and owned, its meaning and role in relationships, and influence on intimacy and privacy. It resembles Hall's (1966) space dimension (intimate, personal, social public).

Trompenaars (1984, 1993) and Trompenaars and Hampden-Turner (1994) differentiated cultures according to *human nature* (universalism/particularism), *nature* (inner-directed/outer-directed), *activity* (achievement status/ascription, analyzing specifics/integrating wholes), *human relationships* (individualism/communitarianism, equality/hierarchy, affective/neutral), and *time* (sequence/synchronization, past/present/future).

The *human nature orientation* is similar to Parsons' (1951) universalism/particularism dimension. The *activity orientation* is similar to Parsons' (1951) achievement/ ascription dimension and diffuseness/ specificity dimension, whereas the *human relationships orientation* is similar to Parsons' (1951) self- and group-orientation, Kluckhohn and Strodtbeck's (1961) individualist versus collateral and lineal dimensions, Stewart's (1971) egalitarian versus hierarchical relations and self-and group-orientation, Hofstede's (1961) individualism and collectivism, and Schein's (1992) individualism and groupism dimensions. The human relationships orientation also differentiates between those who focus on equality (the United States, Canada, Netherlands, Sweden, the United Kingdom) and those who focus on authority (Pakistan, Hong Kong, Indonesia, Thailand, Turkey). The other two cultural orientations identified by Trompenaars and Hampden–Turner are explained below.

The *nature orientation* dimension differentiates between those who are inner-directed versus outer-directed. Members of some cultures are internally motivated in their behavior; believe they can control life, including nature (the United States, the United Kingdom, Canada). Members of other cultures are externally motivated and listen to nature (Hong Kong, Japan, Korea, China).

The *time orientation* dimension indicates the differences between those for whom it is important to plan, do things fast in a sequential manner, and be on-time (the United States, English-speaking countries), and those whose activities are synchronous, who do many things at once, believe time is elastic, and use the past to advance the future (China).

Maznevski (1994) distinguished among cultures on the basis of orientation toward human nature (good/evil, changeable), nature (subjugation/mastery/harmony), activity (doing/being, containing and controlling), and human relationships (individual/collective, hierarchical), as per Kluckhohn and Strodtbeck (1961).

6.2.9.9 Schneider and Barsoux's cultural assumptions

Schneider and Barsoux (1997) identified cultural assumptions according to "relationships with the environment" and "relationships among people." The relationships with the environment or (external adaptation) include assumptions regarding the relationship with nature (control, uncertainty avoidance), the nature of human activity (doing/being, achievement/ascription), and the nature of truth and reality; whereas "relationships among people" (internal adaptation) include assumptions regarding human nature (good versus evil), the nature of human relationships (importance of relationships over task achievement, importance of details versus general rules, relationships with superiors and subordinates – hierarchy, and relationships with peers – and individualism/collectivism). There are also assumptions which relate to both relationships with the environment and relationships with people; these relate to space (personal/physical), language (high-low context) and time (monochronic/polychronic, past, present, future).

6.2.9.10 Inglehart's cultural dimensions

Inglehart (1997) developed a cultural map of the world showing 43 societies on two main dimensions of cross-cultural variation of "modernization" and "postmodernization." These two dimensions reflect the key values of 60 000 respondents examined in the 1990 World Values Survey. These two dimensions are:

1. *Traditional authority* vs *Secular-rational authority*. This dimension reflects emphasis on obedience to traditional authority (usually religious authority), adherence to family and communal obligations, and norms of sharing; versus a secular worldview in which authority is established by rational-legal norms.
2. *Survival values* vs *Well-being values*. This dimension focuses on values of the welfare state, scarcity of resources; hard work and self-denial, versus postmodern values emphasizing the quality of life, emancipation of women and sexual minorities, and self-expression.

The clusters that result from positioning countries with these dimensions show inherent consistency: Latin America, Catholic Europe, Eastern Europe, northern Europe, and English-speaking countries are grouped as could be expected based on our understanding of the major political or religious influences that affected them.

6.2.9.11 Minkov's World Value Survey

In addition to five Hofstede's (1980, 2001) cultural dimensions, Minkov (2007) proposed three new dimensions: Exclusionism versus Universalism, Indulgence versus Restraint (IVR), and Monumentalism versus Flexumility (later called Self-Effacement) (MON).

Exclusionism stands for a society which allows people for describing themselves in categories that are unique upon situation. *Universalism* stands for a society which allows people for using universal rules and standards to describe themselves and objects, regardless of the situation. *Indulgence* stands for a society which allows free gratification of desires and feelings, especially those that have to do with leisure, travel, spending, consumption and sex. *Restraint*, the opposite, stands for a society which controls such gratification and where people feel less able to enjoy their lives. *Monumentalism* stands for a society which rewards people who are proud and unchangeable. *Self-effacement* stands for a society which rewards humility and flexibility.

A comparison of the major cultural dimensions described in this chapter is presented in Table 6.8. While Table 6.8 identifies many similar dimensions that are used to differentiate among cultures, Figure 6.1 shows the relationships between these dimensions. Figure 6.1 points to the central role of Kluckhohn and Strodtbeck's (1961) dimensions that represent the major dimensions for the analysis of cultural differences and form the basis upon which all other dimensions have been developed.

Table 6.8 A Comparison of Distinct Cultural Orientations Towards the World and People

Parsons (1951)	Differentiated cultures according to choices an individual makes prior to engaging in action
Universalism–particularism	Modes of categorizing people or objects (general/specific)
Ascription–achievement	Ways of treating people or objects in terms of qualities ascribed to them (inherent/measurable results)
Diffuseness–specificity	Types of responses to people or objects (holistic/particular)
Affectivity–affective neutrality	The degree to which people seek gratification and express emotions (immediate/self-restraint)
Instrumental–expressive	Nature of the goals people seek in interactions with others (means to another goal/an end goal)
Self-collective orientation	Individual/group needs
Kluckhohn and Strodtbeck (1961)	Differentiated cultures on the basis of orientation towards:
Human nature	Human beings may be perceived as good, a mixture of good and evil, or evil; changeable, unchangeable
Nature	Humans may be subjected to nature, live in harmony with nature, or control nature
Activity	Cultures may be 'being', 'being-in-becoming', or 'doing'
Time	Past, present, and future
Relationship among people	Individual (the individual goals take primacy over group goals), collateral (group relationship), linear (hierarchical relationship)
Space	Public, private, mixed
Stewart (1971)	Differentiated cultures according to orientation towards the world and people
Activity orientation	How people view actions and how they express themselves through activities (being/becoming/doing)
Social relations orientation	How people relate to one another (formal/informal, egalitarian/hierarchical, direct/indirect)
Self-orientation	How people view themselves, what motivates their actions, who is valued and respected (group/self-orientation, changeable/not changeable

Table 6.8 (*Continued*)

World orientation	How people locate themselves in relation to the spiritual world and nature (subjugation to nature/living in harmony with nature/controlling nature)
Hall (1976, 1977, 1983)	Differentiated cultures on the basis of different communication styles
Context	The level of information included in a communication message (low/high context)
Information flow	The structure and speed of messages between individuals (covert/overt messages)
Language	High context cultures (LCC) versus low context cultures (HCC)
Space	Ways of communicating through handling of personal space (public/private)
Time	Different perceptions and orientations towards time (monochronic cultures (MTC) versus polychronic cultures (PTC))
Hall (1960, 1966, 1973), Hall and Hall (1987)	Differentiated cultures on the basis of orientation towards the world and people
Human nature	Agreements (spoken/written)
Human relationships	Amount of space, possessions, friendship, communication
Relation to time	Past/future; monochromic/polychromic
Activity orientation	Change is desirable/risky
Space orientation	Public/private
Hofstede (1980, 2001), Hofstede and Bond (1984)	Differentiated cultures on the basis of cultural dimensions such as:
Power distance (PDI)	The extent to which society accepts social inequality
Uncertainty avoidance (UAI)	The extent to which people feel threatened by ambiguous situations
Individualism–collectivism (IDV)	The extent to which individual goals and needs take primacy over group goals and needs
Masculinity–femininity (MAS)	The extent to which people value work and achievement versus quality of life and harmonious human relations; the extent to which gender roles are differentiated
Long-short term orientation (LTO)	The extent to which the Chinese values apply in the country in which they reside (long-term time orientation)

Table 6.8 (*Continued*)

Argyle (1986)	Differentiated cultures according to the degree of formality and physical contact between people
Formality	Formal/informal cultures
Touch	Contact/non-contact cultures
Bond and Chinese Culture Connection (1987)	
Confucian work dynamism	The extent to which countries act according to Confucian philosophy
Schein (1992)	Differentiated cultures according to orientation towards the world and people
Human nature	Evil/good/mixed
Relations with nature	Control/harmony/subjugation
Human activity	Doing/being/being-in-becoming, work/family/personal
Human relationships	Individualism/groupism, participation and involvement, role relationships
Time	Planning/development, discretionary time horizons (function/occupation/rank), temporal symmetry, pacing; past/present/near or far-future; monochronic/polychronic
Reality and truth	Physical/social/individual; high/low context, moralism/pragmatism
Space	Intimacy/personal/social/public; high/low status
Triandis (1994)	Differentiated cultures according to constraints placed on people's behavior
Structural tightness	The degree to which the norms, rules and constraints are placed on people's behavior (tight/loose)
Trompenaars (1984, 1993), Trompenaars and Hampden-Turner (1994)	Differentiated cultures according to orientation towards the world and people
Human nature	Universalism/particularism
Nature	Internal/external, inner/outer directed
Activity	Achievement/ascription, analyzing/integrating
Human relationships	Individualism/collectivism and communitarianism; equality/hierarchy; affective/neutral
Time	Sequential/ synchronic, past/present/future

Table 6.8 (*Continued*)

Maznevski (1994)	Differentiated cultures according to orientation towards the world and people
Human nature	Good/evil, changeable
Nature	Subjugation/mastery/ harmony
Activity	Doing/being, containing and controlling
Human relationships	Individual/collective, hierarchical
Schneider and Barsoux (1997)	Differentiated cultures on the basis of relationships with the environment (external adaptation) and relationships among people (internal adaptation)
Relationship with nature	Control, uncertainty avoidance
Human activity	Doing/being; achievement/ascription
Human nature	Good/evil
Human relationships	Social/task orientation; particularism/ universalism; hierarchical; individualism/ collectivism
Space	Personal/physical
Language	High/low context
Time	Monochronic/polychronic; past/present/ future
Inglehart (1997)	Differentiated cultures based on the understanding the major political or religious influences that affect them
Traditionalism–seculiarism	The extent to which people obey traditional (religious) authority versus seculiarism
Survival–well being	The extent to which people value the welfare state, hard work and sacrifice versus quality of life and self-expression
Minkov (2007)	Differentiated cultures based on the ability to feel unique, enjoy life and be flexible
Exclusionism–universalism	The extent to which people can describe themselves in unique versus universal categories
Indulgence–restraint	The extent to which people feel able to enjoy their lives
Monumentalism–self-effacement	The extent to which society rewards flexibility and humility

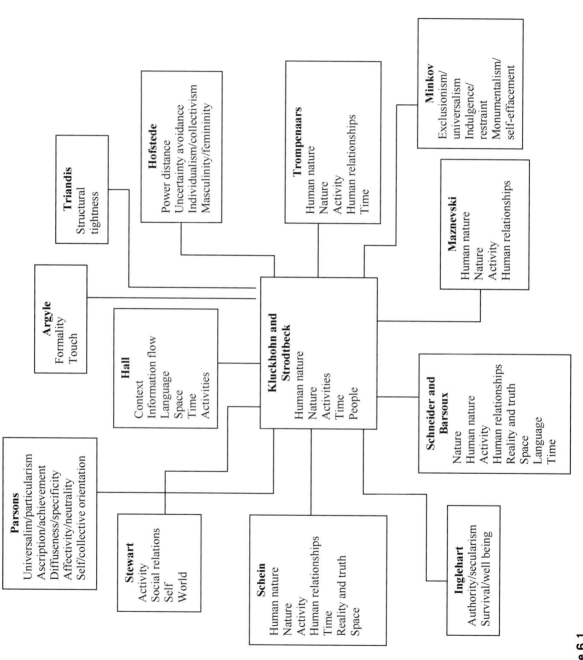

Figure 6.1

Key Dimensions of Culture

SUMMARY

Values are culturally determined standards of socially desirable behavior. They are superior in differentiating cultures and explaining cultural differences. They characterize people within the same culture and distinguish those from other cultures. There are two types of values: instrumental and terminal. There are direct and indirect methods and techniques for measuring values. The Rokeach Value Survey (1973) is accepted to be the best method for measuring values. Hofstede's (1980) cultural dimensions and Kluckhohn and Strodtbeck's (1961) cultural orientations are the measurements most known for distinguishing cultures.

DISCUSSION POINTS AND QUESTIONS

1. What cultural elements distinguish between cultures?
2. Which cultural elements are the most significant indicators of cultural differences?
3. Which cultural elements should be used to be able to successfully compare cultures?
4. What are the major cultural differences between collectivistic and individualistic cultures?
5. What are the major differences in communication in individualistic and collectivistic cultures?
6. Why is a social status a major issue in high-power-distance cultures, but not in low-power-distance cultures?
7. How does uncertainty influence the way people communicate?
8. How does the communication context influence the way people communicate?
9. Which cultural orientation is the most influential on the development of social relations in all cultures, and why?
10. Find two examples that demonstrate how Hofstede's (1980) cultural dimensions can cause clashes in a social interaction between tourists and hosts with different cultural backgrounds.
11. Explain the differences between your own attitudes and behavior and those of the US citizens with respect to human nature; the external environment; social interaction; and orientation towards activities, work, leisure, space, and time.
12. Find situations where your understanding of cultural differences might help solve issues and problems between (1) tourists and hosts, and (2) tourists of various nationalities spending vacations together in a Caribbean resort.

EXERCISES

1. In groups, write four key words that describe your national culture. Ask members of the groups to describe what they think your national culture is by using key words. Compare the results in an open discussion format.

(a) Think of four values that are important in your culture and four values you think are important in the US culture.

My culture: Value 1, ... 2, ... 3, ... and 4 ....

The US culture: Value 1, ... 2, ... 3, ... and 4 ....

(b) Form small groups of students from various countries. Determine which four values are most important in their culture. Compare values that are important in your culture and theirs.

My culture: Value 1, ... 2, ... 3, ... and 4 ....

Their culture: Value 1, ... 2, ... 3, ... and 4 ....

(c) Ask your colleagues which four values they think are the most important in your culture and that of the United States. Do groups from different cultures choose different values to describe your culture? The US culture? What do their descriptions of the two cultures tell you about the two cultures?

CASE STUDY 6.1 The US Culture

The following characteristics of the US Americans were found:

Evaluative and moralistic: judge objects and people; judgments are simple and concise, that is, either someone is right or wrong, good or bad.

Humanistic and egalitarian: believe in equal rights for all; are generous to charitable causes.

Master over nature and perfectability: develop new technologies and ideas to achieve economic goals and gain knowledge and education.

Materialistic and progress-oriented: place value on material possessions, believe in material and educational progress.

Individualistic and achievers: place emphasis on achievement, strive to obtain goals, are individualistic through competition.

Individualistic and achievers: place emphasis on achievement, strive to obtain goals, are individualistic through competition.

Time oriented: believe time is important, time is money; things are scheduled and run by the clock.

Youthful: want to stay and look young; turn to youth activities.

Active: value hard work.

Efficient and practical: search for improvement, better ways of doing things, solutions and strategies.

Religious and moral: are religious; believe the US culture and way of life is the best and their duty is to make others think and act as Americans.

Social and conform: promote teamwork, social interaction and its benefits.

Source: Mill, R., & Morrison, A. (1985). *The tourism system.* Englewood Cliffs, NJ: Prentice Hall.

WEBSITE LINKS

1. Geert Hofstede: http://www.geerthofstede.nl; http://en.wikipedia.org/wiki/Geert_Hofstede
2. Geert Hofstede's cultural dimensions: http://www.geert-hofstede.com

Since major cultural differences occur in the way people communicate the next chapter will discuss cultural influences on communication.

Cultural influences on intercultural communication

7

The aim of this chapter is to identify cultural influences and differences in communication.

OBJECTIVES

After completing this chapter the reader should be able to:
- Understand the concept of communication
- Explain the influence of culture on communication
- Identify cultural differences in communication
- Understand the concepts of ethnocentrism and stereotyping, and their influences on communication
- Learn about intercultural communication strategies
- Identify ethical dilemmas in intercultural communication

INTRODUCTION

Cultural differences influence the way people communicate across different cultures. The major cultural differences that affect intercultural communication are in verbal and non-verbal communication. This chapter argues that effective intercultural communication is very difficult or even impossible.

7.1 THE CONCEPT OF COMMUNICATION

The term *communication* is difficult to define because it has been used in a variety of ways for different purposes. Among early communication scholars, communication was defined as a process of conveying information from one person to another. This process was differently conceived as a one-way, two-way, or circular process of exchange of information or interactions between a sender, receiver, medium, and message (see Figure 7.1). The objective of the communication process was information transfer. Such communication was fairly easy because the information transferred could be simplified by resorting to gestures.

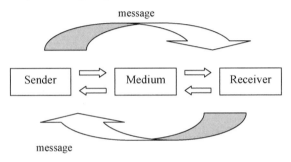

Figure 7.1

Communication Model

Since the 1960s, communication theorists have defined communication as the interpretation of meaning through symbols and signs (Barthes, 1972; Levi-Strauss, 1967; Saussure, 1960) or as a meaning-making process heavily influenced by culture (Berger & Luckman, 1966; Foucault, 1969). Lustig and Koester (1993) summarized these (post)modern definitions into a contemporary definition of communication as a ''symbolic, interpretive, transactional, contextual process in which people create shared meanings'' (p. 25).

- Symbols – which can be words, actions or objects – represent the messages or information that people are trying to communicate;
- Communication is ''interpretative'' because symbols may be interpreted differently at different times by different parties;
- The term ''transactional'' signals that communicators engage in information transaction; they send and receive messages from each other and create meanings during their conversation;
- Communication is ''contextual'' because it takes place within physical, social, historical, and cultural contexts. These contexts influence the purpose of communication, the nature of the relationships between the communication participants, and their behaviors;
- Communication is a ''process'' because meanings (perceptions or feelings that messages create) constantly change;
- ''Shared meanings'' suggests that it is possible to achieve consensus or understanding of each other's meanings.

Lustig and Koester (1993) emphasize in their definition of communication not only the importance of the transfer of messages (as noted in earlier definitions of communication) but also information creation and sharing. A major purpose of communication is achieving the understanding of the transferred messages and their meanings.

The word *communication* means "common," and indicates the ability to obtain common understanding with other people by accepting and sharing their thoughts and experiences. The word *communication* often suggests similarity, agreement, or consensus in the thoughts or experiences shared in communication. For example, the expression "We are on the same wavelength" implies that the meaning of a message is understood and shared between the communication participants. Many definitions of communication imply commonality, which mentions *shared* meanings. Almost all theories and definitions assume it is possible to obtain common understanding with other people by sharing thoughts and experiences. The communication process also includes feedback, which aims to show the degree of understanding of shared information.

Unfortunately, the process of communication is never perfect. In fact, too often the word communication is incorrectly used to imply a level of similarity or agreement in communication. Habke and Sept (1993) characterized communication as a "process of imperfect exchanges." Those authors stated: "A complex thought is encoded in a limited coding system, transferred through unreliable channels, to be coded by another's unpredictable thought process. The encoding process is restrictive, the medium is challenging, the decoding process is far from the encoder's comprehension and control" (p. 421). This definition indicates that communication is a process which is far away from achieving understanding. Communication is not about achieving similarity or agreement. It is about understanding what others are trying to communicate and what their messages mean. Achieving agreement and similarity is not a requirement of communication.

7.2 WHAT IS INTERCULTURAL COMMUNICATION?

Intercultural communication is a communication process in which people from different cultures try to understand what others from different cultures try to communicate and what their messages mean. The term *intercultural* indicates the presence of at least two individuals who are culturally different from each other in their value orientations, preferred communication codes, or expectations from communication. Intercultural communication is often referred to as international communication (Lustig & Koester, 1993).

In a tourism context, intercultural communication is experienced by tourists when they encounter hosts from a foreign culture, and by hosts when they encounter tourists from a foreign culture. The aim of intercultural communication between tourists and hosts is to understand what each party tries to communicate: hosts want to understand the tourists' needs and deliver a product tourists want, and tourists want to communicate their needs to hosts to receive the product they want. They do not need to achieve agreement in their communication or create shared meanings.

7.3 DIFFICULTIES IN INTERCULTURAL COMMUNICATION

The difficulties in intercultural communication are caused by cultural differences. In the process of intercultural communication, tourists and hosts are ''confronted with a culture different from their own in terms of customs, values, standards and expectations'' (Mishler, 1965, p. 555) and adhere to different communication standards. They do not know how to communicate and respond to each other. Communication style that is desirable in the tourists' culture may be inappropriate in the hosts' culture. The greater the cultural difference, the greater the communication difficulties. For example, Sutton (1967) notes that when the cultural differences are large and incompatible, there are fewer cultural commonalities between communication participants; thus their communication becomes more intercultural, difficult, and less efficient; it leads to friction, misunderstanding and misinterpretation. Intercultural communication can become a problem when the degree of cultural differences between communication participants is large enough or significant enough to distort understanding of each other's communication behavior and create different messages and interpretations (Lustig & Koester, 1993). Tourists always experience communication difficulties in contact with hosts due to the cultural differences (Pearce, 1982). Cultural differences cause tourist–host friction, misunderstanding, and often hostility (Bochner, 1982; Bryden, 1973).

Tables 7.1–7.8 present some of the key dimensions of cultural differences that contribute to the difficulties in intercultural communication. These dimensions go far beyond the problems of different vocabularies or sentence structures. They go to the heart of a culture's values and norms, and social expectations.

7.3.1 Verbal signals

Cultural differences in language relate to different languages, dialects, accents, and jargons; making different sounds when speaking; using different sequences of words or a different degree of asking questions and making direct statements. Cultural differences in language also relate to differences in finding the right words or building a proper sentence, and how words are used to create meanings. In different cultures different words are used to form the meaning of ideas. For example, what the British call *chips*, the US Americans call *French fries*. A *boot* to the British means the *trunk* to the US American. Also, in Chinese, Japanese, and Korean cultures there are many words to express various levels of respect toward different social classes, gender, and age groups (Lustig & Koester, 1993).

Different cultures use specialized vocabularies to refer to culturally important features of the environment, like snow in Iceland (Lustig & Koester, 1993) or differentiating the self. For example, in the Chinese language there are ten words for *I* and in the Japanese language there are more than hundred ways to say *I* (Blauner, 1972).

The same words can have different meanings. For example, the words *yes* and *no* can be used differently to signify different meanings. In some Asian cultures, people avoid using the word *no* and giving negative answers because openly disagreeing or saying *no* is considered rude and damaging to social harmony (Elashmawi, 1991). In order to say *no*, Asians use different words, or give no answers to avoid telling a lie, or give pleasing answers even if they are not true. The Chinese confirm a negative statement with a ''yes'' (Leung, 1991). The Japanese have several different ways of saying *no* (DeMente, 1991a). Instead of saying *no* the Japanese may say *perhaps, maybe,* or *I do not know*. Mexican Americans also believe that directly contradicting is rude and disrespectful (Klessig, 1992). Also, in Asian cultures people avoid criticizing in public because it causes loss of face (their own face and others' face) and damages social relationships with those who criticize. The reactions to criticism also differ. For example, when being criticized, the Thai withdraw from conversation, whereas Americans try to defend themselves or increase their cognitive flexibility (Foa et al., 1969).

To African-Americans and Euroamericans it is very important to choose the appropriate words carefully. In Eastern cultures people can communicate by saying nothing. The meaning is in silence or saying as little as possible. They believe that silence is a form of communication. People feel comfortable in silence. For example, Asian cultures, such as Japan, Korea, and China, and Southern African cultures, place more focus on the meaning of silence and on saying nothing or as little as is necessary (Kincaid, 1987). The Japanese emphasize the importance of silence over words. Native Americans believe that silence is a sign of a great person (Johannesen, 1974). In Japan, Korea, and China people are suspicious of those who talk excessively (Lustig & Koester, 1993). Those who talk too much are not respected. On the other hand, US Americans feel under pressure to constantly talk and fill every pause in conversation. US Americans believe that those who are silent are weak and have no opinion, and those who are loud are confident and know their way around.

In different cultures people attach different values to comments. In the United States and Europe people expect comments in a conversation. Euroamericans, for example, make comments in conversations that are related to what the other person has said previously. However, Japanese express views without responding to what the other person has said (Gudykunst et al., 1988; Klopf, 1991).

Some cultures use more verbal communication than others. Direct words and explicit meanings that reflect true intentions and desires are important in Europe and the United States, while in Japan, Korea, China, and South Africa, an indirect style of communication and non-verbal signals are more in use; things are left unspoken (Hall, 1976/1977, 1983; Lustig & Koester, 1993).

In Arab and Latino cultures people use metaphors and proverbs extensively and are very elaborate in communicating (Gudykunst et al., 1988; Lustig & Koester, 1993). This is in contrast with the American and European direct and explicit communication. The North American desire to get to the point can be perceived by Asian people as aggressive or rude (Lustig & Koester, 1993) and even overbearing, especially by Japanese-Americans and Chinese-Americans and Indians who prefer a succinct style of communication, and use understatements, long pauses, and social roles to make their points (Gudykunst et al., 1988). As a result,

Euroamericans may perceive people from Asian, Arab, and Latin cultures as imprecise and confusing (see Table 7.1).

7.3.2 Non-verbal signals

Significant differences among cultures which influence intercultural communication are in the non-verbal cues, such as body movement, eye gaze, and facial expressions, the use of space, and even gestures and postures. For example, those from colder climates maintain larger physical distances when they communicate, whereas those from warmer climates prefer to stand closer. Northern Europeans use a larger communication space, whereas Southern Europeans use a smaller space. As a result, those from the Mediterranean countries are perceived by their Northern neighbors as intrusive and violating privacy, whereas the Southerners perceive Northern Europeans as distant and aloof (Lustig & Koester, 1993).

Cultures differ regarding the acceptable level of physical contact between people in their interpersonal interactions (Argyle, 1986). In *high-contact* cultures, such as those

Table 7.1 Verbal Signals Affecting Intercultural Communication

Cultural characteristics	Communication characteristics	Countries displaying characteristics
Verbal Signals		
Words acknowledge status	Words show respect or disrespect	Japan, China, Korea (Lustig & Koester, 1993)
Complex cultural references	Multiple words to express culturally significant phenomena	Iceland, Japan, China (Leung, 1991)
Customary verbal influences	Contrary meanings emerge (yes means no)	Japan (DeMente, 1991a); China (Leung, 1991)
Words versus silence	Importance of words, formal documents	Europe, the United States, African-Americans (Lustig & Koester, 1993); Greece, Israel, Italy, Arabic countries (Samovar et al., 1998)
	Importance of silence and its meaning	Japan, Korea, China, South Africa (Kincaid, 1987); Swaziland, Zambia, Lesotho (Kincaid, 1987); Japan, India, Native Americans (Samovar et al., 1998); Korea (Yum, 1987); Japan (Tsujimura, 1987)

Table 7.1 (*Continued*)

Cultural characteristics	Communication characteristics	Countries displaying characteristics
Comments	Comments related to previous ones	Europe, the United States (Gudykunst et al., 1988; Klopf, 1991)
	Comments not related to previous ones	Japan (Gudykunst et al., 1988; Klopf, 1991)
Direct (Gudykunst et al., 1988; Gudykunst & Ting-Toomey, 1988; Hall, 1976/1977, 1983)	Explicit verbal messages, use of facts and objectives, direct confrontation, direct expression of one's own needs, true intentions	North America (Dodd, 1998); Europe, the United States, African-Americans (Hall, 1976/1977, 1983; Gudykunst et al., 1988); Japan, Korea (Lustig & Koester, 1993)
Elaborate (Gudykunst & Ting-Toomey, 1988)	Use of metaphors, proverbs and figurative language	Arab and Latin cultures (Gudykunst et al., 1988; Gudykunst & Ting-Toomey, 1988)
Succinct (Gudykunst & Ting-Toomey, 1988)	Understatement, silence, long pauses, precise expression, precise amount of information necessary, only the absolutely necessary is said, no more, no less	Japanese-Americans, Chinese-Americans (Gudykunst et al., 1988; Gudykunst & Ting-Toomey, 1988; Lustig & Koester, 1993)

in the Middle East, Latin America, and Southern Europe, people touch each other in social conversations more, and stand closer to each other than do people from distance or *non-contact* cultures, such as Asia, Northern Europe, or North America (Hecht et al., 1989) who touch less, face each other less directly, and stand further apart (Argyle & Cook, 1976). Arabs, Jews, Eastern Europeans, and Mediterranean people belong to contact or touching cultures, while Germans, English, and other white Anglo-Saxons belong to non-contact cultures because they do not approve frequent touch in social relations (Mehrabian, 1971). Germans, Scandinavians, and Japanese may be perceived as cold by Brazilians and Italians, who in turn may be perceived as aggressive, pushy, and overly familiar by Northern Europeans (Lustig & Koester, 1993).

Cultures differ as to where people can be touched. In Thailand and Malaysia it is forbidden to touch someone's head because the head is considered to be sacred; it is the center of a person's spiritual and intellectual power. Cultures also vary as to who can touch whom. For example, in China, shaking hands among people of the opposite gender is acceptable, whereas in Malaysia, it is not. In Muslim countries, casual touching between members of the opposite sex is forbidden (Lustig & Koester, 1993). In some places there are even legal restrictions against public displays of hugging or kissing, even among married couples.

Cultures vary in the degree of acceptable eye contact. Europeans and North Americans look directly into the eyes of the other person when they are listening, whereas African-Americans look away (Lustig & Koester, 1993). In Europe and America, those who avoid eye contact are regarded either as inattentive or rude. On the other hand, in Japan (and Korea), people do not look each other in the eye much (Morsbach, 1973). Too much eye gaze is considered as disrespectful, threatening, or insulting by Asians (Argyle & Cook, 1976). Japanese and Koreans lower their heads and eyes when speaking to elders or superiors. However, too little gaze is perceived as not paying attention, and being impolite, insincere, dishonest or shy. In Korea and Japan, meanings are conveyed by the eyes (see Table 7.2).

Table 7.2 Non-Verbal Signals Affecting Intercultural Communication

Cultural characteristics	Communication characteristics	Countries displaying characteristics
Non-verbal Signals		
Indirect (Gudykunst et al., 1988; Gudykunst & Ting-Toomey, 1988; Hall, 1976/1977, 1983)	Implicit indirect messages, focus on meanings, use of body language and non-verbal cues, ambiguity, use of intermediaries	Middle East, Latin America (Dodd, 1998); Japan, Korea, China, South Africa (Gudykunst et al., 1988; Hall, 1976/1977, 1983); African-American, Japan, Korea (Lustig & Koester, 1993); African-American, Japan, Korea, Thailand, China (Condon & Yousef, 1975; Stewart, 1971)
Space (proxemics) (Hall, 1976/1977, 1983)	Large physical distance during communication, need for personal space	North Europe, North America (Remland et al., 1992); Great Britain, the United States, Germany, Australia (Gudykunst et al., 1995); Scotland, Sweden, Germany (Hall & Hall, 1990); Japan, China, the United States Americans (Andersen et al., 1990); Northern Europe, Canada (Hall & Hall, 1990)

Table 7.2 (*Continued*)

Cultural characteristics	Communication characteristics	Countries displaying characteristics
	Small physical distance, importance of physical intimacy	Middle East, Africa, Latin America, Southern Europe (Dodd, 1998); South America, Latin America, Southern Europe, Mediterranean region, Arab countries, Indonesia (Andersen et al., 1990); Middle East (Ruch, 1989); Mexico (Condon, 1985)
Contact-cultures (Argyle, 1986)	People touch each other in social conversations	Middle East, Latin America, Southern and Eastern Europe (Condon & Yousef, 1975; Hecht et al., 1989; Stewart, 1971); Mexico (Condon, 1985); Latin America, Middle East, Israel, Greece, Eastern Europe (Samovar et al., 1998)
Non-contact cultures (distance cultures) (Argyle, 1986)	People do not touch each other	Asia, Northern Europe, North America (Hecht et al., 1989; Stewart, 1971; Condon & Yousef, 1975); Japan (Rowland, 1985); Germany, the United Kingdom, Scandinavia (Samovar et al., 1998)
Eye gaze	Look directly into the eyes during conversations	Europe, the United States (Lustig & Koester, 1993)
	Look away, face each other less directly	African-Americans (Lustig & Koester, 1993)

7.3.3 Relationship patterns

One of the most important elements that influences intercultural communication is the interaction style with others. In various cultures people like to know where they stand in relation to others, their social obligations to others, expectations from others, and the role they play in relationships. All these elements guide their interaction and shape communication style. In the *associative* style of communication the focus is on the context of the communication (e.g. psychological, relational, situational, environmental, and cultural) that dictates rules of behavior in a specific situation: where, with whom and how to communicate in particular situations, what should be said and how it should be said. In the *contextual* style of communication the focus is on the status and social roles that people play in relationships with each other. For example, Japanese, Chinese, and Indians emphasize the social role or the community to which a particular person belongs. Their style of communication is formal and focused on status differences (Lustig & Koester, 1993). In China, Korea, and Japan, dress, manners, and self-presentation depend on social status differences.

Eastern cultures employ *lineality* in interpersonal relations and follow strict rules of hierarchical society (Kluckhohn & Strodtbeck, 1961). The focus of social relations is on obedience and loyalty to authority, submission to elders or superior positions, feelings of duty, responsibility, respect, and desire to comply. Confucianism teaches that the superiority of higher status cannot be challenged (Leung, 1991). Eastern cultures are more conforming and people depend more on each other (Doi, 1981). Yau (1988) noted that values important for the Chinese are deference to age and authority.

Eastern cultures also emphasize *collaterality* in interpersonal relations, which is characterized by the ''social order which results from laterally extended relationships'' (Kluckhohn & Strodtbeck, 1961, p. 18), group consensus, group harmony, and concern for the welfare of others. Group orientation and connections are important for the Chinese (Yau, 1988). The Chinese are very socially and psychologically dependent on others (Hsu, 1953, 1971, 1972, 1981). Similarly, Philippino culture emphasizes the importance of being together, emotional closeness with the family, and friendly relations (Bulatao, 1962; Hollnsteiner, 1963; Jocano, 1966). In collateral cultures the style of communication is group-oriented.

In highly *individualistic* Western cultures such as the United States, Australia, the United Kingdom, and Canada the focus is on individual rights and needs, and control over one's own destiny. Importance is attached to freedom, autonomy, initiative, achievement, financial security, the right to private life, and personal opinion (Hofstede, 1980, 2001). Social ties are loose. The style of communication is more personal and casual. On the other hand, in highly *collectivistic* cultures such as Guatemala, Ecuador, Venezuela, Colombia, and Panama in South America, and Indonesia, South Korea, Thailand, and Singapore in Asia, societies are ''we'' oriented and individuality is discouraged. The social ties are tight. The in-group members are expected to look after the other members. The communication style is group-oriented.

Some cultures are characterized by a high degree of *authoritarianism*. Members of these cultures believe in authoritarian leaders and authoritarian social relationships (e.g. Arab countries). They follow strict community rules, the advice of elders, and requests of supervisors. People in these cultures strongly believe that some of them are born to lead and others are born to follow. For example, in Chinese culture deference to authority is considered to be a virtue (Ettenson & Wagner, 1991). The Chinese give an unquestioning respect to parents and the elderly through understanding and expectations of authority (Huyton, 1991). Also, Philippinos and Vietnamese are submissive to authority and desire to comply (Forrest, 1971; Hare & Peabody, 1971).

In *personal* cultures the emphasis is on the individual, who is the center of action and discussion. The style of communication is informal and less status oriented (Lustig & Koester, 1993).

In the *formal* cultures of Asia and Europe, all human behavior is performed according to strict social rules, positions, and seniority. Second names and titles are always used in face-to-face encounters to identify people and their positions in society. Japan, Egypt, Turkey, Iran, and Germany belong to highly formal cultures (Dodd, 1998). These cultures are very concerned about the status differences among people, and their language system requires distinction based on people's degree of social dominance. In Japan, for example, there is a distinction between the *omote* (public, formal) and *ura* (private, informal) style of interaction (Okabe, 1983). On the other hand, in *informal* cultures, such as Australia and the United States, little attention is paid to formal rules, and people have a more casual approach to social relations.

In formal cultures, such as Japan, Thailand, and Korea, bowing and presenting business cards are appropriate forms of greeting. A handshake is appropriate when greeting an American or European. In Europe, addressing other people by their second names and professional titles, such as ''Dr'' or ''Mr'' is expected. In contrast, informal Australians and Americans refer to people by their first names. This, in turn, may be regarded as superficial and impolite by many European and Asian nationalities. In Asian cultures the appropriate and formal address forms are very finely differentiated, according to social status, age and gender.

In some cultures *social bonds* between people are strong, whereas in others they are weak. Members of the individualistic cultures who focus on their own success and are concerned only with the self experience weak social ties. On the other hand, members of the collectivistic cultures who are concerned about the implications of their behavior for others, harmony in relations with others, and both self- and other-face maintenance, experience strong social ties (Hui & Triandis, 1986; Kim & Gudykunst, 1988).

The strength of social bonds determines the way people understand and develop friendships. The understanding of friendship in various cultures differs. For example, individualistic Americans treat friendships as superficial and without obligations, whereas Chinese understand friendships in terms of mutual obligations and reciprocation (Wei et al., 1989). There are also differences in displaying affiliation. In South America, Latin America, Southern Europe, Arab countries and the Mediterranean region people display a high degree of affiliation. In Japan, China, the United States, Canada, and Northern Europe people display a low level of affiliation (Andersen et al., 1990).

Intercultural communication also differs depending on *orientation toward human nature* (Kluckhohn & Strodtbeck, 1961). Western societies that perceive man as good trust each other, whereas Eastern societies that believe that man's nature is good or bad (and often evil) do not trust each other (see Table 7.3).

Table 7.3 Relationship Patterns in Communication Affecting Intercultural Communication

Cultural characteristics	Communication characteristics	Countries displaying characteristics
Associative	Importance of the context	China, Japan, Korea, Vietnam, Mexico, Latin cultures (Hall, 1976)
Contextual (Gudykunst & Ting-Toomey, 1988)	Emphasis on social roles, status, formality, asymmetrical power	Japan, China, India (Gudykunst et al., 1988; Gudykunst and Ting-Toomey, 1988)
Lineality (Kluckhohn & Strodtbeck, 1961)	Hierarchical relationship, submission to superiors, obligations to others, social reciprocity and dependence, importance of status	China (Earle, 1969; Ettenson & Wagner, 1991; Huyton, 1991; Leung, 1991; Meade, 1970; Yau, 1988); Hong Kong (Hsieh et al., 1969); Thailand (Reitz & Graff, 1972); Vietnam (Forrest, 1971); Philippines (Hare & Peabody, 1971; Lynch, 1970)
Collaterality (Kluckhohn & Strodtbeck, 1961)	Group relationships, group consensus, agreement with group norms	China (DeMente, 1991b); Philippines (Bulatao, 1962; Jocano, 1966; Hollnsteiner, 1963; Lynch, 1964, 1970); Thailand (Komin, 1990; Gardiner, 1972); Vietnam (Forrest, 1971)
Individualism (Hofstede, 1980, 2001; Kluckhohn & Strodtbeck, 1961)	Focus on freedom of speech, personal opinion, resolving difficulties, confronting others, human rights, personal position and power, self-references, direct communication, straight talk	The United States, Australia, the United Kingdom, Canada, Netherlands, New Zealand, Italy, Belgium, Denmark (Hofstede, 1980, 2001)
Collectivism (Hofstede, 1980, 2001)	Group orientation, focus on group consensus and decision-making, use of third-party to solve problems and face-saving techniques, group loyalty, personal sacrifice, sense of obligations and responsibilities to others, reciprocation, indirect communication, concern for others	Guatemala, Ecuador, Panama, Venezuela, Pakistan, Indonesia, Taiwan, South Korea, Thailand, Singapore (Hofstede, 1980, 2001)

Table 7.3 (*Continued*)

Cultural characteristics	Communication characteristics	Countries displaying characteristics
Authoritarianism	Acceptance of leaders and followers	Arab countries (Kluckhohn & Strodtbeck, 1961); China (Meade, 1970); Philippines (Hare & Peabody, 1971); Indonesia (Noesjirwan, 1970)
Personal (Gudykunst & Ting-Toomey, 1988)	Parties to communication most important, informal, less status oriented, human beings center of conversation and action	
Formal (Samovar & Porter, 1988)	Communication and behavior is performed according to rules of social etiquette, focus on social status differences, titles and appropriate dress	Japan (Barnlund, 1989); Latin America, Europe (especially Germany), Asia Egypt, Turkey, Iran (Samovar et al., 1998); Germany (Hall & Hall, 1990)
Informal (Samovar & Porter, 1988)	Little attention is paid to rules of communication and social behavior, no focus on social status, titles and manners	The United States, Australia (Samovar et al., 1998)
Fragile people bonds	Low involvement and commitment to long-term relationships and communication, rapidly changing group memberships, direct statement of one's personal needs	The United States, Australia, the United Kingdom, Canada, Netherlands, New Zealand, Italy, Belgium, Denmark, Sweden (Hofstede, 1980, 2001); Germany, Scandinavia, Switzerland, the United States (Hall, 1976/1977, 1983; Ting-Toomey, 1985)
Strong people bonds	High and deep commitment between people, importance of group and responsibilities, easy recognition of the in-group members, lack of confrontation, focus on face saving and social harmony	Japan, Korea, Thailand, China (Stewart, 1971)
Human nature is good (Kluckhohn & Strodtbeck, 1961)	Communication based on trust	Buddhists (e.g. Thailand) (Kluckhohn & Strodtbeck, 1961)

Table 7.3 (*Continued*)

Cultural characteristics	Communication characteristics	Countries displaying characteristics
Human nature is evil (Kluckhohn & Strodtbeck, 1961)	Communication based on distrust	Middle East (Kluckhohn & Strodtbeck, 1961)
Human nature is good and evil (Kluckhohn & Strodtbeck, 1961)	Communication based on trust and distrust	Europe (Kluckhohn & Strodtbeck, 1961)

7.3.4 Conversation style

There are differences in conversation style among cultures. What is perceived as logical, clear, rational, and proper varies considerably between cultures. For example, in *abstractive* cultures, such as Euro-America, the focus is on objective facts; people believe in physical evidence and eyewitness testimony. However, in Chinese and African cultures, physical evidence is discounted. In African cultures, the words of eyewitnesses do not count because no one is regarded as an objective, disinterested party; people believe that if one speaks up about seeing something, one must have a particular agenda in mind (Lustig & Koester, 1993). In *affective-intuitive* cultures, such as Asia or Latin America, the focus is on feelings and emotions, whereas in *axiomatic-deductive* cultures, such as Germany or Switzerland, people follow broad principles from which they deduct facts that they follow.

Conversations differ depending on how direct people are and how they express meanings. For example, in Japanese culture, speakers are required to *circle* around the topic. They indicate only indirectly what they are discussing and what they want the listeners to know. They let the listeners construct the meaning. It is considered rude and inappropriate for the speaker to tell the listener directly the specific point being conveyed (Lustig & Koester, 1993). The Vietnamese also talk around the subject (Forrest, 1971). In contrast, in the English-speaking cultures, speakers are required to be explicit, give clear explanations, and follow *linear logic*; they are responsible for structuring their conversation and creating its meanings. As a consequence, the Japanese or Vietnamese may think of the members of English-speaking societies as rude and aggressive, whereas members of the English-speaking societies may think of the Japanese as imprecise and confusing.

Moreover, Western societies think in linear terms; conversations are organized and always have a beginning and an end. On the other hand, Eastern and Asian cultures think in non-linear terms; conversations have no plan; they are chaotic, limitless, and can be interrupted (see Table 7.4).

Table 7.4 Conversation Styles Affecting Intercultural Communication

Cultural characteristics	Communication characteristics	Countries displaying characteristics
Abstractive	Focus on arguments and facts	Germany, Scandinavia, Switzerland, the United States (Hall, 1976/1977, 1983; Ting-Toomey, 1985)
Affective–intuitive	Involves subjective feelings and emotions instead of facts	China, Japan, Korea, Vietnam, Mexico, Latin cultures (Hall, 1976); Native Americans, Latin Americans, African-Americans (Samovar et al., 1998)
Axiomatic–deductive	Initiated with a broad principle from which deductions and facts follow	Germany, Scandinavia, Switzerland, the United States (Hall, 1976/1977, 1983; Ting-Toomey, 1985)
Circle logic and thinking	Circle around the topic to imply its domain	Japan (Barnlund, 1989); China, Japan, Korea, Vietnam, Mexico, Latin cultures (Hall, 1976); Native Americans, Latin Americans, African-Americans (Samovar et al., 1998); Arabic, Asian and Latin-American cultures (Hall, 1983)
Line logic and linear thinking	Get to the point, clear intentions and explanations of meanings, information is processed in a sequential, segmented, and orderly fashion	The United Kingdom, the United States (Dodd, 1998; Lustig & Koester, 1993); Germany, Austria, Switzerland, the United States (Hall, 1983)
Linear (Dodd, 1998)	Conversation has one theme only, organized with beginning and ending, points and sub-points, evidence stems from logic and empirism	The United States, Great Britain (Dodd, 1998); Great Britain (Mishra, 1982)
Nonlinear (Dodd, 1998)	Has more than one theme, evidence stems from traditional wisdom and authority, heightened by non-verbal communication, lends itself to relationships and personal interaction, events happen, little is planned	India (Kachru, 1988); China (Young, 1982)

Table 7.4 (*Continued*)

Cultural characteristics	Communication characteristics	Countries displaying characteristics
Nonlinear–linear (Dodd, 1998)	One central theme with numerous sub-themes, numerous themes portrayed simultaneously, precise beginning and ending, evidence stems from experience, societal norms and cultural themes	

7.3.5 Interaction style

There are cultural differences in interaction styles. For instance, African-American, Jordanian, Iranian, and Latino interaction style is generally expressive, dynamic and *demonstrative* (Butterfield & Jordan, 1989; Gudykunst et al., 1988). In comparison, Euroamerican style is modest and emotionally *restrained* (Butterfield & Jordan, 1989). Consequently, Euroamericans can be perceived as passive and reserved in conversation with people from more expressive cultures (Lustig & Koester, 1993). Asian cultures are even more reserved and believe in modesty, as opposed to Western cultures that can be perceived by Asians as aggressive and unacceptable. For example, Southern Mediterraneans may be perceived to exaggerate their feelings of grief by Japanese and Thai who hide their sorrows in smile and laughter (Harper et al., 1978). Members of Eastern and Asian cultures often seem to laugh out of context. The Japanese smile often means embarrassment instead of happiness.

Americans usually appear *assertive* and confrontational in their communication style (Samovar et al., 1988). They are direct and loud. Loudness is perceived as strength in the United States. Asians, on the other hand, perceive loudness as aggressiveness. They avoid aggression and try to be calm and humble. They emphasize preserving harmony in relationships, particularly in those that involve conflict and are threats to interpersonal harmony (Zane et al., 1991). Consequently, they also experience greater anxiety in interaction with strangers and guilt compared to Caucasians, regardless of whether they are less assertive or not (Zane et al., 1991).

Social harmony in interpersonal relations is an extremely important value in Eastern cultures that emphasize self-restraint, avoidance of negative opinions, criticism, complaints, disagreeing, not questioning and lack of conflict. Members of Eastern cultures try to ''save face'' and avoid embarrassment (Dodd, 1987). In

China, causing someone else embarrassment is regarded as inappropriate behavior (DeMente, 1991b). Philippinos believe that social disruption, embarrassment and disagreement could bring shame (Lynch, 1970). In Asian cultures, such as Hong Kong, Japan, Thailand, and Vietnam, people do not admit others' failure and do not criticize others in public to protect themselves and others from loss of face. For example, when facing criticism, the Thai keep calm (Gardiner, 1968) or withdraw from the conversation (Foa et al., 1969). The Asian concept of shame and ''saving face'' are in contrast with the Western emphasis on truthfulness or forthrightness. Members of Western cultures believe that saying the truth – being straightforward and transparent – is the right way of achieving social harmony. Also, when being criticized, the Americans blame others for wrong doing or attempt to improve their performance (Foa et al., 1969) rather than keep calm.

Intercultural communication depends on the interaction style. Interactional styles differ depending on the degree to which people feel responsible for the other people (Argyle, 1972). In individualistic cultures people help those who depend on them; whereas in collectivistic cultures helpfulness is a function of reciprocity and mutual responsibilities; the smallest favor must be reciprocated (Berkowitz & Friedman, 1967; Ellis & Ellis, 1989). The Japanese believe people must fulfill their social obligations; those who do not meet their obligations must apologize. Thus, if reciprocation is not possible, the Japanese tend to apologize frequently (Coulmas, 1981). The Japanese also acknowledge their fault even when someone else is at fault, in order to indicate their will to maintain good relations (Wagatsuma & Rosett, 1986). On the other hand, Western societies are less concerned with apologies because they focus more on self-esteem and self-confidence. Americans blame others for their fault even when they know they are at fault. While the Japanese offer compensation for the other person to maintain harmony in relations, Americans give explanations and justify their actions (Barnlund & Yoshioka, 1990).

Asians do not compliment either. They believe compliments can damage social harmony. The Japanese, for example, accept fewer compliments and complain less often than Americans (Barnlund & Araki, 1985).

Members of individualistic cultures tend to be more open and *self-disclosing* about intimate topics than members of collectivistic cultures (Ting-Toomey, 1991). They speak freely about their feelings and personal experiences. Euroamericans disclose more than African-Americans, who in turn disclose more than Mexican-Americans (Littlefield, 1974). On the other hand, members of collectivistic cultures believe that talking about personal feelings violates cultural rules of politeness and respect. It is the role of friends and family members to sense that the other person is hurt or angry, without a person having to express his or her own feelings. Opening themselves to others is an indication of weakness, so that person cannot be trusted. Qualities such as being open, friendly, outspoken, and truthful, are admired in most Western cultures; however, they are less admired in Eastern societies that view Westerners as lacking grace, manners, and cleverness (Craig, 1979) (see Table 7.5).

Table 7.5 Styles of Interaction Affecting Intercultural Communication

Cultural characteristics	Communication characteristics	Countries displaying characteristics
Demonstrative	Emotional, expressive and dynamic	Iran, South America, Latin America, Southern Europe, Mediterranean region, Arab cultures, African-American, Indonesia (Butterfield & Jordan, 1989)
Affective (Gudykunst & Ting-Toomey, 1988)	Emotional, sensitive, intense, dynamic, demonstrative, process oriented, listener focused	African-American, Jordan, Iran, Latino (Gudykunst et al., 1988; Gudykunst & Ting-Toomey, 1988); African-American (Kochman, 1990); African-American (Butterfield & Jordan, 1989); Jordan, Iran, African-American, Latinos (Lustig & Koester, 1993)
Restrained	Modest, passive and reserved	Northern Europe, the United States, Japan, China, Canada (Butterfield & Jordan, 1989); Euroamericans, British (Butterfield & Jordan, 1989; Lustig & Koester, 1993)
	Exaggerated feelings displayed	Southern Mediterranean area (Stewart, 1971; Condon & Yousef, 1975)
Assertive	Aggressive communication style, non-conformity, freedom of expression, directness, taking initiatives in advancing personal interests, disagreement, confrontation, loudness, superficial nature of personal attachments	The United States (Samovar et al., 1998)
Interpersonal harmony	Avoidance of aggression, confrontation, and criticism, calmness, apologetic and humble attitudes, importance of compensation	Thailand (Gardiner, 1968; Foa et al., 1969); Philippines (Gochenour, 1990; Lynch, 1970); Japan (Harris & Moran, 1979; Hendry, 1987; Moeran, 1968); China (Chen & Xiao, 1993; Huyton, 1991); Malaysia (Abdullah, 1993)

Table 7.5 (*Continued*)

Cultural characteristics	Communication characteristics	Countries displaying characteristics
Instrumental (Gukykunst & Ting-Toomey, 1988)	Goal oriented, explicit messages, emotional restrained, sender focused	Euroamericans (Gudykunst et al., 1988; Gudykunst & Ting-Toomey, 1988; Kochman, 1990)
High self-disclosure	Openness, sharing, revealing personal and intimate information about oneself	Germany, Scandinavia, Switzerland, the United States (Hall, 1976/1977, 1983; Ting-Toomey, 1985); Euroamericans (Nishida, 1991)
Low self-disclosure	Not revealing information about oneself	China, Japan, Korea, Vietnam, Mexico, Latin cultures (Hall, 1976); Native Americans, Latin Americans, African-Americans (Samovar et al., 1998); Japan (Nishida, 1991)

7.3.6 Values

Intercultural communication varies depending on cultural values. For example, the *orientation toward nature* (Kluckhohn & Strodtbeck, 1961) plays an important role in intercultural communication. Eastern societies believe people should live in harmony with nature and worship it (China, Japan) or even subjugate to nature (India, South America). The Eastern societies believe that nature and life have been created by God and thus they must protect it. On the other hand, Western societies believe they can control nature. Thus, Eastern societies regard Western societies as unintelligent and biased. Orientation toward nature may cause communication problems between Western and Eastern societies.

The *masculinity (MAS)* dimension (Hofstede, 1980, 2001) distinguishes between cultures, in which there is assertive versus cooperative communication. In the *highly masculine* cultures (Japan, Hungary, Austria) members value achievement, growth, independence and living to work. Communication focuses on extrinsic values, performance, ambition, achieving excellence, money and material possessions. Communication style is more aggressive and formal. There is lack of care for others and the quality of life. People are stressed, and women and men are treated differently. In the *high feminine* cultures (Sweden, Norway, the Netherlands, Denmark), societies that are oriented toward other people and their welfare, focus on intrinsic values, quality of life, family, and harmony. Women and men are treated equally. Communication style is softer and more casual.

Intercultural communication style also depends on *orientations toward activity* (Kluckhohn & Strodtbeck, 1961). Members of the Western cultures that are *doing* and action oriented focus conversations on tasks to be completed and goals to be achieved. Members of the Eastern cultures which are *being* oriented and emphasize passivity, the importance of people, and social harmony at the expense of efficiency, take pleasure in conversation with friends, avoid confrontation, and are tolerant and humble. In the *doing*-oriented societies, (the United States) decisions are driven by economic factors and are task oriented; in the *being*-oriented societies decisions are more emotional and people oriented. Also, members of the societies who value other people highly and enjoy warm relationships with others give more gifts and put more effort into gift selection, than people who exhibit more self-centered and self-concerned values (Beatty et al., 1991). For example, in France gifts should be open and shown, whereas in Japan gifts should be acknowledged and put away (DeMente, 1991a). Societies that are *becoming* oriented believe in evolution and change. The focus of communication in these societies is on innovation, change, and improvements.

Another cultural dimension which affects intercultural communication is *uncertainty avoidance (UAI)* – the extent to which a society feels threatened by uncertain and ambiguous situations (Hofstede, 1980, 2001). In *high uncertainty avoidance* cultures (Greece, Portugal, Guatemala, Uruguay, Japan) people avoid conflict in communication, seek consensus in conversation, and security through written rules, regulations, and face saving. Members of these societies are anxious, aggressive, emotionally restrained and loyal to group decisions. They are often nationalistic and suspicious toward foreigners. In *low uncertainty avoidance* cultures (Singapore, Denmark, Sweden, Hong Kong, the United Kingdom, India, the United States, New Zealand), people tolerate ambiguity and uncertainty in conversations, talk about new ideas, and need few rules as possible to guide them in communication. They believe conflicts and disagreements are natural. They accept foreigners with different ideas and are optimistic about the future.

The *power distance (PDI)* dimension – the extent to which a society accepts the unequal distribution of social power (Hofstede, 1980, 2001) also influences intercultural communication. In *high power distance* cultures (Malaysia, Guatemala, Panama, Philippines, Mexico, China) societies that hold that people are not equal and that everyone has a rightful place, people obey the rules of authority and supervisors; decisions are made autocratically. People use separate forms of communication style, forms of language and ways of addressing those from different social classes. In *low power distance* cultures (Austria, Israel, Denmark, New Zealand, Sweden) societies in which there is no social hierarchy, people consult with each other, use the same communication style for everybody, and focus on independence and personality (see Table 7.6).

Table 7.6 Values Affecting Intercultural Communication

Cultural characteristics	Communication characteristics	Countries displaying characteristics
Mastery of nature (Kluckhohn & Strodtbeck, 1961)	Everything is possible, display of arrogance and power over nature	North America (Kluckhohn & Strodtbeck, 1961)
Live in harmony with nature (Kluckhohn & Strodtbeck, 1961)	People should live in harmony with nature, display of acceptance and respect to nature	Asia, Native Americans (Jaint & Kussman, 1997; Kluckhohn & Strodtbeck, 1961)
Subjugation of nature (Kluckhohn & Strodtbeck, 1961)	We should not try to change destiny, we should accept it, people ruled by nature	India, South America (Kluckhohn & Strodtbeck, 1961)
Idiologism	Communication should always be set within the context of ideological principles (religious, political, social and legal)	
Pragmatism	Precise and practical issues must be addressed to solve problems and achieve concrete results	
Masculinity (Hofstede, 1980, 2001)	Focus on assertiveness, achievement, ambition, inequality, competition, material values	Japan, Hungary, Austria, Venezuela, Italy, Switzerland, Mexico, Ireland, China, the United Kingdom, Germany, Colombia, Philippines (Hofstede, 1980, 2001)
Femininity (Hofstede, 1980, 2001)	Focus on cooperation, social accommodation, quality of life, service to others, sympathy for unfortunate, equality, intrinsic values	Sweden, Norway, Netherlands, Denmark, Finland, Chile, Portugal, Thailand, Guatemala, South Korea, Spain (Hofstede, 1980, 2001)
Doing cultures (Hofstede, 1980, 2001)	Focus on activity, accomplishments, change, control, task completion, goals achievement, getting things done, competition	The United States (Kluckhohn & Strodtbeck, 1961); Euroamericans (Lustig & Koester, 1993)

Table 7.6 (*Continued*)

Cultural characteristics	Communication characteristics	Countries displaying characteristics
Being cultures (Hofstede, 1980, 2001)	Focus on non-action, passivity, acceptance, defensiveness, social harmony, taking pleasure in conversation with friends, tolerance, humility, avoidance of open confrontation, spirituality, contemplation, meditation	Hinduism (India), Buddhism (Thailand) (Kluckhohn & Strodtbeck, 1961); Greece, African-American, India (Lustig & Koester, 1993)
Becoming cultures (Hofstede, 1980, 2001)	Belief in evolution and change, spontaneous activity	Native Americans, Europe, Mexico and Latin cultures (Kluckhohn & Strodtbeck, 1961); Native Americans, South Americans (Lustig & Koester, 1993)
Low uncertainty avoidance (Hofstede, 1980, 2001)	Tolerance for conflict, ambiguity, foreigners with strange behaviors and new ideas, lack of conformity and compromise	Singapore, Denmark, Sweden, Hong Kong, the United Kingdom, Ireland, Malaysia, India, China, Philippines, the United States, Indonesia, New Zealand, Canada (Hofstede, 1980, 2001)
High uncertainty avoidance (Hofstede, 1980, 2001)	Avoidance of conflict, disagreement, desire for consensus, conformity, security through written rules and procedures, importance of face saving	Greece, Portugal, Guatemala, Uruguay, Belgium, Poland, Japan, Peru, Argentina, France, Spain, South Korea, Turkey (Hofstede, 1980, 2001)
Low power distance (Hofstede, 1980, 2001)	Equality, sex roles the same, no social hierarchy	Austria, Israel, Denmark, New Zealand, Ireland, Sweden, Norway, Finland, Switzerland, the United Kingdom, Germany, Australia (Hofstede, 1980, 2001)
High power distance (Hofstede, 1980, 2001)	Social hierarchy and status, autocratic and directive decision-making, separate forms of language for different social classes, formal addressing people	Malaysia, Guatemala, Panama, Philippines, Mexico, Venezuela, China, Indonesia, India, Singapore (Hofstede, 1980, 2001)

7.3.7 Time orientation

The cultural differences in valuing time (Hall, 1983; Kluckhohn & Strodtbeck, 1961) have a significant influence on intercultural communication. In the Western *monochronic* time system, people and human relations are time dependent. People follow procedures and undertake only one task at any time, for example, they interact only with one or a few individuals at one time. They believe time is a commodity and that interruptions are not acceptable. For example, Euroamericans focus their attention first on one thing and then move on to something else. In a *polychronic* time system (Spanish-speaking cultures in Central and South America, Eastern cultures), human relations do not depend on time. Although people do several things at the same time, they always have time to talk to friends and relatives. They believe appointments can be broken and deadlines do not have to be met. Families and friends are more important to them.

Western societies perceive time in linear–spatial terms; they believe there is a past, a present, and a future. Societies that are *past-oriented* (Eastern societies, China, Great Britain, Native Americans) focus on the wisdom of older generations, worship ancestors and have strong family traditions. Traditions and the past guide their conversations and decision-making. Experiences are understood only by reference to past traditions. They also attach relatively small importance to time schedules and punctuality. They perceive time as circular rather than linear (e.g. Indonesian) or limitless. *Present-oriented* societies (Philippines and many Central and South American countries) treat the present and current experiences as most important. People take pleasures in conversations with friends. *Future-oriented* societies (Euroamericans) believe that tomorrow is in their own hands. They are project-oriented, make long-term plans, and sacrifice current pleasures for the sake of the future. They do not have much time for families and friends (see Table 7.7).

7.3.8 Context orientation

Context refers to the level of information included in a communication message. Context can be used to distinguish between different styles of communication. In *low-context* cultures *(LCC)* (Australia, the United States) most of the information is explicit and contained in verbal messages. There is a tendency to emphasize facts, line logic, and clear intentions. There is a need for explicit rules, guidelines, and policies that explain how to behave. In *high context* cultures *(HCC)* (China, Japan, Korea, Vietnam) most information is coded in the non-verbal, contextual message. The focus is on meanings, spiral logic, discretion in expressing one's own opinions (Ting-Toomey, 1991), and use of an indirect communications (Gudykunst et al., 1988; Hall, 1976). Since the HCC value face saving, honor, shame and obligations, they also use negotiations and smoothing strategies to manage interpersonal conflicts (Kim & Gudykunst, 1988). They are reserved, non-confrontational, and more cautious in initial interactions with strangers. They also make more assumptions based upon people's cultural background. They expect others to sense the rules of behavior (Dodd, 1987) (see Table 7.8).

Table 7.7 Time Orientation as it Affects Intercultural Communication

Cultural characteristics	Communication characteristics	Countries displaying characteristics
Monochronism (Hall, 1976/ 1977, 1983)	Time is highly organized, linear, segmented, manageable, task and procedures oriented, importance of appointments and schedules, only one task is undertaken at any time, communication and interaction only with a few individuals at one time, interruptions not acceptable	Germany, Austria, Switzerland, the United States (Hall, 1983); the United States, Great Britain, Canada, Germany (Dodd, 1998); Germany (Hall & Hall, 1990)
Polychronism (Hall, 1976/ 1977, 1983)	Time is flexible and open, responsive to the needs of people, several things are being done at the same time, appointments can be broken, deadlines unmet, simultaneous interaction with several people, interruption in conversation acceptable, communication style spontaneous and unstructured, importance of people	Arabic, Asian and Latin America (Hall, 1983; Dresser, 1996); Latin America, Africa, Middle East, Southern Europe (Dodd, 1998); Indonesia (Harris & Moran, 1996, 1979); Japan (Brislin, 1983)
Past orientation (Kluckhohn & Strodtbeck, 1961)	Importance of tradition and previous experience, past should be the guide for conversation, interaction, making decisions and determining truth	China, Japan, Great Britain (Kluckhohn & Strodtbeck, 1961); China, Greece, Japan, France (Samovar et al., 1989)
Present orientation (Kluckhohn & Strodtbeck, 1961)	`The present is enjoyed and accepted for what it is, what is real exists now, people take pleasure in conversation with friends	Philippines, Mexico, Latin America (Kluckhohn & Strodtbeck, 1961)
Future orientation (Kluckhohn & Strodtbeck, 1961)	Project orientation, importance of long-term plans, tomorrow is in people's hands, appreciation of the achievements of science, control over the consequences of own actions	The United States (Kluckhohn & Strodtbeck, 1961)

Table 7.8 Context Orientation as it Affects Intercultural Communication

Cultural characteristics	Communication characteristics	Countries displaying characteristics
High-context cultures (HCC) (Hall, 1976/1977, 1983; Kim & Gudykunst, 1988; Ting-Toomey, 1991)	Covert and implicit Non-verbal, contextual messages Focus on meanings Spiral logic Group orientation Distinct in-groups and out-groups Reserved reactions Non-confrontational attitudes Face saving and social relationships orientation Smooth and concealing strategies to elevate conflict, negotiation, reciprocity	China, Japan, Korea, Vietnam, Mexico, Latin cultures (Hall, 1976; Ting-Toomey, 1991); Japan (Dodd, 1998); Japan, China, Korea, African-Americans, Native Americans, Latin Americans (Samovar et al., 1998); Japan, African-Americans, Mexico (Stewart, 1971; Condon & Yousef, 1975)
Low-context cultures (LCC) (Hall, 1976/1977, 1983; Kim & Gudykunst, 1988; Ting-Toomey, 1991)	Overt and explicit Verbal detailed messages expressed in specific words Focus on clear intentions and facts Linear logic Individualistic orientation Flexible in-groups and out-groups Readily observable and explicit reactions Confrontational attitudes Action and solution orientation Direct and controlling strategies to deal with conflict, face-to-face negotiation	Germany, Scandinavia, Switzerland, the United States (Hall, 1976/1977, 1983; Ting-Toomey, 1985); Germany, Scandinavia, Switzerland, North America, France (Samovar et al., 1998); Germany, Sweden, Great Britain (Stewart, 1971; Condon & Yousef, 1975)

7.4 IS INTERCULTURAL COMMUNICATION POSSIBLE?

Communicating in a culturally different context can be very difficult or even impossible for the following reasons. There is a very large number of complex dimensions on which cultures differ and which may create difficulties in intercultural communication (see Chapter 6 and Table 6.8). The number of combinations of these cultural dimensions is very large. The differences in any of the cultural dimensions can contribute to different perceptions of the effectiveness of communication. Some differences may cause more problems than others. Others may be very attractive and draw attention (e.g. foreign accent).

There is no universally accepted tool yet to measure the degree of cultural differences among various societies. The existing tools are often questioned and there are calls for developing new measuring scales.

It is impossible to achieve a complete understanding of all cultural differences in a multicultural context. The vast linguistic differences that distinguish one language from another make individuals see and experience the world differently. It is virtually impossible to achieve proficiency in all of the verbal and non-verbal codes used in intercultural communication. Although one may learn a foreign language and its grammar to be able to understand those who speak a different language, communicating in another language can be tiring and frustrating.

It is very difficult to translate effectively and successfully between languages. Translations and interpretations by multilingual guides, whom tourists must rely upon to bridge the intercultural communication gap, can never really be adequate. Not all concepts and meanings can be translated. Only individuals who grow up in a bilingual environment and are familiar with both cultures and their languages can use words and categories effectively to communicate accurately.

In tourism, culturally different tourists and hosts are often unskilled in the communication rules of each others' culture. Thus, most intercultural tourist–host encounters are characterized by communication difficulties. However, it has been argued that communication between culturally different tourists and hosts does not have to be characterized by difficulties. These difficulties may be minimized or even eliminated by learning rules of the foreign culture and cultural understanding of how and why the natives communicate the way they do. It has been argued that by learning other culture and language one may be able to share and understand the experiences of the natives. However, in order to make sense of the behaviors of those who are culturally different, and understand how to successfully deal with them, deep understanding of the foreign communication rules is needed. This, in turn, requires a broad knowledge of historical, political, economic, religious and educational practices of a foreign culture: the natives' values, beliefs, attitudes, and thought patterns. Such knowledge can never be complete, and knowledge of others' rules can be understood only in relative terms.

It has also been argued that obtaining cultural knowledge, learning cultural skills and being tolerant, empathetic and sensitive to cultural differences guarantees effective intercultural communication. Unfortunately, knowledge of various cultures and foreign languages, learning cultural skills and being tolerant and empathetic do not guarantee successful intercultural communication either. Cultural differences among individuals are not the sole influences on intercultural communication. There are many geographical, demographic, socio-economic, psychographic, political and religious considerations that influence the communication process between people. Intercultural communication depends upon the personality and traits of the individuals involved in communication, their social skills, ability to identify not only what people think but what they actually do in intercultural communication, regardless of the cultures represented. In addition, various inter-group factors may be present, such as a desire to defend one's own socio-cultural group identity, which could jeopardize or even block successful intercultural communication.

Communication among people is extremely difficult if not impossible. According to German philosopher Heidegger (1962), each person is unique and has unique experiences. Thus, people cannot understand the experiences of others. Creating and sharing experiences and meanings is impossible because people cannot create and share meanings. When a person identifies his or her own experiences with others, that person gives up individuality and identity for the sake of ''communication''. When people just transfer information they share *imagined* agreement, which is not real communication. People artificially construct their communication in order to feel connected with others and identify with a community (Nancy, 1991). When people try to define themselves as different from the people whom they really are supposed to identify (e.g. community) misunderstanding and conflict always occurs.

Real and authentic communication is not about sharing meanings; it is about the ability to see, acknowledge and respect the difference and uniqueness of other people rather than similarities or commonalities. Real communication is about the ability to see how different people are, so that they can appreciate their own and others' uniqueness. Real communication is about the ability to open themselves and see multiple identities and perspectives.

When people communicate, they focus on different aspects of their experiences. Although some of their experiences have common aspects, their significance and importance to people is different. Thus, people's experiences are not exactly the same (Heidegger, 1962). Even colors have different significance. For example, for Koreans and Japanese white color signifies mourning and grieving, while for Europeans signifies purity. Consequently, because the experiences of foreign tourists are very much different from the experiences of their hosts, intercultural communication in tourism is impossible. However, what is possible is achieving approximation of communication and experiences.

Intercultural communication may be distorted by people's tendencies to develop stereotypes, and prejudices, or to be subjective, ethnocentric, negative, and even racist. These may generate tensions, isolation, and antagonism between culturally distinct groups.

7.5 ETHNOCENTRISM

The concept of ethnocentrism comes from the Greek words *ethos*, people or nation, and *ketron*, center, which means being centered on one's cultural group. Ethnocentrism is a belief in one's own cultural superiority; that the customs, traditions, beliefs and behavioral practices of one's own culture are better than those of other cultures or at least ought to be. Other cultures are either ignored or treated as inferior. Ethnocentrics judge and interpret behavior of others, regardless of their culture, according to their own rules and values. They perceive those from other cultures who behave and do things differently as being bad-mannered and wrong.

Why are people ethnocentric?

People are ethnocentric because they feel good about themselves when they know that others' behavior can be evaluated according to their own values. However, knowing that there are also other cultural standards means that they must admit that their ways of living are not necessarily effective in a culturally diverse environment and thus they have more to learn.

Why is ethnocentrism a problem?

People who believe in their own cultural superiority are not able to objectively assess other cultures and those who are different; they interpret and judge others' behavior according to their own values. Ethnocentrism limits people's ability to understand the symbols and meanings used by other cultures. Ethnocentrism also tends to exaggerate cultural differences by highlighting the most distinct differences in beliefs and practices and ignoring others. Ethnocentrism limits an effective intercultural interaction and communication because it does not allow for understanding those who are different. Ethnocentrism leads to cultural arrogance, avoidance, withdrawal, faulty attribution (stereotyping), and even prejudice and discrimination. Extreme ethnocentrism may lead to conflict and even warfare (Rogers & Steinfatt, 1999).

7.6 STEREOTYPING

Stereotyping refers to the attribution of certain traits, labeling and perceptions of people on the basis of common characteristics, or judgments about others on the basis of their specific characteristics or group membership. Stereotypes can be developed on the basis of culture, occupation, age, race, ethnicity, religion, sexual orientation, or any number of other categories. Stereotypes generalize about a group of people on the basis of only a few individuals who belong to the group. People use stereotypes when they meet new people, are faced with a new situation, or lack depth of knowledge about the group.

In many European nations, especially the United Kingdom, US Americans are stereotyped as brash, ignorant, self-centered, and obese. This is probably due to the perception of the American diet and the popularity of American fast food franchises such as McDonalds and Burger King (which has fueled America's obesity crisis). US Americans are also stereotyped as wearing baseball hats and comfortable clothes, watching basketball games, drinking Coca Cola, and eating hamburgers, French fries, and pizzas. Some people perceive US Americans as the Wild West cowboys.

Germans are stereotyped as aloof, cold, precise, and punctual. People often think of Germans as perfectionists who follow the rules, drink beer, sing and listen to folk music, and walk around in funny clothes. Asians are stereotyped as being ''exotic'', ancient, spiritual, mystical, and full of ancient wisdom. Italians are stereotyped as food and fashion lovers, whereas French are perceived as good lovers and kissers. Arabs are portrayed as belly dancers or billionaires.

There are positive and negative stereotypes. The examples of positive stereotypes are: all Asians are smart, all Latinos dance well, all Whites are successful, and all Chinese and Japanese are hard-working, quiet, and achievement-oriented. The examples of negative stereotypes are: all Asians are sneaky, all Latinos are on welfare, and all Whites are racist. Tourists are stereotyped as rich, loud, and insensitive to host community needs; hosts are stereotyped as poor and exploited by tourists (Frankowski-Braganza, 1983).

People develop stereotypes when they are unable or unwilling to obtain all of the information they need to make fair judgments about new people or situations. Stereotypes allow for making quick generalizations. Often people innocently create stereotypes. Many stereotypes are developed through personal experiences, by reading books and magazines, seeing movies or television, or talking to friends and families and gossiping. In many cases, stereotypes are reasonably accurate and have some ''kernel of truth'' in them.

Importance of stereotypes

In tourism, stereotypes are used to describe tourists and locals. Stereotypes can influence perceptions tourists and hosts hold of each other (MacCannell, 1984). Positive stereotypes may attract tourists, whereas negative stereotypes may detract tourists. For example, stereotypes of Tahitian women as beautiful attract many tourists (Petit-Skinner, 1977).

Stereotypes allow for distinguishing various categories of tourists (Pi-Sunyer, 1978), guiding hosts and tourists in their mutual interaction, and explaining their behavior. Stereotypes are useful because they can show a way to interact during superficial and short-term tourist–host relationships (Frankowski-Braganza, 1983).

In many destinations, residents have developed specific stereotypes of the tourists by nationality. For instance, the Japanese tourists are stereotyped as traveling in groups, bowing to everybody they meet, and spending and photographing heavily (Cho, 1991). Korean tourists are stereotyped as being proud of their identity, willing to accept everything that has similarities to the Korean way of life, and insisting on going to Korean restaurants (Business Korea, 1991). American tourists are stereotyped as being cautious, calculating, purposeful, and careful with money (Brewer, 1984). Swedish tourists are characterized as being misers, and French and Italians as excessively demanding (Boissevain & Inglott, 1979).

Weaknesses of stereotyping

Many stereotypes are inaccurate and do not acknowledge differences and exceptions to general rules (Scollon & Scollon, 1995). The negative attributes are often emphasized, whereas the positive are ignored. Stereotyping leads to errors in interpretation of others' behavior and harmful effects in categorizing and labeling people (Lustig & Koester, 1999). Stereotyping limits the understanding of human behavior (Scollon & Scollon, 1995). Stereotypes can be a source of serious misunderstanding. Negative stereotypes can create distrust, lead to discrimination, and result in rude and hostile behavior (Fridgen, 1991) and impede social interaction (Jandt, 1998). Negative stereotypes can promote prejudice and discrimination of those who are from cultures other than one's own (Lustig & Koester, 1995) and even lead to persecution. Stereotypes can be reduced by learning about other cultures and subcultures.

7.7 PREJUDICES

Prejudice is defined as a bias for or against something formed without sufficient basis or being aware of the relevant facts of a case or event. Prejudice is developed before receiving information about the issue on which a judgment is being made. Often prejudice is referred to as intolerance of or hostility toward members of a certain race, religion, or group. Today, the word is widely used to refer to any hostile attitude towards people based on their race.

Allport (1954) developed the Allport's Scale of Prejudice and Discrimination that measures the degree of prejudice in a society. This scale consists of five stages. At the first stage, called Antilocution, people talk and make jokes about others (usually minority groups) in terms of negative stereotypes and images. Their behavior is usually harmless but sets the stage for more severe signs of prejudice. At the second stage, called Avoidance, people avoid those in a minority group. Although they do not impose any physical harm on anyone, they intend to psychologically harm the minority group by isolating it. At the third stage, called Discrimination, the majority group is trying to harm the minority group by denying it opportunities and services and preventing it from achieving goals such as getting jobs or education. At the fourth stage, Physical Attack, the majority group damages properties and carries out violent attacks on individuals from a minority group. Finally, at the fifth stage, Extermination, the majority group seeks elimination of the minority group. This example shows how the negative stereotypes can create discrimination against those who are from different cultures or race groups.

7.8 RACISM

Racism is a belief that all members of a particular racial group possess specific characteristics or abilities that distinguish it as being either superior or inferior to another racial group(s). Racism involves the idea that one's own race has the right to rule or dominate other races. Racism has been a motivating factor in social discrimination, racial segregation, hate speech and violence.

The term *racial discrimination* refers to ''any distinction, exclusion, restriction or preference based on race, color, descent, or national or ethnic origin which has the purpose or effect of nullifying or impairing the recognition, enjoyment or exercise, on an equal footing, of human rights and fundamental freedoms in the political, economic, social, cultural or any other field of public life'' (Part 1 of Article 1 of the United Nation International Convention on the Elimination of All Forms of Racial Discrimination, 1966).

In 2001, the European Union banned racism along with many other forms of social discrimination in the Charter of Fundamental Rights of the European Union. Article 21 of the charter prohibits discrimination on any ground such as race, color, ethnic or social origin, genetic features, language, religion or belief, political or any other opinion, membership of a national minority, property, disability, age or sexual orientation and also discrimination on the grounds of nationality. Racial discrimination is illegal in many countries.

7.9 STRATEGIES FOR IMPROVING INTERCULTURAL COMMUNICATION

For intercultural communication to be successful, people need to open themselves to new experiences. They should become more flexible, willing to accept other viewpoints without judging or dismissing them. This kind of openness is very important to those working in the tourism industry. Both international tourists and local hosts are exposed to new people, ideas, behaviors, and ways of thinking, different from their own. In order to benefit from new ideas and experiences they need to give these ideas and experiences a chance, not dismiss them just because they are new or strange. They do not necessarily have to accept the new ideas and agree with them. However, they need to be non-judgmental in order to give the other party a fair go and to ensure that their communications are effective.

When tourists and hosts recognize and accept their own uniqueness and differences they will less likely to blindly follow some common pattern of behavior and thinking. They will be more likely to make up their own minds about how new things are. This will help them to see an alternative perspective. They will also be more likely to recognize that their own viewpoint is not the only one or the best one. They will become more cautious and more likely to think before speaking. They will be encouraged to listen more carefully, to study and analyze each other more thoroughly, and to evaluate their own perspectives more thoughtfully. This is likely to make them more effective as intercultural communicators.

7.10 THE ETHICS OF INTERCULTURAL COMMUNICATION

A decision should be made about how much the tourists and hosts should change their behaviors to fit the beliefs, values and norms of those with whom they interact. Is it the responsibility of tourists to adjust their behaviors and communication to cultural norms of the host society, or is it the responsibility of the host society to adjust its behavior and communication to the tourists? There is an old saying "When in Rome, do as the Romans do." This saying clearly suggests that tourists should change their behavioral patterns while visiting new cultures. However, this rule should also be adopted by hosts. Both parties should conform to each other's cultural standards and show respect for their cultures. Such behaviors would allow both sides to interact and communicate on some kind of genuine basis.

The ethical dilemma in intercultural communication is to what degree one should adapt behaviors to another culture. Should both parties engage in behaviors that they regard as wrong or unacceptable in their cultures? What are the benefits of intercultural communication? Are the outcomes of intercultural communication positive? At what point do tourists and hosts lose their own sense of self-identity? At what points do they become hostile to each other? Although the potential benefits of intercultural communication and interaction with foreign individuals are great, certain outcomes may be negative, for example, excessive consumption of natural resources, development of negative stereotypes or prejudice, or harassment. If the outcomes are negative, should intercultural interaction and communication between tourists and hosts be encouraged? Should international tourism and travel be encouraged? Is it ethical to expose locals to different cultural standards, knowing that the outcomes of such exposure can be negative or even damaging? Is it ethical to travel to another country if one does not speak foreign languages or is prejudiced and nationalistic? Is it ethical to ask local hosts to give up on their local standards and adjust to foreign standards? Is it ethical to ask tourists to give up on their standards and adjust to local standards? Is it ethical for a person from one culture to encourage a person from another culture to communicate and interact if they disregard each other's cultural values and beliefs? These questions must be asked. There are no simple answers to any of these questions.

SUMMARY

Intercultural communication is a process in which people from different cultures try to understand what others from different cultures are trying to communicate. Intercultural communication is never perfect. The difficulties are caused by cultural differences in verbal and non-verbal signals, relationship patterns, conversation and interaction styles, cultural values, and time and context orientations. Communicating in a culturally different context can be very difficult due to a very large number of complex dimensions on which cultures differ, the impossibility of achieving a complete understanding of all cultural differences and translating effectively between languages. Tourists and hosts are unskilled in the communication rules of each other's culture. Obtaining cultural knowledge, learning skills, and being tolerant and sensitive to cultural differences are not sufficient for successful intercultural communication. Various geographical, psychographic, political and religious factors need to be taken into account as well as the personal traits of the individuals involved. Inter-group factors, ethnocentrism, stereotyping and racism preclude one from successful intercultural communication. For successful intercultural communication, people need to open themselves to new experiences and accept their own and other's uniqueness and differences. Intercultural communication creates various ethical dilemmas.

DISCUSSION POINTS AND QUESTIONS

1. What are stereotypes and how do they affect people's lives?
2. Think of some events in your life that were influenced by stereotypes and biases. What were the outcomes of these events?
3. How can the media (newspapers, television, movies) help to develop stereotypes?
4. Do you think certain groups are more subject to stereotyping than others? If so, why?
5. What do you think an individual can do to help reduce bias and stereotyping?
6. How can the media (newspapers, television, movies) help to reduce stereotypes?

CASE STUDY 7.1 Courtesy and Politeness in Thailand and Australia

The Thai people are very attentive and try to please everyone. They say whatever is needed to conform to norms of social etiquette, respect and politeness, and avoid unpleasantness and conflict. In contrast, Australians believe in absolute truth that does not depend on a situation. Thai people rarely say ''please'' or ''thank you'' as the Thai words of politeness carry the ''please'' element. As a result, English-speaking individuals think the Thai are demanding, but the Thai-speaking people think they are making a polite request. The Thai also use the smile instead of polite words. This is in contrast with the Australians, who use the words ''please'' and ''thank you'' commonly. In Thailand, respect is shown to all of higher status and age, including objects of everyday life such as books, hats, umbrellas, elephants and rice, which are associated with knowledge, the head, royalty, religion, and life. This is in contrast with Australia, where people are less respectful and do not have as many sacred symbols.

Source: Reisinger, Y., & Turner, L. (1998). *Cultural differences in tourism: A Lisrel analysis of Thai tourism to Australia.* Paper presented at the International Tourism and Hotel Industry in Indo-China and Southeast Asia Conference, Phuket, Thailand, June 4–6, 1998.

WEBSITE LINKS

1. Stereotypes: http://homepages.rtlnet.de/krkarwoth/stereotypes.html#What_are_stereotypes_
2. Examples of stereotypes: www.ask.com
3. The dangers of stereotyping: http://www.culturalsavvy.com/stereotyping.htm

Since cultural differences occur in the way people interact the next chapter will discuss the concept of social interaction and the cultural differences in social interaction.

Cultural influences on social interaction

8

The aim of this chapter is to identify cultural influences and differences in social interaction.

OBJECTIVES

After completing this chapter the reader should be able to:
- Define the concept, purpose, and major features of social interaction
- Explain the concept of social interaction in tourism and identify its types and determining factors
- Explain the concept of intercultural social interaction, its dimensions and types
- Draw a model of social interaction in a cross-cultural context
- Explain contact hypothesis and its outcomes
- Discuss difficulties associated with intercultural interaction
- Explain the concept of culture shock, its types, symptoms, and phases

INTRODUCTION

Cultural differences influence the way people interact. Interaction between those who are from different cultural backgrounds is characterized by difficulties and depends upon the degree of their cultural dissimilarity. Culture shock is one of the most recognized difficulties encountered in a foreign culture.

8.1 THE CONCEPT OF SOCIAL INTERACTION

Social interaction refers to the everyday interaction between people. Social interaction is a "personal association taking place under certain circumstances ... and covers a wide range of behaviors from observation of members of the other group without any communication, to prolonged intimate association'' (Cook & Sellitz, 1955, pp. 52–53). Social interaction also can take forms of a friendly greeting, a brief meeting, conversation, long-term relationship, and friendship. Social interaction occurs in different situations, at work, home, in the residential neighborhood, between children, adults, college students, doctors, bus drivers, and others. The main purpose of social interaction is to associate with other people in specific contexts, engage in conversation, exchange views and experiences, learn about each other, find social connections, develop relationships, and so forth.

Main features of social interaction

According to the Analysis of Social Situations Theory, the major features of social interaction are goals, rules, roles, repertoire of elements, sequence of behavior, concepts and cognitive structure, environmental setting, language and speech, and difficulties and skills (Argyle et al., 1981) (see Table 8.1).

Each social interaction has potential to be successful or a failure depending upon the individuals' motivations to interact, whether they follow socially accepted rules of behavior, know their rights and obligations, are able to use verbal and non-verbal signals appropriately to the specific situation, and know how and when to behave appropriately. Individuals also need to have some knowledge and understanding of the environment in which their interaction occurs, and be able to speak and use language appropriately. The interpersonal, linguistic, memory, and body-language skills determine whether individuals experience difficulties in interaction. Those who have these skills can interact smoothly, while those who do not have these skills usually experience difficulties.

Table 8.1 Major Features of Social Interaction

Analysis of Social Situations Theory

- Goals, which motivate social interaction
- Rules, which regulate social interaction so that the goals can be achieved
- Roles, which determine the duties, obligations or rights of the participants
- Repertoire of elements, which represent verbal and non-verbal behavioral cues appropriate to the situation
- Sequences of behavior, which specify order of appropriate behavior
- Concepts and cognitive structure, which individuals need to possess to behave effectively
- Environment, in which the interaction occurs
- Language and speech that make individuals understand what is happening and how to behave in the interaction, e.g. how things are said, vocabulary, social variations in language
- Difficulties and skills, which require specific skills (perceptual, motor, memory, linguistic) to be properly understood

Source: Argyle, M., Furnham, A., & Graham, J. (1981) *Social situations*. Cambridge: Cambridge University Press.

8.2 SOCIAL INTERACTION IN TOURISM

Social interaction in tourism occurs as the tourist travels in planes and buses, stays in hotels, dines in restaurants, visits tourist attractions, goes shopping or to nightclubs, talks to tour guides, watches local street life, or observes local dances. Social interaction in tourism occurs between various categories of tourists and hosts. Tourists can be of different types depending on the degree of institutionalization of their travel arrangements, form of travel, motivation, preferences for activities, personality, type of holiday, traveler's status, and so forth (see Table 8.2).

Table 8.2 Typology of a Tourist

Type	Characteristics	Author
Sunlust	Travels for rest and relaxation	Gray (1970)
Wanderlust	Travels to learn	
Institutionalized	Desires comfort, relies on the tourism industry to take care of him/her	Cohen (1972, 1974)
organized mass tourist	Travels on organized package holidays, has minimal contact with the local community and very little opportunity for developing a meaningful tourist–host relationship, is surrounded by environmental bubble, social contact limited to service providers	
individual tourist	Uses similar facilities but also wants to visit other places not included in organized tours	
Non-institutionalized	Follows own path and has little contact with the tourism industry	Cohen (1972, 1974)
explorer	Travels independently, wants to have contact with and experience local community	
drifter	Does not seek any contact with other tourists, wishes to live with the host community	

Table 8.2 (*Continued*)

Type	Characteristics	Author
Pleasure-seeker recreationalist diversionary	Travels for recreational purposes, desires entertainment and relaxation Wishes to escape the routine of everyday life	Cohen (1979)
Pilgrimage tourist experiential experimental existential	Seeks an authentic experience, does not totally identify with local culture Wishes to seek an alternative but does not become totally immersed in a foreign culture Becomes totally immersed in the foreign culture	
Charter tourist, Mass tourist, Incipient mass tourist, Unusual tourist, Off-beat tourist, Elite tourist, Explorer	They gradually progress from (charter) tourists who arrive by plane in large numbers to enjoy their holiday to the few tourists who explore new areas and fully accept local culture (explorers)	Smith (1989)
Interactional tourist *Cognitive-normative tourist*	Interacts with the destination, area, region, or site based on the desire for familiarity and the level of institutionalization Has specific motivations for outdoor activities, e.g. eco-tourists	Cohen (1972), Lowyck et al. (1992), Murphy (1985)
Ecotourists activity-based motivation-based	Dominant activities include watching wildlife, walking on trails Motivated by natural attractions such a birds, wildlife, cultures and hilltribes, scenery, waterfalls	Hvenegaard (2002)

Table 8.2 (*Continued*)

Type	Characteristics	Author
High-activation (high energy) extrovert	Needs a variety of activities and options to choose from and non-tourist atmosphere	Fiske and Maddi (1961)
Low activation (low energy) introvert	Seeks packaged products and service that emphasizes a relaxing atmosphere, comfort, several choices and familiarity of the destination and products	
Psychocentric	Anxious, inhibited, non-adventurous, inner-focused, with lower income level, seeks comfort, safety, familiarity, travels to short-haul destinations, prefers packaged tourist and touristy areas	Plog (1974)
Midcentric	Makes up the middle of the continuum, travels for relaxation and pleasure or for change; the largest group of tourists	
Allocentric	Adventurous, self-confident, curious, outgoing, with higher income level, seeks new experiences, novelty, challenge, excitement, travels to long-haul exotic destinations, prefers unstructured vacations, wants to get involved with local cultures	
High-energy traveler	Active, prefers high levels of activities, many activities	Plog (1979)
Low-energy traveler	Less active, prefers fewer activities	
Venturer	Seeks and explores, wants to be a first user	Plog (1987)

Table 8.2 (*Continued*)

Type	Characteristics	Author
Pleasure-seeker	Desires luxury and comfort in all aspects of travel	
Impulsive traveler	Wants to do things immediately, makes quick decisions, does not plan, spends heavily	
Self-confident	Wants to do unique things, e.g. selects unusual places, unique destinations or activities	
Planful	Plans a trip in advance, looks for bargains and pre-packaged tours	
Masculine	Action-oriented, seeks outdoors, travels by car, takes many things with them	
Intellectualist	Has special interests in cultural activities, likes to explore and discover, sees plays and goes to museums	
People oriented	Desires to be close to people, experiences cultures of the world, sociable, often disorganized, impulsive venturer	
Venturer	Intellectual leader, explores the world, seeks excitement and new experiences, achiever, self-confident, successful, values interests more than comfort and financial gains, seeks new destinations before others have discovered them, likes to discover, adapts to the local area and native foods, uses less adequate accommodation, feels comfortable in foreign cultures, is not afraid of those who speak different languages	Plog (2002)

Table 8.2 (*Continued*)

Type	Characteristics	Author
Dependable	Indecisive, anxious, seeks safety and comfort, uses name-brand products with established identity, travels to well-known overdeveloped destinations, returns to the same destinations each year, likes sun and fun sports, home atmosphere, fast-food restaurants, movie, theatres, routine, listens to what others around suggest to do, travels less than venturer	
Solitary traveler	Individualist, self-oriented, travels independently to pursue own interests	Mehmetoglu (2004)
Group or package traveler	Collectivist, other-oriented, travels to seek companionship, relationships or the needs that can be met with other travelers	

The typology of a tourist is further accentuated when one starts crossing cultural borders (domestic versus international). Also, in many parts of the world tourists are called sojourners, travelers, and visitors, and they are often treated as guests (Nozawa, 1991). For example, in the South Pacific, where tourists are treated as ''guests'' rather than tourists (Vusoniwailala, 1980), much social interaction between tourists and locals is based on the concepts of social obligation, including reciprocity. Western tourists often do not understand this concept of reciprocity and do not fulfill expected obligations; this leads to the exploitation of hosts.

Hosts can be local residents, indigenous residents, investors, developers, and those who provide a service to tourists (e.g. hoteliers, front office employees, waiters, shop assistants, custom officials, tour guides, tour managers, and taxi and bus drivers). The service providers are often called ''professional hosts'' (Nettekoven, 1979).

Social interaction in tourism can take place between a (1) tourists and other tourists (international, domestic), (2) tourists and services providers, (3) tourists and local residents, (4) tourists and indigenous residents/providers, (5) tourists and imported workers, and (6) tourists and investors. Social interactions in tourism may consist of (1) personal meetings when tourists and residents find themselves side by side at an attraction, or participate in mutual activities, (2) enquiries in the tourist information centers or at the front office when the two parties come face to face during the process of information exchange, and (3) business transactions when tourists purchase goods and services from residents at shops, restaurants, or airlines (DeKadt, 1979).

8.2.1 The nature of tourist–host social interaction

The tourist–host interaction is usually brief and temporary. The tourist usually stays in the destination for a short time, so there is no opportunity to develop meaningful relationships between tourists and hosts. The traditional hospitality can be overused, and interaction can be open to exploitation. The interaction is unequal and unbalanced in terms of its meanings for both sides. Tourists and hosts have different social status, play different roles, and have different goals. Tourists are to be served, whereas hosts are the servers; tourists are at leisure, whereas hosts are at work; tourists are motivated by leisure, whereas hosts are motivated by financial gains. As a result, they develop different attitudes and behavior toward each other. Tourists and hosts have also different access to wealth and information, commitment and responsibilities, and socio-economic position and cultural identity. The visible wealth of the tourists often leads to jealousy, hatred, and exploitation. The tourist–host contact is superficial, not intensive, lacking spontaneity. The contact is commercial, limited mostly to business transactions and transformed into a source for economic gain. However, at the same time it requires friendliness and concern for service quality for the purpose of profit. The contact is formal depending on whether tourists and hosts (1) meet together at the place of tourist attraction, (2) exchange information and ideas, and whether (3) tourists buy goods and services from hosts. The first and third types of interaction are more common and formal. The tourist–host contact is also competitive, involves an element of dreams, demands new experiences, and is ambiguous (Cohen & Cooper, 1986; DeKadt, 1979; Din, 1989; Hoivik & Heiberg, 1980; Jafari, 1989; Nettekoven, 1979; Sutton, 1967; Van den Berghe, 1980; Van den Berghe & Keyes, 1984).

8.2.2 The context of tourist–host social interaction

Tourist–host interaction takes place in the (1) spatial (e.g. physical space shared by the tourist and host or physical distance, social status of interactants, rules of behavior they have to conform to), (2) temporal (e.g. length of time tourists stay in the destination, the time of the contact itself, different roles played by interactants), and (3) communicative (e.g. the ability to speak each other's language and understand non-verbal behavior), and (4) cultural (e.g. different cultural values, perceptions, attitudes, willingness of both to share their values and experiences) contexts.

Temporal and spatial context

The tourist–host contact occurs when there are opportunities for contact, which allow participants to interact, get to know each other, and understand one another. If no opportunity exists, no contact occurs. However, due to the specific nature and the unfavorable conditions under which the tourist–host contact takes place, this contact provides little opportunity for deep interaction. Any contact which is transitory, superficial, unequal and subjected to exploitation, mistrust, and stereotype formation does not provide any opportunity for engaging in a meaningful interaction. The maximum opportunities for tourist–host encounters occur in places of tourist attractions where tourists are isolated in the ''tourist ghettos'' and encounter ''professional hosts'' (service providers) (Nettekoven, 1979). Also, more intensive interaction is more likely to develop between tourists and tourists rather than tourists and locals or ''professional hosts.''

The degree of involvement in social interaction depends on the interpersonal attraction of participants (Triandis, 1977), especially their cultural similarity. The greater similarity in cultural backgrounds, the more attracted interactants are to each other and more intense is their contact.

The personal characteristics of tourists and hosts, such as tolerance, enthusiasm, interests, generosity, welcoming attitudes, willingness to listen and understand each other's needs, and mutual respect increase the chances for mutual interaction. On the other hand, resentment, disrespect, lack of appreciation for each other's cultural background, arrogance, and sense of superiority decrease the chances for interaction.

Social interaction between tourists and hosts also depends upon their motivation to interact. Unfortunately, many tourists and hosts encounter each other without being motivated to it. Some tourists prefer to interact with fellow tourists rather than with hosts. Other tourists like to engage in conversations with hosts in shops or restaurants and exchange information about their own countries, but without committing themselves to further interaction. Some tourists like to get involved in conversation but with no further commitments. Only a few tourists may like to interact, engage in deep and long conversations, get to know each other better, share personal experiences, and develop long-term friendships.

In addition, goals and purposes of the interaction play an important role in the decision to interact. Tourists who are at leisure treat their interaction with hosts as experience and are more likely to seek social encounters. In contrast, hosts who are at work are more likely to seek financial gains in the interaction. Since the relationship between tourists and local hosts is based on ''economic exchange'' their interaction may involve tension, stress and even conflict.

Social interactions between tourists and hosts are governed by rules of social behavior. These rules concern introductions, greetings and farewells, names and titles, behavior in public places, and so forth. These rules provide guidelines on how to behave in socially and culturally different situations and are culturally determined (see Chapter 9).

Further, the development of social interaction depends upon the status of the participants, mutual interests, activities, and common goals (Bochner, 1982; Sellitz & Cook, 1962; Triandis & Vassiliou, 1967). If one participant's status is lowered or motivation is different, interaction may not occur.

The social interaction increases when it is perceived as rewarding (Triandis, 1977) or when its benefits are perceived to outweigh costs. The greater the rewards received from the interaction (pleasure, joy, satisfaction), and the fewer the costs (superficiality, stress), the more likely the interaction will take place in the future. The assessment of the perceived costs and benefits depends upon the cultural similarity and differences between participants. The more culturally similar interactants are, the more likely they perceive their interaction as rewarding. The more culturally different interactants are, the more likely they perceive their interaction as costly.

The resources that are exchanged in tourist–host interaction such as money, goods, services, love, status and information also determine interaction. The perceived value and significance of the exchanged resources depend upon cultural beliefs and norms. For example, in Polynesia, hospitality is reciprocated by gifts, food, crafts, financial contribution to the hosts or by hosting in return (Berno, 1999). Western tourists rarely understand the concept of long-lasting rewards for hosts that result from their transactions (Van den Berghe, 1994).

Communication context

People interact socially with those whom they can effectively communicate with. The communication between people who are similar is more effective than communication between those who are dissimilar. People usually do not try to have contacts with strangers (Gudykunst & Kim, 1997) because their communication with strangers is not as effective as they would wish it to be.

Cultural context

Cultural values significantly influence social interaction. Cultural values determine motivations for interactions, participants' interests, perceptions of status, the importance of personal goals, activities, willingness to cooperate or compete, personal attractiveness, and communication style. Rewards and resources exchanged in social interaction are more likely to be perceived as having value if they are familiar to the perceiver. For example, financial gains are not perceived as having value by the Polynesian hosts, and reciprocation is not regarded as being important by Western hosts (Berno, 1999).

Culture encourages the development of specific attitudes toward people. The intensity of these attitudes influences the development of social relations. Those with more positive attitudes tend to be more active in social relations, and those with less positive attitudes tended to be less active (Festinger & Kelly, 1951). Negative attitudes create reservation, suspicion, dissatisfaction and lack of understanding and thus discourage from the development of interactions. Negative attitudes often create antagonistic relationships, stereotypes, and prejudices. The more a person is prejudiced, the less likely the person is involved in interaction. However, prejudice does not mean avoidance of contact; even highly prejudiced people seek contact with others.

Culture also encourages the development of different perceptions of people. When a person perceives another positively, he or she is likely to be perceived by the other positively and vice versa (Triandis, 1977). Thus, mutual positive perceptions enhance social interaction, and negative perceptions reduce it.

The cultural familiarity and similarity facilitates interactions because it reduces uncertainty and anxiety. People develop social relations with those who are relatively similar: members of their own culture. People who belong to the same cultural group or know each other are more likely to interact than people who belong to different cultures or do not know each other (Triandis, 1977). Also, people prefer to develop social contact with those with a similar background, even if they are not their friends, rather than with those with a different cultural background. Therefore, the cultural similarity between tourists and hosts is a very important factor deciding about their social interaction.

Perceived cultural similarity depends on cultural values. Those who perceive their values to be similar are more likely to interact socially than those who perceive their values to be dissimilar. Large differences in the perceived cultural value system inhibit interaction (Feather, 1980a). Perceived cultural similarity affects mutual attraction and liking. Those with similar cultural values are likely to like each other and interact together. However, cultural dissimilarity can also be an important factor attracting people to each other and result in reduction in social barriers.

There are also other factors that influence tourist–host contact, such as different types of travel arrangements, the role of the culture broker (e.g. tour guide), the type and stage of tourism development, and the number of tourists and hosts at the destination visited. For example, at the maturity stage of destination development (Butler, 1980), a number of undesirable social impacts emerge, including crime, resident irritation with tourism and overcrowding, and a reduction in the willingness of hosts to interact socially with tourists. The above identified factors are not examined because their discussion exceeds the scope of this book. However, they should be examined in future cross-cultural tourism studies.

8.3 INTERCULTURAL SOCIAL INTERACTION

Intercultural interaction refers to the direct face-to-face encounter between individuals from different cultures. The intercultural interaction usually involves interactions between individuals from two different cultures who are culturally different in terms of their values, communication style, expectations, perceptions, rules of behavior, and the way they view the world. They live in different cultures, speak different languages, and use different symbols of communication. This type of interaction is experienced by tourists when they travel from a home culture to the foreign host culture and by hosts when they meet tourists from a culture different form their own. An example of intercultural interaction is the interaction between the US American and Asian cultural groups.

The term intercultural is often confused with interethnic and interracial, intracultural and cross-cultural. *Interethnic* and *interracial* interactions refer to interactions between members of different ethnic and racial groups who are members of the same nation or state. The *intracultural* interaction refers to interaction between individuals from a similar culture.

The *cross-cultural interaction* refers to the interaction between individuals from more than two cultural groups and involves a comparison of interactions among people from the same culture to those from other cultures (Lustig & Koester, 1999). An example of cross-cultural interaction is the interaction between members of the US American and Asian populations, which represent several distinct cultural groups.

8.3.1 Dimensions of intercultural encounters

The intercultural encounters depend upon two dimensions: the time (length of the encounter) and the purpose of travel (motives for engaging in encounter). Intercultural encounters may occur in various settings and involve international tourists, students, immigrants, business people, foreign workers, diplomats or refugees. For each tourist, business person, immigrant, or student, there are hundreds of other people with whom they s/he will interact. Each encounter, regardless of whether voluntary or forced, short- or long-term, involves different behaviors and expectations.

8.3.2 Interculturalness of social interaction

Social interactions can be arranged in order from least intercultural to most intercultural (see Figure 8.1). Encounters in which individuals are culturally very similar to one another are least intercultural, whereas the encounters in which the individuals are culturally very different from one another are most intercultural (Lustig & Koester, 1999).

Least
Intercultural -- Most Intercultural

Figure 8.1

A Continuum of Interculturalness

Source: based on Lustig, M., & Koester, J. (1993). *Intercultural competence.* New York: Harper Collins College Publishers

Every social encounter is intercultural to a certain degree because every interacting person is different in terms of cultural background and other characteristics.

8.3.3 Degree of interculturalness

The interculturalness of social encounter depends not just on the presence or absence of cultural differences, but the degree of difference between those involved in encounter (Kim & Gudykunst, 1988). The degree or the extent of difference might range from very small to extreme. As the degree of difference increases, the level of interculturalness increases (Sarbaugh, 1988). Samovar and Porter (1991) presented these differences along a minimum–maximum dimension and reported that the maximum cultural difference is between Asian and Western cultures. The members of cultural groups with maximum cultural groups speak different languages, follow different religious beliefs, have different experiences and perceptions, and see their worlds differently, as opposed to the members of similar cultural groups. However, similar cultural groups might also be dissimilar (to some extent) because they may consist of various sub-cultural groups with divergent beliefs, values, and attitudes (e.g. French Canadians and English Canadians).

8.4 TYPES OF INTERCULTURAL INTERACTION

There are different types of intercultural interaction depending upon the degree of their interculturalness, or similarities and differences in the cultural backgrounds of the individuals. There are encounters when the cultural background of individuals is (1) the same, or similar; (2) different, but the differences are small and supplementary; and (3) different, and the differences are large and incompatible (Sutton, 1967). In the first two types of encounter, individuals have similar backgrounds and share cultural commonalities; the level of interculturalness in their encounter is low, they understand each other accurately, and their social contact is most effective. In the third type of encounter, participants are separated by large cultural differences and their interaction is more difficult and less efficient (Sutton, 1967). As the cultural differences among the contact participants increase, their encounter becomes more intercultural and may lead to friction, misunderstanding, and misinterpretation that inhibit interaction. The greater the differences among the two cultures, the greater the probability that their encounters will lead to friction and misunderstanding (Triandis, 1977) because it is more likely that they distort the meaning of a person's behavior; as a result information exchanged and communication become less effective.

However, some cultural groups can be culturally similar and dissimilar at the same time. Although the US Americans, English, Canadians, and Australians belong to Western cultures and speak English, they have diverse values, beliefs, and attitudes toward life. Thus, the interculturalness of the social encounters largely depends upon the significance of the cultural differences among the individuals, rather than their presence. When the cultural differences are small or insignificant, intercultural encounters are not affected by cultural differences. However, when the cultural differences are large and significant, the probability that intercultural encounters will lead to cultural problems and conflicts is high. In the destinations where the majority of tourists are foreigners, the residents usually perceive the tourists to be very different from them. On the other hand, in the destinations where the majority of tourists are domestic tourists, the residents perceive the tourists to be similar or the same (Pizam & Telisman-Kosuta, 1989).

8.5 MODEL OF CROSS-CULTURAL SOCIAL INTERACTION

Figure 8.2 presents a model of social interaction in a cross-cultural context. This model is based on Porter and Samovar's (1988) model of intercultural communication process. The figure shows three distinct shapes that represent three different cultures: cultures A, B and C. Culture A and culture B are more similar, while culture C is less similar to culture A and culture B. Within each culture A, B, and C, there are inner forms which represent the individual (a) who is "traveling" between the three cultures and is influenced by each culture. The influence of three cultures on an individual is

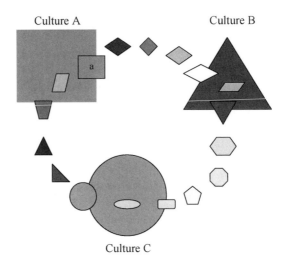

Figure 8.2

The Cross-cultural Interaction Model

Source: based on Reisinger, Y., & Turner, L. (2003). *Cross-cultural behaviour in tourism: Concepts and analysis* (p. 27). Burlington, MA: Butterworth-Heinemann; Porter, R., & Samovar, L. (1988). Approaching intercultural communication. In L. Samovar, & R. Porter (Eds.), *Intercultural communication: A reader* (5th ed., p. 22). Belmont, CA: Wadsworth.

represented by the differing shapes and colors of the individual. Although the shape and color of the dominant culture A and the individual are initially the same (culture A is the culture of origin of the individual) the shape and color of the individual change once s/he visits other cultures. When an individual from culture A leaves its culture and reaches culture B, his or her behavior (shape) changes because of the influence of a culturally different society (B). The degree to which culture influences an individual from culture A and an individual from culture B is a function of the dissimilarity of cultures A and B. Similarly, when an individual from culture B leaves it and reaches culture C, his or her behavior also changes because of the influence of a culturally different society (C). The extent to which culture influences an individual from culture B and an individual from culture C is a function of the dissimilarity of cultures B and C.

8.6 CONTACT HYPOTHESIS

The "contact hypothesis" relates to social contact between individuals from different cultural groups (e.g. Allport, 1954; Cook, 1962). The contact hypothesis suggests that social interaction between people of different cultural backgrounds may result in positive and negative outcomes. In terms of positive outcomes this contact may result in mutual appreciation, understanding, respect, tolerance, liking, development of positive attitudes, and reduction of ethnic prejudices, stereotypes, and racial tension; and improvement of the social interactions between individuals. It also contributes to cultural enrichment and learning about others (Bochner, 1982; Cohen, 1971; UNESCO, 1976).

However, the same contact may also develop negative attitudes, prejudices, stereotypes, misunderstanding, increased tension, hostility, suspicion, clashes of values, conflict, disharmonies, exclusion from mutual activities, feeling the sense of a social barrier and inferiority, difficulty in forming friendships, problems of adjustment, self-rejection, resentment, irritation, frustration and stress, communication problems, the loss of a sense of security and emotional well-being, and ethnocentrism. Social contact between culturally different people can even be a threatening experience; participants may feel like outsiders, intruding, undermining values of the other culture (Argyle et al., 1981; Biddlecomb, 1981; Bochner, 1982; Boissevain, 1979; Brewer, 1984; Cohen, 1982; DeKadt, 1979; Doxey, 1976; Evans-Pritchard, 1989; Hall, 1984; Lynch, 1960; Petit-Skinner, 1977; Pi-Sunyer, 1978, 1982; Sutton, 1967; Taft, 1977; Triandis & Vassiliou, 1967). Such contact may inhibit future social interaction. The more frequent the social contact between people of different cultural backgrounds, the more negative feelings they may develop (Anant, 1971).

8.7 CONTACT HYPOTHESIS IN TOURISM

Contact between culturally different tourists and hosts can lead to enhancement of tourists' and hosts' attitudes toward each other, learning about the others' culture, and development of a positive attitude. When tourists are friendly, respectful, and show an interest in the host society, local residents can develop pride in their local culture, socialize with tourists, and learn their language. Those who have longer contact with each other may develop more favorable attitudes toward each other. Tourist–host contact may also result in exchange of correspondence and gifts, the development of personal relationships and even friendships (Bochner, 1982; Boissevain, 1979; Pearce, 1982, 1988).

On the other hand, the contact between tourists and hosts of different cultural backgrounds is the most superficial form of cultural encounter (Hofstede, 1997). Tourists' and hosts' perceptions of each other are highly distorted; hosts develop their perceptions of tourists on the basis of symbols such as clothing or music, and tourists develop their opinions of hosts on the basis of the outcomes of their mutual commercial exchange. These perceptions may create communication problems and result in negative change of attitudes.

Tourist–host contact may also generate conflict of values. For example, the non-Islamic tourists who pursue Western liberal values by wearing inappropriate dress or drinking alcohol contradict the Islamic religion and break domestic social and cultural rules. Such a situation leads to the development of unwelcoming attitudes by the hosts of Arab States towards tourists and tourist isolation, separation, and segregation from the host community. When tourists violate local values, they may also experience victimization, including verbal and physical abuse and may also be robbed and cheated.

The contact between tourists and hosts from different cultures can also create communication and health problems, preoccupation with safety, or luggage organization (Downs & Stea, 1977; Pearce, 1977, 1982).

In less developed countries, where cultural differences between tourists and hosts are greater than in more developed countries, the negative effect of direct tourist–host contact may be greater. Rich tourists who visit Third World countries often have little respect for local values. Therefore, tourists are perceived as aggressive and insensitive, and they are exploited, assaulted, and victimized (Pearce, 1982, 1988).

8.8 DIFFICULTIES IN CROSS-CULTURAL INTERACTION

In social interactions in which individuals are confronted with a culture different from their own, many situations are unfamiliar to them. They do not know what behavior is desirable and appropriate; nor do they know what to say and do. The main difficulties in social interactions that occur in a cross-cultural context are in (a) interpersonal communication (verbal and non-verbal), and (b) social behavior. The difficulties in verbal communication occur due to the differences in peoples' verbal skills, such as language fluency, polite language usage, and expressing attitudes, feelings, and emotions. The difficulties in non-verbal communication occur due to the differences in non-verbal skills, such as facial expressions, eye gaze, spatial behavior, touching, posture, and gesture. The difficulties in social behavior occur due to the differences in rules and patterns of social behavior, such as greetings, self-disclosure, and making or refusing requests (Bochner, 1982) (see Chapter 9). For instance, in Western cultures people talk about their feelings and emotions, as opposed to Asian cultures where people believe that revealing personal feelings violates cultural rules of politeness and respect. In Asian cultures it is believed that friends and family members should sense the other person's feelings. Also, each culture has its specific rules of proper introduction, expressing opinions, showing respect, and even eating habits. For instance, different customs of handling cutlery or keeping a wine glass can cause irritations and be grounds for misunderstanding and interaction difficulties.

Cultural differences in verbal and non-verbal communication and rules and patterns of social behavior influence tourists' and hosts' perceptions of each other. Those who have communication and interpersonal skills can effectively interact in their home culture. However, they may lack the same skills and be unable to interact smoothly in a foreign culture. As a result, tourists and hosts from different cultures may develop negative perceptions of each other. Thus, cultural differences are important factors influencing interaction difficulties and mutual perceptions.

Social interaction between tourists and hosts, however, does not have to be characterized by difficulties. These difficulties may be minimized or even eliminated when tourists and hosts are aware of their differences and try to understand them. The potential difficulties in intercultural interaction between tourists and hosts can be identified and managed by using a framework of a Coordinated Management of Meaning (CMMT) Theory (discussed in Chapter 3), which argues that the successful intercultural interaction needs to achieve a degree of understanding at six different levels of communication and interaction, such as verbal and non-verbal behavior, speech acts, episodes, relationships, life script, and cultural patterns (Cronen & Shuter, 1983).

8.9 CULTURE SHOCK

Culture shock is one of the difficulties most experienced by individuals encountering foreign cultures (Adler, 1975; Bochner, 1982; Oberg, 1960; Taft, 1977) as well as difficulties experienced by international tourists when traveling abroad. Culture shock refers to an unpleasant surprise or shock when an individual is confronted with the unknown and the ''foreign.'' The shock occurs because expectations of the individual do not coincide with reality. The shock is caused by an inability to cope in a new cultural environment, respond to unfamiliar stimuli, confront different ways of life and doing things, ask questions and understand the answers and even recognize food (Rogers & Steinfatt, 1999). Culture shock occurs when individuals visiting a foreign culture experience the ''loss of equilibrium,'' or ''loss of familiar signs and symbols of social intercourse,'' because of the differences in foreign culture (Craig, 1979, p. 159), lack knowledge of how to behave in a new culture (Oberg, 1960), and suffer from the difficulties with adjustment to a new environment. As more people from different cultures travel around the world and experience difficulties with the unknown foreign cultures, culture shock is becoming part of their everyday vocabulary.

8.9.1 Symptoms of culture shock

Visiting or working in a new culture can produce a variety of reactions. Table 8.3 presents major symptoms of culture shock.

The visitor in a foreign culture behaves like a child who has to learn the simplest things once again, often with difficulties. This normally leads to feelings of helplessness, disorientation, distress and even hostility towards the new environment. Due to culture shock, many visitors to a foreign country can become physically or mentally ill, remain so homesick that they have to return home quickly, or even commit suicide (Hofstede, 1997).

8.9.2 Types of culture shock

There are several types of culture shock:

- *Role shock:* occurs due to lack of knowledge about the rules of behavior (Byrnes, 1966)
- *Language shock:* occurs due to problems with an unfamiliar language and an inability to communicate properly (Smalley, 1963)
- *Culture fatigue:* occurs due to tiredness and the need for constant adjustment to a new cultural environment (Taft, 1977)
- *Transition shock:* occurs due to negative reaction to change and adjustment to a new cultural environment, inability to interact effectively within a new environment (Bennett, 1977)

Table 8.3 Symptoms of Culture Shock

Absent-minded and far-away stare	Frustration
Anger about foreign practices	Humiliation
Anxiety	Inappropriate social behavior
Confusion about one's own values, role, self-identity	Incompetence
	Insomnia
Craving	Isolation
Criticism of the new country	Irritation
Decline in initiatives	Fatigue
Decline in a work quality	Loneliness
Depression	Loss of appetite
Disgust	Negative feelings toward hosts
Disorientation	Nervousness
Embarrassment	Over-dependence on being with one's own nationals
Emotional and intellectual withdrawal	
Excessive washing of hands	Preoccupation with cleanliness and worries
Extreme concern over drinking the water, eating local food	Refusal to learn a new language
	Self-doubt
Fear of physical contact with anyone in the new country	Sense of loss arising from being removed from one's familiar environment
Fear of socializing	Skin irritation and slight pains
Feelings of being rejected by the members of the new environment	Strain caused by the effort to adapt to the new environment
Feelings of deprivation in relation to friends, status, professions and possessions	Stress on health and safety
Feelings of helplessness, not being able to cope and deal competently within the new environment	Terrible longing to be back home
	Use of alcohol and drugs
Feelings of rejecting members of the new culture	

Sources: Bochner (1982), Brislin and Pedersen (1976), Oberg (1960), Taft (1977).

- *Re-entry shock:* occurs due to the emotional and physiological difficulties experienced upon returning home from overseas (Gullahorn & Gullahorn, 1963).

8.9.3 How long does culture shock last?

Most people think of culture shock as a short experience in a foreign place. Few realize that its effects can be much deeper and more prolonged if they are not dealt with effectively. The greater the feelings of helplessness, anxiety, or worry, the longer the visitors experience culture shock. This suggests that in order to reduce the culture shock, one must deal with its symptoms when they appear.

8.9.4 Culture shock and social interaction

Culture shock has an adverse effect on intercultural interaction and communication: both become less effective. Participants of intercultural interaction may interpret others' anger and frustration as hostility or hate. The larger the degree of cultural differences between the contact participants, the larger the culture shock they may experience, the less information is exchanged, and the less effective is their interaction.

8.9.5 Culture shock in tourism

It is falsely believed that tourists do not experience culture shock, or experience it to a lesser degree than the longer-stay visitors, such as diplomats, guest workers, or even business people. The fact is that many reactions of tourists visiting foreign cultures are not different from those of other foreign visitors. Many tourists experience culture shock when they travel to a foreign culture and encounter taxi drivers, front office employees, shop assistants, and customs officials. Tourists do not know what to expect from the foreign hosts and hosts do not know what to expect from tourists. Hosts often behave in ways that are strange to tourists, and tourists behave in ways which are not understood by hosts. The same behavior may be considered appropriate in one culture, and inappropriate or even rude in another. Tourists often do not know how to greet others in a foreign culture, what is appropriate to say in conversation, or how much to tip the waiter. Many social situations are confusing to them and make the trip difficult. Therefore, in order to interact successfully with the hosts of a foreign society, tourists might have to adapt to local rules, customs, and values.

Also, not only tourists experience culture shock, but also the host population. Both the encounters may be stressful because they are confronted with new values and behavior. However, when the host population has limited exposure to foreign cultures, the sociocultural and psychological impact of tourists on hosts is greater (Pearce, 1982, 1988).

8.9.6 Phases of culture shock

Going abroad or working internationally puts an individual through a cycle of distinct phases of culture shock. According to Oberg (1960), there are four phases of culture shock. The first phase is the *honeymoon phase*, characterized by fascination and optimism: visitors see all encounters in the new place as exciting, positive, and stimulating. Life in the new culture is viewed as providing opportunities for learning, socializing, and enjoying life. Visitors are open and curious, ready to accept whatever comes. They do not judge anything and suppress minor irritations. They concentrate on the nice things to do, see, and experience, such as the food, landscape, people, and the country. The second phase is the *hostility phase*, characterized by visitors' negative attitudes toward the host society and increased contact with fellow sojourners. At this stage visitors are annoyed and irritated by new ways of doing things, rules, and customs. They are not willing to adapt all new elements of a foreign culture. They are disappointed and do not want to integrate into a new culture. They contact only fellow visitors. The third phase is the *recovery phase*, characterized by the visitors' increased ability to cope in the new environment. Visitors begin to learn and understand new ways of life in a foreign culture. The forth phase is the *adjustment phase*, characterized by acceptance and enjoyment of the new cultural environment. Visitors feel comfortable and confident in the new environment and accept it.

A very similar pattern of culture shock was introduced by Gullahorn and Gullahorn (1963), who proposed a U-curve of cultural adjustment or satisfaction with sojourn, consisting of four stages: (1) *initial optimism*; (2) *subsequent disappointment*; (3) *adaptation*; and (4) *gradual recovery*. The U-curve has been extended to the W-curve (Gullahorn & Gullahorn, 1963; Trifonovitch, 1977) by introducing an additional stage of a *re-entry* (return home). As a result, the following stages of culture shock, change, and adaptation were proposed:

1. *Honeymoon stage:* travelers prepare themselves for travel, are excited and full of optimism about visiting a new culture; their expectations are high.
2. *Hostility stage*: travelers arrive to a new culture and start experiencing a new environment. They discover cultural differences between the new and home culture, feel frustrated, stressed and disappointed because they are unable to solve problems in familiar ways. They reject the new culture; seek out people from the home culture.
3. *Humor stage*: visitors adjust to the new culture, accept differences, begin to appreciate the new culture, spend less time with people of the home country, interact more with locals, learn the local language and habits, and even joke in a foreign language. Visitors become adjusted to the new culture.
4. *At home stage*: visitors look forward to returning home, regret they have to leave the new culture, and become happy about returning home.
5. *Reverse culture shock*: travelers experience re-entry shock upon return to the home culture. They feel that the home culture has changed; they are unable to cope in the home environment, feel confused, alienated and become depressed.
6. *Readjustment stage*: travelers learn to cope with the problems at home (see Figure 8.3).

Both culture shock and reverse shock show that culture is not only an extremely important influence on human behavior but also a very useful learning experience. By experiencing culture shock and reverse shock, an individual can gain important understanding about more than one culture and its relativism and thus become better aware of cultural differences and better prepared for a next sojourning experience (Rogers & Steinfatt, 1999).

Experiencing culture shock is not a weakness or an indication of future international failure. Quite the opposite, it is normal to experience culture shock in all its forms. Those who experience culture shock and reverse shock are the most culturally effective because they are most aware of themselves and their emotions, and the differences between themselves and others, and thus are able to adapt more effectively later on. Experiencing culture shock is part of a successful adaptation process; it can significantly facilitate the process of cultural acculturation and assimilation.

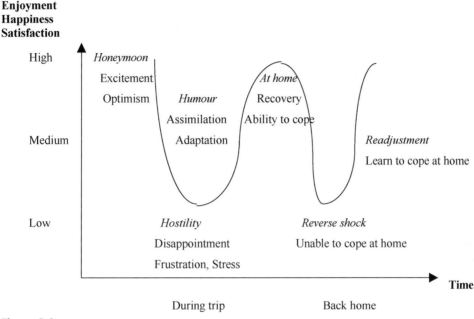

Figure 8.3

The U-curve and W-curve of Cultural Change and Adaptation over Time

Source: Reisinger, Y., & Turner, L. (2003). *Cross-cultural behaviour in tourism: Concepts and analysis* (p. 60). Burlington, MA: Butterworth-Heinemann.

Hofstede (1997) presented an acculturation curve of a change in sojourner's feelings that consists of:

1. Short Phase 1 *Euphoria*: individuals experience pleasant feelings, the excitement of traveling to and seeing new places.
2. Long Phase 2 *Culture shock*: individuals experience the different way of living in the new environment.
3. Longest Phase 3 *Acculturation*: individuals learn to function in a new cultural environment, adapt some of the local values and customs, become more confident and develop social relationships.
4. Phase 4 *Stable state*: individuals reach a stable state of mind. They may either (a) remain negative towards a foreign environment and continue feeling alien; (b) remain feeling the same as at home and consider oneself as being bi-culturally adapted; or (c) remain more positive towards a foreign environment, as compared to home, and become like ''natives'' (see Figure 8.4).

8.9.7 Intensity and duration of culture shock

The intensity and duration of culture shock depend on the degree of cultural differences between the visitor and host's cultures, the cultural knowledge of the individual, the ability

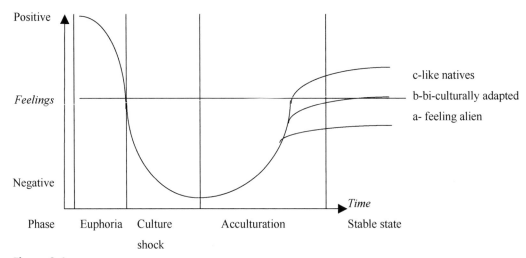

Figure 8.4

The Acculturation Curve

Source: based on Hofstede, G., & Hofstede, G. J. (2005). *Cultures and organizations: Software of the mind* (Revised and expanded 2nd ed.). New York: McGraw; Jansen, D. (2004). Developing the intercultural competence of engineering students: a proposal for the method and contents of a seminar. *World Transactions and Technology Education*, *3*(1), 23–28; Weiss, T. (2004). Safe mode of cultural orientation. Presentation at Sea Border Central seminar, 30 January 2004; http://www.more.fi/files/IOM_Presentation.ppt.

to adjust, motivation and frequency of overseas travel, number of friends in a host community, type of travel arrangements, the length of stay in the foreign country, interpersonal and foreign language skills, personality, and many others. For example, the greater the degree of the cultural differences between tourists and hosts, the more intense could be culture shock. Some tourists may experience culture shock at the initial stage only; others may never leave the ''honeymoon'' or ''euphoria'' stage. In particular, when the length of stay in a foreign culture is very short, tourists may feel only excitement about new experiences fulfilling their motivations. On the other hand, others may feel constantly confused. Also, those who frequently visit foreign cultures or have a better cultural knowledge can cope more easily with culture shock. Those with better social and language skills can adjust more quickly. However, even those who have good communication and interpersonal skills of own culture may find it difficult to cope and adjust in a foreign culture.

   The individuals who stay in a foreign culture for a short period of time can experience all stages of culture shock. Others who stay longer (e.g. several years) may experience each stage of culture shock over a longer period of time (e.g. year) or even longer before they adapt or completely acculturate or assimilate. Tourists who visit a large number of cultures in a short time could be in constant shock (Taft, 1977) because they have little chance to quickly adapt to each new culture. Those who have friends in a host community, experience less culture shock than those with no friends (Sellitz & Cook, 1962). However, not every type of tourist experiences culture shock. Organized mass tourists do not have to experience culture shock at all. The organized pre-purchased packages and guided tours provide an environmental bubble which limits opportunities for mass tourists for direct contact with a new culture and foreign hosts, and protects them from experiencing stress and anxiety. In contrast, the individual non-institutionalized type of a tourist who wishes to experience new culture and seeks contact with the host community may experience more culture shock.

8.9.8 Doxey's Irridex ''Irritation Index''

The most well known theory on how hosts and guests interact, directly related to the theory of culture shock, is Doxey's Irridex or ''Irritation Index'' (Doxey, 1976). According to Doxey's theory, when there is no touristic activity in the region, hosts are curious and interested in tourists (*Euphoria stage*); tourists are welcome, and hosts are delighted and excited about tourists' presence. However, when the number of tourists increases, they are taken for granted; contact between tourists and hosts becomes more formal and locals become indifferent towards tourists; they do not know whether to welcome tourists or not (*Apathy stage*). When the number of tourists reaches maximum level, tourism development reaches the saturation stage and the rate of tourism growth is expected to be even higher, hosts become concerned over price rises, crime, and tourist rudeness, and cultural rules being broken and eventually irritated by tourists' presence; tourists are perceived as an annoyance (*Irritation* or *Annoyance stage*). When tourists are blamed for all wrongdoings in the host society, and are seen as lacking human values, hosts become hostile towards them. Hosts start to believe tourists can be exploited (*Antagonism* or *Hostility stage*). Eventually, hosts call for actions which would offset the negative impacts of tourism development (see Figure 8.5).

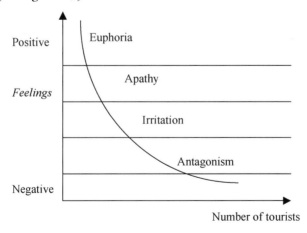

Figure 8.5

Doxey's Irridex ''Irritation'' Index

Source: based on Doxey, G. (1976). A causation theory of visitor-resident irritants, methodology, and research inferences. In the *6th annual conference proceedings of the travel and tourism research association: The impact of tourism* (pp. 195–198). San Diego, CA.

SUMMARY

The concept of social interaction refers to personal associations taking place in different forms and contexts. The major factors determining social interaction in tourism are (a) temporal and (b) spatial (the nature of the tourist–host contact itself and the social character of the situation in which the contact occurs, including the opportunity for contact, the place in which contact takes place, characteristics of individuals, their motivation, interpersonal attraction, social status, activities and interests, interaction purpose, rules of social behavior, attitudes, social skills, perceived costs and benefits derived from interaction, resources that are exchanged), (c) communication (effectiveness), and (d) cultural (values, attitudes, perceptions, cultural familiarity and similarity).

Intercultural interaction depends upon the degree of its interculturalness, which is determined by the degree of cultural differences between participants. The contact hypothesis suggests that contact between tourists and hosts of different cultural backgrounds may result in positive and negative outcomes. Similarity in cultural background facilitates interaction between tourists and hosts; dissimilarity reduces it. Tourists and hosts from different cultural backgrounds can experience difficulties in their social interaction. Most difficulties occur due to cultural differences in communication and rules of social behavior. Culture shock is one the most recognized difficulties encountered by travelers in a foreign culture. Tourists experience culture shock when they travel to a foreign culture. Many symptoms of culture shock have been identified. There are several stages of culture shock.

DISCUSSION POINTS AND QUESTIONS

1. Explain the concept of social interaction and how it can be applied in a tourism context.
2. Identify the unique characteristics of the tourist–host contact.
3. Give examples showing that the social interaction between tourists and hosts from different cultures results in positive and negative outcomes.
4. Describe the stages of culture shock. Do you think that every traveler must experience culture shock?
5. Is culture shock an evidence of an international experience failure? If not, why not?
6. What are the advantages of experiencing culture shock?

CASE STUDY 8.1 Shanghai Night or Nightmare?

In summer 2005 Chuyen and her three fellow students from Thailand, Vietnam, and India went to Shanghai. Chuyen had heard about Shanghai from movies. Many interesting films were produced in Shanghai. Chuyen was excited to see beautiful Huangpu River and experience the ''Shanghai night.''

Shanghai's modern look was far beyond Chuyen's imagination. High-rise buildings, highways, and commercial centers were everywhere. The well-designed parks, the beautiful view of the Huangpu River, the old quarter of the city with old-style houses added to its charm and beauty. The taxi drivers spoke some English and the taxi fares were cheap. Chuyen and her friends fell in love with the city ''at first sight.'' They walked long the streets sightseeing, dining, taking photographs, and shopping. However, as the proverb says ''beauty is only skin deep.''

The first night, when they walked along the Huangpu riverbank, an artist approached Chuyen and asked if she wanted him to paint her portrait. Chuyen asked about the price and was assured it would cost her 4 Yuan; the artist even showed his four fingers to confirm the price. However, after the portrait was finished Chuyen could not recognize any feature of her face. The artist demanded 40 Yuan for his work explaining that he mistook ''four'' for ''forty'' because his English was not good enough.

The second night, Chuyen and her friends went out to eat at a local restaurant. The price of the meal was 4 Yuan per dish. While they were enjoying their meals the seller brought the bill for the amount of 200 Yuan! Chuyen asked the seller to re-calculate the bill. The seller dropped the price to 98 Yuan. Ketchup, spices and fish sauce had been counted as main dishes.

On the third day, Chuyen and her friends went for a tunnel tour under the Huangpu River. A package tour included a visit to aquarium, a ''magic sound'' room, and the sex culture exhibition: total cost 35 Yuan. Unfortunately, the aquarium was full of artificial fish and the ''magic sound'' resembled the sounds of rain and lightning – all ordinary daily life sounds, including Chinese language sounds.

On the fourth day, the group went shopping in a market. One of Chuyen's friends bought a shirt for 100 Yuan; the seller's price was 300 Yuan. Chuyen and her friends noted that other people bought the same shirt for only 25 Yuan! They were unaware that they should bargain and buy the shirt cheaper. They did not know how to bargain and felt cheated.

Today, Chuyen has a mixture of good and bad memories of Shanghai. Although the Chinese government heavily promotes Shanghai as an attractive tourism destination, her trip was spoiled by bad experiences with local people. Cheating on tourists always brings short-term benefits. Chuyen decided not to come back to Shanghai. She would also not recommend it to her friends. She felt her money was stolen from her.

WEBSITE LINKS

1. Social interaction: http://en.wikipedia.org/wiki/Social_interaction, http://www.hawaii.edu/powerkills/TCH.CHAP9.HTM
2. Culture shock: http://en.wikipedia.org/wiki/Culture_shock, http://kidshealth.org/teen/your_mind/emotions/culture_shock.html

Since the way people interact is determined by social rules the next chapter will discuss the concept and cultural differences in rules of social behavior.

Cultural influences on rules of social interaction

*The aim of this chapter is to identify cultural differences
in rules of social interaction.*

After completing this chapter the reader should be able to:
- Understand the concept of rules of social behavior
- Identify different types of rules of social behavior
- Explain the influence of culture on rules of social behavior
- Understand the consequences of breaking the social rules
- Identify cultural differences in social rules

INTRODUCTION

Rules of social behavior play a central role in human interactions. Their role is to maintain harmonious social relations. Rules of social behavior are culturally determined. Knowledge of the rules governing social relationships in a cross- or intercultural context is an important element for improving social relationships.

9.1 RULES OF SOCIAL INTERACTION

An important feature of social interaction between tourists and hosts and also a source of their interaction difficulties, especially in a cross-cultural context, is rules of social behavior, sometimes called rules of social interaction. Rules of social interaction are **225** guidelines and standards that direct behavior of the individuals in relationships; they indicate how people ought or ought not to behave in various situations and contexts, what is appropriate and inappropriate behavior in a specific situation, and what behavior is accepted and what is prohibited. Rules of social interaction provide the meaning of a behavior within a specific situation; they make interaction easier and more understandable to others. They organize and regulate interaction between individuals to achieve public order and social harmony. Rules are also used to evaluate and predict the future behavior of others.

Rules of social interaction are created by mutual consent of society. Behavior that conforms to socially accepted rules is regarded as appropriate. Rules depend upon the social situation and context in which interaction occurs. Rules may be subjected to different interpretations and thus they can be broken. Many rules cannot be enforced by law (e.g. implicit rules).

9.2 ORDERS AND TYPES OF RULES

There are three orders of rules. The first order relates to rules of social etiquette. The second order relates to rules of social relations (how to develop social relations and maintain social hierarchy) (Harre, 1974). The third order relates to rules of self, for example, self-presentation or self-performance, and shows how to create self-image (Goffman, 1969). There are also different types of rules of social interaction (see Table 9.1).

Argyle, Graham, and White, (1979) studied the rules of 25 social situations and found that rules "should be friendly" and "should keep to pleasant topics of conversation" apply to all social situations. The universal rules of social interaction that

Table 9.1 Types of Rules of Social Interaction

Type	Example
Interpersonal	Should be polite, nice to each other
Task	Should help
Require reward	Should support
Prevent conflict	Should cooperate and not complain
Rules for actions	Should wake up early
Rules for conduct	Should be disciplined
Enabling	Should speak when asked
Restricting	Should not be loud when others talk
Explicit (written spoken, direct, known by the majority)	School and work rules
Implicit (implied and indirect)	Rules of social etiquette; these are implied and indirect
Formal	Public and institutional regulations
Informal	For private gatherings

Table 9.1 (*Continued*)

Type	Example
Verbal behavior	Should use direct and specific words when talking to others
Non-verbal behavior	Should keep physical distance when talking to others
Situation	Indicate how to greet each other (e.g. should shake hands), exchange gifts, initiate conversation, what to talk about during conversations, or the mood that is appropriate
Relationship	Indicate how to behave in relation to guests, strangers, or friends
Universal	Apply to nearly all situations and cultures (e.g. should be friendly, should keep to pleasant topics of conversation)
Specific	Show how to behave in specific situations

tourists and hosts should follow are to be polite, honest, open, friendly, genuine, and respectful (Pearce, 1988).

9.3 RELATIONSHIP RULES

Relationship rules govern social relationships. They can be formal, directly stated (explicit), coded in a written or spoken language, and well-known, for example, public or institutional regulations. They can also be informal, indirectly stated (implicit), and learned through socializing or observing others. In involuntary relationships the behaviors need to be regulated by explicit rules. Thus, in collectivistic cultures in which the relationships are involuntary, there are many formal and explicit relationship rules. On the other hand, in voluntary relationships the behaviors do not need to be guided by formal rules. Thus, in individualistic cultures there are many informal relationship rules. In tourism, social interaction between tourists and locals or service providers is a form of voluntary relationship; thus there is less need to regulate it by formal rules; the informal and implicit rules play a more important role in this interaction.

9.4 CULTURAL INFLUENCES ON RULES OF SOCIAL INTERACTION

Rules of social interaction are influenced by the cultural values of those who participate in these interactions. Since culture determines the rules of social relationships, rules vary according to the national culture of the contact participants (Mann, 1986). Members of similar cultures who follow similar social rules understand their rules, whereas members of different cultures who have different rules may not understand each others' rules. For example, different cultures have different rules for defining, establishing, and maintaining social relations, greetings, beginnings of conversation, farewelling, expressing opinions, intimacy, politeness, dissatisfaction and criticism, understanding friendship, joking, showing warmth, apologizing, telling the truth, taking initiatives and responsibility, feelings of obligations, confronting others, avoiding embarrassment, perceiving a sense of shame, frankness, persistency, reasoning, exaggerations, attitudes toward social status, physical proximity and privacy, using social space and time, acceptable volume of interaction, gift-giving, tipping, eating, drinking, and entertaining guests. There are cultural differences in rules regarding bodily contact, eye and body movements, external appearance and self-presentation, (Argyle, 1967, 1972; Argyle et al., 1978; Dodd, 1987; Goffman, 1963; Gudykunst & Kim, 1984; Hall, 1966, 1983; Jensen, 1970; Nomura & Barnlund, 1983; Wei et al., 1989).

Since different cultures have different rules of behavior, the expectations and meanings of these rules also differ across cultures. As a result, members of different cultures may misunderstand and misinterpret the rules of other cultures. This can lead to confusion, and generate tension and even conflict. Many international tourists whose cultural background differs from the one of local residents report difficulties in interaction with local hosts due to differences in rules of social behavior. Even different ways of handling forks and knifes as well as eating habits can cause irritation (Stringer, 1981).

9.5 UNDERSTANDING RULES OF SOCIAL INTERACTION

Understanding the rules governing social interaction is extremely important. Such understanding can enable both parties to share and understand their experiences and facilitate the development of mutual relationships. Understanding rules of social interaction of the foreign culture, however, requires a deep understanding of the verbal and non-verbal patterns, and how and why the foreigners interact the way they do. This, in turn, requires the broad knowledge of historical, political, economic, religious and educational environment of the parties involved, including their values, beliefs, attitudes, and thought patterns. It is impossible to understand the culturally different behaviors without understanding the rules that govern these behaviors. Since international tourism creates many opportunities for interactions between tourists and hosts, there is a need to learn the rules of their behavior.

9.6 BREAKING RULES

Many people are unaware of the cultural differences in the rules of behavior and as such they often either break the rules or ignore them. Tourists often break social rules on the streets, in shops, banks, at meal times, and at religious services by inappropriate clothes, gestures, or language. Tourists break the social rules because they do not know the rules of the visited country. Their stay in the receiving countries is usually short and temporary and thus they do have a very little opportunity to learn about the rules of proper interaction with hosts. Consequently, the host community develops stereotypes of tourists as being ignorant, rude, and disrespectful. Breaking rules leads to deterioration of the tourist–host relationships. Compliance with others' social rules is necessary for developing smooth interpersonal relationships.

9.7 CROSS-CULTURAL DIFFERENCES IN RULES OF SOCIAL INTERACTION

Members of collectivistic and high uncertainty avoidance cultures have many rules concerning the out-groups because they are more cautious about strangers. Members of collectivistic and high power distant cultures have many formal rules for hierarchical work relationships and social relationships; they spend lots of time cultivating social relationships and reciprocating social information. In contrast, members of individualistic and low power distance cultures spend most of the time on self-disclosure and exchanging information on their private life (Gudykunst et al., 1988). As a result, members of individualistic cultures have fewer rules regulating self-disclosure than members of collectivistic cultures. Also, in collectivistic cultures there are many rules related to harmonious relations as these cultures emphasize group harmony, unlike individualistic cultures that emphasize self-assertion and self-reliance (DeRivera, 1977). In collectivistic cultures, where people avoid public confrontations and negative criticism, there are many rules prohibiting public criticism. In individualistic cultures people are less concerned with public criticism. Members of high uncertainty avoidance cultures also have many rules supporting conforming behavior as opposed to the members of low uncertainty avoidance cultures, who tolerate violation of formal rules of behavior. In addition, in masculine cultures there are more rules of performance than rules maintaining harmonious relations.

Asian cultures, such as Japan or Hong Kong, have many rules dealing with public and human interaction, regulating conflict, avoiding public disagreement and criticism, restraining emotions, saving face, hierarchy and power differences, obeying people in authority, exchanging obligations, repaying debt, gift-giving and receiving, prohibiting jokes, teasing, and teaching positive regard, respecting privacy, parents, ancestors, and obligations (Argyle et al., 1986; Befu, 1971; Benedict, 1967; Morsbach, 1977). The Japanese have many formal rules regulating public interactions (Doi, 1973), relations with supervisors and subordinates at work, restraining and obedience rules and rules concerned with loyalty, group harmony, conflict avoidance and ''face saving'' (Lebra, 1976).

SUMMARY

Rules of social relationship play a very important role in human interactions. Their role is to coordinate behavior, avoid conflict, and maintain harmonious interactions. There are universal and culture-specific rules of social behavior. There are differences in rules of social behavior among various cultures. Knowledge of the rules of social behavior governing inter- or cross-cultural tourist–host interaction is an important element for improving tourists' and hosts' relationships with each other.

DISCUSSION POINTS AND QUESTIONS

1. What is the role of rules of social behavior?
2. Identify five rules of social interaction that are universal in all cultures, and five that are different.
3. Identify universal rules of social interaction that should be followed by tourists and hosts in their social interaction.
4. Identify cultural differences in rules of social interaction related to Hofstede's (1980) four cultural dimensions, that is, individualism and collectivism, power distance, uncertainty avoidance, and masculinity and femininity.
5. Describe and explain the behavior of persons from other than your own cultures in the area of social and professional interaction.
6. Cultures differ when it comes to entertaining business visitors. What is done in your culture to entertain guests?

CASE STUDY 9.1 Universal and Specific Rules of Social Relationships

British researchers (Argyle & Henderson, 1984, 1985a, 1985b; Argyle et al., 1985, 1986) examined the relationship rules in England, Italy, Hong Kong, and Japan, by asking the respondents to rate the importance of common and specific relationship rules on a nine-point bipolar scale. Relationships rules were found to be important elements of social relationships in all four cultures. Many cultures had similar rules. Numerous similarities in rule endorsement among the four cultural groups were identified. For instance, there were consistent rules for professional formal relationships such as watching one's personal appearance, showing courtesy and respect, and avoiding social intimacy. The universal rules highly endorsed across most of the social relationships and common to all situations were: (a) one should respect others' privacy; (b) one should look the other person in the eye during conversation; (c) one should not discuss what is said in confidence; (d) one should or should not indulge in sexual activity; (e) one should not criticize the other in public; and (f) one should repay debts, favors, or compliments no matter how small. The only rule endorsed for all social relationships in all four cultures was respect for privacy. However, this rule might have different meanings in different cultures. There were also specific rules for social relationships in the four cultures. For instance, the rules for close friendships endorsed in Japan were quite different from those endorsed in Italy. The Japanese placed less emphasis on the expression of emotion, opinions, showing affection, and requesting help and advice than did Italians. There was a difference in rules relating to intimacy. In the Eastern clusters there were more rules about obedience, avoidance of conflict and saving face, maintaining harmonious relations, restraining emotional expressions, and ''losing face'' because of the importance of self-presentation. In Hong Kong rules about showing respect for parents were important. In Japan there were more rules for hierarchical work relations, fewer for family, more rules concerned with avoidance of conflict and out-groups. The Japanese did not have many rules about exchange of rewards (Argyle et al., 1986) which was not supported by the well-known custom of gift exchange in Japan (Morsbach, 1977). This could be explained by the fact that the study had a British origin and it did not include Japanese specific rules concerning such things as expressing humility, using indirect form of refusal, asking strangers personal questions, and not expressing personal opinions (Naotsuka & Sakamoto, 1981).

WEBSITES

1. Social etiquette in Australia: http://www.convictcreations.com/culture/socialrules.htm
2. Dress and behavioral rules in Islamic countries: http://www.enel.ucalgary.ca/People/far/hobbies/iran/dress.html

Since the rules of social behavior affect perceptions of service, the next chapter will discuss the concept of service and cultural differences in service perception.

Cultural influences on service 10

The aim of this chapter is to explore the influence of national culture on service and identify cultural differences in service perception.

OBJECTIVES

After completing this chapter the reader should be able to:
- Understand the concept of service, service quality and satisfaction with service
- Understand the role and importance of cultural influences on service
- Identify cultural differences in service perception among various nations

INTRODUCTION

National culture is an important factor influencing expectations and perceptions of service quality and satisfaction with service. Different cultural groups attach different importance to service quality criteria. The examples of cultural differences in service quality perceptions and expectations are presented.

10.1 THE CONCEPT OF SERVICE

Services are intangible activities or benefits one party can offer to another; they do not result in the ownership of anything. Services are provided in every sector of the economy: retailing, wholesaling, transportation, telecommunication, finance, health, education, and many other sectors, including tourism, hospitality, and leisure. Tourists create demand for a wide range of services, such as transportation, communication, accommodation, catering, attractions, activities, entertainment, and information (e.g. language interpretation and translation). These services cater directly to tourist needs. **233**

Tourists also create demand for indirect services, such as financial, medical, insurance, retailing, wholesaling, cleaning, printing, drinking water, sewerage, and electricity. Without indirect services, the provision of direct services would be impossible. As a result, a tourism product is mostly a service rather than a tangible product.

10.2 SERVICE ENCOUNTER

The focus of service is on the service process, performance, or service encounter, which has been defined as the (1) interaction between the customer and the firm or service provider; (2) a period of time during which a provider and a consumer confront each other; and (3) a ''moment of truth'' – a moment during which customers evaluate how closely their service expectations are met. What happens between a customer and a provider during this ''moment of truth'' determines the quality of the services offered to a customer, and a customer's satisfaction with service.

10.3 SERVICE CLASSIFICATION

The degree of personal contact with the service encounter allows for distinguishing among different types of services, such as (1) maintenance-interactive (characterized by little interaction between the provider and customer because of little risk in trans-actions, e.g. in fast food restaurant services); (2) task-interactive (characterized by a higher degree of interaction because of greater risk in transaction; customers depend upon the service providers for information and expertise, e.g. banking services, brokerage services); and (3) personal-interactive services (require the most intense inter-action between the provider and customer, a high degree of customization, information exchange, and trust, e.g. tourism and hospitality services) (Mills, 1986).

10.4 KEY CHARACTERISTICS OF SERVICE

Services are characterized by intangibility, heterogeneity, inseparability, perishability, lack of ownership, and the importance of people and their characteristics.

Intangibility

Services are intangible; they cannot be seen, tasted, felt, heard, or smelled before purchase. As a result, it is difficult to evaluate and compare them. A customer buys experiences (e.g. the hotel atmosphere, the way the customer is treated at the front desk), benefits (e.g. physical comfort of a hotel bed, or psychological, such as enjoy-ment and happiness) and memories, rather than a tangible product. Most services offer a combination of intangible and tangible elements of service. For example, restaurants offer an intangible product in the form of atmosphere or advice on food and beverage selection, as well as a tangible product in the form of food. Airlines offer intangible elements in the form of transportation, and tangible elements in the form of aircraft, food, seat, pillows, and blankets. The hotels offer intangible elements, such as the atmosphere of a hotel lobby, and tangible elements, such as the design and architecture of a hotel. Service evaluation depends on the individual customer's preferences, and the importance attached to tangible and intangible elements of service. Different cultural groups attach different importance to tangible and intangible elements of service. For example, the Japanese tourists have the lowest expectations from tangibles (physical facilities and surroundings, equipment, and appearance of personnel) when compared to tourists from the United Kingdom, the United States, Australia, and Taiwan (Mok & Armstrong, 1998).

Heterogeneity

Services are highly variable (heterogeneous); they vary because they are delivered by people-to-people. Each service experience is different depending upon who performs it, when it is performed, and the circumstances under which it is performed (e.g. demand, seasonality). The provider's performance fluctuates on a daily, weekly, and even monthly basis and depends on the provider's moods and feelings as well as professional skills. Similarly, service depends on the customer to whom it is offered. The consumers' and providers' socio-demographic, economic, psychological, and cultural profiles affect the way the service is performed, delivered and evaluated. In particular, the cultural background is of critical importance, as it determines the provider's and the consumer's perceptions of what a high standard of service is, and the consumer's needs and expectations from service. It is difficult to achieve consistency of service performance and uniformity in service quality. As a result, services must be customized for each consumer group or situation. Different cultural groups require different levels and types of customized services. For example, a good hotel room in Australia for the Japanese tourist must have a big bath and slippers, whereas for the British tourist it must have an ocean view and air-conditioning. It is a challenge to provide services to culturally different customers whose needs and standards may be different from those of the providers.

Inseparability

Tourism services are sold first and then produced and consumed simultaneously. For example, a passenger first purchases an airline ticket and then consumes the in-flight service as it is produced. A tourist who wishes to go on vacation must travel to the destination to consume the services offered at the destination. Thus, tourism services require simultaneous presence of the customer and service provider during their production and consumption. As a result, tourism services are offered during the tourist's interaction with providers. The quality of this interaction is of critical importance for service evaluation. Different cultural groups attach different importance to the quality of personal interactions. For example, the collectivistic Asian cultures attach relatively more importance to the quality of the interpersonal element of service than physical facilities or equipment, whereas individualistic Western cultures pay more attention to service promptness, reliability, and tangible elements of service.

Perishability

Tourism services are perishable; they cannot be stored. They must be consumed at the point of production. For example, it is not possible to save the spare seat on a flight that is leaving today and move the whole flight experience from today to tomorrow if tomorrow's flight is overbooked. The unsold airline ticket cannot be used at a later date because the unsold service is ''lost.'' Once the plane departs, the empty seats cannot be sold. Similarly, the unsold hotel room cannot be stored and used one night later. Although most tourism and hospitality services cannot be stored, some hospitality sectors can store part of their service process. For example, restaurants can store their meals for a limited period of time. However, they cannot store the entire dining experience by saving spare capacity on a Friday evening for the Saturday evening peak.

Since tourism services are short-lived, airlines must try to fill all seats on all flights, hotels must fill all rooms each night, and restaurants must fill all seats each evening. The value of their services exists only when the travelers fly, spend overnight at the hotel and dine in the restaurant. For this reason, it is imperative to make appropriate adjustments to the cultural needs for the level and range of services offered to airline passengers or hotel and restaurant guests in order to secure their demand for services.

Ownership

The purchase and consumption of hotel or airline services does not result in ownership of airlines or hotel chains. When travelers purchase airline services, they purchase a temporary right to a transportation service. However, they do not purchase the right to own the service or the title to that service. The traveler can own only the benefits of the transportation service (e.g. the flight experience, in-flight entertainment, the memory of the flight attendant's smile, or the opportunity to socialize with other travelers), not the service itself. But when the traveler arrives at the destination, he/she owns only an old ticket and boarding card. As a result, the price that the traveler pays for tourism services is the price for the benefits and experiences received, including the provider's welcoming attitude, friendliness, and smile. However, there are considerable differences among cultural groups in attaching importance to the service benefits and experiences, and thus willingness, to pay for particular services. While Asian tourists attach relatively more importance to the manner in which the service provider delivers the service, Western tourists attach more importance to what the customer actually receives from the service.

People-based and personality-dependent

Tourism, hospitality, and leisure services are provided by people and for people. The people (providers and consumers) are part of the service process and experience. The behavior of providers and consumers can ruin or enhance the service experience. The providers' emotions, skills, knowledge, and the way they perform service determine consumers' experiences with the service. Providers who show personal interest in the customer, are appreciative of the customer, tactful, attentive, responsive, caring, prompt, honest, and neatly dressed enhance the service experience. Similarly, customers who show an interest in the provider's culture, ask questions, and are friendly and respectful can also enhance the service experience. However, if the travel consultants are rude and unwelcoming, tourists may not purchase a package tour. If the guests are unable to communicate their needs adequately, front office employees may not be able to guarantee their guests a hotel room with an ocean view.

10.5 IMPORTANCE OF SERVICE PERCEPTIONS

The tourism and hospitality industry relies heavily on the positive perceptions of people providing services to tourists: restaurateurs, hotel staff, flight attendants, salespeople and cashiers in shops, waitresses, and tour guides. The tourist's perceptions of the service providers determine the overall perceptions of the tourism product quality. The best quality of attractions, accommodation, transportation, amenities, and activities will not attract tourists if the service quality is poor and tourists feel unwelcome.

The service providers' characteristics influence customers' perceptions of service. If the providers are friendly, tactful, and respectful, the services are perceived positively, whereas when the providers are rude, slow, and uncaring, the services are perceived negatively. Negative perceptions of service deter tourists from visitation and discourage repeat purchases, whereas positive perceptions of service encourage tourists to buy the product again.

However, perceptions of services are very subjective and depend upon the individual cultural profile and cultural standards that define high quality services. When the customers' cultural expectations and needs are met, service quality is perceived as good, but when the cultural expectations are not met, service quality is perceived as poor.

10.6 CULTURAL DIFFERENCES IN EXPECTATIONS FROM SERVICE

The national culture of tourists and hosts influence expectations from service and what is perceived to be a proper treatment of guests (Sheldon & Fox, 1988; Wei et al., 1989). What is regarded to be good quality service in Europe or the United States (individualistic cultures) may not be regarded as such in Japan or China (collectivistic cultures). For instance, in China the host ignores the expectations of the guests. The hosts escort their guests everywhere, provide them with a very tight itinerary, and do not leave any opportunity for guests to experience Chinese life on their own. The Chinese believe that occupying every moment of the guests' time is demonstrating courtesy. However, Western tourists from Europe or the United States may perceive such hospitality as being very uncomfortable and an intrusion of privacy. On the other had, Japanese hosts, anticipate the guests' needs in advance and take care of the affairs of their guests and even try to fulfill them beyond needs (Befu, 1971). The Japanese believe that the hosts shall know best what the guests' needs are. Such an attitude toward service and guests may also be frustrating for Western tourists who think they know best what their needs are. Western tourists may also regard Japanese hospitality as uncomfortable. On the other hand, the Western tradition of not anticipating the guests' needs in advance and giving the guests "free time" to do whatever they wish to do may be perceived negatively by the Japanese tourists and affect their satisfaction with the hospitality of the Western host. The cultural differences in expectations from services among tourists and providers may develop many negative perceptions.

Considerable differences in expectations from service were found among airline passengers from Japan, Korea, China, and the United States in areas such as duty-free purchases, availability of in-flight reading materials, and requests for additional food and beverages. For example, Japanese passengers exhibited the highest tendency to treat attendants with respect, and Chinese and Korean passengers exhibited the highest tendency to hinder work of attendants due to frequent demands (Kim & Prideaux, 2003).

10.7 SERVICE QUALITY AND VALUE

Service quality refers to the appropriateness of assistance and support provided to a customer and the value and benefits received for the price paid. It is difficult for tourists to judge the quality of the intangible service. The only reliable evaluation criteria are the price and the physical environment in which the service is offered. However, the price cannot always be used as a measure of evaluation as it is set up by a producer and does not reflect the perceived value and benefits for individual consumers. The difficulty of defining a service quality is also enhanced by its subjective nature. Moreover, most tourism services are high in experience properties, which can only be assessed after purchase or during consumption (e.g. taste, credibility, atmosphere, friendliness, meals) and credence properties, which cannot be assessed confidently even after purchase and/or consumption (e.g. competence, reputation, security). As a result, tourism services are the hardest to evaluate or even impossible to evaluate even after purchase (Darby & Karni, 1973; Nelson, 1974).

In order to facilitate the evaluation of service quality, several distinct quality dimensions were identified: (1) physical (physical aspects of the service); (2) corporate (organization's image or profile); (3) interactive (derives from the interaction between contact personnel and the customer) (Lehtinen & Lehtinen, 1982); (4) procedural (mechanistic in nature, the quality of selling and distributing a product to a customer); (5) convivial (interpersonal in nature, emphasizes the service providers' positive attitudes to customers, appropriate verbal and non-verbal skills) (Martin, 1987); (6) technical (what the consumer actually receives from the service as a result of the interaction with the service provider); and (7) functional (the manner in which the service provider delivers the service to a customer) (Gronroos, 1984). The interactive, convivial and functional dimensions are interpersonal in nature. These dimensions refer to the provider's characteristics, such as showing interest in the customer, being friendly, appreciative, suggestive, tactful, attentive to customer needs, willing to help, so the customer can feel liked, respected, relaxed, comfortable, important, even pampered and, most importantly, welcomed. The interactive, convivial, and functional dimensions of service quality are vital to the assessment of the overall quality of service (Parasuraman et al., 1985, 1986; Urry, 1991).

The 10 most popular criteria used by consumers in assessing service are reliability, responsiveness, competence, access, courtesy, communication, credibility, security, understanding and knowing the customer, and tangibility. These criteria were grouped into five major dimensions of service quality: tangibles, reliability, responsiveness, assurance, and empathy (Parasuraman et al., 1985, 1986).

The importance attached by consumers to service quality criteria and dimensions differs among various cultures. For example, it was found that tourists from the United Kingdom, United States, Australia, Japan, and Taiwan had different expectations for the tangibles and empathy dimensions in terms of hotel service. Asian tourists attached more importance to the empathy dimension, whereas Western tourists attached more importance to tangibles and reliability (Mok & Armstrong, 1998). Members of the status-conscious societies attach more importance to the formality of service than egalitarian societies, whereas members of the individualistic societies attach more importance to personalization of service than collectivistic societies (Winsted, 1999).

Significant differences in service evaluation were found among members of low- and high-masculine cultures. Those from low-masculine cultures (e.g. Brazil, Taiwan) who were more sympathetic toward others evaluated airport facilities more positively and were more loyal to airlines. Those from the high-masculine cultures, who were more assertive and judgmental and had less concern for the feelings of others gave lower ratings of airline service quality and were less loyal to airlines. Also, those from low-masculine societies reported satisfaction more often, whereas those from high-masculine societies reported dissatisfaction more often. The reason was that individuals from low-masculine societies might be more willing to disregard perceived shortcoming of service and criticize less when compared to others from more masculine societies (Crotts & Erdmann, 2000). Also, Pakistani passengers were found to be far more patient that other customers when a carrier serving London to Pakistan was delayed for departure for seven hours. Most British passengers demanded to be transferred to another airline after three hours, and American passengers threatened to sue the airlines after four hours (Crotts & Erdmann, 2000). Pakistan (50) scored lower on the Hofstede's masculinity index than the United Kingdom (66) and the United States (62).

10.8 SERVICE SATISFACTION

While service quality is concerned with the attributes of service and the development of positive perceptions of service, satisfaction refers to the psychological outcome deriving from service experience, or customer's feelings and emotions developed in response to an evaluation of service and service experience. Usually a high quality of service, which develops positive service perceptions, results in high satisfaction, whereas poor quality of service develops negative perceptions of service and dissatisfaction. Thus, service quality determines customer satisfaction, and both are vastly dependent upon the perceptions of the quality of service encounter.

Often, the service providers' attitudes to the customer, verbal skills, knowledge of the customer needs and wants may give the customer more satisfaction than the pure mechanistic delivery of service. Thus, positive social interaction between a service provider and customer may generate high satisfaction with service, and compensate the low quality of mechanistic service.

The importance of service quality dimensions to consumer satisfaction differs among various cultures. For example, Winsted (1999), who analyzed the importance of service dimensions in the United States and Japan, found that Japanese consumer satisfaction with service was influenced by formality of service, whereas the US consumer satisfaction was influenced by personalization of service. Choi and Chu (2000) found that Asian travelers' satisfaction derived mainly from the value factor, whereas Western travelers' satisfaction was influenced by the room quality factor.

10.9 DO CULTURAL DIFFERENCES ALWAYS MATTER?

It is generally assumed that the national culture of the service provider and customer influence the evaluation of service quality and satisfaction with service because national culture teaches about the acceptable standard of service and how to perform service. Thus, individuals from different cultures evaluate service performance differently and have different expectations and perceptions of service requiring specific attention to different elements of services. As a result, problems may arise in intercultural service encounters in which service providers and customers are from different cultural backgrounds and have different views of what the service quality means. The mismatch may be between service quality expectations and perceptions of customers from foreign cultures, and quality expectations and perceptions of domestic providers. Understanding the cultural differences in attaching importance to various service quality dimensions could help in determining the types of service expected by culturally different customers.

However, expectations and perceptions of service quality depend on cultural proximity or cultural distance between providers and customers. Cultural distance among various nations was classified along a continuum from global to local. In between these two extremes there is a vast range of subcultures that equally govern tourist behavior and influence perceptions of service quality. Each type of distance has a different influence on the perceptions of service quality and satisfaction with service. The closer tourists' culture is in terms of experiencing cross-cultural service encounter, the more critical tourists are in terms of perceiving and judging service quality and satisfaction. The further away tourists are from experiencing the cross-cultural, the less demanding and more tolerant they tend to be regarding service quality (Weiermair, 2000).

Also, cultural differences seem to be important only for certain specific service quality dimensions. Tourists are more tolerant and less critical of experiences involving authentic products/services (e.g. local service, food, entertainment, appearance of people). Tourists are more critical about services with shared values such as transportation services, security, aesthetics, freedom of choice or variety and fun, accessibility of services, and specific tourist activities, such a shopping. These are evaluated similarly (more critically) regardless of cultural proximity or distance (Weiermair & Fuchs, 1999).

The increase in travel exposure and experience leads to globally universal and converging service quality demands, particularly with respect to technical quality dimension (as opposed to functional) (Gronroos, 1984). Transportation services, both to and from the destination, are perceived, evaluated, and judged as important to all tourists due to globally shared values and standards. In particular, convenience of travel, punctuality of travel schedules, and customer orientation are of importance (Weiermair & Fuchs, 2000). Cultural differences play a more important role in influencing perception and evaluation of such service quality criteria as waiting times and queuing, added service components and the choice of transportation mode (Becker & Murmann, 1999).

SUMMARY

Services are intangible activities or benefits one party offers to another. Services are characterized by intangibility, heterogeneity, inseparability, perishability, and lack of ownership. They are people-based and personality-dependent. There are cultural differences in service expectations, evaluation, and satisfaction. Different cultural groups attach different importance to service quality criteria and dimensions. However, cultural differences seem to matter only for specific service-quality dimensions. The increase in travel exposure leads to globally universal quality demands with respect to some quality dimensions.

DISCUSSION POINTS AND QUESTIONS

1. Does national culture influence consumers' evaluation of travel services? If yes, why?
2. Identify some differences in service in different cultures.
3. Give some practical examples of how national culture influences satisfaction with services.

> **CASE STUDY 10.1 Chinese Travelers in France**
>
> The opening of China's borders has allowed Chinese people to travel abroad. France is a very popular tourism destination for Chinese travelers. Unfortunately, the products and services offered in France are not yet fully customized for Chinese travelers. The increasing number of the Chinese visitors to France is concerned about the service in hotels, restaurants, and airports.
>
> Chinese travelers avoid risk when traveling abroad; they usually purchase organized pre-paid tour packages and travel in groups; they seek familiarity and safety, and like to eat in Chinese restaurants. When they are taken to French restaurants they are disappointed; they complain and refuse to tip. Also, they do not understand why they cannot smoke in public areas.
>
> French tourism professionals must better understand the Chinese culture to be able to customize their products/services and meet the Chinese travelers' needs. Currently, actions are being taken to help to communicate with Chinese travelers. In Paris, Chinese signs are being introduced in places of tourist attractions. Promotional brochures and tourist guides are printed in Mandarin, and the industry personnel is learning Chinese phrases. Audio-guides in Mandarin are frequently used. The Accor and InterContinental hotel chains offer tea sets, Chinese newspapers and Asian-style breakfast to the Chinese travelers craving for comforts of their homes.
>
> Chinese outbound travel is expected to grow in the next few years. The cultural differences between European countries and China present a real challenge. The tourism representatives have to develop sensitivity to Chinese needs and use the cultural knowledge when designing products to meet the Chinese cultural expectations and traditions.

WEBSITE LINKS

1. Cultural differences: Service: http://neuropetravel.suite101.com/blog.cfm/cultural_differences_service

Since in a global competitive world people and businesses are expected to behave in an ethical manner the next chapter will discuss the concept of ethics and cultural differences in ethics.

Cultural influences on ethics

11

The aim of this chapter is to explain the concept of ethics and identify cultural differences in ethical behavior.

OBJECTIVES

After completing this chapter the reader should be able to:
- Understand the concept of ethics and ethical behavior
- Explain the importance of ethics in tourism
- Define ethics in a cross-cultural context
- Explain cultural influences on ethical behavior
- Understand the most debatable business ethical issues
- Identify the main conflicting ethical behavior practices and ethical dilemmas
- Learn about ethical theories and frameworks dealing with ethical dilemmas
- Identify strategies for managing ethical dilemmas
- Learn about the Global Code of Ethics for Tourism

INTRODUCTION

In today's global and very competitive environment people and businesses are expected to behave in an ethical manner and follow ethical standards of behavior. These standards are dictated by ethical norms. Various ethical norms are commonly held by people around the world, such as those that condemn murder, theft, lying, and so on. These norms are central to human existence and to life in society. However, there are norms that are viewed as ethical in one country and unethical in another country. The challenge is to behave in an ethical manner and follow the ethical standards dictated by local hosts. If businesses and people do not behave in an ethical manner, they may face negative consumer or public reactions and even government prosecution that can generate negative publicity and even litigation (Saee, 2005).

THE CONCEPT OF ETHICS

What is ethics? Ethics is the set of universally accepted moral principles and values that govern the behavior of a person or group in terms of what is right and wrong. Ethics is concerned with how people think about and behave towards each other; how the consequences of their decisions and behavior impact human life (Saee, 2005).

What is business ethics? Business ethics is about the rightness or the wrongness of business practices. Business ethics is guided by principles of commercial relationships (Dirksen & Kroeger, 1973) and right and moral standards applied within an enterprise (Holt & Wigginton, 2002) that indicate what is good and right for business (Hoffman & Moore, 1990).

What is the difference between ethics and morality?

Ethics is the basis for developing a system of morality and the moral laws that evolve from ethics. Morality is the activity that governs appropriate human conduct in a given culture (Churchill, 1982). People's behavior is guided by moral rules and obligations that show how to behave. People have many moral obligations in their lives. For example, it is a moral obligation to care for parents and children, and even to support one's country.

How is ethical behavior developed?

Ethical behavior is developed by people through their physical, emotional, and cognitive abilities. People learn ethical behavior from families, friends, experiences, religious beliefs, educational institutions, and media (Saee, 2005). Business ethics is shaped by societal ethics.

What is ethical behavior?

Ethical behavior is that which is socially responsible. Socially responsible behavior is that which enhances the human welfare and interest of society as well as the organization. Examples of socially responsible behavior are obeying the law, telling the truth, showing respect for people, not harming anyone or anything, acting responsibly, fighting for human rights, guaranteeing product safety, protecting the environment, or protecting local culture and heritage (Saee, 2005). Examples of socially irresponsible behavior are bribery and extortion, patent and copyright infringement, lying and deceit about product performance and safety, use of substances harmful to the environment, international environmental pollution, discrimination, dangerous working conditions, violations of promises, misleading advertising and financial reporting, and distorting images (Saee, 2005). Nowadays, people and businesses are expected to be socially responsible and adapt ethical manners. The concept of Corporate Social Responsibility is increasingly accepted by companies. Private and public organizations now publish annual reports that include the goals, strategies, and achievements of social responsibility.

Is ethical behavior the same as legal behavior?

Certain ethical behaviors are illegal, such as strikes or activities of environmentalists who often break laws in order to protect the environment. Also, many unethical behaviors such as cheating or lying to a customer are not illegal, but they can lead to negative outcomes (being rejected by a customer). People and businesses must not only behave ethically but also act according to moral law. Thus, ethical behavior must also be legal.

How can ethical business behavior be achieved?

Ethical business behavior can be achieved through respecting the human rights of consumers, employees, honoring the local host culture and local people, supporting the ecosystem and consumer safety, cooperating with the local government in developing new industries and enforcing just institutions (laws and regulations), paying a fair share of taxes, following the local laws when operating in a cross-cultural environment, not harming anyone intentionally, contributing to the host country's development, and practicing the golden rule, ''Do as you would be done by others.''

11.1 ETHICS IN TOURISM

Ethics is very important for international tourism. Ethics and social responsibility are the foundation of successful sustainable tourism development. Ethical behavior in tourism requires understanding and promoting ethical values common to humanity, tolerating and respecting the diversity of religious and moral beliefs, observing the social and cultural traditions and practices of all people, including those of minorities and indigenous people, protecting natural environment and cultural heritage, safeguarding tourists against crime, assaults, or other threats such as defective products, unethical behavior of sales representatives, guaranteeing them safety and security, providing them with accurate and reliable information, assisting with their particular needs, and protecting tourism facilities. Ethical behavior in tourism also requires protecting the industry employees from unethical practices (e.g. unsafe work environment), protecting businesses from unethical behavior of employees, (e.g. harming the good name of the business) and from unethical competitors (e.g. price fixing). Ethical behavior requires protecting society (e.g. against disregard for social and cultural values or economic fraud) and protecting the value system of the society (Saee, 2005). Everyone involved in tourism development – individuals, organizations, and society – must behave ethically in order to enhance the society and the individual's welfare.

Ethics is extremely important in tourism marketing, especially in effective segmentation, communication of appropriate destination messages, creation of awareness of the nature of a tourist resource and destination image, and realization of the fragility of the environment (Wheeler, 1995). For example, businesses often use promotional techniques and view pricing as the main factor in attracting an additional numbers of tourists. The impact of such activities on the environment is very visible and ranges from the destruction of wildlife species, erosion of footpaths in national parks, and the destruction of coastlines by high-rise development. Travel brochures often promise sunny, clean, non-crowded destinations in order to create a positive destination image in the mind of potential tourists. However, businesses also have the responsibility to ensure that such images are consistent with reality and do not disappoint tourists (Wheeler, 1995).

The development of tourism on a large scale brings environmental and socio-cultural disruptions. The right question to ask is whether tourism development and encouraging tourists to travel around the world are ethical. Some have doubts about it. An ethical response to the environmental problems caused by mass tourism is green or eco-friendly tourism, which supports small-scale controlled developments that are in harmony with the environment and target more sensitive, educated, and ethical travelers. The concept of green or eco-friendly tourism calls for saving species, looking after the countryside, preserving the world's culture and heritage, abandoning materialistic and egoistic values and moving towards caring, sharing, being socially, culturally, and environmentally sensitive, and making morally right choices (Wheeler, 1995). Consequently, the concept of green tourism is ethical and socially responsible.

Urban destinations are themselves increasingly paying attention to the environment. For example, under the leadership of Prince Albert, the Principality of Monaco makes efforts towards sustainable development. The main tourism business in Monaco, the *Société des Bains de Mer*, owner of hotels, restaurants, resorts, spas, and the world-famous Monte Carlo Casino, has recently been actively involved in developing an environmental charter to reduce energy consumption and gas emissions. But is attracting luxury jet travelers from the world over consistent with such environmental concerns?

The tourism industry has a long way to go on the path toward corporate social responsibility. Travelmole reported in a 2008 story (http://www.travelmole.com) that: VisitBritain, the marketing agency for British tourism, has a clearly stated policy to green the whole of the British tourism offer. The organisation's mission is to "Take Green Tourism from Niche to Mainstream by 2010" and its tag line states "Promoting Sustainable Businesses – Encouraging Responsible Visitors". It couldn't get much more straightforward than that. However, of England's 59 000 known tourism establishments (hotels and visitor attractions), currently just 300 have expressed interest in VisitBritain's Green Tourism beginner accreditation scheme – Green Start.

11.2 ETHICS IN A CROSS-CULTURAL CONTEXT

In a cross-cultural context, such as international tourism, ethics is a difficult term to explain and adapt. In an international context, ethics refers to a very complicated set of social and cultural obligations and responsibilities that often cannot be easily fulfilled in a way consistent with the norms and values placed upon ethics in the domestic environment. What is ethical behavior in one country can often be viewed as unethical in another country (Saee, 2005). For example, present-giving in the Middle East is accepted as ethical, whereas in the Western world, it is considered bribery and unethical. Thus, in the international environment, ethical problems may arise due to cultural differences in perceiving what is right and wrong.

11.3 CULTURAL INFLUENCES ON ETHICAL BEHAVIOR

Differences in ethical behavior are due to different cultural, social, and economic factors (Buller et al., 1991). Culture, in particular, influences business ethics and social responsibility. Culture represents a set of standards for what is right and wrong, produces different expectations and ethical norms, and therefore dissimilar behaviors. People learn their ethical norms and values from their cultural environments. As a result, individuals from different countries, nations, or wider cultural groups differ with respect to their moral and ethical intentions (Srnka, 1997).

Cultural values are especially strong predictors of ethical behavior. Cultural values determine what is ethical and what is not ethical. Thus, in different cultures there are different ethical values. Consequently, ethical decisions are difficult to make when different cultural values are followed (Srnka, 1997). Cultural values also affect perceptions of ethical dilemmas.

What is ethical behavior depends on circumstances and is affected by culturally determined social obligations and ties of an individual (de Bettignies, 1991, cited in Schneider & Barsoux, 1997). For example, in Western countries, such as the United States, ethical decisions are considered to be personal and require personal responsibility, accountability, morality, and self-criticism. Ethical behavior is defined in terms of an individual who "has to live with himself or herself rather than with others." "Ethics is considered as a question of personal scruples, a confidential matter between individuals and their consciences" (Vogel, 1992). On the other hand, in Europe and Asia, ethical decisions are considered to be more "consensual." In Asia, for example, ethical behavior and morality are defined in terms of others, interdependence rather independence (Markus & Kitayama, 1991). It is believed that those who do not belong to the group and do not share the same values are not concerned for the welfare of the group and thus are not given an opportunity to make a business.

Culture influences how ethics is defined and judged. For example, in the United States, ethics is viewed as universal; the same rules of ethical behavior apply to everyone. These rules are explicit (low-context culture), presented in written forms and displayed throughout the company; everyone should comply with these rules. In contrast, in France no one needs written rules of ethical behavior because these rules traditionally were developed hundreds of years ago and passed from generation to generation; French learned the ethical rules transmitted from their ancestors; they knew how they should conduct themselves in their lives (Vogel, 1992).

Cultures influence the application of the business codes of conduct (Schneider & Barsoux, 1997). A code of conduct is ''a statement setting down corporate principles of ethics, rules of conduct, codes of practice or company philosophy concerning responsibility of employees, shareholders, consumers, the environment or any other aspects of society external to the company'' (Langlosis & Schlegelmilch, 1990). Nearly all US firms have codes of conduct; 51% of the German firms and only 30% of the French firms have codes of conduct.

The content of the codes of conduct differs among cultures. For example, the European codes of conduct focus on employees' attitudes and behaviors towards the company (the collective), while the US codes focus on company policy towards employees (the individual). For US firms it is important to treat employees with fairness and equity, and ensure equal opportunity rights, while for the French and British firms it is important to stress the significance of employees to the organization, a sense of their belonging and collective goals. While German firms emphasize shared responsibility, reliability, and loyalty as well as technology and innovation, the French focus on customer-relations (Schneider & Barsoux, 1997).

There are differences in resolving ethical dilemmas among nations. The US managers are more likely to consult with their bosses than Hong Kong managers, whereas Hong Kong managers are more likely to discuss the issue with friends. These differences show evidence of greater collectivism among the Hong Kong managers when compared to those in the United States: sharing information, group consensus, conformity, and loyalty. Laws and regulations appear to be unnecessary in Hong Kong; public exposure and loss of face are considered sufficient punishment for unethical behavior (Becker & Fritzsche, 1987).

However, culture is not the only important determinant of business ethical decision-making. There are also other factors such as gender, age, education, religion, politics, and institutional factors that determine people's perceptions of what is right and what is wrong.

11.4 THE MOST DEBATABLE BUSINESS ETHICS ISSUES

Today, the most debatable ethical issues in business are: (1) Should the goal of a business be profit or ethics? (2) Is it ethical or unethical to make a profit? (3) Is profit more important than ethics? (4) Should ethics be a necessity in conducting international business? (5) Are there universal rules of ethics and can they be applied? (6) Is it possible to define what is ethical in a global world? (Schneider & Barsoux, 1997). The answer to these questions is: it all depends on culture.

Should the goal of a business be profit or ethics?

In many Western cultures the main goal of businesses is profit maximization. Nearly 50% of US American managers chose profit accumulation as their main goal (Trompenaars, 1993). Western work ethics teaches that it is moral to make money and work for profit; organizations and managers should be driven by the "bottom line," financial gains, and self-interest. However, in France, working for profit is sometimes viewed with suspicion. French people believe that social status and prestige do not derive from what the person does or earns; rather, it involves who the person is, the person's culture/education, and his/her relationships and family connections (ascription versus achievement). In Russia, under Communist ideology, making profit was treated as being selfish and unethical. In Japan, a major goal of business is taking care of stakeholders and employees. Only 4% of the Japanese chose profit as the main business goal (Trompenaars, 1993). However, today, in a globalized and very competitive world there is a growing number of Western companies that promote the well-being of society and are concerned about their social responsibilities and stakeholders (Schneider & Barsoux, 1997); the same is true of Asian companies that promote making money. One must note, however, that the meaning of profit is interpreted differently in different cultures (Schneider & Barsoux, 1997).

Is it ethical or unethical to make a profit?

Many US Americans think about profit as a "bottom line." They believe it is ethical to close factories, lay off workers, and neglect obligations towards them in order to maintain financial gains. However, Europeans and Asians believe that such behavior may be unethical; it proves the lack of social conscience. Further, many Americans and Australians frequently change jobs for an increase in pay or promotion. In Japan and other Asian countries, job changes are less frequent and seen as immoral. However, today, when European and Asian countries face economic recession and increased competition, they also opt for restructuring and downsizing. This creates anxiety and fear among employees who lose jobs and social benefits. As a result, the companies that behaved ethically in the past may now behave unethically in the face of increased globalization and competition (Saee, 2005).

Is profit more important than ethics?

In different cultures companies have different ways of doing business; they pursue different goals. Some companies believe that making profit is more important than being socially responsible. Other companies believe that social responsibility is more important than profit, and they sacrifice their economic gains. For example, Levi Strauss pulled its $40 million business out of the lucrative Chinese market to protest against human rights violations in China (Schneider & Barsoux, 1997). Other companies argue that being socially responsible depends on profitability. By producing and selling more, they boost their profits, create employment in the local community, and contribute to its development. There are also companies that are financially successful by following the social responsibility principles. For example, companies such as The Body Shop or cosmetic companies make huge profits by selling ''natural'' products and following the policy of ''no animal testing.''

Should ethics be a necessity in conducting international business?

Some believe that ethics is a fundamental necessity in conducting business; ethical behavior is a moral responsibility and the basis of a free society and a free economy (Schneider & Barsoux, 1997). No free society or free economy can survive without ethics (Simon, 1976). However, what is ethical and necessary in business is understood differently across national cultures. For example, the concept of human rights has a different meaning in the West and Asia. According to the Asian view, Western ethical rules, democracy, and freedom of expression are undesirable because they provoke conflicts, encourage instability, and lead to chaos; therefore, they have to be rejected. Asian leaders want to operate their own way, ''the Asian way.'' They argue that developing Asian countries need authoritarian governments, social hierarchy, and discipline. The rights of individuals must be respected as long as they do not affect the greater rights of the community and country. Western standards of human rights, understanding democracy, and attitudes toward environmental protection are inappropriate, especially since Asia is on the rise and the West is declining (Mallet, 1994). An illustration of this cultural antagonism was clearly observed in 2008, as Westerners protested Chinese practices and threatened to boycott the Beijing Olympics.

Are there universal rules of ethics and can they be applied?

It is believed that there are universal rules of ethics, such as honesty, integrity, protection of society, customers, employees, the environment and children, giving a fair share to everyone, providing equal opportunities and access to products and markets, and not protecting home interests. These universal rules should be followed by all nations. However, although these rules may be successfully applied in the Western culture, which relies on performance, Asian cultures that rely on relationships, personal networks, and belonging may not share the same rules. For example, Western and Asian cultures have different understandings of fairness. Asian cultures do not accept the Western rule of ''fair share'' based on performance, whereas Western cultures do not accept the Asian rule of ''fair share'' in the context of a family or parent–child relationship (Schneider & Barsoux, 1997). Consequently, globalization that requires nations to follow universal rules of ethics causes culture clashes in the way businesses are conducted, and challenges many business principles as well as cultural assumptions.

Is it possible to define what is ethical in a global world?

It is not possible to define what is ethical in a global world. What is ethical and moral is culturally determined and depends upon culturally established meanings and symbols. In collectivistic cultures, ethical behavior is determined by the greatest benefits for the largest number of people, social hierarchy, social role and status, family connections and group consensus. In individualistic cultures ethical behavior is determined by the benefits for an individual, equality, freedom, and democracy. In order to understand what is universal ethical behavior one must first learn about the similarities and differences in people's ethical behavior and what culture-specific behavior is. One must identify different cultural assumptions and understand the reasons for specific behavior; one should not impose cultural assumptions on others (Schneider & Barsoux, 1997).

11.5 CONFLICTING ETHICAL BEHAVIOR AND PRACTICES IN TOURISM AND HOSPITALITY: ETHICAL DILEMMAS

In a global economy, companies increasingly operate and travelers increasingly visit diverse social and cultural environments that create many ethical conflicts. Conflicts arise when foreign companies or tourists are confronted with local norms and behaviors, and fail to take into consideration the complexity of cultural values or religious traditions and beliefs of the host country, and vice versa. For example, a conflict arose when McDonald's decided to enter the Indian market, counting on its "fast food global formula": cooking French fries in beef fat and selling beef burgers without realizing that almost 1 billion of the Indian Hindu population worship cows as holy creatures. Thus, what is an ethical practice in the foreign country may not be ethical in the host country.

When two or more practices conflict and there is no clear right or wrong, this is the moment when cross-cultural conflicts turn into dilemmas. The main ethical dilemmas that have direct relevance to the tourism and hospitality industry are bribery and corruption, gender and racial discrimination, sexual harassment, exploitation of child labor, child sexual harassment, violation of human rights, harming natural resources, selling of unhealthy food, false and misleading advertising, nepotism, and even software piracy.

Bribery

Bribery is remuneration for the performance of an act that is inconsistent with the work contract or the nature of the work one has been hired to perform. Bribery is not universally accepted as an illegal, immoral, or unethical business practice. In fact, bribery is sometimes the only way of doing business in certain cultures (Worthy, 1989). Bribery is a common ethical business practice in the developing nations of Asia, Africa, and the Middle East. French and German managers often consider bribery a necessity – the price of doing business – whereas American managers view such behavior as illegal, unethical, and against company policy (Becker & Fritzsche, 1987). In France, Belgium, Greece, Germany, and Luxembourg, deducting foreign bribes as business expense is a legal practice. However, American executives can be prosecuted within the United States if they are found guilty of bribery in another country (Vogel, 1992).

Corruption

Corruption is the misuse of authority for personal gain, which need not be monetary. Corruption includes bribery, nepotism, extortion, dishonestly appropriating goods, usually money, by one to whom the money has been entrusted (embezzlement), and utilization of resources and facilities which do not belong to the individual for his own private purposes (Muzaffar, 1980). While many Asian countries consider corruption a necessity for conducting business, American executives see such behavior as unethical and illegal.

Gender discrimination

One of the areas in which individualistic and collectivistic nations differ most is that of gender equality. There is still discrimination between women and men in terms of their social role, responsibilities, working conditions, travel opportunities, and pay. For example, in the United States and other developed countries, there are laws protecting women against discrimination. Many senior administrative positions are held by women. For example, in Norway, nearly 50% of senior administrative positions are held by women. On the other hand, in Japan, Korea, and Saudi Arabia, there is gender inequality; men are favored over women for senior positions in business organizations and renumeration. In Saudi Arabia, women, in the name of strongly held religious and cultural beliefs, are not allowed to serve as corporate managers; their role is strictly limited to education and health care (Ferro, 2004). In Korea, better employment opportunities and salaries are for men, even when women are more skilled and talented (DeMente, 1991c).

In many developed countries women are protected by equal opportunity legislation (e.g. the United Kingdom); however, women are often asked during employment interviews about their plans to start families and make child arrangements. In Italy, women are discriminated against in the workplace despite the issuing of Equal Treatment of Men and Women Act (ETA) (Saee, 2005).

In some countries women travel less than men due to their traditional responsibilities. They are often discouraged and even constrained in their travel. Women travelers can also be discriminated against. For example, they may not have access to some services if unaccompanied by males. Single women are not allowed to enter Saudi Arabia, to get a visitor visa, they must be accompanied by their husbands.

Sexual harassment

Attitudes towards sexual harassment vary among cultures. For example, while French and Spanish women believe that complimenting a woman, touching her gently, and flirting with her on a casual basis is acceptable and even desirable in social relationships, American women believe that such behavior is unacceptable and represents a significant threat to women.

Exploitation of child labor

In poor countries some companies hire underage children as cheap labor. Many children are employed as kitchen-hands, cleaners, shoe polishers, and sale representatives. In developing countries, with their very high levels of unemployment, poor living conditions, and high poverty, this is a legitimate practice; however, in the developed world such practice is unacceptable.

Child sexual abuse

In poor countries it is a common practice to sell underage children for sexual practices. In some developing countries, the commercial sexual exploitation of children is related to foreign child sex tourism. The possibility of relatively high earnings, low value attached to education and cultural obligation to help support the family make children vulnerable to physical and sexual abuse, drug abuse, child pornography and molestation. In the developed world such practices are unacceptable and called barbaric.

Nepotism

It is a frequent practice of companies in developing countries to favor relatives regardless of their abilities or suitability to work. For example, some companies in India and Asia offer their employees' children the chance to join the company once they have completed school, even when other applicants are more qualified than employees' children. In the Indian context strong family connections, privileges, and family relationships are legitimate practices, but in Western countries such favoritism is regarded unacceptable.

Environmental and ecological concerns

The attitudes toward environmental degradation and environmental responsibilities vary among different cultures. For example, while the majority of French and German managers may believe that pollution does not harm the environment, American managers believe that pollution is a significant threat to the environment (Saee, 2005). However, the increased awareness of environmental issues and global warming appears to be changing attitudes towards such concerns worldwide.

False information

Lying and providing other companies and customers with false information is a complex ethical dilemma. For example, lies, misleading information in travel brochures, and distorted media images are frequently used in advertising. However, nations differ in their attitudes toward lying and deception. While in collectivistic cultures such as Malaysia or Hong Kong, misleading advertising is considered acceptable, in individualistic cultures such as the United Kingdom, Australia, and the United States, misleading advertising presents a major problem.

Similarly, nations differ in their attitudes toward copyright violations. In Canada, the United States, and Europe, copyright violations are unethical. However, in Indonesia or Thailand copyright violations are acceptable. Many Indonesian and Thai businesses pirate copyrighted materials such as books, software, or DVDs and sell them in shops; this is regarded as acceptable and legal. They believe that they need cheap books and software to enhance their knowledge and thus assist their countries in future development (Saee, 2005). On the other hand, Japan and the Philippines strongly oppose software piracy. Also, while padding expense accounts is considered a very unethical practice by Hong Kong Chinese and Malaysian managers, it is considered more of an ethical issue by American managers (McDonald & Zepp, 1988).

Acceptance versus avoidance of social responsibility

The ways companies conduct businesses to protect the welfare of society differ among nations. Some companies believe that their only responsibility is to make money for their stockholders. Other companies believe that they have responsibilities other than making profit. These responsibilities include giving back to the society in the form of sponsoring charities and educational scholarships, donating items, knowledge, and expertise, providing free services to the special needs groups, conserving and protecting the environment, producing eco-friendly products, creating working standards and rules that adhere to the standards of developed countries, producing safe products, providing international assistance, and treating effluent and waste in an environmentally sound manner (Sanyal, 2001).

11.6 THEORIES AND FRAMEWORKS DEALING WITH ETHICAL DILEMMAS

There are several theories and frameworks that explain why certain behavior is believed to be ethically right or wrong. These theories are: (1) theology, (2) deontology, (3) the theory of justice, and (4) cultural relativism (Phatak, 1997; Saee, 2005).

Theology teaches that a behavior is socially accepted as long as it produces the desired consequences or outcomes (e.g. promotion at work, increased market share). There are two key theological approaches: egoism and utilitarianism. *Egoism* teaches that it is ethical to maximize individual self-interest, whereas it is immoral to behave contrary to self-interest (Hoffman & Moore, 1990). Every individual should seek self-interest regardless of what his or her interest is (money, social prestige, or power). *Utilitarianism* teaches to maximize the ''greatest good for the greatest number of individuals.'' This theory is unjust, however, because it assumes that one can use the goods of the minority for the benefit of the majority (http://en.wikipedia.org/wiki/Utilitarianism).

Deontology teaches that one should behave according to one's own sense of duty (*Deon*, in Greek, means duty) rather than concern for consequences or outcomes (Mill, 1957). People's sense of duty dictates their morality. A universal moral duty is to ''do the right thing.'' For example, it is everyone's duty to behave according to a moral law and treat others with respect and dignity as an end and not as the means to reach the end. It is also everyone's moral duty not to harm another person even if the end aim is good.

The *theory of justice* teaches that people and businesses should follow three principles that guide making ethical decisions: to be equitable, fair, and impartial (Phatak, 1997).

Cultural relativism theory teaches that there is no right or wrong way of behaving because what is right or wrong is relative and depends on culture. Every culture has different standards of what is right and wrong. These standards depend on the customs, practice, and laws of a particular culture or society. Since cultures are different, the acceptable behaviors are also different; there is no universally acceptable behavior. Also, there are no better or worse standards. One should always follow the rules and standards of a specific culture and not judge these standards. For example, each world religion, such as Buddhism, Christianity, Confucianism, Hinduism, Judaism, and Islam, has its rules on the right ways to behave; no one should criticize or undermine these rules.

Cultural relativism theory teaches to follow the local rules, habits, and norms according to the motto ''When in Rome, do as the Romans do.'' People should adapt; when they do not, they may lose important networks and privileges. However, one must remember that following the socially and culturally acceptable rules of the host culture may be illegal and against the ethical standards of the home culture (e.g. corruption is acceptable in Italy, but it is not acceptable in the United States). As a result, when operating in the international context one should always follow the ethical standards and legal rules of both cultures – host and home cultures.

There are also so-called rule-based theories. For example, *fundamentalism* teaches to follow the rules of the Bible, Koran, and Torah, as well as various prophets. *Universalism* teaches to follow the same universal rules, duties, and obligations, which all people should conform to. This theory ignores differences and calls for maintaining one's own norms in different societies and cultures. According to this theory, people should behave everywhere exactly as they behave at home in the name of universal principles that transcend local customs. There is only one list of acceptable rules; one is immoral if he or she violates these rules. The theory of universalism denies the existence of national or sub-national ethics and imposes a ''one-fit-for-all-approach'' (Ferro, 2004).

11.7 STRATEGIES FOR MANAGING BUSINESS ETHICAL DILEMMAS

Many principles of ethical behavior acceptable in the home environment cannot be adapted in the host-country environment. The dilemma is whether to impose home-country or host-country rules. There is an argument that individuals and businesses should not be forced to obey the laws of a host society; certain rules of the host society may make dealings in the foreign environment difficult. On the other hand, some may find themselves in big trouble when not following foreign rules and laws. Following the rule "When in Rome, do as the Romans do" (e.g. corruption is acceptable in Italy) has proved to cause serious troubles for foreign companies.

Although foreign tourists and companies are guests in host countries and must conduct themselves according to the foreign countries' rules (Schmidt, 1980) by complying with local rules travelers and foreign companies can also contribute to social problems between themselves and locals. The question arises whether it is better to refuse or to follow local rules. In order to answer this question, travelers and managers of companies must first learn about their own cultural background and that of their company, industry, or host country. They need to create a framework of what is ethical/unethical in each country (home and host country), decide about the appropriate criteria for judging ethical behavior in each country, identify the areas of differences, understand the reasons for these differences, and then develop mutually acceptable ethical standards. For example, doing business in Russia under the Communist regime was difficult due to political and economic uncertainty. Although making profit was seen immoral and selfish in Russia, both Russian and the US managers followed mutually acceptable ethical values of honesty, integrity, trust, and fairness (Schneider & Barsoux, 1997).

While certain ethical standards are universal, others are culturally specific: reciprocity (gift-giving), profit maximization, or social welfare. These culturally specific ethical standards reflect the importance particular societies place on what is good for the group versus the individual, on achievement versus belonging, and on social harmony versus adherence to abstract principles. The recommendation is to identify the differences in ethical behavior and evaluate them against certain universal moral principles (Stark, 1993).

Also, in order to solve ethical dilemmas in this world, it is proposed to create a common set of ethics (Schneider & Barsoux, 1997). However, although individuals and businesses will probably follow a certain set of universal ethical rules, the decisions taken in specific nations will most likely be culturally determined. Those from individualistic cultures will look after themselves; those from collectivistic cultures will look after others. Those from low-context cultures will follow explicit and written ethical standards; those from high-context cultures will follow the standards that are implicit and shared by members of a community. Those from the universalistic cultures will follow the rules applied to everyone; those from particularistic cultures will pay more attention to the circumstances and people involved (Schneider & Barsoux, 1997).

Although decision-making in different nations will remain culturally determined, it is believed that sooner or later globalization will require a convergence of rules of ethical behavior and shared, universally accepted moral rules. Global tourism and hospitality managers will have to accept the cultural differences and diversities of people, share others' values, despite their different interpretations (e.g. human rights, freedom, democracy) and adjust their own ethical standards when trying to survive or seeking to make decisions in different cultures.

11.8 GLOBAL CODE OF ETHICS FOR TOURISM

The World Tourism Organization (WTO) developed universal codes of ethical behavior for tourism and tourism providers called the Global Code of Ethics for Tourism (GCET). The GCET sets a frame of reference for the responsibility and sustainable development of world tourism in the new millennium. It draws inspiration from many similar declarations and adds new principles and industry codes that reflect the changing society of the 21st century. The Code has been developed following the opportunistic tourism developments that had harmful impacts on local people. The Code outlines ''the rules of the game'' that should guide destinations, governments, tour operators, developers, travel agents, workers, and travelers themselves in order to achieve sustainability. The codes identify political, economic, environmental, social, and cultural principles that tourism shareholders must follow in order to behave ethically. The aim of the universal code of ethics in tourism is to minimize the negative impact of tourism on the environment, host communities, and cultural heritage, and to maximize the potential benefits for the residents of the areas visited as well as for the private sector.

The Code consists of 10 articles that synthesize most of ethical concerns raised to tourism development. The first article emphasizes that all actors in tourism development and tourists themselves should observe the social and cultural traditions and practices of all peoples, including national minorities and indigenous people. The Code condemns the exploitation of other people in any form, notably sexual, and stresses that tourism policies should benefit local communities, contribute to preserving and embellishing heritage, and allow traditional crafts and folklore to flourish. The summary of all 10 articles is presented in Case Study 11.1 below.

SUMMARY

Ethics is the set of moral principles that guides the behavior of people and business. Ethics is the foundation of human existence. Ethical behavior is a socially responsible behavior that enhances the human welfare and interest of society and organizations. What is ethical behavior in one culture can be unethical in another culture. The most debatable business of ethical dilemma is whether profit is more important than social responsibility. The most conflicting ethical behaviors in tourism include bribery and corruption, gender and race discrimination, sexual harassment, exploitation of child labor, child sexual abuse, environmental degradation, providing false or misleading information, and avoidance of social responsibility. Differences in ethical behavior are due to cultural factors. Global tourism managers operating in an increasingly competitive world must accept differences in ethical behavior and adjust their own ethical standards when making decisions in different cultures.

DISCUSSION POINTS AND QUESTIONS

1. What is ethics and why is ethical behavior important?
2. Why is the understanding of ethics important to international tourism managers?
3. Why does the tourism and hospitality industry need business ethics?
4. ''What is ethically wrong in one culture may be acceptable in another culture.'' Critically discuss and give examples.
5. What are the most debatable ethical dilemmas and most conflicting ethical issues in the world?
6. Give examples of ethical and unethical behavior in your national culture and compare it with other cultures. Give reasons for differences in this behavior.
7. Search the Internet for annual reports on corporate social responsibility for hospitality and tourism companies such as TUI and ACCOR. Identify the major social and environmental issues that these companies focus on.

CASE STUDY 11.1 Global Code of Ethics for Tourism

Article 1: Tourism's contribution to understanding and respect

1. The understanding and promotion of the ethical values common to humanity, tolerance and respect for the diversity of religious, philosophical and moral beliefs, are the foundation of responsible tourism; stakeholders and tourists should observe the social and cultural traditions and practices of all peoples, including those of minorities and indigenous peoples.
2. Tourism activities should be conducted in harmony with the traditions of the host regions and in respect for their laws, practices and customs.
3. The host communities and local professionals should acquaint themselves with and respect the tourists who visit them and find out about their lifestyles, tastes and expectations.
4. It is the task of the public authorities to protect tourists and their belongings, provide them with safety and security, information, insurance, and assistance; any attacks, assaults, or threats against tourists or industry workers as well as the destruction of tourism facilities or cultural or natural heritage should be condemned and punished in accordance with their respective national laws.
5. Tourists and visitors should not commit any criminal act, behave offensively, injure the local populations, or damage the local environment, should refrain from all trafficking in illicit drugs, arms, antiques, protected species and products and substances that are dangerous or prohibited by national regulations.

6. Tourists and visitors are responsible to acquaint themselves with the characteristics of the countries to be visited, the health and security risks inherent in travel and behave in such a way as to minimize those risks.

Article 2: Tourism as a vehicle for individual and collective fulfillment

1. Tourism, relaxation, sport, and access to culture and nature should be planned, it is an irreplaceable factor of education, tolerance, and learning about the differences between people and cultures and their diversity.
2. Tourism activities should respect the equality of men and women and promote human rights.
3. The exploitation of human beings in any form, particularly sexual conflicts with the fundamental aims of tourism should be penalized by the law.
4. Travel for purposes of religion, health, education, and cultural or linguistic exchanges are particularly beneficial forms of tourism, which should be encouraged.
5. The introduction into curricula of education about the value of tourist exchanges, their economic, social and cultural benefits, and also their risks, should be encouraged.

Article 3: Tourism, a factor of sustainable development

1. All the stakeholders should protect the natural environment to achieve continuous and sustainable economic growth for present and future generations.
2. Saving rare and precious tourism resources such as water and energy, as well as avoiding waste production, should be given priority.
3. A more even distribution of holidays should be sought to reduce the pressure of tourism activity on the environment and enhance its beneficial impact on the industry and economy.
4. Tourism infrastructure and activities should be designed and programmed to protect the natural heritage and preserve endangered species of wildlife.
5. Nature tourism and ecotourism should respect the natural heritage and local populations.

Article 4: Tourism, a user of the cultural heritage and contributor to its enhancement

1. Tourism resources belong to the common heritage and all communities in whose territories they are situated have rights and obligations to them.
2. Tourism policies and activities should be conducted with respect for the artistic, archaeological, and cultural heritage.
3. Financial resources derived from visits to cultural sites and monuments should be used for the development and embellishment of this heritage.
4. Tourism activity should be planned to allow cultural products to survive and flourish.

Article 5: Tourism, a beneficial activity for host communities

1. Local populations should share equitably the economic, social, and cultural benefits they generate from tourism activities.
2. Tourism policies should raise the standard of living of the populations of the regions visited and meet their needs.

3. Special attention should be paid to the specific problems of coastal areas and island territories and to vulnerable rural or mountain regions.
4. Tourism professionals should carry out studies of the impact of their development projects on the environment and natural surroundings.

Article 6: Obligations of stakeholders

1. Tourism professionals have an obligation to provide tourists with objective and honest information on their places of destination and the conditions of travel.
2. Tourism professionals should show concern for the security and safety, accident prevention, health protection and food safety of those who seek their services.
3. Tourism professionals should contribute to the cultural and spiritual fulfillment of tourists and allow them, during their travels, to practice their religions.
4. The authorities of the generating and the host countries should ensure that the necessary mechanisms are in place for the repatriation of tourists in the event of the bankruptcy of the enterprise that organized their travel.
5. Governments have the right – and the duty – especially in a crisis, to inform their nationals of the difficult circumstances, and the dangers they may encounter during their travels abroad.
6. The press should issue honest and balanced information on events and situations that could influence the flow of tourists.

Article 7: Right to tourism

1. All the world's inhabitants have the right to access to the discovery and enjoyment of the planet's resources.
2. The universal right to tourism must be regarded as the corollary of the right to rest and leisure, including reasonable limitation of working hours and periodic holidays with pay.
3. Social tourism, which facilitates widespread access to leisure, travel, and holidays, should be developed with the support of the public authorities.
4. Family, youth, student, and senior tourism and tourism for people with disabilities, should be encouraged and facilitated.

Article 8: Freedom of tourist movements

1. Tourists and visitors should be free to move within their countries and from one State to another.
2. Tourists and visitors should have access to all forms of communication, local administrative, legal, and health services and consular representatives of their countries of origin.
3. Tourists and visitors should benefit from the same rights as the citizens of the country visited concerning the confidentiality of the personal data and information concerning them.
4. Visas or health and customs formalities should be adapted to facilitate to the maximum freedom of travel and widespread access to international tourism.
5. Travelers should have access to allowances of convertible currencies needed for their travels.

Article 9: Rights of the workers and entrepreneurs

1. The fundamental rights of salaried and self-employed workers in the tourism industry and related activities should be guaranteed under the supervision of the national and local administrations.
2. Salaried and self-employed workers in the tourism industry have the right and the duty to acquire appropriate training and be given social protection;
3. Any natural or legal person, with the abilities and skills, should be entitled to develop a professional activity in the field of tourism under existing national laws.
4. Exchanges of experience offered to executives and workers, from different countries should be facilitated to foster the development of the world tourism industry.
5. Multinational enterprises of the tourism industry should not exploit their positions; they should avoid becoming the vehicles of cultural and social models artificially imposed on the host communities.
6. Partnership between generating and receiving countries contribute to the sustainable development of tourism and an equitable distribution of the benefits of its growth.

Article 10: Implementation of the principles of the Global Code of Ethics for Tourism

1. The public and private stakeholders in tourism development should cooperate in the implementation of these principles and monitor their effective application.
2. The stakeholders in tourism development should recognize the role of international institutions, among which the World Tourism Organization ranks first.
3. The stakeholders should refer any disputes concerning the application or interpretation of the Global Code of Ethics for Tourism for conciliation to the World Committee on Tourism Ethics.

WEBSITE LINKS

1. Business ethics: http://www.business-ethics.com
2. World ethics http://www.ethicsworld.org
3. Tourism ethics http://www.world-tourism.org/code_ethics/eng.html
4. http://knowledge.wharton.upenn.edu/category.cfm?cid=11

The next part will discuss the concept of tourist behavior and identify cultural differences in tourist buying behavior.

Tourist Behavior

4

*This part provides a comprehensive understanding of the concept of tourist
behavior and identifies cultural differences in tourist buying behavior.*

Human behavior: its nature and determinants

The aim of this chapter is to introduce the concept of human behavior and its different theories. The aim is also to explain the concept and nature of tourist behavior and the importance of studying tourist behavior in a cross-cultural context.

OBJECTIVES

After completing this chapter the reader should be able to:
- Understand the concept of human behavior and its many facets
- Identify environmental factors that influence human behavior
- Learn about the major theories of human behavior
- Identify the basic needs that drive human behavior
- Identify factors influencing human needs
- Explain the nature and meaning of tourist behavior
- Understand the importance of studying tourist behavior in a general sense as well as in a cross-cultural context
- Understand the benefits of learning about tourist behavior in a cross-cultural context

INTRODUCTION

Tourism is always associated with human nature. The tourism industry is based *on* people – run *by* people and *for* people. Success in the industry depends on the performances of those who are either directly or indirectly associated with the industry. These can be local residents of the host country, those who work in the industry **265** and provide services to tourists, tourists themselves, developers, investors, marketers, and managers. The industry capitalizes on the diversity of human personalities, skills, and abilities. Understanding human beings and the influence their behavior has on industry operations is necessary if the tourism industry is to flourish in the future.

Human behavior is very diverse and complex. It is difficult to examine and understand why people behave the way they do. People's behaviors and their worldviews are determined by their background, lifestyle, and needs. Often we try to assess others without a deep enough understanding of the influences their background has on their actions. In tourism, we try to understand why people travel, what they want to enjoy, and how they want to spend their money. Appreciation of where tourists originate, the environment from which they come, how they make travel decisions, and which elements determine their travel decisions are all fundamental factors that determine the success of the tourism industry. Failing to understand tourists and people associated with them is a serious mistake that may lead to negative consequences for tourists and the industry as a whole. Misinterpretation, misunderstanding, perception distortion, or developments of negative experiences are some of the examples of negative consequences. The ultimate result of such problems could be a decrease in tourism demand or repeat visitation, a consequent drop in sales and profitability, and often business failure.

12.1 THE CONCEPT OF HUMAN BEHAVIOR

The concept of *human behavior* refers to the manner in which human beings act and conduct themselves; the ways in which they work and play, react to the environment, perform their functions and responsibilities, and do things in their daily lives. Let us examine the major aspects of human behavior and the factors that influence that behavior.

Mind, body and spirit

There are three major aspects of human behavior: mind, body, and spirit (Huitt, 2003) (see Figure 12.1). Mind (sometimes called human personality) has three dimensions: (1) *cognition* (knowing, understanding, thinking, acting), (2) *affect* (attitudes, predispositions, emotions, feelings), and (3) *conation* (intentions to act and behave, reasons for doing, volition, will) (Eysenck, 1947; Miller, 1991). Cognition is a process of gaining knowledge and understanding; the process of perception and knowing; the process of encoding, storing, processing, and retrieving information from an environment. According to *Merriam-Webster's Collegiate Dictionary*, cognition is ''the act or process of knowing in the broadest sense; specifically, an intellectual process by which knowledge is gained from perception or ideas.'' Cognition is generally associated with thought or action and the questions of ''what'' (e.g. What is the meaning? What happened?) (Huitt, 1999a).

Affect is a feeling that results from intense sentiments, desires, or emotions, such as love, fear, and hate, or a state of agitation or disturbance taking place within an

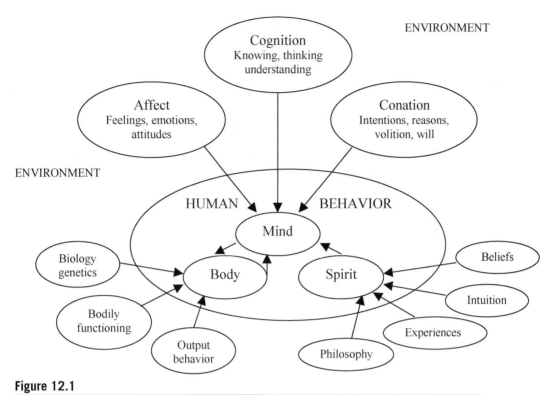

Figure 12.1

Major Aspects of Human Behavior

individual's mind. Affect also refers to the emotional interpretation of perceptions, information, or knowledge. It is generally associated with the question ''how'' (e.g. How do I feel about this? How did it happen?). Affect is usually associated with one's positive or negative attitudes, perceptions or statements about people, objects, ideas, etc. (Huitt, 1999b). One can have favorable or unfavorable attitudes, perceptions, or feelings about other people or objects.

Conation refers to the connection of knowledge and affect to behavior and is associated with the question ''why'' (e.g. Why did you go there? Why did it happen?). Conation is closely associated with one's will, and affects the freedom to make choices about what to do (Mischel, 1996). Conation refers to the intentional and personal motivation of behavior (Bandura, 1997); human behavior cannot be explained without understanding conation (Miller, 1991). It is critical to understand how knowledge (cognition) and emotion (affect) affect human behavior (conation) (Bagozzi, 1992).

In addition, the development and functioning of the mind is influenced by bodily and spiritual factors (see Figure 12.1). Body is represented by (1) biological or genetic factors, (2) bodily functioning, and (3) overt behavior (Skinner, 1953). The mind receives information from the body and sends information to body. The mind influences behavior through the body. While some argue that the mind (psychological) and the brain (biological) are related to each other (when the brain ceases to function, the mind ceases to function as well), others believe the mind and the brain are separate entities (the mind functions separately from brain; the mind has a spiritual or meta-physical aspect). According to the latter theory, human beings and their behavior are not limited to their physical bodies. Human beings have a soul or spirit that influences the functioning of the mind and that continues to exist after the body dies. Spiritual factors are religious beliefs, intuitions, personal experiences, or even philosophy. They are critical to the development of mind and how people learn, think, feel, reason, and make their decisions. Spiritual factors have a profound influence on human behavior. In fact, spirituality defines who the people are as human beings (Huddleston, 1993), why they are, and where they are going (Huitt, 2003). The above theory is important to today's tourism, which is characterized by an increasing demand around the world for spiritual experience, an important motive for travel. Spiritual tourism is one of the new types of tourism based on the assumption that there is more to life than what one can see or understand.

In summary, there are five major components of human behavior:

1. Cognitive – responsible for gaining knowledge and learning, and perceiving, storing, processing, and retrieving information
2. Affective – responsible for developing feelings, perceptions, and thoughts (before and after they are processed cognitively)
3. 'Conative – responsible for making choices, personal motivation, and intentions (directing and managing input and output functioning) (inner and outer behavior)
4. Spiritual – responsible for inert behavior (input of the individual), that is, developing beliefs, intuition, and experiences, and determining how human beings approach the unknown, how they relate to the sacred
5. Behavioral – responsible for overt behavior (output of the individual) (Huitt, 2003).

12.2 ENVIRONMENTAL FACTORS INFLUENCING HUMAN BEHAVIOR

Human behavior is influenced by a variety of environmental factors that play an important role in the development of human beings and are also influenced by human behavior themselves. The various environments that influence human beings can be examined at different levels. The first level, called *micro*, has the most immediate influence on individual behavior and development. It includes the family, local neighborhood, or community institutions (e.g. schools, religious institutions), peer groups, and the specific culture of the family and community. The second level, called *meso*, includes the intermediate influences of social institutions, professional groups, and industries involved in such activities as transportation, entertainment, health organizations, etc. The third level, called *macro*, includes the influences of national regions and changes in the local economy, politics, culture, social system, or demographics. The fourth and the highest level, called *supra*, has the most remote influences on the individual behavior and includes the impacts of international regions and global changes. At this level the behavior of individuals, families, communities, and societies is influenced by international and global trends in economics, information technology, political and socioeconomic systems and their developments, religion, and ethnicity (see Figure 12.2).

Supra- and macro-environments represent the *wider environments*; meso- and micro-environments represent the *closer environments*. Supra-, macro-, meso- and micro-environments differ in the ways in which they influence human behavior and the way human behavior influences them. For example, the family (micro), social institutions (meso), national economy (macro), and international and global trends (supra) all influence human behavior. Likewise, human behavior influences the local neighborhood and community and peer groups (micro), professional groups and industries (meso), local politics and social life (macro), as well as international and global developments (supra). In addition, all four environmental levels influence each other; they cannot exist in isolation from each other. For example, the health institutions (meso) have immediate influence on the family and friends' health behavior, and at the same time they themselves depend on the national trends in economics and

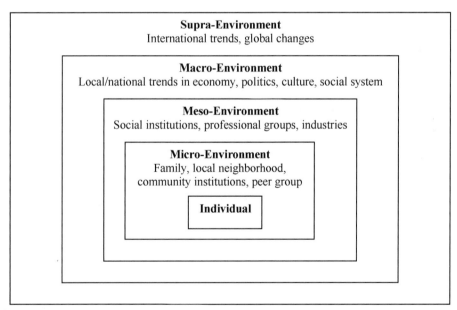

Figure 12.2

Levels of the Environment Influencing Human Behavior

Source: based on Huitt, W. (2003). A systems model of human behavior. *Educational Psychology Interactive*. Valdosta, GA: Valdosta State University. Retrieved from http://chiron.valdosta// whuitt/materials/sysmdlo.html; Srnka, K. (2004). Culture's role in marketer's ethical decision making: An integrated theoretical framework. *Academy of Marketing Science Review*, 8(3); http://www.amsreview.org/articles/srnka01-2004.pdf.

politics. Similarly, advances in information technology (supra) have had a profound effect on communication in international communities and regional industries (macro), institutions (meso), families (micro), and the individual itself. The closer environments (meso and micro) influence human behavior in day-to-day interactions on a continuous basis (e.g. schooling, family, friends), and the wider environments influence human behavior on a less frequent and regular basis (e.g. politics, industries). Similarly, human behavior itself impacts closer environments (family, neighbors) on a more regular and constant basis, as well as the wider environments (industry, national economy) on a less intense basis (Srnka, 2004).

In sum, human behavior develops as a result of the:

1. Interrelationships between the mind (cognition), affect (feelings), and conation (will)
2. Influence of biological, genetic, and spiritual factors
3. Influence of the environment in which human behavior occurs; and
4. Feedback from the environment as a result of an individual's behavior (Huitt, 2003).

12.3 THEORIES OF HUMAN BEHAVIOR

One of the most important factors that influence human behavior is motivation. *Motivation* can be defined as an internal state or condition (sometimes described as a need, desire, or want) that activates or energizes behavior and gives it direction (Kleinginna & Kleinginna, 1981a,b) and leads to behavior that aims at satisfying needs (Lussier, 1990). Motivation can be categorized as either extrinsic (external to the individual) or intrinsic (internal). Intrinsic sources of motivation can be subcategorized as body/physical, mind/mental (e.g. cognitive, affective, conative) or transpersonal/spiritual (see Figure 12.3). Behavior will not occur unless it is motivated or energized by a specific need.

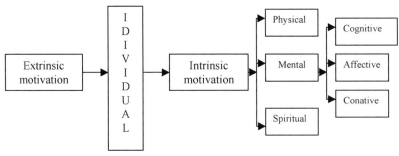

Figure 12.3

Categories and Sources of Motivation

Source: based on Huitt, W. (2001). *Motivation to learn: An overview*. Valdosta, GA: Valdosta State University. Retrieved from http://chiron.valdosta//whuitt/col/motivation/motivate.html.

12.3.1 Cause-Motive-Behavior-Goal Theory

According to the Cause-Motive-Behavior-Goal theory (Leavitt, 1978; Leavitt et al., 1990), human behavior has three important characteristics:

1. Behavior is *caused* (behavior does not happen; it is caused by factors that an individual may not even be aware of).
2. Behavior is *directed* (behavior has its aims; all individuals aim at achieving certain goals regardless of whether they are conscious of these goals or not).
3. Behavior is *motivated* (motives determine an individual's actions and what individuals do; they provide the energy to achieve goals).

A cause, a motive, and a goal depend on each other. When a person has a reason to engage in certain behavior, this reason creates a need, want, or energy that directs or motivates that person to achieve a certain goal. Once a goal is achieved, the reason for behavior ceases to exist. Elimination of the reason eliminates the motive, which eliminates the behavior. For example, when a thirsty person satisfies his/her own thirst, he/she no longer has a need (motive to drink) and does not seek water. By eliminating thirst (cause), the person ceases to seek water (motive). Leavitt's (1978) and Leavitt et al.'s (1990) model for understanding the relationship between a cause, motive, and a goal is illustrated in Figure 12.4.

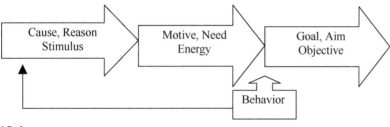

Figure 12.4

Cause-Motive-Behavior-Goal Model (Leavitt, 1978, Leavitt et al., 1990)

Unfortunately, Leavitt's (1978) and Leavitt et al.'s (1990) model does not hold when needs are difficult to fulfill or when they can be only partially fulfilled (e.g. a need for safety during a war). There are also environmental factors, such as the influence of social context (e.g. people, tensions, frustrations, stress, conflicts) that may interfere with the model. Moreover, individuals vary greatly in behavior, motivation, and goals because they have different abilities, skills, and capabilities. Each individual reacts differently to environmental influences under different circumstances. Similarly, each individual has different reasons to develop a motive, and a different energy level (a different degree of motivation) to respond to the environmental stimuli.

12.3.2 Maslow's Hierarchy of Needs

According to Maslow's Hierarchy of Needs (1954), human behavior depends upon the needs human beings want to satisfy. All human beings have five major types of needs: *physiological* (the need for air, water, food, comfort, waste elimination, temperature control, sleep, and sex); *safety and security* (the need for protection, order, and stability, and the freedom from fear of physical danger); *social* (the need for love, family, family affiliation, and social acceptance); *ego* (the need for achievement, competency, recognition, approval, status, good reputation, and fame); and *self-fulfillment* (the need for personal development and growth, self-actualization, and challenge). These five types of needs exist in a hierarchy as shown in Figure 12.5. The most basic need is survival itself: to eat, sleep, and have shelter. The highest order need is the need for self-actualization, personal development, and growth. Only when the lower-order needs of physical safety are satisfied do human beings become motivated by the higher-order needs of personal growth and self-fulfillment. For example, only when physiological needs for food and shelter are met is a person able to think about social or recreational needs.

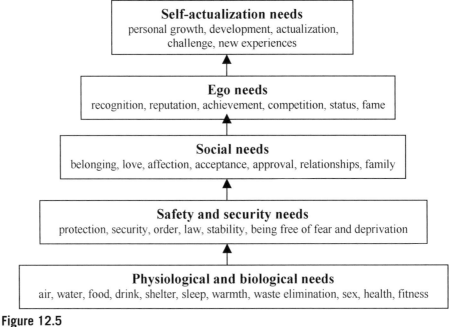

Figure 12.5

Maslow's Hierarchy of Needs (original 5-Stage Model)

Once certain needs are satisfied, they do not motivate the individual any longer. For example, the thirsty person who satisfied her own thirst by drinking a glass of water is no longer motivated by thirst because she is no longer thirsty. Similarly, the person who feels safe and free of danger is no longer motivated to look for shelter because she is no longer concerned about safety.

The five types of needs identified in the Maslow's Hierarchy of Needs can be grouped into *deficiency* needs and *growth* needs. Within the deficiency needs, each lower need must be satisfied before an individual will move to the next higher level. If a deficiency need is detected, the individual will act to remove the deficiency. If the deficiency needs are met, an individual is ready to act upon the growth needs.

In Maslow's initial five-stage model (see Figure 12.5) there was only one growth need – a self-actualization need. Individuals who are motivated by self-actualization seek personal development, growth, challenges, and new experiences. In his later model, Maslow differentiated the growth needs of self-actualization; he identified two lower-level growth needs prior to the general level of self-actualization (Maslow & Lowery, 1998) and one higher-level beyond that level (Maslow, 1971). The first two lower-level growth needs are *cognitive* need (the need to know, understand, explore) and *aesthetic* needs (the need for beauty, harmony, balance, symmetry, order). The one higher-level need beyond self-actualization is *transcendent* need (the need to help others to find self-fulfillment and realize their potential) (see Figure 12.6).

Transcendent needs refer to the needs of all people in the entire world rather than to those of a single individual. Transcendent needs may include the needs to connect to something beyond the self-ego. It may involve helping others and advocating human rights, anti-discrimination, social justice, environmental preservation and conservation, ethics, universal religion, living in harmony with each other and the earth, and appreciating nature, art and music. In order to meet these needs, many humans change their behavior from an external expression of themselves to an inner change and spiritual journey. Many feel a need to experience divine energy, the transcendence of the entire universe, life after death, karma, invisible energy that surrounds objects and human bodies, and psychic powers, whereas others feel a need to heal themselves and others. As one becomes more self-transcendent, one becomes wiser. The identification of the transcendent needs that are the highest levels of human needs is Maslow's most important contribution to the study of human behavior and motivation.

Maslow's model can be used to predict human behavior. When one knows where an individual is on the needs hierarchy, one can determine the next level of needs the individual will be seeking to fulfill. Unfortunately, the model is often criticized for not applying to all life situations. Different people have various needs; some require less sleep, food, and relationships than do others. Some may be satisfied with the higher-level needs, whereas others may be satisfied with the lower-level needs. Some people may need other people to fulfill certain needs (e.g. a need for wide social networks). Others may have to learn not to have certain needs (e.g. eating sweets, traveling overseas) and instead find different ways of satisfying them (e.g. eating fruits, traveling domestically). This does not mean that the person does not have these needs; rather, he or she is refraining from them.

Further, some people differ as to the order in which they try to satisfy their needs. For example, some may not be concerned about safety and security needs and may wish to fulfill the social needs immediately after satisfying the physiological and biological needs. Some people may also have multiple needs on the same day or at the same moment. For example, within the same day an individual may be motivated by

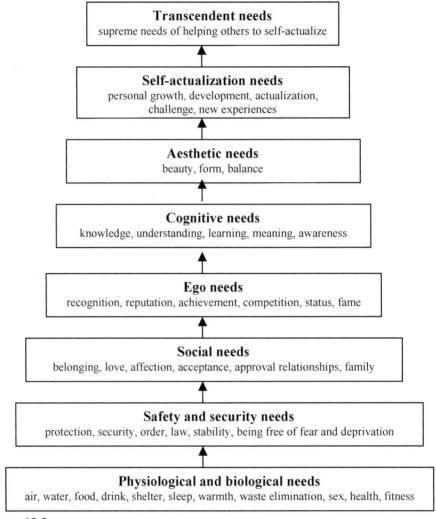

Figure 12.6

Maslow's Hierarchy of Needs (8-Stage Model)

Note: The original model of Maslow's Hierarchy of Needs comprised five different types of needs, was developed between 1943 and 1954, and published in 1954. In 1970 and 1990 the model was modified. The 1970 model comprised seven types of needs, and the 1990 model comprised eight types of needs (see figure).

Source: Haney, W. (1992). *Communication and interpersonal relations: text and cases* (6th ed.). Homewood, IL: Irwin. http://www.businesssballs.com/maslow/htm.

several types of needs. The same person may be thirsty and hungry, concerned about personal safety on a street, desire social acceptance among friends, and seek recognition and advancement at work. Moreover, the same person may also want to contribute to humanity and environmental protection.

It is also possible that one person may be motivated by several needs of the same level and/or several levels of needs simultaneously. It is also possible that there may be a conflict of needs when a person has very strong and urgent needs, and wants to fulfill a need immediately (e.g. a need for warmth, sleep) but cannot satisfy all needs simultaneously. The conflict of human needs often occurs between physiological and safety–security needs, social and ego needs, or ego- and self-fulfillment needs. For example, an ambitious person's need for achievement can conflict with the need for social relations at work. In this case, the person may have to suppress her/his ambition in order not to damage social relationships with co-workers. Alternatively, the person may have to suppress the need for social relationships with co-workers in order to fulfill the need for professional recognition and enhanced work status.

Despite the criticism, Maslow's Hierarchy of Needs is currently one of the most widely accepted motivational theories. It is used to identify what motivates an individual and what kinds of information the individual seeks at different need levels. For example, individuals at the lowest level seek *coping* information to meet their basic needs. At the safety level individuals seek *helping* information to understand how they can be safe and secure. At the social-needs level individuals seek *enlightening* information to meet their belonging needs. At the esteem level of needs individuals seek *empowering* information to develop their ego. Finally, at the growth level of cognitive, aesthetic, and self-actualization needs, individuals seek *edifying* information to connect to something beyond them or to edify others (Norwood, 2000) (see Figure 12.7).

Figure 12.7

Maslow's Hierarchy of Needs and Information Sought at Different Needs Levels

Motivational needs are related to a variety of human personalities. Personalities differentiate people according to how they relate to each set of needs. One of the most frequently cited aspects of personality in the literature is that of introversion and extraversion. An introvert may seek personal development, knowledge, or enhancement of specific skills, whereas an extrovert may want to assist others in the development of their competencies. An introvert at the social level may seek personal acceptance and inclusion in a group (belongingness), whereas an extrovert at the same level may pay attention to how others value that membership (esteem). At the self-level actualization an introvert may try to satisfy his own psychological and biological needs, whereas an extrovert may be concerned with connectedness with others and security.

12.3.3 Alderfer's ERG Theory

According to Alderfer (1972), lower-level needs do not have to be completely satisfied before upper-level needs become motivations. Also, if an individual is unable to meet upper-level needs the person will regress and lower-level needs become the major determinant of their motivations.

12.3.4 Herzberg, Mausner, and Snyderman's Two-Factor Theory

Herzberg et al.'s (1962) theory of human behavior relates to work environment. They suggested that fulfilling some human needs does not always lead to satisfaction. In a work environment, there are two important aspects of all jobs: (1) job content – what people do in terms of job tasks and (2) job context – the work setting in which they do it. Job content is associated with the ''motivators,'' and job context or environment is associated with ''hygiene factors.'' When job content motivators (e.g. recognition, advancement) can fulfill the growth needs of the individual, then job satisfaction occurs. When motivators cannot fulfill the growth needs, then job dissatisfaction occurs. However, the same does not apply to hygiene factors. When job context hygiene factors (e.g. salary, working conditions) cannot satisfy the individual, then job dissatisfaction occurs. However, when hygiene factors satisfy the individual, neither dissatisfaction nor satisfaction can occur.

Herzberg et al.'s (1962) theory is often called the motivator-hygiene theory. In sum, the theory argues that meeting the lower-level needs (hygiene factors) of individuals does not motivate them to exert effort, but only prevents them from being dissatisfied. Only if higher-level needs (motivators) are met individuals can be motivated. ''Nothing wrong with a service'' (the absence of dissatisfiers) is not enough to satisfy a customer; intrinsic satisfaction must be present to motivate a purchase (satisfiers must be present).

12.3.5 Expectancy Theory

According to Vroom's (1964) Expectancy theory, in order for people to become motivated, three factors are needed: *expectancy* (perceived probability of success or outcome of behavior, expectations), *instrumentality* (the perception that the first outcome of behavior (e.g. success) will be associated with the second outcome (e.g. reward); and *valence* (the extent to which the expected outcomes are attractive or unattractive; the value assigned to outcomes of behavior, the value of obtaining a goal). These three variables must be present for people to become motivated. If an individual expects or believes he or she can achieve a goal, and sees a connection between his/her own activity and the achievement of that goal (e.g. enhancement of self-ego), then the individual will be motivated to engage in that activity. However, if even one of these motivators is non-existent (e.g. instrumentality and valence are high, but expectancy is absent), the person will not be motivated.

12.3.6 Cognitive Dissonance Theory

The Cognitive Dissonance theory (Festinger, 1957) stated that individuals can change their own behavior when trying to fulfill two or more conflicting needs. For example, when there are conflicts between values or actions among human beings, those individuals will behave in a specific way to resolve these conflicts. They will change their behavior and thinking, which in turn will lead to even bigger change in their needs and behavior. However, Murray (1938) argued that human needs change independently. The desire to satisfy one need does not necessarily explain the desire to fulfill the other need. For example, the desire to travel does not necessarily explain the need for food or drink.

12.3.7 Reinforcement Theory

The Reinforcement theory (Skinner, 1969) holds that pleasant outcomes tend to generate repeated behavior, whereas unpleasant outcomes do not generate repeated behavior. For example, a satisfied tourist can come back to the same destination, whereas a dissatisfied tourist will go somewhere else. Thus, in order to motivate a specific behavior (e.g. repeat visitation) one has to strengthen positive outcomes of this behavior. In other words, in order to make the tourist purchase the same product, marketers have to emphasize the positive and pleasant outcomes that the tourist experiences with that product.

12.3.8 Equity Theory

The Equity theory suggests that individuals engage in social comparisons by comparing their efforts and rewards with those of relevant others. The perception about the fairness of the rewards influences their motivation. The ratio of efforts to rewards must be the same for them as it is for others to whom they compare themselves if they are to be motivated.

12.3.9 McClelland's Learned Needs Theory

According to McClelland (1953), human behavior depends on motives developed in respective cultures. Humans learn about their needs from their cultures, which dictate what needs are important, and what needs should be fulfilled first, and why. For example, British tourists traveling to Australia usually prefer an ocean-view hotel room, whereas Japanese tourists choose hotels offering big bath tubs and slippers.

The theories of human behavior presented above allow us to understand human reactions to the environmental stimuli, and to learn how to influence, control, and predict human responses. These theories represent considerable potential for our understanding of tourist behavior. There are, of course, other theories of human behavior that can be further identified in the literature.

12.4 BASIC NEEDS OF HUMAN BEHAVIOR

Apart from Maslow (1954), who distinguished among five types of human needs (physiological, safety and security, social, ego, and self-fulfillment), there are other types of needs that drive human behavior. Murray (1938) classified human needs into six categories: (1) *achievement* (to accomplish and achieve something difficult), (2) *dominance* (to control, organize, dominate others), (3) *autonomy* (to have a sense of independence), (4) *affiliation* (to have relationships with other people and groups), (5) *play* (to relax, enjoy, feel excitement, have fun, laugh, joke, be happy, amuse oneself, entertain oneself, avoid serious tension), and (6) *cognizance* (to explore, be aware, comprehend, observe, ask questions, satisfy curiosity, look, listen, inspect, read, and seek knowledge).

Herzberg et al. (1962) identified two kinds of human needs: (1) *growth* needs and (2) *avoidance* needs. Growth needs can be satisfied by motivators such as achievement, recognition, responsibility, advancement, or work itself. Avoidance needs can be fulfilled by hygiene factors, such as salary, interpersonal relations, working conditions, policy and administration, or supervision.

Alderfer (1972) distinguished between the *existence* needs that include all the forms of material and psychological desires (similar to Maslow's physiological and safety categories), *relatedness* needs that involve relationships with others (comparable to aspects of Maslow's belongingness and esteem needs), and *growth* needs that imply focus on oneself and one's environment and attainment of one's potential (associated with Maslow's esteem and self-actualization needs).

McClelland (1976) identified three basic human needs: (1) *achievement* (a need for taking responsibility, challenge), (2) *affiliation* (a need for establishing, maintaining, and repairing social relationships; for having warm, friendly associations with others), and (3) *power* (a need for acquiring a reputation, controlling one's environment, and influencing others). According to McClelland, there are two types of power needs: *socialized* power, which is used in the interests of the group, the organization, etc.; and *personalized* power, which is used in the interests of the self, often at the expense of the group.

Ryan and Deci (2000) identified three types of human needs: the needs for autonomy, competence, and relatedness. Nohria et al. (2001) argued that there are four basic human needs: (1) to acquire objects and experience, (2) to bond with others, mutual care, and commitment, (3) to learn and make sense of the world and of oneself, and (4) to defend oneself and loved ones from harm. The Institute for Management Excellence (2001) identified nine human needs: (1) security, (2) adventure, (3) freedom, (4) exchange, (5) power, (6) expansion, (7) acceptance, (8) community, and (9) expression.

12.5 FACTORS INFLUENCING HUMAN NEEDS

Various demographic, socio-cultural, economic, geographic, and psychological factors drive people in their pursuits to fulfill their own needs. These factors create motivational patterns that influence human behavior (see Figure 12.8).

12.6 THE CONCEPT OF TOURIST BEHAVIOR

The concept of tourist behavior can be explained in relation to topics associated with consumer behavior. *Consumer behavior* is the behavior that consumers display in selecting, purchasing, using, and evaluating products, services, ideas, and experiences that they expect will satisfy their needs and desires. Consumer behavior is the behavior that consumers display in the decision-making process when facing several alternatives or choices.

The study of tourist behavior concerns the ways in which tourists select, purchase, use, and evaluate travel products, services, and experiences. *Tourist behavior* studies attempt to understand and explain how tourists make decisions to spend available resources, such as time, money, and effort, on travel-related products and services. The study of tourist behavior is the study of a tourist's (1) mind, comprising cognition (thinking, knowing, understanding, perceiving, storing, processing, and retrieving information from the environment); affect (feelings, emotions, attitudes, predispositions); and conation (intentions to act and behave in a specific way, reasons for doing things, willingness and volition); (2) body in terms of overt behavior; (3) spirit; (4) environment, which influences tourist behavior; and (5) feedback, what a tourist receives from the environment.

12.7 THE NATURE OF TOURIST BEHAVIOR

The study of tourist behavior is interdisciplinary in nature; it is based on concepts and theories about people that have been developed by social scientists in diverse disciplines, such as:

- Psychology (the study of an individual)
- Sociology (the study of groups of individuals and their social relations)

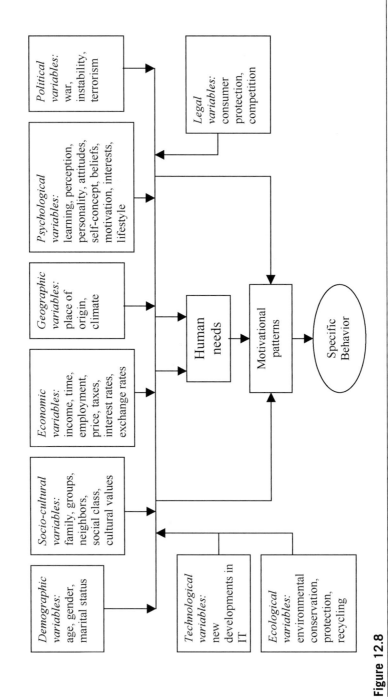

Figure 12.8

Factors Influencing Human Needs

- Social psychology (how an individual operates in groups, how he/she interacts with others)
- Anthropology (how society influences the individual)
- Economics (how the individual behaves to maximize benefits in the purchase of goods and services)
- Marketing (how to create and keep customers)
- Management (how to plan and organize the product, and how to motivate the individual so he/she can achieve satisfaction; how to influence the individual's consumption decisions to design effective management strategies).

The study of tourist behavior is also based on concepts borrowed from:

- Leisure and recreation (how an individual recreates physically and mentally)
- Geography (how the earth's climate, population, vegetation and land use influence the individual)
- Urban and regional planning (how to plan and develop cities, towns, and urban communities to provide an individual with a comfortable living environment)
- Transportation (how to efficiently transport passengers to maximize their comfort and safety)
- Law (what legal principles and policies emanate from a government and apply to people)
- Agriculture (how to cultivate the land–forestry, and farming), and
- Education (how to acquire knowledge and training).

The approach to tourist behavior will vary according to the disciplinary perspective, as presented above. No matter the perspective used, the objective of understanding tourist behavior is to better respond to the needs of increasingly diverse tourists and to better manage the growing numbers of tourists that travel suppliers and destinations attract, so as to establish mutually beneficial relationships.

12.8 THE MEANING OF TOURIST BEHAVIOR

Tourist experiences and their meanings vary from person to person. There are several reasons for this. First, there are many types of tourists, and their characteristics come in many different categories: demographic (e.g. age, gender, marital status, stage of life), social (e.g. social class), economic (e.g. income, spending patterns, employment), cultural (e.g. values, norms, customs), geographic (e.g. origin, trip destination), psychographic (e.g. personality, needs, attitudes, lifestyle, emotions, preferences, benefits sought), and behavioral (e.g. buyer status, buying rates, activities, experiences). Each type of tourist has different priorities, preferences and behavior. Therefore, dealing with multiple types of tourists means dealing with their multiple and diverse behaviors.

Second, tourists try to meet their multiple needs and wants in numerous contexts: socially, culturally, geographically, economically, and politically. These contexts are very diverse in nature and provide many different opportunities for tourists to express their behavior in multiple ways.

Third, although many demographic, economic, or socio-psychological variables that are used to characterize tourists are common to many tourists (e.g. lifestyle, interests, and income), the ways by which individual tourists express themselves are very different. Tourists have a very large and diverse number of goals, priorities, and preferences that determine how they behave and why they behave the way they do. For example, although the backpacker traveling to exotic destinations and the group of elderly tourists on a trip have a common motivation, sightseeing, both types of travelers express different behaviors because they are influenced by differences in age, social status, spending power, values, and interests. The backpacker might be interested in outdoor recreation, live entertainment, and socializing with natives, whereas elderly tourists might like to travel to destinations close to home and experience indoor activities in a peaceful, relaxing atmosphere.

12.9 THE IMPORTANCE OF STUDYING TOURIST BEHAVIOR

There are diverse reasons why it is important to study tourist behavior. First, in order to make better strategic decisions, marketers and managers must learn what tourists buy and why, where, and how they make their purchases; what types of destinations tourists like to travel to; and what types of travel arrangements, accommodations, and amenities they prefer. Are they interested in authentic or staged attractions? Do they want to play sports or gamble? What encourages and discourages them from traveling? How long are they prepared to stay away from home on their trips? How much are they prepared to spend? Tourism marketers and managers must know what types of tourists buy specific holiday destinations, products, and services. Are these tourists active or comfort oriented? Are they extroverted, outgoing, and venturesome, or introverted and shy? What motivates them to buy? How do they search for products? What product attributes do they look for? What benefits do they seek and for what reasons? How do they search for information? What information do they seek about the product/destination? How do they evaluate and select among alternatives? What choices do they make? Who does influence tourists' choices? How likely are they to revisit the same destination and use the same travel products and services? The answers to all these questions can provide tourism marketers and managers with important information to help design strategies that will better respond to the needs of travelers. For example, when tourists feel dissatisfied with their choice of a holiday spot, perhaps because of a lack of service or information about available activities, they may decide not to visit the same destination in the future. They may express their dissatisfaction to their friends and relatives and discourage them from future purchase. Tourists may never come back to the same destination again, limiting their own future selection decisions. Understanding why tourists do not purchase specific products and services is as important as understanding why they purchase others.

In addition to studying tourist evaluations of the travel products, marketers have to know what tourists do with their new purchases. For example, after tourists purchase a product, do they use it (e.g. do they travel to Hawaii and stay in a resort?), or sell or rent it (e.g. time share)? The answers to these questions are important to marketers, who must match their offerings to the frequency with which tourists buy the products.

If marketers understand tourist behavior and decision making, they will also be able to predict how future tourists will react to new products and services, information, and environment that stimulate them to behave as they do. Marketers who understand the nature of tourist behavior and the process of tourist decision-making have great competitive advantage in the marketplace.

12.10 THE IMPORTANCE OF STUDYING TOURIST BEHAVIOR IN A CROSS-CULTURAL CONTEXT

The massive growth of international tourism over the last 50 years is an indicator of people's increased mobility. Globalization, economic development, and political changes leading to the opening of China and Eastern Europe have significantly increased the number of tourists who are crossing national borders. The increasing high demand for international tourism will expose future tourists to culturally different societies. It will bring many diverse cultures together, offer many wonderful opportunities for meeting people from distant continents and countries, and provide many occasions for cross-cultural contact around the world. A large number of people will travel to experience different cultures, taste different foreign food, observe fashion, or listen to foreign music, but mostly to expose themselves to different people, lifestyles, customs, and traditions, and to trade and conduct business.

The 2020 forecast shows that culturally diverse visitors will be the future targets of the international tourism industry. This will create many challenges for the industry as it attempts to globally standardize its products and at the same time attract culturally bound visitors. It will become crucial for the industry to develop a thorough understanding of culturally distinct tourists and to identify cultural differences and similarities between them and the locals.

If the industry is to flourish in the future, it must undertake the important task of learning the foreign languages of the international tourist markets. However, cultural differences are not limited to language, food or clothing. Cultural differences are particularly related to cultural values, needs, preferences, and attitudes. These differences are experienced in a variety of human interactions, including forms of address, body language, gestures, time orientation, religious beliefs, and many others. Failure to understand these differences can lead to serious consequences, such as insults, uncomfortable situations, misunderstandings, misinterpretations, and conflicts between people. For example, the simple rejection of a cup of coffee or tea could be perceived as being rude. Declining an invitation or being late can be considered an affront. Similarly, setting deadlines and time schedules or asking visitors to travel at a specific time can be considered offensive and threatening. In order to successfully attract and satisfy international visitors, and to avoid making cultural mistakes and blaming others for having bad manners or being arrogant, future industry employees must learn to identify cultural differences between international tourist markets: What is acceptable behavior and what is not?

Learning about the cultural differences in international visitor behavior represents a key factor in effective segmentation, targeting and promotion to the specific foreign markets. For example, while all women are interested in shopping, Asian women (office ladies) are particularly known for being interested in traveling for the purpose of shopping; they spend heavily on brand-name handbags and luxury items (see Case Study 12.1). Thus, although women travelers might share some interests, there are obviously differences among them. As a result, although there might be similarities among international tourists, there are obvious differences among them. However, contrary to general belief, many international tourists are also similar in numerous ways. Cultural similarities, if properly identified, can be vital in clustering tourists in terms of their profiles. For example, while separate advertising strategies might need to be designed by the airlines to appeal to culturally distinct markets, the first- or business-class passengers may be persuaded by the same messages emphasizing luxury and upscale facilities. Success of marketing in culturally distinct markets is influenced by how different and similar are the beliefs, values, and customs that govern the selection and use of the product in the various markets.

This book supports the notion that cultural differences as well as similarities among international tourists are important marketing tools. Earlier chapters describe the underlying differences and similarities that exist among people of different cultural backgrounds and the external cultural influences that differentiate them into distinct market segments. These cultural distinctions among international tourists should lead to tailoring marketing strategies to specific segments of tourists based on their cultural needs.

12.11 BENEFITS OF UNDERSTANDING TOURIST BEHAVIOR IN A CROSS-CULTURAL CONTEXT

12.11.1 Tourism industry perspective

Understanding tourist behavior in a cross-cultural context is very important because it facilitates learning about international tourists, recognizing differences between tourists and locals, designing more effective marketing strategies that successfully target the specific group of international tourists, and implementing these strategies. The greater the differences between international tourist markets, the more advisable it is to use distinct and culturally tailored strategies in each market. If the cultural values, beliefs and customs of specific markets differ significantly, then a highly individualized marketing strategy must be developed for each market. On the other hand, if there are cultural similarities among tourist markets, then a similar marketing strategy may be used for all markets.

Identifying cultural similarities and differences among the international tourist markets allows the tourism industry to understand that tourist behavior is culture bound and that culture deeply affects tourist behavior and the operations of the whole industry. Understanding the cultural background of the target market, being sensitive to cultural differences, and accepting and respecting these differences help to minimize cross-cultural marketing and management mistakes, enhance tourist holiday experiences and satisfaction, increase tourism demand for a travel product, improve business profitability and, consequently, contribute to the success of the tourism industry.

If the tourism industry is to survive in the global economy, it must address tourists from a cultural point of view. Globalization destroys cultural characteristics, identity, and attractiveness of tourism products, and homogenizes the total international tourist market. Capitalizing on national cultures and cultural diversity of international tourists can be the major step to the future success of the international tourism industry. Effectively dealing with culturally different tourists and their national cultures will allow the tourism industry to flourish in the next decades.

Since cultural differences are potential grounds for cultural misunderstanding and conflict between tourists and locals, understanding which cultural differences have the most detrimental effects on tourist behavior is vital to managing the relationship between guest and host.

12.11.2 Tourist perspective

It is important to tourists to learn about the culture of local hosts. Cultural understanding of locals helps tourists to adjust their behavior to the unfamiliar environment in which they travel. Many tourists experience culture shock when they get off the plane. They do not understand the foreign language. They do not know how to ask for help, how much to tip, how to order a meal, or what is appropriate to say in a new culture. Unable to understand the behavior of locals, tourists can feel annoyed, upset, and even insulted. Although initially tourists may feel excited about the opportunity to see and experience different destinations, after a while they can get stressed by their inability to deal with the new environment. To reduce the stress and hassle of organizing their trips many tourists travel in groups. As a result, they do not have much contact with the locals. However, there is an increasing number of tourists who like to travel independently and experience a "cultural difference."

Many of the travelers do not know what to expect in a foreign place and what it means to experience cultural problems. They ask family and friends for their advice. Unfortunately, someone else's experiences can be very subjective and misleading. To avoid anxiety, unpleasantness, disappointment or even insult, the best strategy is to learn and understand aspects of the local culture. Knowledge of the local culture and behavior helps tourists develop confidence and creates a sense of well-being, control, and competency. Understanding foreign culture aids the tourist in knowing how to behave in certain situations. Understanding locals' behavior, customs, dress style, and eating and sleeping habits can also be an interesting educational experience. For instance, while visiting China, tourists can learn that Chinese food can be very different in Western countries than it is in China. While visiting the United States, tourists can learn that it is customary to receive a glass of icy water before a meal. If tourists seek genuine educational experiences, understanding foreign culture can help them to view the foreign culture more objectively, gain more positive experiences, and even change their negative attitudes.

12.11.3 Local resident perspective

It is also important to local hosts to learn about the culture of international tourists. Cultural understanding of international tourists helps locals to respond to the culturally determined needs of tourists. Many locals have difficulties when talking to international tourists; they do not understand the tourists' language; hence they do not know what tourists are asking or what they want to do. Although locals rely on the services of translators and tour guides, they often experience communication and interaction difficulties with international tourists. Lack of understanding of tourist behavior makes the locals feel incompetent in providing services to tourists, and this can be frustrating and stressful.

Knowledge of the tourist culture and behavior helps locals to develop a sense of confidence and pride that they are able to provide the product tourists enjoy. Locals do not have to totally adjust their behavior to match the tourists' cultural expectations. The cultural uniqueness of the local culture can be very attractive to tourists. Rather, locals should accept and respect the tourist culture. Observing the behavior of international tourists, talking to tourists, listening to their needs and preferences, and learning about their habits can help the locals avoid cultural mistakes. For example, it is perfectly appropriate to ask a Euroamerican male tourist about his wife. However, this would be a breach of social etiquette for a male from the United Arab Emirates.

One of the most important benefits of cultural understanding of tourist and host behaviors is the development of favorable impressions tourists and locals can make on one another. Most people are sensitive about foreigners' perceptions of their culture. If one is enthusiastic or does have interest in and even knowledge about another's culture, this may be interpreted as an interest and respect and a signal that one's culture is worth learning about and thus is treated as being superior. Those who show active interest and involvement in foreign cultures are usually perceived as being polite, respectful, and knowledgeable. People usually respond very warmly to those who show interest in their culture. If tourists and locals show even slight awareness of each other's culture or at least willingness to learn, they may develop favorable impressions of each other and even friendship. Developing personal relationships is essential to getting anything done in many foreign cultures. Moreover, if people sense a respect for others' cultures, then they do anything to build genuine social and professional relationships (Hooker, 2003).

SUMMARY

Human behavior develops as a result of transactions among mind (thinking, feeling, willing), body (biology, genetics), spirit (beliefs, experiences, intuition), the influence of micro-, meso-, macro-, and supra-environments on the individual, and feedback from the environment. Human behavior occurs only when it is motivated by a need that energizes toward achieving goals. Many different types of needs have been identified. According to Maslow (1954), when the lower-order needs are fulfilled, human beings become motivated by higher-order needs. Satisfied needs cease to motivate. Alderfer (1972) noted that when the upper-level needs cannot be met, the lower-level needs become major motivators. Herzberg et al. (1962) suggested that fulfilling some of the needs does not always lead to satisfaction. Vroom (1964) suggested that having goals and seeing a connection between own activity and the achievement of the goals is a motivator factor. Festinger (1957) stated that individuals can change their behavior to fulfill conflicting needs. Skinner (1969) argued that pleasant outcomes generate repeated behavior. McClelland (1953) argued that humans acquire motives from their cultures, which dictate what needs are important to fulfill first and why.

Tourist behavior has different meanings; it is very diverse, multi-dimensional, and interdisciplinary in nature. Tourist behavior can be examined in relation to topical areas associated with consumer behavior.

Currently, the tourism industry is facing an unprecedented growth worldwide. Culturally diverse visitors will be the future targets of the international tourism industry. Learning about and understanding the cultural background of international tourists has become a top priority for the tourism industry. A cultural approach to tourist behavior gives a richer and more robust portrait of tourist behavior than any other discipline. Such a cultural approach to marketing is critical to the long-term success of the tourism industry.

DISCUSSION POINTS AND QUESTIONS

1. What are the major aspects of human behavior? How do they relate to each other?
2. What factors influence human behavior?
3. Does Maslow's Hierarchy of Needs account for human behavior? What do you think of various shortcomings of the model?
4. In your own experience, are tourism professionals in your country sensitive to cultural differences? Identify examples to prove your point.
5. Do you think marketers and managers should adapt a cultural approach to the study of tourist behavior? What arguments can you suggest to support the study of tourist behavior in a cross-cultural context?
6. Have you traveled outside your home country? If yes, identify some of the differences in cultural values, behavior, and travel patterns that you noted between people in your home country and a country you visited.

CASE STUDY 12.1 The Asian Woman's Shopping Experience: New Research from Thailand

Shopping patterns and motives differ between the United States and Asia. In industrialized economies such as the US consumers shop to relieve stress or find a bargain. American women buy for emotional satisfaction. They buy small gifts for themselves that symbolize ''life's little luxuries.'' They often purchase things they want but do not need. Thus the products do not always satisfy their direct functional needs. Also, American women seek premium-priced brand names because they want to make a statement about their social status. American women are proud of being able to buy top-quality designer products cheaply. Many Americans treat shopping as a daily routine; some are obsessed with shopping.

Asian women, on the other hand, do not shop for emotional and self-actualization purposes, or for the purpose of finding a luxury bargain. They are just discovering the thrill of shopping and are approaching routine shopping as fun rather than as emotional therapy or obsession. Today, in South East Asia more women are joining the work force and becoming financially independent. Asian women treat shopping as the opportunity to show their new wealth or to socialize with friends.

In many South East Asian countries, women place a high value on shopping in luxury malls. While shopping at malls is taken for granted by Western women, in South East Asia shopping malls have existed for only a decade and are perceived as social-status venues. Young, single Asian women attach high importance to strolling through the mall and showing off their wealth by purchasing expensive handbags, clothes, and jewelry. In Japan, collecting designer handbags has become a fetish among young, bargain-conscious women, especially those who are still in school and concerned about the price. Asian women also treat shopping at malls as social events with friends.

Many single women in Bangkok work hard and spend their free time shopping. They go on brand-shopping sprees four times a month and purchase low-priced items, such as toys and casual clothes.

Shopping as a lifestyle will continue to grow in Asia, especially among women from the growing middle class.

Source: *Asian Market Research News*. Retrieved June 20, 2003, from [http://www.asiamarketresearch.com/news/000309.htm]

WEBSITE LINKS

1. Maslows' Hierarchy of Needs, http://www.businessballs.com/maslow/htm
2. Consumer behavior and culture: Consequences for global marketing and advertising, http://www.sagepub.com/booktoc/aspx?pid=9647&sc=1
3. Food in Chinese culture, http://www.askasia.org/frclasrm/readings/r000044.htm
4. Dating cultural gaps, http://www.harbus.org/news/365215.html
5. How to market your product internationally? http://www.lfpackage.com/international_marketing.htm

In order to understand tourist buying behavior, one must first learn consumer buying behavior. The next chapter will discuss the concept of consumer buying behavior.

Consumer buying behavior

The aim of this chapter is to describe consumer buying behavior and decision process.

INTRODUCTION

Consumer buying behavior is influenced by numerous factors. Decision-making questions such as what, why, how, where and when consumers buy are influenced by three major conditions: (1) environmental factors, (2) the buyer's factors, and (3) the buyer's responses factors (see Figure 13.1).

There are three types of environmental factors: (1) the environmental stimuli that are beyond the consumer's control (e.g. demographic, cultural, social, geographic, economic, historic, legal, political, technological, competitive stimuli); (2) the market stimuli that are largely under the control of marketing managers (e.g. company, customers, suppliers, intermediaries, publics); and (3) the marketing efforts, which refer to the marketing, pricing, distribution, and promotion of products and services, as well as people who deliver them. The environmental factors influence the buyer's factors.

There are three types of buyers' factors: (1) the buyer's personal characteristics, (2) the buyer's psychological characteristics, and (3) the decision process. The buyer's **289**

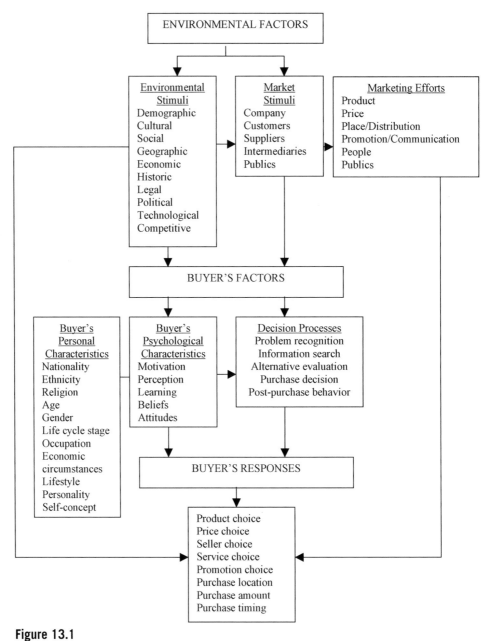

Figure 13.1

Consumer Buying Behavior Process

personal characteristics include nationality, ethnicity, religion, age, gender, lifecycle stage, occupation, economic status, lifestyle, personality, and self-concept. The buyer's psychological characteristics include motivation, perception, learning, beliefs, and attitudes. Both personal and psychological characteristics of the buyer affect the decision process, i.e. the way buyers identify their needs, seek information, select criteria for product evaluation, evaluate products, make the purchase decision, and feel about the purchase. The decision process consists of five major steps: (1) problem recognition, (2) information search, (3) alternative evaluation, (4) purchase decision, and (5) post-purchase behavior.

The buyer's personal and psychological characteristics and the decision process influence buyer's responses such as product selection, pricing acceptance, seller and service choice, reactions to product promotion, purchase location, amount, and timing (see Figure 13.1).

13.1 ENVIRONMENTAL FACTORS

13.1.1 Environmental stimuli
Demographic environment

The major demographic factors that influence buyers' behavior are those that define buyers as individual consumers as well as populations. These factors include age, gender, education, occupation, socio-economic status, marital status, and life stage. Of particular importance are trends and developments in population growth, age mix, dispersion, density, and diversity. The current world population is over 6 billion, and it is predicted that by 2020 it will reach 8–10 billion. Currently, the world population experiences problems of overcrowding, pollution, declining quality of natural and cultural resources, and deteriorating quality of life. These problems will intensify in the future. As a result, many consumers will seek a simpler life; move to smaller apartments and cheaper houses in less populated communities; buy second homes in less developed countries; choose less extravagant, sophisticated, and stressful lifestyles; and travel in a more environmentally friendly way.

Most of the population growth takes place in less developed countries, which account for 70% of the world's population. The lowest growth occurs in the developed world, particularly, in Italy, Poland, Switzerland, and Sweden. In the United States, the most rapid population growth is noted in the South and Southwest. The areas with the highest growth will become the future tourism-generating regions and require a wide variety of travel products and services.

The population age mix varies, and ranges from extremely young and fast-growing populations (e.g. Mexico) to elderly and slow-growing populations (e.g. Japan and Italy). Of all age-group segments, the 34–54 and over 65 groups experience the largest growth. They will become the important tourism markets whose needs have to be adequately met in the future.

The world population is highly dispersed due to population migrations within and between countries that resulted from the break up of the Soviet bloc, the ethnic turmoil in the Balkans and Middle East, the formation of the European Union, and the opening of borders between Central and Eastern European countries. The world population is also highly concentrated along sea and ocean shores and big, urban metropolitan areas.

Diverse population groups distinguish themselves on the bases of their different nationalities, ethnicities, races, religions, and various demographic and cultural factors. In the United States, Australia, and Canada, people come from virtually all nations. The United States, initially called a ''melting pot,'' now called a ''salad bowl'' society, has ethnic groups that maintain their ethnic differences, neighborhoods, cultures, and traditions. These trends indicate where consumers will be and what types of people will become future consumers of travel and tourism goods.

Major demographic trends that will significantly change the buying behavior of Western consumers in years to come are: (1) an increasing world population; (2) a relatively low birth-rate; (3) a decline in the numbers of teenagers and children; (4) an aging population and the creation of the ''Silver Century''; (5) aging Baby Boomers in the United States and a shift to older, more mature consumers (aged 35–54); (6) an increased life expectancy; (7) delayed retirement; (8) the increasing influence of baby boomers' values and attitudes; (9) a focus on maintaining a younger, healthier, more active lifestyle; (10) increased mobility (geographical, social, and professional); (11) geographic population shifts (from cities to suburbs and ''micropolitan areas''); (12) widening geographic differences between cities, suburbs, and rural areas; (13) the transformation of marriage, professional career, and parenting; (14) changing family structure (more singles, more childlessness, later marriages, higher separation and divorce rates, more unmarried working women; (15) an increasing number of gays, lesbians, and same gender households; (16) shifting birth trends (older mothers, fewer pregnant teenagers); (17) the increasing importance of women as decision-makers; (18) increased educational levels; (19) increased white collar population (higher percentage with high school education, fewer blue-collar workers; (20) increases in numbers of both legal and illegal immigrants, many of whom exhibit high birth-rates; (21) increasing ethnic and racial diversity mix; (22) rising Hispanic and Asian influence; and (23) declining Western influence.

For example, it is envisaged that women will raise families in the later stages of their life cycles, opting instead to be more mobile and to travel more, either for personal or professional reasons. The number of working women, especially in high administrative and managerial positions, will be constantly rising in the developed world. Evidence suggests that women will represent half of the business world. Women will also travel more in the future than men (Staats et al., 2006). Women's desire for future travel is an effect of an emerging cohort of working women with travel experience; university graduate women, in particular, are aware of the professional benefits of travel (Staats et al., 2006). In the past, women traveled less than men because they were perceived as unable or unwilling to travel due to family commitments (Adler, 1993; Markham et al., 1986). Today, travel provides women with important opportunities for career development and networking.

Further, it is also envisaged that families with small children will seek child-oriented destinations and vacation facilities such as child-care centers. There will be a growth in customized travel products for people of the same gender living and traveling together. Children returning home after graduating from college may seek luxury gifts for their parents in the form of travel, as gestures of appreciation. An increasing number of immigrants will require products that meet their cultural and religious needs (ethnic food, clothing, arts and crafts, or religious books). Table 13.1 shows the major consumer demographic segments and their future purchasing needs.

Other factors that can bring a change in consumer buying behavior and create new marketing opportunities, especially in the United States (but already visible in other countries) are (1) changing nature of work (more focus on information technology and automized services), (2) increasing obesity among adults and children (inappropriate diet due to time pressure, eating more outside), (3) awareness of health problems, (4) increasing demand for low-carbohydrate diets, (5) pressure to be seen as different from others, (6) increasing pace of life and demand for slower and more rewarding life, (7) increasing demand for pleasures of life and indulgence, (8) need for emotional escapes and more social contacts, and (9) need for safety and security.

The major market segments, mostly in an American context, that may significantly create new opportunities for travel and tourism and influence the direction of future marketing efforts are identified in Table 13.2.

Cultural environment

Culture is the fundamental determinant of a person's wants and behavior. The major cultural factors that influence people's buying behavior are values, beliefs, language, religion, customs, traditions, and family relations. Culture determines what kind of clothes people buy, what food they eat, how they dress, and what they do with their leisure time. Culture defines people's needs for products and services. Culture dictates which products to buy and avoid, where to buy and how often, what sources of information to rely upon, whether to be rigid or flexible in the acceptance of new ideas, what criteria to use in evaluating products, and what type of service to accept. Distinct cultural groups of consumers have different value systems based on different life experiences and situations and thus have different product expectations and preferences, expenditure patterns, and responses to promotional messages. Retailers need to be aware how national cultures influence consumers' purchasing needs and patterns. Learning about national cultures of distinct groups of consumers can help to develop more effective and successful products for culturally different consumer segments.

By the year 2020 half the world's population will be living in mainland China, India, the former Soviet Union, the United States, and Indonesia. These regions will be the major sources of potential consumers. Understanding cultural differences among these

Table 13.1 Future Consumer Segments and Their Buying Needs

Segment	General characteristics	Buying needs
Adult-centered families	Older parents with children	Educational travel, travel close to home
Blended families	Remarried with children from other marriage, need to start from the beginning	Need everything, including vacations
Boomerang kids	Children returning home after college, have high discretionary income, often pay nothing for accommodation and food	Gifts for parents in form of travel, weekend getaway, cruise trips
Dual income families	Both spouses work	Convenience and luxury, expensive travel, clothes, haircuts, manicures, massages, facials, elegant briefcases, jewelry
Empty nesters	Families with no children	Luxury items, exotic and adventure travel, sporty cars, designer clothing
Expanded families	Parenting stepchildren, grandchildren, elderly parents, grandparents, spouses, ill relatives, may include adopted children	Purchases depend on interests and needs
Friends as families	Friends being virtual family members bonded by companionship and compassion	Gifts, weekend getaway together, cruise trips
Grandparent families	Families with multiple grandparents	Intergenerational products catering to young and old, comfortable all-inclusive trips with educational focus
Multigenerational or vertical families	Several generations alive at once	User-friendly products for all ages and abilities, extended family vacations, multiple-generation trips, scheduled events and dinners, each sponsored by different family members

Table 13.1 (*Continued*)

Segment	General characteristics	Buying needs
Solo fliers	Single either married or not, enjoy the solitary lifestyle, mostly older women, widowed or divorced	Products and services that help to look and feel good, and maintain problem-free life, security, e.g. health clubs, wellness and spa products, healing services, travel insurance, educational information
Soul mates	Live in long-term relationships, financially stable	Luxury items such as retreat trips, cruises, spas, restaurants

Source: items adapted from Dychtwald, M. (2003) *Cycles: How we will live, work and buy.* New York: Free Press.

various international consumer markets is imperative. For example, in some countries, due to different cultural traditions, there are different attitudes to distinguish gender groups, especially roles and rights of men and women. For example, most Asian and Islamic countries exhibit male preference. In China, a male preference is manifested by the widespread abortions of female fetuses. In Saudi Arabia the socio-economic status of women is downgraded. Women attend separate schools and are restricted from working outside the home. Women who are permitted to work are restricted to having contacts with women only. Women are also prohibited from driving cars or riding in taxis without a male escort. The patriarchal structure also dominates in Hispanic communities.

Cultural differences in roles and responsibilities lead to different needs in terms of travel behavior. For example, in the countries where women's responsibility is to take care of children and depend on men as breadwinners, women are more constrained in their travel than men. They are discouraged from independent travel because this is a masculine activity unsuitable for women (Henderson et al., 1988). On the other hand, in Western cultures women are more independent, and travel frequently for vacation and business purposes.

In some countries, there are also significant cultural differences in types of jobs and salaries regarded as appropriate for women and men. For example, in Sweden, nearly half of administrative and managerial positions are held by women, compared to less than 5% in Spain. In many countries around the world women are disadvantaged in terms of pay and working conditions. Consequently, understanding cultural differences in attitudes toward genders can help to determine and predict women and men's travel behavior in selected countries, for example, what products they will seek, how they will react to promotional ads, or who will make a purchasing decision.

Table 13.2 Future Important Market Segments

Baby Boomers: mature "fifty-something" segment, born between 1946 and 1954, represents about 80 million well educated, wealthy, and mobile people with interest in discovery, exploration, leisure products, vacation, adventure, cruises, and luxury. Want to stay active and youthful, seek healthcare products and physical activities. Demand activities, services and equipment that maintain physical fitness (e.g. sports, recreation, gyms, weight-loss clinics, diet products). Seek health and wellness products that foster being healthy and looking young (e.g. health clubs, retreat camps, spas, cosmetics). Interested in comfortable lifestyles, casual sport clothing and shoes. Need travel-friendly products (e.g. light and small), pharmaceuticals, medical and healing services, assisted traveling and shopping facilities. Demand convenience, quality, and safety. Require travel insurances, financial services, second homes, cars, home care products, and educational information.

Generation X: born between 1965 and 1976, represents 45 million young and freedom-minded individuals who lived in the age of AIDS during recession and corporate downsizing, who are environmentally and socially oriented, less materialistic, looking for quality of life and satisfaction rather than professional career and promotion. Sceptical and cynical, however, value honesty and low prices. Like recreation activities such as hiking or biking.

Generation Y: born between 1977 and 1994, represents 80 million of North Americans who have grown up surrounded by computers and digital media. Fluent with computers, Internet and digital technology (N-Gens or Net generation). Likes comfort, simplicity, and fast food. Sometimes called Echo boomers.

Generation M: the Internet or Google generation. Have also grown up with computer technology and whose first source of knowledge is the Internet; a search engine Google being the most popular one. Distinct from previous generations that grew up before the widespread availability of the Internet, and whose major sources of knowledge were books and conventional libraries. Sometimes called Generation Xbox, iPod and the instant-messaging generation.

Millennial Generation: youngest generation, born between 1978 and 1982 and ending in 2003. Are the children of the Baby Boomers.

Generation D: digital generation of young computer wizards. Very comfortable with digital devices and digital culture.

Generation Now: three- to five-year-old children who understand technology, request own iPods, fast foods, fast TV, and instant gratification. Never had to wait for much.

Sandwich Generation: have finished raising their children, are caring for their aging parents, have become parents to their parents. Struggling to pay college tuition for their children and having to deal with the housing, financial, medical and emotional problems of their parents. Some are in their 30s or 40s, caught between the needs of their growing children and their parents. Others are in their 50s or 60s, planning for relaxation and travel.

Generation XL: children or young adults who are overweight because they gave up a balanced diet and regular exercise to dedicate themselves to their dot-com jobs. Mainly college students who eat too much of the wrong food and have too little activity and unhealthy lifestyle. On their way to health problems such as diabetes, heart attacks, and strokes.

Social environment

Consumer buying behavior is influenced by social factors such as social class, social stimuli, family, social roles and social status. Social classes are groups of a society whose members share similar values, interests, status or position based on amount and type of income, occupation, area of residence, interests, opinions, and lifestyle preferences. Social classes include upper-uppers, lower-uppers, upper-middles, middle class, lower-middle, upper-lowers and lower-lowers. Only 1% of the population is located in the upper-upper stratum, 12% in the upper-middle stratum, and 9% in the upper-lower stratum. Within the same social class people tend to behave alike. However, distinct social classes behave differently and show different product and brand preferences for clothing, home furniture, appliances, electronics, cars, travel, recreation, and leisure activities.

Social stimuli or influence can be interpersonal and intrapersonal. Interpersonal stimuli refer to (1) larger social and cultural groups to which people belong or would like to belong (e.g. family, friends, or interests, gender- and age-based groups, or membership groups) and (2) smaller peer and reference groups. In general, there are three major categories of reference groups that have influence on people's behavior and decision-making. These are the groups to which (1) the individual already belongs; (2) the individual would like to belong, called *aspirational groups* (e.g. sport clubs); and (3) the individual would not like to belong to, called *dissociative groups* (e.g. groups of people who take drugs and drink alcohol). The aspirational groups create pressures to conform to their norms, and influence an individual's attitudes and self-concept. The strength of this influence depends on the values and norms of the groups and those who would like to belong to them.

Intrapersonal stimuli refer to needs, perceptions, and attitudes that characterize and shape an individual's behavior. The individuals differ and create distinct market segments because they are influenced by different needs and attitudes that affect their behavior. For example, the mature consumer segment (people 65 years and over) differs from the young consumer segment (less than 35 years of age); seniors usually demand health and convenience products, while youngsters seek more excitement and adventure.

Family significantly influences people's buying behavior. The family consists of parents, children, grandparents, aunts, uncles, and cousins, all of whom influence an individual's values, attitudes toward religion, politics, the economy, personal lifestyle, and even ambition. The spouses and children usually have a more direct influence on the individual's behavior than any other group. Families vary in terms of size, strength, and cohesion depending upon the cultural orientation of their members. For example, Norwegian and Swedish families are smaller, while Italian, Greek, and Chinese families are bigger. In Mediterranean and Latin American countries the family represents the most important social group, and it exerts the strongest influence over its members' behavior. In ethnic Greek and Korean communities the very strong family ties manifest themselves in cooperative family business ventures (e.g. family restaurants, family-run shops).

Families also vary in terms of their economic status, religious beliefs, political orientation, or attitudes toward roles and responsibilities, for example, wife, husband, or child. Some families are husband dominant, while others are wife dominant. In some families, purchasing decisions are made jointly by husband and wife, while in others, they are made separately. In some families husbands are responsible for purchasing cars and making financial investments, while wives are responsible for buying food, kitchen ware, cleaning products, personal clothing, and cosmetics; joint decisions are made about annual vacations, schooling, housing and entertainment. In many families children have a significant influence upon parents' purchases.

A social role refers to the activities that a person is expected to perform in a family or society (e.g. the role of son, daughter, husband, wife, teacher, or doctor). Each social role determines an individual's behavior. For example, mothers are expected to take care of their children. The social roles are influenced by external surroundings. For example, children spending vacations with parents in a luxury hotel behave differently than when they travel with other children at a school camp.

Each social role reflects a social status given to an individual by a society. People usually buy products and services that show their status in society. For example, a factory worker and lawyer have different social statuses. A factory worker buys comfortable and casual clothes, while a lawyer buys brand clothing, elegant briefcases, and luxury cars to emphasize the difference in social status. Similarly, business travelers expect to fly first or business class; flying economy class would mean losing their social standing.

Geographic environment

The major geographic variables that affect people's buying behavior are the natural resources, such as water, forests, beaches, wildlife, coral reefs, clean air, vegetation, and land use. Most tourists purchase holiday trips to destinations that offer distinctly different geographical environments than their place of residency. For example, many North European tourists travel to Southern Europe to warm themselves up in warm climates along the Mediterranean Sea. Further, various geographic areas are characterized by different climates, economies, politics, religious affiliations, and customs and thus offer distinct lifestyles, values and culture. For example, the Northeast area of the United States offers a very busy and stressful pace of life. Similarly, in Europe, Germany offers a scheduled and rigid lifestyle. On the other hand, the Southeast area of the United States, influenced by the growing number of Hispanics, offers a slower, more casual, outdoor lifestyle; the area is known for its entertainment and nightlife. Likewise, Australia offers a casual and relaxed pace of life; the country is known for its social and family orientation and environmental protection.

Economic environment

The major economic factors that affect purchasing and spending power of individual consumers as well as populations are (1) the disposable income (income left after taxes are paid), (2) the discretionary income (income left after taxes, bills and necessities are paid), (3) the price of necessities (e.g. daily food, clothing), and (4) the price of luxury goods (e.g. travel, recreation, education). According to Engel's law, as the disposable and discretionary (spendable) income increases, people spend (1) less on necessities, (2) the same amount on accommodation, except for utilities and electricity, which expenditures decrease, and (3) more on luxury items (e.g. cars, jewelry, travel, yachts). According to the law of price elasticity of demand, as the price of the goods increases, people spend (1) the same amount on necessities and (2) less on luxury items. However, as prices increase, some may spend more on luxury and expensive goods in order to enhance their social status.

The other economic factors that influence people's purchasing and spending patterns are business cycles, inflation, the unemployment rate, the interest rate, the exchange rate, saving policy, debt, credit availability, taxation policy (federal, state), imports and exports. For example, in terms of business cycles, during prosperous times people have higher incomes and thus buy more: they usually spend more on expensive and luxury items. During a recession, consumers have less discretionary income and thus buy less: they usually look for basic and low-priced products. In terms of inflation, serious price increases can cause a decrease in the consumer's purchasing power, or change in their spending patterns (e.g. purchase a bicycle rather than purchase a car, lease rather than buy).

A high unemployment rate reduces consumers' spending and buying. A declining exchange rate (e.g. low local currency) makes local products cheaper, and products purchased overseas more expensive, whereas a rising exchange rate (e.g. high local currency) makes overseas products cheaper and more affordable than local products. High sales taxes on goods and services (e.g. VAT, GST) discourage consumers from spending money and deter them from traveling. For example, currently South and Central American destinations are cheaper than Asian, European or North American because the former have lower sales taxes.

Historic environment

Historical and ancestral ties are important in influencing people's behavior. For example, after the Second World War, many Poles refused to buy German products and travel to Germany. Likewise, due to mutual animosity, Japanese and Koreans often refused to cooperate and engage in various economic and social activities.

Legal and political environment

The legal and political environment that influences people's buying and spending behavior is composed of laws, legislation, policies, regulations, government agencies, and pressure groups. Monetary and fiscal policies determine how much money the government will spend for goods and services, how much is made available to consumers, and how much discretionary income people will have left after their taxes and necessities are paid for. Social legislation determines civil rights, and environmental protection laws determine the extent to which people can use the environment for their purposes, including travel. Government relations with individual industries determine subsidies for agriculture and tourism. Laws address unfair competition, price and consumer discrimination, misleading advertising, and hidden pricing. Rules govern airline deregulation; safeguard children; protect consumer credit; secure food handling and sanitation procedures; regulate alcohol consumption; fix sales, hotel and restaurant taxation; and control packaging and labeling.

Currently, there is an increased emphasis on socially responsible purchases and ethics, such as abandoning smoking in public areas, eliminating drunk driving, treating animals ethically, and buying fair trade products. There is increased attention paid to rights of special interest groups, such as women, senior citizens, people with disabilities, minorities, gays, and lesbians. There are laws protecting the individual consumer's privacy and identity.

Technological environment

The new technology has had a dramatic effect on people's buying behavior. The Internet, sophisticated websites, computerized reservation and payment systems, WebCTs, cell phones, bar codes, ATMs, eBay, Skype, etc., have allowed sellers and consumers to change the ways they communicate and make transactions. For example, any individual with access to the Internet can see and experience products before purchase and obtain information about price, special rates, seasonal discounts, special deals, and purchase conditions, as well as compare prices charged by other suppliers. These websites also enable buyers to purchase the products from the convenience of their home. In addition, technology has created opportunities for telemarketing and TV/computer home shopping.

The most dramatic forces affecting travel and tourism have been the emergence of Global Distribution Systems (such as SABRE in the United States and Amadeus in Europe) and online travel agencies (OLTA) such as Expedia, Travelocity, Opodo, and Orbitz. The technology helps traditional travel agents and enables individual buyers to book and buy their own airline tickets, accommodation, rental cars and travel insurance.

In addition, consumers are increasingly encountering automation in stores. Many stores offer self-scanning and self-checking out. Customers in the United States have begun to use biometric identification to pay for their purchases. The need for cash, checks or credit cards has been eliminated in many stores. Soon, barcodes will be replaced by radio-frequency identification (RFID) technology. Already, mobile phone users are able to surf the web, purchase products and services, and have access to online interpretation when visiting museums. Companies such as SNCF (the French railroad company) and Air France have developed applications allowing their customers to purchase tickets from their mobile phone and register or check in for their trip/flight.

Travel companies are already able to access consumers with personalized text and email messages and target special interest groups such as skiers, golfers, and business travelers with customized offerings. Customers are able to receive wireless messages and suggestions on products and activities related to their personal interests. Technology will allow suppliers to recognize a customer who visits their sites and tailor offers based on previous online behavior or purchases (Katz cited in Dickson & Vladimir, 2004). The wireless technology, including PDAs, cell phones and laptop computers with international reach will be commonly used to shop for products and location-based services.

Although some developments bring opportunities for innovation (biotechnology, computers, telecommunication, robotics), they also threaten people's privacy, simplicity, and quality of life. Society increasingly seeks safety in food, cars, clothing, electrical appliances, transportation, and construction.

Competitive environment

Competitive environment varies depending on the market structure. For example, in a pure market structure, many similar products are offered to many buyers; the slightest increase in product price eliminates demand for it. In the oligopolistic market structure similar products are provided by a few large sellers dominating the market; any decrease in product price is immediately matched by competitors to generate additional sales. In a monopolistic market structure dominated by one provider only (usually government or a private sector) there is no competition; demand is inelastic, allowing prices to rise to sellers' satisfaction and consumers' dissatisfaction.

13.2 BUYER'S FACTORS

13.2.1 Buyer's personal characteristics
Nationality

The behavior of potential buyers is influenced by their nationality and language spoken. National cultures affect what people buy and eat, how they dress, what music they listen to, and where they travel. For example, demand for ethnic food in areas with large numbers of migrants with different nationalities is determined by the tastes and customs of the migrants who live in these areas.

Countries such as Australia, Canada, the United Kingdom, and the United States comprise a very wide range of different nationalities of origin and cultures. While many immigrants to these countries identify with the culture of their host country, many follow their traditional values and rules of conduct and speak native languages to emphasize their own cultural identity.

Ethnicity

Ethnicity refers to the process of identification of human groups within the larger society on the basis of their ethnic characteristics, such as physical attributes, religion, common perceptions and cognitions, values and traditions, and geographical location. For example, African-American, Asian-American, Hispanic, and French-Canadian represent distinct ethnic groups that use their own ethnic symbols to define and differentiate themselves from other ethnic groups. Sometimes the terms *ethnic groups* and *subcultures* are used interchangeably. It is widely assumed that subcultures represent smaller groups within the larger culture. However, some believe that the term *subculture* should be avoided as the connotation of ''sub'' implies the inferiority of the ethnic group.

Religion

Religion represents an important influence on people's buying behavior. Different religious groups have distinct consumption habits and preferences for leisure and entertainment. Religion gives people direction and teaches them what is morally appropriate and what is not. For example, Jews eat kosher food products, and Seventh Day Adventists limit their consumption of meat. Mormons do not purchase tobaccos or liquor, and Evangelical Christians avoid purchasing jewelry. Muslims do not eat pork and generally do not consume alcohol. Hispanics like to purchase clothing and spend heavily on fashion and dancing. Italians spend heavily on food, and African-Americans on music. While African-Americans frequent discos, buy music albums, and do arts and crafts, white Americans like eating out, playing golf, and boating (Blackwell, 1979). Although many of these differences can be explained by religious differences, some may also be explained by income differences.

Age

Age determines the way people behave and the type of goods they purchase. For example, young people (less than 35 years of age) often download music from the Internet, buy fashionable dress and sports equipment, and seek excitement and adventure. On the other hand, seniors (people 65 years and over) still buy music on CDs, usually demand health and convenience products, and buy extra medicine and insurance.

Gender

People's buying behavior and consumption patterns depend upon their gender. Women are known for exhibiting different shopping behavior from men. They love shopping for clothes and accessories, while men are known for their interest in cars and consumer electronics. Women usually decide about grocery shopping and men about the purchase of a car.

Lifecycle stage

The family lifecycle (FLC) is a useful concept that explains how the family influences people's buying behavior and consumption patterns. According to the FLC, a typical family goes through a number of distinct stages in its life; each stage is characterized by different consumption needs and patterns. For example, young married people without children have higher discretionary incomes; they travel and dine out more frequently than do families with children. In the United States, people with children opt for home delivery and take out food.

Occupation

A person's occupation affects his/her behavior and need for goods. For example, business executives usually eat their lunches at a full-service restaurant, while clerical employees bring their lunches from home or purchase them from a nearby quick-service restaurant.

Economic status

A person's economic status affects the choice the person makes and products purchased. For example, people with low discretionary incomes have less savings, do not eat out frequently at restaurants, and do not spend much on entertainment and expensive vacations. Those with higher discretionary incomes spend more on luxury goods, such as jewelry, expensive wines and beers, luxury hotels, and upgraded air travel.

Lifestyle

Lifestyle refers to a person's specific patterns of activities, interests, and opinions (AIO) in areas such as work, leisure, politics, and recreation. Some people follow a very social lifestyle: they surround themselves with friends and relatives. They are outgoing and confident, and frequently travel for social purposes. Others are shy, seek solitude, and travel close to home. While some like peaceful, nature-based activities, such as walking, hiking, and bird-watching, others like risky activities such as bungee-jumping or mountain climbing.

One of the most popular classifications of lifestyles is the VALS (Values and Life-styles) framework, which categorizes American adults into eight groups based on their different lifestyles: (1) believers (17%), who are conservative, conventional, traditional, religious, community- and country-oriented; (2) achievers (14%), who are successful, work-oriented, status-seeking, and satisfied with families and jobs; (3) experiencers (13%), who are young, vital, enthusiastic, impulsive, variety- and excitement-seeking, heavy spenders who buy clothing, fast food, music and videos; (4) strivers (12%), who are striving to find a place in life, unsure about themselves, and low in socio-economic status; (5) makers (12%), who are practical, self-sufficient, trying to experience the world, politically conservative, suspicious of new ideas and resentful of government intrusion into individual rights; (6) strugglers (12%), who are poor, uneducated, low-skilled, elderly, concerned about security and safety, and cautious about consumption; (7) fulfillers (11%), who are mature, well educated, knowledgeable, responsible, satisfied, conservative, practical, recently retired; and (8) actualizers (10%), who are successful, sophisticated, active, and image oriented not in terms of status but taste and character, and have high self-esteem and significant resources.

Personality

Personality refers to a person's distinguishing psychological characteristics that lead to specific responses to the environment and distinguish one individual from another. People with different personalities behave differently and have different needs.

Fiske and Maddi (1961), who introduced activation theory of personality development, identified two major types of personality: (1) high-activation (high-energy) extroverts and (2) low-activation (low-energy) introverts. The high-activation type needs a variety of activities and alternatives to choose from, whereas the low-activation type seeks comfort, familiarity, and fewer choices (e.g. restaurants, hotels).

Self-concept

Self-concept refers to self-image or mental picture of self. Self-image plays a determining role in how people see themselves and what they buy to improve their self-image. For example, people who perceive themselves as outgoing and active are unlikely to be shy, inhibited, and inner-focused. They are extroverted, very social, and open to new ideas and things. Those who are energetic, full of strength and new ideas usually purchase products that attract, or are perceived to be for, young, dynamic, successful people.

Buyer's psychological characteristics

In exploring the influence of intrapersonal factors on buying behavior, we must identify the impact of psychographic factors, such as motivation, perception, learning, beliefs, and attitudes.

Motivation

A motive is a primary factor driving a person's behavior. It is stimulated externally and internally by a need that the individual seeks to satisfy. Every person has some needs and thus behaves and reacts in a way that allows those needs to be fulfilled. A need that goes unsatisfied generates tension that is eliminated once the need is satisfied. The needs a person seeks to satisfy differ depending upon that person's personal characteristics (as discussed above). The major motivation theories were discussed in Chapter 12.

There are primary motives which stimulate needs for consumption of general products such as food products, computers, or travel; and selective motives which stimulate needs for consumption of specific products such as low-calorie food products or Apple computers. Motives must be stimulated in order for an individual to feel a need and behave in a certain way. However, how the motives are stimulated depends on the person's perception of the environment that creates the specific motives.

Perception

Perception is the process by which people create meanings from the selection, organization, and interpretation of stimuli from within themselves (e.g. feelings of stress or frustration) or from the external environment (e.g. travel advertisements). Perceptions differ: for example, one person may perceive a waiter to be casual and unsophisticated, while another person may view the same waiter to be formal and cold. People have different perceptions because they experience the same stimuli or information in different ways, depending upon their personal characteristics and personality. The selection and interpretation of various stimuli varies because people have different sensory abilities.

Learning

Learning arises from experiences and represents changes in people's behavior arising from experience. Most human behavior is learned; thus people can be taught. Learning occurs through stimuli, observation, active participation, socialization, response, and reinforcement. People behave in a certain way and make choices based on the information learned from the environment. For example, tourists select accommodations based on the information obtained from travel brochures, talking to hotel guests, or direct experience with the hotel facilities.

Beliefs

Beliefs are the thoughts people hold about something based on knowledge, faith, or opinion. For example, customers may believe that a certain restaurant's services are the best in town, regardless of whether this is indeed true. Beliefs reinforce images, and people behave depending on their images and what they believe in.

Attitudes

Attitudes describe people's evaluations, feelings, and tendencies to perceive and behave in a consistent way toward certain objects (e.g. clothes, food, music), ideas (e.g. religion, politics), or other people. Attitudes decide whether people are going to like or dislike certain objects, ideas, or people. Attitudes are developed during childhood and are formed and adjusted during adulthood. The degree of adjustment depends upon what an individual learned from the environment, mainly social groups, information received, and past experience. The strength of attitudes depends upon people's motivation and personal characteristics. Attitudes influence product purchases, as well as perceptions of a product's ability to meet needs, enhance self-image, respond to cultural values, and give meanings to beliefs and experiences. Attitudes predict people's behavior. Those with negative attitudes behave differently from those with positive attitudes. Negative attitudes are difficult to change.

13.2.2 Decision process

A buyer's personal and psychological characteristics influence the buyer's decision process (see Figure 13.2). The decision process consists of major five steps: (1) problem recognition, (2) information search, (3) alternative evaluation, (4) purchase decision, and (5) post-purchase behavior. Every buyer must pass through these five stages with every purchase s/he makes.

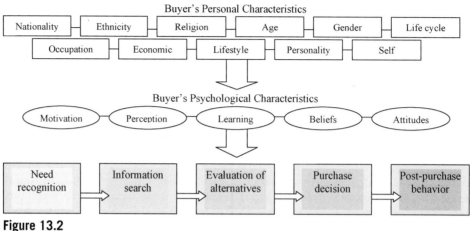

Figure 13.2

The Influence of Buyer's Personal and Psychological Characteristics on the Decision Process

Stage 1

The decision process begins in the first stage, called *Need Recognition*. Potential buyers recognize a need when is faced with a "problem" such as being tired from work and needing some rest. The buyer feels that the best way to eliminate the problem and satisfy the need for rest may be to leave work and go for a trip. The buyer recognizes a *possible need* to travel. If the buyer perceives the tiredness as a problem, s/he is in the *actual state* of buying. If the buyer desires travel as something new to experience, s/he is in a *desired state* of buying.

The recognition of a need or problem can be triggered by internal or external stimuli, e.g. hunger, tiredness, or illness. Potential buyers may have different types of needs or problems that lead them to purchase. Internal and external stimuli often trigger unsatisfied needs that would most likely motivate prospective buyers towards a purchase (e.g. a vacation trip). If the prospective buyer feels a need to relax and recuperate from work, s/he might be motivated to go on vacation to a destination that offers peace and relaxation. However, if the prospective buyer feels a need to learn about South America and become familiar with a new culture (internal stimuli), s/he might be motivated to explore Peru or Argentina. Both needs can be combined with a need to use the opportunity and purchase discounted airfare (external stimuli) or a travel package. It is important to anticipate what kinds of needs or problems prospective buyers have.

Need/problem recognition may be a simple or complex process. *Simple need recognition* occurs frequently and can be dealt with easily and automatically. For example, when a prospective buyer recognizes the need for a drink or daily news, s/he can purchase drinks from a vending machine or magazines from a local newsdealer.

Complex need recognition develops over a longer period of time and may change the actual state buyer to the desired state buyer. For example, after visiting Peru, the buyer may consider traveling to South Africa. The actual state of buying a trip to Peru can turn the buyer into the desired state of buying a trip to South Africa.

Stage 2

In the second stage, called the *Information Search*, potential buyers feel the need to make a purchase, so they begin to search for information about a product. If the need is strong enough, and can be satisfied by a purchase, the buyer will probably not need to search for information and make the purchase at that moment. Otherwise, the buyer will collect information about the product.

Potential buyers can search for information in two ways: (1) some buyers perform a *simple information search*, which allows them to enhance interest in the product and makes them more receptive to product information; or (2) some buyers perform an *intensive and complex information search*, which allows them to search extensively for such information. The extent to which potential buyers engage in an information search depends on such factors as the degree of the buyer's motivation, the amount of information needed and available, the difficulty of obtaining information, the reliability of the information source, the value of the information source to the buyer, the satisfaction with engaging in the search process, and the perceived risk. In high-risk situations (e.g. buying expensive vacations), prospective buyers are likely to engage in intensive and complex information searches; in low-risk situations (buying a daily newspaper), buyers are more likely to use very simple searches. Other factors that are likely to increase consumers' pre-purchase information search are presented in Table 13.3.

Potential buyers can obtain information from either internal or external sources. Buyers can also search for information actively or passively. The active way of searching for information includes referring to past information or personal experiences; using memory, which might provide some answers to make the choice (internal sources); asking friends for advice; reading brochures; and consulting others who have experience with a product (external sources). The passive way of searching for information does not highly involve the buyer in a purchase; rather the buyer learns about the product from watching TV commercials, listening to the radio, or looking at billboards beside the road. The consumer is actively involved in the search for information when s/he really needs the product.

Potential buyers seek more external information and engage in a more extensive information search if they have no prior experience with a product or have very little experience. In this case they are actively involved in the search. Buyers may contact personal sources of information (e.g. ask for advice from friends and relatives, use word of mouth), marketing (promotion, advertising), neutral sources (e.g. travel agent, tour guides), or refer to those who have had experience with the product before. The more relevant past experience the potential buyers obtain, the less external information they need and the less extensively they have to search.

Table 13.3 Factors Influencing Pre-Purchase Information Search

Buyer's factors	Socio-demographic characteristics (e.g. age, gender, education, occupation, social class, lifecycle stage)
	Psychographic characteristics (e.g. personality, such as extrovert/introvert or perfectionist/generalist; motivations; beliefs; attitudes; interests; lifestyle; self-image)
	Cultural characteristics (e.g. values, traditions, customs, attitudes toward risk, importance of family and social groups)
	Economic status (e.g. income, mortgages, taxes to pay, access to credit)
Product factors	Type of product (necessity versus luxury), price, brands, different features, demand, product visibility and competitiveness, availability of alternatives, novelty, packaging, labeling
Situation factors	Ecological considerations (past experience, frequency and type of purchase)
	Economic considerations (e.g. inflation, recession, interest rate, exchange rate)
	Technological considerations (e.g. new developments in information technology, access to the Internet, eBay, availability of online websites)
	Political considerations (e.g. wars, political instability, terrorism)
	Legal considerations (e.g. warranties, guarantees, consumer protection)
	Competitive considerations (e.g. market structure, number and size of competitors)

Information sources can be classified as either (1) personal or impersonal and (2) commercial or non-commercial. Personal commercial sources include endorsements from sales representatives, dealers, or agents. Personal non-commercial sources include endorsements from families, relatives, friends, neighbors, acquaintances, or co-workers. Impersonal commercial sources include commercial advertising, direct mail, product packaging, and displays. Impersonal non-commercial sources include newspaper and magazines articles, travel reports, restaurant reviews, editorials in travel sections, and consumer-rating organizations.

There are also experiential sources of information that include examining, using, touching, smelling, or tasting the product. One of the most powerful methods of obtaining information about a product is word of mouth (e.g. asking friends, professionals, or acquaintances for recommendations). Word of mouth is the most convincing, cost effective, and influential because it is perceived as very credible.

It is important to determine the influence of each source of information on a prospective buyer and to understand how this information can be provided to the buyer (e.g. by disseminating commercial information through advertising on the TV or radio, in professional associations and journals, or by using personal information). By collecting information, potential buyers become aware of the choices and features available for a particular product. The collected information allows the buyers to evaluate a product against the alternatives.

Stage 3

At the third stage of decision-making, called *Alternatives Evaluation*, potential buyers use the collected information to evaluate the product and its available alternatives. At this stage, potential buyers develop a final set of choices and purchase their final selection. How do potential buyers evaluate available alternatives and arrive at the final decision? First, prospective buyers form three different sets of options. The first is a set of available products or brands that potential buyers consider when making their selection. This set is called the *evoked* or *consideration set*. The evoked set usually consists of a small number of products or their brands that potential buyers are familiar with (known products). For example, in travel and tourism the evoked set refers to destinations of which the buyer is aware and from which s/he will probably make a purchase. These destinations appear on the list of alternatives that the potential traveler feels good about and is likely to select.

Prospective buyers exclude certain products and their types from purchase. The set of products excluded from purchase is called *inept set*. Some products are excluded from purchase because they are (1) unknown (e.g. poorly exposed through media and advertising), (2) unacceptable (e.g. have poor features), (3) overlooked (e.g. have not been clearly positioned in the target market), or (4) unable to meet the buyer's needs as fully as the product that has been chosen. These products make buyers feel uncomfortable. For example, in tourism, the inept set is composed of those alternative destinations the potential travelers dislike and thus are unworthy of further consideration. Sometimes products are excluded from purchase because potential buyers are not able to process all information about these products even if such information is readily available.

Prospective buyers may also feel indifferent towards some products or destinations that do not have any special features or benefits to offer. These products compose the *inert set* of products. In tourism, the inert set refers to the destinations the traveler does not care about. Although the potential traveler usually accepts information about these destinations, s/he does not actively seek such information (see Figure 13.3).

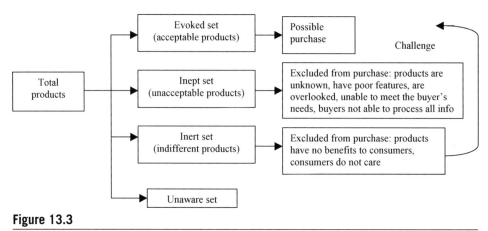

Figure 13.3

Types of Products from which Consumers Make Selection

The challenge for tourism marketers is to move the product from the inert set (indifferent products) to the evoked set (acceptable products).

Prospective buyers tend to create a mental ''list'' of products and destinations, and their features, from which they make their selection. Buyers also develop a set of criteria used to evaluate each product, destination and feature. For example, a businessperson develops a set of criteria for selecting a hotel; s/he considers hotels that offer wireless access to the Internet, a business center with fax and conference phone capabilities, and meeting and conference rooms. If several hotels meet the criteria, business travelers usually choose the one with the most convenient location. Examples of criteria used by potential leisure travelers to evaluate tourism destinations are presented in Table 13.4.

Prospective buyers see products/destinations as bundles of features (attributes). Prospective buyers pay attention to features that are important to them. Buyers evaluate the importance of product/destination features depending upon their needs and wants. For example, women usually attach more importance to the restaurant ambiance and romantic atmosphere, while men attach importance to parking facilities. Since different buyers have different needs, they attach different importance to product/destination features.

Buyers can follow a multi-attribute model of decision making to choose the right product/destination with the right features. Buyers evaluate each feature of the product/destination, add all scores for each product/destination, and obtain the overall score for their features on a 10-point scale (1 – the lowest rating; 10 – the highest rating). In our example, destination C is selected because it scored the highest among all three alternatives (see Table 13.5).

Buyers can also evaluate each feature of the product/destination in its importance relative to the other features. These are called *importance weights*. Buyers compute a weighted or summated score for each product/destination by multiplying each feature's value and importance weight, and adding them together to obtain an overall

Table 13.4 Criteria Used to Evaluate Tourism Destinations

Accommodation (luxury, budget)	Historical attractions (buildings, museums)
Accessibility	Image of the destination
Activities (indoor, outdoor)	Industrial attractions
Amenities (variety and quality)	Local prices
Architecture/buildings	Natural attractions (national parks, wildlife)
Assistance with foreign language	Nightlife (nightclubs)
Atmosphere (relaxing, peaceful)	Opportunity for adventure
Availability of tourist information	Opportunity for socializing with locals
Beaches	Opportunities for shopping
Catering (food and drink)	Opportunity for sightseeing
Cleanliness (clean facilities)	Recreation opportunities and facilities
Cost of airfare or transportation to get to the	Rest and relaxation
destination	Safety and security of the destination
Climate	Scenery and landscape
Cultural attractions (theatres, galleries)	Service quality
Different culture/customs	Social acceptance of residents
Different food and drink	Special events (exhibitions, festivals)
Ease of getting to the destination	Sport activities
Ease of local transportation	Theme parks
Entertainment (live concerts, cinemas)	Tour guides speaking foreign languages
Exotic environment	Transportation (local)
Friendliness of the locals	Unpolluted environment

Table 13.5 Example of Ratings for Hypothetical Destinations

Destination attribute	Destination A	Destination B	Destination C
Accommodation	6	7	10
Activities	10	8	10
Catering	6	6	10
Cleanliness	5	7	10
Image	5	8	10
Natural attractions	4	9	8
Shopping	3	7	8
Total	39	52	66

Note: evaluations are on a 10-point scale (1 = very low rating; 10 = very high rating).

score for the total product/destination. Buyers choose the product/destination that scores highest among the alternatives. Table 13.6 shows how a potential traveler evaluates three different destinations in terms of accommodation, catering, and attractions on a 10-point scale (1 – the least important; 10 – the most important). Attractions are more important to the traveler than accommodation and catering; s/he assigns an importance weight of 0.6 to destination A and B, and a weight of 0.5 to destination C. Destination A offers the best attractions as compared to destination B (9) and destination C (8). The buyer multiplies the attribute values and importance weights, adds them, and obtains a score of 9.9 for destination A ($6 \times 0.3 + 7 \times 0.3 + 10 \times 0.6 = 9.9$), 7.3 for destination B ($7 \times 0.2 + 5 \times 0.1 + 9 \times 0.6 = 7.3$), and 7.2 for destination C ($8 \times 0.3 + 4 \times 0.2 + 8 \times 0.5 = 7.2$). Destination A is selected because it scored the highest among all three alternatives (see Table 13.6). So, if we know the importance weights that prospective buyers attach to the destination features, we can predict destination choice.

Table 13.6 Destination Purchase Decision: Attribute Criteria

Destination	Accommodation		Catering		Attractions	
	Value	Importance weight	Value	Importance weight	Value	Importance weight
A	6	0.3	7	0.3	10	0.6
B	7	0.2	5	0.1	9	0.6
C	8	0.3	4	0.2	8	0.5

Note: Importance weight is assigned on a scale from 1 to 10 (1 = not important at all; 10 = very important).

The evaluation of the product/destination features that the buyer perceives to be the most important can be used to characterize the buyer's purchasing behavior. For example, if the buyer assigns the highest score to product/destination prestige, this might indicate that the buyer is status oriented. On the other hand, if the consumer attaches the most importance to a low price, this might reveal that the buyer is saving/economy-oriented.

Buyers develop images about the products/destinations available. Buyers rank these products/destinations and their features, following the theory of selective perception, distortion, retention, and anticipated satisfaction level with each product and its feature. As a result of this process, prospective buyers develop attitudes toward product/destination features, identify the specific products/destinations that they may consider, and form purchase intentions.

Often buyers lack information about a product or its features because of inadequate promotion or advertising, or their own memory problems. Some products/destinations can be evaluated only after they have been used and experienced (e.g. tourism destinations can be evaluated only after visitation). In order to deal with missing information, buyers may (1) delay the final purchasing decision to find additional information, (2) make a purchase using the available information, (3) choose a product/destination that better serves his/her needs to accommodate missing information, or (4) infer the missing information. The buyer may also lower his/her expectations and purchase the best available alternative, or seek further information about the additional alternatives. If the product is a discretionary (e.g. extra handbag) or luxury item (e.g. vacation travel), buyers may postpone the purchase.

There are also numerous other situational factors that can influence product/destination evaluation and the final purchase decision. These include physical surroundings (e.g. weather, or hotel décor); social surroundings (e.g. people with whom one travels, such as children on a plane or in a hotel); time and seasonality of travel; time pressure; travelers' moods; different roles people play in buying decisions; degree of readiness to buy and state of buying; and levels and types of buying decisions.

Also, people play different roles in buying decisions:

- The *initiator*: this is the person who first recognizes the need for the product and services (e.g. the need for vacation) and initiates the purchase.
- The *influencers*: these are people who influence the decision about which product to buy (e.g. where to travel).
- The *decider*: this is the person who has authority for a final purchasing decision and decides whether to buy or not to buy (e.g. whether to go on vacation or not to go).
- The *purchaser*: this is the person who authorizes payment for the product or spends money on it (e.g. buys travel package).
- The *users*: these are the people who actually use the product (e.g. travel for vacation).

When a family is considering purchasing a trip to a summer resort, often the husband, wife, and the children are involved in the decision. The wife can be the first person who recognizes the need for a family vacation and initiates the buying process. Children can greatly influence the parents' decision; the family can travel only during the school break. The husband can decide whether to purchase a trip. After he authorizes the payment, the whole family can actually travel to the resort and enjoy their vacation.

The different roles people play in the buying decision imply that people have different needs and seek different benefits. In the vacation purchase, the wife may be the initiator of the decision and seek the relaxation aspect. However, the husband may be concerned about the price. While parents are concerned about children having a good vacation, children are most interested in having fun. Although they are not deciders or the purchasers, they are influencers and users.

Prospective buyers may be at different stages of readiness to buy (Rogers, 1995), especially when a product/destination is new on the market. There are five types of buyers, each with a different attitude to buying and different degree of readiness to buy a new product/destination. These types include:

- *Innovators* are the first buyers. They are eager to buy new products and travel to new destinations. They are price insensitive and venturesome. They want to be the first to travel to new destinations and try to have new products. If they like it, they spread the positive word of mouth about it to later users. Innovators represent the smallest portion of the market.

- *Early adopters* are the second, after innovators, who want to experience new destinations and try new products. If the new product is successfully accepted by innovators, early adopters invest in it. They are early opinion leaders. They represent a small portion of the market.
- *Early majority* are interested in new products/destinations; however, they wait-and-see to determine whether the new products/destinations are just a short-term trendy fad or can really enhance their lives. The early majority adopt the new product (travel to a new destination) before an average person does. They represent a large group of the market.
- *Late majority* are similar to early majority; however, they are more skeptical. They want to see whether the product/destination has an established reputation before they purchase it. They adopt the new product (travel to a new destination) after most people have tried it (or travel to it).
- *Laggards* are not interested in new products. They are skeptics and tradition bound; they are the last customers to buy new products. They represent a high proportion of the market.

It is important to understand the buyers' attitudes toward purchasing new products and traveling to new destinations. People differ in accepting new ideas and buying new products, particularly if they do not have enough information about the product and a buying decision is extensive and complex; this makes a purchase risky. Information passed from innovators and early adopters about the product may reduce later buyers' perceived risk.

The degree of involvement of an individual in decision-making and the effort needed to make a decision can also vary. There are three levels of involvement in a buying decision. Each level requires a different type of decision to be made.

Routinized or *habitual decision-making* takes place when buyers have some experience with the product, well-established criteria with which they evaluate the product, and a sufficient information about it. Routinized decision-making involves low-cost, low-risk, low-involvement decision-making; purchase is made impulsively or habitually (e.g. daily simple purchases such as buying daily newspapers or soft drinks). A prospective buyer is usually aware of or knows the product and thus does not need to search for extra information and engage in alternative evaluation. After trial the buyer adopts the product.

Limited decision-making takes place when buyers are familiar with a product and have established the criteria for product evaluation. However, they are not familiar with all product features and have not decided yet which product they prefer. Consequently, buyers search for additional information to learn more about the product features that differentiate it from the other products they are considering. Limited decision-making involves higher-cost, higher-risk and higher involvement decision-making; the purchase is made after collecting additional information.

Extensive or *complex decision-making* occurs when there are a large number of products with which buyers are not familiar and alternatives to choose from. Although buyers have established the criteria for product evaluation, they do not know how to evaluate a specific product, or feature. As a result, buyers need more information to evaluate a product, or feature. Extensive decision-making involves high-cost, diverse high-risk, and high involvement decision-making. A buyer usually gets involved in many stages of decision-making, starting from developing product awareness and knowledge, enhancing interest in it, searching for information, evaluating its alternatives, engaging in product trial and finally adopting the product.

Stage 4

At the *Purchase Decision* stage buyers develop intentions to purchase. They may make three types of purchase: *trial purchase, repeat purchase, and a long-term commitment purchase*. A buyer opts for a trial purchase when s/he purchases a product for the first time, often without commitment. At this stage the buyer explores and evaluates the product by purchasing a smaller quantity than usual. For example, before travelers purchase a new time share about which they are uncertain, they want to experience it. Initially, they purchase one bedroom for one week and spend a short vacation in a newly purchased accommodation. They often receive a free week's vacation as a motivation to buy. This offer substantially influences the initial trial of products.

When buyers are happy about the trial, and the product meets their approval, they are willing to purchase it again in large quantities or more frequently. At this stage buyers are likely to repeat the purchase (e.g. buyer buys more time share weeks). When the product brand name is of high quality (e.g. Marriott time share), buyers may go for a repeat purchase and develop product loyalty which guarantees long-term commitment to it.

Two types of variables can influence the final purchase decision: (1) attitudes of others and (2) unanticipated situational factors. The strength of the influence of others' attitudes depends upon the intensity of these attitudes, buyers' characteristics, personality, purchase motivation, and the closeness of the others to the buyers. For example, the attitudes of family usually have the most direct and strongest influence on the buyer's decision. The unexpected factors that can influence buyer decision can include price changes, motivation change, or increased risk of purchase. For example, when the buyer perceives high purchase risk s/he may postpone the purchase, collect additional information, or settle for another product.

There are many types of risks that prospective buyers may perceive and experience during the process of purchasing and consuming the tourism product. Numerous types of risks were identified in the travel context (see Table 13.7). For example, the perceived risk of natural disasters or terrorism can deter tourists from visiting destinations such as Asia and the Middle East. The high crime rate can impact on the desirability of some cities as tourist destinations. Travelers postpone their trips and seek more information on destinations, or go to destinations which are perceived as being safer.

Table 13.7 Types of Risk Associated with Tourism

Type of risk	Examples
Crime	Possibility of being robbed, becoming a subject of rape or murder
Cultural	Possibility of experiencing difficulties in communicating with foreigners, cultural misunderstanding, inability to adjust to a foreign way of life and standards
Equipment	Possibility of mechanical, equipment, organizational problems occurring during travel or at destination (transportation, accommodation, attractions)
Financial	Possibility of not obtaining value for money; losing or wasting money if travel expectations are not fulfilled
Health	Possibility of becoming sick while traveling or at the destination
Performance	Possibility of not receiving holiday benefits due to the travel product or service not performing well
Physical	Possibility of being physically injured, includes danger and injury detrimental to health (accidents)
Political	Possibility of becoming involved in the political turmoil of the country being visited
Psychological	Possibility that travel experience will not reflect traveler's personality or self-image, damage self-image, reflect poorly on personality
Satisfaction	Possibility of not achieving personal satisfaction and/or self-actualization with travel experience
Social	Possibility that vacation choices or activities will be disapproved by friends, families, associates; losing or lowering personal and social status, appearing unfashionable
Terrorism	Possibility of being involved in a terrorist act such as airplane or personal hijacking, bomb explosion or biochemical attack
Time	Possibility that travel experience will take too much time, product will not perform on time; traveler will lose or waste time

Sources: Basala, S., & Klenosky, D. (2001). Travel style preferences for visiting a novel destination: A conjoint investigation across the novelty-familiarity continuum. *Journal of Travel Research*, *40*, 172–183; Dimanche, F., & Lepetic, A. (1999). New Orleans tourism and crime: A case study. *Journal of Travel Research, 38*(1), 19–23; Sonmez, S., & Graefe, A. (1998b). Determining future travel behavior from past travel experience and perceptions of risk and safety. *Journal of Travel Research*, *37*(2), 171–177; Reisinger, Y., & Mavondo, F. (2006). Cultural differences in travel risk perception. *Journal of Travel and Tourism Marketing, 20*(1), 13–31.

Stage 5

At the *Post-Purchase Behavior* stage following a purchase, buyers must decide whether to repurchase a product (e.g. revisit a destination) or buy other products (e.g. select other destination). This decision is significantly influenced by the buyer's evaluation of the product/destination and post-purchase satisfaction with it. The buyer compares his/her own experiences with the product with initial expectations. There are three possible outcomes of these evaluations:

(a) Buyers' expectations match buyers' experiences with the product, resulting in neutral feelings;

(b) Buyer's experiences (product performance) exceed his/her expectations, causing confirmation of expectations, which leads to satisfaction with purchase; and

(c) Buyers' expectations exceed his/her experiences (product performance), causing disconfirmation of expectations, which leads to dissatisfaction with purchase.

If the product/destination performance exceeds buyer's expectations (experiences are greater or better than expectations), the buyer is likely to experience *positive cognitive dissonance*. However, if the product/destination performance does not match buyers' expectations (expectations are greater than experiences) the buyer is likely to experience discomfort, called *negative cognitive dissonance*.

It is important to match or even exceed a buyer's expectations (deliver what buyers expect to get and what they perceive they get) to make the buyer satisfied or very satisfied. However, in today's global and very competitive world, it becomes increasingly important to deliver better value and create greater satisfaction than competitors do. Today, the buyer needs to be delighted rather than just satisfied. Delighting the buyer can be achieved by delivering an element of surprise to a purchase (what the buyer expects to get and what the buyer gets to perceive) in the form of offering, for example, a free-of-charge service or a free lunch. It is also important to help buyers experience less sacrifice by offering them what they really want rather than what they settle or agree for. Focusing on the buyer's feelings and emotions will make the buyer feel cared for. Caring is essential to customer loyalty. When buyers feel valuable and cared for they go out of their way to be long-term loyal to the product. Only by focusing on the buyer's emotions and showing care for the buyer can the element of delight be delivered and long-term loyalty be inspired. Consequently, delivering superior value means incorporating both rational and emotional components of a product. Purchasing decisions influenced by emotions are deeper and longer-lasting than those based on rational thought alone.

The effect of positive cognitive dissonance is a satisfied or even delighted buyer who is more likely to buy a product again (e.g. repeat destination visitation), become loyal to it, spread positive word of mouth, recommend it to others, spend more on it, and cherish it in a memory for a long time. Delighted customers are likely to be the best advertisements for products/destinations.

The effect of negative cognitive dissonance is a dissatisfied buyer who may stop buying the product permanently or temporarily (e.g. stop traveling to the same destination). The dissatisfied buyer may also return the product to the seller (e.g. return an airline ticket), complain to friends, families, reference groups, and associates, and discourage them from the same purchase. In addition, the unhappy buyer may ask for a refund or product exchange (e.g. change a hotel room), or decide to sell the product, (e.g. sell time share), or trade it. Some unhappy customers may give the product to someone else (e.g. unwanted gift), store it, or convert it into something else. In case of a high level of dissatisfaction buyers may also initiate a lawsuit.

In order to avoid or decrease negative dissonance (the unfavorable gap between expectations and experience), buyers often take steps to reduce the uncertainty that they might have about their selection by (1) trying to convince themselves that their decision was wise, (2) seeking more information that reinforces the purchase and supports the choice, (3) persuading friends to purchase the same product, or (4) contacting other owners to reassure themselves of their decisions.

13.3 OTHER THEORIES OF CONSUMER DECISION-MAKING

There are also other theories of and approaches to how consumers make decisions. Most of them have three basic stages of movement, from a low level to a high level of response. At the lowest level of response, called *cognitive stage*, buyers think about the product, become aware of it, and develop knowledge of its attributes and benefits. At the higher level of response, called *affective stage*, the buyer develops feelings toward the product and perceptions of it. If the perception of the product is positive, then the buyer develops a liking, interest, or positive attitude toward the product. A positive attitude is developed when the benefits of the product match the buyer's needs and wants. After evaluating various product alternatives, the buyer develops a preference or desire for a specific product and becomes convinced that its benefits will meet his/her needs and wants. At the final stage, called *behavioral stage*, the potential buyer still has the opportunity to evaluate the barrier to purchase (e.g. lack of money, lack of transportation). Once the barrier is overcome the buyer makes the choice and buys the product.

SUMMARY

Consumer buying behavior is a process influenced by (1) environmental factors such as (a) environmental stimuli that are beyond the consumer's control (e.g. demographic, cultural, social, economic stimuli); (b) market stimuli under the control of marketing managers; and (c) marketing efforts. The process is also influenced by (2) buyer's factors such as (a) personal characteristics (e.g. nationality, religion, age, gender, occupation); and (b) psychological characteristics (e.g. motivation, perception, learning, beliefs, attitudes). Both personal and psychological characteristics of the buyer affect the decision process, which consists of five stages: (a) problem recognition, (b) information search, (c) alternative evaluation, (d) purchase decision, and (e) post-purchase behavior. The buyers' characteristics and decision process influence the buyer's responses to purchase.

Buyers can obtain product information from internal and external sources. They can search for information in an active or passive way. They form three different sets of product options: evoked, inept and inert. Buyers see products/destinations as bundles of features and evaluate the products/destinations according to the importance of these features to buyers. Buyers can play various roles in a buying decision: the role of initiator, influencer, decider, purchaser, or user. Prospective buyers may also be at a different stage of readiness to buy a new product. Innovators, early adopters, early majority, late majority, and laggards have different attitudes to buying new products. In addition, buyers can engage in three different types of decision-making: routinized, limited, and extensive. Buyers may make three types of purchase: trial, repeat, and long-term. There are many types of risks that perspective buyers may perceive and experience during the purchasing process. If a buyer's experiences with product/destination are better than expected, the buyer experiences positive cognitive dissonance. If a buyer's expectations are greater than experiences, the buyer experiences negative cognitive dissonance. The theories of consumer decision-making consist of three stages: cognitive, affective, and behavioral.

DISCUSSION POINTS AND QUESTIONS

1. Describe how the political and legal environment influences (a) buying time shares in Hawaii, and (b) buying an airline ticket.
2. Describe how the socio-economic and cultural environment influences (a) buying a meal in a local restaurant and (b) buying a cinema ticket.
3. Do people from your own culture differ from other cultures in consumption patterns? Show and explain some differences in their (a) needs and wants; (b) information search (e.g. attitudes to different promotional techniques); (c) motivation to buy things; (d) product evaluation (e.g. attitudes to specific product qualities, spending patterns on different products, attitudes to owing products, brand awareness); (e) making choices (e.g. style of shopping, brand loyalty, preferences for packaging, buying online, attitudes to discounts, bargaining and complaints, importance of product features); (f) post-purchase behavior (e.g. attitudes toward re-sail, rental, give away, re-use).
4. How do tourists from different cultures shop? Why do they shop the way they do? Explain Japanese shopping behavior by identifying specific Japanese cultural traits.
5. Identify different travel products that you believe would require an intensive pre-purchase information search. Then, identity the specific characteristics of these products that make an intensive pre-purchase search likely.
6. Develop a list of destination features that you will use as the purchase criteria in evaluating different regions you plan to visit next year.

WEBSITE LINKS

1. Skriloff, L. (1999). The 1.5 Generation: A New Window to the Multicultural Market. *Multicultural Marketing Resources*, Inc. http://www.multicultural. com/archives/articles/99_56_mmr.htm
2. Break the resistance of consumer buying behavior: http://sbinformation.about. com/od/advertisingpr/a/behavior.htm
3. Marketing factors: consumer buying behavior: http://www.associatedcontent. com/article/19593/marketing_factors_consumer_buying_behavior.html
4. http://www.udel.edu/alex/chapt6.html

The next chapter will identify cultural differences in tourist buying behavior.

Cultural influences on tourist buying behavior

14

The aim of this chapter is to identify cultural differences in tourist buying behavior and decision process.

OBJECTIVES

After completing this chapter the reader should be able to:

- Identify the influence of national culture on tourist personal and psychological characteristics
- Understand the influence of national culture on need recognition, information search, product evaluation, purchase decision and post-purchase behavior
- Explain the influence of national culture on buyer's feelings and emotions and the factors which are beyond the purchasing decision

INTRODUCTION

To date, research in the area of cross-cultural differences has identified numerous behavioral differences among tourists from different cultural groups. For example, cultural differences have been identified in the following categories: tourist motivation (Ahmed & Krohn, 1992; Jang & Cai, 2002; Kozak, 2002; Laing & Crouch, 2005; Sangpikul, 2008; You et al., 2000); preferences for travel services (Crotts & Erdmann, 2000; Crotts & Pizam, 2003); information search (Chen, 2000a; Money & Crotts, 2003); planning and purchases of international vacations (Money & Crotts, 2003), trip characteristics (Richardson & Crompton, 1988; Sussmann & Rashcovsky, 1997), destination perceptions (Reisinger & Mavondo, 2006a); image (Litvin et al., 2004); social interaction (Reisinger & Turner, 1997a, **321**

1997b, 1998a, 1998b, 1998c, 1999a, 1999b, 2002a, 2002b); perceptions of travel risk, anxiety and safety (Dolnicar, 2005; Mitchell and Vassos, 1997; Reisinger & Mavondo, 2005, 2006a, 2006b); travel behavior (Litvin et al., 2004); perceptions and stereotypes of tourists (Pizam & Jeong, 1996; Pizam & Reichel, 1996; Pizam & Sussmann, 1995; Pizam & Telisman-Kosuta, 1989; Pizam et al., 1997); perceptions and satisfaction with service quality (Mattila, 1999b, 1999c; Reisinger & Turner, 1999a, 1997a; Tsang & Ap, 2007; Weiermair, 2000), perceptions of hotel facilities (Bauer et al., 1993; Choi & Chu, 2000; Mattila, 1999a), evaluation of travel services (Crotts & Erdmann, 2000), and consumption patterns (Rosenbaum & Spears, 2005).

Numerous studies have identified cultural differences among international tourists in attaching importance to accommodation (Becker & Murmann, 1999; McClearly et al., 1998; Sussmann & Rashcovsky, 1997), travel information (Sussmann & Rashcovsky, 1997), service (Liu et al., 2000; Mattila, 1999b, 1999c), service in hotels (Armstrong et al., 1997, restaurants and food establishments (Becker & Murmann, 1999; Sheldon & Fox, 1988), and many others.

The above studies have shown that tourist behavior and travel patterns are culture-specific (You et al., 2000). As Pizam and Sussmann (1995) put it, behavioral differences among international tourists are attributable to cultural influences. Below are the examples of some studies that have identified cultural differences in tourist behavior and suggested that national cultures of tourists influence their behavior, selection of tourism destinations, products and services, and decision-making. However, before the effect of national culture on tourist behavior is discussed, the influence of national culture on tourist personal and psychological characteristics is identified.

14.1 CULTURAL INFLUENCES ON BUYER'S PERSONAL CHARACTERISTICS

14.1.1 Gender roles

Gender roles vary across cultures. For example, there are behavioral differences between men and women that reflect the culturally determined differing roles of men and women. In some cultures, the traditional values indicate the need for women to stay at home and take care of children. In these cultures women depend on men as breadwinners: A women's responsibility is to take care of a family and home; as a result, women are more constrained in their travel than men (Jackson & Henderson, 1995). For example, in Mexican-American families, men dominate women more than in Anglo families (Imperia et al., 1985). The woman's role is to stay at home, be a wife and a mother, and sacrifice for the family (Gonzales, 1982). A woman is expected to protect her children and be submissive toward her husband (Rosen & La Raia, 1972). In comparison, the gender roles of Anglo-Americans are more autonomous and egalitarian (Woodside & Motes, 1979). In other cultures (e.g. Arab cultures), women are discouraged from engaging in certain activities such as sport or independent travel because these activities are perceived as being masculine and unsuitable for women (Henderson et al., 1988). In Western cultures (e.g. the United States, the United Kingdom) women are independent and travel frequently for holiday and business purposes.

14.1.2 Lifestyle and activities

Lifestyle refers to shared values, interests, opinions, attitudes, and behavior. Lifestyle reflects individual preferences for products and services, destinations and travel-related lifestyle.

Travel-related lifestyles vary across cultures. In the feminine cultures, people feel more connected to their homes and places of residency than in masculine cultures. Members of feminine cultures like to travel around the home and spend less money on accommodations, whereas members of the masculine cultures like to travel to more distance destinations, stay in hotels, and spend more on accommodations.

Travel preferences vary across cultures. For example, American college students prefer, more than Japanese students, to travel with a small number of people, and visit adventurous and different destinations. Japanese students, on the other hand, favor individually arranged travel more than American students. American and Japanese students also differ in their preferences of the allocentric type of travel (distant travel). The more collectivistic Japanese students are, the less likely they prefer allocentric types of travel and the more likely they prefer psychocentric types of travel (close to home) (Sakakida et al., 2004).

Korean tourists differ from Japanese tourists in their travel patterns. Korean tourists travel as part of a group and use the packaged tour because it is an easy and quick way to arrange travel (Kim & Prideaux, 1998). Korean tourists are more adventurous than the Japanese in choosing tourism activities and more impulsive in purchasing (March, 1997). Korean tourists also have significantly shorter decision timeframes than Japanese travelers (Iverson, 1997).

National culture affects tourists' preferences for length of stay at a destination, expenditures, and preferences for accommodation and facilities. For example, Japanese tourists prefer short holidays, while Europeans prefer longer holidays (Ritter, 1987). Japanese travelers are more likely to use all-inclusive packages for vacations, while German tourists use resorts that include facilities such as beaches, skiing, golf, and tennis (Dybka, 1988). Mainland Chinese visitors travel in groups more than the American visitors. Mainland Chinese visitors to Hong Kong also engage in shorter trips (four nights), whereas American visitors have a total trip duration of more than 13 nights. In addition, the Mainland Chinese visitors spend less on vacations than the American visitors (Yoo et al., 2004).

American tourists prefer socializing with other nationals more than tourists from Japan and Korea (Pizam & Jeong, 1996). Japanese tourists are reluctant to try new cuisine when on vacation (Sheldon & Fox, 1988). Tourists from low UAI cultures, such as Germany, and tourists from high UAI cultures, such as Japan, differ in information-search patterns, trip-planning time horizons, travel-party characteristics, and trip characteristics (Money & Crotts, 2003).

National culture also explains differences in tourists' activities (e.g. Pizam & Jeong, 1996; Pizam & Sussmann, 1995; Sheldon & Fox, 1988). Muslims and Arabs are less active, more leisure-oriented, and more socially oriented than Europeans. Since cultural norms dictate that they protect women, they look for privacy in recreation leisure. Gender segregation prevents Muslims and Arabs from participating in many forms of activities, such as sport and play, commonly found in Europe and America (Groetzbach, 1988).

National culture explains differences in shopping. Members of the individual cultures, such as the United States, Canada, and Australia, treat shopping as a recreational or bargain-hunting activity, whereas members of collectivistic cultures, such as Asia, may treat shopping as a social activity. While customers in individualistic cultures go to a mega malls and big stores to do a bulk of shopping, Europeans and Asians make their daily routine visits to small nearby supermarkets (DeMooij, 2004).

Further, research suggests differences in tipping behaviors of casino guests from five cultural groups: Japanese, Korean, Chinese (Mainland Chinese, Taiwanese, Hong Kong Chinese), Westerners (US Americans and Europeans) and Others (mainly Sri Lankan, Philippine, Bangladeshi, Thai, and Malaysian). The Chinese exhibit the most disruptive behavior, while the Japanese are the least disruptive. The Japanese and Koreans have the greatest tendency to tip the dealer, and the Japanese are the most likely to tip the drink waitresses, while the Chinese and minority guests rarely give tips. Also, Chinese guests have the highest tendency to purchase drinks from the bar, whereas Japanese guests prefer to order drinks from waitresses. Japanese guests are also the most likely to consume alcoholic drinks in contrast to Chinese guests (Kim et al., 2002).

Moreover, national culture influences tourists' destination choice (McKercher & duCross, 2003; O'Leary & Deegan, 2003). People from high individualistic cultures tend to choose culturally similar destinations, while people from high collectivistic countries tend to choose culturally dissimilar destinations (Jackson, 2001). This is because people from highly individualistic countries are less interdependent with their in-groups and have greater need for affiliation (Franzoi, 1996).

14.1.3 Personality

Personality is the sum of distinct qualities and characteristics of a person, such as abilities, skills, motives, or values that lead to a consistent response to the environment. Each person has a specific personality that influences his or her behavior. However, personality can differ across cultures.

In collectivistic cultures in Asia, South America, and Africa, where people depend on one another, their behavior depends on the social context. A person is a part of social networks and relationships. On the other hand, in individualistic cultures, a person's behavior depends on that person and is determined by that person's personality.

National culture influences the type of person attracted to a destination, activities pursued, and risk aversion (McKercher & Chow, 2001). Plog (1990, 2002) suggested that collectivists in the East are psychocentric – less adventurous and attracted to culturally proximate destinations that are familiar and non-threatening. Individualists in the West are in general allocentrics and venturers; they are more adventurous and are attracted to culturally distant destinations. Similarly, sunlusts (Gray, 1970), institutionalized (organized and individual) tourists (Cohen, 1972, 1974), recreational tourists (Cohen, 1979), mass tourists (Smith, 1989), low-activation tourists (Fiske & Maddi, 1961), pleasure seekers (Plog, 1987), dependables (Plog, 2002), and group or package tourists (Mehmetoglu, 2004) are attracted to destinations that offer familiarity, home atmosphere, routine, comfort, and the safety of packaged products and services (see Chapter 8). Traditionally, such tourists are represented by a collectivistic-oriented personality who is either other-oriented and travels to seek companionships and relationships or whose needs can be met with other travelers.

On the other hand, wanderlusts (Gray, 1970), non-institutionalized (explorers, drifters) tourists (Cohen, 1972, 1974), experiential and experimental tourists (Cohen, 1979), off-beaten-track tourists (Smith, 1989), eco-tourists (Hvenegaard, 2002), high-activation tourists (Fiske & Maddi, 1961), self-confident tourists (Plog, 1987), venturers (Plog, 2002) and solitary travelers (Mehmetoglu, 2004) are attracted to unusual destinations that offer novelty, learning, authentic experiences, opportunities to immerse in foreign culture, a variety of activities and options to choose from, and a non-touristic atmosphere in which one can travel independently and pursue his or her own interests (see Chapter 8). Traditionally, such tourists are represented by an individualistically oriented personality who is self-oriented and travels for the purpose of satisfying his or her own needs.

There are multiple personality types for tourists, and these types explain preferences for destinations. However, since human nature is very complex, tourist personality can be so very different that no single theory can explain the needs of all tourists.

14.1.4 The self concept

The concept of self plays an important role in the behavior of an individual. The sense of self determines who the individual is. The concept is influenced by the cultural context in which the individual grows up and affects an individual's perceptions, evaluations, and values. The concept of self is related to the concepts of personality, identity, and attitude. In the individualistic cultures, which focus on individual autonomy, self-identity, and being different from a group, the self is independent. In collectivistic cultures, which focus on people's dependency in very complex hierarchical social relationships and being like a group, the self is dependent on others (DeMooij, 2004).

Consequently, people from individualistic cultures see themselves as independent, whereas those from collectivistic cultures see themselves as a part of a greater group. Individualists such as North Americans tend to focus on positive self-evaluation and their own uniqueness, whereas collectivists such as Asians focus on self-criticism, modesty, humility, and self-improvement. In North America, self-criticism and focus on negative characteristics of self are perceived as the lack of ability to be self-sufficient, independent and make one's own way in the world (DeMooij, 2004).

In the collectivistic cultures such as the Philippines, Korea, or Thailand, the development of the self is achieved through the group, social acceptance, and social image. For Americans, social acceptance and self-image achieved through the group is not so much important. Americans are not concerned so much about opinions of others; instead they rely more on the self, their own individual value system, and their personal opinions.

14.2 CULTURAL INFLUENCES ON BUYER'S PSYCHOLOGICAL CHARACTERISTICS

14.2.1 Motivation and needs

The degree of importance of motives and needs is influenced by national culture. For example, it was found that the Asian and Caucasian visitors have different motivations for attending a Cultural Expo in Korea (Lee, 2000). British and German tourists have different motivations for and satisfaction levels with visits to Mallorca and Turkey (Kozak, 2001, 2002). Those from masculine cultures are usually more motivated by material success, position and social status, exotic vacations, and luxury resorts. Those from individualistic cultures are motivated by hedonism, convenience, the pursuit of pleasure, thrill, enjoyment, stimulation, having fun, and self-satisfaction. Those from collectivistic cultures are motivated by socializing and group activities, in particular, nature-based activities. Those from high-power-distance cultures are motivated by social status and image. Those from feminine cultures are motivated by family vacation and time spent with friends.

Also, culture itself plays a vital role in motivating international tourists to undertake travel (Hanquin & Lam, 1999; Kim & Chalip, 2004; McGehee et al., 1996; Oh et al., 1995). For example, culture was identified as an important destination attribute and reason for traveling (McKercher & duCross, 2003) and an important motive for the Australian leisure travel market to the United States (McGehee et al., 1996). A large proportion of Australian tourists seek to increase knowledge by experiencing a different culture (Oh et al., 1995).

14.2.2 Perception and image

Different cultural groups perceive differently (Mayo & Jarvis, 1981). National culture influences local residents' perceptions of international tourists (Pizam & Sussmann, 1995; Richardson & Crompton, 1988). For example, the Japanese are perceived as traveling in groups, bowing to everybody, spending heavily, constantly photographing (Cho, 1991), taking short holidays to avoid separation from the family, and expecting facilities and services for larger groups (Ritter, 1987). Koreans are perceived as loyal to their cultural identity, unwilling to accept other than Korean ways of living, being proud of their Confucian philosophy, traveling in groups, spending freely (Cho, 1991), and traveling in a loose and unplanned manner relative to the Japanese and Americans, who travel in a rigid and planned manner (Pizam & Jeong, 1996).

National culture influences tourists' perceptions of local residents (Hoffman & Low, 1981). The perception of service personnel is a primary way in which visitors form perceptions and make judgments about their destinations and residents (Wei et al., 1989). However, perceptions of service quality vary across cultures. For example, Asian-Pacific and European-American visitors to Hong Kong perceive service quality differently (Luk et al., 1993). European, Asian and English Heritage cultural groups significantly differ in their perceptions of service quality obtained in the Hong Kong hotel industry (Armstrong et al., 1997).

National culture leads to different perceptions of what constitutes proper guest treatment. For example, according to the Chinese, hosts should escort their guests everywhere and provide them with a very tight itinerary; this, they believe, is courteous and high-quality service (Sheldon & Fox, 1988). Japanese hosts take care of the affairs of their guests in advance and even fulfill their needs beyond expectations (Befu, 1971). The Japanese believe that the hosts know best what the guests' needs are. However, Western tourists perceive such hospitality as uncomfortable, intrusive, or lacking trust.

National culture also affects the tour guides' perceptions of similarities and differences between international tourists. For example, Pizam and Sussmann (1995) proposed that British tour guides perceive Japanese, French, Italian, and American tourists as differing in 18 out of 20 behavioral characteristics related to social interactions, activity preferences, bargaining, knowledge of destination, and commercial transactions. Japanese tourists are the most distinctive, whereas Italian tourists are the most like the other nationalities. The Italians and French are very similar to each other in their behavior, followed by the Americans and Italians. French and American tourists are the least similar.

Pizam and Jeong (1996) noted that Korean tour guides perceive Americans as the most distinct among Japanese, American, and Korean tourists. Koreans and Japanese are the most similar to each other, followed by Japanese–Americans. American and Japanese tourists know more than Koreans about foreign destinations. Koreans are more interested in artifacts than people, while Americans and Japanese are more interested in people than in artifacts.

According to Pizam and Jeong (1996), Americans are perceived as the most interested in people, novelty, desire to be near nature and to visit national parks and national monuments. They plan their trips rigidly and meticulously and prefer long trips. They are the most sociable, adventuresome, and active of the three nationalities (probably due to high risk-taking). In contrast, both Koreans and Japanese like to travel to foreign destinations that are relatively close to home, but Koreans prefer longer trips than the Japanese. Koreans and Japanese are also the least active and reserved in new social situations (probably due to their collectivistic and high-uncertainty-avoidance characteristics). Koreans and Japanese also buy more souvenirs than Americans to commemorate their visit to a particular destination and fulfill social obligations by letting the loved ones left at home know they have not been forgotten. In addition, Japanese and Koreans travel in groups and bargain more than Americans.

Koreans are the least interested in people and the least adventurous in food. They are skeptical and distrustful. They conduct their trips in a loose and unplanned manner. Japanese are the most adventurous in food preferences, and they plan their trips rigidly and meticulously, but choose short trips.

Further, national culture influences selective perception. Selective perception refers to observation of the selected reality related to own needs, feelings, and beliefs only. People perceive what they want to perceive. They usually perceive what is similar to their cultures and according to their cultural standards. In individualistic cultures people perceive that everybody has similar values, notice similar cues, respond to similar stimuli, and interpret messages similarly. In collectivistic cultures, on the other hand, people's perceptions depend on the social context. Although members of the individualistic and collectivistic cultures can see the same people and objects, their interpretation of others and objects can be different because of the situation in which the interpretation occurs. Thus, perceptions are very subjective. Consequently, misunderstanding between those from individualistic and those from collectivistic cultures may occur.

Image is how others perceive and evaluate a person or an object (e.g. how others perceive a destination). Each cultural group develops its own unique images and has its own specific definition of a positive image. In collectivistic Asian cultures, images of people, groups, objects, or genders portrayed in the media are different than in individualistic Western cultures. For example, in Korea, positive self-image and identity are associated with belonging to high-status families. In Western cultures, self-image and others-identity is assessed based on personality and individual characteristics, such as age or occupation, and mostly material possessions. In many Western societies people buy self-image and social status. People buy tangible goods, such as cars, luxury apartments, jewelry, or luxury travel to develop a specific image and show they are from a higher social class. However, in France, numerous Asian cultures, and India, people believe they cannot buy social status or self-image; self-image and status are inherited. In these cultures, self-identity and image are assessed based on family and ancestors' connections, and traditions.

In addition, in Western cultures, importance is attached to the images of those who are successful. Much emphasis is put on external appearance, which it is believed to lead to success, happiness, and greater self-esteem. However, in Asian cultures, external appearance is of less importance; success and happiness are measured by the quality of social relations.

14.2.3 Learning and knowledge

Learning varies by culture. In individualistic Western cultures, the focus of learning is on logical and verbal skills. In Japan, learning is understood in terms of social competence, sociability, and ability to sympathize with others. In Africa, learning refers to achieving wisdom – learning how to be trustworthy, social attentive, and responsible. The goal of learning in individualistic Western cultures is achievement, whereas in collectivistic cultures it is lifelong learning. In collectivistic cultures, knowledge and education are treated as among the most important investments in life, whereas in individualistic cultures people believe in different types of achievement, such as the ability to make money and buy material goods (DeMooij, 2004).

Differences in learning are determined by different communication styles. In low-context-direct culture, learning is more abstract, separated from the social environment, and based on verbal skills. In high-context and indirect cultures, learning is more contextual, linked to the social environment, and based on non-verbal skills.

14.2.4 **Attitudes**

People's attitudes are influenced by their cultural values. Attitudes have affective (feelings, emotions one experiences in response to an attitude object) and cognitive (attributes, functions, knowledge, learning) components. In Western cultures, attitudes help to gain knowledge, organize one's environment and provide frames of reference. ''Proper'' attitudes help people to achieve success, maximize rewards, enhance life enjoyment, and minimize the costs and hardships. In collectivistic cultures, where situational factors influence behavior, attitudes help to fulfill social-identity functions and obligations. People are more constrained by situations in their behavior, more under pressure to behave in a socially accepted manner and take into account attitudes of others. In individualistic cultures people are less constrained by social situations and are under less social pressure when developing attitudes. They take into account personal attitudes when making decisions (DeMooij, 2004).

Attitudes vary across cultures. For example, there are important differences in attitudes toward food. For British and Japanese tourists, food is the most important part of a good vacation. For Australians it is ranked third, for Germans it is fifth, and for the French food is not at all important (Sheldon & Fox, 1989). Those from high-uncertainty-avoidance cultures have more negative attitudes to pre-cooked food because they are more concerned about the purity and quality of food than those from low-uncertainty-avoidance cultures, who frequently purchase and consume fast food (DeMooij, 2004). Culture also influences eating habits. According to Robertson (1987), Americans eat oysters but not snails; French eat snails but not locusts; Zulus eat locusts but not fish; Jews eat fish but not pork; Hindus eat pork but not beef; Russians eat beef but not snakes; Chinese eat snakes but not people; The Jelas of New Guinea find people delicious!

There are important differences among national cultures in attitudes toward success. Those from individualistic and high masculine culture, such as the United States, the United Kingdom, Germany, and Austria, see their success in the possessions of material goods. Those from higher-uncertainty-avoidance cultures define their success and happiness more in terms of stability and social security (Austria, Germany, Japan) than material possessions. Those from feminine cultures emphasize more the quality of life (e.g. family gatherings, spending time with family) (DeMooij, 2004).

Culturally different people have different attitudes toward nationals of specific countries. Those who have positive or negative attitudes toward a particular country show favorable or unfavorable responses to its nationals. Often, Japan is admired for its technological development and the Japanese are seen as technologically competent people. Germany is regarded as a country of precision and rules, and Germans are perceived as detailed, reliable, and disciplined. France and Italy are known for good food and fashion. Thus, French and Italians are seen as good-food lovers and experts in style and design. America is known for offering opportunities, freedom, and independence. Consequently, Americans are perceived as freedom-loving people. Europe is known for its history and culture, and Europeans are known for their culture.

According to Kang and Moscardo (2006), even attitudes toward environmental protection and conservation are culturally influenced. For example, Korean, Australian, and British tourists differ in attitudes toward responsible tourist behaviors. The Korean tourists are the most likely to spend time before they travel studying or collecting information about the environment of the destination, the lifestyle of the local residents, and environmentally friendly tours and places to stay. They also seek to participate in environmental education programs while traveling and agree to spend some money on environmental conservation and preservation.

14.2.5 Attribution

Attribution refers to searching for causes of a certain phenomenon or behavior. Once one knows the causes of behavior one can predict and explain the behavior of other people. According to the Attribution Theory (Heider, 1958), every individual assigns certain attributions to explain behavior of self or others. These attributions are either internal or external. The internal attribution refers to findings causes within the individual, and external attribution refers to finding causes outside the individual. In individualistic culture people assign causes of their behavior to internal attributes, such as personality characteristics, and predict behavior of others based on their personality traits and past behavior. In collectivistic cultures people assign causes of their behavior to situational factors and predict behavior of others based on situational context.

14.3 CULTURAL INFLUENCES ON BUYER'S DECISION PROCESS

The effect of national culture on the buying process and decision-making is demonstrated below.

14.3.1 Need recognition

People's needs vary from one culture to another. People across cultures may do or buy the same things or travel to the same destination for different reasons. For example, the Mainland Chinese and the Americans travel to Hong Kong for different reasons. Mainland Chinese visit Hong Kong more for business/meeting purposes; American visitors come for vacation/leisure purposes (Yoo et al., 2004). People may also do or buy different things or travel to different destinations for the same reasons. For example, some people may travel to winter ski and tropical resorts for the same reason: rest and relaxation.

Although the same needs may exist in different cultures, the degree of importance people attach to these needs may vary. For example, the need for conformity is one of the significant differences between individualistic and collectivistic cultures. Collectivists are more willing to conform to a group and consider the influence of their behavior on other people. Individualists behave according to their own needs and perceived personal gains. Also, people in Confucian collectivistic cultures must meet social expectations of others in order to preserve their face and the face of others. They may lose face if their behavior does not meet the minimal socially acceptable standard. For example, the need for gift-giving in Korea and the United States differs. Koreans give more gifts on more occasions and have a bigger gift budget than Americans. Koreans are motivated by group-conformity pressure and face-saving, whereas Americans are motivated by altruism (Park, 1998). Koreans believe that if they do not give gifts on special occasions to members of in-groups, they may not stand up to others' expectations.

Also, collectivistic consumers make purchases to become similar with members of their in-groups, while individualistic consumers make purchases to differentiate themselves from others. While Western individuals make purchases to satisfy personal needs and emphasize their own personality and distinctiveness, the collectivists follow the principles of modesty, self-effacement, and moderation: They do not want to stand out in the group. For example, Chinese consumers are usually not demanding and tend to have few desires. Due to the importance of thrift, their awareness of their needs is restrained and the needs themselves are limited. Chinese consumers are more often in actual state of buying rather than desired state of buying, which is in contrast to the individualistic consumers who are often in desired state of buying.

14.3.2 Information search and choice of information sources

National culture influences the use of external travel information sources. In high-power-distance cultures and uncertainty-avoidance-cultures, most consumers seek information from personal sources. However, the studies show that this is not always the case. For example, tourists from Japan, South Korea, and Australia traveling to the United States have different preferences for external information sources (Chen, 2000a). Business travelers from highly collectivistic Japan and Korea rely heavily on tour companies, corporate travel offices, travel guides, and advice from friends and relatives. Business travelers from the individualistic Australian society prefer obtaining their information directly from the airlines and state/city travel offices (Chen, 2000a). The Japanese rely more heavily on the print medium as an information source when compared to Germans, who rely more on word-of-mouth advice from family and friends (Mihalik et al., 1995).

National culture influences the preferences for commercials. American consumers from low-context cultures prefer commercials with high levels of information (Taylor et al., 1997). In the United States, individualistic consumers can be attracted to advertisements that emphasize individualistic benefits and are persuasive, whereas collectivistic consumers, such as the Chinese, can be attracted to advertisements that focus on family or in-group benefits (Aaker & Maheswaran, 1997). Because of the value of family and group orientation, Chinese consumers heavily rely on word-of-mouth (WOM) communication. Chinese also rely more on past experiences of one's own and others than Americans (Moore, 1998). Due to the high tendency to respect authority, Chinese believe that official media are most trustworthy.

In South Korea, the dominance of collectivism influences the use of the Internet more than in the individualistic United States. Koreans spend more time online to show a high level of conformity with their peers, whose behavior and opinions are regarded as reference points (Park & Jun, 2003). US Americans use the Internet to rely upon themselves to do the majority of the information search.

14.3.2.1 The role of reference groups

The cultural orientation toward individualism/collectivism has the strongest influence on the role of reference groups in purchasing decisions. In collectivistic cultures people do not belong to groups, clubs and associations as they do in individualistic cultures. The influence of reference groups is much less important to collectivists than individualists and those from high uncertainty cultures. Members of high-uncertainty-avoidance cultures respect professional groups more than do low-uncertainty-avoidance cultures (DeMooij, 2004).

The influence of reference groups varies with the type of product purchased. If a product is expensive and luxurious, such as a travel product, the opinions of reference groups are more important than when the product purchased is a necessity. In individualistic cultures, the influence of reference groups and peers is higher for public than for private goods. In collectivistic cultures, the influence of peers inside the group is stronger due to the extended families; numerous family members can influence the individuals' decision-making. However, the influence of peers and reference groups outside the family groups is weaker. In contrast, in individualistic cultures the family influence is limited to private products (DeMooij, 2004).

14.3.2.2 The role of opinion leadership

The role of opinion leaders varies across cultures. In strong-uncertainty-avoidance cultures, leaders, experts, and professionals are likely to be listened to and followed. Similarly, in masculine cultures the opinion of successful leaders, experts, professionals, and popular people are respected and listened to. In collectivistic cultures, opinions of elders and senior executives are more relevant and respected than in individualistic cultures. In high-power-distance culture, the opinion of those who hold power is important.

The sources of obtaining information by opinion leaders vary across cultures. In individualistic cultures the opinion leaders receive their information from external sources, such as the media; in collectivistic cultures, they receive information from internal sources, such as social networks. In collectivistic cultures the information received from the media is regarded as less reliable than the information received from social networks (DeMooij, 2004).

14.3.2.3 Family decision-making

The degree of influence of family is stronger in collectivistic cultures than in individualistic cultures because of the dependency on other family members. In South Korea, the extended family, neighbors and friends have greater influence on purchase decisions than in the United States (Park & Jun, 2003).

In Japan, when choosing a tourist destination, all members of the families participate in the decision. The chosen destination should be preferred by everyone to preserve group harmony (Reisinger & Turner, 1997c, 1999a).

14.3.2.4 Buying roles

In collectivistic cultures purchasing decisions are made collectively, in consensus with the group, family, friends, and colleagues. Friends and colleagues have more influence on consumers than media and advertising or sales people. Parents and grandparents initiate, influence and decide about the purchases. Children are taught to follow parental guidelines. In individualistic cultures, decisions are made on an individual basis. Although parents can be involved in decision-making, children are taught to have their own opinions and decide about their own needs. Children often initiate and influence the purchases. In high power distance cultures, elders and seniors play an important role in decision-making. They often influence and decide about the final purchases.

In Hispanic families, husbands dominate in the more important decision phases and decide what to buy, whereas wives dominate in the minor phases and suggest the purchase (Kenkel, 1961). Husbands decide about purchasing cars or travel, and wives decide about purchasing home appliances (Webster, 1994). Husbands decide about important and functional product attributes, such as price, while wives concentrate on minor and aesthetic product attributes, such as color (Davis, 1970; Woodside & Motes, 1979). Although North Americans also possess masculine and feminine traditional roles that determine who buys what, these roles are not so rigid as in the collectivistic cultures.

14.3.2.5 Level of decision-making

There are variations in the individual's involvement in the purchase decision and level of decision-making across cultures. In the collectivistic and high-context cultures, individuals actively gather information and make decisions. The context of making decisions is more important than verbal messages to convince the consumer to buy. The level of decision-making is more extensive than in individualistic cultures. The focus is on the development of dependency and feelings in order to draw the consumer's attention. In individualistic cultures, the focus is on arguments and rational aspects of the decision-making (DeMooij, 2004).

In individualistic and low-uncertainty-avoidance cultures, individuals are not so much involved in the decision-making process. The level of decision is more routine and limited. Purchases are often made on impulse. People go to shops with no intentions to buy, yet they always buy something. Such impulsive buying in individualistic cultures is related to the need for variety, novelty, stimulation, and thrill. On the other hand, in collectivistic cultures, where the focus is on interdependence, emotional control, and moderation, purchases are more planned (DeMooij, 2004).

Lee (2005) noted that Chinese consumers conduct internal and external information searches and compare alternatives as much as possible; impulse purchases are not likely to happen. ''Compare three shops before purchasing'' is the most widely accepted approach of information searching in China. Before making a final buying decision, Chinese consumers spend a lot of time browsing, and therefore are disinclined to convenience or impulse buying. Chinese consumers fully plan or partially plan their purchasers. The waste of money is shameful and should be avoided (Gong, 2003).

14.3.2.6 Buying new products

The adaption of new products and acceptance of ideas varies across cultures. In individualistic and low-uncertainty cultures, adaption of new ideas and products, and traveling to new places and meeting new people happens faster than in collectivistic and high-uncertainty-avoidance cultures. In individualistic cultures, people want more choice and novelty; thus new ideas, products, and behavior are initiated and even demanded. The reason for such behavior is the drive for achievement and success. Without new ideas and change one cannot enhance one's own social standing and self-esteem, and compete and succeed. In collectivistic cultures, the adaption of new ideas and products is slower. People are cautious about new ideas, traveling to new places, and meeting new people. In low-uncertainty-avoidance cultures, the percentage of early adapters is higher than in high-uncertainty-avoidance cultures. In high-uncertainty-avoidance and collectivistic cultures there is a higher percentage of late adapters.

For example, in Japanese cultures (high collectivistic and high-uncertainty-avoidance) people are very cautious about new products, ideas and strangers. Also, Chinese consumers are reluctant to try new products or services, and traveling to new destinations due to risk aversion. Chinese consumers tend to enjoy available things and use products that are out of date but still in good condition. It is unlikely for a Chinese consumer to change brands or destinations for more novelty or variation. It is said that Chinese are slow in accepting new products. However, since the Chinese belong to a low-uncertainty-avoidance culture, they seem to be the least cautious about adaption of something that is new.

14.3.3 **Criteria and product evaluation**

National culture influences assigning different importance weightings to the five SERVQUAL dimensions of service quality (Furrer et al., 2000). Customers with a Western cultural background rely more on tangible cues from the physical environment than customers with an Asian cultural background. The hedonic dimension of the consumption experience is more important for Western consumers than for Asians (Winsted, 1999).

According to Tsaur et al. (2005), there are differences in all dimensions of service quality among three cultural groups: persons of English Heritage, Asians, and Europeans. Accordingly, the English-Heritage group perceives better service quality for "tangibles," "reliability," "assurance," and "empathy" than the Asian and European groups. The English-Heritage group relies more on tangible cues from a physical environment to evaluate service quality than Asians and Europeans. The English Heritage and European groups are more "loyal" in their behavioral intentions than the Asian group, and the English Heritage group is also more willing to pay more for service than the Asian and European groups.

Quality of interpersonal relationships is a key factor in determining the Asian customers' service-encounter evaluation, while Western customers place more emphasis on goal completion, efficiency, and time saving. Asian tourists give significantly lower ratings for all the relational quality service attributes compared to their Western counterparts. Asian tourists assess service in terms of staff understanding the guest's problems and needs, dependability of service, and effective responsiveness. On the other hand, Western tourists assess service in terms of the ability of service providers to develop an atmosphere of welcoming and willingness to help, which suggests that Western tourists seek more intangible aspects of service that are over and above basic service provision. (Tsang & Ap, 2007).

Since Asian countries are characterized by large power distance, they also require the providers to pay attention to social hierarchy. Since Western customers are characterized as having small power distance, customers accept less status differences and expect more egalitarian service (Mattila, 1999b, 1999c). For example, routine Western customer–employee service encounters do not satisfy Korean guests because they ignore the importance of status differences. Koreans expect a formal relationship in a service encounter, especially in upscale, expensive restaurants. Koreans avoid unnecessary involvement in service encounters; they do not desire familiarity with service providers whose social status differs from their own. Korean service providers are required to show respect for social distance and avoid expressions of familiarity, which is in contrast to Americans (Kong & Jogaratnam, 2007).

Expectations from service also vary across cultures. For example, the Japanese are more demanding and have higher service expectations than other international tourists. Japanese tourists demand more attention and care than American tourists (Ahmed & Krohn, 1992). The Japanese also have higher expectations in terms of detail, aesthetics, quality, and service (Turcq & Usunier, 1985).

Tourists from Great Britain, the United States, Australia, Japan, and Taiwan have different expectations for hotel service quality. It was found that British tourists have the highest expectations, followed by tourists from the United States, Australia, Taiwan, and Japan. Japanese tourists have the lowest expectations for the tangible and the empathic dimensions of service quality. The Taiwanese tourists also have lower expectations for the empathic dimensions in terms of providing, caring, and giving individual attention to the tourist (Mok & Armstrong, 1998).

Preferences for service timing also vary across cultures. International guests in casual restaurants have different preferences for service timing. American tourists accept a longer waiting time prior to seating, whereas guests from Hong Kong accept a longer waiting time for the check upon the conclusion of the meal. US guests perceive a prolonged wait for the check to be a sign of neglectful service (Becker & Murmann, 1999).

In general, it was found that tourists from individualistic cultures demand more efficient, prompt, and error-free service than those from collectivistic cultures, where orientation toward people and sincerity shown by service employees is the most important concern. Individualistic customers have higher expectations of assurance from service providers than collectivistic customers because they expect service providers to give them confidence about the service they are receiving (Donthu & Yoo, 1998). However, it was also argued that individualists maintain a distance between themselves and the service providers, and use the tangible elements of service to reduce the closeness of the interaction (Furrer et al., 2000). Individualists also consider personalized service as being important relative to those in collectivistic cultures, where consistency is more important than personalized treatment (Kong & Jogaratnam, 2007).

Further, it was found that tourists coming from countries with greater cultural distance are less demanding and more tolerant in evaluating service quality (Weiermair, 2000). For example, Asian visitors to Hong Kong are more critical in judging the service they receive than their Western counterparts because the culture of Asian tourists is much closer to that of Hong Kong.

Buyers from Western countries place greater emphasis on product attributes designed to offer curiosity, utility (e.g. exploration of new product offerings) than buyers from Asian countries (Jones & McCleary, 2005).

Studies show that culturally different consumers have different perceptions of products made in different countries, and these diverse perceptions have impact on alternative evaluations (Lee, 2005). For example, Chinese consumers regard imported products as better than domestic ones (Tai, 1998). Chinese have more favorable attitudes toward imported consumer products than domestic ones for attributes such as quality, design, innovation, customer service, and overall value (Lee, 2005).

The acceptable price range for Chinese consumers is narrower than that for Westerners (Gong, 2003), partly due to the relatively lower purchasing power of Chinese consumers compared to Westerners, combined with Confucian cultural influences and the strong role of thrift. However, due to the influence of large power distance and collectivism, Chinese consumers tend to put heavy weight on the social risks involved in purchasing, especially when the purchase activities are related to gift-giving. Chinese also believe that a "cheap product is never good"; purchasing a cheap product may cause buyers to lose face and harm the relationship between individuals (Lee, 2005). They also think that cheap products have quality problems or other defects.

Moreover, national culture influences the evaluation of travel services (Crotts & Erdmann, 2000) and destinations. In general, visitors from Western cultures tend to rate their experiences at vacation destinations higher than those from Eastern cultures, but the strength of their ratings is not consistent. Even though visitors from Western cultures rate their satisfaction highest, the likelihood of returning to the same destinations is relatively low in comparison to other cultures (McCleary et al., 2006).

14.3.4 Purchase decision

Culture is being recognized as a major reason why people in different countries make different decisions (Hofstede, 1980; Kluckhohn, 1951; Rokeach, 1973a,b). Individualists make decisions differently than the collectivists. Individualists are in control of their decisions, while collectivists allow others to make decisions for them. In fatalistic cultures people leave the decisions to uncontrollable higher-order forces such as God, luck, or faith. In some other cultures, people postpone decisions (*manãna* syndrome = do it tomorrow) (DeMooij, 2004).

Individualists make decisions on an individual basis, while collectivists make decisions in consensus with the group. Individualists attribute their behavior to their personal characteristics and emotions; their buying behavior is more emotion driven. Collectivists, on the other hand, attribute their behavior to situational factors; their buying behavior is less emotional and more rational (McDonald, 1995; Usunier & Lee, 1996).

Studies on Chinese purchasing behavior show that the Chinese have deep roots in Confucianism and emphasize thrift, diligence, and value consciousness. Thrift is highly advocated and the Chinese people "save for a rainy day" instead of "living for today" or "buying now and paying later." It is socially desirable to save money and be a meticulous shopper in China (Lee, 2005). Chinese consumers are saving oriented. Borrowing money is widely seen as shameful because it means living beyond one's means. Chinese have an aversion toward using credit; they prefer to purchase products with cash instead of credit cards (Gavin, 1994). Chinese consumers watch what they buy and how they spend their hard-earned money. For the Chinese, shopping is mainly a planned, calculated task to perform. Chinese consumers are more conservative, utilitarian, and functionally oriented when compared with Western counterparts (Li, 1998). It is believed that consumers who keep using the old products never become repeat purchasers or users.

14.3.4.1 Purchase risk

A number of studies have shown that perceived risk varies across countries (Goszczynska et al., 1991; Hoover et al., 1978; Verhage et al., 1990). For example, risk perceptions significantly vary between the People's Republic of China (PRC), the United States, Germany and Poland (Weber & Hsee, 1998). American, Mexican, Dutch, Turkish, Thai and Saudi consumers are different in their risk perception for consumer products (Yavas et al., 1992).

Tourists from highly risk-adverse cultures behave differently than tourists from low-risk- avoidance cultures. For example, Japanese travelers engage in risk/uncertainty-reducing behaviors by seeking pre-trip information from Travel Channel members, purchasing pre-paid tour packages, traveling in larger groups, staying for shorter periods, and visiting fewer destinations than the Germans (Money & Crotts, 2003). The higher the cultural distance between visitor and host cultures, the higher the likelihood that the international visitor engages in more risk-reducing travel behaviors through the use of travel packages, tour operators and traveling in larger numbers on shorter trips to fewer destinations (Crotts, 2004).

Litvin et al. (2004) noted that tourists from the high UAI cultures (Japanese and Greek) acquire more information from friends, relatives, state and city travel offices, and tour operators than tourists from low UAI cultures (the Germans and British), who use travel guides and information obtained from marketing-dominated sources, such as advertisements on TV and radio. High UAI tourists also spend fewer days on trip planning, whereas those from low UAI cultures find pleasure in trip planning and choose to spend more time in arranging its details. The less-risk-avoidant tourists are more likely to travel alone, or travel with fewer parties than tourists from high UAI cultures. Those from high UAI cultures purchase significantly more pre-packaged travel tours, whereas those from low UAI cultures are more likely to rent cars. High UAI tourists visit fewer destinations and spend fewer nights in the visited country and during the length of their journey, as compared with low UAI tourists (Litvin et al., 2004).

Travelers of different nationalities may perceive the same risk differently (Richardson & Crompton, 1988). There are significant differences in perceived risk between American and Chinese-Malaysian students when choosing Australia as a holiday destination (Summers & McColl-Kennedy, 1998) and among international tourists traveling to Israel (Fuchs & Reichel, 2004). Tourists from the United States, Hong Kong and Australia perceive more travel risk, feel less safe and are more anxious and reluctant to travel than tourists from the United Kingdom, Canada, and Greece (Reisinger & Mavondo, 2006b).

Risk perceptions influence perceptions of safety (Reisinger & Mavondo, 2005). Safety perceptions also vary across cultures. For example, international tourists attending the 2000 America's Cup in Auckland, New Zealand, placed a higher importance on safety than domestic tourists (Barker et al., 2003). Chinese visitors feel relatively safe and Japanese visitors feel relatively unsafe compared with European visitors. The Japanese are more interested in security attributes of tourism products than North American and European business groups (Suh & Gartner, 2004). Also, the needs for safety versus adventure differ among Japanese, Korean and American tourists (Pizam & Jeong, 1996).

14.3.5 Post-purchase behavior/decision

14.3.5.1 Satisfaction

The degree to which consumers achieve satisfaction or experience dissatisfaction (cognitive dissonance) is greatly influenced by national culture. In collectivistic societies, customer satisfaction often depends on trust, caring, shared duty and long-term commitment, such as provision of services beyond contract terms, attending to all concerns, expressing gratitude for the relationships and rewards loyalty, and placing customer interests at times above those of the firm. In individualistic societies it is believed that customer satisfaction depends on efficiency, promptness and error-free service.

However, it was found that for American diners' satisfaction the personalization of service is important, whereas for Korean diners individual recognition and personalization are less important. Koreans believe that service providers should be punctual, respectful, courteous, and caring, rather than personal. Koreans are also most likely to return to a restaurant where they have previously enjoyed their dining experiences (Kong & Jogaratnam, 2007).

It was also found that those who reside in high cultural distance (CD) countries (with more cultural differences between visitor and host cultures) and travel in fully prepackaged tours (to minimize potential friction) report higher satisfaction with travel experience and probability of repeating a visit than those who do not. Those who reside in low CD countries and engage in free and independent travel report higher satisfaction and repeat visit intent compared to those with more structure in their visit (Crotts & McKercher, 2006). Those from highly masculine societies have also higher dissatisfaction than those from low-to-moderate masculine societies (Crotts & Erdmann, 2000).

14.3.5.2 Loyalty and commitment

According to the reinforcement theory, pleasant outcomes tend to generate repeat behavior, whereas unpleasant outcomes do not generate repeated behavior. In order to motivate consumers for repeat purchase or visitation, one has to develop positive perceptions to enhance their satisfaction. Satisfaction, in turn, does produce loyalty and commitment.

Customer loyalty and commitment vary across cultures. The difference in customer loyalty depends on the levels of expected and perceived satisfaction after the experience. For example, collectivistic buyers are usually more loyal and committed in their buying behaviors than individualistic buyers. The Chinese and Koreans may even sacrifice themselves for the benefits of others. However, Philippino consumers were found to be less loyal than American consumers (Sun et al., 2004). A lower level of customer loyalty for Philippinos can result from a lack of brand savvy in comparison to Americans and being less financially satisfied. Also, tourists from less masculine cultures are more loyal when evaluating travel services, while tourists from more masculine societies report strong customer defection (Crotts & Erdmann, 2000).

14.3.5.3 Criticism and complaints

Dissatisfied consumers can (1) voice their dissatisfaction, (2) spread negative word of mouth, (3) switch to another product, or (4) take legal action. In collectivistic cultures, where the focus is on maintaining social harmony and loyalty, consumers hesitate to complain by voicing their complaints or taking legal action when they experience post-purchase problems.

For example, the Chinese are less likely than the Americans to conduct a formal complaint for a faulty product (Lowe & Corkindale, 1998). The Chinese believe that nature has a way by which all things become what they are, and that it is not wise to hold too tightly onto what one has gained or lost (Chan, 1963). The Chinese also believe in Yuan (Karma): things that are far beyond one's control. While in the individualistic cultures people desire to seek control over their life, the Chinese submit to their own individual fate–fatalism. They generally have low expectations toward the purchased product and attribute failure of the product to fate rather than to the company or manufacturers (Yao, 1988).

The desire to maintain social harmony discourages Chinese consumers from showing their dissatisfaction. Even if they want to complain, they express themselves in a vague way. Chinese believe that a complaint to a certain degree is a manifestation of not making a wise decision. Also, one can lose face in front of others if no positive outcome from the complaint is obtained (Lowe & Corkindale, 1998).

Since Confucianism requires individuals to adapt to the context, control emotions, avoid competition and conflict, and maintain harmony (Lee, 2005), the Chinese follow the principles of modesty and humility which tend to increase Chinese consumers' level of tolerance with dissatisfaction (Lowe & Corkindale, 1998). However, they are more likely to spread a negative word of mouth to in-group members. In contrast, in individualistic and masculine cultures, consumers often complain widely and even take legal actions.

Tourists from higher-uncertainty-avoidance cultures have also a higher intention to praise and compliment the service providers if they experience positive service quality. If they experience a problem, they show a lower intention to switch to another service provider, to give negative word of mouth, or to complain (Liu & McClure, 2001).

However, the study shows that young Taiwanese consumers are more likely to switch restaurant providers than the US consumers. Switching to other service providers allows them to look for new ways to satisfy the need for curiosity, novelty and variety, express their individuality, achieve stimulation in consumer choices, and escape from collectivistic, rigid core cultural values. Taiwanese are less likely than US consumers to complain face-to-face about poor service in order to avoid hurting another person's face, causing shame and embarrassment (Lin & Mattila, 2006). According to Confucian beliefs, people should be guided in their lives by forgiveness and compromise to maintain social harmony. In contrast, North Americans who focus on their individual needs believe that a person in control of his or her own destiny is more likely to voice dissatisfaction than a Taiwanese counterpart (Hui & Au, 2001).

Other studies show that in response to unsatisfactory service in a hotel Americans are more likely to stop patronizing the hotel, complain to hotel management, and warn family and friends. Japanese, on the other hand, are less likely to complain to management and tell friends and relatives about unsatisfactory experiences (Huang et al., 1996).

Complaint behavior also varies across cultures. For example, guests in hotel restaurants in Hong Kong, SAR, are more likely to complain about the food tastiness, temperature and freshness than the Houston guests in Houston, Texas, United States. The Hong Kong guests also complain more about the noise level, while the Houston guests complain more about temperature and décor of hotel restaurants. Service efficiency, greetings, attentiveness, and helpfulness are the top service attributes about which guests complain; however, they are also rated differently; the Hong Kong guests rate ''greetings'' higher than the Houston guests (DeFranco et al., 2005).

14.3.5.4 Product disposal

National cultures have profound affect on what the consumers do with a product after the purchase. For example, the collectivistic consumers who follow the value of thrift and modesty are more likely to use the product as long as it works and delivers benefits. They also save old products for later or give the products away to children or families. In contrast, the individualistic consumers who follow the value of pleasure and immediate gratification are more likely to dispose of an old or used product and buy a new one. European consumers are more likely to repair a product rather than dispose of it. Members of cultures which are more prone to repairs and reuse than to replacement and buying new products cannot be relied upon as repeat purchasers.

14.3.6 Beyond the purchase decision

14.3.6.1 Memories and meanings

Culture affects memory. Those who are from the same culture better remember significant activities and events in their life that are consistent with their cultural background. Those from similar cultures also use similar cues to memorize messages. For example, Asian speakers from high context cultures, such as the Chinese, rely more on visual representation, whereas English speakers from low context cultures rely more on verbal sounds. Visualization facilitates memory in high-context cultures such as Chinese and Japanese, while explicit repetition of the same word facilitates memory in low-context cultures (DeMooij, 2004).

Preferences and meanings also vary across cultures. For example, in Europe, white is associated with purity and weddings, whereas black is associated with mourning. In contrast, in Japan, white is associated with mourning, and black is associated with happiness. In Japan, China and Korea, purple is associated with expensive, whereas in the United States purple is associated with inexpensive (DeMooij, 2004).

14.3.6.2 Emotions and feelings

Emotions such as pain, joy, sadness, anger, fear, stress, or excitement represent a very important concept in tourism. Tourism is all about feeling better mentally, physically, and spiritually. Emotional responses to consumption of tourism services can explain satisfaction and repeat patronage or destination visitation. Emotions are learned by growing up in a culture or by exposure to the culture. Emotions are culturally dependent. Although many emotions, such as happiness, fear, anger, or sadness, are universal, people in different cultures express emotions differently.

Emotions can be expressed visually (by using mimics and face expressions), vocally (by using voice), and by using other senses (smell or touch). A smile can be used to express happiness in one culture, or distrust in another culture, or even an invitation for a social interaction in another culture. In collectivistic societies people control their emotions and often suppress expressions of negative feelings, displeasure or dissatisfaction because it would negatively reflect on their in-group. They always try to express politeness. In collectivistic cultures the display of emotions depends on the context and belonging to a group. Expression of anger and frustration is more easily tolerated in individualistic than in collectivistic cultures. In low-uncertainty-avoidance cultures people have less control over the expressions of emotions, whereas in high- uncertainty-avoidance cultures people display emotions and often show embarrassment and guilt.

For example, in Japan, criticizing or complaining in public is a serious breach of social etiquette. In contrast, expressing feelings and thoughts in public and praising good and loud talkers is a normal practice in the West. In Japan, a humble, apologetic attitude is an appropriate way of showing emotions. Openly expressing emotions is regarded as rude. Westerners are perceived as too cold, too objective, and uncaring about the emotional aspect of personal relations. Those who talk too much and raise their voices are perceived to be insincere and creating friction.

In Indonesian society the expression of emotions, negative and positive, is very rare, as they disrupt the smooth flow of relationships (except in the presence of family members and close friends). Expressions of love are also not accepted in public. In contrast, Australians have less control over the expression of negative and positive feelings, and more informal behavior is accepted (Reisinger & Turner, 1997b).

In collectivistic culture, emotions are more relational and social, whereas in individualistic cultures emotions are more individual. In collectivistic cultures emotions are ''other focused'' (e.g. sympathy, shame, feelings of interpersonal communion, feelings of social obligations, sense of saving face), whereas in individualistic cultures, emotions are ego-focused (e.g. anger, frustration, pride) (DeMooij, 2004).

Anger, happiness and sadness are expressed differently in Western and Asian cultures. In Western cultures people smile when they are happy, cry when they face grief, and open their mouth and eyes when they are surprised. In Asian collectivistic cultures, people often smile or laugh to hide sorrows, embarrassment or shame. Such a smile is not a reflection of happiness. In Asian collectivistic cultures people often cry when they are happy.

Emotional responses to negative service encounters differ across cultures. While UK customers blame service employees for failing to provide the required customer service, African customers who emphasize the need to conform to rules and expect the sellers to be as helpful emphasize feelings of sadness (humiliation and embarrassment). Such feelings are more likely to influence switching service providers (Smith, 2006).

In some cultures emotional words include multiple feelings. For example, the Japanese *jodo* include emotions such as anger, happiness, and sadness as well as consideration, and calculations. The German *Schadenfreude* means malicious delight, enjoying other people's suffering or bad luck (DeMooij, 2004).

Understanding the concept of emotions can help to determine the quality of the individual's motivations, needs, experiences and the outcomes of these experiences. However, emotions can be accurately understood only by members of the same national culture.

SUMMARY

Numerous studies identified behavioral differences among tourists from different cultural groups. These studies suggest that national culture influences the individual's personal characteristics, such as gender roles, lifestyle and activities, personality, and self, as well as psychological characteristics, such as motivations and needs, perceptions and image, learning, knowledge, and attitudes. National culture influences tourist's decision process, including need recognition, information search and choice of information sources, product/destination evaluation and post-purchase behavior. National culture decides how the following influence the tourist: reference groups, opinion leaders and families. It also determines buying roles, levels of decision-making, and preferences for new products/destinations. National culture influences the tourist's perceptions of purchase and travel risk, loyalty and commitment to a purchase, and its criticism. Finally, national culture affects emotions and feelings that decide about the tourist's needs and experiences, and the outcomes of these experiences.

DISCUSSION POINTS AND QUESTIONS

1. How does tourist personality influence the tourist destination choice and tourist behavior?
2. Which variables (motivation or personality) can best explain the needs of international tourists? Justify your response and give examples.
3. How does culture impact the nature of travel? (destination selection, purpose of travel, travel arrangements, travel timing and schedule, length of stay, spending patterns, companionship, activities, interests, risk taken)?

CASE STUDY 14.1 Japanese Tourist Behavior

Cultural background strongly influences Japanese tourist consumer behavior. For instance, the Japanese select a holiday destination differently from a domestic tourist in Australia. In order to maximize the benefits of their holidays, Japanese carefully pre-plan their travel arrangements. They examine all alternative destinations, their pros and cons, and consider various pricing policies to save additional funds. As a result, in the pre-purchase stage of consumer behavior Japanese spend a lot of time on decision-making. The process of their decision-making is longer when compared to Western consumers. On the other hand, the purchase stage itself is speedier than in Western countries because Japanese try to avoid offending and disturbing the harmony of the group (Ziff-Levine, 1990). In the evaluation stage, Japanese assess the products and services consumed depending on the situation and personal relationships. The Japanese holiday satisfaction level is always weighted against the degree of the Japanese reluctance to express negative emotions.

In contrast, the process of decision making of an average Australian tourist is shorter in the pre-purchased stage. Australians do not spend much time on deciding about their holiday destinations. Their holidays are often unplanned, worry free and relaxed. They are also designed around the individual needs. However, the purchase stage is longer because Australian tourists often shop around to get the best deal in various travel agencies. In the evaluation stage, Australians express their holiday dissatisfaction openly and directly; they often argue and refer to facts.

Source: Reisinger, Y., & Turner, L. (1999a). A cultural analysis of Japanese tourists: challenges for tourism marketers. *European Journal of Marketing*, *33*(11–12), 1203–1227.

CASE STUDY 14.2 Cultural Influences on Tourist Behavior

Helen was working the tourist information centre in Flåm, Norway. She met many tourists from all over the world. She noticed differences between different nationalities of tourists in their behaviors. According to Helen, tourists from different cultures have different demands regarding accommodation, food services, attractions, activities, etc. One day Helen talked to an American lady who came to the tourist information to share her positive impressions about the guest house. The American lady considered the service to be excellent and the rooms to be cosy and charming. She would definitely come back to Flam next year. Helen was pleased to hear this. However, later, that very same day, an English lady came into the office. She found the guest house to look like a prison, the rooms too dark and small, and the service non-existent. The lady asked for the address of the Norwegian tourism authorities so she could write them a letter of complaint about how horrible the guest house was. The next day, a Dutch lady who had stayed in the guest house before wrote a postcard to the tourist office attaching a photograph of her in front of the waterfalls. She thanked the office for her lovely stay.

WEBSITE LINKS

1. Dealing with cultural differences in tourism and hospitality: http://www.vea.com.au/Product.aspx?id=376
2. Tourism and cultural differences: http://rielworld.com/2007/05/29/tourism-and-cultural-differences/
3. Representing foreign nationals: http://representingforeignnationals.blogspot.com/2008/02/cultural-differences-conviction-of.html

The next part will compare the cultural orientations of the selected international societies.

Cross-Cultural Comparison

5

Part Five compares cultural orientations of international societies.

Cultural differences among international societies

15

The aim of this chapter is to summarize and compare core cultural values and behavior of the selected international societies.

After completing this chapter the reader should be able to:

- Identify major cultural differences and similarities among African, Asian, Australian, European, Indian, Latin and North American and the Middle East societies
- Compare the major cultural value orientations and behaviors of the selected regions

INTRODUCTION

This chapter concentrates on the major cultural patterns and behaviors in Africa, Asia, Australia, India, Europe, Latin and North America, and the Middle East. Numerous countries are selected and their values and behaviors compared. The values common to specific cultural groups are highlighted.

15.1 AFRICA

The most important unit of African society is the family, which in most cases includes the extended family or tribe. African family life centers in villages, where food is gathered. The village elders are leaders; they judge and dictate the rules. The family tribe provides the rules for acceptable behavior, individual rights, duties, marriage, **349** inheritance, and succession. Africans believe that people and social relationships come first. Friendships based on trust and sincerity are highly valued. People accept that everyone is a friend unless otherwise proved. Showing respect is the key element for social harmony. Elders are given the most respect; young people are not expected to express opinions. Africans are warm, friendly, relaxed, and informal. They are never in a hurry; they view time as flexible. They like to sit and talk to get know each other better before they discuss business. Time is unlimited; what cannot be done today can be accomplished tomorrow. The concept of time is, however, changing in big cities. In Africa, corruption is common; it is related to poverty, inadequate pay, and bad working conditions (Harris et al., 2004).

15.2 **ASIA**

Common Asian values

A number of values are common to most Asian cultures. These are social hierarchy; respect for elders, parents, ancestors, and traditions; importance of the family and family ties as a source of personal self-worth; differentiation between in-groups and out-groups; social harmony; a sense of obligation and shame; face-saving, group consensus, loyalty, cooperation, indirectness, ambiguity, silence, and emotional restraint (Dodd, 1995), patience, avoidance of strong emotions, having connections, self-respect, and reputation (Tung cited in Joynt & Warner, 1996). Group orientation, discipline, importance of education, protocol, avoidance of conflict and moral responsibility are also important.

China

The People's Republic of China has a population of 1.3 billion. The name of the country means ''center of the world''. As a result, Chinese people think of their culture as the center of human civilization and hold themselves in high esteem. The Chinese culture has been influenced by the teachings of Confucianism, Taoism, and Buddhism. China is a hierarchical society, people believe in authority and subordination. They follow the formal rules of social etiquette; social status is important. The important personal characteristics are determination, calmness, honor, persistence and patience. Chinese culture is group-oriented; group activity, consensus, cooperation, support and loyalty are vital for social harmony. Chinese culture is high-context culture. Chinese understand non-verbal signals and use them frequently to send the true meanings in conversation. Chinese are long-term oriented; they are interested in long-term benefits. They are bound by their tradition and proud of ancestors. They negotiate and talk through an intermediary or a third party. They do not believe that the signing of a contract is a completed agreement; circumstances may change. They reciprocate invitations and gifts (Harris et al., 2004).

Chinese are punctual, dress formally, and address others by their second names or titles. They use business cards in introductions and follow a proper etiquette. They are reserved, respectful and sensitive. The concept of privacy does not exist; they often ask questions about salaries or incomes, personal information is frequently discussed. They avoid displaying affections, keep a distance when speaking, do not touch, and do not appreciate loud behavior (Harris et al., 2004).

The four most important terminal values of Chinese are true friendship, wisdom, freedom, and mature love, whereas the four least important terminal values are family security, a comfortable life, an exciting life, and salvation. The four most important instrumental values are being ambitious, broadminded, intellectual, and courageous, whereas the four least important instrumental values are being forgiving, helpful, clean, and obedient (Feather, 1976, 1980b). Table 15.1 lists the major cultural differences between Chinese Mandarin-speaking and Australian societies.

Table 15.1 Cultural Differences Between Mandarin-Speaking Tourists and Australian Hosts

Mandarin-speaking tourists	Australian hosts
Orientation toward group	Orientation toward individual
Focus on being together	Focus on being independent
Hierarchy	Egalitarianism
Importance of age and position	Importance of accomplishment
Importance of group activities and obedience	Importance of hard work and capabilities
Non-materialistic values first	Materialistic and hedonistic values first
Focus on being dependent	Focus on being self-reliant
Privacy does not exist	Focus on privacy
Focus on punctuality	Focus on flexibility
Formal dress	Informal dress
Seek relationships	Seek agreement
Focus on social harmony	Focus on getting the best deal quickly
Focus on formal etiquette	Focus on informal behavior
Tradition of gift-giving	No tradition of gift-giving
Emotions are suppressed	Emotions are displayed
Implicitness	Explicitness
Risk-avoiding	Risk-taking
Focus on obligation	Focus on standing out

Source: Reisinger, Y., & Turner, L. (1998). Cultural differences between Mandarin-speaking tourists and Australian hosts and their impact on cross-cultural tourist-host interaction. *The Journal of Business Research*, *42*(2), 175–187.

Indonesia

Indonesia has a population of about 232 million. The major ethnic groups are Javanese and Sundanese. Indonesia is the largest Islamic country in the world; nearly 90% of the population is represented by Muslims. Generally, people adhere to the village law

(*Adat*) rather than the rules of the Koran. The society is hierarchical. Indonesians follow the rules of social hierarchy in all personal relationships; they show respect to superiors. The family is the basic unit of life. Indonesians are group-oriented; they conform and abide. They avoid confrontation, making someone ashamed, insulted, or embarrassed. Criticizing or contradicting a person in front of others is avoided because it causes one to lose face. People talk indirectly. Asking personal questions and touching in public are forbidden. People greet by nodding the head; they avoid using the left hand. They do not like to be pressured; they believe in ''rubber time'' that is flexible and unlimited (Harris et al., 2004). Table 15.2 lists the major cultural differences between Indonesian and Australian societies.

Japan

Japan has a population of about 130 million. More than 99% of it is represented by Japanese. Traditionally, Japan is a very noble country which values honor, pride, and perseverance. However, the Japanese culture is slowly changing; it is following values of the contemporary world. The major religions are Shintoism and Buddhism. Japanese put a great emphasis on the group, the family, and belonging and loyalty. They show respect for social classes, authority, and elders. They try not to harm anyone; rather, they save their own face as well as others' in order to preserve social harmony. They avoid praising, complementing and criticizing. They do not stand out from a group. Japanese use indirect, vague communicating style; they focus on the context rather than content of a verbal message. Non-verbal language is more important to them than verbal expressions. They leave sentences unfinished so others can make a conclusion. The Japanese language is full of nuances; it has various degrees of courtesy and respect for different social classes. Third party is used in introductions and deals to create trust between individuals. Japanese follow the custom of using business cards (*meishi*) that identify their owner's professional titles. Cards are usually translated into English. Formality prevails. Bowing is a traditional form of greeting. Japanese are time conscious and punctual. They also follow a tradition of obligatory gift-giving; gifts are given at any social event and must be reciprocated. Japanese like order, cleanliness, and discipline. They are sensitive to what others think or expect of them. They avoid risk; they require physical and psychological security. They have difficulties dealing with strangers and foreigners. Many experience a difficulty to adapt and feel alienated (Frager, 1970). They laugh when they are happy and sad. They are insular. They value education, new technological developments; they have pride in their work. They work hard.

The Japanese give consideration to the effect of their behavior on others. When on vacation, Japanese tourists are activity-oriented unlike the Western tourists who travel to do nothing. Shopping is very important to them. The Japanese attach importance to obligatory gift-giving and polite inexplicitness; they avoid humiliation, try not to offend, or disturb the harmony of a group. Trust and relationship building are vital to their existence (Ziff-Levine, 1990). A high standard of service is critical to Japanese satisfaction (Reisinger, 1990).

Table 15.2 Cultural Differences Between Indonesian Tourists and Australian Hosts

Indonesian tourists	Australian hosts
Family orientation	Self-orientation
Group orientation	Individual orientation
Emphasis on community, togetherness, sociability	Emphasis on individualism and privacy
Focus on dependence, obedience, welfare of others	Focus on independence, challenge, self-interest
Emphasis on physical and emotional closeness	Emphasis on privacy
No exclusive friendships	Strong exclusive friendships
Focus on consensus	Individual decision-making
Focus on duty and obeying the will of the group	Focus on individual autonomy and initiative
Group responsibility for actions	Moral responsibility for own actions
Social hierarchy	Egalitarianism
Age grading	No age grading
Respect for elders and their advice	No respect for elders and their advice
Correct form of behavior	Direct and open manner of behavior
Indirect expression of opinions	Direct expression of opinions
Control of emotions, avoidance of disagreement	Open disagreement
Smooth interpersonal relations	Efficiency and promptness
Risk avoidance	Risk-taking
Greetings followed by unhurried conversation	Brief greeting without conversation
Social rituals involve meals	Meals are not part of socializing
Time is stretchable	Time is money
Avoidance of hurry, frequent lateness	Hurried use of time, punctuality
Absence of stress	More stress and anxiety
Importance of formal dress	Informal dress
Frequent smiling in social encounters	Smiling used to express genuine pleasure
Eye contact avoided in formal encounters	More frequent eye contact
Frequent body contact	Body contact avoided
Smaller physical distance	Larger physical distance
Restrained gesticulation	Unrestrained gesticulation
Use of left hand avoided	Free use of either hand
Restrained feet and leg movement	Free leg movement

Source: Reisinger, Y., & Turner, L. (1997). Cross-cultural differences in tourism: Indonesian tourists in Australia. *Tourism Management, 18*(30), 139–147.

   Numerous studies have been done on Japanese culture. It was noted that Japanese are courteous, moral, loyal to others (*gimur*), have a sense of obligation and duty (*giri*), try to save face (*kao*), avoid others' shame and humility, follow correct protocol of presentation, do not display emotions, participate in rituals, and use non-verbal communication. The Japanese value peacefulness, passivity, reciprocal obligation, and hierarchical structure (Isomura et al., 1987). They are expected to subordinate individual interests to the group, cooperate with one another, and remain loyal to the group (Moeran, 1984). Their behavior is formal to reduce conflict and embarrassment and maintain harmony. *Seishin* spirit teaches them self-discipline, order, sacrifice, dedication, hierarchy, loyalty, responsibility, goodwill, and group activity; they must be beautiful for themselves and others, and disregard material disadvantages (Moeran, 1984). The spirit stresses the importance of duty (*giri*), indebtedness (*on*) and obligation (Lebra, 1976). Buddhism teaches the Japanese to live in harmony with nature. A stranger is not an enemy but a friend, and the aim is to reach consensus and compromise (Schinzinger, 1983).

Confucianism and Buddhism prescribe collectivism, a hierarchical structure of authority, status and obedience of superiors (Chinese, Japanese, Korean, and Indo-Chinese). The importance of the social hierarchy in Japanese culture can be explained in terms of high scores on power distance and masculinity, and low scores on individualism. Differences in status dictate different non-verbal behavior (Matsumo & Kudoh, 1987). Japanese culture is characterized by a high degree of collectivism; it emphasizes conformity, belongingness, empathy, and dependence (Benedict, 1946; Lebra, 1976; Nakane, 1973). The Japanese value courage, a sense of justice, love, companionship, trust, and friendship; they are concerned with war and peace (Triandis, 1972). The Japanese do not value comfort; they value self-adjustment, advancement, and serenity.

The Japanese are group-oriented; they emphasize harmony in interpersonal relations, solidarity, loyalty, and belongingness to society. That society is closed to outsiders (Mourer & Sugimoto, 1979). They differentiate between what they say and actually do, between *tatemae* (outside behavior) and *honne* (real intentions), between formal and informal behavior. They avoid giving negative answers to not to hurt others. They have several ways of saying ''no''. They depend on each other, cooperate, suppress open conflict and competition, and strive for group welfare (Kracht & Morsbach, 1981). They perceive Westerners as ''odd'' people due to their focus on individualism. They remove shoes before entering house. Table 15.3 presents some of the insights on the cultural differences between Japanese and Australian cultural characteristics.

Malaysia

The country has a population of about 23 million. The major ethnic groups are Malay, Chinese, and Indian. Islam is the predominant religion. The Koran dictates the rules of behavior and business activities. People are expected to pray five times a day, fast during the Ramadan, and make a trip to Mecca. People do not eat pork or drink alcohol. People believe they should live in harmony with nature or subjugate themselves of it. They are concerned with the present: the future is vague and unpredictable; the past has happened. They have a strong sense of fatalism. They are not motivated by careers and professional success; rather, long-lasting relationships with friends and families. The needs of families and friends are more important than self-centered needs, such as

Table 15.3 Cultural Differences Between Japanese and Australian Characteristics

Japanese cultural traits	Australian cultural traits
Social hierarchy, submission to elders and superiors	Social hierarchy, inequality is minimized
Respect for age, wisdom, higher social position	Little respect for age, wisdom, seniority
Social harmony	Individual opinions, beliefs, positions
Avoidance of conflict and competition	Tolerance for ambiguity, new ideas, different behaviors
Avoidance of risk	Taking risk
Strong group bonds, long-term relationships	Weak social bonds, temporary social relationships
Group needs and goals	Individual needs and goals
Group consensus	Individual opinions, importance of arguments and facts
Process oriented	Results oriented
Long-time oriented	Short-time oriented
Importance of *who*	Importance of *what*
Family and social groups	Materialism, possession, financial status
Dependency on others; co-existence with others	Democracy, equality, advancement, achievements
Non-verbal communication	Verbal communication
Difference between *what* is said and *how* it is said	Importance of *what* is said
Behavior according to strict social rules	Little attention paid to formal rules of social behavior
Hold back emotions in public	Display emotions in public
Silence as a symbol of power and strength	Silence as a symbol of weakness
Obligatory gift-giving	No obligatory gift-giving

the accumulation of money and material possessions. People are not materialistic; however, they work hard. The social status is important to them and the basic rules of behavior are obeyed. The most important rules of behavior are respect, courtesy, affection and love for one's parents; also harmony in the family, the neighborhood, and society. Bowing is a traditional form of greeting. Certain gestures are not permitted. For example, patting a child on the head or calling for a taxi by using the fingers of the right hand (Harris et al., 2004) are not acceptable.

Pakistan

More than 95% of the Pakistani are Sunni Muslim. Islam is the state religion. There are minority groups, such as Christians, Hindu, Afghans, and Parsi. Pakistanis are warm and hospitable. Family and friends are important to them. Personal honor is critical. They have a flexible approach to time. They do not eat pork or drink alcohol. They do not touch food with the left hand. They remove shoes before entering someone else's house and bring gifts. They follow the rules of formal introduction, and expect hand-shakes and business cards. Women wear the *burqah*, which covers their bodies from head to foot (Harris et al., 2004).

The Philippines

There are more than 85 million people in the Philippines, mostly Christian Malay-sians. The languages spoken are Philippino, English, and Chinese. Philippinos are friendly, hospitable, and warm. They focus on large, extended families. They do not criticize another person in public because shame is the greatest insult. In order to avoid shame, the Philippinos also avoid competition, change, and innovation. They try to save face at any cost. They are sensitive. They believe in fate and destiny rather than merit. They demand loyalty and are flexible about time. They value the concept of individualism; they want to be treated as individuals. Honor, good reputation and respect are important values. They follow tradition and believe in reciprocal obli-gation. Even thought they may not mean what they say, they say it in order to maintain appearances. Personal relationships are established before the business deal is made. People use a handshake (for men) or a kiss (for women) to greet each other (Harris et al., 2004).

South Korea

Korea's population is less than 50 million. In terms of ethnic groups, the country is pretty homogenous. Half of the population is represented by Christians and half by Buddhists. Koreans believe in inequality among people based on virtue, loyalty to authority, and filial piety to parents and sincerity to friends. They are committed to personal relations (Kim, 1988). There is little evidence of individualism (Bellah, 1970). The society and relationships are hierarchical. Proper interpersonal relationships are the most important; each person has either a lower or higher position. Spending time with people is more important than spending time making money. Koreans are hum-ble, and honor others. Confucianism teaches them to put public needs above private. The concept of privacy hardly exists. Respect is given to elders and their every wish is catered to. Sending elderly to elder-care facilities (as happens in the United States) is considered barbaric. Protocol is extremely important; rules of social etiquette are strongly observed. Slapping someone on the back or putting an arm around a person is considered unacceptable. Korean greets each other by bowing or shaking hands. Second names, professional titles, and positions are used when addressing others. People do not worry about keeping up with time. Koreans give gifts on many occa-sions. Koreans are indirect in communication; they avoid saying ''no''. ''Yes'' may not mean an agreement or intention to comply. People avoid saying ''no'' to avoid hurting someone else's feelings. Written contracts are important as in the West; oral contracts are accepted (Harris et al., 2004).

Thailand

Thailand means "the land of the free". About three quarters of the population is represented by Thai; Chinese is a minority group. Buddhism is an official religion. Thailand is a hierarchical society; people give respect to elders, teachers, and those in higher positions. Rules of social etiquette are followed. Family is the most important unit of society. Relationships between people are based on interdependence, trust, and cooperation. Social harmony is a virtue. People do not criticize and complain; they are humble, polite, and understanding (Harris et al., 2004). The nine major Thai values are smooth interpersonal relationships, grateful relationships, interdependence, the ego, flexibility and adjustment, religion orientation, education and competence, fun and pleasure, and achievement–task orientation (Komin, 1990). Table 15.4 lists the major cultural differences between Thai and Australian societies.

Vietnam

Vietnam has a population of more than 80 million, of which about 90% are Vietnamese. The largest minority is Chinese. Vietnamese people maintain strong family relationships which provide financial and emotional support. They place a great deal of importance on relationships and visiting people. They follow formal rules of addressing others by either shaking hands or bowing; official titles and positions are used to address others. They do not show affection in public, and do not touch the heads of young children (Harris et al., 2004).

15.3 AUSTRALIA

Australia is the sixth largest country in the world, with a population of nearly 20 million. More than 90% of all Australians are represented by Caucasian ethnic groups who descend from European ancestry (Dutch, Estonian, French, German, Greek, Italian, Latvian, Lithuanian, Polish, and former Yugoslavian). The Asian ethic groups represent less than 10% of the population and include Chinese, Indonesian, Korean, Malaysian, Polynesian, Taiwanese, Vietnamese, and Cambodian. The remaining percentage of Australians is the Aborigines, the original inhabitants of Australia.

Although Australians speak English, their English is different from American, British, or Canadian English. Australians frequently use slang and shorten words. They speak openly and directly, which often makes strangers feel that they are being attacked (Harris et al., 2004). They try to be politically correct to avoid hurting anyone's feelings. They dislike social classes and differences, and value close friendships. Mateship is valued. Mateship is a form of true friendship related to loneliness, hardship of outback life, need for companionship, joint activities, support, equality, and conformity to group norms (Encel, 1970).

Australians like sport and respect good sportsmanship. Australians praise those successful in sport, and are critical and less respectful of successful intellectuals ("tall

Table 15.4 Cultural Differences Between Thai and Australian Characteristics

Thai cultural traits	Australian cultural traits
Smooth interpersonal relationships	Exclusive interpersonal relationships
Smile as an expression of politeness	Verbal expression of politeness
Concern about others' feelings	No concern about others' feelings
Respect for elders	No respect for elders
Focus on religious and spiritual beliefs	Focus on logic and science
Truth is relative	Truth is absolute
Focus on fun and pleasure	Focus on hard work
Focus on social relationships	Focus on assertion and task
Success perceived in social and religious terms	Success perceived in terms of achievement and money
Family orientation	Independent, self-sufficient
Group orientation, interdependence	Individual orientation
Importance of status, seniority, hierarchy	Egalitarianism
Risk avoidance	Risk-taking
Self-control and self-restraint	Unreserved behavior
Criticism avoidance	Acceptance of constructive criticism
Avoidance of questions	Frequent critical questioning
Face-saving	No face-saving
Strong sense of self-ego	Weak sense of self-ego
Eye contact not frequent	Frequent eye contact
Restrained use of left hand	Free use of either hand
Formal introduction conforming to status	No formal introduction protocol
Greetings with a smile	Greetings with ''hello''
Frequent smiling as a social function	Smiling used to express genuine pleasure
Addressing by title and first name	Addressing by first name
Enquiries about age and earnings accepted	Enquiries about age and earnings impolite
Inclusive personal relations	Exclusive personal relations
Superficiality	Need for a deep meaning
Humility	Self-confidence
Gratefulness and reciprocation	Selfishness
Situation orientation	System and principles orientation
Importance of self-presentation	Self-presentation less important
Importance of external presentation	External presentation less important

Source: Reisinger, Y., & Turner, L. (1998). Cultural differences in tourism: A Lisrel analysis of Thai tourism to Australia. Paper presented at the *International Tourism and Hotel Industry in Indo-China and Southeast Asia Conference*, Phuket, Thailand, June 4–6, 1998.

poppies''), whose accomplishments they tend to play down and devalue (Encel, 1970; Sharp, 1992). Australians admire the ''Aussie battler'' and those who stand out against authority (Feather, 1986b). Australians are less concerned about safety and security at the personal and national levels due to the country's affluence and stability. Rather they are more concerned with love, affiliation, self-definition, and self-fulfillment (Feather, 1975, 1980b, 1986a; Feather & Hutton, 1973).

Australians enjoy life. They "work to live," not "live to work". Although they feel close to their British ancestors, they are not reserved; they are outgoing, relaxed, and informal. They greet each other by shaking hands, waving, or saying a simple "Hello, how are you?" They usually use first names to address someone. They are relatively open in expressing their feelings (Harris et al., 2004).

The four most important terminal values for Australians are happiness, inner harmony, freedom, and true friendship, whereas the four least important terminal values are pleasure, social recognition, national security, and salvation. The four most important instrumental values for Australians are being honest, loving, being broadminded, and being cheerful; the four least important instrumental values are being logical, polite, clean, and obedient (Feather, 1976, 1980b). Australian contemporary values are those of achievement, success, activity, work, humanitarianism, democracy, equality, aggressiveness and independence, all deriving from a value of self-reliance (Elashmawi, 1991). Lipset (1963) found that Australians are more egalitarian but less achievement oriented, universalistic and specific than Americans. Australians place importance on friendships and equality more than Americans and Israelis. Feather (1975) noted that Australians are more achievement oriented than Canadians and Israelis. Family, security, happiness and intellectual values are less important to Australians than to the other groups. Leading an exciting life; appreciating the world of beauty, inner harmony, mature love, and friendships; and being cheerful are all more important to them than to Americans. Having a comfortable life, salvation and ambition are less important than to Americans (Feather, 1975).

15.4 EUROPE

Important European values

Currently, the European Union encompasses more than 400 million people. The majority of the population is Caucasian. Europeans speak German, Romance, and Slavic languages. According to Harris et al. (2004), Europeans have an inherent interest in the quality of life. Historically they had to fight their neighbors, and they think in the context of the past. They have suffered and survived many wars, plagues, and government changes; they have a sense of survival. Long-term survival is more important to them than money. They have a sense of social responsibility. They desire education and security, and mistrust authority. They observe formal rules and titles in oral and written communication. They like new ideas and new ventures that lead to the enhancement of their quality of life.

The four most significant European values that dominate the European culture are pragmatism, rationalism, holism, and humanism (Lessem & Neubauer, 1994). However, European countries are quite different from each other in terms of their value orientations. Table 15.5 shows the evaluation scores, which represent the relative positions of

Table 15.5 Evaluation of the European Countries on the Hofstede and Hofstede's (2005) Cultural Dimensions

Country	Power Distance	Uncertainty Avoidance	Individualism	Masculinity	Long-Term Orientation
Austria	11	70	55	79	31
Belgium total					38
Belgium Flemish	61	97	78	43	
Belgium Walloon	67	93	72	60	
Bulgaria	70	85	30	40	
Croatia	73	80	33	40	
Czech Republic	57	74	58	57	13
Denmark	18	23	74	16	46
Estonia	40	60	60	30	
Finland	33	59	63	26	41
France	68	86	71	43	39
Germany	35	65	67	66	31
Great Britain	35	35	89	66	25
Greece	60	112	35	57	
Hungary	46	82	80	88	50
Ireland	28	35	70	68	43
Italy	50	75	76	70	34
Luxembourg	40	70	60	50	
Malta	56	96	59	47	
Netherlands	38	53	80	14	44
Norway	31	50	69	8	44
Poland	68	93	60	64	32
Portugal	63	104	27	31	30
Romania	90	90	30	42	
Russia	93	95	39	36	
Serbia	86	92	25	43	
Slovakia	104	51	52	110	38
Slovenia	71	88	27	19	
Spain	57	86	51	42	19
Sweden	31	29	71	5	33
Switzerland					40
French	70	70	64	58	
German	26	56	69	72	
Turkey	66	85	37	45	

*A high score on a dimension indicates a high ranking on that dimension, e.g. scores high in ranking represent the most individualistic countries, whereas scores low in ranking represent the most collectivistic ones.
Source: Hofstede, G., & Hofstede, G. J. (2005). *Cultures and organizations: Software of the mind* (Revised and expanded 2nd ed.). New York, USA: McGraw-Hill.

the selected European countries on Hofstede and Hofstede's (2005) cultural dimensions. A high score on a dimension indicates a high position in that dimension. The most individualistic European countries are the United Kingdom, the Netherlands, Hungary, Belgium, and Denmark; the most collectivistic are Portugal, Bulgaria, Romania, Greece, and Turkey. High on power distance are Slovakia, Russia, and Romania. Low on power distance are Austria and Denmark. The highest on uncertainty avoidance and the most threatened are Greece, Portugal, Malta, Russia, and Belgium; the lowest on uncertainty avoidance are Denmark, Sweden, the United Kingdom, and Ireland. The most masculine are Slovakia, Hungary, Austria, Italy, and Switzerland; the most feminine are Sweden, Norway, the Netherlands, Denmark, Finland, and Portugal. The highest on long-term orientation are Hungary, the Netherlands, and Slovakia, followed by Sweden and Germany; the lowest are the Czech Republic and Norway.

Greece is one of the countries that scored highly on collectivism and very highly on uncertainty avoidance. Sweden is the most feminine country. The Germanic countries are characterized by smaller power distance and weak-to-medium uncertainty avoidance. In the Germanic group the extreme country is Denmark, characterized by very small power distance and very weak uncertainty avoidance. Belgium, on the other hand, is characterized by a quite high uncertainty avoidance. The United Kingdom and Ireland are close to Germany but they are low on both power distance and uncertainty avoidance dimensions. Germany is more collectivistic than the United Kingdom. It was noted that Germans value cooperation, mutual support, team spirit, avoidance of conflict, and punctuality. However, the degree of formality in Germany is extreme. Germans address others and conduct themselves in a very formal manner; they use titles and identify people by their positions in social structures (Samovar et al., 1988).

In terms of the Confucian Work Dynamism dimension, Sweden, Poland, and Germany are in the middle rank on the Confucius long-term orientation (Chinese Culture Connection, 1987). Their value orientations are in between the long-term orientation (persistence, ordering relationships by status, thrift, having a sense of shame) and short-term orientation (personal stability, protecting "face," respect for tradition, reciprocation).

The most universalistic cultures can be found in the United Kingdom, Germany, and Sweden; and the most particularistic in France (Hampden-Turner & Trompenaars, 1993). Countries in which people are inner directed are the United Kingdom and Germany; countries with outer-orientation are Sweden, the Netherlands, and France. The most analytical are the United Kingdom, the Netherlands and Sweden; the most integrative are France and Germany. Countries in which status is gained by achievement are the United Kingdom, Sweden, Germany and the Netherlands; the country in which status is ascribed is France. Countries that view time as sequential are Sweden, the Netherlands, the United Kingdom and Germany; that country that views time as synchronized is France.

France

France's population is about 60 million. The French are mostly Roman Catholic. They are concerned with such values as honor, integrity, liberty, equality, and fraternity.

They are religion tolerant and appreciate diversity. They are individualistic in nature. They want to be and seen different, unique, and special. They are very status conscious. Although they like power, they dislike competition. The French are proud of their cultural heritage and language. They focus on the quality of life; they work to live rather than live to work. They love life. They attach great importance to vacations and free time. They are casual and flexible in terms of time; they enjoy leisure and socialization, good food and wine. They are inner-oriented and base their decisions on feelings and emotions. They are often indirect in conversations, which are meant to entertain. They talk more freely about sex; however, they avoid talking about money, jobs, and salaries, which are perceived to be not the business of others. French people are friendly, humorous, and often cynical; they want to be liked and they want to impress. They attach importance to appearance and good taste. They judge others on the basis of personality (Harris et al., 2004).

Germany

Germany has a population of more than 82 million. Most Germans are Roman Catholics. They are known for being hard working, reserved, disciplined and cold in behavior. They are meticulous, methodical, precise (linear thinking), well organized, and efficient. They have one of the highest standards of living in the world and can afford buying luxuries. They are very punctual and formal, and use an official form of address when addressing others in public. They are title conscious. They maintain large distance between themselves. They are restrained in their body movements and follow rules of polite behavior. For example, talking to someone with your hands in your pockets, or sitting with the bottom of the shoes facing another person is unacceptable (Harris et al., 2004).

Italy

Italy has a population of about 60 million. The major ethnic groups are Italians, with small groups of Germans, French, Slovenes, Albanians and Greeks. They are primarily Roman Catholic. They are family and relationships oriented. Having a big family and network of friends is most important. Italians are more being-oriented rather than doing-oriented. Individuals are valued by not what they do for living but how they do and who they are. Although they like to be individualistic they do depend on each other. Although initially they are formal in relationships, they are warm, and like to hug, embrace, and kiss each other. The rules of social hierarchy must be followed; status and titles are important. Image is the key element in all areas of life, including dress and behavior. Good appearance is of great importance. Italians compete in appearance and lifestyle. Italian culture is high-context culture; language is elaborate and musical. People talk a lot and engage in heated discussions. Italians are emotional, expressive, and affectionate. They discuss secrets in public. They have a very well developed system of non-verbal gestures. They are very creative and can find solutions to any problem; they are very good at getting around and beating the system. Since they do not like to take risks, they have to follow thousands of laws and regulations. Italians are fatalistic and believe in destiny. They always do several things simultaneously. In the more industrial North, they are more punctual; in the South they are more flexible about time, relaxed about the appointments and schedules (Harris et al., 2004).

Poland

Poland, the biggest country in Central Europe, has a population of about 40 million. The majority are Roman Catholics. Polish people are very religious. They are proud of their history and cultural heritage and being the home country of their beloved Pope John Paul II. Polish people enjoy freedom of speech, press, and assembly. They are tolerant of different cultures and religions. Poland has survived many wars and communism. They mistrust authority. Polish people have a strong sense of survival and justice. They desire peace and security. They follow the accepted rules of behavior; social etiquette is important to them. They are individualistic. Everyone has his or her own opinion. They like to debate, fight for good causes and individual rights. They are hospitable and open, especially towards foreigners. In the past, Poland experienced a large migration to the United States and currently to EU countries.

Russia

Russia has about 145 million people. In the past, Russian individualism, personal gains and self-interest were traditionally discouraged. People had to sacrifice and subjugate to the state that had a control over their life. Young Russians were taught discipline and subordination. Russians suffered from a sense of inferiority. The society was very hierarchical. They were passive and believed in the governing class. They needed authority to establish order. They distrusted outsiders and anyone outside the circle, particularly foreigners. In business, Russians were noted for patience and stalling; they did not accept compromise. They constantly sought concessions and used connections and influences, and exchanged favors.

Currently, after the collapse of the Soviet Union, the Russian people are trying to rebuild rich Russian tradition and culture. Although the Russian economy is booming, it is also experiencing chaos, which is generating a fear of the unexpected among those who are at the bottom of a social class. After heavy casualties during the wars, Russian people avoid risk and danger, and search for stability, certainty, and order (Jandt, 1998). Russian values reflect more feminine than masculine values; people attach importance to friends, family life, social relations, and cultural life rather than money. Love, ethics, morality, and feelings are taught as being important values in life. Although in public people are reserved and use formal ways of address, privately they are expressive and emotional. They dislike the Western attitude toward materialism, time, and pace of life. The younger generations strive to be more educated and cosmopolitan. Russians are very hospitable people.

In general, Russian values reflect both Asian and European values. Russian people attach great importance to social harmony and relationships with others. They worship the past and present more than the future. They are pessimistic due to experiencing hardship for long decades. They believe people are bad or a mixture of good and evil. They believe they cannot control the environment (Jandt, 1998). At the same time, they seek the Western values of personal rights, individualism, and freedom. Today Russians have become more individualistic, risk-taking, and masculine. They seek identity, want to be unique, and enjoy all the pleasures of the Western world.

Spain

Spain has more than 40 million people. The major religious group is Roman Catholic, and minority is Muslim. The Spanish enjoy their life; they focus on life quality; they work to live rather than live to work. They are proud of their own heritage, and enjoy companionship, music, and good food. People do not follow the rules of the clock; they have time for families and friends. Gender roles are differentiated, and children are pampered. Spanish people are very friendly, hospitable, and warm; it is easy to establish relationships with them. They are also emotional, affectionate and lively – often chaotic in discussions (Harris et al., 2004).

United Kingdom

The United Kingdom has more than 60 million people. The major ethnic groups are English, Welsh and Scottish. They are traditional, conventional, reserved, and distant; they avoid direct conflicts and do not complain. They tend to downplay situations that may cause conflict. Respect and deference is shown to superiors and appropriate distance is used in communication and social interactions. Family names and titles are used. Manners and good etiquette are followed on all occasions (Harris et al., 2004).

15.5 INDIA

India has a population of 1 billion. Hinduism is the major religion that dominates the culture and all personal and business relationships. India has a huge variety of languages, customs and cultural beliefs. There are 15 official languages, including English, with more than 1400 dialects. Family and friends are of great importance. People are expected to sense others' needs and help to meet these needs. India is a hierarchical society; people respect those of higher social positions and use titles to address others. The rules of social etiquette are followed. People do not ask personal questions and do not display affection in public. Hindu people are mostly vegetarian; they do not eat beef and do not drink alcohol. Drinking alcohol is considered degrading. People eat with their hands. The left hand is considered unclean; the right hand is used for eating. The American style of backslapping is not acceptable. Women should not be touched in public. Hindu people like to bargain for goods and services (Harris et al., 2004).

15.6 LATIN AMERICA

Common Latin American values

Latin America has a population of nearly 400 million. Major cultural groups are represented by Native Indians (Mayan, Incas, Aztecs), Europeans (mostly Spanish), Africans, and Asians, especially Polynesians and Japanese. Many countries in Latin America differ widely in terms of their socio-economic status, education, history, governance, and the behavior and values of the people. The major cultural similarities among the Latin American countries are the influence of the Catholic Church, the value of the family, and the differentiation between male and female roles (Harris et al., 2004).

Mexico

Mexico is one-fourth the size of the United States and has a population of more than 103 million. Major ethnic groups are of indigenous, Mestizo and European descent. About 90% of the Mexican people are Roman Catholic. Mexicans are warm and hospitable. Their culture is people-oriented, and less task-oriented. Mexicans value strong family and strong social relationships. They like to socialize and take time for conversation. Although they are relaxed and leisure-oriented, many are hard working. They are proud of their own heritage and culture. They believe individual achievements are not as important as a person's soul or spirit. Although they value equality and democracy, they are also status-, age-, and gender-conscious. They are concerned with protocol; they address others by using official titles, such as *senor* or *don*, as a sign of respect. They are traditional and have high moral values. They believe money is not the only determinant of social status; honesty and decency are more important. They respect the past and enjoy the present. They believe nature has been created by God, and only God can influence or change it. The future is determined by God's will (Harris et al., 2004).

Mexican culture is a high-context culture; messages are sent through non-verbal language, such as hand movements, and emotional expressions. People like closeness; they stand close to each other and often touch each other. Mexicans have a polychronic attitude toward time; they do many things simultaneously. They are relaxed about time; they do not allow time schedules to interfere with their friends and families. Although they believe it is important to be on time for meetings, they also agree that one should always expect to wait. They avoid risk and believe in a written document (Harris et al., 2004).

Brazil

Brazil has a population of about 176 million. About 55% of the people are white descendants of the Portuguese, German, Italian, Spanish and Polish; 40% are mixed; and 6% black. More than 50% of the population is young – under 20 years of age. People are warm, hospitable, emotional, affective, sensitive, generous, and receptive to foreigners. Brazilians are not prejudiced against any skin color or nationality. For them social relationships are more important than individual achievements. Extended family, usually male-dominated, is the single most important social institution. They believe in social hierarchy and appropriate forms of greetings. They are concerned about their appearance. They treat business relationships as personal relationships. They think time is flexible. They like to talk about their families. They avoid controversial subjects. They are not always direct. Their communication style is expressive and focused on details. They are high-contact communicators; they use a lot of non-verbal communication, such as eye contact. They like to interrupt in discussions. They do not follow formal rules and procedures; those who do are perceived as unimaginative and lacking intelligence. They are often late; time is not important to them. Their speaking distance is close (Harris et al., 2004).

15.7 MIDDLE EAST

Common Arab values

The most important values of Arab people are dignity, honor, and reputation. Losing face or being ashamed is avoided. Arabs are loyal to family, courteous, and good communicators. They put people and country needs first. They seek close personal relationships. They emphasize the importance of good listening skills. It is customary for men to kiss each other on both cheeks. Islamic teachings forbid eating pork, drinking alcohol, gambling, and prostitution. Men are allowed to marry more than one woman, whereas a woman may marry only one man. The Koran teaches to be modest in appearance; people have to cover arms and shoulders. The feminist movement is quickly emerging within the Arab cultures, alongside Islamic fundamentalism (Harris et al., 2004).

Saudi Arabia

Saudi Arabia is the heartland of Islamic culture. Approximately 90% of the Saudi people are Arabs; the rest are Afro-Asian. The Kingdom's population is 24 million. Islam permeates Saudi life. The royal family controls the top government positions and the nations' wealth. Arab society places great emphasis on honor, and shame that must be avoided. Shame means a loss of power and influence. Families depend upon each other. Arabs are concerned about their families, clan, tribe, and country.

They seek connections and networking. Arab women are not part of the socialization process and networking. Bargaining is a norm. Arabs dislike imposing Western time frames and work schedules. Communication with Arabs is complex; Arab language is high-context and uses lots of non-verbal cues such as gestures, facial expressions, eye browsing, eye contact, standing close, etc. ''Yes'' may mean ''no'' or ''maybe''. Swearing is unacceptable. It is unacceptable to engage in conversation about religion, politics, and Israel. Drinking alcohol is prohibited. Pointing fingers at someone or showing the soles of the feet when seated are considered rude (Harris et al., 2004).

United Arab Emirates

The UAE is a Middle Eastern federation of seven states situated in the southeast of the Arabian Peninsula in Southwest Asia on the Persian Gulf. The UAE, rich in oil and natural gas, has become highly prosperous after gaining foreign direct investment funding in the 1970s. UAE has the most diverse populations in the Middle East; 19% of the population is represented by Emirati, 23% by other Arabs and Iranians, 50% by South Asians and 8% by expatriates (includes Westerners and East Asians). Islam dominates all aspects of life. According to official ministry documents, 76% of the total population is Muslim, 10% is Hindu, 9% is Christian, and 5% is Buddhist. The official language is Arabic. The society is divided into two social categories: the nationals and the foreign immigrants. Citizens are subdivided into classes; the ruling sheikhly families hold the political power and wealth.

The UAE has the highest gender imbalance among any nation in the world; there are more than twice the number of males than females. Although officially men and women have equal rights and opportunities, patriarchy is still visible in social life. Women do not play a significant role in political and religious life; men receive employment preferences. Arranged marriages are the preferred patterns however this tradition is changing.

The largest city Dubai is the one of the 'hottest' tourist destinations of the present and future. It is the only emirate of the UAE with both a Hindu Temple and a Sikh Gurdwara. Christian churches are also present in the country. Emiratis are tolerant toward other religions.

Emiratis are known for their hospitality; they feel honored when receiving guests and socializing with friends and relatives. Guests are welcomed with coffee and fresh dates and incense is passed around.

Muslims greet each other with ''Assalamo Alaikum,'' which means ''May peace be upon you and may God's blessings be with you''. This greeting makes Muslims aware that they have to spread love and peace wherever they go. If someone calling himself a Muslim and a follower of the Holy Prophet does not promote peace and love in his actions and does not follow this teaching, he cannot be a true follower of the Holy Prophet (http://www.cyborlink.com/besite/uae.htm). Muslims pray five times a day, asking God for his love.

Visitors are expected to abide by local standards of modest dress code however do not adopt native clothing. Most of the body must remain covered. Shoes are removed before entering a mosque or any other building. Alcohol and pork are not consumed. When greeting, men touch nose-to-nose while shaking hands, and women kiss each other on each cheek. First names are not used. Respect and courtesy are shown to elders. Gender segregation is evident; men are entertained in large living rooms, while women entertain friends in the home. The left hand is considered unclean and reserved for hygiene. People do not point at another person, do not cross legs when sitting, and do not show the bottom of the shoe or foot. The ''thumbs up'' gesture is considered offensive. Gifts are appreciated and open in private. It is impolite to refuse a gift. Gifts should not include alcohol, perfume containing alcohol, pork, personal items, knives, and images of nude women. The subject of women and Israel are avoided in conversations. Communication is slow with periods of silence. ''Yes'' usually means ''possibly''. Meetings are commonly interrupted. Those who ask most questions are likely to be the least important. Decisions are made by silent observers (http://www.cyborlink.com/besite/uae.htm).

15.8 NORTH AMERICA

Canada

Canada has a population of about 32 million. It is a bilingual and multicultural society. It consists of two dominant cultural groups: the English Canadian and French Canadian. The English Canadian culture dominates in most of the provinces where the official language is English, whereas the French Canadian culture dominates in Quebec, where the official language is French. There are strong minority ethnic groups of German, Scandinavian, Asian, Dutch, Ukrainian, Polish, and Italian in Canada. Other ethnic groups are represented by those of British Isles and French origin, other Europeans, Amerindian, Asians, Africans, Arabs and those with mixed background. Canada has also a large percentage of the refugees from India and Pakistan. The biggest influx of refugees is from Hong Kong.

Canadians are proud of their country; they do not like to be compared to the other ''Americans''. Canadians are friendly and more reserved than US Americans. They respect authority and formalities, do not support individualism, and prefer cooperation over competition. They are patriotic, law-abiding, and proud of their heritage. They like peace and order. They are bound by time schedules and deadlines, and they appreciate promptness. They welcome foreign businesses and immigrants. The family is the center of society. They tend to confront conflict.

English Canadians tend to focus on theoretical issues. They are more cooperative and less concerned with protocol and ceremony, whereas French Canadians are more focused on practical issues, more individualistic and competitive. They focus on relationship building, and observe formalities and rules of social etiquette. English Canadians are low-context communicators; they send message by the words spoken and they are less concerned with protocol. French Canadians are high-context communicators; they use non-verbal means in addition to spoken words to communicate (Harris et al., 2004).

The United States

The United States is the fourth largest nation in the world, with a population of nearly 300 million. More than 70% of all the populations is represented by White ethnic groups, followed by African-Americans, Hispanics, Asians, Alaskan natives, Hawaiians and other Pacific Islanders. The United States is a multicultural society; it contains many ethnic groups whose cultures mixed together and melted into the culture of the United States. Two words – ''salad bowl'' and ''mosaic'' – are used to describe the nation in which different cultures combine together to form a diverse country.

The country is experiencing latinization. Its character and communication are affected by the influx of those from Latin America. Although English is the official language, Spanish is emerging as a second language, especially in the Southwest, California, Florida, and Puerto Rico. The country consists of two societies: white people and people of color. There are huge regional differences in lifestyles and attitudes. For example, the eastern part of the United States is more established, conservative, organized and deteriorating; the western part of the nation is more casual, innovative and flexible. Table 15.6 presents the major values of people in the United States, as identified in the literature.

Table 15.6 Major Values and Orientations of the US Population

Value/characteristics	Description
Active	Motivated to stay active and do something; busy, live fast, use resources
Believe in equality	Believe in equal opportunity for everyone, regardless of gender, class, race
Believe in success	Believe in achievement and goals attainment; successfully dominate the natural environment and space
Competitive, aggressive	Competition is healthy, driven by success, want to be the best
Democratic	Believe everyone is equal and has the same rights to freedom of expression, success, and material well-being
Efficient	Want good planning, organization, search for easier, better and more efficient ways of doing things

Table 15.6 (*Continued*)

Value/characteristics	Description
Egalitarian	Believe all people are equal
Explicit	Direct, straightforward, open, specific
Fighters	Fight for freedom and causes, such as protecting endangered species and the environments
Freedom loving	Fight for democracy, resent control or interference
Friendly	Friendships are social, commitments are short, friends are shared, relationships are loose
Future oriented	Future is bigger and brighter
Generous	Like to share, altruistic, generous in their charity and community services, involved in foreign aid and refugee assistance programs
Goal oriented	Believe can achieve anything
Highly organized and believe in institutions	Like organized and secure society
Humanitarian	Pay attention to social welfare, charity and voluntary work
Ignorant	Not interested in the outside world
Individualistic	Control own destiny, do own things; everyone is responsible for own actions; everyone is unique; the interests of the individual are important
Informal	Reject traditional idea of social class, differences and privileges, spontaneous
Materialistic	Consumption oriented, desire comfort, judge others by their material possessions; believe in material world rather than spiritual
Non-contact	Avoid embracing in public, maintain certain physical and psychological distance with others
Optimistic, believe in progress	Want change, improvement, "the new"; explore possibilities, focus on the future which is "bigger and brighter," everything is possible
Rational	Search for reasons, science makes everything possible to accomplish
Self-promoting	Motivated to show own success and achievements
Self-reliant	Believe they can control own destiny, do own thing
Short-term view	Want quick results now

Table 15.6 (Continued)

Value/characteristics	Description
Task, goal and achievement oriented	One can accomplish anything; fulfillment comes from personal achievement; world and nature can be controlled; future can be planned and controlled
Value time	Time conscious, time is limited, time is commodity, lineal, precise
Verbal	Use language and verbal cues to express intentions and meanings
Work and doing oriented	Motivated by work and ''doing'' things, work is a means for recognition, money and power; activities and performance determine self-identity; have strong work ethic
Value education	Value education as a means of self-development
Youth oriented	Fitness and wellness-oriented, health cautious, want to feel and look young

SUMMARY

Although there are similarities within the cultural groups, cultural value patterns and behavior in Africa, Asia, Australia, Europe, India, Latin and North America (Canada and the United States), and the Middle East differ among these groups.

DISCUSSION POINTS AND QUESTIONS

1. Are there any similarities in cultural value patterns among Asia, Australia, Canada, Europe, and the United States?
2. Compare similarities and differences in the ways different cultural groups, societies and cultures meet human needs and concerns.
3. Is globalization leading to greater similarities between cultural groups?
4. Should tourism managers and marketers be aware of cultural similarities and differences for their various markets? Explain how understanding the cultural specificities of one market will lead to marketing adjustments in the context of a hotel's services.

CASE STUDY 15.1 Managing in Asia: Cross-cultural Dimensions

There are common themes that determine economic success in Asia. Business people in Japan, Korea, China, Hong Kong, and Taiwan draw their inspiration in the formulation and execution of business strategies from several ancient works. Themes that underlie Asia's success are listed in detail below.

1. *The Art of War* by Sun Tzu's identifies six components to success in military warfare: (1) the moral cause; (2) leadership; (3) temporal conditions, including the four seasons, the changes in weather, wind and tidal conditions; (4) the terrain; (5) organization and discipline; and (6) use of espionage.
2. *The Book of Five Rings* by Miyamoto Musahi's identifies several paths to success: (1) to grasp relationships between matters and view situations from multiple perspectives; (2) to seek knowledge and information; (3) to be patient; (4) to train and discipline oneself; (5) to disguise one's emotions and true intentions; (6) to possess flexibility; (7) to use diversion as an attack strategy; (8) to divide and conquer; and (9) to assess the terrain.
3. *The Three Kingdoms* by Lo Kuan-chung describes intrigues, strategies, ploys and alliances used by the leaders to gain control over China after the collapse of the Han dynasty (206 BC–AD 220).
4. *The Thirty-Six Stratagems* describes the principles of military strategies and their applicability in business and interpersonal relationships.

Major principles guiding the East Asian approach to business:

1. Engage in "mind games"; develop hidden messages to counteract the perceived message sent by the other party.
2. Use diplomatic means (negotiations, discussions, intermediaries) to resolve a confrontation.
3. Use non-diplomatic means (open warfare, litigation) to resolve confrontation.
4. Wage war against a well-established opponent.
5. Transform an adversary's strength into weakness.
6. Transform one's own weaknesses into strengths.
7. Follow the rule "relax while the enemy exhausts himself".
8. Believe that misfortune and fortunes can be reversed; all events occur in cyclical patterns, as opposed to the discrete phases as perceived by the West.
9. Engage in deception to gain a strategic advantage (e.g. create illusion, pretend to be greater than your really are, pretend to have more than you really have). In East Asia, deception has a neutral meaning; it is believed one should engage in it if it brings a greater good. This is in contrast to the Western belief that deception is immoral and wrong.
10. Play the fool: "Pretend to be a pig in order to eat the tiger," "play dumb while remaining smart," and "inflict injury on yourself to win the enemy's trust" and make the other party become complacent and let his/her guard down.
11. Understand contradictions so perceived weakness can become strength, and vice versa.
12. Compromise and use moderation. Allow an opponent for a small gain to obtain a greater prize. Gift-giving, lavish entertainment and bribes facilitate desired outcome.

13. Strive for total victory.
14. Do not be complacent or careless during good times.
15. Think about the long-term implications of your action.
16. Take advantage of misfortunes of a competitor.
17. Make the best of what you have for the moment.
18. Run away when faced with defeat. Escape is better than the death. With escape there is always change to regain your strength or position (China). If there is no escape, death is preferred (Japan).
19. Be flexible and adapt to changing conditions and fortunes (e.g. strategies can change as the circumstances change.
20. Gather intelligence and information about competitors (spying, business espionage, spreading erroneous information to mislead the opponent are acceptable practices).
21. Learn about the key players and partners to discover their true intentions.
22. Understand the relationships among matters/situations so they can be put to good use. The use of spiral and non-linear logic is common in East Asia.
23. Be patient: focus on long-term implications of actions, develop and nurture human relationships, wait for the right time.
24. Avoid emotions because they can distort logical thinking. However, provoke strong emotions among competitors to bring their downfall. Use women and sensual entertainment to achieve desired outcome in business transactions.

Source: Tung, R. (2002). Managing in Asia: Cross-Cultural dimension. In M. Warner & P. Joynt (Eds.), *Managing across cultures: Issues and perspectives* (pp. 137–142). London: Thomson Learning.

WEBSITE LINKS

1. Cultural profiles throughout the world; developed to assist Canadians in understanding immigrants http://www.cp-pc.ca/english.
2. Cultural Profiles. ''They are in-depth national cultural portals, created in partnership with national governments around the world. They showcase national culture, encourage and facilitate international dialog and exchange in the arts, heritage, media, libraries, archives and tourism sectors, and help to promote international cultural tourism.'' http://www.culturalprofiles.net/.

The last part will explain the importance of being multiculturally competent in a contemporary global world.

Multicultural Competence

This part explains the importance of being multiculturally competent in a contemporary global world.

Multicultural competence in a global world

16

The aim of this chapter is to answer the question of what it means to be multiculturally competent and what skills are needed to become multiculturally competent.

OBJECTIVES

After completing this chapter the reader should be able to:
- Understand the concept of multicultural competence and its domains
- Understand factors influencing multicultural competence
- Identify the skills needed for becoming multiculturally competent
- Become aware of multiculturalism assessment techniques
- Understand the opportunities and challenges multicultural competence provides in a contemporary world

INTRODUCTION

The questions that are explored in this chapter are: What is multicultural competence? What are the domains of multicultural competence? What are the major characteristics and elements of each domain? What are the stages the individual has to go through to become multiculturally competent? What are the instruments that can be used to assess multicultural competencies? The cultural skills needed for being multiculturally competent are identified. A self-assessment tool for measuring multicultural competence is presented. The importance of multicultural competence is explained.

16.1 THE CONCEPT OF MULTICULTURAL COMPETENCE

The term *multicultural competence* is now widely used in the field of marketing, communication, management, and international business. However, it is still not widely understood; nor do scholars agree upon a common definition. The concept of multicultural competence is often referred to as *multicultural competency*. There are also several other labels used in addition to multicultural competency: *cross-cultural competence (y)*, *intercultural competence (y)*, *cross-cultural/intercultural/cultural effectiveness*, and *cross-cultural/intercultural/cultural communication competence (y)*. The reference to *communication competence (y)* is inappropriate because it refers to communication competence (y) only. Multicultural competence is more than communication competence.

What most scholars do agree upon is that multicultural competence refers to the ability of the individual to behave appropriately and effectively in interactions between individuals from different cultures, or the development of competence in another culture and proficiency in its language, both of which enable the individual to provide the opportunity for powerful reflections into one's own native worldview and those of others. Numerous factors must be present in order for an individual to become multiculturally competent and be able to interact effectively in a multicultural environment.

16.2 DOMAINS OF MULTICULTURAL COMPETENCE

Figure 16.1 presents a preliminary conceptual model of multicultural competence. According to Figure 16.1, multicultural competence consists of four domains: cognitive, affective, behavioral, and environmental. These domains allow individuals to

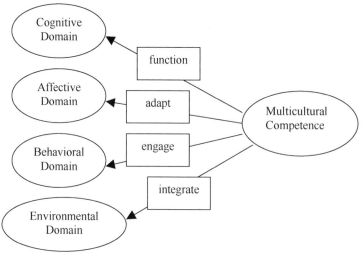

Figure 16.1

A Conceptual Model of Multicultural Competence

effectively function, adapt, engage, and integrate into another culture. The cognitive domain refers to knowledge and explains how individuals acquire and categorize cultural knowledge. The individual who has knowledge of a new culture and its people is able to function in this culture. The affective domain refers to emotions, feelings, and attitudes attained through knowledge. The individual who develops positive feelings and attitudes towards a new culture is able to adapt to a new culture. The behavioral domain refers to the abilities and skills related to specific cultural behavior. The individual who has specific abilities and skills is able to effectively engage in a new culture. The environmental domain refers to relationships between individuals and the environment. The individual who knows the cultural orientation of a new environment is able to fully integrate into this environment.

16.2.1 Cognitive domain

The cognitive domain refers to the acquisition of cultural knowledge and consists of (1) knowledge, (2) awareness, (3) language, and (4) learning (see Figure 16.2). Those who have cultural knowledge of a specific culture can function in that culture because they have the enhanced ability to minimize misunderstandings with others from another culture. Knowledge can be general or specific. Culture-general knowledge includes the knowledge of the concept of culture, its components, purpose, various domains, and value systems, how values are learned, frameworks for understanding and

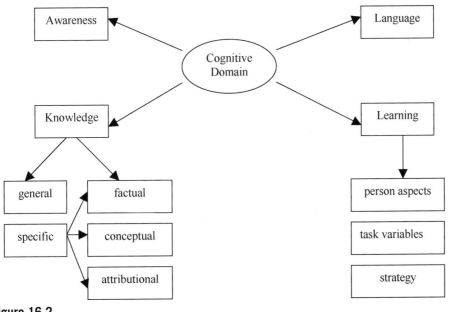

Figure 16.2

The Cognitive Domain of Multicultural Competence

comparing different cultures, the influence of cultural differences on human behavior, culture shock and conflict, perceptions and stereotyping. Culture-general knowledge also includes knowledge of the economic, political, legal, social, financial, and technological environment in which individuals operate (Johnson et al., 2006). Culture-general knowledge prepares individuals for learning how to learn, provides a broader experience, and makes it easier to learn about culture-specific knowledge. Culture-general knowledge is a foundation for the acquisition of culture-specific knowledge (Nonaka & Takeuchi, 1995).

Culture-specific knowledge refers to knowledge about another culture: its geography, economy, legal system, history, religion, values, norms, customs, traditions, cultural practices, ''what to do and what not to do,'' and the language of the culture. Culture-specific knowledge can be (1) factual (knowledge of the facts of a country's history, geography, political system, economic system, institutions, and social structure); (2) conceptual (understanding the value system of a specific cultural group and its influence on people's behavior); and (3) attributional (a heightened awareness of appropriate behavior, knowledge of how to correctly attribute the behavior of individuals in the target culture) (Byram, 1997).

Awareness (of self and others) is the key factor on which effective and appropriate multicultural interactions depend. Those who are aware of their own culture and its values, traditions, and norms can become aware of and understand the culture and values of others. Awareness develops through exploration, experimentation and experiences. Awareness leads to deeper knowledge, skills, attitudes, and emotions. Awareness is very important to multicultural competence because it makes the individual aware of selfhood, and of his or her relation to others. Gaining knowledge is the most important task of education.

Culture-specific knowledge also includes knowledge of one's own language and language of others. Language is a road map to perception, interpretation, thinking, and expressions. Those who speak their native language well can learn languages easily and communicate with and understand people of other cultures.

The cognitive domain also includes learning. Learning refers to the process of acquisition of knowledge, or meta-cognitive knowledge. Learning involves obtaining knowledge about (1) person aspects, (2) task variables, and (3) strategy. The personal aspects (intra- and inter-individual, universal) deal with how people learn about other people and how they view themselves and others. Learning about the personal aspects is extremely important for social interactions. The task variables deal with how the person who is learning about the culture deals with the nature of information being acquired and the complexity of this task. The strategy deals with how people use the acquired knowledge and what they do with it (Earley & Ang, 2003).

16.2.2 Affective domain

Cultural knowledge, awareness, and learning are necessary but not sufficient for performing effectively in a multicultural setting. Individuals who want to be multiculturally competent must also be motivated to use the knowledge available. The affective domain refers to feelings and emotions; it is also called the emotional or feeling domain, or attitude domain. It allows the individual to adapt to a new culture. The affective domain consists of (1) motivations to use the acquired knowledge, (2) sensitivity to cultural differences, (3) attitudes toward a new culture and those from different cultural backgrounds, and (4) personal characteristics that help a person use the acquired cultural knowledge (see Figure 16.3). In terms of motivation, the individual may be competent in a multicultural environment not because s/he has cultural knowledge but because s/he is motivated to acquire new cultural knowledge, and learn about new ways of life and people. The individual must also be sensitive to cultural differences and understand that one's own culture is not the only culture, not the most prestigious culture; there are other cultures that must be understood and accepted. Having positive attitudes toward those who are culturally different, and showing interest in and respect for their traditions, history and ways of doing things, are part of the affective domain. There are also personality traits or attributes, in addition to internal values, norms, and beliefs of one's home culture, that are needed for effective multicultural competence. The examples of these personality traits are having respect of others; being tolerant of cultural differences; having courage to interact with others; being able to accept risk and ambiguity in dealing with culturally different people; being able to manage conflict, handle emotions (emotional intelligence), and adapt to and accept others (cultural

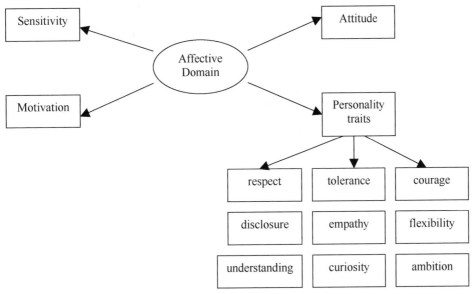

Figure 16.3

An Affective Domain of Multicultural Competence

intelligence); and being empathetic, flexible, understanding, curious, ambitious, patient, persistent, passionate about other cultures, willing to suspend judgments, able to self disclose and open to others and establish interpersonal relationships (social intelligence). There may be dozens of other desirable attributes a multiculturally competent person should possess, yet it is still not known which attributes are most essential. It is assumed that the combination of a wide range of these attributes is necessary if one is to be able to adapt to a multicultural environment.

16.2.3 Behavioral domain

The behavioral domain frequently refers to skills and abilities needed in order to use cultural knowledge (see Figure 16.4). This domain allows the individual to engage in a new cultural environment. In the literature there is considerable overlap between skills, abilities (sets of specific skills) and aptitudes (individual capacities to acquire additional abilities in a specific skill-set); it is not always necessary to distinguish clearly among them. The skills part of the behavioral domain include communication skills (language and non-verbal), social skills (relationship, interpersonal), comparative skills (being able to compare values of different cultures), task-completion skills, or affective skills (human warmth skills). Abilities include the ability to adjust to a new cultural, social or political environment, understand others, establish relationships, see and understand the world from others' perspectives, deal with stress, manage anxiety,

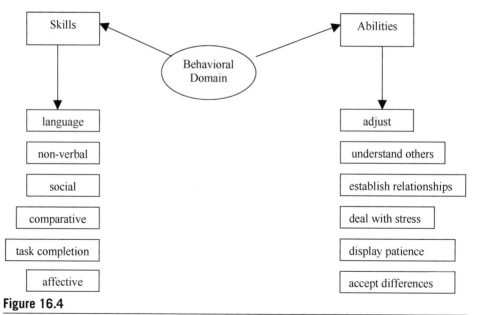

Figure 16.4

A Behavioral Domain of Multicultural Competence

reduce risk, display patience, deal with misunderstanding, solve problems, avoid problems, resolve conflicts, work cooperatively with others, and accept different ways of doing things. Again, there may be dozens of other abilities necessary to effectively deal within a multicultural environment. Although it is still not known which abilities are more essential for being multiculturally competent, it is probably a combination of a wide range of abilities that allow the individual to effectively engage in a multicultural environment.

16.2.4 Environmental/interactional domain

Multicultural competence is not only about having cultural knowledge, positive attitudes and feelings about other cultures, and specific skills and abilities. The multiculturally competent individual must also be able to integrate into a multicultural environment. Environmental domain is an interactional domain that allows people to integrate into a new cultural environment. This domain consists of (1) social interactions, (2) relationships with nature, and (3) orientation toward time (see Figure 16.5). Social interactions explain how people interact with each other: whether they focus on equality or accept social hierarchy (PD); whether they conform to a group or focus on self-interest (IDV); whether they avoid risk and strangers or accept newcomers and new experiences (UAI); whether they focus on being competitive and aggressive or emphasize the quality of life (MAS); or whether they see men's nature as good or bad. Relationships with nature explain how people interact with nature: whether they worship and live in harmony with it, or whether they control or subjugate of it. The orientation toward time explains how people perceive and interact with time: whether they view time as flexible or as a usable resource and commodity; what attitudes they have toward working hours, schedules and appointments; and what importance they attach to time schedule versus human relationships.

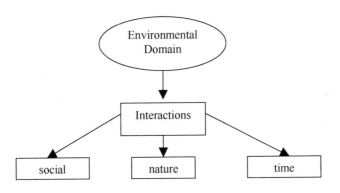

Figure 16.5

An Environmental Domain of Multicultural Competence

16.3 OTHER FACTORS INFLUENCING MULTICULTURAL COMPETENCE

Cultural factors are not the only causes of success or failure in gaining multicultural competency. There are also moderating variables, such as age, gender, context (work, social), or political and economic factors that determine the ability of an individual to effectively deal in a multicultural environment. Members of different socio-economic and cultural systems have different understandings of what constitutes competence, and use different definitions and have different interpretations of the multiculturalism concept. Cultural distance between the tourist and host culture also plays an important role in the ability of the individual to function, adapt, engage in and successfully integrate into another culture. As the cultural distance increases, the difficulties people face when encountering others from different cultures increase and the ability to adapt to a new culture decreases. Issues such as stereotyping and ethnocentrism (imposing one's own values on someone else, belief that one's own values are the most important) block the individual abilities to become multiculturally competent. In addition, the extent to which an individual can be trained to acquire required knowledge and skills is important for achieving multicultural competence.

16.4 MULTICULTURAL COMPETENCE AS A PROCESS

Contacts with people from other cultures and speaking other languages provide excellent opportunities for fostering multicultural competence development. Multicultural competence development is an on-going process; once the process begins, it can last for a lifetime. An individual is always in the process of becoming aware, learning, acquiring knowledge, and developing some feelings and attitudes; s/he is never completely multiculturally competent. New challenges always occur despite the fact that the individual may constantly develop and expand his or her own competencies.

Becoming multiculturally competent depends on the stages the individual has to go through and the degree to which s/he adapts to a second culture. The individual may (1) reject the target culture, (2) learn to operate in a native-like fashion (accepted by the host society), (3) adjust to two (or more cultures) and become bilingual–bicultural or multilingual–multicultural (adjusted and accepted), (4) adjust to a foreign culture and lose original identity (forced or voluntarily assimilation), and (5) question his or her identity as a member of any group (state of anomie, loosening clear ties to either culture) (Fantini, 2000).

16.5 MULTICULTURAL COMPETENCE DEVELOPMENT LEVELS

There are four developmental levels of multicultural competence:

Level 1 *Educational traveler*: participates in short-term exchange programs, 4–6 weeks

Level 2 *Sojourner*: is exposed to a foreign culture for a longer period of time, e.g. semester abroad programs, international internships of long duration, 4–8 months

Level 3 *Professional*: staff who work in intercultural or multicultural context, e.g. multinational companies directors

Level 4 *Intercultural/multicultural specialist*: individuals involved in training, educating, consulting, advising international students, overseas directors, and cross-cultural trainers (Fantini, 2000).

16.6 MULTICULTURALISM ASSESSMENT TECHNIQUES

Various instruments may be used to assess multicultural competencies such as Cross-Cultural Adaptability Inventory (CCAI) (Kelley & Meyers, 1992), American Council on the Teaching of Foreign Languages (ACTFL), Language Proficiency Scale (LPS) (Liskin-Gasparro, 1982), Your Objectives, Guidelines and Assessment (YOGA) (Fantini, 1995, 1999, 2006). The quantitative instruments include the Inter-cultural Development Inventory, the Cultural Intelligence Scale, and the Multicultural Personality Questionnaire (Abbe et al., 2007). Qualitative assessment instruments such as scenario-based assessments are also useful tools to gain insight into multicultural competence. Table 16.1 presents the example of self-evaluation for assessing one's own

Table 16.1 A Self-Evaluation Form for Assessing Multicultural Competence

	Educational traveler	Sojourner	Professional	Intercultural/ multicultural specialists
Culture-general knowledge				
Culture-specific knowledge				
Cultural awareness				
Foreign language proficiency				
Culture learning				
Motivation to learn about new culture				
Sensitivity to cultural differences				
Attitude to new culture				
Personality traits				
Skills				
Abilities				
Social interactions				
Orientation to nature				
Orientation to time				

Note: Rating from 0 (no competence) to 5 (very high competence).

multicultural competence at various stages of its development. Respondents can be asked to rate themselves in each of the areas from 0 (no competence) to 5 (very high competence).

16.7 AN EDUCATIONAL CHALLENGE

Multicultural competence presents a challenge for educators and learners. It offers the chance of gaining a broader view of our world, seeing the world through the eyes of others, understanding the limitations of one's own perspective, experiencing other culture(s) and communicating through another language. It provides opportunities for individuals to experience a different view point and an appreciation for both differences and similarities among human beings, and understanding that one's own perspective is not the only perspective; there are many other views of our world. Multicultural competence allows one to understand others on their own terms, which, in turn, depends upon an appreciation of one's own culture and heritage. The development of multicultural competence and foreign languages is the core of global education and competence as well as mindedness, which allows for affective understanding of the totality of humanity rather than nationalism of particular countries or regions of the world.

SUMMARY

The concept of multicultural competence refers to the ability of the individual to effectively function, adapt, engage and integrate in another culture. Multicultural competence consists of four domains: cognitive, affective, behavioral and environmental. The cognitive domain consists of knowledge, awareness, language and learning. The affective domain consists of motivation, sensitivity, attitude and personality traits. The behavioral domain consists of skills and abilities. The environmental domain consists of social interactions, as well as interactions with nature and time. There are various other factors, except for culture, that influence multicultural competence. Multicultural competence is a process that depends upon the stages and degree to which an individual adapts to a second culture. The development of multicultural competence and foreign languages is the core of global competence and education.

DISCUSSION POINTS AND QUESTIONS

1. What is multicultural competence?
2. What factors influence multicultural competence?
3. Why is multicultural competence an important element of today's education?

> **CASE STUDY 16.1 One Practical Solution to Overcoming the Language Barrier**
>
> Japan is among the top three international inbound visitor markets to Vietnam. Japanese visitors love to listen to Vietnamese traditional music, buy traditional crafts, and enjoy the specialties of well-known Vietnamese chefs. Although Japanese tourists are keen to experience the Vietnamese culture, the language represents a cultural barrier to this market. When in Vietnam, Japanese tourists prefer to communicate in their mother tongue and demand Japanese language-speaking tour guides. However, in Vietnam there is a shortage of qualified tour guides who speak Japanese. There are only two professional guides serving Japanese tours in Hochiminh city (ITPC, 2005). One of the reasons is the lack of education and training of Vietnamese tour guides. The school programs do not respond to the needs of the Vietnamese tourism industry. Students are lacking practical knowledge of industry operations and do not learn languages of their international visitors. Dealing with the demanding Japanese tourist market is more difficult than dealing with other international tourist markets. The ability to communicate in tourists' native languages is a pre-requisite for working in the tourism industry. Tour operators should provide their employees with foreign language courses, language scholarships, and internship opportunities. To become qualified tour guides, industry employees should learn about tourist cultural behavior and language.

WEBSITE LINKS

1. Excellence in diversity awareness and education: http://www.dtui.com
2. Diversity in practice: Becoming culturally competent: http://www.centre4activeliving.ca/publications/wellspring/2006/oct/oct06.pdf
3. National Center for Cultural Competence at Georgetown University: http://gucchd.georgetown.edu/nccc/
4. Gestures: Their origin and meanings: http://bernd.wechner.info/Hitchhiking/Thumb/
5. French language: gestures: http://french.about.com/library/weekly/aa051801b.htm
6. The Game of Tarof: An extensive look into the custom from an Iranian's perspective: http://en.wikipedia.org/wiki/Intercultural_competence

Conclusion

This book suggests that significant cultural differences in behavior and decision-making exist among the international tourist markets. Considering that the international tourist industry is expected to continue to grow and aim at diverse cultural groups of tourists, industry professionals must increasingly meet the needs and expectations of those cultural groups. As the industry grows, opportunities for misinterpretation and misunderstanding of tourists' needs may be enhanced. In order to avoid cultural tensions and frustration and successfully deal with international tourists, industry practitioners must recognize and understand the importance of cultural differences in meeting international tourists' needs.

National culture is an excellent tool for explaining differences in tourist behavior, better than nationality. Today, tourists have multiple nationalities and their culture of origin may be totally different from their nationality or country of birth or residence. In many countries there are different groups of people who wish to maintain their cultural heritage. Thus, national culture is a better variable than nationality or country of birth or residence in distinguishing among tourist behavior.

Tourism marketers and managers need to learn and understand how national cultures affect tourist behavior. National culture has an impact of many aspects of tourist behavior, from needs recognition to service perceptions and repeat visitation. Understanding national cultures of international tourists can assist in making better marketing and management decisions and serving tourist more effectively and efficiently. Ignoring culture's influence and cultural sensitivity and awareness may result in tourist dissatisfaction and the loss of business and declining profitability.

This book calls for fully embracing national cultures of future travelers in order to make them feel comfortable. If the tourism products or services do not adequately satisfy tourists' cultural needs and fail to address the cultural values of the tourist society, marketers and managers must revise and/or adjust their product offerings. It is not suggested here that the total tourism product should be adjusted to match the tourists' cultural standards. Many international tourists travel overseas to experience foreign countries and learn about their cultural uniqueness. Rather it is suggested that marketers and managers need to address each international tourist market from a cultural point of view prior to marketing to it.

Also, national culture should be always used with other variables, such as age, gender, marital status, or socio-economic status, to properly understand tourist behavior. However, although these variables may affect tourist behavior, national culture is a very important, if not the most important, variable responsible for differences in tourist behavior.

Understanding cultural make-up of the future travelers and adjusting business strategies to their psyche will be the pathway to future success. More investigation in the area of cultural differences among various nationalities in the tourism context is needed.

REFERENCES AND FURTHER READING

Aaker, J., & Maheswaran, D. (1997). The effect of cultural orientation on persuasion. *Journal of Consumer Research, 24,* 315-328.

Abbe, A., Gulick, L., & Herman, J. (2007). *Cross-cultural competence in army leaders: A conceptual and empirical foundation,* U.S. Army Research Institute, Washington, DC.

Abdullah, A. (1993). *Understanding the Asian workforce. The Malaysian experience.* Paper presented at the 20th Annual Conference of the Asian Regional Training and Development Organization. Jakarta, Indonesia, November.

Abe, H., & Wiseman, R. (1983). A cross-cultural confirmation of the dimensions of intercultural effectiveness. *International Journal of Intercultural Relations, 7,* 53-67.

Adler, P. (1975). The transition experience: An alternative view of culture shock. *Journal of Humanistic Psychology, 15*(4), 13-23.

Adler, N. (1993). Gender differences in job economy: The consequences of occupational segregation and authority position. *Sociological Quarterly, 34,* 449-465.

Ahmed, Z., & Krohn, F. (1992). Understanding the unique consumer behavior of Japanese tourists. *Journal of Travel and Tourism Marketing, 1*(3), 73-86.

Ajzen, I., & Fishbein, M. (1977). Attitude-behavior relations: A theoretical analysis and review of empirical research. *Psychological Bulletin, 84,* 888-918.

Akpinar, S. (2003). Globalisation and tourism. *Journal of Travel and Tourism Research, 1*(1/2), 22-39.

Alderfer, C. (1972). *Existence, relatedness and growth,* Free Press, New York.

Allport, G. (1954). *The nature of prejudice,* Doubleday Anchor/Addison-Wesley Publishers, New York/Reading, MA.

Allport, G., Vernon, P., & Lindzey, G. (1951/1960). *A study of values: A scale for measuring the dominant interest in personality,* Houghton Mifflin Co, Boston.

Allport, I. (1979). *The nature of prejudice,* Addison-Wesley, Reading, MA.

Anant, S. (1971). Ethnic stereotypes of educated North Indians. *Journal of Social Psychology, 85,* 137-138.

Andersen, P., Lustig, M., & Andersen, J. (1990). Changes in latitude, changes in attitude. The relationships between climate and interpersonal communication predispositions. *Communication Quarterly, 38,* 291-311.

Argyle, M. (1967). *The psychology of interpersonal behavior,* Penguin Books Ltd, Harmondsworth.

Argyle, M. (1972). Nonverbal communication in human social interaction. *Nonverbal communication,* Hinde, R. (Ed.)., Royal Society and Cambridge University Press, London.

Argyle, M. (1978). *The psychology of interpersonal behaviour,* (3rd ed.). Penguin Books, New York.

Argyle, M. (1981). Intercultural communication. *Social skills and work,* Argyle, M. (Ed.)., MethuenBennett, London, pp. 1977.

Argyle, M. (1986). Rules for social relationships in four cultures. *Australian Journal of Psychology, 38*(3), 309-318.

Argyle, M., & Cook, M. (1976). *Gaze and mutual gaze,* Cambridge University Press, Cambridge.

Argyle, M., & Henderson, M. (1984). The rules of friendship. *Journal of Personal and Social Relationships, 1,* 211-237.

Argyle, M., & Henderson, M. (1985a). *The anatomy of relationships: and the rules and skills needed to manage them successfully,* Heinemann, London.

Argyle, M., & Henderson, M. (1985b). The rules of relationships. *Understanding personal relationships,* Duck, S., & Perlman, D. (Eds.)., Sage, London and Beverly Hills, CA, pp. 63-84.

Argyle, M., Shimoda, K., & Little, B. (1978). Variance due to persons and situations in England and Japan. *British Journal of Social and Clinical Psychology, 17,* 335-337.

Argyle, M., Graham, J., & White, P. (1979). The rules of different situation. *New Zealand Psychologist, 8,* 13-22.

Argyle, M., Furnham, A., & Graham, J. (1981). *Social situations,* Cambridge University Press, Cambridge.

Argyle, M., Henderson, M., & Furnham, A. (1985). The rules of social relationships. *British Journal of Social Psychology, 24,* 125-139.

Argyle, M., Henderson, M., Bond, M. H., Iizuka, Y., & Contarello, A. (1986). Cross-cultural variations in relationship rules. *International Journal of Psychology, 21,* 287-315.

Armstrong, R., Mok, C., Go, F., & Chan, A. (1997). The importance of cross-cultural expectations in the measurement of service quality perceptions in the hotel industry. *International Journal of Hospitality Management, 16*(2), 181-190.

Asante, M. (1989). *Handbook of international and intercultural communication,* Sage, Newbury Park, CA.

Asante, M., & Gudykunst, W., (Eds.). (1989). *Handbook of international and intercultural communication,* Sage, Newbury, CA.

Augustyn, M., & Ho, S. (1998). Service quality and tourism. *Journal of Travel Research, 37*(1), 71-75.

Bagozzi, R. (1992). The self-regulation of attitudes, intentions, and behavior. *Social Psychology Quarterly, 55*(2), 178-204.

Baier, K. (1969). What is value? An analysis of the concept, *Values and the future. The impact of technological change on American values,* Baier, K., & Rescher, N. (Eds.)., The Free Press, New York.

Bailey, J. (1991). *Managing organizational behavior,* (2nd ed.). John Wiley and Sons, Brisbane.

Bakhtin, M. (1981). *The dialogic imagination: Four essays by M.M. Bakhtin.* Michael E. Holquist (Ed.). Caryl Emerson & Michael Holquist (trans.). Austin: University of Texas Press.

Ballah, R., Madesn, R., Sullivan, W., Swindler, A., & Tripton, S. (1985). *Habits of the heart: Individualism and commitment in American life,* University of California Press, Berkeley.

Bandura, A. (1997). *Self-efficacy: The exercise of control,* W.H. Freeman, New York.

Barker, M., Page, S., & Meyer, D. (2003). Urban visitors' perceptions of safety during a special event. *Journal of Travel Research, 41*(4), 355-361.

Barnlund, D. (1989). *Communicative styles of Japanese and Americans: Images and realities,* Wadsworth, Belmont, CA.

Barnlund, D., & Araki, S. (1985). Intercultural encounters: The management of compliments by Japanese and Americans. *Journal of Cross-Cultural Psychology, 16,* 9-26.

Barnlund, D., & Yoshioka, M. (1990). Apologies: Japanese and American styles. *International Journal of Intercultural Relations, 14*(2), 193-206.

Barthes, R. (1972). *Mythologies,* Jonathan Cape, London.

Barton, A. (1969). Measuring the values of individuals. *Dynamic social psychology,* Dean, D.G. (Ed.)., Random House, New York.

Bauer, T., Jago, L., & Wise, B. (1993). The changing demand for hotel facilities in the Asia Pacific region. *International Journal of Hospitality Management, 12*(4), 313-322.

Beard, J., & Ragheb, M. (1983). Measuring leisure motivation. *Journal of Leisure Research, 15*(3), 219-228.

Beatty, S., Kahle, L., & Homer, P. (1991). Personal values and gift-giving behaviors: A study across cultures. *Journal of Business Research, 22*(2), 149-157.

Becker, C., & Murmann, S. (1999). The effect of cultural orientation on the service timing preferences of customers in casual dining operations: An exploratory study. *Journal of Hospitality Management, 18,* 59-65.

Becker, H., & Fritzsche, D. (1987). A comparison of the ethical behavior of French and German managers. *Columbia Journal of World Business, 22*(4), 87-95.

Befu, H. (1971). *Japan: An anthropological introduction,* Harper and Row, New York.

Belk, R. (1988). The Third World consumer culture. *Research in Marketing*, (Suppl. 4), 103-127.

Bellah, R. (1970). *Beyond belief: Essays on religion in a post-traditional world*, Harper and Row, New York.

Benedict, R. (1946). *The chrysanthemum and the sword*, Houghton Mifflin, Boston.

Benedict, R. (1967). *The chrysanthemum and the sword*, Houghton Mifflin, Boston, MA.

Bennett, J. (1977). Transition shock: Putting culture shock in perspective. *International and Intercultural Communication Annual*, Jain, N., (Ed.)., Vol. 4, pp. 45-52.

Berger, C. (1979). Beyond initial interactions. *Language and social psychology*, Giles, H., & R.Clair, R. (Eds.)., Basil Blackwell, Oxford.

Berger, C., & Calabrese, R. (1975). Some exploration in initial interaction and beyond: Toward a developmental theory of interpersonal communication. *Human Communication Research*, *1,* 99-112.

Berger, P., & Luckman, T. (1966). *The social constriction of reality*, Penguin, Harmondsworth.

Berger, J., & Smith, P. (1971). *Ways of seeing*, Penguin, New York.

Berger, J., & Zelditch, M., (Eds.). (1985). *Status, rewards and influence,* Jossey-Bass, San Francisco.

Berkowitz, L., & Friedman, P. (1967). Some social class differences in helping behavior. *Journal of Personality and Social Psychology*, *5,* 217-225.

Berno, T. (1999). When a guest is a guest: Cook Islanders view tourism. *Annals of Tourism Research*, *26*(3), 656-675.

Berry, J. (1980). Social and cultural change. *Handbook of cross-cultural psychology: Social psychology*, Trandis, H., & Brislin, R., (Eds.)., Allyn and Bacon, Boston, *Vol. 5*, pp. 211-279.

Berry, J. (2003). Conceptual approaches to acculturation. *Acculturation: Advances in theory, measurement, and applied research*, Chun, K., Organista, B., & Marin, G. (Eds.)., American Psychological Association, Washington, DC, pp. 17-37.

Berry, J., & Sam, D. (1997). Acculturation and adaptation. *Handbook of cross-cultural psychology: Social behaviour and application*, Berry, J., Segall, M., & Kagicibaci, C., (Eds.)., Allyn and Bacon, Boston, *Vol. 31*, pp. 291-326.

Biddlecomb, C. (1981). Pacific tourism: Contrasts in values and expectations. *Pacific Conference* Churches. Suva, Fiji: Lota Pasifica Productions.

Blackwell, R. (1979). *Consumer behavior*, College of Administrative Science. Ohio State University.

Blauner, R. (1972). *Racial oppression in America*, Harper Collins, New York.

Bochner, S. (1982). *Cultures in contact: Studies in cross-cultural interaction*, Pergamon Press, Oxford, New York.

Boissevain, J. (1979). The impact of tourism on a dependent Island: Gozo, Malta. *Annals of Tourism Research*, *6*(1), 76-90.

Boissevain, J., & Inglott, P. (1979). Tourism in Malta. *Tourism: Passport to development?* DeKadt, E. (Ed.)., Oxford University Press, Oxford.

Bond, M. and Chinese Culture Connection (1987). Chinese values and the search for culture-free dimensions of culture. *Journal of Cross-Cultural Psychology*, *18*(2), 143-352.

Boorstin, D. (1961). *The image: A guide to pseudo-events in America*, Harper and Row, New York.

Boyacigiller, N. (1990). The role of expatriates in the management of interdependence, complexity, and risk in multinational corporations. *Journal of International Business Studies*, *21*(3), 357-383.

Braithwaite, V., & Law, H. (1985). Structure of human values: Testing the adequacy of the Rokeach Value Survey. *Journal of Personality and Social Psychology*, *49,* 250-263.

Brewer, J. D. (1984). Tourism and ethnic stereotypes: Variation in a Mexican town. *Annals of Tourism Research*, *11*(3), 487-501.

Brislin, R. (1993). *Understanding culture's influence on behavior*, Harcourt Brace Jovanovich, Orlando.

Brislin, R., & Pedersen, P. (1976). *Cross-cultural orientation programs*, Wiley/Halsted, New York.

Brislin, R., Lonner, W., & Thorndike, R. (1973). *Cross-cultural research methods*, John Wiley and Sons, New York.

Brislin, W. (1983). Cross-cultural research in psychology. *Annual Review of Psychology, 34,* 363–400.

Bryden, J. (1973). *Tourism and development: A case study of the commonwealth Caribbean,* Cambridge University Press, New York.

Bulatao, J. (1962). Philippine values: The Manileno's Mainsprings. *Philippine Sociological Review,* January-April, 7–26.

Buller, P., Kohls, J., & Anderson, K. (1991). The challenge of global ethics. *Journal of Business Ethics, 10*(10), 767–775.

Burnham, M., Hough, R., Karno, M., Escobar, J., & Telles, C. (1987). Acculturation and lifetime prevalence of psychiatric disorders among Mexican Americans in Los Angeles. *Journal of Health and Social Behavior, 28,* 89–102.

Burns, P. (2003). Brief encounters: Culture, tourism and the local-global nexus. *Tourism in the age of globalization,* Wahab, S., & Cooper, C. (Eds.)., Routledge, London.

Business Korea,. (1991). The way of Korean travelling. Koreans are so strange? *Business Korea, 9*(2), 29.

Butler, R. (1980). The concept of a tourism area cycle of evolution. Implications for management of resources. *Canadian Geographer, 24,* 5–12.

Butterfield, M., & Jordan, F. (1989). Communication adaptation among racially homogeneous and heterogeneous groups. *Southern Communication Journal, 54,* 265.

Byram, M. (1997). *Teaching and assessing intercultural communicative competence,* Multilingual Matters, Clevedon, UK.

Byrnes, F. (1966). Role shock: An occupational hazard of American technical assistants abroad. *Annals of the American Academy of Political and Social Science, 368*(1), 95–108.

Cai, D., & Rodriguez, J. (1997). Adjusting to cultural differences: The intercultural adaptation model. *Intercultural Communication Studies, 6,* 31–42.

Callan, R. J. (1990). Hotel award schemes as a measurement of service quality – an assessment by travel industry journalists as surrogate consumers. *International Journal of Hospitality Management, 9*(1), 45–58.

Chan, W. (1963). *The way of Lao Tse,* Bobbs-Merrill, New York.

Chen, G., & Xiao, X. (1993). *The impact of harmony on Chinese negotiations.* Paper presented at the Annual Convention of the Speech Communication Association, Miami Beach, Florida, November.

Chen, J. S. (2000a). Cross-cultural differences in travel information acquisition among tourists from three Pacific-Rim countries. *Journal of Hospitality and Tourism Research, 24,* 239.

Chen, J. (2000b). A case study of Korean outbound travelers' destination images by using correspondence analysis. *Tourism Management, 22*(4), 345–350.

Chinese Culture Connection. (1987). Chinese values and the search for culture-free dimensions of culture. *Cross-Cultural Psychology, 18,* (2), 143–164.

Cho, S. (1991). The ugly Koreans are coming? *Business Korea, 9*(2), 25–31.

Choi, T., & Chu, R. (2000). Levels of satisfaction among Asian and Western travellers. *International Journal of Quality and Reliability Management, 17*(2), 116–131.

Chua, E., & Gudykunst, W. (1987). Conflict resolution style in low- and high-context cultures. *Communication Research Reports, 4,* 32–37.

Churchill, L. (1982). The teaching of ethics and moral values in teaching: Some contemporary confusions. *Journal of Higher Education, 53*(3), 296–306.

Clark, T., & Pugh, D. (2001). Foreign country priorities in the internationalization process: A measure and an exploratory test on British firms. *International Business Review, 10*(3), 285–303.

Cohen, E. (1971). Arab boys and tourist girls in a mixed Jewish-Arab community. *International Journal of Comparative Sociology, 12*(4), 217–233.

Cohen, E. (1972). Towards sociology of international tourism. *Social Research, 39*(1), 164–182.

Cohen, E. (1974). Who is a tourist? A conceptual clarification. *Sociological Review, 22*(4), 527–555.

Cohen, E. (1979). A phenomenology of tourist experiences. *Sociology, 13,* 170-201.

Cohen, E. (1979). A phenomenology of tourist experiences. *Sociology, 12,* 179-202.

Cohen, E. (1982). Marginal paradises: Bungalow tourism on the Islands of Southern Thailand. *Annals of Tourism Research, 9*(2), 189-228.

Cohen, E. (1988). Authenticity and commoditization in tourism. *Annals of Tourism Research, 15,* 371-386.

Cohen, E. (1993). The heterogenization of a tourist art. *Annals of Tourism Research, 20,* 138-163.

Cohen, E. (1995). Contemporary tourism: Trends and challenges. Sustainable authenticity or contrived post-modernity? *Change in tourism: People, places, processes,* Butler, R., & Pearce, D. (Eds.)., Routledge, London, pp. 12-29.

Cohen, E., & Cooper, R. L. (1986). Language and tourism. *Annals of Tourism Research, 13*(4), 533-563.

Collier, M. (1988). A comparison of conversations among and between domestic culture groups: How intra- and intercultural competencies vary. *Communication Quarterly, 36,* 122-144.

Collier, M., & Thomas, M. (1988). Cultural identity: An interpretative perspective. *Theories in intercultural communication,* Kim, Y., & Gudykunst, W. (Eds.)., Sage, Newbury Park, CA, pp. 99-122.

Condon, J. (1985). *Good neighbors: Communicating with the Mexicans,* Intercultural Press, Yarmouth, ME.

Condon, J., & Yousef, F. (1975). *An introduction to intercultural communication,* Bobbs-Merrill, Indiana-polis, IN.

Cook, S. (1962). The systematic analysis of socially significant events: A strategy for social research. *Journal of Social Issue, 18*(2), 66-84.

Cook, S., & Sellitz, C. (1955). Some factors which influence the attitudinal outcomes of personal contact. *International Sociological Bulletin, 7,* 51-58.

Coulmas, F. (1981). Poison to your soul: Thanks and apologies contrastively viewed. *Conversational routine,* Coulmas, F. (Ed.)., Mouton, The Hague.

Cox, T., & Blake, S. (1991). Managing cultural diversity: Implications for organizational competitiveness. *Academy of Management Executive, 5*(3), 45-56.

Craig, J. (1979). *Culture shock! What not to do in Malaysia and Singapore, how and why not to do it,* Times Books International, Singapore.

Crompton, J. (1979). Motivations for pleasure vacation. *Annals of Tourism Research, 6,* 408-424.

Cronen, V., & Shuter, R. (1983). Initial interactions and the formation of intercultural bonds. *Intercultural communication theory,* Gudykunst, W. (Ed.)., Sage, Beverly Hills, CA.

Crotts, J. (2000). Consumer decision making and prepurchase information search. *Consumer behavior in travel and tourism,* Pizam, A., & Mansfeld, Y. (Eds.)., Haworth Press, Binghamton, NY (p. 157).

Crotts, J. (2004). The effect of cultural distance on overseas travel behavior. *Journal of Travel Research, 43,* 83-88.

Crotts, J., & Erdmann, R. (2000). Does national culture influence consumers' evaluation of travel services? A test of Hofstede's model of cross-cultural differences. *Managing Service Quality, 10*(6), 410-422.

Crotts, J., & McKercher, B. (2006). The adaptation to cultural distance and its influence on visitor satisfaction: The case of first-time visitors to Hong Kong. *Tourism Analysis, 10,* 385-391.

Crotts, J., & Pizam, A. (2003). The effect of national culture on consumers' evaluation of travel services. *Journal of Tourism, Culture and Communication, 4*(1), 17-28.

Culler, J. (1981). Semiotics of tourism. *American Journal of Semiotics, 1,* 127-140.

Cushner, K., & Brislin, W. (1995). *Intercultural interactions: A practical guide,* (2nd ed.). Sage, New York.

Czinkota, A., & Ronkainen, I. (1993). *International marketing,* (3rd ed.). The Dryden Press, Orlando.

Damen, L. (1987). *Culture learning: The fifth dimension in the language classroom,* Second Language Professional Library, Addison-Wesley, Reading, MA.

Dann, G. (1981). Tourist motivation an appraisal. *Annals of Tourism Research, 8*(2), 187-219.

Darby, M., & Karni, E. (1973). Free competition and the optimal amount of fraud. *Journal of Law and Economics, 16,* 67–86.

Davis, H. (1970). Dimensions of marital roles in consumer decision-making. *Journal of Marketing Research, 7,* 168–177.

Debono, S., Jones, S., & van der Heijden, B. (2008). *Managing cultural diversity*, Meyer Sport, Meyer.

DeFranco, A., Wortman, J., Lam, T., & Countryman, C. (2005). A cross-cultural comparison of customer complaint behavior in restaurants in hotels. *Asia Pacific Journal of Tourism Research, 10*(2), 173–190.

DeKadt, E. (1979). *Tourism: Passport to development? Perspectives on the social and cultural effects in developing countries*, Oxford University Press, London.

Delors, J. (1993). *Questions concerning European security*, International Institute for Strategic Studies, Brussels.

DeMente, B. (1991a). *Japanese etiquette and ethics in business*, NTC Business Books, Chicago.

DeMente, B. (1991b). *Chinese etiquette and ethics in business*, NTC Business Books, Chicago.

De Mente, B. (1991c). *Korean etiquette and ethics in business*, Etiquette and Ethics Series, NTC Publishing Group, Lincolnwood, NE.

DeMooij, M. (2004). *Consumer behavior and culture: Consequences for global marketing and advertising*, Sage, Thousand Oaks, CA.

DeRivera, J. (1977). *A structural theory of the emotions*. Psychological Issues 10, Monograph 40.

DeSebastian, L. (2005). *Globalisation and cross-cultural challenge*. ESADE, University Ramon Llull, Barcelona, Spain.

Dimanche, F., & Jolly, D. (2006). The evolution of alliances in the airline industry. *The international handbook on the economics of tourism*, Dwyer, L., & Forsythe, P. (Eds.)., E. Elgar, London, pp. 191–208.

Din, A. (1989). Islam and tourism: Patterns, issues, and options. *Annals of Tourism Research, 16*(4), 542–563.

Dirksen, C., & Kroeger, A. (1973). *Cases in marketing*, (4th ed.). Allyn & Bacon, Boston.

Dodd, C. (1987). *Dynamics of intercultural communication*, William C. Brown, Dubuque, IA.

Dodd, C. (1995/1998). *Dynamics of intercultural communication*, McGraw-Hill, Boston, MA.

Doi, L. (1973/1981). *The anatomy of dependence*, Kodansha International Ltd, New York.

Dolnicar, S. (2005). Understanding barriers to leisure travel – tourist fears as marketing basis. *Journal of Vacation Marketing, 11*(3), 197–208.

Donaldson, T. (1989). *The ethics of international business*, University Press, New York, Oxford.

Donthu, N., & Yoo, B. (1998). Cultural influences on service quality expectations. *Journal of Service Research, 1*(2), 178–186.

Downs, R., & Stea, D. (1977). *Maps in minds – reflections on cognitive mapping*, Harper and Row, New York.

Doxey, G. (1976). A causation theory of visitor-resident irritants, methodology, and research inferences. *6th Annual Conference Proceedings of the Travel and Tourism Research Association,* The Impact of Tourism, San Diego, CA, pp. 195–198.

Dresser, N. (1996). *Multicultural manners*, Wiley and Sons, New York.

Dybka, J. (1988). Overseas travel to Canada: New research on the perceptions and preferences of the pleasure travel market. *Journal of Travel Research, 26*(4), 12–15.

Eagles, P. (1992). The travel motivations of Canadian ecotourists. *Journal of Travel Research, 31*(2), 3–7.

Earle, M. (1969). A cross-cultural and cross-language comparison of dogmatism Scores. *Journal of Social Psychology, 79,* 19–24.

Earley, P., & Ang, S. (2003). *Cultural intelligence: Individual interactions across cultures*, Stanford Business Books, Stanford, CA.

Elashmawi, F. (1991). Multicultural management: New skills for global success. *Tokyo Business Today, 59*(2), 54–56.

Ellingsworth, H. (1988). A theory of adaptation in intercultural dyads. *Theories in intercultural communi-cation*, Kim, Y., & Gudykunst, W. (Eds.)., Sage, Newbury Park, CA, pp. 259-279.

Ellis, W., & Ellis, M. (1989). Cultures in transition: What the West can learn from developing countries. *The Futurist, 23*, 22-25.

Encel, S. (1970). *Equality and authority*, Tavistock, London.

Errington, S. (1998). *The death of authentic primitive art and other tales of progress*, University of California Press, Berkeley.

Ettenson, R., & Wagner, J. (1991). Chinese versus US consumer behavior: A cross-cultural comparison of the evaluation of retail stores. *Journal of International Consumer Marketing, 3*(3), 55-71.

Evans-Pritchard, D. (1989). How they see us: Native American images of tourists. *Annals of Tourism Research, 16*(1), 89-105.

Eysenck, H. (1947). *Dimensions of personality*, Routledge & Kegan Paul, London.

Fantini, A. (1995, 1999). *Assessing intercultural competence: A YOGA Form*. Brattleboro, VT: School for International Training, Unpublished.

Fantini, A. (2000).A central concern: Developing intercultural competence. *About our institution*, Fantini, A. (Ed.), SIT Occasional Papers Series. Brattleboro, VT: The School for International Training, pp. 25-42.

Fantini, A. (2006). 87 assessment tools of intercultural competence [Electronic version]. Brattleboro, VT: School for International Training. Retrieved June 20, 2007 from http://www.sit.edu/publications/docs/feil_appendix_f.pdf.

Fayed, H., & Fletcher, J. (2002). Globalization of economic activity: Issues for tourism. *Tourism Economics, 8*(2), 207-230.

Feather, N. (1975). *Values in education and society*, Free Press, New York.

Feather, N. (1976). Value systems of self and Australian expatriates as perceived by indigenous students in Papua New Guinea. *International Journal of Psychology, 11*, 101-110.

Feather, N. (1980a). Value systems and social interaction: A field study in a newly independent nation. *Journal of Applied Social Psychology, 10*(1), 1-19.

Feather, N. (1980b). Similarity of values systems within the same nation: Evidence from Australia and Papua New Guinea. *Australian Journal of Psychology, 32*(1), 17-30.

Feather, N. (1986a). Value systems across cultures: Australia and China. *International Journal of Psychology, 21*, 697-715.

Feather, N. (1986b). Cross-cultural studies with the Rokeach Value Survey: The Flinders Program of research on values. *Australian Journal of Psychology, 38*(3), 269-283.

Feather, N., & Hutton, M. (1973). Value systems of students in Papua New Guinea and Australia. *International Journal of Psychology, 9*(2), 91-104.

Fennett, D. (2006). *Tourism ethics*. Clevedon: Channel View Publications.

Ferro, N. (2004). Cross-country ethical dilemmas in business: A descriptive framework. Social Science Research Network Electronic Paper Collection: http://papers.ssrn.com/abstract_id=501805.

Festinger, L. (1957). *A theory of cognitive dissonance*, Row, Peterson, Evanston, IL.

Festinger, L., & Kelly, H. (1951). *Changing attitudes through social contact*, University of Michigan, Institute for Social Research, Ann Arbor.

Firth, R. (1989). Second introduction: 1988. *A diary in the strict sense of the term*, Malinowski, B. (Ed.)., Stanford University Press, Stanford.

Fiske, D., & Maddi, S. (1961). *Functions of varied experience*, Dorsey, Homewood, IL.

Foa, U., Mitchell, T., & Lekhyananda, D. (1969). Cultural differences in reaction to failure. *International Journal of Psychology, 4*(1), 21-26.

Fodness, D. (1994). Measuring tourist motivation. *Annals of Tourism Research, 21*(3), 555-581.

Forgas, J. (1983). Episode representations in intercultural communication. *Theories in intercultural communication*, Kim, Y., & Gudykunst, W. (Eds.)., Sage, Newbury Park, CA, pp. 186-212.

Forrest, D. (1971). Vietnamese maturation: The lost land of bliss. *Psychiatry, 34,* 111-139.

Foucault, M. (1969). *What is an author? In textual strategies: Perspectives in post-structuralist criticism,* Methuen & Co, New York.

Frager, R. (1970). Conformity and anticonformity in Japan. *Personal and Social Psychology, 15,* 203-210.

Frankowski-Braganza, A. (1983). *Host/guest interaction and its impact on social identity.* Ph.D. Thesis, Department of Anthropology, Indiana University.

Franzoi, S. (1996). *Social psychology,* Brown and Benchmark, Madison.

Fridgen, J. (1991). *Dimensions of tourism,* The Educational Institute of the American Hotel and Motel Association, Orlando.

Friedman, J. (1995). Global system, globalization and the parameters of modernity. *Global modernities,* Featherstone, M. (Ed.), Sage, London.

Fuchs, G., & Reichel, A. (2004). Cultural differences in tourist destination risk perception: An exploratory study. *Tourism - An International Interdisciplinary Journal, 52*(1), 21-37.

Furnham, A., & Bochner, S. (1986). *Culture shock: Psychological reactions to unfamiliar environments,* Methuen, London (p. 56).

Furrer, O., Liu, B., & Sudharshan, D. (2000). The relationship between culture and service quality perceptions: Basis for cross-cultural market segmentation and resource allocation. *Journal of Service Research, 2*(4), 355-371.

Gallois, C., Franklyn-Stokes, A., Giles, H., & Coupland, N. (1988). Communication accommodation theory and intercultural encounters: Intergroup and interpersonal considerations. *Theories in intercultural communication,* Kim, Y., & Gudykunst, W. (Eds.), Sage, Newbury Park, CA, pp. 157-185.

Gallois, C., Franklyn-Stokes, A., Giles, H., & Coupland, N. (2005). Communication accommodation in intercultural encounters. *Theories in Intercultural Communication,* Kim, Y., & Gudykunst, W. (Eds.), Sage, Newbury Park, CA.

Gardiner, G. (1972). Complexity training and prejudice reduction. *Journal of Applied Social Psychology, 2,* 326-342.

Gardiner, H. (1968). Expression of anger among Thais. *Psychologia, 11,* 221-228.

Gavin, M. (1994). China's super spenders. *The China Business Review, 21*(3), 5.

Gee, C., Makens, J., & Choy, D. (1997). *The travel industry,* (3rd Ed.). The Wiley and Sons, New York.

Ger, G. (1992). The positive and negative effects of marketing on socio-economic development: The Turkish Case. *Journal of Consumer Policy, 15*(3), 229-254.

Ger, G., & Belk, R. (1999). Accounting for materialism in few cultures. *Journal of Material Culture, 4*(2), 183-204.

Gioseffi, D., (Ed.). (1963). *On prejudice: A global perspective,* Doubleday, New York.

Gnoth, J. (1997). Tourism motivation and expectation formation. *Annals of Tourism Research, 24*(2), 283-304.

Gochenour, T. (1990). *Considering filipinos,* Intercultural Press, Yarmouth, ME.

Goffman, E. (1963). *Behavior in public places,* Free Press, Glencoe, Ill.

Goffman, E. (1969). *The presentation of self in everyday life,* Allen Lane, Penguin, London.

Gong, W. (2003). Chinese consumer behavior: A cultural framework and implications. *Journal of American Academy of Business, 3*(1/2), 373-384.

Gonzales, A. (1982). Sex roles of the traditional Mexican family. *Journal of Cross-cultural Psychology, 13,* 330-339.

Gordon, L. (1960). *Survey of interpersonal values,* Science Research Associates, Chicago.

Goszczynska, M., Tyszka, T., & Slovic, P. (1991). Risk perception in Poland: A comparison with three other countries. *Journal of Behavioral Decision Making, 4,* 179-193.

Graburn, N. (1976). Introduction. *Ethnic and tourist arts: Cultural expressions of the fourth word,* Graburn, N. (Ed.), University of California Press, Berkeley, pp. 1-32.

Gray, H. (1970). *International travel: International trade health*, Lexington Books, Lexington.

Groetzbach, E. (1988). Erholungsverhalten und Tourismusstile am Beispeil Orientalischer Lander. *Berichter und Materialen Institut fur Tourismus*, Ritter, W., & Milelitz, G. (Eds.)., Freie Universitat, Berlin.

Gronroos, C. (1984). *Strategic management and marketing in the service sector*, Chartwell Brett, London.

Grunewald, R. (2002). Tourism and cultural revival. *Annals of Tourism Research, 29,* 1004-1021.

Gudykunst, W. (1983). Similarities and differences in perceptions of initial intracultural and intercultural encounters. *Southern Speech Communication Journal, 49,* 49-65.

Gudykunst, W. (1985). A model of uncertainty reduction in intercultural encounters. *Journal of Language and Social Psychology, 4,* 79-97.

Gudykunst, W. (1988). Uncertainty and anxiety. *Theories in intercultural communication*, Kim, Y., & Gudykunst, W. (Eds.)., Sage, Newbury Park, CA, pp. 123-156.

Gudykunst, W. (1998). *Bridging differences: Effective intergroup communication*, (3rd Ed.). Sage, Thousand Oaks, CA.

Gudykunst, W. (2005). An anxiety/uncertainity management theory of effective communication. *Theorizing about intercultural communication*, Gudykunst, W. (Ed.)., Sage, Thousand Oaks, CA, pp. 292.

Gudykunst, W., & Kim, Y. (1984). *Communicating with strangers: An approach to intercultural communication*, Addison-Wesley Publishers, Reading, MA; Random House, New York.

Gudykunst, W., & Kim, Y. (1997). *Communicating with strangers: An approach to intercultural communication*, (3rd ed.). McGraw-Hill, Boston, MA: New York, NY.

Gudykunst, W., & Nishida, T. (1983). Social penetration in Japanese and North American friendships. *Communication yearbook*, Bostrom, R., (Ed.)., Sage Publications, Beverly Hills, CA, Vol. 7.

Gudykunst, W., & Nishida, T. (1986). The influence of cultural variability on perceptions of communication behavior associated with relationship terms. *Human Communication Research, 13,* 147-166.

Gudykunst, W., & Ting-Toomey, S. (1988). *Culture and interpersonal communication*, Gudykunst, W.B., Ting-Toomey, S., & Chua, E. (Eds.)., Sage Publications, Newbury Park, CA.

Gudykunst, W., Yoon, Y., & Nishida, T. (1987). The influence of individualism–collectivism on perceptions of communication in ingroup and outgroup relationships. *Communication Monographs, 54,* 295-306.

Gudykunst, W., Ting-Toomey, S., & Chua, E. (1988). *Culture and interpersonal communication*, Sage Publications, Newbury Park, CA.

Gudykunst, W., Ting-Toomey, S., Sudweeks, S., & Steward, P. (1995). *Building bridges: Interpersonal skills for a changing world*, Houghton Mifflin, Boston.

Guirdham, M. (1999). *Communication across cultures,* MacMillan Press, Hundmills, Basingstoke, Hampshire, pp. 211.

Gullahorn, J., & Gullahorn, J. (1963). An extension of the U-curve hypothesis. *Journal of Social Issues, 19*(3), 33-47.

Gundara, J. (2000). *Interculturalism, education and inclusion*. Paul Chapman, London.

Habke, A., & Sept, R. (1993). Distinguishing group and cultural influences in inter-ethnic conflict: A diagnostic model. *Canadian Journal of Communication, 18*(4), 415-436.

Hair, J., & Anderson, R. (1972). Culture, acculturation and consumer behavior: An empirical study. *Conference Proceedings of American Marketing Association*, 423-428.

Hall, D. (1984). Foreign tourism under socialism: The Albanian ''Stalinist'' model. *Annals of Tourism Research, 11*(4), 539-555.

Hall, E. (1955). The anthropology of manners. *Scientific American, 182*(4), 84-88.

Hall, E. (1959/1973). *The silent language*, Doubleday and Fawcett Company, Garden City, New York.

Hall, E. (1960). The silent language in overseas business. *Harvard Business Review*, May 1.

Hall, E. (1966). *The hidden dimension*, Doubleday and Fawcett Company, Garden City, New York.

Hall, E. T. (1983). *The dance of life: The other dimensions of time*, Doubleday, New York.

Hall, M. (2003). Territorial economic integration and globalization. *Tourism in the age of globalization*, Wahab, S., & Cooper, C. (Eds.)., Routledge, London.

Hall, S. (1990). Cultural identity and disapora. *Identity, community, culture, differences*, Rutheford, (Ed.)., Lawrence and Wishart, London, pp. 237-247.

Hall, E., & Hall, M. (1987). *Hidden differences: Doing business with the Japanese*, Anchor Press/Doubleday, Garden City, New York.

Hall, E., & Hall, M. (1990). *Understanding cultural differences*, Intercultural Press, Yarmouth, ME.

Hampden-Turner, C. & Trompenaars, F. (1993). *The seven cultures of capitalism: Value systems for creating wealth in the United States, Japan, Germany, France, Britain, Sweden, and the Netherlands*. Doubleday, New York.

Hampden-Turner, C., & Trompenaars, F. (1996). *Managing across cultures: Issues and perspectives*, Joynt, P. (Eds.)., International Thomson Business Press, North Yorkshire, UK.

Hampden-Turner, C., & Trompenaars, F. (1998). *Riding the waves of culture: Understanding diversity in global business*, McGraw, New York.

Haney, W. (1992). *Communication and interpersonal relations: Text and cases* (6th ed.) Homewood, IL: Irwin. Retrieved from http://www.businesssballs.com/maslow/htm.

Hanquin, Z., & Lam, T. (1999). Analysis of mainland Chinese visitors' motivations to visit Hong Kong. *Tourism Management, 29,* 587-594.

Hare, A., & Peabody, D. (1971). Attitude content and agreement set in autonomy authoritarianism. Items for U. S., African, and Philippine university students. *Journal of Social Psychology, 83,* 23-31.

Harper, R., Wiens, A., & Matarazzo, J. (1978). *Nonverbal communication: The state of the art*, Wiley, New York.

Harre, R. (1974). Some remarks on 'rule' as a scientific concept. *Understanding other persons*, Mitschel, T. (Ed.)., Blackwell, Oxford.

Harris, P., & Moran, R. (1979). *Managing cultural differences*, Gulf Publishing Company, Houston, Texas.

Harris, P., Moran, R., & Moran, S. (2004). *Managing cultural differences: Global leadership strategies for the 21st Century*, (6th ed.). Elsevier-Butterworth-Heinemann, Burlington, MA.

Havel, V. (1994, July 8). The new measures of man. *New York Times*, p. A27.

Hecht, M., Andersen, P., & Ribeau, S. (1989). The cultural dimensions of nonverbal communication. *Handbook of interpersonal and intercultural communication*, Asante, M., & Gudykunst, W. (Eds.)., Sage, Newbury Park, California.

Heidegger, M. (1962). *Being and time*, Harper & Row, New York.

Heider, F. (1958). *Psychology of interpersonal relations*, Wiley, New York.

Henderson, K., Stalnaker, D., & Taylor, G. (1988). The relationships between barriers to recreation and gender - role personality traits for women. *Journal of Leisure Research, 20*(1), 69-80.

Hendry, J. (1987). *Understanding Japanese society*, Croom Helm Ltd, London; New York.

Herbig, P. (1998). *Handbook of cross-cultural marketing*, The Haworth Press, New York.

Herbig, P., & Dunphy, S. (1998). Culture and innovation. *Cross-cultural Management: An International Journal, 5*(4), 13-21.

Herzberg, F., Mausner, B., & Snyderman, B. (1962). *The motivation to work*, (2nd ed.). Wiley, New York.

Hoffman, D., & Low, S. (1981). An application of the profit transformation to tourism survey data. *Journal of Travel Research, 20*(2), 35-38.

Hoffman, W., & Moore, J., (Eds.). (1990). *Business ethics: Readings and cases in corporate morality*, McGraw-Hill, New York.

Hofstede, G. (1980). *Culture's consequences: International differences in work-related values*, Sage Publications, Beverly Hills, CA.

Hofstede, G. (1991/1997). *Cultures and organizations. Software of the mind*, McGraw-Hill International, New York.

Hofstede, G. (2001). *Culture's consequences: Comparing values, behaviours, institutions and organizations across nations*, (2nd ed.). Sage Publications, Thousand Oaks.

Hofstede, G., & Bond, M. (1984). Hofstede's culture dimensions: An independent validation of Rokeach's Value Survey. *Journal of Cross-Cultural Psychology, 15,* 417–433.

Hofstede, G., & Hofstede, G. J. (2005). *Cultures and organizations: Software of the Mind.* Revised and expanded 2nd ed. New York: McGraw-Hill, USA.

Hoivik, T., & Heiberg, T. (1980). Centre-periphery tourism and self-reliance. *International Social Science Journal, 32*(1), 69–98.

Holden, A. (2003). In need of new environment ethics for tourism. *Annals of Tourism Research, 30*(1), 94–108.

Hollnsteiner, M. (1963). Social control and Filipino personality. *Philippine Sociological Review, 11,* 184–188.

Holt, D., & Wigginton, K. (2002). *International management,* Harcourt College Publishers, New York.

Hooker, J. (2003). *Working across cultures,* Stanford University Press, Stanford.

Hoover, R., Green, R., & Saegert, J. (1978). A cross-national study of perceived risk. *Journal of Marketing, 42*(3), 102–108.

Hoyle, R., Pinkley, R., & Insko, C. (1989). Perceptions of social behavior: Evidence of differing expectations for interpersonal and intergroup interaction. *Personality and Social Psychology Bulletin, 15,* 365–376.

Hsieh, T., Shybut, J., & Lotsof, E. (1969). Internal versus external control and ethnic group membership: A cross-cultural comparison. *Journal of Consulting and Clinical Psychology, 33,* 122–124.

Hsu, F. (1953). *Americans and Chinese: Two ways of life,* Akerland-Schuman, New York.

Hsu, F. (1971). Filial piety in Japan and China. *The Journal of Comparative Family Studies, 2,* 67–74.

Hsu, F. (1972). *Americans and Chinese,* Doubleday Natural History Press, New York.

Hsu, F. (1981). *Americans and Chinese: Passage to differences,* (3rd ed.). University Press of Hawaii, Honolulu.

Huang, J., Huang, C., & Wu, S. (1996). National character and response to unsatisfactory hotel service. *International Journal of Hospitality Management, 15*(3), 229–243.

Huddleston, J. (1993). Perspectives, purposes, and brotherhood: A spiritual framework for a global society. *Transition to a global society,* Bushrui, S., Ayman, I., & Laszlo, E. (Eds.)., Oneworld, Oxford, pp. 142–150.

Hui, C., & Triandis, H. (1986). Individualism-collectivism: A study of cross-cultural researcher. *Journal of Cross-Cultural Psychology, 17*(2), 225–248.

Hui, M., & Au, K. (2001). Justice perceptions of complaint handling: A cross-cultural comparison between PRC and Canadian customers. *Journal of Business Research, 52*(2), 161–173.

Huitt, W. (1999a). Conation as an important factor of mind. *Educational psychology interactive.* Valdosta, GA: Valdosta State University. Retrieved September 30, 2005, from http://chiron.valdosta.edu/whuitt/col/regsys/conation.html.

Huitt, W. (1999b). The effective system. *Educational psychology interactive.* Valdosta, GA: Valdosta State University. Retrieved October 3, 2005, from http://chiron.valdosta.edu/whuitt/col/affsys.html.

Huitt, W. (2001). *Motivation to learn: An overview.* Valdosta, GA: Valdosta State University. Retrieved from http://chiron.valdosta//whuitt/col/motivation/motivate.html.

Huitt, W. (2003). A systems model of human behavior. *Educational psychology interactive.* Valdosta, GA: Valdosta State University. Retrieved October 3, 2005, from http://chiron.valdosta.edu/whuitt/materials/sysmdlo.html.

Huntington, S. (1996/2003). *The clash of civilizations and the remaking of world order,* Simon and Schuster, New York.

Huyton, J. (1991). *Cultural differences in HE: The example of Hong Kong students in British educational systems/institutions.* Paper presented at the International Association of Hotel Management Schools Spring 1991 Symposium, East Sussex, Brighton, April 4–5.

Hvenegaard, G. (2002). Using tourist typologies for ecotourism research. *Journal of Ecotourism, 1*(1), 7–18.

Imperia, G., O'Guinn, T., & MacAdams, E. (1985). Family decision-making role perceptions among Mexican-American and Anglo wives: A cross-cultural comparison. *Advances in Consumer Research*, Hirschman, E., & Holbrook, M., (Eds.)., Association for Consumer Research, Provo, UT, *Vol. 12*, pp. 71–74.

Inglehart, R. (1997). *Modernization and postmodernization: Cultural, economic and political change in 43 societies*, Princeton University Press, Princeton.

Institute for Management Excellence. (2001). The nine basic needs. *Online Newsletter*. Retrieved October 3, 2005, from http://www.itstime.com/print/jun97p.htm.

Iso-Ahola, S. (1982). Towards a social psychology of tourism motivation: A rejoinder. *Annals of Tourism Research, 9*, 256–261.

Isomura, T., Fine, S., & Lin, T. (1987). Two Japanese families: A cultural perspective. *Canadian Journal of Psychiatry, 32*(4), 282–286.

Iverson, T. (1997). Japanese visitors to Guam: lessons from experience. *Journal of Travel and Tourism Marketing, 6*(1), 41–54.

Jackson, M. (2001). *Cultural influences on tourist destination choices of 21 Pacific Rim nations*. Paper presented at the CAUTHE national research conference Australia, pp. 166–176.

Jackson, E., & Henderson, K. (1995). Gender-based analysis of leisure constraints. *Leisure Sciences, 17*(1), 31–51.

Jafari, J. (1987). Tourism models: The socio-cultural aspects. *Tourism Management, 8*(2), 151–159.

Jafari, J. (1989). Sociocultural dimensions of tourism: An English language literature review. *Tourism as a factor of change: A sociocultural study*, Bystrzanowski, J. (Ed.)., European Coordination Centre For Research and Documentation in Social Sciences, Vienna.

Jafari, J. (1996). Tourism and culture: An inquiry into paradoxes. *UNESCO/AIEST Proceedings of round table culture, tourism and development: Critical issues for the XXst century*, UNESCO/AIEST, Paris, pp. 31–34.

Jaint, N., & Kussman, E. (1997). Dominant cultural patterns of Hindus in India. *Intercultural communication: Reader*, (8th ed.)., Samovar, L., & Porter, R., (Eds.)., Wadsworth, Belmont, CA.

Jandt, F. (1998). *Intercultural communication: An introduction*, (2nd ed.). Sage Publications, Thousand Oaks, CA.

Jang, S., & Cai, L. (2002). Travel motivations and destination choice: A study of British outbound market. *Journal of Travel and Tourism Marketing, 13*(3), 111–133.

Jansen, D. (2004). Developing the intercultural competence of engineering students: A proposal for the method and contents of a seminar. *World Transactions and Technology Education, 3*(1), 23–28.

Jensen, J. (1970). *Perspectives on oral communication*, Holbrook Press, Boston, MA.

Jocano, F. (1966). Variation in Philippine values: A Western Bisayan case study. *South East Asian Quarterly, 4*, 49–74.

Johannesen, R. (1974). The functions of silence: A plea for communication research. *Western Speech, 38*, 25–35.

Johnson, J., Lenartowicz, T., & Apud, S. (2006). Cross-cultural competence in international business: Toward a definition and a model. *Journal of International Business Studies, 37*, 525–543.

Jones, D., & McCleary, K. (2005). An empirical approach to identifying cross-cultural modifications to international hospitality industry sales training. *Journal of Travel and Tourism Marketing, 18*(4), 65–81.

Joynt, P., & Warner, M. (1996). *Managing across cultures: Issues and perspectives*, International Thomson Business Press, North Yorkshire, UK.

Kachru, Y. (1988). Writers in Hindi and English. *Writing across languages and cultures: Issues in contrastive rhetoric*, Purvis, A. (Ed.)., Sage, Newbury Park, CA.

Kahle, L. (1986). The nine nations of North America and the value basis of geographic segmentation. *Journal of Marketing, 50,* 37–47.

Kahle, L., & Timmer, S. (1983). A theory and a method for studying values. *Social values and social change,* Kahle, L.R. (Ed.)., Praeger, New York.

Kang, M., & Moscardo, G. (2006). Exploring cross-cultural differences in attitudes towards responsible tourist behavior: A comparison of Korean, British and Australian tourists. *Asia Pacific Journal of Tourism Research, 11*(4), 303–320.

Katz, J. (2004). The future of Internet travel-building loyalty and making sites relevant. *The complete 21st century travel and hospitality marketing handbook,* Dickson, B., & Vladimir, A. (Eds.)., Pearson, Englewood Cliffs, pp. 459–468.

Kelley, D., & Meyers, J. (1992). *The cross-cultural adaptability inventory,* Intercultural Press, Yarmouth, ME.

Kenkel, W. (1961). Husband-wide interaction in decision-making and decision choices. *The Journal of Social Psychology, 54,* 255–262.

Kim, Q. Y. (1988). Korea's Confucian heritage and social change. *Journal of Developing Societies, 4*(2), 255–269.

Kim, Y. (1985). Communication and acculturation. *Intercultural communication: A reader,* Samovar, L., & Porter, R. (Eds.)., Wadsworth Publishing, Belmont, pp. 379–387.

Kim, M., & Wilson, S. (1994). A cross-cultural comparison of implicit theories of requesting. *Communication Monographs, 61,* 210–235.

Kim, N., & Chalip, L. (2004). Why travel to the FIFA World Cup? Effects of motives background. *Tourism Management, 25,* 695–707.

Kim, S., & Prideaux, B. (1998). Korean inbound tourism to Australia – a study of supply-side deficiencies. *Journal of Vacation Marketing, 5*(1), 66–81.

Kim, S., & Prideaux, B. (2003). A cross-cultural study of airline passengers. *Annals of Tourism Research, 30*(2), 489–492.

Kim, S., Prideaux, B., & Kim, S. (2002). A cross-cultural study on casino guests as perceived by casino employees. *Tourism Management, 23*(5), 511–520.

Kim, Y., & Gudykunst, W. (1988). *Theories in intercultural communication. International and intercultural communication annual,* Sage Publications, Newbury Park, CA, Vol. 12.

Kincaid, D. (1987). Communication east and west: Points of departure. *Communication theory. Eastern and Western perspectives,* Kincaid, L. (Ed.)., Academic Press, San Diego.

Kleinginna, P., & Kleinginna, A. (1981a). A categorized list of motivation definitions with suggestions for a consensual definition. *Motivation and Emotion, 5,* 263–291.

Kleinginna, P., & Kleinginna, A. (1981b). A categorized list of motivation definitions with suggestions for a consensual definition. *Motivation and Emotion, 5,* 345–379.

Klessig, J. (1992). The effect of values and culture on life support decisions. *Western Journal of Medicine, 157,* 316–322.

Klopf, D. (1991). *Intercultural encounters: The fundamentals of intercultural communication,* (2nd ed.). Morgan, Englewood Cliffs, NJ.

Kluckhohn, C. (1951). Values and value orientations in the theory of action. *Toward a general theory of action,* Parsons, T., & Shils, E.A. (Eds.)., Harvard University Press, Cambridge, pp. 388–433.

Kluckhohn, C. (1956). Toward a comparison of value-emphases in different cultures. *The state of the social sciences,* White, L.D. (Ed.)., University of Chicago Press, Chicago, pp. 116–132.

Kluckhohn, F., & Strodtbeck, F. (1961). *Variations in value orientations,* Harper and Row, New York.

Knowles, T., Diamantis, D., & El-Mourhabi, B. (2001). *The globalisation of tourism and hospitality: Strategic perspective,* Thomson Learning EMEA, Ltd, London.

Knutson, B. J. (1988). Ten laws of customer satisfaction. *Cornell Hotel and Restaurant Administration Quarterly, 29*(3), 14–17.

Kochman, T. (1990). Force fields in black and white communication. *Cultural communication and intercultural contact*, Carbaught, D., & Hilsadle, M. (Eds.)., Lawrence Erlbaum, New Jersey.

Komin, S. (1990). Culture and work-related values in Thai organizations. *International Journal of Psychology*, *25*(5), 685–704.

Kong, M., & Jogaratnam, G. (2007). The influence of culture on perceptions of service employee behavior. *Managing Service Quality*, *17*, 275–297.

Korzenny, F., & Korzenny, B. (2005). *Hispanic marketing: A cultural perspective*, Elsevier, Oxford, UK.

Kottak, C. (2007). *Windows on humanity*, McGraw Hill, New York (pp. 209, 423).

Kozak, M. (2001). Comparative assessment of tourist satisfaction with destinations across two nationalities. *Tourism Management*, *22*(4), 391–401.

Kozak, M. (2002). Comparative assessment of tourist motivations by nationality and destinations. *Tourism Management*, *23*, 221–232.

Kracht, K., & Morsbach, H. (1981). Transcultural understanding and modern. *Fourth Symposium Sponsored by Tokai University*, Ruhr University, Bochum.

Kraft, C. (1978). Interpreting in cultural context. *Journal of the Evangelical Theological Society*, *21*(4), 357–368.

Kroeber, AL., & Kluckhohn, C. (1952). *Culture: A critical review of concepts and definitions* Papers of the Peabody Museum of American Archaeology and Ethnology, Harvard University Press, New York, Random House, 47, 1, p. 223.

Kroeber, L., & Kluckhohn, C. (1967/1985). *Culture: A critical review of concepts and definitions*, Vintage, Random, New York.

Kroger, R., Cheng, K., & Leong, I. (1979). Are the rules of address universal? A test of Chinese usage. *Journal of Cross-Cultural Psychology*, *10*, 395–414.

Laing, J., & Crouch, J. (2005). Extraordinary journeys: An exploratory cross-cultural study of tourists on the frontier. *Journal of Vacation Marketing*, *11*(3), 209–223.

Langlosis, C., & Schlegelmilch, B. (1990). Do corporate codes of ethics depend on national character? Evidence from Europe and the United States. *Journal of International Business Studies*, *21*, 519–539.

Leavitt, H., & Bahrami, H. (1988). *Managerial psychology: Managing behavior in organizations*, The University of Chicago Press, Chicago.

Leavitt, H., Pondy, L., & Boje, D., (Eds.). (1990). *Readings in managerial psychology*, (3rd ed.)., University of Chicago Press, Chicago.

Lebra, T. (1976). *Japanese patterns of behavior*, The University Press of Hawaii, Honolulu.

Lee, C. (2000). A comparative study of Caucasian and Asian visitors to a cultural Expo in an Asian setting. *Tourism Management*, *21*, 169–176.

Lee, S. (2005). An application of a five-stage consumer behavior decision-making model: An exploratory study of Chinese purchasing of imported health food. Master of Business Administration Research Project, Simon Fraser University, Burnaby, BC, Canada.

Lee, W. (1988). *Becoming an American consumer: A cross-cultural study of consumer acculturation among Taiwanese, Taiwanese in the United States and Americans*, Communications. University of Illinois, Urbana-Champaign (p. 116).

Lehtinen, U., & Lehtinen, J. R. (1982). *Service quality: A study of quality dimensions*. Working Paper. Service Management, Institute Helsinki, Finland.

Lessem, R., & Neubauer, F. (1994). *European management systems: Towards unity out of cultural diversity*, McGraw-Hill, London.

Leung, E. (1991). *Cross-cultural impacts in classroom situations from a student perspective*. Paper presented at the International Association of Hotel Management Schools Spring 1991 Symposium, East Sussex, Brighton, April 4–5.

Leung, K., & Bond, M. H. (1984). The impact of cultural collectivism on reward allocation. *Journal of Personality and Social Psychology, 47,* 793-804.

Levi-Strauss, C. (1971). Race and culture. *International Social Science Journal, 23*(4), 608-625.

Li, C. (1998). *China: The consumer revolution,* John Wiley, Singapore.

Liebes, T., & Katz, E. (1990). *The export of meaning: Cross-cultural readings of Dallas,* Oxford University Press, New York.

Lin, I., & Mattila, A. (2006). Understanding restaurant switching behavior from a cultural perspective. *Journal of Hospitality and Tourism Research, 30*(1), 3-15.

Lipset, S. (1963). The value patterns of democracy: A case study in comparative analysis. *American Sociological Review, 28,* 515-531.

Liskin-Gasparro, J. (1982). *ETS oral proficiency testing manual,* Educational Testing Service, Princeton. NJ.

Littlefield, R. (1974). Self-disclosure among some Negro, white, and Mexican-American adolescents. *Journal of Counseling Psychology, 21*(2), 133-136.

Litvin, S., Crotts, J., & Hefner, F. (2004). Cross-cultural tourist behaviour: A replication and extension involving Hofstede's uncertainty avoidance dimension. *International Journal of Tourism Research, 6,* 29-37.

Liu, R., & McClure, P. (2001). Recognizing cross-cultural differences in consumer complaint behavior and intentions: An empirical examination. *The Journal of Consumer Marketing, 18*(1), 54-75.

Liu, B., Sudharshan, D., & Hamer, L. (2000). After-service response in service quality assessment: A real-time updating model approach. *Journal of Services Marketing, 14*(2), 160-177.

Lowe, A., & Corkindale, D. (1998). Differences in cultural values and their effects on responses to marketing stimuli. *European Journal of Marketing, 32*(5), 843-867.

Lowyck, E., Van Langenhove, L., & Bollaert, L. (1992). Typologies of tourist roles. *Choice and demand in tourism,* Johnson, P., & Thomas, B. (Eds)., Mansell, London.

Luk, S., Leon, C., Leong, W., & Li, E. (1993). Value segmentation of tourists' expectations of service quality. *Journal of Travel and Tourism Marketing, 2*(4), 23-38.

Lussier, R. (1990). *Human relations in organizations,* Richard Irvin, Homewood, IL.

Lustig, M., & Koester, J. (1993/1999). *Intercultural competence: Interpersonal communication across cultures,* Harper Collins College Publishers, New York.

Lynch, K. (1960). *The image of the city.* Cambridge, MA: Cambridge.

Lynch, F. (1964). Lowland Philippine values: Social acceptance. *Four readings on Philippine values,* (2nd ed.)., Lynch, F., (Ed.)., Ateneo de Manila University Press, Quezon City.

Lynch, F. (1970). Social acceptance reconsidered. *Four readings on Philippine Values,* (3rd ed.)., Lynch, F., & de Guzman, A., (Eds.)., Ateneo de Manila University Press, Quezon City.

MacCannell, D. (1953). Fundamentals of tourist motivation. *Tourism research and critique and challenges,* Pearce, D., & Butler, R. (Eds.)., Routledge, London, New York.

MacCannell, D. (1973). Staged authenticity: Arrangements of social space in tourist settings. *American Journal of Sociology, 79,* 589-603.

MacCannell, D. (1984). Reconstructed ethnicity: Tourism and cultural identity in Third World communities. *Annals of Tourism Research, 11*(3), 375-391.

MacCannell, D. (1989). *The tourist. A new theory of the leisure class,* Schocken Books, New York.

Madrigal, R., & Kahle, L. (1994). Predicting vacation activity preferences on the basis of value-system segmentation. *Journal of Travel Research, 32*(3), 22-28.

Malinowski, B. (1988). *Eine wissenschaftliche Theorie Der Kultur,* (3rd ed.). Suhrkamp, Frankfurt/Main.

Mallet, V. (1994). Confucius or convenience? Asian leaders say their ideology must be taken seriously by the west, but critics say the philosophy is cynically self serving. *Financial Times,* 26.

Malloy, D., & Fennell, A. (1998). Ecotourism and ethics: Moral development and organizational culture. *Journal of Travel Research, 36*(4), 47-56.

Mann, L. (1986). Contributions to cross-cultural psychology: An introduction. *Australian Journal of Psychology, 38*(3), 195-202.

March, R. (1997). Diversity in Asian outbound travel industries: A comparison between Indonesia, Thailand, Taiwan, South Korea and Japan. *International Journal of Hospitality Management, 16*(2), 231-238.

Markham, W., Bonjean, C., & Corder, J. (1986). Gender, out-of-town travel and occupational advancement. *Sociology and Social Research, 70,* 156-170.

Markus, H., & Kitayama, S. (1991). Culture and the self: Implications for cognition, emotion and motivation. *Psychological Review, 98*(2), 224-253.

Marsella, A., DeVos, G., & Hsu, F. (1985). *Culture and self-Asian and Western perspectives,* Tavistock, New York.

Martin, W. (1987). A new approach to the understanding and teaching of service behavior. *Hospitality Education and Research Journal, 11*(2), 255-262.

Maslow, A. (1954/1970). *Motivation and personality,* Harper, New York.

Maslow, A. (1971). *The further reaches of human nature,* Viking Press, New York.

Maslow, A., & Lowery, R., (Eds.). (1998). *Toward a psychology of being,* (3rd ed.)., Wiley, New York.

Mason, P. (2003). *Tourism impacts, planning and management,* Butterworth–Heinemann, Burlington, MA.

Matsumo, D., & Kudoh, T. (1987). Cultural similarities in the semantic dimensions of body postures. *Journal of Nonverbal Behavior, 11,* 166-179.

Mattila, A. (1999a). An analysis of means-end hierarchy in cross-cultural context: What motivates Asian and Western business travellers to stay at luxury hotels? *Journal of Hospitality and Leisure Marketing, 6*(2), 19-28.

Mattila, A. (1999b). The role of culture in the service evaluation process. *Journal of Service Research, 1*(3), 250-261.

Mattila, A. (1999c). The role of culture and purchase motivation in service encounter evaluations. *Journal of Service Management, 13*(4/5), 376-389.

Matveev, A., & Milter, R. (2004). The value of intercultural competence for performance of multicultural teams. *Team Performance Management, 10*(5/6), 104-111.

Matveev, A., & Nelson, P. (2004). Cross-cultural communication competence and multicultural team performance. *International Journal of Cross-Cultural Management, 4*(2), 253-270.

Mayo, E., & Jarvis, L. (1981). *The psychology of leisure travel: Effective marketing and selling of travel service,* CBI, Boston.

Maznevski, M. (1994). *Synergy and performance in multi-cultural teams.* Unpublished doctoral dissertation, University of Western Ontario.

McCleary, K., Choi, B., & Weaver, P. (1998). A comparison of hotel selection criteria between U.S. and Korean business travelers. *Journal of Hospitality and Tourism Research, 22*(1), 25-38.

McCleary, K., Weaver, P., & Hsu, C. (2006). The relationship between international leisure travellers' origin country and product satisfaction, value, service quality and intentions to return. *Journal of Travel and Tourism Marketing, 21*(2-3), 117-130.

McClelland, D. (1953). *The achievement motive,* Appleton-Century-Crofts, New York.

McClelland, D. (1976). Power is the great motivator. *Harvard Business Review,* 100-111.

McDonald, G., and Zepp, R. (1988). Ethical perceptions of Hong Kong Chinese business managers. *Journal of Business Ethics, 7*(11), 835-845.

McDonald, K. (1995). Focusing on the group: Further issues related to western monogamy. *Politics and the Life Sciences, 14,* 38-46.

McGehee, N., Loker-Murphy, L., & Uysal, M. (1996). The Australian international pleasure travel market: Motivations for a gendered perspective. *The Journal of Tourism Studies, 7,* 45-57.

McKercher, B., & Chow, B. (2001). Cultural distance and participation in cultural tourism. *Pacific Tourism Review, 5,* 23-32.

McKercher, B., & duCross, H. (2003). Testing a cultural tourism typology. *International Journal of Tourism Research*, *51*(1), 45–58.

McLeod, D. (2004). *Tourism, globalization and cultural change: An island community perspective*, Channel View, New York.

Mead, R. (1998). *International management*, (2nd ed.). Blackwell, Oxford.

Meade, R. (1970). Leadership studies of Chinese and Chinese-Americans. *Journal of Cross-Cultural Psychology*, *1*, 325–332.

Meethan, K. (2001). *Tourism in global society: Place, culture, consumption*, Palgrave, New York.

Mehmetoglu, M. (2004). A typology of tourists from a different angle. *International Journal of Hospitality Tourism Administration*, *5*(3), 69–90.

Mehrabian, A. (1971). *Silent messages*, Wadsworth, Belmont, CA.

Melko, M. (1969). *The nature of civilizations*, Porter Sargent, Boston.

Merriam-Webster's collegiate dictionary (11th ed.). (2003). Springfield, MA: Merriam-Webster.

Mihalik, B., Uysal, M., & Pan, M. (1995). A comparison of information sources used by vacationing Germans and Japanese. *Hospitality Research Journal*, *18*(3), 39–46.

Milbraith, L. (1980). *Values, lifestyles and basic beliefs as influences on perceived quality of life*, UNESCO, Paris.

Mill, J. S. (1957). *Autobiography*, Liberal Arts Press, New York.

Miller, A. (1991). Personality types, learning styles and educational goals. *Educational Psychology*, *11*(3–4), 217–238.

Miller, G., & Steinberg, M. (1975). *Between people*. Chicago: Science Research Associates.

Mills, P. (1986). *Managing service industries: Organizational practices in a post-industrial economy*, Ballinger, New York.

Minkov, M. (2007). *What makes us different and similar: A new interpretation of the world values survey and other cross-cultural data*, Klassika I Stil, Sofia, Bulgaria.

Mirels, H., & Garrett, J. (1971). The Protestant ethic as a personality variable. *Journal of Consulting and Clinical Psychology*, *36*, 40–44.

Mischel, W. (1996). From good intentions to willpower. *The psychology of action*, Gollwitzer, P., & Bargh, J. (Eds.)., Guilford, New York, pp. 197–218.

Mishler, A. (1965). Personal contact in international exchanges. *International behavior: A social-psychological analysis*, Kelman, H. (Ed.)., Holt, Rinehart and Winston, New York.

Mishra, A. (1982). Discovering connections. Gumpers, J. (Ed.). *Language and social action. Cambridge Psychology*, 1, 325–332.

Mitchell, V., & Vassos, V. (1997). Perceived risk and risk reduction in holiday purchases: A cross-cultural and gender analysis. *Journal of European Marketing*, *6*(3), 47–80.

Moeran, B. (1968). Individual, group and Seishin: Japan's internal cultural debate. *Japanese culture and behavior*, Lebra, T., & Lebra, W. (Eds.)., University of Hawaii Press, Honolulu.

Moeran, B. (1984). Individual, group and seishin: Japan's internal cultural debate. *Man*, *19*, 252–266.

Mok, C., & Armstrong, R. (1998). Sources of information used by Hong Kong and Taiwanese leisure travellers. *Australian Journal of Hospitality Management*, *3*(1), 31–35.

Mok, C., & Armstrong, R. (1998). Expectations for hotel service quality: Do they differ from culture to culture? *Journal of Vacation Marketing*, *4*(4), 381–391.

Money, R., & Crotts, J. C. (2003). The effect of uncertainty avoidance on information search, planning, and purchases of international travel vacations. *Tourism Management*, *24*, 191–202.

Moore, E. (1998). Competitive judgments in a business stimulation: A comparison between American and Chinese business students. *Psychology and Marketing*, *15*(6), 547–562.

Morris, C. (1956). *Varieties of human value*, University of Chicago Press, Chicago.

Morsbach, H. (1973). Aspects of non-verbal communication in Japan. *Journal of Nervous and Mental Disease*, *157*, 262-277.

Morsbach, H. (1977). The psychological importance of ritualized gift exchange in modern Japan. *Annals of the New York Academy of Sciences*, *293*, 98-113.

Moum, T. (1980). *The role of values and life-goals in quality of life*, UNESCO, Paris.

Mourer, R., & Sugimoto, A. (1979). *Some questions concerning commonly accepted stereotypes of Japanese society*. Research paper No. 64, Australian-Japan Economic Relations Research Project, Sydney.

Muller, T. (1991). The two nations of Canada vs. the nine nations of North America: A cross-cultural analysis of consumers' personal values. *Journal of International Consumer Marketing*, *1*(4), 57-79.

Murphy, P. (1985). *Tourism: A community approach*, Methuen, London.

Murphy, L. (2001). Exploring social interactions of backpackers. *Annals of Tourism Research*, *28*(1), 50-67.

Murray, H. (1938). *Explorations in personality*, Oxford, New York.

Muzaffar, C. (1980). Schneider, S., & Barsoux, J. (Eds.). (1997). *Managing across cultures*. (Chapter 10). Hartfordshire: Prentice-Hall.

Nakane, S. (1973). *Japanese Society*, Penguin, New York.

Nancy, J. (1991). *The inoperative community*, University of Minnesota Press, Minneapolis.

Naotsuka, R., & Sakamoto, N. (1981). *Mutual understanding of different cultures*, Taishukan, Tokyo.

Nelson, P. (1974). Advertising and information. *Journal of Political Economy*, *82*(4), 67-86.

Nettekoven, L. (1979). Mechanisms of intercultural interaction. *Tourism: Passport to development?* DeKadt, E. (Ed.)., Oxford University Press, London, pp. 135-145.

Nishida, T. (1991). *Sequence patterns of self-disclosure among Japanese and North American students*. Paper presented at the Conference on Communication in Japan and the United States, Fullerton, CA, March.

Noesjirwan, J. (1970). Attitudes to learning of the Asian student studying in the West. *Journal of Cross-Cultural Psychology*, *1*, 393-397.

Noesjirwan, J. (1978). A rule-based analysis of cultural differences in social behavior: Indonesia and Australia. *International Journal of Psychology*, *13*(4), 305-316.

Nohria, N., Lawrence, P., & Wilson, E. (2001). *Driven: How human nature shapes our choices*, Jossey-Bass, San Francisco.

Nomura, N., & Barnlund, D. (1983). Patterns of interpersonal criticism in Japan and the United States. *International Journal of Intercultural Relations*, *7*(1), 1-18.

Nonaka, I., & Takeuchi, H. (1995). *The knowledge-creating company: How Japanese companies create the dynamics of innovation*, Oxford University Press, Oxford.

Norwood, G. (2000). Maslow's Hierarchy of Needs. *The truth vectors (Part 1)*. Retrieved October 3, 2005, from http://www.deepermind.com/20maslow.htm.

Nozawa, H. (1991). *Host-guest relations in international tourism: How education can help establish a positive host-guest scenario*. Paper presented at the New Horizons Conference, University of Calgary.

O'Leary, J., & Deegan, J. (2003). People, pace, place: Qualitative and quantitative images of Ireland as a tourism destination in France. *Journal of Vacation Marketing*, *9*(3), 213-226.

Oberg, K. (1960). Culture shock: Adjustment to new cultural environments. *Practical Anthropology*, *7*, 177-182.

Ogden, D., Ogden, J., & Schau, H. (2004). Exploring the impact of culture and acculturation on consumer purchase decisions: Toward a microcultural perspective. *Academy of Marketing Science Review*, available at: www.amsreview.org/articles/ogden03_2004.pdf, No. 3.

Oh, H., Uysal, M., & Weaver, P. (1995). Product bundles and market segments based on travel motivations: A canonical correlation approach. *International Journal of Hospitality Management*, *14*, 123-137.

Okabe, R. (1983). Cultural assumptions of East and West: Japan and the United States. *Intercultural communication theory: Current perspectives*, Gudykunst, W. (Ed.)., Sage Publications, Beverly Hills, CA.

Olmedo, E. (1979). Acculturation: A psychometric perspective. *American Psychologist, 11,* 1061–1070.

Padilla, A., (Ed.). (1980). *Acculturation: Theory, models and some new findings,* Westview Press, Boulder, CO.

Parasuraman, A., Zeithaml, V., & Berry, L. (1985). A conceptual model of service quality and its implications for future research. *Journal of Marketing, 49,* 41–50.

Parasuraman, A., Zeithaml, V., & Berry, L. (1986). *SERVQUAL: A multiple-scale item for measuring consumer perceptions of service quality,* Marketing Institute, Cambridge, MA.

Parasuraman, A., Zeithaml, V., & Berry, L. (1988). SERVQUAL: A multiple-scale item for measuring consumer perceptions of service quality. *Journal of Retailing, 64,* 12–40.

Park, C., & Jun, J. (2003). A cross-cultural comparison of Internet buying behavior effects of Internet usage, perceived risks, and innovativeness. *International Marketing Review, 20*(5), 534–553.

Park, S. (1998). A comparison of Korean and American gift-giving behaviors. *Psychology and Marketing, 15,* 577–593.

Parsons, T. (1951). *The social system,* Free Press, Glencoe, IL.

Parvis, L. (2007). *Understanding cultural diversity in today's complex world,* Parvis Press, New York.

Payne, D., & Dimanche, F. (1996). Towards a code of conduct for the tourism industry: An ethics model. *Journal of Business Ethics, 15,* 997–1007.

Pearce, P. (1977). Mental souvenirs: A study of tourists and their city maps. *Australian Journal of Psychology, 29,* 203–210.

Pearce, P. (1982). *The social psychology of tourist behaviour.* International Series in Experimental Social Psychology. Vol. 3. Oxford: New York Pergamon Press.

Pearce, P. (1988). *The Ulysses factor: Evaluating visitors in tourist settings,* Springer-Verlag, New York.

Pearce, P. (1995). From culture shock and culture arrogance to culture exchange: Ideas towards sustainable socio-cultural tourism. *Journal of Sustainable Tourism, 3*(3), 143–154.

Pearce, W., & Cronen, V. (1980). *Communication, action and meaning: The creation of social realities,* Praeger, New York.

Pelto, P. (1968). The difference between ''tight'' and ''loose'' societies. *Transaction, 1,* 37–40.

Pennington-Gray, L., & Reisinger, Y. (2005). Do U.S. tour operators educate the tourist on culturally responsible behaviors? A case study for Kenya. *Journal of Vacation Marketing, 11*(3), 265–284 [Special issue on ''Leisure Travel Trends: Cultural Differences, National Trends''].

Peric, V. (2005). Tourism and globalization. *Proceedings of the 6th International Conference of the Faculty of Management Koper,* Congress Centre Bernardin, Slovenia, November 24–26.

Petit-Skinner, S. (1977). Tourism and acculturation in Tahiti. The social and economic impact of tourism on Pacific communities (1982). *Cultures in contact: Studies in cross-cultural interaction,* Bochner, S. (Ed.)., Pergamon Press, New York.

Phatak, A. (1997). *International management: Concepts and cases,* Irvwin, New York.

Phillips, H. (1965). *Thai peasant personality,* University of California Press, Berkeley, CA.

Pi-Sunyer, O. (1978). Through native eyes: Tourists and tourism in a Catalan Maritime community. *Hosts and guests,* Smith, V. (Ed.)., University of Pennsylvania Press, Philadelphia.

Pi-Sunyer, O. (1982). The cultural costs of tourism. *Cultural Survival Quarterly, 6*(3), 7–10.

Pi-Sunyer, O., & Smith, V. (1989). Changing perceptions of tourism and tourists in a Catalan resort town. *Hosts and guests: The anthropology of tourism,* (2nd ed.)., Smith, V., (Ed.)., University Press, Philadelphia, pp. 187–199.

Pizam, A. (1999). Cross-cultural tourist behavior. *Consumer behavior in travel and tourism,* Pizam, A., & Mansfeld, Y. (Eds.)., Haworth, Binghamton, pp. 393–411.

Pizam, A., & Calantone, R. (1987). Beyond psychographics – values as determinants of tourist behavior. *International Journal of Hospitality Management, 6*(3), 177–181.

Pizam, A., & Jeong, G. (1996). Cross-cultural tourist behavior: Perceptions of Korean and tour guides. *International Journal of Tourism Management, 17*(4), 277-286.

Pizam, A., & Mansfeld, Y., (Eds.). (1999). *Consumer behavior in travel and tourism,* Haworth, Binghamton.

Pizam, A., & Reichel, A. (1996). The effect of nationality on tourist behavior: Israeli tour guides' perceptions. *Journal of Hospitality and Leisure Marketing, 4*(1), 23-49.

Pizam, A., & Sussmann, S. (1995). Does nationality affect tourist behavior? *Annals of Tourism Research, 22*(4), 901-917.

Pizam, A., & Telisman-Kosuta, N. (1989). Tourism as a factor of change: Results and analysis. *Tourism as a factor of change: A socio-cultural study*, Bystrzanowski, J., (Ed.)., European Coordination Centre for Documentation in Social Sciences, Vienna, *Vol. 1*, pp. 149-156.

Pizam, A., Jansen-Verbeke, M., & Steel, L. (1997). Are all tourists alike regardless of nationality? The perceptions of Dutch tour guides. *Journal of International Hospitality Leisure and Tourism Management, 1*(1), 19-40.

Plog, S. (1974). Why destination areas rise and fall in popularity. *The Cornell hotel and Restaurant Administration Quarterly, 14*(4), 55-58.

Plog, S. (1979). *Where in the world are people going and why do they want to go there?* Paper presented at The Tiangus Touristico Annual Conference, Acapulco, Mexico.

Plog, S. (1987). Understanding psychographics in tourism research. *Travel, tourism and hospitality research*, Ritchie, B., & Goeldner, C. (Eds.)., John Wiley, New York, pp. 203-213.

Plog, S. (1990). A carpenter's tool: An answer to Stephen, L.J., Smith's review of psychocentrism/allocentrism. *Journal of Travel Research, 28*(4), 43-45.

Plog, S. (2002). The power of psychographics and the concept of venturesomeness. *Journal of Travel Research, 40*(3), 244-251.

Porter, R., & Samovar, L. (1988). Approaching intercultural communication. *Intercultural communication: A reader,* (5th ed.)., Samova, L., & Porter, R., (Eds.)., Wadsworth Publishing Company, Belmont, CA.

Potter, C. (1989). What is culture and can it be useful for organizational change agents? *Leadership and Organization Development Journal, 10*(3), 17-24.

Rao, A., & Schmidt, S. (1998). A behavioral perspective on negotiating international alliance. *Journal of International Business Studies, 29*(4), 665-689.

Ratz, T. The socio-cultural impacts of tourism. Budapest University of Economic Sciences http://www.ratztamara.com/impacts.html.

Redding, G., & Martyn-Johns, T. (1979). Paradigm differences and their relation to management, with reference to Southeast Asia. *Organisational functioning in a cross-cultural perspective*, England, G., Neghandi, A., & Wilpert, R. (Eds.)., Comparative Administration Research Unit, Kent State University, Kent, Ohio.

Redfield, R., Linton, R., & Herskovits, M. (1936). Memorandum for the study of acculturation. *American Anthropologist, 38,* 149-152.

Reisinger, Y. (1990). *The perceptions of Australian hosts by Japanese tourists*, Unpublished Master's Thesis, Faculty of Business, Victoria University of Technology, Melbourne, Australia.

Reisinger, Y. (2001). Unique characteristics of tourism, hospitality and leisure services versus goods. *Service quality management in hospitality, tourism and leisure*, Kandampully, J., Hsu, C., & Sparks, B. (Eds.)., Haworth Hospitality Press, New York; London; Oxford, pp. 15-50.

Reisinger, Y. (2006). Shopping in tourism. Buhalis, D., & Costa, D. (Eds.). *Tourism business frontiers: Consumers, products and industry.* Oxford, UK: Elsevier.

Reisinger, Y., & Mavondo, F. (2005). Travel anxiety and intentions to travel internationally: Implications of travel risk perceptions. *Journal of Travel Research, 42*(3), 212-224.

Reisinger, Y., & Mavondo, F. (2006a). Cultural consequences on travel risk perception and safety. *Tourism Analysis, 11*(4), 265-284.

Reisinger, Y., & Mavondo, F. (2006b). Cultural differences in travel risk perception. *Journal of Travel and Tourism Marketing, 20*(1), 13-31.

Reisinger, Y., & Steiner, C. (2006a). Reconceptualising object authenticity. *Annals of Tourism Research, 33*(1), 65-86.

Reisinger, Y., & Steiner, C. (2006b). Reconceptualising interpretation: The role of tour guides in authentic tourism. *Current Issues in Tourism, 9*(6), 481-498.

Reisinger, Y., & Turner, L. (1997a). Tourist satisfaction with hosts: A cultural approach. Comparing Thai tourists and Australian hosts. *Pacific Tourism Review, 1*(2), 147-159.

Reisinger, Y., & Turner, L. (1997b). Cross-cultural differences in tourism: Indonesian tourists in Australia. *Tourism Management, 18*(3), 139-147.

Reisinger, Y., & Turner, L. (1997c). Asian and Western cultural differences: The new challenge for tourism marketplaces. *28th Annual Travel and Tourism Research Association Conference (TTRA),* Norfolk, Virginia Beach, June 15-18, pp. 110-125.

Reisinger, Y., & Turner, L. (1998a). Asian and Western cultural differences: The new challenge for tourism marketplaces. *Journal of International Hospitality, Leisure and Tourism Management, 1*(3), 21-35.

Reisinger, Y., & Turner, L. (1998b). Cross-cultural differences in tourism: A strategy for tourism marketers. *Journal of Travel and Tourism Marketing, 7*(4), 79-106.

Reisinger, Y., & Turner, L. (1998c). Cultural differences between Mandarin-speaking tourists and Australian hosts and their impact on cross-cultural tourist-host interaction. *Journal of Business Research, 42*(2), 175-187.

Reisinger, Y., & Turner, L. (1999a). A cultural analysis of Japanese tourists: Challenges for Australian tourism marketers. *European Journal of Marketing, 33*(11-12), 1203-1227.

Reisinger, Y., & Turner, L. (1999b). A cultural approach to destination marketing: Analysis of Thai tourism to Australia. *Tourism - An International Interdisciplinary Journal, 47*(2), 92-107.

Reisinger, Y., & Turner, L. (2000). Japanese tourism satisfaction with destination attributes: Gold Coast versus Hawaii. *Journal of Vacation Marketing - An International Journal for the Tourism and Hospitality Industries, 6*(2), 299-317.

Reisinger, Y., & Turner, L. (2002a). Cultural differences between Asian tourist markets and Australian hosts, Part 1. *Journal of Travel Research, 40*(3), 295-315.

Reisinger, Y., & Turner, L. (2002b). Cultural differences between Asian tourist markets and Australian hosts, Part 2. *Journal of Travel Research, 40*(4), 374-384.

Reisinger, Y., & Turner, L. (2003). *Cross-cultural behavior in tourism: Concepts and analysis,* Butterworth-Heinemann, Burlington, MA.

Reitz, H., & Graff, G. (1972). Comparisons of locus of control categories among American, Mexican, and Thai workers. *Proceedings of the 80th Annual Convention of the American Psychological Association, 7,* 263-264.

Remland, M., Jones, T., & Brinkman, H. (1992, October). *Interpersonal distance, body orientation and touch in the dyadic interactions of Northern and Southern Europeans.* Paper presented to the Speech Communication Association, Chicago.

Richards, G. (1996). *Cultural tourism in Europe,* CABI, Wallingford.

Richards, I. (1936). *The philosophy of rhetoric,* Oxford, London.

Richardson, S., & Crompton, J. (1988). Vacation patterns of French and English Canadians. *Annals of Tourism Research, 15*(3), 430-435.

Ritter, W. (1987). Styles of tourism in the modern world. *Tourism Recreation Research, 12*(1), 3-8.

Ritter, W. (1989). On deserts and beaches: Recreational tourism in the Muslim world. *Tourism Recreation Research, 14,* 3-10.

Ritzer, G. (1993). *The McDonaldization of society,* Forge Press, Thousand Oaks, CA.

Ritzer, G., & Liska, A. (1997). McDonaldization and post-tourism: Complementary perspectives on contemporary tourism. *Touring cultures – transformations of travel and theory*, Rojek, C., & Urry, J. (Eds.)., Routledge, London, pp. 96–109.

Robertson, I. (1987). *Social psychology*, Prentice Hall, Englewood Cliffs.

Robertson, R. (1995). Time space and homogeneity-heterogeneity. *Global modernities*, Featherstone, M. (Ed.)., Sage, London.

Robinson, M. (1998). *Tourism management: Tourism and cultural conflicts*, CABI Publishing, Wallingford.

Rogers, E. (1995). *Diffusion of innovations*, (4th ed.). Free Press, New York.

Rogers, E., & Steinfatt, T. (1999). *Intercultural communication*, Waveland Press, Prospect Heights, IL.

Rokeach, M. (1973a). *The nature of human values*. New York: Free Press.

Rokeach, M. (1973b/1979). *Understanding human values: Individual and societal*. New York: Free Press.

Ronen, S. (1986). *Comparative and multinational management*. New York: John Wiley & Sons.

Ronen, S., & Shenkar, O. (1985). Clustering countries on attitudinal dimensions: A review and synthesis. *Academy of Management Review*, *10*(3), 435–454.

Rosen, B., & La Raia, A. (1972). Modernity in women: An index of social change in Brazil. *Journal of Marriage and the Family*, *34*, 353–360.

Rosenbaum, M., & Spears, D. (2005). Who buys what? Who does what? Analysis of cross-cultural consumption behaviours among tourists in Hawaii. *Journal of Vacation Marketing*, *11*(3), 235–247.

Ross, G. (2003). Ethical beliefs, work-problem-solving strategies and learning styles as mediators of tourism marketing entrepreneurialism. *Journal of Vacation Marketing*, *9*(2), 119–136.

Rowland, D. (1985). *Japanese business etiquette: A practical guide to success with the Japanese*, Warner Books, CA.

Ruch, W. (1989). *International handbook of corporate communication*, McFarland, Jefferson, NC.

Ryan, R., & Deci, E. (2000). Self-determination theory and the facilitation of intrinsic motivation, social development and well-being. *American Psychologist*, *55*(1), 68–78. Retrieved October 3, 2005, from http://www.psych.Rochester.edu/SDT/publications/documents/2000RyanDeciSDT.pdf.

Saee, J. (2005). *Managing organizations in a global economy: An intercultural perspective*, Thomson Corporation, Mason, Ohio.

Sakakibara, E. (1995). The end of progressivism: A search for new goals. *Foreign Affairs*, *74*, 8–14.

Sakakida, Y., Cole, S., & Card, J. (2004). A cross-cultural study of college students' travel preferences: A value-oriented perspective. *Journal of Travel and Tourism Marketing*, *16*(1), 35–41.

Saleh, F., & Ryan, C. (1992). Client perceptions of hotels: A multi-attribute approach. *Tourism Management*, *13*(2), 163–168.

Samovar, L., & Porter, R. (1988). *Intercultural communication: A reader*, (5th ed.). Wadsworth Publishing Company, Belmont, CA.

Samovar, L., & Porter, R. (1991). *Communication between cultures*, Wadsworth Publishing Company, Belmont, CA.

Samovar, L., Porter, R., & Jain, N. (1981). *Understanding intercultural communication*, Wadsworth, Belmont, CA.

Samovar, L., Porter, R., & Stefani, L. (1988). *Communication between cultures*, Wadsworth Publishing Company, Belmont, CA.

Sangpikul, A. (2008). Travel motivations of Japanese senior travellers to Thailand. *International Journal of Tourism Research*, *10*(1), 81–94.

Sanyal, R. (2001). The social clause in trade treaties: Implications for international firms. *Journal of Business Ethics*, *29*, 379–389.

Sapir, E. (1964). *Culture, language, and personality: Selected essays*, Mandelbaum, D.G. (Ed.)., University of California Press, Berkeley and Los Angeles, CA.

Sarbaugh, L. (1988a). A taxonomic approach to intercultural communication. *Theories in intercultural communication*, Kim, Y., & Gudykunst, W. (Eds.)., Sage, Newbury Park, CA, pp. 22–40.

Sarbaugh, L. (1988b). *Intercultural communication*, Transaction Books, New Brunswick, New Jersey.

Sarbaugh, L., & Asuncion-Lande, N. (1983). Theory building in intercultural communication: Synthesizing the action caucus. *Intercultural communication theory*, Gudykunst, W. (Ed.)., Sage, Beverly Hills, pp. 45–60.

Saussure, F. (1960). *Course in general linguistics*, P. Owen, London.

Schein, E. (1992). *Organizational culture and leadership*, Jossey-Bass Publishers, San Francisco.

Schinzinger, R. (1983). Imitation and originality in Japanese culture. *Japan Quarterly, 30,* 281–288.

Schmidt, E. (1980). *Decoding corporate camouflage: U.S. business support for apartheid*, Institute for Policy Studies, Washington, DC.

Schneider, S., & Barsoux, J.-L. (1997). *Managing across cultures*, Prentice-Hall, New York.

Scholte, J. (2000). *Globalization. A critical introduction*, Palgrave, London.

Schrerer, K., Wallbott, H., & Summerfield, A. (1986). *Experiencing emotions: A cross-cultural study*, Cambridge University Press, Cambridge.

Schwartz, S. (1990). Individualism-collectivism: Critique and proposed refinements. *Journal of Cross-Cultural Psychology, 21,* 139–157.

Schwartz, S. (1994). Are there universal aspects of the structure and content of values? *Journal of Social Issues, 50*(4), 19–45.

Scollon, R., & Scollon, S. (1995). *Intercultural communication: A discourse approach*, Blackwell, Cambridge, MA.

Scott, W. (1965). *Values and organizations: A study of fraternities and sororities*, Rand McNally, Chicago.

Segall, M. H. (1986). Culture and behavior: Psychology in global perspective. *Annual Review of Psychology, 37,* 523–564.

Segall, M., Dasen, P., Berry, J., & Poortinga, Y. (1990). *Human behavior in global perspective: An introduction to cross-cultural psychology*, Pergamon Press, New York.

Sellitz, C., & Cook, S. (1962). Factors influencing attitudes of foreign students toward the host country. *Journal of Social Issue, 18*(1), 7–23.

Shafranske, E., & Malony, H. (1990). Clinical psychologists' religious and spiritual orientations and their practice of psychotherapy. *Psychotherapy, 27,* 72–78.

Sharp, I. (1992). *Culture shock – A guide in customs and etiquette*, Times Books International, Australia. Singapore.

Sharpley, R. (1994). *Tourism and tourist motivation*, Tourism, tourists and society. University of Luton, Bedfordshire, UK (pp. 96–126).

Sheldon, P., & Fox, M. (1988). The role of foodservice in vacation choice and experience: A cross-cultural analysis. *Journal of Travel Research, 27*(3), 9–15.

Shih, D. (1986). VALS as a tool of tourism market research: The Pennsylvania experience. *Journal of Travel Research, 24*(2), 2–11.

Shiraev, E., & Levy, D. (2004). *Cross-cultural psychology: Critical thinking and contemporary applications*, Pearson, Boston, New York.

Simmel, G. (1908). Group expansion and the development of individuality. *George Simmel on individuality and social forms*, Levine, D. (Ed.)., University of Chicago Press, Chicago 1971.

Simon, W. (1976). A challenge to free enterprise. *The ethical and economic freedom*, Hill, I. (Ed.)., American Viewpoint, Chapel Hill, NC, pp. 405–406.

Skinner, B. F. (1953). *Science and human behavior*, Macmillan, New York.

Skinner, B. F. (1969). *Contingencies of reinforcement: A theoretical analysis*, Prentice-Hall, Englewood Cliffs, NJ.

Smalley, W. (1963). Culture shock, language shock, and the shock of self-discovery. *Practical Anthropology, 10,* 49-56.

Smith, A. (2006). A cross-cultural perspective on the role of emotion in negative service encounters. *The Service Industries Journal, 26*(7), 709-726.

Smith, B. (1969). *Psychology and human values,* Aldine, Chicago.

Smith, V. (1978). *Hosts and guests,* Blackwell, Oxford.

Smith, V. (1989). *Hosts and guests: The anthropology of tourism,* (2nd ed.). University of Pennsylvania Press, Philadelphia.

Sofield, T. (2000). Re-thinking and re-conceptualizing social and cultural issues of tourism development in South and Southeast Asia Institute for Sustainability and Technology Policy. http://www.sustanaibility. murdoch.edu.au/casestudies/Case_Studies.

Spengler, O. (1937/1985). Werner, H. (Ed.). *The decline of the West.* English abridged edition prepared by Arthur Helps from the translation by Charles Francis Atkinson. New York: Oxford University Press [1926, 1928, 1932].

Spitzberg, B., & Cupach, W. (1984). *Interpersonal communication competence,* Sage, Beverly Hills, CA.

Srnka, K. (1997). *Ethik in marketing,* Vienna University, Vienna.

Srnka, K. (2004). Culture's role in marketer's ethical decision making: An integrated theoretical framework. *Academy of Marketing Science Review, 8*(3),http://www.amsreview.org/articles/srnka01-2004.pdf.

Staats, S., Panel, P., & Cosmar, D. (2006). Predicting travel attitudes among university faculty after 9/11. *The Journal of Psychology, 140*(2), 121-132.

Stark, A. (1993). What is the matter with business ethics? *Harvard Business Review,* 38-48.

Steiner, C., & Reisinger, Y. (2006). Understanding existential authenticity. *Annals of Tourism Research, 33*(2), 299-318.

Stewart, E. (1971). *American cultural patterns: A cross-cultural perspective,* Regional Council for International Education, Pittsburgh.

Stewart, R. (1971). Cross-cultural personality research and basic cultural dimensions through factor analysis. *Personality, 2,* 45-72.

Stringer, P. (1981). Hosts and guests: The bed and breakfast phenomenon. *Annals of Tourism Research, 8*(3), 357-376.

Suh, Y., & Gartner, W. (2004). Perceptions in international urban tourism: An analysis of travelers to Seoul, Korea. *Journal of Travel Research, 43,* 39-45.

Summers, J., & McColl-Kennedy, J. (1998). Australia as a holiday destination: Young Americans' vs. Chinese Malaysians' decision-making. *Journal of Hospitality and Leisure Marketing, 5*(4), 33-55.

Sun, T., Horn, M., & Merritt, D. (2004). Values and lifestyles of individualists and collectivists: A case study on Chinese, Japanese, British and US consumers. *Journal of Consumer Marketing, 21*(5), 318-331.

Sussmann, S., & Rashcovsky, C. (1997). A cross-cultural analysis of English and French Canadians' vacation travel patterns. *International Journal of Hospitality Management, 16*(2), 191-208.

Sutton, W. (1967). Travel and understanding: Notes on the social structure of touring. *International Journal of Comparative Sociology, 8*(2), 218-223.

Svanberg, I., & Runblom, H. (1988). *Det margkulturella Sverige. En hundbok om etniska grupper och minoriteter. The multicultural Sweden. A handbook on ethnic groups and minorities.* Varnamoc Centrum for moltietnisk forskning och Gidlunds forlag.

Swarbrooke, J., & Horner, S. (2007). *Consumer behavior in tourism,* Butterworth-Heinemann/Elsevier, Burlington, MA.

Szalai, A. (1972). *The use of time: Daily activities of urban and suburban residents in twelve countries,* Mouton and Co, The Hague, Netherlands.

Taft, R. (1977). Coping with unfamiliar cultures. *Studies in cross-cultural psychology 1,* Warren, N. (Ed.)., Academic Press, London.

Tai, S. (1998). Factors affecting advertising approach in Asia. *Journal of Current Issues and Research in Advertising*, *20*(1), 33-45.

Tajfel, H. (1978). Social categorization, social identity, and social comparison. *Differentiation between social groups*, Tajfel, H. (Ed.)., Academic Press, London.

Taylor, C., Miracle, G., & Wilson, R. (1997). The impact of information level on the effectiveness of US and Korean television commercials. *Journal of Advertising*, *26*(1), 1-18.

Taylor, H. (1974). Japanese kinesics. *Journal of the Association of Teachers of Japanese, 9,* 65-75.

Thiederman, S. (1989). Overcoming cultural and language barriers. *Public Management, 71,* 19-21.

Ting-Toomey, S. (1985). Towards a theory of conflict and culture. *Communication, culture and organizational processes*, Gudykunst, W., Steward, L., & Ting-Toomey, S. (Eds.)., Sage, Beverly Hills, CA, pp. 299-321.

Ting-Toomey, S. (1991). Intimacy expressions in three cultures: France, Japan, and the United States. *International Journal of Intercultural Relations, 15,* 29-46.

Tiryakian, E. (1974). Reflections on the sociology of civilizations. *Sociological Analysis, 35,* 125.

Triandis, H. (1972). *The analysis of subjective culture*, Wiley-Interscience, New York.

Triandis, H. (1977). *Interpersonal behavior*, Brooks/Cole Publishing Company, Monterey, CA.

Triandis, H. (1988). Collectivism versus individualism: A reconceptualization of a basic concept in cross-cultural social psychology. *Personality, cognition, and values: Cross-cultural perspectives of childhood and adolescence*, Bagley, C., & Verma, G.K. (Eds.)., MacMillan, London.

Triandis, H. (1994). *Culture and social behavior*, McGraw-Hill, New York.

Triandis, H. (1995). *Individualism-collectivism*, Boulder, CO, Westview.

Triandis, H., & Vassiliou, V. (1967). Frequency of contact and stereotyping. *Journal of Personality and Social Psychology, 7,* 316-328.

Triandis, H., Bontempo, R., Villareal, M., Asai, M., & Lucca, N. (1988). Individualism and collectivism: Cross-cultural perspectives on self-ingroup relationships. *Journal of Personality and Social Psychology, 54,* 323-338.

Trifonovitch, G. (1977). Culture learning/culture teaching. *Educational Perspectives, 16*(4), 18-22.

Trompenaars, F. (1984). *The organisation of meaning and the meaning of organisation - a comparative study on the conceptions and organisational structure in different cultures*. PhD thesis, University of Pennsylvania.

Trompenaars, F. (1993). *Riding the waves of culture: Understanding cultural diversity in business*, Brealey, London.

Trompenaars, F., & Hampden-Turner, C. (1994). *Riding the waves of culture: Understanding cultural diversity in business*, Nicholas Brealey, London.

Tsang, N., & Ap, J. (2007). Tourists' perceptions of relational quality service attributes: A cross-cultural study. *Journal of Travel Research, 45,* 355-363.

Tsaur, S., Lin, C., & Wu, C. (2005). Cultural differences of service quality and behavioral intention in tourist hotels. *Journal of Hospitality and Leisure Marketing, 13*(1), 41-63.

Tsujimura, A. (1987). Some characteristics of the Japanese way of communication. *Communication theory: Eastern and Western perspective*, Lawrence, D. (Ed.)., Academic Press, San Diego.

Turcq, D., & Usunier, J. (1985). Les Services au Japon: l'Efficacite: Par la Non-Productive. *Revue Francaise de Gestion*, 12-15.

Tylor, E. B. (1874). *Primitive culture: Researches into the development of mythology, philosophy, religion, art and custom*, Holt, New York.

UNESCO. (1976). The effects of tourism on socio-cultural values. *Annals of Tourism Research, 4*(2), 74-105.

UNESCO. (2002). UNESCO Declaration on Cultural Diversity. Retrieved from <http://unescdoc.unesco.org/images/0012/001272/127160m.pdf>.

Urriola, O. (1989). Culture in the context of development. *World Marxist Review, 32,* 66-69.

Urry, J. (1991). The sociology of tourism. *Progress in tourism, recreation and hospitality management,* Cooper, C. P., (Ed.)., The University of Surrey, England, *Vol. 3,* pp. 48-57.

Usunier, J., & Lee, J. (1996). *Marketing across cultures,* Prentice Hall, New York.

Usunier, J., & Lee, J. (2005). *Marketing across cultures,* Prentice Hall, Essex.

Van den Berghe, P. (1980). Tourism as ethnic relations: A case study of Cuzco, Peru. *Ethnic and Racial Studies, 3*(4), 375-392.

Van den Berghe, P. (1994). *The quest for the other,* University of Washington Press, Seattle.

Van den Berghe, P., & Keyes, C. (1984). Introduction: Tourism and re-created ethnicity. *Annals of Tourism Research, 11*(3), 343-352.

Verhage, B., Yavas, U., & Green, R. (1990). Perceived risk: A cross-cultural phenomenon? *International Journal of Research Marketing, 7*(4), 297-303.

Vogel, D. (1992). The globalization of business ethics: Why American remains distinctive. *California Management Review, 35,* 30-49.

Vroom, V. (1964). *Work and motivation,* Wiley, New York.

Vusoniwailala, L. (1980). Tourism and Fijian hospitality. *Pacific tourism as Islanders see it,* Rajotte, F., & Crocombe, R. (Eds.)., University of the South Pacific, Suva, Fiji.

Wagatsuma, H., & Rosett, A. (1986). The implications of apology: Law and culture in Japan and the United States. *Law and Society Review, 20*(4), 461-498.

Wagner, U. (1977). Out of time and place - mass tourism and charter trips. *Ethnos, 42,* 38-52.

Wahab, S., & Cooper, C., (Eds.). (2003). *Tourism in the age of globalization,* Routledge, London.

Weber, E., & Hsee, C. (1998). Cross-cultural differences in risk perception, but cross-cultural similarities in attitudes towards perceived risk. *Management Science, 44*(9), 1205-1217.

Webster, C. (1994). Effects of Hispanic ethnic identification on marital roles in the purchase decision process. *Journal of Consumer Research, 21,* 319-331.

Wei, L., Crompton, J. L., & Reid, L. M. (1989). Cultural conflicts: Experiences of US visitors to China. *Tourism Management, 10*(4), 322-332.

Weiermair, K. (2000). Tourists' perceptions towards and satisfaction with service quality in the cross-cultural service encounter: Implications for hospitality and tourism management. *Managing Service Quality, 10*(16), 397-407.

Weiermair, K., & Fuchs, M. (1999). Measuring tourist judgments on service quality. *Annals of Tourism Research, 26*(4), 1004-1024.

Weiermair, K., & Fuchs, M. (2000). The impact of cultural distance on perceived service quality gaps: The case of Alpine tourism. *Journal of Quality Assurance in Hospitality and Tourism, 1*(2), 59-76.

Weiss, T. (2004). *Safe mode of cultural orientation.* Presentation at Sea Border Central Seminar, 30 January 2004. http://www.more.fi/files/IOM_Presentation.ppt.

West, J., & Graham, J. (2004). A linguistic-based measure of cultural distance and its relationship to managerial values. *Management International Review, 44*(3), 239-260.

Wheeler, M. (1995). Tourism marketing ethics: An introduction. *International Marketing Review, 12*(4), 38-49.

Whorf, B. (1956). *Language, thought, and reality: Selected writings of Benjamin Lee Whorf,* MIT Press, Cambridge, MA.

Wierenga, B., Pruyn, A., & Waarts, E. (1996). The key to successful Euromarketing: Standardization or customization? *Journal of International Consumer Marketing, 8*(3-4), 39-67.

Williams, A. (2002). *Understanding the hospitality consumer,* Butterworth-Heinemann, Oxford.

Williams, R. M. (1970). *American society. A sociological interpretation,* (3rd ed.). Knopf, New York.

Williams, R. (1976/1983). *Keywords: A vocabulary of culture and society.* Rev. Ed. New York: Oxford University Press, pp. 87-93 and 236-238.

Williams, R. (1979). Change and stability in values and value systems: A sociological perspective. Rokeach, M. (Ed.) (2000). *Understanding human values*. Free Press: New York.

Winsted, K. (1997). The service experience in two cultures: A behavioral perspective. *Journal of Retailing*, 73(3), 337–360.

Winsted, K. (1999). Evaluating service encounters: A cross-cultural and cross-industry exploration. *Journal of Marketing Theory and Practice*, 7(2), 106–123.

Woodside, A., & Motes, W. (1979). Perceptions of marital roles in consumer decision processes for six products. *American Marketing Association Proceedings*, Beckwith, N. (Ed.)., American Marketing Association, Chicago, pp. 214–219.

Worthy, F. (1989). When somebody wants a payoff. *Fortune*, 13.

Wright, G., & Phillips, L. (1980). Cultural variation in probabilistic thinking. *International Journal of Psychology*, 15, 239–257.

Wright, G., Phillips, L., Whalley, P., Chao, G., Ng, K., Tan, I., & Wisudha, A. (1978). Cultural differences in probabilistic thinking. *Journal of Cross-Cultural Psychology*, 9, 285–299.

Wuthnow, R. (1994). *God mammon in America*, Free Press, New York.

Yao, O. (1988). Chinese culture values: Their dimensions and marketing implications. *European Journal of Marketing*, 22(5), 44–57.

Yavas, U. (1987). Correlated of vacation travel: Some empirical evidence. *Journal of Professional Services Marketing*, 5(2), 3–18.

Yavas, U., Verhage, B., & Green, R. (1992). Global consumer segmentation versus local marketing orintation: Empirical findings. *Management International Review*, 32(3), 265–272.

Yoo, J., McKercher, B., & Mena, M. (2004). A cross-cultural comparison of trip characteristics: International visitors to Hong Kong from Mainland China and USA. *Journal of Travel and Tourism Marketing*, 16(1), 65–77.

You, X., O'Leary, J., Morrison, A., & Hong, G. (2000). A cross-cultural comparison of travel push and pull factors: United Kingdom versus Japan. *International Journal of Hospitality and Tourism Administration*, 1(2), 1–26.

Young, L. (1982). Inscrutability revisited. *Language and social identity*, Gumperz, J. (Ed.)., Cambridge University Press, Cambridge.

Yum, J. (1985). *The impact of Confucianism on communication: The case of Korea and Japan*. 35th Annual Conference of the International Communication Association, Honolulu.

Yum, J. (1987). Korean philosophy and communication. *Communication theory: Eastern and Western perspectives*, Kincaid, D. (Ed.)., Academic Press, New York.

Yum, J. (1988). Network theory in intercultural communication. *Theories in intercultural communication*, Kim, Y., & Gudykunst, W. (Eds.)., Sage, Newbury Park, CA, pp. 239–258.

Zane, N., Sue, S., Hu, L., & Kwon, J. (1991). Asian-American assertion: A social learning analysis of cultural differences. *Journal of Counseling Psychology*, 38(1), 63–70.

Zavalloni, M. (1980). Values. *Handbook of cross-cultural psychology: Social psychology*, Triandis, H. C., & Brislin, R., (Eds.)., Allyn and Bacon, Boston, *Vol. 5.*

Ziff-Levine, W. (1990). The cultural gap: A Japanese tourism research experience. *Tourism Management*, 11(2), 105–110.

Index

A

Abilities, 195, 379, 382, 383
Abrahamic religions, 92, 96
Abstractive cultures, 178
Acculturation
    assimilation continuum, 76, 80
    curve, 220
    definition, 73
Active strategies, 57
Addressee focus, 63
Adjustment phase, 218
Adult-centered families, 294
Aesthetic needs, 273
Affect, 266
Affective
    domain, 380
    intuitive cultures, 178
    stage, 318
Affectivity–affective neutrality dimension, 128
Affiliation, 74, 278
Africa, 349–350
African-Americans, 32, 40, 115–116
Age-based subcultures, 107
Alderfer's ERG Theory, 276
Alternative evaluation, 291, 305
Amadeus, 16
American
    consumerism, 25, 27
    soap operas, 19
Antagonism or hostility stage, 75, 218, 221
Antilocution, 194
Anxiety/uncertainty management theory, 57–59
Apathy stage, 221
Arab values, 366
Argumentation style, 121
Argyle's cultural differentiation, 151–152
Ascription–achievement dimension, 128, 156
Asia, 97, 350–357
Asian
    civilizations, 104
    cultures, 134, 175, 180, 229, 236
Asian-American market, 116, 117
Aspirational groups, 297
Assertive cultures, 140, 150, 183, 239
At home stage, 218
Attitudes, 305, 329
Attribution, 330, 380
Australia, 357–359

Australian cultural traits, 355, 358
Australian hosts, 351, 353
Authenticity, 11, 20, 21, 69
Authoritarianism, 174, 177
Autonomy, 278
Avoidance needs, 278
Awareness, 380
Axiomatic–deductive cultures, 178

B

Backpacker traveling, 282
Backslapping, 365
Becoming cultures, 130, 133, 186
Behavioral domain, 379, 382, 386
Behavioral stage, 318
Being-oriented societies, 184
Beliefs, 88, 93–94, 305
Blended families, 294
Body movements, 121
Bond's Confucian cultural patterns, 150–151
Boomerang kids, 294
Bottom line, 249
Brand image, 18
Brazil, 89, 366
Breaking rules, 228–229
Bribery, 251–252
British passengers, 239
Buddhism, 91, 92, 93, 94, 97, 101, 352, 354, 357
Business, goal of, 249
Business cycles, 299
Business ethics, 244, 248–249
Buyer's factors, 289, 301
    decision process, 289
    personal characteristics, 289
    psychological characteristics, 289
Buying new products, 314, 319, 334
Buying roles, 333

C

Canada, 368–369
Case study, 28–29, 258–261
Caucasian(s), 32, 33, 107, 180, 326, 357, 359
Caused behavior, 271
Cause-motive-behavior-goal
    model, 271
    theory, 271
Child-care centers, 293
Child labor, exploitation of, 253

419

Child sexual abuse, 253
China, 242, 350–351
Chinese culture connection, 150, 158
Chinese friendly, 36
Christian civilization, 101
Christianity, 92–94, 96, 97, 101
Civilization, 91, 101, 103
Civilization culture, 98, 100
Closer environments, 269–270
Cluster analysis, 114
Cocacolonization, 17
Code of conduct, 248
Code systems, 56
Cognition, 266
Cognitive
    anthropologists, 86
    dissonance, 339
    dissonance theory, 277
    domain, 379
    knowledge, 88
    stage, 318
Cognizance, 278
Collaterality, 174
Collectivism, 113, 133, 140, 149, 154, 176, 332, 354
Collectivistic
    Asians, 150
    consumers, 331
    cultures, 51, 227, 251
    and high power distant cultures, 229
    and high uncertainty avoidance cultures, 229
Collectivistic(s), 149
Colonizing nations, 26
Commodity, 70
Communication
    associative style of, 173
    contextual style of, 174
    convergence, 61
    definition, 166
    difficulties, 24, 168, 190
    ethics, 196
    intercultural, 155, 167
    maintenance, 61
    model, 166
    non-verbal, 355
    process, 166
    style, 168
    verbal, 136
Communication Accommodation Theory, 60–63
Communication Resourcefulness Theory, 50
Competitive
    advantage, 24
    environment, 243
Complaint behavior, 341

Complex thought, 167
Conation, 266, 267
Conflicts, 78, 251
Confucian
Confucianism, 340, 356
Confucian Work Dynamism, 150, 151, 158, 361
Constructivist theory, 64
Consumer behavior, 279
Consumer buying behavior, 289
Consumer buying behavior process, 290
Consumer decision-making theories, 318
Consumerism, 21
Contact
    cultures, 152
    hypothesis, 212–213
    tourism, hypothesis in, 213
Context orientation, 187
Continuum, 56, 76
Convergence strategy, 62
Conversation
    structure, 121
    style, 178
Coordinated Management of Meaning Theory, 214
Coping information, 275
Copyright violations, 254
Corporate social responsibility, 245, 258
Corruption, 252
Cosmopolitan culture, 26, 28
Country of birth, 110
Country of residence, 100, 109, 110
Covert messages, 135
Criticism and complaints, 340–341
Cross-cultural
    context, ethics in, 247
    differences, 149
    interaction, 209
    interaction, difficulties in, 214
Cultural
    adaptation, 74–75
    adjustment, 75
    Americanization, 25–27
    antagonism, 250
    arrogance, 68
    assimilation, 75–77
    assumptions, 154–155
    authenticity, 20, 21
    awareness, 21, 41
    background, 19, 211
    borrowing, 71
    changes, 70
    clash, 25–27, 250
    commoditization, 20
    comparison, 155, 156

competence, 41
conflicts, 78-79
context, 208
convergence, 19
deterioration, 20, 21
difference, 35
dimensions, 127-128, 161
disappearance, 16-17, 25-27
divergence, 19
diversity, 31-41, 113, 285
emergence, 15-16, 22
erosion, 20, 67-68
expectations from service, differences in, 237
heterogenization, 19
identity, 25, 53-54, 110-111
influences, 225-229, 233-241, 243-257, 321-343
loss, 20, 21
marketing, 70
practices, 19, 36, 38, 67-79
regions, 91-92
resistance, 22
rules, differences in, 228
sensitivity, 35, 381
standardization, 196, 237, 328
target market, background of, 285
theories, 19
transformation, 58, 70
values, 122-160, 208, 209, 246, 247, 371
Cultural differences, 21, 165, 190, 211
    in communication, 120-121
    definition, 86, 208
    diffusion, 71
    dimension, 5
    diversity, 32, 40
    drift, 72
    elements, 71
    environment, 293
    ethical behavior, influences on, 247
    familiarity, 209
    fatigue, 215
    features, 71
    goods, 38
    groups, 211
    heritage, 38
    homogenization, 17
    hostility, 68
    hybridization, 19
    identity, 54, 110
    influences, 248
    pattern, 63
    perceptions, 60
    powers, 26
    relativism, 255

    rights, 38
    rules of behavior, 121-122
    shock, 190, 215-221
    shock and social interaction, 217
    shock in tourism, 217
    social behavior rules 121-122
    social categories, 121
    social interaction, influences on rules of, 227
    sources of, 119-122
    specific knowledge, 380
    standards, 255
    tourism, shock in, 217
    uniqueness, 286
    value dimensions, 127
    values, 119, 208, 247
Cultural distance
    countries, 339
    definition, 111
Cultural Identity Theory, 110-111
Culture
    characteristics, 105-106
    dimensions, 127, 160
    levels, 98-100
    measurement, 113-114
    purpose, 104-105
    types, 98-100, 104
Culture shock
    intensity and duration of, 219-421
    phases of, 217-219
    symptoms of, 215, 216
Customer satisfaction, 240, 339

D

Debatable business ethics issues, 248-249
Decision-making, level of, 333-334
Decision process, 289, 291, 330
Declaration, 37-38
Deficiency needs, 273
Degree of interculturalness, 210-211
Demographic factors, 291-293
Demographic projections, 39
Demonstration effect, 77-78
Demonstrative cultures, 180, 182
Deontology, 255
Deterritorialization, 4
Development time, 153
Diffuseness-specificity dimension, 128, 154
Direct and explicit communication, 169
Directed behavior, 271
Discretionary income, 298-299, 302
Discrimination, 194, 195, 252
Disposable income, 298
Dissociative groups, 297

Distinct individuals, 52
Distinctiveness theory, 111
Divergence strategy, 62
Diverse group(s), 32, 97
Diversity, 32, 34–35, 42
    benefits, 35
    challenges, 40
    development, 37
    future, 39–40
    importance, 37–38
    influence, 35–36
    interpretation, 33–34
    measure, 34
Doing-oriented societies, 184
Dominance, 278, 332
Double-income couples without kids, 11
Doxey's Irridex, 221
Dual income families, 294

E

Early adopters, 314
Early majority, 314
Eco-friendly tourism, 246
Economic benefits, 79
Economic dimension, 5
Economic environment, 298–299
Economic status, 303
Edifying information, 275
Educational traveler, 384–385
Eight-Stage Model, 274
Emiratis, 367
Emotional domain
Emotions and feelings, 342–343
Empowering information, 275
Empty nesters, 11, 294
Encouraging education, 37
Enculturation, 77
Engel's law, 299
Enlightening information, 275
Environment
    degradation, 8
    dimension, 5
    domain, 383
    and ecological concerns, 253
    factors, 268, 289
    issues awareness, 253
    levels, 268–270
    stimuli, 271, 278, 289, 291–301
Episode Representation Theory, 51–52, 276
Equity theory, 277
Ethical
    behavior, 244, 245, 247, 248
    development, 244
    frameworks, 254–255

issues, 248
practices, 245
principles of, 256
strategies, 256
theories, 254
Ethical business behavior, 245
Ethical decisions, 247
Ethical dilemma(s), 196, 248, 251
Ethical norms, 243, 247
Ethical standards, 243, 256
Ethics
    concept, 244–245
    context, 247
    cultural influences, 243–257
    definition, 244
    issues 248-251
    and morality, 244
    necessity, 250
    tourism, 251–254
Ethnicity, 301–302
Ethnic groups, 351, 365, 368
Ethnic subcultures, 107
Ethnocentric people, 192
Ethnocentrism, 35, 192
    problem, 192
Europe, Muslim population, 98
European Union, 22
Evaluation criteria, 238
Evaluation of service quality, 238
Exchanged resources, 208
Exclusionism, 155
Existence needs, 278
Expanded families, 294
Expectancy theory, 276–277
Expectancy violation theory, 53
Expectations theory, 52–53
Expectations and perceptions of service quality, 240
Experiencing culture shock, 218
Experiential, 11, 309
Extensive or complex decision-making, 315
Extermination, 194
External factors, 53
Extrovert, 203, 276

F

Face Negotiation theory, 59
Factors influencing human needs, 265, 279
Fair share, 245, 250
False information, 254
Family
    culture, 99, 100
    decision-making, 333
    life, 302, 349
Feminine cultures, 184, 323, 326

Five-Stage Model, 272
Forced acculturation, 74
Foreign
    culture, visitor in, 215
    tourists and companies, 256
Foreignness, 60
Formal cultures, 133, 151, 175
France, 361–362
Friends as families, 294
Friendship, 350, 353, 354
Functional culture, 99
Functionalists, 86
Fundamental freedoms, 38, 195
Fundamentalism, 255, 366
Future-oriented societies, 187

G

Gender
    -based subcultures, 107
    definition, 100, 106
    discrimination, 252
    imbalance, 367
    roles, 322–323
    segregation, 324
Generation
    culture, 99
    D, 296
    M, 296
    now, 296
    X, 296
    XL, 296
    Y, 296
Geographic environment, 298
Geographical subcultures, 107
Germany, 362
Gimur, 353
Giri, 353, 354
Global
    challenge, 31
    consumer, 15
    distribution systems, 300
    identity crisis, 111
    products, 16, 17, 25
    tourism managers, 24
    village, 25
    world ethics, 251
Global Code of Ethics for Tourism, 257
Globalization 3, 23, 250
    benefits, 6–8
    concept, 3–6
    culture, 15–23
    examples, 9–10
    forms, 9–10
    limitations, 23–24
    roots, 3–6
    tourism industry, 8–15
Glocalization, 23
Grandparent families, 294
Group-oriented cultures, 143
Growth needs, 273, 276, 278

H

Hall's cultural differentiation, 134–138
Harmonious interaction, 37
Health problems, awareness of, 293
Hedonism, 326
Helping information, 275
Herzberg, Mausner and Snyderman's Two Factor
        theory, 276
Heterogeneity, 19, 235
Heterogenization culture, 19
High
    -context cultures, 134, 170, 187, 189
    culture, 91
    masculine cultures, 239
    power distance culture, 51, 184, 333
    uncertainty avoidance cultures, 59, 184, 229,
        342
Hinduism, 93, 364
Historic environment, 299
Hofstede's cultural dimensions, 113, 147, 148
Holism, 359
Homogenous country, 18
Honeymoon phase, 217–218
Honne, 354
Horizontal
    collectivistic cultures, 140
    cultures, 140
    individualistic cultures, 140
Host
    culture, 104
    definition, 205
    societies, 72
Hostility phase, 217–218
Hotel corporations, 9
Human
    activities orientation, 130
    environment, 86
    nature orientation, 154
    rights, 38
Human behavior
    aspects of, 266–267
    basic needs of, 278–279
    components of, 268
    definition, 266
    development, 270
    factors influencing, 268–270, 279
    theories, 270–278

Humanism, 359
Humor stage, 218

I

Identity, 21, 22, 53-54, 110-111
Imagined agreement, 191
Imperialism, 34
Increasing migration, 39
India, 364-365
Indian religion, 92, 96
Indian–Pakistani conflicts, 78
Indicative factors, 53
Individual
    culture, 100
    reality, 153
    rights, 250
Individualism (IDV) dimension, 139
Individualistic cultures, 149, 150, 174, 181, 227,
        251
Indonesia, 351-352
Indonesian tourists, 353
Industry culture, 99
Inflation, 299
Informal cultures, 133, 151, 175
Information search, 291, 307, 331-332
Information sources, 308, 331-332
Information technology, 8-9
In-groups, 135-136
Inglehart's cultural dimensions, 155
Intercultural
    interaction, 209-210
    model, 211-212
    types, 211
Interculturalness
    degree, 210-211
Interpersonal interaction
    harmony, 132, 150, 180, 182
Initial orientation, 62
Inner-oriented, 362
Innovators, 313-314
Inseparability, 235-236
Islam, 91-94, 96-98, 101, 102, 354, 355, 366, 367
Instrumental value, 124, 351
Instrumental-expressive dimension, 129
Instrumentality, 277
Intangibility, 234-235
Intangible components, 90
Interaction
    definition, 190
    purposes of, 207
    style, 180-183
Interactional domain
Interactive strategies, 57

Intercultural
    adaptation, 59
    communication, 120, 167
        difficulties in, 168
        ethics of, 196
    competence, 378
    encounters, 50, 210
    interaction, 49, 209
    networks, 55
    theories, 49
Intercultural/multicultural specialist, 385
Interculturalism, 34
Interethnic and interracial interactions, 209
Inter-group, 53
International context, 247
International tourists, 228, 284-287
Internationalization, 4
Internet, 6, 9
Interpersonal interaction, 49
Interpretative communication, 166
Intracultural interaction, 209
Introvert, 276
Involvement, degree of, 207, 314
Irreligious people, 97
Irritation
    or annoyance stage, 221
    index, 221
Islamic civilization, 104
Israeli–Palestinian conflicts, 78
Italy, 362-363

J

Jainism, 92, 94
Japan, 352-354
Japanese civilization, 102
Japanese cultural traits, 352-355
Japanese tourist behavior, 344
Japanese tourists, 193, 235, 238, 278, 323, 327, 329,
        335, 336, 387
Job content, 276
Judaism, 93, 97, 98

K

Kao, 353
Kluckhohn and Strodtbeck's value orientation,
        129-132
Knowledge, 50, 52, 53, 267, 286, 328-329
Korean tourists, 193, 323, 327, 330

L

Laggards, 314
Language, 135
Language shock, 215

Last-minute-purchase, 10
Late majority, 314
Latin America, 103, 365-366
Latin American civilization, 103
Learning
    definition, 284, 305
    and knowledge, 328-329
Legal
    behavior, 245
    and political environment, 299-300
Life script, 63
Lifecycle stage, 302
Lifestyle
    and activities, 323-324
    definition, 303
Limited decision-making, 314
Lineality, 174
Linear
    interpersonal, 131
    logic, 178
Linguistic differences, 190
Linguistic relativity, 120
Local
    cultures, 16-17, 67-68
    resident perspective, 286
Long-term orientation, 151
Long-term perspective, 105
Loudness, 180
Low
    -context culture, 134, 187, 248
    masculine cultures, 239
    power distance cultures, 184
    uncertainty avoidance cultures, 184
Loyalty and commitment, 339

M
Macdonaldization, 17, 74
Macro level, 268
Malaysia, 354-355
Manana syndrome, 337
Mandarin-speaking tourists, 351
Market
    aggregation, 25
    stimuli, 289
Marketers, 16, 86, 282
Masculine cultures, 140, 183, 326
Masculinity (MAS) dimension, 140, 183
Maslow's Hierarchy of Needs, 272-276
Mass culture, 91
Mateship, 357
Maznevski's cultural differentiation, 152-154
McClelland's learned needs theory, 278
Meaning of Meaning Theory, 54

Meishi, 352
Memories and meanings, 341
Mental process, 88
Meso level, 268
Mexico, 365
Microcultures, 115
Micro level, 268
Middle East, 366-368
Millennial generation, 296
Mind, body and spirit, 266
Mind, functioning of, 267, 268
Minkov's World Value Survey, 155-160
Misleading advertising, 251, 254
Mixed culture, 91
Modern
    communication, 26
    technology, 15
Monochronism, 188
Monumentalism, 155
Moralistic cultures, 153
Mosaic, 369
Motivated behavior, 271
Motivation
    categories and sources of, 270
    definition, 270
    and needs, 326
    theories, 304
Motivator-hygiene theory, 276
Multiculture
    assessment techniques, 385-386
    competence, 377-378, 384
    development levels, 384-385
    domains of, 377, 378-379
    educational challenge, 386
    environment, 41
    factors influencing, 384
    immigration, 32
    process, 384
Multiculturalism policies, 34
Multiethnic, 32
Multigenerational families, 294
Multilingual guides, 190
Multinational organization, 40
Mutual knowledge, 37

N
Nation
    culture, 85, 233
    economies, 6
Nationalism, 22
Nationality
    definition, 109
    subcultures, 107

Nature dimension, 152
Need(s)
    conflict of, 275
    recognition, 330
Need for
    emotional escapes, 293
    more social contacts, 293
    safety and security, 293
Negative
    attitudes, 208, 217
    consequences, 266–268
    perceptions, 237
    stereotypes, 193–194
Network theory, 54–55
Nepotism, 253
Non-contact cultures, 152, 171
Non-linear, 138, 178
Non-utilitarian values, 18
Non-verbal communication, difficulties in, 214
Non-verbal signals, 170–173
Normative patterns, 56
North America, 368–371

O

Occupation, 303
Opinion leadership, role of, 332–333
Organizational culture, 100
Orientation towards
    activity, 138, 184
    human nature, 137, 175
    nature, 129, 183
Original art, 67
Orthodox civilization, 102
Out-groups, 135, 137
Outsourcing, 7
Overt messages, 135
Ownership, 39, 233, 236

P

Padding expense accounts, 254
Pakistan, 355–356
Pakistani passengers, 239
Parsons' pattern variables, 127–129
Particularistic orientation, 128
Passive strategies, 57
Past-oriented societies, 187
People-based and personality-dependent, 237
Perceived cultural similarity, 209
Perception(s)
    definition, 89
    and image, 326–328
    of services, 36, 327

Perishability, 236
Person aspects, 380
Personal cultures, 175
Personality, 276, 303–304, 324–325
Personalized power, 278
Persuasion style, 121
Philippines, 356
Physiological and biological needs, 272
Play, 278
Poland, 363
Polarization, 7, 20
Political
    dimension, 5
    phenomenon, 106
Polychronism, 188
Polychronic time system, 187
Positive
    social interaction, 240
    stereotypes, 193
Post-purchase behavior, 317, 339–341
Power distance (PDI) dimension, 139, 184
Pragmatic cultures, 153
Pragmatism, 185, 359
Prejudice, 194
Present-oriented societies, 187
Problem recognition, 291, 306
Purchase
    beyond, 341–343
Product
    customized, 13, 18–19
    disposal, 341
    evaluation, 335–337
    standardized, 18–19
Professional
    culture, 99
    definition, 385
    group, 100
    hosts, 205
Profit and ethics, 249–250
Profit making, 249
Providers, 237
Provider's performance, 235
Pseudo-artifacts, 69
Psychological state, 62, 121
Public-space cultures, 136
Purchase
    decision, 291, 315, 337
    risk, 337

R

Race culture, 99
Racial discrimination, 195

Racial subcultures, 106
Racism, 195
Rationalism, 359
Readjustment stage, 218
Real and authentic communication, 191
Reciprocal obligation, 354, 356
Reciprocity, 205
Recovery phase, 217-218
Recreational needs, 272
Re-entry shock, 216
Reference groups, 332
Regional cooperation, 23
Regional culture, 99
Reinforcement theory, 277, 339
Relatedness needs, 278
Relationship
    building, 352
    patterns, 105, 173-178
    rules, 227
Religion, 92, 96-98, 302
Religious
    group, 364
    subcultures, 107
Restrained cultures, 149, 182
Resident perspective, 286
Retail sector, 9
Reverse culture shock, 218
Rich tourists, 214
Risk perceptions, 338
Risk-adverse cultures, 338
Role shock, 215
Roman Catholicism, 97
Rule-based theories, 255
Rules, orders of, 226
Rules of
    breaking, 228-229
    cultural influences, 225-229
    differences, 54, 121
    order, 226-227
    social behavior, 121, 207, 225
    social interaction, 225-228
    types, 226-227
    understanding, 228
Russia, 363-364

S

Safety and security, 272, 273, 278
Salad bowl, 292, 369
Sandwich generation, 296
Satisfaction, 339
Saudi Arabia, 366-267
Schein's cultural differentiation, 152-154

Schneider and Barsoux's cultural assumptions,
    154-155
Secular-rational authority, 155
Segmentation, 27, 246, 284
Seishin, 354
Self
    -actualization, 272, 273, 275, 316
    -collective orientation dimension, 129
    -concept, 291, 297, 304
    -criticism, 247, 325, 326
    -effacement, 155, 159
    -fulfillment, 272, 273, 278
    -orientation, 133, 140, 156
    -rating, 114
Senor, 365
Sense of self, 87, 110, 196
Sensitivity, 12, 35, 381
Service
    characteristics of, 234-236
    classification, 234
    definition, 233
    encounter, 234
    evaluation, differences in, 239
    experience, 235
    focus of, 234
    perceptions, importance of, 237
    providers' characteristics, 237
    quality, 238
        dimensions, 240
        evaluation of, 238
    satisfaction, 240
Sexual harassment, 253
Shared meanings, 166
Shinto, 92, 94
Short-term orientation, 151
Sikhism, 93
Silence, 169
Skills, 35, 41, 50, 52, 63, 151, 214, 220, 382
Social
    anthropologists, 86
    behavior, difficulties in, 214
    bonds, 175
    categories, 121
    dimension, 5
    group, 105
    harmony, 132, 180
    interaction, 190
    interaction between tourists and hosts, 207
    interaction, features of, 200
    interaction increment, 207
    interaction, interculturalness of, 210
    interaction model, 211-212

interaction nature, 206
interaction potential, 200
interaction, purpose of, 200
network(s), 55
phenomenon, 105
reality, 153
role, 176, 252, 298
status, 53, 177, 206
strength of, 175
Social Network Theory, 54
Social responsibility, acceptance versus avoidance
    of, 254
Social situations theory, analysis of, 200
Socialized power, 278
Sociocultural disruptions, 246
Software piracy, 251, 254
Sojourner, 217, 219, 385
Solo fliers, 295
Soul mates, 295
South Korea, 176, 185, 356
Spain, 360, 364
Spanish-speaking Americans, 116
Spiritual factors, 267, 268, 270
Stage
    1, 306-307
    2, 307-309
    3, 309-315
    4, 315-316
    5, 317-318
Staged attractions, 69, 282
Standardization, 8, 18, 24
Status-conscious societies, 239
Stereotypes, importance of, 193-194
Stereotyping, 192-194
    weaknesses of, 94
Stewart's cultural patterns, 132-134
Stranger theory, 59
Strategic decisions, 282
Strategy, 285, 372, 380
Subculture, 106-108
Subjugation of nature, 185
Sunni–Shia split, 98
Supra level, 268
Supraterritoriality, 4, 7
Survival values, 155
Sustainable tourism, 13, 245
Symbols, 166, 197, 301
Symbols and meanings, 86, 89, 192
Symptoms of culture shock, 215, 216

T

Tangible components, 90
Task variables, 380

Tatemae, 354
Taxonomic Approach, 56
Technological dimension, 4, 5, 27
Temporal and spatial context, 206-208
Ten most popular criteria, 239
Terminal values, 124, 126, 351, 359
Thai cultural traits, 358
Thai tourists, 197, 358
Thailand, 144, 146, 197, 357
Theology, 254
Theories
    and framework, 254-255
    of human behavior, 270
Theory of justice, 255
Thumbs up, 368
Tight cultures, 151
Time orientation, 130, 138, 187
Time orientation, effects on intercultural commu-
    nication, 188-189
Today's tourism, 268
Tour operators, 9, 12, 257, 338
Tourism
    culture, 104
    definition, 8
    development, 245, 246, 257
    ethics, global code of, 257
    ethics in, 245
    and hospitality industry, 237
    industry, 246, 265-266
    industry perspective, 284
    marketers, 282
    marketing, 246
    services, 236
    services, value of 236
    social interaction in, 201
Tourist, 201
    consumption, 21
    culture, 104
    demand, 234
    experiences, 69, 217, 282, 285
    hosts, 206
    host contact, 206, 213
    host encounters, 207
    host interaction, 206
    host social interaction, context of, 206
    and local hosts, 207
    perspective, 285
    societies, 72
    typology, 201-205
        personal characteristics of, 207
Tourist behavior
    benefits, 284-286
    concept, 279

importance, 282-283
meaning, 281-282
nature, 279-281
study, importance of, 279, 283-284
understanding, 284-286
Traditional authority, 155
Traditional hospitality, 206
Traditional values, 20
Transactional signals, 166
Transcendent need(s)
definition, 273
identification of, 273
Transcontextual, 26
Transculturation, 73
Transition shock, 215
Travel brochures, 246, 254, 305
Travel exposure and experience, 241
Treatment of men and women act (ETA), 252
Tribe subcultures, 107
Trompenaar's cultural differentiation, 152-154
2020 forecast, 283
Types of
culture shock, 215-216
intercultural interaction, 211
needs, 272-274, 278
social interaction, 226-227
tourists, 281, 282

U

U-curve and W-curve, 219
Uncertainty avoidance dimension, 139
cultures, 323, 338
definition, 184
tourists, 338
Understanding
foreign culture, 240, 285
rules of social interaction, 228
tourists, 266
Unemployment rate, 299
UNESCO Declaration on Cultural Diversity, 37-38
United Arab Emirates, 367
United Kingdom, 364
United States, 369-371
Universal
culture, 98
ethics rules, 250

moral duty, 255
social interaction, 226
Universalism, 255
Universalization, 4, 5
Unwelcoming attitudes, 213
Utilitarianism, 254, 255

V

Valence, 277
Value
affecting intercultural communication, 185-186
classification, 124-125
definition, 183-186
differences, 123-124
dimensions, 127-128
laden, 106
measurement, 125-127
orientation, 124
studies, 127
surveys, 126
system, 123-124
types, 124
Verbal communication
definition, 120
difficulties in, 214
Verbal signals, 168-170
Vertical cultures, 140
Vietnam, 357, 387
Voluntary acculturation, 74

W

Well-being values, 155
Western
civilization, 101, 103
industrialized nations, 70
monochronic time system, 187
work ethics, 25, 249
Westernization, 4, 5, 17
Wider environments, 269, 270
Women travelers, 252, 284
Word-of-mouth communication, 332
World orientation, 134, 157
World Tourism Organization, 257, 261
World trade, 5, 24